Once again, Charles van Onselen offers us a remarkable book, though this one is especially ambitious and expansive. Through the exploits and experiences of John Hays Hammond – relatively unknown but immensely consequential – van Onselen reveals to us the political economy of late nineteenth and early twentieth century capitalism and state formation as it should be seen: transnational, imperial and very much a product of alliances between states and private capitalists. Historians of South Africa, the United States and Mexico will see connections and a world they have never before glimpsed and understand a historical stage of 'globalisation' in new ways. *The Cowboy Capitalist* is a brilliant contribution to historical scholarship as well as a reminder of van Onselen's master story-telling and riddle solving.

Steve Hahn, Pulitzer Prize-winning author, New York University

Charles van Onselen's richly informative and gripping *Cowboy Capitalist* offers intrigue, betrayal and suspense worthy of a spy thriller in a deeply documented account of international entrepreneurial capitalism, labour exploitation and political conspiracy in the age of imperialism. Above all, this epic biography of California native John Hays Hammond enriches transnational history by illuminating the influence of American mining engineers, the US South's filibustering past and San Franciscan/Western vigilantism on the infamous Jameson Raid in 1895–96 to overthrow Paul Kruger's South African Republic. No one reading this mesmerising tri-continental tale will ever look at the US informal empire, the Boer republic or British imperialism in southern Africa in quite the same way again.

Robert May, Purdue University

The Cowboy Capitalist is one of those rare but exciting books that explode what we long believed we knew about a historical event and present us with a new and compelling reinterpretation that will rejuvenate and define future debate. There has long been tired consensus that the Jameson Raid of 1895 was a capitalist conspiracy hatched by Cecil Rhodes and the Rand mining magnates, with the tacit support of Downing, to impose their agenda on Kruger's obscurantist republic. In his enthralling reassessment of the Jameson Raid, Charles van Onselen brings the hard-nosed but fascinatingly complex American entrepreneur John Hays Hammond to the fore. With his extensive holdings in the gold mines and with his important business and political connections in the United States, Hays Hammond was active in promoting the United States' informal empire during the 1890s. Van Onselen shows that Hays Hammond's leading, but previously downplayed, role in planning the Jameson Raid was integral to this expansionist agenda, and he repositions the Jameson Raid as an international capitalist conspiracy in which US interests, alongside British ones, played a pivotal role.

John Laband, Wilfrid Laurier University

This is a fantastic read. Bloody hell. Charles van Onselen has given us a master class in historical revisionism. With forensic detail, a global cast and compelling argument, this book delivers a dynamic new history of the murky world of late nineteenth century imperialism in southern Africa, culminating in a new transnational history of the infamous Jameson Raid. John Hays Hammond has finally met his match.

Joanna Lewis, London School of Economics

This wonderfully readable book is also a work of profound scholarship by one of the finest historians working today. Charles van Onselen writes with a Tolstoyian control over complex narrative and the contested human condition. Justly famous for giving voice to the marginalised individuals and social classes in South Africa, here he brings alive the political and financial ruling classes who shaped an Anglo-American world of colonial empires and finance capital from the 1880s to the 1930s. His overt subject is the life of Californian John Hays Hammond (1855–1936) – the entrepreneurial American millionaire, brilliant mining engineer, freebooting expansionist and über political animal – who played a crucial (yet curiously neglected) role in the Jameson Raid conspiracy. But his grand narrative sweeps over a fast-changing trans-Atlantic and African world through fifty years of Western colonialism, in which global ideologies of culture and capital, race and 'manifest destiny' gripped the mindsets of generations. John Hays Hammond indeed personified this 'revolutionary capitalism' in an era of geo-political transformations. While researching the Age of Rhodes, Kruger and Chamberlain might now seem like working an exhausted Rand mine, Charles van Onselen shows that we are only at the beginning of a new understanding of the modern South Africa story within the international dynamics of global history.

Deryck M Schreuder, University of Sydney

One version of the Jameson Raid – that it was a British imperialist conspiracy to topple Paul Kruger's Boer republic – has stood for many years. Now, South Africa's finest and most formidable historian has taken a swipe at the rock of historical certainty, splintering it. In this rich and complex revision of historical understanding of the botched coup of 1895, Charles van Onselen's twist is to depict it as a testy, competing Anglo-American lunge at imperial expansion. Who knows, had the frontier posse of John Hays Hammond prevailed, the Transvaal might well have toppled into Washington's paws as a southern African version of the Philippines or the Dominican Republic. Enjoyably argumentative, *The Cowboy Capitalist* displays in abundance the trademark talent of its author – his blistering combination of depth, breadth, authoritative scholarship, combativeness and wit. A brilliant book which makes an old imperial story fresh and surprising, it will be essential reading both for those new to its topic and for those who think that they know the wider history of South Africa and America in the 1890s.

Bill Nasson, University of Stellenbosch

The Cowboy Capitalist

CHARLES VAN ONSELEN

The Cowboy Capitalist

John Hays Hammond, the American West and the Jameson Raid

Jonathan Ball Publishers

JOHANNESBURG & CAPE TOWN

© Text Charles van Onselen 2017
© Published edition 2017 Jonathan Ball Publishers

Published in South Africa in 2017 by
JONATHAN BALL PUBLISHERS
A division of Media24 (Pty) Ltd
PO Box 33977
Jeppestown
2043

ISBN 978-1-86842-738-3
EBOOK ISBN 978-1-86842-739-0

Twitter: www.twitter.com/JonathanBallPub
Facebook: www.facebook.com/JonathanBallPublishers
Blog: http://jonathanball.bookslive.co.za/

Cover by Michiel Botha
Design and typesetting by Triple M Design, Johannesburg
Maps by Philip Stickler
Printed and bound in Malaysia by Times Offset (M) Sdn. Bhd.
Set in 10,75pt/13pt Bembo Std

For those in search of history without borders

Contents

MINING

BLASTING

UNDERMINING

REFINING

List of Maps

Looking Up From the
Last of History

One day, a decade ago, I was paging through the brittle sheets of old newspaper runs, hoping to pick up the scent of something that I had been working on for some time. Late in January 1895, an Englishman, a petty criminal from Stoke-on-Trent, had been executed by a one-armed Irishman from Manchester in an unpretentious boarding house at the lower end of Commissioner Street, Johannesburg. The executioner was a charismatic gangster, the murder brazen and the sequel so bizarre – a celebration in a restaurant – that it excited a good deal of press attention. The outrage that followed among resident English nationals was predictable, and I followed the trail with the routinised attention of the professional historian until I came across a totally unexpected report.

In early March 1895, Fred Hamilton, editor of *The Star*, gave generous coverage to a meeting at which the town's citizens had elected a leading mine owner, Lionel Phillips, to chair a 'Vigilance Committee'. What piqued my interest was the fact that 'Vigilance Committees' were not an integral part of the late 19th-century English political repertoire. Vigilance committees were American frontier phenomena, populist responses, more characteristic of the Wild West. I was aware that in 1895 the town boasted a fair number of engineers and miners from California but thought little more of it until, a few editions later, I came across a half-page article written by an anonymous 'American' entitled 'Vigilance Committees – A Famous Association', recalling the San Francisco Vigilance Committee of 1851. All that I concluded from this, however, was that there had been some behind-the-scenes manoeuvring involving influential American and English mining industry leaders who might have been keen to exploit public discontent

1

about the always ineffectual state of policing in Johannesburg during one of its periodic 'crime waves'. To me, it looked very much like a 'dead' idea.

Alas, that naive reading prompted no further, let alone rigorous, questioning by me for some years. I did, however, have the wit to file it in that part of my memory marked 'puzzling historical connections'. Then, on a snowy morning in Cambridge, Massachusetts, in 2012, I ran out of the material necessary to prompt my next paragraph and, reluctant to abandon the day's work, decided to walk across the square to a nearby second-hand bookshop. In search of inspiration, I moved through the section on United States history and there, left by the great god Coincidence at a height so as not even a partially-sighted old fool might miss it, was George R Stewart's *Committee of Vigilance: Revolution in San Francisco, 1851*. I suddenly recalled that, in the filing cabinet of my mind, Stewart's work fitted under 'puzzling connections' rather than 'American History'. I flipped through the table of contents, checked the price, looked up and noted that snow flurries were starting to obscure the outline of a favourite coffee shop refuge. The price of the book was rung up and I dragged Stewart along with me to share a mug of coffee.

It was a touch selfish because I had little to offer by way of conversation, even though he could probably teach me a great deal. After all, San Francisco, like Johannesburg, was once at the centre of a great mining industry, and just as Chelsea buns in summer attract the blackest flies so, in booming economies, does gold pull in the darkest of criminals.

Coffee left unattended soon goes cold, and a second cup had to be ordered. Reading about San Francisco's 1851 'revolution' triggered a minor earthquake in the cortex, sending shock waves through what had been reasonably stable foundations of a view of Johannesburg's own shorter-lived Vigilance Committee of 1895. From Stewart it became clear that a popularly endorsed 'Vigilance Committee' constituted no less than a variant on a coup d'état; it was, in fact, a unilateral declaration of independence at city level. Middle-class citizens were, in effect, taking on the established centralised authority, as well as the local law-breakers. The nation-state's writ to enforce 'law or order' from a recognised base of power no longer ran locally. A town controlled by a militant vigilance committee was, in truth, an independent city-state.

Viewed from *that* perspective, the Johannesburg Vigilance Committee was enormously significant. Only nine months later, there was an attempt to foment a 'revolution' in the town as a prelude to toppling the Kruger government by those involved in the plot, which culminated in the disastrous Jameson Raid. And there were links between the Johannesburg Vigilance Committee and the Raid. Not only had Phillips chaired the Vigilance Committee but he had also been one of four sentenced to death for their role in a 'Reform Committee' that was not so much intent on 'reform' as in ushering in 'revolutionary' change.

All that such thinking did, however, was to lead me into a cul-de-sac. If the Johannesburg committee had been a sort of political dry run for the Jameson Raid conspirators, then the notion was unlikely to have been that of Phillips – an Englishman. No, the person behind the idea and the article in *The Star* was not only an 'American' – as the by-line suggested – but probably a Californian, one with roots in San Francisco. And, from that sprung a more exciting and radical idea still. If the Johannesburg committee and the Jameson Raid *were* connected, then perhaps that same San Franciscan had put together much of the larger template underpinning the Jameson Raid? After all, the idea of a doctor leading 500 men on horseback in a gallop over hundreds of miles of veld to effect a 'revolutionary' outcome was faintly barmy by 1895. Where else had men intent on expanding the British Empire resorted to such wild adventurism? It smacked more of the American West, of a cowboy or a filibustering expedition than of a serious attempt by British imperialists to overthrow a Boer government.

Chances were that if I discovered who the moving spirit behind the Johannesburg committee was, I might also find the man who had contributed most to the idea of staging the failed coup of 1895, and perhaps then uncover something that had been eluding historians for 120 years: the principal architect behind the Jameson Raid. By the time I recalled that there had been an American sentenced to death for his part in the Raid, and that his name was Hammond, the seed had long since sprouted and I could detect the first green shoots. Johannesburg and San Francisco were undoubtedly connected. But was John Hays Hammond a Californian, and was he San Franciscan? Had the snow been ten feet deep, I would still have rushed to the library.

The *Autobiography of John Hays Hammond* was published, in New York City, in two volumes, in 1935. I tore into chapter one, 'Heritage of a Californian', and within minutes it was clear that not only was he born in San Francisco, but also that the 'Hays' in his name came from a charismatic uncle, Colonel John 'Coffee' Hays, a former Texas Ranger, a veteran of the Mexican-American War, and the town's first Sheriff. A glance at the index in Stewart's book confirmed that Colonel Hays had been actively involved in several key events linked to the San Francisco Committee of Vigilance. Just four pages later, Hammond recounted how, as a child, former members of that committee were in and out of the family home. The very next chapter, 'A Boy on the Frontier', made it clear that Coffee Hays, along with Hammond's father, Major RP Hammond, another Mexican-American War veteran, had had decisive roles in the young Hammond's upbringing in San Francisco and, across the bay, in nearby Oakland.

But there, much to my frustration, the trail linking Johannesburg to San Francisco ran dead. I could find no more clues in Californian history that might plausibly link the towns to the cognitive architecture that underlay the wider Jameson Raid plot. I read both volumes of Hammond's *Autobiography*, noting his role in the hoped-for 'revolution', including a plan to abduct State President, Paul Kruger, and seize the arsenal at Pretoria. Alas, neither of these schemes resonated with anything in his memoirs; in fact, there was not even a hint of a meaningful parallel. But then the penny dropped. If Hammond had *not* explicitly linked the idea of the Johannesburg Vigilance Committee to that of San Francisco and wished to hide his thinking in *that* regard, why would he not do the same when it came to any of the supplementary initiatives he had planned?

From that insight, two related ideas were born. First, in regard to his role in the Jameson Raid and for which he had been sentenced to death, it was not so much what was in Hammond's autobiography that was important, but what was left *out* – so as not to reveal any San Franciscan or other borrowings in his thinking. Second, in order to find what hidden links there might have been in the history of the two mining towns and the Jameson Raid would require extensive research. Only then might I establish which events in his boyhood, adolescence or his life before reaching Johannesburg, in 1894, could *not* have failed to leave their mark on Hammond and which he had then deliberately left out of a life story doctored so as to place him centre stage, as a courageous and innovative hero.

The idea that 500 mounted 'raiders' galloping in from a neighbouring territory could overthrow the South African Republic resonated with my understanding of American filibusters, that is, private armies raised in the United States to invade and assume control of states either in the Caribbean or Central America during the 1850s. But, since Hammond was born in 1855, it meant that such events could only have been 'experienced' by him via the men in his family. But what if Colonel Hays and Major RP Hammond, the boy's role models, had been involved with one of the major filibuster leaders of the 1850s? That would surely be significant.

I found an appropriately sharp historical work to probe for an artery connecting members of the extended Hammond family to the leading filibusters of the day; within hours the blood was in the vial and it tested positive. In the early 1850s, William Walker, 'the grey-eyed man of destiny', had been based in San Francisco where he and RP Hammond were both active, on the same side, in a fractious local branch of the Democratic Party. Moreover, both Hammond Snr and Coffee Hays had played dubious official roles – as Collector of Customs and Sheriff, respectively – when Walker and a party of armed supporters had slipped out of the port aboard the brig *Arrow* and set off to invade Mexico, where they established the short-lived 'Republic of

Lower California' (1853–1854). Clearly, the idea of a foreign force invading a neighbouring republic, by whatever means for whatever reason, was one that the extended Hammond family would have been familiar with.

But in 1852 Hammond was not yet of this world, and not even Walker's shenanigans up and down Central America provided a template for Dr Jameson's wild dash. Filibustering was in the mix when it came to the troubles on the Witwatersrand in 1895 – and the same word was used when reported on at the time – but the linkage remained distant and unpersuasive unless, as with the San Francisco Vigilance Committee, it could somehow be shown to have resonated with not only 'Americans' in Johannesburg but also the elusive one himself.

By the time that the American Civil War broke out, in 1861, young Hammond was seven years old and likely to have developed a few impressions of his own as to what was going on in San Francisco. The question was, what exactly *had* gone on at that time in a town with a sizeable population of Southerners, many of whom, like members of the extended Hammond family, held political sympathies that were hardly secret? I found another scholarly scalpel, made a small incision and collected a second sample that also tested positive.

In 1861, those Southerners in San Francisco set up a shadowy oath-bound 'Committee of Thirty' that plotted to capture the city and state for what they hoped could be turned into a 'Pacific Republic' that would divert its gold supplies to underwrite the Confederate war effort. 'Our plans,' suggested one of the principal conspirators, 'were to paralyze all organised resistance by simultaneous attack.'[1] Taken in the round, the Committee of Thirty's conspiracy in San Francisco mirrored some of the major elements in the coordinated, integrated and sequenced components of the Reform Committee's plot to seize the state arsenal in Pretoria and assume control of Johannesburg in 1895.

But mastering theory – even revolutionary theory – did not take a man very far in America in the 1890s. In a decade that for the most part took a dim view of idealists, and that paved the way politically for the arrival of Teddy Roosevelt and the Rough Riders, it was courage and fighting ability, as displayed on the field of battle or in the profession of mining engineering by 'practical men', that was expected to lead the way. It was such men who were most readily feted in Gilded Age society.

What made John Hays Hammond so special was that he was the embodiment of a 19th-century revolutionary capitalist. He was capable of analysing how, in theory, the economy and the state should best be aligned in order to extract the maximum amount of profit for self and private enterprise, and then of applying the lesson in the most practical way possible. And, when current practice failed to address, or violated the needs of, theory he could,

and did, intervene directly in the 'real' world to change the existing arrangements – be they economic, political or social – so as to achieve an outcome
that was nothing short of revolutionary.[2]

His 'twin brother' in all this, his constant partner in crime against the state
on two continents, and the terror of organised labour everywhere from the
mid-1880s until his death, in 1903, was a man born into the same cohort
as Hammond, in Los Angeles, in 1855. His name was Victor M Clement.
The twins' deeply personal experience of bloody industrial warfare, fought
against anything from railway companies to trade unionists, started in
Mexico but was raised to the level of national importance in the Coeur
d'Alene, in Idaho, in the early 1890s – just before the two fled to southern
Africa.

Under Hammond's leadership, a select group of the biggest producers
in the Coeur d'Alene organised themselves into a secretive Mine Owners'
Association (MOA), which sometimes operated relatively openly and
legally, arguing its case through the courts. But, just beneath this veneer of
professional authenticity lurked a beast of industrial savagery bereft of most
notions of decency, fairness, ethics or morality. Front organisations devoted
to skewed interpretations of 'law and order' were established up and down
the valleys. Editors and newspapers were bought to produce class-based
propaganda directed against mineworkers operating under oppressive company policies focused pre-eminently on cutting rather than holding wages.
The illegal importation of firearms for use by small company-based armies,
Pinkerton agents, informers and spies completed the MOA's repertoire.

So powerful and sustained was Hammond and the mine owners' attack
on working-class living standards in Idaho that it contributed, in no small
measure, to the birth, in 1893, of what, arguably, went on to become the
most militant and violent trade union ever seen in the history of the United
States of America – the Federation of Western Miners, which was later
briefly affiliated to the Industrial Workers of the World. Revolutionary capitalists could spawn their own revolutionary workers.

By the time Hammond reached the Johannesburg goldfields, in 1894, he
was head-and-shoulders above all others in terms of mining expertise. With
some justification, he presented himself as the best in his field and succeeded
in becoming the highest paid engineer in the world, as well as a significant
partner in several local mining ventures. Hammond, however, was not only
a mining engineer; he was also a social engineer, one who desired total control over all the factors of production, including labour, in order to maximise
profit. He blended history, theory and significant practical experience into
an explosive mixture of revolutionary capitalism. A ball of fire had rolled in
through the door of a room stacked to the ceiling with political dynamite.

In late 1894, John Hays Hammond, Cecil Rhodes and Leander Starr

Jameson undertook a mining safari though Matabeleland, in the southern part of territory controlled by the British South Africa Company (also
known as the 'Chartered Company') and which later became the strangely
named country of Rhodesia and, much later still, Zimbabwe. The leader
of the expedition, Rhodes, already a millionaire and Prime Minister of the
Cape Colony, was in an agitated frame of mind. The economic fortunes of
the Chartered Company, to the extent that they were based on gold mining, and as was about to be confirmed by Hammond, were not all that rosy.
Moreover, as the British Empire's most ardent continental strategist, Rhodes
was being thwarted at every turn through southern Africa. His attempt to
purchase Delagoa Bay in adjacent Portuguese East Africa, not unlike earlier
unsuccessful attempts by the United States to purchase Cuba, had come
to naught. Moreover, President Kruger and his *Zuid-Afrikaansche Republiek*
(South African Republic) was militantly opposed to even the idea of entering into a tentatively mooted southern African economic federation. And, as
if all that was not bad enough, Hammond – still bruised by his experiences
in the Coeur d'Alene – added more tales of woe about revolutionary static
building up on the Witwatersrand goldfields.

If Rhodes was the 'dreamer' in an exceptionally close partnership, then
Jameson was the doer. What Leander Starr Jameson lacked in terms of
insight and political sophistication – and there was a good deal wanting – he
made up for it through action, courage and decisiveness. He was admiring
of American masculinity and, as a young man, had paid a short visit to the
United States, where his family had distant kin. Together, he and Rhodes
formed a formidable combination, each checking or prompting the other
in a complex balancing act. When it came to bravado and self-confidence,
however, Jameson had just passed through a long and very fruitful season of
renewal. In 1893, with the aid of Major FR Burnham, the famous American
frontiersman and Indian fighter he had employed as chief scout, Jameson
and troops armed with Maxim machine guns had defeated spear-wielding
Ndebele tribesmen in order to enforce their authority throughout the territory the Chartered Company laid claim to.

The fact that the Rhodes-Jameson partnership was slightly out of kilter
in 1894 strengthened Hammond's hand during the camping trio's debates
because he could assume the role of either action man or deep thinker
with equal alacrity and conviction. But, being unwilling to choose between
the two roles unless it became necessary, he played both. With the Coeur
d'Alene wind at his back, he laid out an analysis of a revolutionary political climate developing among unenfranchised white miners along the
Witwatersrand, and then coupled it to a depressing analysis of the unreasonable cost factors bearing down on a vulnerable gold-mining industry.[3]
Unless the Rand mine owners were willing to co-opt the emerging muscle

power of the unenfranchised white workers and employ it directly so as to usher in a sympathetic administration in Pretoria, they would continue to bleed profits as well as have to cope with the possibility of insurgent, radical trade unionism.

Rhodes and Hammond did not always agree on questions of political economy. There were several sharp exchanges as to what characterised the essence of true democratic representation, or whether tariffs – a subject of enduring American interest – advanced or retarded industrialisation.[4] Nor was Rhodes fully convinced by Hammond's argument that the Witwatersrand was ripe for a revolution, one which, if not appropriated early on, might be controlled either by the other mining houses or by a white populist constituency. Indeed, so sceptical was Rhodes that it was only some weeks later, after he and Jameson had both paid visits to Johannesburg to take their own in-depth soundings of the situation, that he finally conceded that Hammond had a point. What Rhodes did *not* tell Hammond, however, was that what he found was that the most dangerous revolutionary elements of all on the Rand were Americans, republicans, men hostile to a future in the British Empire.[5]

It was later conceded directly by Jameson, and indirectly by Rhodes, but for reasons that had to do with his fumbling during the Johannesburg uprising only grudgingly, and in part, by Hammond, that the 1894 Matabeleland mining safari was the *fons et origo* of what came to be known as the 'Jameson Raid'. It was there, north of the Limpopo, where three revolutionary romantics swapped notes about courage and initiative, that the longer-term threat posed by American economic expansionism and its cultivation of a new zone of influence in southern Africa collided with the politics of British imperialism for the first time; it was there, over a smoky fire that Californian history conjured up images of abducting political rivals, of filibustering expeditions, of seizing arsenals, occupying cities and declaring new republics; and it was there, on the evening breeze, that the Coeur d'Alene whispered a pointed warning about the Witwatersrand.

The broad outlines of the plot agreed to by the triumvirate were, with the support of several strategically placed mine owners extended, modified and refined over the 14 months that followed. The venture was financially underwritten by Rhodes, who also persuaded Alfred Beit and leading members in his mining house to support the scheme. Rhodes assumed responsibility for educating Joseph Chamberlain, Secretary of State for the Colonies in Westminster, about the prospects for extending the British Empire and eliciting his covert support for the operation. Jameson and Hammond were left to deal with arming and providing for the respective strike forces both beyond and within Johannesburg, and agreed to be cross-wired in such a way that neither of the two could order an armed strike or response without the prior approval of the other.

The original conspirators looked forward to the formation of a 'provisional government', which, while being significantly more sympathetic to industrial than to agricultural interests, would do so without excluding entirely the republic's indigenous Afrikaner-Dutch farming constituency. The would-be revolutionists not only wished to avoid a prolonged civil war with the formidable Boer commandos but also to ensure the continued functioning of agricultural markets that fed the growing mining population of the Witwatersrand. To this end, the mine owners identified a few well-placed urban insiders, led by Advocate EA Esselen, and cultivated them as a set of Pretoria-based collaborators. It was hoped that from within this Boer fifth column, composed largely of 'Progressive' supporters of General PJ Joubert and bitterly opposed to the Kruger administration, would emerge the potential members of a 'provisional government'.

The dollop of 'Anglo-Saxon' cultural bonding agent that had held the basic American expansionist and British imperialist components of the triumvirate together in the Matabeleland bush, however, proved unequal to the local, regional and international strains imposed upon it once political temperatures mounted. Jameson, poised on a thin strip of land on the margins of Bechuanaland, peeled away, first from Hammond whom he began to suspect of having lost his nerve and stalling unnecessarily, and then, thinking that a quick blow might yet deliver the main prize to his hesitant hero in Cape Town, from Rhodes. The Raid, unauthorised, and by then out of sequence with the 'revolutionary' acts supposed to precede it, ended in a fruitless display of bravado on the West Rand.

The failure of the Jameson Raid cost Rhodes his position as Prime Minister of the Cape Colony, but in broad terms he paid little for his involvement in the plot. Suffering from a long-standing heart condition, he died, in Muizenberg, in 1902. After a well-publicised trial in London, Jameson endured a brief term of imprisonment and then, remarkably, went on to become Prime Minister of the Cape (1904–1908). British imperialists knew how to look after their own and how to manage defeat.

After a trial in Pretoria, in 1896, at which he and three others were sentenced to death, Hammond and his wife, Natalie Harris, successfully orchestrated an impressive political campaign in the United States that not only helped ensure the commutation of his death sentence but, in effect, also allowed him to buy his way out of having to serve a term in prison for high treason. To some it seemed appropriate that a jacket-and-tie capitalist 'revolutionary', as opposed to a 'political' revolutionary in uniform, could buy his way out of trouble. Money could solve most problems.

In Washington, DC, the American elite's cross-party support for the well-connected Hammond in his hour of need came not only from the Secretary of State, Richard Olney, but also from several influential Southerners, including John T Morgan, Grand Dragon of the Ku Klux Klan in Alabama and a six-term representative of his state in the US Senate. For all that, however, many others took the view that Hammond was the handmaiden of Rhodes and that, by assisting the arch-imperialist in his attempt to overthrow what was a sister republic, he had acted dishonourably and done great violence to American democratic values.

Hammond might have slipped the hangman's noose, but, worryingly for an ambitious man, he had also lost caste in certain quarters of the United States and become *persona non grata* for having played what looked like an imperialist game on behalf of the old enemy. The irony in this was that when it came to American political adventurism abroad, Hammond was *leading* the way rather than lagging behind. Just months after his trial in Pretoria, America annexed Hawaii and invaded Cuba and the Philippines as the United States' sphere of economic influence and expansion gave way to a formal empire of its own after 1898. True, Hammond was a man, not a state, but in the mid-1890s he embodied the ethos of the times just as William Walker had back in the 1850s.

In 1896, with so much hostility and suspicion in America about his decision to back the imperialists – rather than they him, as Rhodes later acknowledged – Hammond felt it unwise to return directly to the United States. His position was made worse by a rumour that began to do the rounds in London and New York to the effect that the Johannesburg 'Reform Committee' had been guilty of 'cowardice' for not having gone to Jameson's aid at Krugersdorp.[6]

Hammond used four years of self-imposed exile in London, from 1896 to 1899, to great effect, consciously rehabilitating his damaged personal and political reputation. He deliberately ingratiated himself with the American Ambassador to the Court of St James's, John M Hay, in order to open a line of access to the transatlantic elite and to sell his own, self-aggrandising version of the attempted coup in southern Africa. It was a version listened to with growing attention as British-Boer relations, set on a destructive course by the Jameson Raid, deteriorated steadily.

More pertinently, Hammond assiduously cultivated the company and friendship of one of the leading journalists and novelists of the epoch, his fellow American, Richard Harding Davis. Davis, a purveyor of tales of bravery and heroism to American readers of the popular 'yellow' press, used his fiction and non-fiction writings to champion Hammond's cause during the exile years, helping set him up for a smoother return to elite circles in the United States, in 1899, than Hammond might otherwise have enjoyed.

In 1897, Davis authored two works that cast Hammond in the principal heroic role. The first, extolling his 'moral as well as physical courage' was the non-fictional *Dr Jameson's Raiders*, which, published in New York City, placed the Jameson Raid in a grand American tradition while simultaneously linking it to contemporary developments on the eve of the Spanish-American War.[7] In the second, the novel *Soldiers of Fortune*, published to great acclaim in New York, the engineer hero Robert Clay – whose father 'was a filibuster' – mimed many aspects of Hammond's career, right down to a short spell on the Kimberley diamond mines. Finally, in the same year, Natalie Harris used her non-fictional account, *A Woman's Part in a Revolution*, published in London, to argue the case that her husband was in no way responsible for the Raid debacle and that, motivated only by a profound sense of duty, he had emerged with his honour intact.

When Hammond returned to America, in late 1899, he found that popular attitudes regarding direct political intervention and vigorous economic expansionism had to some extent caught up with his own robust inclinations as expressed in southern Africa half a decade earlier. And, by the time that Theodore ('Teddy') Roosevelt became President, in 1901, Hammond and the Republican Party were marching in unison and his career in its 'progressive' wing and in public affairs was about to take off.

The definitive moment and move came from Hammond, in 1904, when he contrived to renew a distant friendship from his days at Yale with William Howard Taft – then still Governor-General of the Philippines – over lunch at a New York club. Taft, conservative and legal-minded, was, it was rumoured, the coming man, having already been picked by Teddy Roosevelt as his successor in the White House. From then on Hammond and Taft, the one more ambitious than the other, grew ever closer, to hunt in a pack. By the time Taft was elected President, in 1908, Hammond had run a very public but unsuccessful campaign, one without historical precedent at Republican conventions, to gain the party's endorsement as Taft's vice-presidential running mate. The fact that Hammond did not become the Vice President mattered less than it might have. In 1911, Taft gave John Hays Hammond and Natalie Harris the gift of a lifetime. Hammond was made the United States' Special Ambassador at the coronation of King George V and Queen Mary. The Hammonds' rehabilitation within the Anglo-American elite was complete.

Not holding official office in Washington suited Hammond. It allowed him to operate from within the shadows of 1600 Pennsylvania Avenue, to slip in an out of the White House at will as a member of President Taft's informal 'golf cabinet'. In a way, it also mirrored the behind-the-scenes role Hammond had played with Prime Minister Rhodes, in 1894–1895. And, whether he knew it or not, Taft was at political risk. It is instructive to note how the commentators of the day felt that, throughout Taft's one-term presidency (1909–1913), much of Mexican policy, and even US troop movements on the border, could be traced back to Hammond.

All such border activity could hardly be attributed to Hammond alone, even if he, along with other leading American capitalists, such as Daniel Guggenheim, were heavily invested in mines and oil in Mexico. But neither could it be dismissed out of hand. In 1909, shortly before the outbreak of the Mexican Revolution (1910–1920) Hammond, FR Burnham and others had acquired a valuable concession in the north-western state of Sonora. The ill-fated Yaqui Delta Land and Water Company, covering 60 000 hectares, had, like Rhodes's Chartered Company, been identified by Hammond as a site for colonisation by his compatriots. Infiltrated and surrounded by revolutionaries, and at one stage protected by a 500-strong private army, the Yaqui estate was, for several years, managed much like a militarised settler colony in Africa before it was eventually sold, in 1927. Hammond had taken modern American mining expertise fused with frontier experiences to Africa in the late 19th century and then, in the early 20th century, used some of his southern African capitalist adventures to inform the administration, management and defence of a new colonising initiative in revolutionary northern Mexico.

It was Taft's successor, the Democrat Woodrow Wilson (1913–1921), assisted by his éminence grise and fixer, Colonel Edward M House, who perhaps saw through Hammond most clearly, witnessing the millionaire engineer's gradual public transformation from interventionist capitalist to national elder statesman advocating the wisdom of international peace. But even through Wilson's eight years in office, Hammond and Natalie Harris continued to wield curiously disproportionate political, economic and social influence up and down the East Coast, and in Washington in particular. The failed coup d'état on the Witwatersrand in 1895, however, never ceased to haunt Hammond.

He wrestled continuously with the problem of how it had destroyed his relationship, if not with Rhodes himself then with his sidekick, Jameson, and how the entire debacle had called into question his courage and judgment, let alone how it had bedevilled the political future of southern Africa. In 1918, at age 63, Hammond had another run at the problem, employing the journalist Alleyne Ireland to relate 'The True Story of the Jameson Raid as told to me by John Hays Hammond' in two articles in the prestigious *North American Review*. Hammond's take, modified to meet wartime ideology, ended predictably: his actions, in 1895, had been fully justified.[8]

Hammond's influence, although declining as he aged, continued to be felt through the Republican administrations of Warren Harding (1921–1923), Calvin Coolidge (1923–1929) and Herbert Hoover (1929–1933). Despite being offered prestigious positions within the state machinery, one or two of which he accepted, Hammond refused to accept high public office, preferring to play his accustomed behind-the-scenes role and preparing a two-volume autobiography that, he hoped, would provide the definitive account of his role as a benevolent, far-sighted and fair-minded capitalist, as a statesmen rather than a politician, and, above all else, as a patriotic and principled American spreading 'civilisation' and progress.

By the time that he died at age 81, in 1936, Hammond had prepared the way to be eulogised by many sectors of an admiring American public. 'Although he was never a candidate for public office and refused several appointive offices such as cabinet positions,' it was noted in one obituary, 'he exerted a powerful influence in politics and statecraft in the United States and in the British Empire.'[9] In the same obituary and others, it was also duly noted that Hammond had not been in sympathy with the Jameson Raid. He had succeeded in confounding the past.

In one distant corner of the British Empire, however, Hammond's death appeared to have attracted little or no interest, which was odd. In South Africa it had, by then, long been taken as an article of faith that the Jameson Raid had been the single most destructive event ever experienced in 'white' politics through the region as a whole. Moreover, it was also accepted that the Jameson Raid had detonated a chain reaction in the region's formal politics – the Anglo-Boer War (1899–1902), the British reconstruction regime (1902–1905), the handing back of power to Afrikaner nationalists in 1907 and the hurried formation of the Union of South Africa in 1910.

What was *not* accepted in America, in Britain or in South Africa in 1936, or for half a century and more thereafter, was the fact that each of these connected, sequential steps aggravated the devastating political, economic and social consequences for African, Asian and Coloured South Africans, who were denied the chance of acquiring meaningful citizenship in the country of their birth. The Jameson Raid helped set South Africa on course for the development of a modern, industrialised mining economy that was dependent on a politically enslaved, economically exploited and socially impoverished African proletariat.

And while he was hardly responsible for all that followed, there was indeed one person who might have been held to account for having set off the initial explosion that led to this chain reaction of political disasters. He was an American, a mining engineer, a man whose attitudes and historically-derived experience when it came to questions of political, racial and social engineering could be traced back to the antebellum South and the Civil War, and his name was John Hays Hammond. The time has come for those interested in such things to re-examine the Jameson Raid and place it not only within the context of British imperialism and its collision with Afrikaner nationalism, but also against the much broader background of American economic expansion in the late 19th century. In a benighted country, such as South Africa, fatally attracted to ethnic or racial nationalism rather than class as an organising principle capable of producing social justice, we need to be reminded that we were, and are still, citizens of the world and in serious need of more convincing explanations of a largely self-created plight.

The Mother Lode

CHAPTER ONE

North Atlantic Revolutions and South African Realities

Plotting Urban Insurrection in an Agrarian Economy

SEPTEMBER 1894

By the mid-19th century, economic growth was starting to deliver unprecedented benefits to the urban middle classes on either side of the North Atlantic. By contrast, the semi-arid interior of southern Africa was still an agricultural backwater, barely able to sustain farmer-hunters of European descent, let alone nurture a tiny white middle class element in a few isolated towns north of the Orange River.

It was the discovery of diamonds around Kimberley, in the late 1860s, and gold, near Johannesburg, on the Witwatersrand, in the late 1880s that changed everything. The two events set hitherto distant northern and southern cousins, with markedly different cultural, educational, industrial and political legacies, on a collision course that proved to be as brief as it was traumatic. The primary misalignment, the unusual perceptions that it gave rise to, and the way in which these led to the disastrous Anglo-Boer War (1899–1902), arose from fateful discussions that took place between three men around campfires during a six-week safari to assess the value of gold mining properties spread through the bush of Matabeleland, between mid-August and late September 1894. Those deliberations changed the course of southern Africa's history for a hundred years and more. They also helped apply the finishing touches to an already aggrieved ethnic edge of a small, white, Afrikaner-Dutch ruling class that, in the post-bellum period, continued to perceive its members as serial victims of northern imperialist ambitions and therefore entitled to take control of their destiny, free of interference, in the construction of a racist state.

The three travellers in Matabeleland were an American, an Englishman

John Hays Hammond PHOTO: LIBRARY OF CONGRESS

Cecil Rhodes

Leander Starr Jameson

and a Scot – proudly and self-consciously 'Anglo-Saxon' and born within 18 months of one another, in San Francisco, in Bishop's Stortford and Edinburgh, in the mid-1850s. Their fathers, although of vastly different means, were professionals – a soldier-turned-surveyor and land-speculator, a vicar in the Anglican Church, and a lawyer. All had been raised at a time when revolutionary wars on both sides of the Atlantic were still within living memory, and when capitalism and imperialism were rapidly enveloping the world through rail and telegraphic networks. Their sons, perhaps predictably, were graduates of three great universities – Yale, Oxford and University College, London – the one a mining engineer, the second an arts graduate, the third a medical doctor.

Richly endowed in terms of class, education and financial well-being, the friendships of the Anglo-Saxons – who enjoyed the services of a 'Coloured' butler-valet during their extended travels through the bush – were further underwritten by membership of prestigious clubs, by Freemasonry and by a penchant for capitalist-political conspiracies, oath-taking and secret societies. And, as befitted men in a frontier-gobbling age, in which the success of the nation-state was calibrated by the formal extension of the empire by force, or through the informal conquest that came via aggressive economic expansion, all three were deeply admiring of heroes who demonstrated a propensity for action rather than talk, displayed great courage or 'pluck', and who behaved in ways that were identifiable as being simultaneously gentlemanly and masculine.

All three men, circling 40 years of age, were already spectacularly successful by the standards prevailing in an increasingly pervasive Anglophone world. The American, in awe of the Englishman, was the highest paid mining engineer in the world and never shy of mentioning the fact to anyone who inquired. The Englishman, a millionaire, owned the largest diamond mining company in the world and had ambitions to expand his holdings on the Witwatersrand with the help of the engineer. In a world where money and political power were lifelong partners he was also the Prime Minister of the Cape Colony. The Scot, much taken with the American and so close to the Englishman that one modern analyst has suggested that they might have been lovers, had given up practising medicine a few years earlier so as to provide practical assistance to the latter's dream of imperial expansion through the African continent. Only months earlier, the diminutive Scot had become an instant hero of the frontier when he had orchestrated the military defeat of Ndebele tribesmen whose erstwhile domain the party were then traversing. The Englishman, who had acquired the rights to a Chartered Company bearing the royal seal, even before the indigenous people had suffered their first defeat, had made the Scot the administrator of a territory larger than the Low Countries. It was a touring party not much given to suppressing personal or political ambition. In short, the travellers saw themselves as part of an emerging transatlantic elite destined to take 'civilisation' and enlightened rule to the lesser 'races' of the world, including the benighted Boers of southern Africa, whom nature had blessed with the richest goldfields on the planet.[1]

These latter-day musketeers, John Hays Hammond, Cecil Rhodes and Leander Starr Jameson, took it as self-evident that the future of the entire region would eventually be determined by the administration and government of the goldfields, which, rather perversely, were locked into the *Zuid-Afrikaansche Republiek* (ZAR), or South African Republic, overseen by the formidable President SJP 'Paul' Kruger with the help of a poorly educated Afrikaans-Dutch-speaking agrarian elite ill-suited to presiding over an emerging industrial economy.

The three were also *ad idem* that Kruger's rural notables could not, and probably should not, be allowed to prevail over a modernising urban dispensation which, if it was not already doing so, might unleash new and challenging class-based forces that, if ignored or neglected, might give rise to a new republic, one dominated by an insurgent white working class, which in turn might be poorly disposed to the rest of Anglophone southern Africa and perhaps to British imperial interests throughout the wider region.

The question was thus not so much as to whether or not there would be a revolution in the South African Republic – there almost certainly would be one – but *when* it would occur and *who* might best seize control of it so as to steer a new, second-generation republic into a loosely federated economic structure that would inevitably come to dominate the political future of the subcontinent. It was a daring, transatlantic political thought transposed to an African context and one capable of producing an outcome of global significance. The timing and nature of the change coming to the South African Republic could certainly be argued back and forth, but what was clearly not worth debating at length was who might be best suited to steering the process.

When the three friends stared into the campfire smoke of Matabeleland, it was Hammond, who had only recently fled the United States and who was still indirectly involved in a bitter, unresolved industrial war between mining capitalists and mineworkers in the Coeur d'Alene region of Idaho, who most readily perceived the spectre of revolution in Johannesburg. And, because he outlived his co-conspirators and the revolution failed, Hammond later denied that he had stoked the fears of his companions. In truth, he probably had thought Idaho and talked Witwatersrand.[2]

Rhodes, a Prime Minister and the man with the most to lose should the predicted revolution go wrong, was not easily convinced by Hammond's tales, since he had recently experienced other setbacks in the quest to realise his geopolitical dreams for the region. In 1891, he and Jameson had made an unsuccessful attempt to wrest the port of Beira from the Portuguese so as to provide his Chartered Company with an East Coast outlet. More recently, he had failed to persuade the Portuguese to sell him Delagoa Bay (today Maputo) so as to acquire a port and seal off the landlocked ZAR.[3] For all that, Rhodes and Jameson were sufficiently intrigued by Hammond's prognostications to agree to visit the republic and take soundings as to the likelihood of there being a revolution from below.

Exploratory visits to the South African Republic by Rhodes and Jameson, in late 1894 and again in early 1895, appeared to confirm Hammond's view about a nascent upheaval. There can be little doubt that the seed of the original idea of a full-scale revolution, one stoked and appropriated by a capitalist vanguard composed of mine owners – a notion that bore a few striking similarities to the industrial war being waged in the Coeur d'Alene – was the brainchild of Hammond. Likewise, it was Hammond, rather than Rhodes or Jameson, who, in 1895, borrowed freely from the experiences of San Francisco at the outbreak of the American Civil War, in 1861, and from the history of that city's Vigilance Committee of 1851, as he expanded, refined and sold his idea of an urban 'revolution' to the other mine owners on the Witwatersrand.

There should then be no confusion around, or elision of, the notions of 'reform' and 'revolution' in what later became incorrectly characterised as the 'Jameson Raid'. The fourth Earl Grey, a director of the Chartered Company and later an administrator of its sprawling central African domain, was intimately acquainted with Rhodes's geopolitical thinking through-out the 1890s. At the time of Rhodes's death, in 1902, both the Earl and Hammond happened to be in New York City. Questioned by a reporter, Grey was adamant. 'I do want to make it clear,' he said, 'that my friend [Rhodes] hoped by an effective coup d'état to destroy at a blow Krugerism.' In a fit of candour, Hammond added that, when it came to the 'unfortunate Jameson Raid', Rhodes 'has received far more blame than he deserves' – quite so.[4]

That noted, Hammond was always at pains to deny that it was *he* who placed the idea of an imminent revolution on the Witwatersrand on the agenda during the 1894 Matabeleland expedition. In his memoirs, he sug-gested 'it would have been presumptuous of me, who had been in Africa not quite a year, to have undertaken to give a true picture of the political conditions in Johannesburg to Rhodes and Jameson, who had been in the country for many years'.[5] It was undoubtedly true that Rhodes and Jameson probably knew more about 'the political conditions in Johannesburg', but it was also true that, of all things in the world, the one thing that Hammond never lacked was presumptuousness. Yet, somehow, between these three well-educated graduates, they *did* seriously misread the revolutionary potential of the Witwatersrand. That, in turn, raises a key question for us: what exactly were the underlying strengths and weakness of the ZAR in the 1890s? In order to appreciate fully the events that came to constitute the 'Jameson Raid', we need to explore the anatomy of the Kruger state.

★ ★ ★

The remote origins of the South African Republic lay in the Cape Colony, as a part of a response to Britain's abolition of slavery. In the late 1830s, a substantial number of discontented Boer farmers, who saw their future bound to forms of pastoral agricultural production that were reliant on cheap, if not chattel, black labour, trekked north and settled beyond the Vaal River. As men and women of Dutch, French and German origin and in possession of a rudimentary biblical education, many remained unconvinced of the advances of the Enlightenment and of urban-based market economies. A frugal lifestyle was underwritten by subsistence farming and, depending on time and place, some seasonal hunting.

On the Highveld, the trekkers founded a domain of hundreds of thousands of square miles in which the last independent African chieftaincy was conquered only on the eve of the 20th century. Small isolated and self-contained farming communities were served by the flimsiest of state structures, erected around the need for a coordinated strategy for conquest, defence and security. As late as 1895, the positions of Commandant-General, responsible for mobilising Boer commandos comprised of mounted sharpshooters, and Superintendent of Native Affairs, were combined and held by just one man, General PJ (Piet) Joubert. A broad-brush constitution proclaimed it as an explicit article of faith that there was to be no equality between blacks and whites in matters of either church or state.

An elemental, landlocked polity – embodying a conscious withdrawal from the modern world – was served by a largely archaic body of law. The legal system of the republic, which among other things determined the circumstances under which force could be legitimately used, was based largely on a codified and simplified form of Roman-Dutch law from the 17th century.[6] The state's instruments of compliance – the courts, the police and prisons system – were out of alignment with one another and badly underdeveloped, reflecting the imperfections of the constitution and an antiquated legal system. The resulting conflicts, between the State President and the legislature on the one hand, and the judiciary on the other, were reflected in the tempestuous career of Justice JG Kotzé (1849–1940). Appointed to the

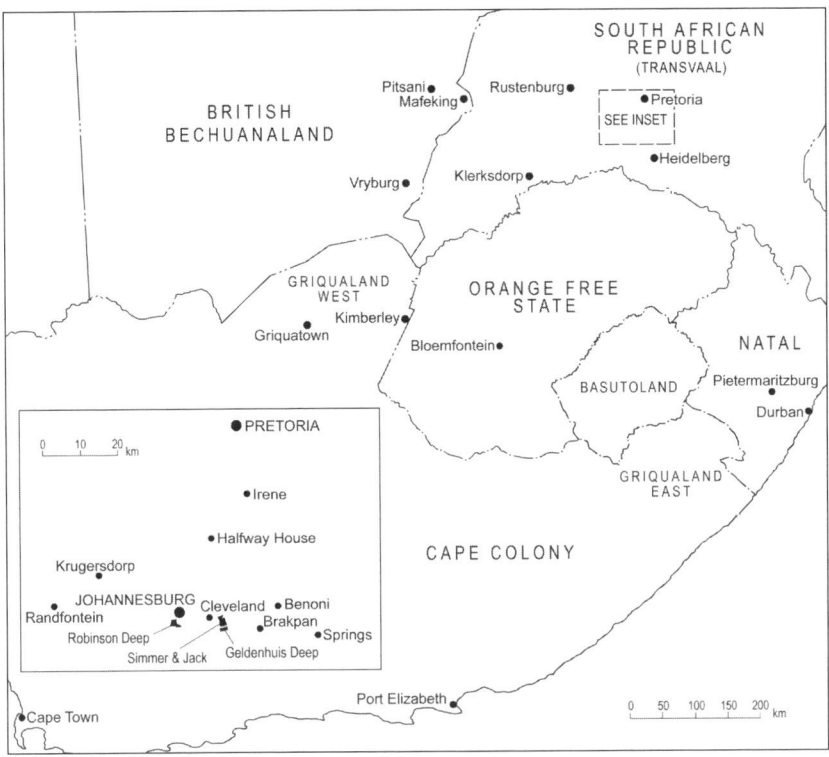

Southern Africa and the Witwatersrand, 1895

High Court in 1877, at the tender age of 26, and referred to famously as the 'boy judge' by Anthony Trollope, John Gilbert Kotzé, trained at the Inns of Court in London, and went on to become the Chief Justice just four years later. Thereafter he was often at odds with Kruger, whose respect for judicial independence could be arbitrary when it was not conditional. In 1893, the ambitious but principled young Kotzé opposed Kruger in the presidential election without resigning from office and, in 1897, was dismissed as Chief Justice when he insisted that the courts had the right to test the legality of laws, including mining law, against the constitution.[7]

In much the same way and for many of the same reasons, it was the executive position of State Attorney – equivalent in status to a modern Minister of Justice – that proved most difficult for the State President to fill satisfactorily. After the discovery of gold, younger, better-educated, legal practitioners who had trained abroad proved difficult to align with the demands of constituents locked into an older agricultural economy.

Military conquest, the main if not the sole muscle of an aspirant state that lacked a standing army even after the Jameson Raid, also helped shape the structure and efficiency of the early police and prison administrations. Accustomed largely to dealing with rural crime in country districts, the inadequately trained police force had a notably 'flat' organisational structure characterised by few ranks and limited professional specialisation. Neither the police nor the prison service had the experience, or the need, to cope with criminals drawn from urban, industrial dispensations. In 1891, the Governor of the Pretoria prison and almost his entire staff were dismissed on grounds of corruption, and in 1894 the Commissioner of Police wrote an open letter to the press in which he 'acknowledged the *rottenness* of the entire police force, but decline[d] to accept the disgrace attached thereto having striven to reorganise the same, but failed through lack of support'.[8]

For a decade after the first 'War of Independence', in 1881, deficiencies in the law-enforcement agencies of a state rooted in the soil left small towns in the ZAR vulnerable to assault from both bandits and gangs devoted to organised crime. In early 1887, the 'Irish Brigade' – a group of roving bandits composed of deserters from the British garrison in Natal – produced a week of frontier mayhem when it occupied Eureka City, a short-lived mining hamlet on the outskirts of Barberton. The invasion precipitated a reorganisation of the local police force, but only months later, in 1888, the same bandits, turned urban gangsters, took over Johannesburg for a murderous weekend that forced the emergence of a dedicated 'detective department' on the Rand. Then, late in 1891, the core of the self-same old Irish Brigade caused the Kruger government to mobilise the small, and until then largely ceremonial, State Artillery, to prevent an attempt at a mass prison breakout and to suppress an organised 'mutiny' in the Pretoria prison.[9] These examples of the weakness of the state were not lost on those members of the 'Reform Committee' who later participated in the planned urban insurrection in Johannesburg meant to trigger Jameson's incursion.[10]

If the legal framework of the republic dated back to the Cape in the 17th century, then its ramshackle prisons were better suited to dealing with indigenous African cattle thieves than European immigrants intent on accelerating a gathering industrial revolution. The penal system was, if not lingeringly medieval, then decidedly pre-modern. An unstated assumption that there was a primary connection between crime and skin colour meant that the use of crudely constructed cells, hard physical labour, shackles, leg irons, stocks, public whippings and hangings all proved to be significantly longer-lived in the South African Republic than in the surrounding British colonies or in far-off Europe.[11]

An unwillingness to abandon outmoded forms of punishment, directed originally and principally at rural African offenders, gave rise to additional ideological and political problems when these were extended to urban white criminals after the proclamation of the Witwatersrand goldfields in

1886. The use of stocks, abandoned in England in 1872, remained in use for black and white prisoners alike in the ZAR in the mid-1890s. Flogging, which had fallen into disfavour in the Royal Navy in the mid-19th century and which was officially suspended in 1881, was, controversially, extended to include white offenders in the ZAR in 1892. The last public hanging in England was that of the Fenian, Michael Barratt, in 1868, and it was only the prospect of yet another open-air execution, that of a pair of Irish highwaymen in Pretoria, in 1891, that persuaded President Kruger, amid an appeal for a reprieve, to abandon public hangings.[12]

Yet, despite these signs of sluggish social development there was nothing in the Protestantism of the Afrikaner-Dutch political elite that militated against the accumulation of wealth by individuals or excluded the possibility of the collective development of markets for agricultural products. The trekboers may have left behind the commercial markets of the Cape when slavery was abolished in 1834 but, as they were soon to discover, the market had never fully left them. The discoveries of diamonds and gold reminded the Boer elite about the profit that more proximate markets might hold for those intent on pursuing progressive forms of commercial agriculture and developing an independent state underpinned by a modern transport infrastructure. Indeed, it was the first mineral discoveries that prompted an attempt – doomed to failure for want of capital – to construct a railway link between the isolated, landlocked republic and nearby Portuguese Delagoa Bay.

The Boer elite's idea of developing a state underwritten by a dominant agricultural economy that helped feed a secondary industrial base, whose urban centres provided a commercial outlet for the produce of its constituents, thus went back to the 1870s, and *pre-dated* the discovery of the largest gold reserves in the world on the Witwatersrand. This rural-urban model of economic development was not without precedent or success in the northern hemisphere, and it was firmly embraced by Afrikaner notables as the diamond industry grew through the 1870s.

The notion of driving a privileged agricultural sector while simultaneously developing a more rounded economy received a fillip in the mid-1870s and early 1880s with the arrival in the South African Republic of two notable East European Jewish entrepreneurs. AH Nellmapius, an Austro-Hungarian, and Samuel Marks, a Lithuanian, were both familiar with the policy of concession-granting in Tsarist Russia, where first-time producers were provided with monopolistic access to markets until such time as a more diversified economy took root in a state dominated overwhelmingly by small-scale agricultural producers.

In 1881, immediately after the first War of Independence and before the discovery of substantial gold deposits at Barberton, Nellmapius convinced

President Kruger of the desirability of granting him a concession for a distillery. 'The First Factory' – *Het Eerste Fabrieken* – would have the exclusive right to manufacture spirits from fruit and grain, provided by Boer producers, for a modest local market. The idea of granting concessions in order to privilege a politically dominant agricultural sector over a secondary industrial development that spawned its own urban markets became a central, if controversial, tenet of economic policy in the South African Republic.

But the logic and thinking behind this controversial paradigm imploded barely five years later. The discovery of gold on the Witwatersrand, in 1886, meant that, within months, the mining industry became not only the principal contributor to the economy of the ZAR, easily surpassing the still nascent agricultural sector, but also a major competitor for, and employer of, cheap black labour. Concessions, intended to further progress in agriculture, now became extended to goods or services that directly or indirectly affected the prospects of the mining industry and stymied the interplay of international market forces.

The damage caused by the mineral explosion, however, went beyond commercial agriculture; it threatened to shatter the political foundations of the Boer state. Prior to 1886 and the rise of immigrant-dominated Johannesburg, the semi-feudal ZAR was characterised by an extraordinary congruence between its small-scale economic and political machinery. Pretoria was, simultaneously, the centre of political *and* economic power. After the discovery of gold on the Witwatersrand, however, power was split into its constituent elements, with political and judicial power continuing to reside almost exclusively in Pretoria, and economic power shifting steadily towards industrialising Johannesburg.

Thus, after 1886 there was a potentially fatal disjuncture in the state between land-hungry, vernacular-speaking, Afrikaner-Dutch nationalists drawn from farming backgrounds and entrenched in Pretoria, and more middle-class, cosmopolitan, English-speaking, quasi-liberal elements, devoted to commerce and industry based in Johannesburg and the adjacent satellite towns. Lacking the carefully constructed circuit board necessary for the functioning of a balanced political economy, one capable of producing integrated as well as sustained growth, the state was characterised by disparities, as embodied in the politics of Pretoria and economics of Johannesburg. Given imperfect connections in the wiring system linking political to economic power, and the strong charges emanating from the positive and negative terminals, there was constant short-circuiting and the danger of an even bigger explosion.

In the South African Republic, as in most systems characterised by disparities in power and wealth, the classic short-circuiting mechanism was corruption. In developed economies, where wealth is relatively well-entrenched within certain sectors, such as in the United States, money is often used to acquire high political office. In underdeveloped or persistently weak economies, where money is harder to come by, as in parts of Africa, it is high office and the selling of favours that is most often used to acquire wealth. But after 1886 the emerging mine owners of the early Witwatersrand, the so-called Randlords – an aspirant industrial aristocracy in a republic lacking an indigenous nobility – never desired political office for themselves. What they *did* hanker after, however, was extensive political influence over a more compliant and dependent urban-based electorate that might offer them the long-term safeguards necessary to protect their new-found sources of wealth.

The acquisition of the franchise by recent immigrants, who threatened to become numerically preponderant in the republic, and whom the Boers viewed as *Uitlanders* (outsiders) – mere foreign interlopers and opportunists working in an industry that mined a non-renewable source – became a major bone of contention between Pretoria and Johannesburg. In essence, the irresistible force of a rising industrial elite found itself pitted against an immovable object in the shape of an entrenched agricultural ruling class. The undistributed middle that might resolve this impasse lay on the Witwatersrand. Lacking the political clout to effect the economic outcomes they desired, the mining companies and mine owners became vectors of corruption in a state that they never ceased to characterise as being as backward and obstructive as it was antiquated and venal.

The corrupting and manipulative influence of mining money, along with that of concession-hunting speculators, as expressed through bribes, 'gifts' and/or insidious personal loans at favourable rates, was easily detectable. Members of the legislature who would not accept cash incentives for voting in favour of concessions that were no longer bound to further agricultural interests alone but to goods or services destined to help shape the financial well-being of the emerging mining industry – became the recipients of 'presents', a practice that not even the State President found problematic.[13] Leading newspaper proprietors in Pretoria and Johannesburg were bought, or, as they preferred to see it, were 'subsidised', so as to further the political and economic interests of both the government and the frequently oppositional mining industry.[14]

Even leading members of the judiciary, already out of step with the more archaic and intransigent forms of nationalism advocated by Kruger and members of his cabinet, were not immune to indirect influence exercised by the agents of the mining industry through bonds and loans. By March 1894, Lionel Phillips, acting on behalf of H Eckstein & Co, the Rand-based face of the huge finance house of Wernher, Beit & Co, held a bond worth £2 500 on the home of Judge de Korte. In addition to that, the judge had been the beneficiary of other cash grants to the value of at least £500. When de Korte, in a moment of panic issued a further, unauthorised draft of £500 against Eckstein's, Phillips, sensing that the judge's financial predicament might lead to trouble, sent for him and 'asked how he dared draw on us knowing that he had no possible right to. It is useless to describe the painful scene that ensued, suffice it to say that he declared that he did it in a moment of despair and wept in the office.'[15]

De Korte reminded his benefactor that 'when Hermann Eckstein died he did us a favour which could never be repaid', but Phillips, who insisted that the judge had never been suborned, felt that it was probably better 'not to have him in our books'. The only question unanswered was why the company had allowed the judge to get into its debt in the first place.

De Korte's was not the only case worthy of explanation. When the Chief Justice JG Kotzé was dismissed by Kruger, in 1898, he was left owing a debt of several thousand pounds to the mining house by way of loans. So desperate was the former judge's financial situation that, in 1899, in his comeback appearance as an advocate in the same High Court over which he had once presided, Kotzé had to defend Joseph Silver, the Polish-American mastermind behind commercial vice on the Witwatersrand.[16]

The Kruger government, weak from its inception, thus found that while the emerging gold mines were at the heart of a gradual turnaround in its economic fortunes, financial progress came at the cost of living with agents from finance houses who, while complaining publicly about corruption, in private leeched some of the major organs of state of their credibility, efficiency and legitimacy at precisely the historical moment that they were, arguably, in the greatest need of being strengthened.

It was not as if the state lacked ongoing problems, many of which were of its own making. Priding itself on a commando system that allowed for the swift mobilisation of burghers known for their horsemanship and ability as sharpshooters, the government remained largely indifferent to the potential threat posed to it by thousands of unenfranchised immigrant white workers on the Witwatersrand. Some Boers, with one eye on the emerging markets, were, however, no longer as keen as they had once been to abandon their farms for national service. In 1894, amid great controversy, the government had to draft Uitlanders – called upon to provide their own wherewithal – for a military campaign against the unruly Chief 'Malaboch' in the remote northeastern part of the country.[17]

Kruger, always content with the services of a small contingent of State Artillery only, was unwilling to establish a standing army that would be overseen by his consistent political rival for the position of President, Commandant-General Piet Joubert. A degree of smugness became apparent in government. In June 1893, barely 12 months before the outlines of a coup were being sketched by certain of the mine owners in Johannesburg, the State President's scandal-prone Minister of Mines, CJ Joubert, boasted to members of the Volksraad (parliament) that 'he had ruled the Gold Fields for six years without revolution' and that that 'was something extraordinary in the world of Gold Fields'.[18]

Behind the scenes, however, there was less room for complacency. Out in the countryside some of the magazine masters responsible for issuing arms and ammunition to the commandos were corrupt, inefficient or both. The Commandant-General complained that some of the Martini-Henry rifles issued to Boers during campaigns against African chiefs in the 1890s had found their way into the hands of the natives. More pertinently, it was claimed that, in Pretoria itself, the country's main arsenal and the artillery camp that guarded it were poorly administered.[19]

In economic terms, however, the government's greatest bugbear remained a concessions policy conceived before the mining era. Extended uncritically into an industrial sector that it was never designed for, concessions for the manufacture of dynamite and running of the railways were said to press heavily on the cost structures of the Rand's deep-level mines, which required the use of cheap explosives and imported machinery to offset the disadvantage of their low-grade ores.[20] These problems were exacerbated by a pronounced recession in the mining industry in 1889–1892, occasioned by difficulties in working gold-bearing rock drawn from deeper and still less tractable veins. Nor did it help that a government reluctant to imperil the fortunes of long-distance Boer transport riders utilising ox-drawn wagons was in no great hurry to see the arrival on the Rand of railways from British coastal colonies.[21]

The 1889–1892 slump exacerbated pre-existing problems and limited the ability of the government to raise loans at competitive rates of interest. To some Afrikaner patriots, and a fair number of the new mine owners, the State President appeared to have surrounded himself with 'foreign' advisers and experts who were not fully accountable to the legislature. A set of intensely disliked Dutch officials – 'Kruger's Hollanders' – presided over a civil service that was frequently corrupt and inefficient. A group of shady entrepreneurs, the so-called Third Volksraad, led by the Cape-born Irish nationalist, Solomon Gillingham, but often collectively dismissed as 'Jews' because of the influence wielded by Marks and Nellmapius, was instrumental in obtaining questionable concessions, such as that for the manufacture of jam.[22] Weak administrative structures and the uncertain future of the mining industry meant that, whereas a British colony such as Natal could raise loans for development at 3.5 per cent in the early 1890s, the Kruger government was called upon to pay interest at rates of between 4 and 5 per cent for the development of an independent rail network.[23]

These obstacles contributed to the cost of importing food and clothing on the Witwatersrand.[24] Complaints by the white working class about
the high cost of living complemented those coming from mine owners
struggling to contain the huge expenditure necessary to develop deep-level
mines that were slower to deliver dividends than the short-lived, open-cast
diggings of the late 1880s. Predictably, these underlying economic forces
translated themselves into organised political pressure.

In 1891, the Kruger government established a second chamber of the
legislature designed to accommodate the aspirations and grievances of
an unenfranchised immigrant community saddled with difficulties compounded by the depressed state of the economy. But the Second Volksraad,
and more especially so before 1893, was a largely toothless body. It had no
budget, could not authorise expenditure, and its resolutions could be vetoed
in the First Volksraad, which was dominated by an Executive Council in the
thrall of the State President.[25]

Prisoners of their seemingly indivisible Afrikaner-Dutch and Protestant
identities, and shocked by what was emerging among English-speaking
whites in *Duiwelsdorp* – Satan's City – members of the powerful First
Volksraad nevertheless continued to tilt at windmills all along the length of
the Witwatersrand. Efforts to protect the Dutch language by way of some
compulsory instruction in state schools was perceived to be an act of cultural hostility by those who had brought their businesses to southern Africa
but left their hearts in England.[26] Law No 2 of 1889, passed at a time when
old-style prizefighting was making the transition to more 'scientific' boxing
governed by the Marquess of Queensberry's rules, prohibited all contests for
financial reward, thereby contributing to the emergence of an underworld
culture. All betting and horse racing on Sundays was outlawed in 1891, and
by early 1893 the police were staging regular raids on 'gambling hells' all
around Johannesburg's Market Square. Such laws did nothing to win over
members of the white working class or soften the attitude of middle-class
critics.[27]

But white miners, uncertain about the long-term future of the
Witwatersrand goldfields and therefore not unduly concerned about acquiring the vote, sensed that their primary struggle was economic, rather than
political or cultural. They focused their organisational efforts on counter-
acting the emerging centrality of the stock exchange, born in 1887, and the
Chamber of Mines, established in 1891. Once the recession began to lift and
the future of the deep levels looked a little more assured, in late 1892, white
mineworkers responded by founding the Witwatersrand Mine Employees
and Mechanics' Union.[28]

The formation of a miners' union, as part of an undistributed middle with the potential for determining where the longer-term balance of

political power between Pretoria and Johannesburg might lie, alarmed a few commercial and professional elements with imperialist sympathies on the Witwatersrand even if, at first, the mine owners were less concerned. In order to counter the influence of the newly formed trade union, Charles and JW Leonard, advocates and brothers who relied heavily on the Chamber of Mines for most of their fees, responded almost at once by launching the National Union, which agitated for the enfranchisement of the Uitlanders.

The Kruger government, aware of what was at stake, welcomed the development of a working-class foil to the emerging economic muscle of the mine owners and any rumblings coming from the still relatively weak National Union. The high point in cooperation between the government and the new miners' union came in the opening weeks of 1893, when the leaders of the trade union persuaded Volksraad members not to pass a gold thefts bill, sponsored by the Chamber of Mines, that would make severe inroads into the personal liberties of many white workers.[29]

In retrospect, then, it can be seen that the South African Republic experienced what was perhaps its moment of greatest political, economic and social turbulence *before* 1895, during the depression of 1889–1892. During the earliest months of the downturn the last independent, small-scale diggers were turned into craftsmen or miners when they sold their holdings to emerging mining companies with the capital to sit out the gold-recovery crisis and wait on the dividends coming from the deep levels. But the full extent of the social transformation of the industry only became clear in the organisational changes of the latter half of 1892 and first quarter of 1893. If the rural elite that constituted Kruger's government ever was to be subjected to a successful working-class challenge by disillusioned elements drawn from an urban, industrialising milieu, this was more likely to have occurred in 1890–1892 than in 1894–1895, the period identified by mine-owning conspirators.[30] The former period held the seeds of a few street-based disturbances built around populist resentment at the marginalisation of the 'small man' and workers by the banks, building societies and mining companies. The latter period, by contrast, was rooted largely – although not exclusively – in an economic upswing, leaving the agents of the mine owners to plot a top-down 'revolution' with little spontaneous working-class support. The Matabeleland campfire conspirators had missed a boat that may have sailed three years earlier.

The mis-assessment of Johannesburg's revolutionary potential after 1894 could, in part, be traced back to the continued weakness of the police and the state's inability to enforce the law. Benefiting from the completion of a national railway grid and an upturn in the economy, 1894–1895 and most of 1896 witnessed a spurt in the internationalisation of organised crime on the Rand. Criminal syndicates devoted to gold theft, the illicit sale of alcohol and brothel-based prostitution all grew as Irish, east European and American gangsters systematically corrupted members of the police and staff in the office of the public prosecutor.[31]

An unsatisfactory situation was made worse when several white workers were murdered between December 1894 and January 1895. The mine owners' agents, sensing what they thought might well be an upwelling in public disgust – and as we shall see in due course – seized the moment and tested the mood of citizens by establishing a short-lived 'Vigilance Committee'.[32]

But the ongoing weakness of the police force in Johannesburg, where a mushrooming immigrant population and a rapidly developing underworld posed problems that would have challenged most states, was a bit of an anomaly. After a pronounced crisis, in 1890–1892, even the prisons administration, working from an abysmally low base, improved slowly after yet another bribery and corruption scandal, in Pretoria, in 1894.[33]

More important by far, however, was the manner in which, after the depression of 1889–1892, the Kruger state, while steadfastly eschewing the establishment of a standing army, went about systematically developing muscle that might help militate against an armed invasion by British forces, or an urban insurrection by empire loyalists. This subtle, largely unseen, shift in the government's defence policy – from one designed to cope exclusively with challenges posed by independent African chiefdoms in the countryside to one better adapted to dealing with a potential urban enemy within – was effected largely in 1894–1895.

By the time of the retrocession, in 1881, the Kruger state or the British had subdued most independent African chieftaincies, including those of the Pedi and Tswana, where environmental factors limited the capacity to produce food surpluses and maintain strong standing armies. The better-watered, more remote and malaria-infested northeastern parts of the republic, however, provided the indigenous peoples with better opportunities as well as more resources for resistance. By the mid-1890s, however, with the notable exception of Makhado's VhaVenda (who eventually succumbed in 1898), Boer forces had defeated Mojaji (1890–1894), Malaboch's Hanwana (1893–1894) and Makgoba (1895).

Progressively relieved of the need to face African resistance in the countryside, the Kruger government used the economic upturn of 1893–1895 to refine and revise its defence and foreign policies in ways that would render it less vulnerable to urban insurrection or surprise attacks. The tipping point in this transition from rural to urban-based defence and security policies may have come in May 1894, when the conscription of unenfranchised Uitlanders for the campaign against Malaboch occasioned significant resentment among immigrants along the Witwatersrand. After the High Commissioner, Sir Henry Loch, went to Pretoria to ease tensions British demonstrators chanted 'God Save the Queen' and 'Rule Britannia' at the State President, 'unharnessed the horses for Kruger's coach and dragged the coach from the railway station to the hotel'.[34] If the nominal head of state security was compromised in the heart of the republic's political capital, how vulnerable would he be when visiting Johannesburg, the industrial capital, a place with a prior history of humiliating the State President?

It was after this incident and a discussion between Loch and Lionel Phillips, the man who would later join the Matabeleland three to become one of the principal conspirators on the Rand, that petitions from the National Union to acquire the franchise began to be supplemented by bellicose exchanges about the need for Uitlanders to arm themselves.[35]

By autumn 1894, possibly even before the MaJaboch conscription got properly under way, and certainly by the time that the call-up began to cause consternation that May, the Kruger government had paid informers working for it.[36] In spring, mutterings in Johannesburg bars and saloons began to blossom and there was more open talk about the need for men to acquire rifles in order to protect themselves against any further, possibly unreasonable, demands coming from the Boer state. By then the government had already established the first of a few permanent secret service agents – termed 'detectives' for administrative purposes – who were eventually to be paid from a specially created fund that deeply upset the organisers of the National Union.[37]

The presence of new agents soon became known to radical English-speakers with republican sympathies who were becoming willing to act as spies for the Kruger government. In August 1894, the Scottish trade unionist JT Bain – for a moment unemployed and in political limbo – wrote to the Edinburgh-educated State Attorney, Ewald Esselen, seeking an appointment as a 'detective'.[38] Fully a year before the planned insurrection, the Kruger state was laying the foundations of an intelligence service that took on a more dedicated form still in 1895.[39]

But it did not require a Sidney Reilly to keep the Kruger government broadly informed about military preparations north of the border and revolutionary talk along the Rand. The Jameson Raid was one of the worst-kept secrets in military history. As early as March 1895, the *Pretoria News* noted that Rhodes's British South Africa Company was investing heavily in everything from Maxim machine guns – which Jameson saw as all-conquering – to uniforms for a new 'expeditionary force'. [40] South of the border, Hammond, responsible for gathering intelligence for the conspirators, later complained that 'No white community can be safely trusted with a military secret, but untutored black savages will keep one in a silence as of the grave.'[41] And, on 22 December 1895, seven days before the raid, a 'Scottish Uitlander' – possibly JT Bain – wrote to Commandant-General Joubert informing him, almost to the day, when the incursion would occur, where it would set out from, and who the principal instigators were.[42]

Kruger famously observed that, if one wished to kill a tortoise, you had to wait for it to stick out its head before striking. Despite the gossip, consistent rumours and a tiny stream of intelligence, the government, struggling with intra-elite conflicts of its own, was in no hurry to act.[43] It did, however, plan on strengthening its urban defences by making provision for the erection of two forts, one in Johannesburg and the other in Pretoria. Predictably, the announcement of this intention caused anger among some conspirators and more especially those closely involved with the National Union.[44] While plotting to overthrow the government, the Jameson Raid conspirators – not unlike the boy who murdered his parents and then placed himself at the mercy of the court on the grounds that he was an orphan – were greatly outraged when the state sought to defend itself.

The cost of erecting the forts, estimated to be in excess of £250 000, not only reflected the shift in focus of the government's defence policy – from rural-black to urban-white – but also how rapidly the state had gathered in economic strength after the 1889–1892 depression. Extensions to the rail network that placed the Rand within easier reach of coastal ports, and the development of the new, deeper-level mines, both contributed to the improving situation. Small deficits in 1891 and 1892 gave way, in 1893, to a surplus of about £500 000, and by 1894–1895 the surplus was close on £1 million a year.[45]

The republic's growing financial well-being reflected a steady increase in taxable revenue derived from accelerated immigration, growing urban markets for rural producers and a steadily diversifying economy. Indeed, the sustained upswing that culminated in the 'Kaffir Boom' of 1895 began to call into question the foundational economic beliefs of the state, namely, the primacy of an agricultural sector that relied on concessions at the expense of a more open, if not a totally free, market as the principal driver of the republic's long-term development. The impetus of industrial capitalism on the Witwatersrand and the need for market forces to be allowed freer play became ever more apparent to the Volksraad but perhaps not to its founding father. In May 1894, the State President strongly supported the granting of a concession for the manufacture of jam to Solomon Gillingham, leader of the shadowy, unofficial 'Third Volksraad'. But his advocacy merely brought to a head the gathering opposition to the idea of concessions. In August, members of the Second Volksraad, representing the interests of the Uitlanders, decided 'by 14 votes to 9 to reject all concessions'. The real hammer blow, however, fell that same September when even members of the all-powerful First Volksraad – including, no doubt, some fruit producers – voted down the granting of the jam concession.[46]

After that, the concessions policy died a lingering death. The growing disfavour with which it was viewed, however, reflected two related, developing trends: a growing appreciation of the free market by Boer legislators and producers who were less and less averse to accumulating capital; and the gradual erosion of the gerontocratic, patriarchal, near-feudal dominance and style exercised by President Kruger and his cohort over the various branches of the legislature.

The first signs of mounting burgher discontent with Kruger's policies dated back to the recession and, predictably, came from the younger, university-educated legal scholars – all constitutionalists, democrats and patriots. In 1890, Ewald Esselen, a leading figure in the South African students' association at Edinburgh University in the early 1880s and later, briefly, counsellor and secretary to Kruger, resigned his position as a High Court judge and returned to private practice to devote himself more fully to oppositional politics.[47] Among his initiatives was helping to found 'Young South Africa', a nationalist ginger group almost certainly inspired by its 19th-century predecessor, 'Young Ireland', and of a piece with the 'Young Turks' that came to jolt the Ottoman order in 1908.[48]

Unlike Esselen, JG Kotzé, the 'boy judge', did not resign from his official position as Chief Justice but nevertheless opposed Kruger's policies when he stood against him in the election for State President in 1893. It is probably also significant that both Esselen and Kotzé based themselves in the Potchefstroom constituency, a prosperous farming district enjoying easy access to the markets of the Witwatersrand and which boasted a small local newspaper strongly opposed to Kruger.[49]

The effect of market-induced vagaries during the recession was not, however, confined to one or two critical Afrikaner-Dutch intellectuals or members of the judiciary; it went well beyond that, into the realm of popular political perceptions. The old, grey-bearded members of the First Volksraad, while not wanting to be seen as disloyal to their President, were nevertheless aware of Johannesburg's shrinking during the economic contraction of the mines, of a rise in ill-feeling among Boers and Uitlanders and of an increase in crime in adjacent rural areas as the usual suspects fled the towns and made their way to Kimberley.[50]

Kruger, as ever reading the times, was not slow to respond. In 1890, he had led the drive to establish the Second Volksraad, not only to hear and deflect Uitlander aspirations and grievances more effectively, but to help contain mutterings within the ranks of his own supporters. But the underlying discontent would not go away and, in July 1891, many Boer notables were among the 60 persons present when a new organisation, the Unie van de Zuid Afrikaansche Republiek, was founded, in Pretoria, with the President's blessing. The object of the short-lived union was 'to foster co-operation between white residents of all nationalities established in our

Republic, with full respect for the laws of the land and determination to uphold the independence of the State'.[51]

The need for such an organisation had probably never been more pressing. Despite the emergence of a second chamber, the recession had triggered two rounds of the most pronounced short-circuiting yet seen between political power and wealth. First, in 1890, a concession awarded to Barend Vorster, a member of the First Volksraad, for a line of rail supposedly linking Komatipoort to gold discoveries at Leydsdorp led to bribery, corruption and market manipulation on a truly spectacular scale. By 1899, barely 70 miles of the notorious Selati railway had been laid.[52]

The roots of the second round, the 'stands scandal', lay in Satan City. In early 1889, the state auctioned off a block of potentially valuable land in the Hospital Hill area of Johannesburg but, given the times, not all the property was sold, leaving unsold a sizeable remnant that fell under the administration of the Minister of Mines, CJ Joubert. In 1892, as the economy started to turn, Joubert – heavily in debt to the mine owners Lewis & Marks, JB Robinson and H Eckstein & Co – agreed that the unsold property be divided up and the lots sold through private sale rather than by public auction. With Kruger's nationalists firmly in control of the legislature and unlikely to be dislodged at the polls, members of the Executive Council – effectively the cabinet – the First, Second and sinister 'Third Volksraad' all played a part in the looting that followed and that eventually became the subject of a commission of inquiry.[53]

But, as the 'stands scandal' partly illustrated, in politics, as in life, actions can have unintended consequences. Conceived of during the depression largely as a talking shop, it was Esselen and his supporters in the Second Volksraad that proved most vocal about a scandal that also fed into an election year. And as the economic tide rose during 1893–1895, so did the fortunes of Kruger's opponents, who grew in both number and quality not only in the Second Volksraad but in the old First as well.[54]

Indeed, by 1895, the state's legislative chambers were characterised by a virtual dual-party system, with increasingly beleaguered hard-line Kruger loyalists being vigorously opposed by modernising 'Progressives'. The Matabeleland conspirators and some Rand mine owners might rail to the outside world about the conservative old State President, but in private and in public even the National Union jingoes had to concede that the system of government was changing. Pretoria held power and Johannesburg the purse strings, but the opening-up of useful informal conduits meant that a few members of the Volksraad were amenable to representations from the industrial heartland and the administration was more supple than it had been. The first shoots of a more responsive white, male democracy of sorts were beginning to take root among even some burgher constituencies.

These young shoots meant that, by 1895, both the granting of concessions and much of the type of corruption orchestrated through the 'Third
Volksraad' had seen its heyday. There were signs that some in the Kruger
administration, previously locked into the Old Testament, were gradually
coming to terms with not only the trade union representatives of the dominant industry but also some of the more alien and exotic manifestations
of immigrant, white, Victorian working-class culture on the Witwatersrand.

Laws limiting or outlawing betting on horses, gambling or prizefighting
were never rescinded, but the return of the good times saw the state take
a more pragmatic view of working-class pastimes, which, between 1893
and 1895, remained largely free from the predations of professional criminal
syndicates. The result was that, after 1893, the state in effect tolerated boxing
matches – supposedly not for gain – that were governed by the Marquess
of Queensberry Rules rather than the old and outdated London prize fight
rules. Some of the same sort of tolerance was extended to bookmakers
when, in 1893, many of the mining towns in the republic fell prey to a so-
called sweepstake mania.[55]

It was not as if these were the only examples of 'common sense' ever to
break out among the agencies of the Kruger administration. As far back
as 1890, when Kruger fell foul of demonstrators during an early visit to
Johannesburg, the local chief of police had been smart enough to withdraw
all the Boer members of his force so that the mob, to its surprise, was 'held
back largely by Colonial, English and Irish "bobbies"'.[56]

Looking back, then, it can be seen that the Kruger government's pre-
Witwatersrand economic policies were poorly adapted to cope with the
recession of 1889–1892 and contributed to the anger, alienation and frustration of mine owners and the emerging white working class alike. By 1893,
however, and most certainly by 1894–1895, over a matter of months the
situation on the Rand goldfields had undergone a profound change that
mining capitalists and thousands of white miners alike were beginning to
benefit from significantly in economic, political and even social terms. The
marked downturn in the economy in the early 1890s, followed by a steep
upturn in 1893–1894, which reached its high point in 1895, had not only
heightened the rapidly developing market awareness of the Afrikaner-Dutch
citizenry and a Boer elite elected into office by burghers who enjoyed a voting monopoly, but had also given rise to a new and evolving openness and
suppleness when it came to policies of reform.

It was as if a Boer republic founded on agriculture and long trapped in
a post-slavery dream state had woken suddenly to discover that its British
imperial enemies had not disappeared but that it was now surrounded by
urban markets that offered ready outlets for its surplus production. The
Transvaal Boers had not gone to market, the market had come to them, and

they were not slow in realising the opportunities that it offered. As Calvinist republicans rooted to the soil and in danger of being swamped by industry, they needed inspiration for the tasks that lay ahead from other Protestants, farmers who had once rejected British rule and had had to adapt to an enclosing industrial and manufacturing world. But there, too, as in the case of the market, they did not need to go out and find the Americans. By the time the republic awoke, in 1893–1894, the Americans were already among them in considerable numbers, and among them was John Hays Hammond.

CHAPTER TWO

American Sway and Acquisitive Ways

Capitalist Culture and the Foundations of the Witwatersrand

C 1890–1899

Historians have, for a century or more, been persistently one-eyed in the way that they have presented and analysed the causes of the 'Jameson Raid'. If not most, then many have chosen to view the 'Raid' through Anglo-centric spectacles only, perceiving it to be of overwhelming interest to those concerned with British expansionism and the coming of the Anglo-Boer War three years later. It is an understandable but limiting approach, offering but a partial explanation. It is an approach that has taken in generations of British and South African students whose worlds revolve around a Westminster-Whitehall axis more than they do the Witwatersrand, let alone the United States of America.

Interestingly, it is an illusion that was also passed on successfully to some historians of Afrikaner nationalism who, for their own reasons, have seldom looked beyond Perfidious Albion – in the shape of Joseph Chamberlain or that arch-imperialist villain, Cecil Rhodes – in their search for causes that contributed to the suffering and recovery of their people. For the most part, there has also been a strange lack of interest in the 'Raid' on the part of historians interested in American expansionism.[1]

What is perhaps most puzzling about all this unintentional misdirection or silence by historians is the fact that two of the three principal conspirators in the failed coup did not mince words when it came to suggesting a second – parallel – axis around which to analyse the 'Raid' and broaden our understanding of the complex causes behind the failed insurrection. One of them was John Hays Hammond himself. In 1911, speaking at a banquet in London marking the coronation of King George V, Hammond, growing more confident as the Raid slipped into history, abandoned his usual caution and stated openly that, when it came to events leading up to the Raid and the failed insurrection, 'the chief agitators were Americans'.[2] Nor was Hammond the only one of the main conspirators to hold that view. In 1902, Rhodes confided to his friend, WT Stead, that Americans were in the vanguard of a potentially revolutionary movement, and that if he had failed to act he would have lost control of events that might culminate in a new republic poorly disposed to the British Empire.[3]

As has been famously argued, the 'lost causes' of the Jameson Raid may indeed have lain, in part, with the owners of the new deep-level mines on the Witwatersrand. But we will be remiss if we do not take seriously the views of the chief conspirators who, between them, did most to finance, plan and take care of the logistics for the proposed uprising on the Rand in 1895. How exactly had Americans managed to insert themselves into the political vanguard of the Kruger republic?

★ ★ ★

The history of secular – as opposed to religious – thinking in the evolution of Afrikaner nationalist ideology and, more especially, in regard to the influence of the American struggle for independence from British rule has yet to be fully sketched. It would be surprising, however, if the American War of Independence (1775–1783), the publication of Thomas Paine's *Common Sense* (1776) or the adoption of the American Constitution (1788) all passed without comment or notice in 18th-century Dutch circles at the Cape of Good Hope. After all, long before one Atlantic-facing city became New York, in 1664, it was New Amsterdam.

It is unlikely that those Boers who abandoned Britain's Cape Colony in the late 1830s bore no knowledge of the American fight for freedom, including the right to own slaves, as they trekked into the southern African interior in their search for an escape from a world closing in on them.[4] Indeed, it has been suggested that the infamous clause in the South African Republic's founding document, which stipulated that there was to be no equality in matters of church or state between blacks and whites, had been inspired by the constitutions of states in the American Deep South. Moreover, it is claimed that even before the trekkers set off for the north some unknown Boer leaders stated that 'We desire to establish our new settlement on the same principles of liberty as those adopted by the United States of America' but 'under our burgher law'.[5]

The young man who did eventually get to draft the constitution of the Zuid-Afrikaansche Republiek, MW Pretorius, would perhaps have had even more reason for giving thought to the founding of the United States when he became the first president of the country, in 1857. When Pretorius settled on a site for a new town, in 1855, he named it Pretoria-Philadelphia, which not only honoured his father and uncles, but also resonated with the American struggle for independence. What is clear is that, in 1877, Paul Kruger was in no doubt that the United States, a champion of liberty in the face of British imperialism, should be among the countries lobbied for support in the face of Britain's annexation of the Transvaal. 'I like and trust true Americans,' Kruger told a visitor a few years later. 'They are,' he suggested, 'a magnificent people because they favour justice.'[6]

It may also be significant that, when two Afrikaner-Dutch freebooter republics emerged briefly beyond the southwestern borders of the South African Republic, and joined in 1883–1885, they became 'The United States of Stellaland'. Interestingly, there too Cecil Rhodes became involved when he persuaded the British government that the upstart 'United States' threatened the Road to the North and had it forcibly dismantled.[7]

Rhodes had strong reservations about the American constitution's suitability for the governance of the United States, let alone its applicability in colonial situations. Indeed, it was one of the points that he and Hammond disagreed about. 'You Americans,' he lectured Hammond – during their Matabeleland rambles in 1894 – 'have stubbed your toe on the rock called equality.' 'Democracy,' Rhodes stated emphatically, 'is greater than equality; it should mean justice for all.'[8]

'Justice', of course, was what the Kruger government was in search of. But the Boer rejection of any form of liberty circumscribed by British imperialists and a yearning for a republic rooted in agriculture and Calvinism – a dream still largely intact after their First War of Independence, in 1881 – was at risk from the moment gold was discovered in the eastern Transvaal shortly thereafter. And it took less than 36 months from the time of the discovery of gold on the Witwatersrand, in 1886, for President Kruger to realise that the idea of an exclusively burgher republic wedded to the soil was unsustainable and that he would need to look around for new structures that might accommodate the presence of Uitlanders in the emerging urban centres.

It is almost certain that, during this search for a new model that could be adapted or grafted on to the existing republican constitution, Kruger would have consulted the man he had appointed as Chief Justice, in 1881, JG Kotzé. Kotzé was an admirer of many aspects of the American constitution and so it may well have been the Chief Justice's thinking, that, in part, was being articulated when, in establishing the Second Volksraad in 1890, the State President claimed that the idea of having two chambers 'was working well in the United States and in Europe, the only difference being that the same people [the burghers] would choose both the chambers'. Likewise, the notion of having mid-term elections, agreed to by the Volksraad, was an idea first formulated across the Atlantic, in Philadelphia.[9]

But, as Kruger discovered, the American constitution was a multi-faceted instrument and the Chief Justice, who harboured presidential aspirations of his own, was not beyond drawing on it to further his own ambitions. On 10 August 1892, shortly before the presidential elections, Kotzé addressed an open letter to Kruger, published in Pretoria's *De Volksstem*, suggesting that 'A State President should not serve longer than, at the most, two terms of office. The example of Washington, the first president of the great republic of North America should be emulated.' But if Kruger proved to be hard of hearing on this issue, then there were other opinion-makers in the patriotic press with reservations about the ways that the Americans and others conducted their elections. Thus, the same loyalist newspaper criticised the 'Americanised methods' adopted by those running the Joubert campaign during the presidential election that followed, and there were widespread fears of the emergence of a dual-party system that might, over time, come to divide the *volk*.[10]

The Boer elite's admiration of the American Constitution was thus hemmed in by rural conservatism both before and after 1895. The origins of the United States of America, like the South African Republic, may have lain in an agricultural economy but, by the 1880s, it had long been evident that the future of America lay in urban industrialisation and international trade. The usefulness of the United States Constitution as a model for a country where the long-term future of deep-level mines and the ways in which mining might be made to articulate with agriculture was by no means clear. But even as these caveats and doubts were being expressed by the burgher representatives in Pretoria, the economy and society of Johannesburg and the Witwatersrand – the cutting edge of modernity in the South African Republic – were becoming 'Americanised' in ways that Rhodes feared. As happens, politics lagged some distance behind the economy.

The rise of America as a manufacturing power in the latter part of the 19th century, one capable of rivalling Britain and Germany, was inexorable and especially noticeable during the closing decade. In 1890, American manufactured products accounted for a mere 17 per cent of the country's exports, but by 1900 the figure stood at more than 30 percent.[11] Seen from the United States, the southern African market accounted for but a tiny part of this growth. But, viewed from southern Africa and especially the ZAR, the growth in imports of capital goods – in the shape of mining machinery – food and manufactured products, destined for Johannesburg, was truly spectacular. In 1897, it was estimated that US exports to South Africa had, from a standing start, quadrupled within a decade. That might have been a serious underestimate. From exports worth about $1 million a year, in 1890,

American exports increased to the point where, by 1898, they were considered to be worth closer to $20 million a year. It was a trade that was a source of growing concern to British businessmen in particular.[12]

In the early 1890s, as gold mining on the Rand shifted from the adits, tunnels and inclined shafts of the late 1880s to deeper-level mines, heavy-duty mining machinery, imported duty-free, accounted for by far the largest part of the ZAR's imports. Of the $6 million worth of heavy mining machinery deployed on the Rand in 1893, fully half, it was estimated, had been imported from the US. Twelve months later, Hammond's agents travelled the length and breadth of America buying compressors, drums, electrical hoists, power drills and pumps from the leading suppliers of the day for the 20 engineers who reported to him at Consolidated Gold Fields. But EP Allis, General Electric and Ingersoll-Rand were not the only firms to benefit from the Rand mines.[13]

An exponentially increasing number of boxes, cross-cuts, haulages, shafts and stopes in the subterranean rat-runs and workplaces of the underground workings required constant shoring-up with an endless supply of strong, reliable timber. The Transvaal Highveld, grass-rich and tree-poor, had to import most of its timber requirements from Tacoma, Washington, or from Australia.[14] American engineers and Cornish miners shared the view that no southern African timber, cultivated or natural, was up to the special demands of deep-level mining.[15]

The Lingham Trading & Timber Company was founded in Johannesburg in 1893.[16] Its owner, Frederick R Lingham, went on to become a member of the 'Reform Committee', and imported so much timber from Puget Sound throughout the decade and beyond the South African War that he established his own shipping line, as well as a flour mill and a wharf at Lourenço Marques.[17] Within 12 months of Lingham's opening his business, another firm of timber exporters, operating out of Mobile, Alabama, contemplated entering the trade.[18]

By the late 1890s, three shipping companies were operating freighters between the United States and South Africa. At times, there were as many as five vessels a day unloading American goods in Cape Town harbour. But so limited were South African exports that, once offloaded, the steamships were compelled to sail on, round the Cape, in the hope of acquiring sufficient cargo in Australia and India to cover the costs of their return journey.[19]

In the South African Republic, the imprimatur of the United States was hardly confined to the goldfields. From 1886 to 1895, before the rail grid was complete, the American presence was evident in transport. The Abbott Downing Company, of Concord, New Hampshire, supplied scores of the same stagecoaches that had once done the famous gold runs in California.[20] Most electric tram cars, from Cape Town to Pretoria, were

Philadelphia-made. But it was another American creation that entirely seduced the Boer elite.

Working out of South Bend, Indiana, Studebaker Brothers, Carriage and Wagon Manufacturers, had their fortunes consolidated during the Civil War when they supplied the Union Army with a wide range of rugged horse-drawn vehicles. By the 1880s, the company had a splendid modern outlet on Michigan Avenue, in Chicago. Their lightly constructed, extremely robust, high-bodied, four-wheeled, horse-drawn carriages, known as 'spiders', were the last word in comfort and style, and were in great demand throughout America. For the new Boer political elite, in Pretoria, the spider became a dream come true.

In 1891, spiders became the bribe of preference as Barend Vorster, a member of the First Volksraad, set out to corrupt several members of the Raad to secure the Selati Railway concession. So conspicuous and so successful was Vorster's campaign that, in insider and press circles, the word 'spider' became almost synonymous with venality.[21] Spiders were considered to be superior to the traditional, bone-jarring Cape cart, and so energetically did John Hays Hammond advocate the advantages of the luxurious American vehicle that, in 1894, he succeeded in persuading Rhodes to switch to the spider. Thereafter, Hammond claimed, the Studebaker product became the favoured form of conveyance for the better-off across Rhodesia.[22]

The growing number of freighters entering Table Bay in the early to mid-1890s were, however, not only unloading capital goods for the mines, or luxury items destined for Johannesburg and Pretoria. Indeed, by quantity, perhaps even by value, agricultural implements, alcohol, clothing, cutlery, flour, oil, printed cotton, processed food and shoes became ever more important after the upturn in the economy in 1893.[23]

Despite the Kruger government's tariffs on agricultural products and imported foodstuffs – tariffs that were immediately suspended during the Jameson Raid – a huge surge in wheat production in the American Midwest in the latter half of the 19th century found a natural outlet in the ZAR. The climate of the republic meant it was unable to grow all the wheat necessary to supply its burgeoning urban population, and so American imports of wheat into southern Africa ballooned throughout the 1890s, much of it making its way to the Witwatersrand. In 1893, American exports of wheat to South Africa were said to be worth $350 000; by 1896 the figure was $3 million, and by 1898 it had reached a staggering $6 million.[24] The losers in this production war were the BaSotho and Boer grain producers of the Orange Free State.

Questions of tariffs and economic development also featured in the camp-fire discussions of the would-be revolutionaries in Matabeleland in 1894, and occasioned a notably sharp exchange between Rhodes and Hammond.

Rhodes criticised the Americans for having imposed a heavy duty on diamonds from De Beers during the previous year. It hurt because, by the early 1890s, about a quarter of all diamonds from the Kimberley mines were being exported to the United States. Hammond, a man with a profound personal and financial interest in American silver mines, knew exactly why the tariff had been imposed on De Beers diamonds. The American felt that the collapse in silver prices, in 1893, could, in large measure, be attributed to the Rothschilds – bankers with a powerful interest in De Beers. American silver producers – of whom Hammond had been one – had persuaded 'Congress to have a tariff placed on the De Beers diamonds in reprisal against the Rothschilds'.[25] Rhodes, deeply displeased by this move, vigorously criticised American tariff policies.

Hammond responded by defending US economic policies and, waving a red rag at the bull, told Rhodes that Britain and its colonial markets were sorely in need of tariff protection if they were to develop more fully. What followed is worthy of repeating in full, not least because Hammond could recall it all so clearly 40 years later:

> Rhodes, who had been brought up under free trade principles, became much excited and lost his temper. I, therefore, ended the discussion by stating firmly; 'When you can discuss this matter as one gentleman with another, I shall resume my argument. Your attitude is childish!'
>
> Without saying a word, Rhodes picked up his blankets and moved off about fifty feet from where he, Dr Jameson and I had already spread our blankets for the night. Jameson, who, with all his fondness for Rhodes, knew his temperamental weaknesses, smiled at me and said, 'He'll get over it.'[26]

But did Rhodes 'get over it'? Perhaps not. By then he and Hammond had disagreed not only about the American Constitution and ways that it might possibly be relevant to southern Africa and the troublesome Kruger state, but also about the United States' economic policies. On the contrary, it could have been these stark differences in political outlook between the two that did most to persuade Rhodes of the profound dangers that a revolution on the Witwatersrand, led and 'largely manned by Americans', posed to his own ambitions for British imperial expansion, and that prompted him to take part in the slowly evolving conspiracy.[27]

The journey through Matabeleland brought home to Rhodes that he had acquired the services of a Jekyll and Hyde monster – a technical expert he desperately needed to expand and protect his financial kingdom but one who, simultaneously, placed his long-term plans for a federated economic union in southern African in the gravest jeopardy. Hammond – engineering genius by day, political saboteur by night – presided over the Witwatersrand, where he and many of his American compatriots who ran the mining industry would need to be 'roped in'.

Rhodes was not alone in thinking deeply about the emerging American influence in Johannesburg, let alone southern Africa. In 1894, someone who would have known all about Hammond's extraordinary doings back in Idaho in the early 1890s, Jim Wardner, toured the Witwatersrand. Upon his return, Wardner briefed members of the United States Congress about expanding trade opportunities in southern Africa. 'There was one thing that particularly attracted my attention,' he told readers in the US, 'and that was the growing popularity of American ways and manners, and especially of American goods.'[28]

There was ample anecdotal evidence to back him up. The best-paid white miners on the Rand, many of them Cornish 'hard-rock' men – long-distance migrant workers, Celts, who did not perceive themselves as being part of the mainstream 'English' working class – were impressed by American products. At about the same time that Wardner was passing through the country, IW Schlesinger – who later became a southern African entrepreneurial millionaire – was making his way from New York to Johannesburg. Within months, Schlesinger was benefiting from the steep economic upturn and earning between ten and fifteen thousand pounds in commission each year as a representative of the 'Equitable Insurance Company' of New York selling life policies to miners dying of occupational lung diseases.[29]

Howard Hillegas, American correspondent for the *New York World*, detected the same gathering undercurrent of concern in British circles that so troubled Rhodes. 'In public, editors and speechmakers in Cape Town, Natal and the Transvaal spend hours in deploring the progress of Americanism in South Africa,' Hillegas once observed, 'but in their clubs and libraries they study and discuss the causes which led to American progress.'[30]

Nowhere in southern Africa was creeping 'Americanism' more evident than in Johannesburg. Within months of its proclamation, the settlement was being described – a touch prematurely perhaps – as an 'American city'.[31] The names of several mine properties and the adjoining suburbs bore the footprints of the US, with Cleveland, Denver and Selby being the obvious markers. In the plushest new neighbourhood, Doornfontein, the main thoroughfare was Saratoga Avenue, and a good part of the conspiracy to start an urban revolution was plotted in 'Saratoga House', the home of Frank Rhodes. In the centre of the town, the foremost hotel for many years, Height's, which bore the name of its Mississippi-born proprietor, boasted the longest 'American Bar' in town. Other dives, such as the 'Californian Hotel' and the most popular saloons, such as the 'Silver King', named after a mine of the same name in Arizona, were thus designated to attract patrons who had prior experience of the great American West.

But, as Jim Wardner noted during his brief visit to Johannesburg, 'American ways and manners' went well beyond those to be found on open display in the town's bars and hotels. Some of it came directly out of the Wild West. While the Kruger government had, from an early date, made it an offence to import rifles into the country – something that proved to be a major stumbling block for those planning the urban insurrection in 1895 – it had always been taken as a God-given right that, in a racially contested frontier society white men might bear concealed sidearms. And so they did, with American Colt or Smith & Wesson revolvers being the most popular weapons.[32]

In September 1893, *The Star* newspaper complained that 'there is scarcely a row that occurs on the Rand which does not immediately entail the production of a revolver'.[33] And it was not just the Americans, of whom there were between two and three thousand in the early 1890s, who brandished revolvers. Many Cornish and English miners were equally quick on the draw – a pleasing feature that the Jameson Raid plotters hoped would play into their hands when their revolt started.[34]

Like its eastern Transvaal predecessor, Barberton, early Johannesburg could conjure up images of a mid-century Californian mining camp. Men not only *saw* the town as something out of the Wild West, but also had their perceptions reinforced through reading the stories of a man who captured the flavour of the old West and who Jack Hammond had known personally – Bret Harte.[35] In Johannesburg, Harte's novels were so well known that the police magistrate referred to them in open court and local newspaper reports often alluded to the American writer.[36] Nor did Harte's work escape the notice of Percy FitzPatrick, who became Secretary to the 'Reform Committee' and, in 1907, author of *Jock of the Bushveld*. 'What struck me about him,' FitzPatrick noted of his fictional character, 'Rocky Mountain Jack', 'was the long Colt revolver, carried on his hip; and for two days the "gun" as he called it, conjured up visions of Poker Flat and Roaring Camp.' But not all was fiction in Johannesburg.

As with most 19th-century gold rushes, the Witwatersrand had attracted its fair share of bums, casual labourers, hobos, navvies and professional criminals of American origin. In Johannesburg, they were noteworthy in the late 1880s and early 1890s and embarrassed their more respectable countrymen. 'Highwaymen, pickpockets, illicit gold buyers, confidence men and even train-robbers were active,' Hillegas recalled a decade later, 'and for several years served to discredit the American colony.'[37]

Those in the low life may have given up on God, but God had not given up on them. From the late 1880s, through the recession of 1889–1892 and until the eve of the South African War, in 1899, a thin thread of Americanised evangelical Christianity could be detected among the urban poor – black and white – in Johannesburg. In 1890, some visiting African Americans approached General Piet Joubert and, through him, the State President, as 'citizens of a sister Republic', to explore the possibility of founding a church. A year later, Kruger was present – and apparently moved – by a 'negro spiritual' as rendered by the McAdoo singers in a Pretoria theatre.[38] By the late 1890s the African Methodist Episcopal Church, born in the United States and perceived as potentially subversive of the racial order, was making its presence felt along the Witwatersrand.[39]

Likewise, it did not take long before the Afrikaner-Dutch, already softened up for an evangelical approach by their own Dutch Reformed Church, responded to American evangelism.[40] By 1897, there was a 'Divine Healing Home' in the racially mixed working-class suburb of Jeppe in which scepticism about the supposed benefits of industrialisation and modern medicine was openly expressed. The Seventh Day Adventists, too, established a foothold in inner Johannesburg in the late 1890s.[41]

The process of 'Americanisation' was not without paradoxes of its own. Indeed, at the apex of social life in Johannesburg, the leading American couples, including John Hays Hammond and his wife, Natalie Harris, took the sobriquet 'Randlord' to heart and did their level best to turn themselves into a European-style aristocracy that even visiting British noblemen might find acceptable.

The Hammonds ran their home on baronial, if not monarchical lines.[42] Among notable guests were Baron Rothschild, Sir Charles and Lady Halle, Lord James Bryce and, bringing up the republican rear, Mark Twain. Not surprisingly, then, the couple found social life in Johannesburg to be 'brilliant' and on a par with that of London, Paris or Washington, DC. Nor would their domestic staff have been out of place in the world's leading cities. Natalie Hammond remembered that, on the Rand, in addition to employing a former Rothschild chef, their staff included 'a French governess, an English secretary, a Malay coachman, a Hottentot groom, a Zulu cow herd, a Kaffir gardener, a Scotch laundress, two English maids, a French cook and a coolie scullion'.[43] The heads of the two Hammonds, enthusiastic 'revolutionaries', were filled with quasi-aristocratic notions.

The Hammonds were not the only American couple to live out a mock-British cum European lifestyle. There were at least a half a dozen American engineers, including two of Hammond's closest associates in the insurrection conspiracy, who led similar, though more modest existences. Captain Thomas Mein, manager of the Robinson Mine, and his gregarious Irish wife offered dressed lobster at dinner parties that went on so long that couples could dance to the accompaniment of a violin and guitar between courses.[44]

All these genteel indulgences were, however, constructed atop rock-solid financial platforms deriving from a mining industry based on the skilled labour of thousands of white workers and tens of thousands more black workers working for bare subsistence wages. And, precisely because the wealth of these influential Americans derived largely from their technical expertise – as manifested in the day-to-day workings of the gold mines – historians have developed a tendency to see them only as mining 'engineers', 'experts' or 'managers'.[45] They are worthy of any of those designations, but, in truth, for Hammond and the half-dozen professionals closest to him, along with the others who went on to make up a full team of 20 or more, such titles concealed more than they revealed. History has cast them as technocrats when, in truth, they were far more like mine-owners-in-the-making than professionals.[46] In order to understand fully why so many Americans got closely involved in the 'Reform Committee', we have to look beyond their formal qualifications.

Hammond was a man with an insatiable appetite for money who, for all his wealth, never sought to insert himself into the great American tradition of public philanthropy. His philosophy was brutal and direct – 'charge all the traffic would bear, or almost the limit'.[47] Part of a new era of scientifically based mining and allied industries, he felt that the time for modesty had passed. The engineer was destined 'to invade the sphere now monopolized by the employer and capitalist and eventually become, in fact, himself the master'.[48]

When Hammond entered into a contract with the diamond magnate Barney Barnato, in 1893, he commanded an annual salary of $50 000 – equivalent to approximately $1.3 million dollars today. Six months later, on taking up a new, two-year contract with Rhodes, he insisted on an annual starting salary of $75 000 ($2 million), 2 per cent of the profits of Consolidated Gold Fields as well as the right to take on any other consulting work as might come his way.[49] Indeed, at this point Hammond no longer saw himself as an 'engineer'; his work was, he said, 'more commercial and financial than technical'. And indeed it was. In October 1895, at a time when he was embroiled in the conspiracy to overthrow the Kruger government, he was actively calculating his wealth and already planning a short sabbatical: 'I am making money fast,' he wrote to a member of his wife's family, 'and expect to have about $750 000 [$20 million] well in hand by the end of this year – then shall take a rest in London but go on adding to my pile until I reach the million mark [$27 million] – which should not take many months.'[50] And, on leaving South Africa after the attempted coup had failed, Hammond, more mine owner than mining engineer, turned to his wife – who came to sport an amethyst ring given by Queen Elizabeth I to Sir Walter Raleigh, as well as a necklace of rubies that once belonged to Marie Antoinette and noted, 'Revolutions are expensive games to play.'[51]

Indeed they are, but while he was undoubtedly the pre-eminent mining expert implicated in the conspiracy to overthrow the Kruger government, he was only one of about 50 American engineers on the Rand of whom over half were, like him, Californians. He set the tone for these men, saw to it that all those working for Rhodes, and especially his close friends Thomas Mein and Victor Clement, were well paid and encouraged them to make certain that, as it was for him, profit-sharing was an integral part of their remuneration packages. By 1895, American mining engineers, many of whom had been recruited personally by Hammond, enjoyed almost total control of the technical aspects of the great mining houses of the day, such as Wernher, Beit & Co and its local face, H Eckstein & Co, and Cecil Rhodes's Consolidated Gold Fields.

The net result was that they, like Hammond, made a financial killing during the five to ten years spent on the Witwatersrand goldfields. Like Hammond, these were men increasingly involved in the 'commercial and financial' aspects of the industry. Most started out as technocrats but they were, in truth, capitalists, the core of which – had Hammond's coup succeeded – might have constituted the kernel of a new industrial class with republican sympathies that might well have challenged President Kruger and the poorly educated rural elite over which he presided. Instead, as we shall note, in due course, once their hoped-for urban insurrection failed and Hammond's plan for a special constitutional dispensation for the Witwatersrand had evanesced, they were little more than a set of international smash-and-grab capitalists, rich men who exported their wealth, with little affection for or loyalty to their decade-long home nor any sign of public benefit – like almost every one of the Randlords.[52] Back in the US, they may have gone on to become multi-millionaires but everyone knew that, in terms of capital, it was southern Africa that had given them a head-start.

It is difficult to know how much money Victor M Clement, manager of the Simmer & Jack Mine, lifelong business associate, colleague, friend and co-conspirator of Hammond's, took with him on leaving the South African Republic, but, when he died it was reported in California – where the calibration of such things was taken seriously – that he had 'made a large fortune in South Africa'.[53] The manager of the Robinson Mine, Thomas Mein, another leading American conspirator, left with about £90 000 – the equivalent of about £9 million in 2014 – and, not surprisingly, died a millionaire in the country of his birth. Charles Butters, wealthy engineering conspirator, left the Rand with about $100 000 ($2.5 million) and bought a mine back in the US. JS Curtis, another of the conspirators, also went home to buy a mine.[54]

Interestingly, a few of the leading American engineers on the Rand who did *not* partake in Hammond's conspiracy to overthrow the Kruger government, indeed one or two who actively opposed the conspirators, seem to have made even more money than his lieutenants. Henry C Perkins was said to have left town with an astounding £25 000, while Hennen Jennings was waiting to collect the equivalent of £100 000 before he was willing to leave in the late 1890s. Ernest Wiltsee recalled that, in the year of the Raid, he cleared $50 000 on a single deal, and that, separately, an initial speculative investment of $250 in property during the great 'Kaffir Boom' of 1895, had yielded him $187 500 ($5 million). American engineers helped launch scientific gold mining in southern Africa, but several left with their wallets bulging.[55]

The fact that a significant number of the 50 American engineers on the Rand during the mid-1890s became involved in a conspiracy to overthrow the government of the day and/or left the South African Republic as very wealthy men could be attributed to a range of factors – some personal, others structural – mere features of the times. Most were highly intelligent, well-educated men with degrees from leading universities in California or 'out east', at Harvard or Yale. Some, like Hammond, had furthered their education as mining experts at the famous *Königlich-Sächsische Bergakademie* (Royal Saxon Mining Academy) in Freiberg, Germany.

Insight, personality and professionalism contributed greatly, possibly over-whelmingly, to their successes, but so, too, did chance – the luck of being born into the right cohort, increased international mobility and the discov-ery of the world's largest gold deposits in an age and place untrammelled by the need for passports and visas. But, once all these factors have been discounted, what needs to be understood is that they were also drawn into a profession where the need for confidentiality, discretion, privacy and trust was both necessary and in-built. In an age free from legislation governing what is now termed 'insider trading', the positive virtues of the profession could easily mutate into conspiracies, not only commercial and financial, but also, in extremis, outright political plotting.

Determining lines of easy access and egress, getting to know the lie of the land, mapping, planning transport and logistics, prospecting and reconnoi-tring in unfamiliar terrain or foreign countries were the stock-in-trade of mining engineers. Hammond and his intrepid wife personally mapped out what they considered to be the best route for the Jameson Raiders to follow into the heartland of the South African Republic. Clement, Mein and oth-ers on his staff were centrally involved in arms procurement, gun-running, smuggling and the laying-in of food supplies should Johannesburg ever be besieged by the Boers.[56]

Likewise, accustomed to being retained by the great financiers of the day to scout out new propositions or discover the true worth of exist-ing properties amid total secrecy, mining engineers were adept at using codes to convey sensitive market-related information via the telegraph. In Johannesburg, the would-be revolutionaries settled on the Bedford McNeil Mining Code as their secret cipher, even though it turned out to be far more widely available than they suspected.[57] But, that aside, it is clear that there were many quasi-military dimensions to the engineering profession, something that Hammond was only too aware of and prided himself on. It was not by chance that, in the 'war conscious Missouri Mines class of 1916', the instructor told his charges that those 'who managed mines and metallurgical works' were the 'subalterns, captains and colonels of our army', and that men like Herbert Hoover and Hays Hammond are 'our generals'.[58]

By the mid-1890s, however, corruption, good communications, market intelligence, international mobility, military-like organisation, secret codes and an appetite for money on a gargantuan – American – scale was no longer the exclusive preserve of those who oversaw the underground workings in the ZAR. It was also the hallmark of New York gangsters who, having fled the crackdown that followed on the Lexow Commission in 1894, were taking control of the Witwatersrand underworld and organised crime and who would dominate it throughout the late 1890s.

Johannesburg, a male-dominated frontier settlement for most of the late 1880s, was by 1893 a substantial mining centre characterised by the presence of ostensibly single, well-paid immigrant white workers who outnumbered women by two to one. News of an expanding new market for commercialised prostitution undergoing explosive growth in terms of moneyed males soon spread to those port cities of the Atlantic world dominated by Americanised East European criminal syndicates who controlled much of the international trafficking in 'white slaves'.

By 1894, pimps and prostitutes with assumed names like 'Jack Rand' and 'Sadie Afrikaner' were already spreading the good news on the streets of New York, and by the end of the following year there were two dedicated 'American' brothels in central Johannesburg. This lucrative trade in sexual services continued to grow at a brisk pace throughout the mid-nineties. In 1898, the criminal mastermind behind much of it, Joseph Silver, constituted the 'American Club' of pimps and white slavers in which he, as President, was supported by a Secretary – alias 'Joe Gold' – who helped convene formal underworld meetings replete with careful minute-taking. It will also be recalled that, when he was prosecuted, in 1899, Silver was defended by the indebted ex-Chief Justice, Kotzé.[59]

Looking back, then, by 1895 Johannesburg and the Witwatersrand had become if not *the* prime international site for mining and under-mining – criminal, economic and political – then, at the very least, the undisputed continental capital of conspiracy, untrammelled greed and intrigue. It would have provided a challenge to any modern state, let alone one presided over by a hard-pressed rural elite confronted by an industrial explosion of epic proportions in its heartland. And at the heart of the new state's misfortune lay American interests, with roots that spread as far apart as California and New York State.

By the mid-1890s Rhodes, the archetypal British imperialist, had good reason to be concerned about the prospects of there being an urban revolution led and 'manned by Americans' that might produce a republican outcome over which he had little or no political control.[60] But the greatest irony was that the most notable revolutionary among the Americans was a *soi-disant* Californian cowboy-turned-reckless capitalist adventurer who was in day-to-day control of his own Consolidated Gold Fields Company. As John Hays Hammond himself pointedly reminded his fellow countryman, the journalist Poultney Bigelow, in 1896: 'Out of the 60-odd members of the Reform Committee, 11 were Americans, which you will see, is a large percentage.'[61] Indeed, and so it was.

CHAPTER THREE

The Makings of Cowboy Jack

John Hays Hammond and the Wild West

1855–1883

John Hays ('Jack') Hammond was conceived at a time, and raised in a place, where almost everyone had to a greater or lesser extent succumbed to gold fever. Born in San Francisco, in 1855, the illness among the pioneering 'forty-niners' had barely stabilised when he entered the world.

His father, Major Richard Pindell Hammond, originally of Maryland, then Arkansas, and a graduate of West Point, as well as a veteran of the Mexican-American War of 1846–1848, was directed to the then remote San Francisco in 1849. Prey to the money bug almost from the moment he arrived, RP Hammond used his army-acquired surveying skills during off-duty hours to identify and map 'waste land' and plot the sites of prospective residential areas and towns.[1] So influential and promising a pursuit was this that, within 24 months of his arrival he, too, succumbed to the fever and, in 1851, resigned from the army. After that, the rise of Hammond senior, an extremely ambitious man, was almost inexorable.[2]

The following year he was elected Speaker of the House, and at various times thereafter was also President of the boards of Education and Police Commissioners of the city. But RP Hammond's big financial break came, in 1853, when Franklin Pierce, perhaps the worst president in American history but a comrade-in-arms during the Mexican-American War, used his presidential patronage to reward army friends. A Northern Democrat with some Southern sympathies, Pierce offered Hammond the lucrative position of Collector of Customs in San Francisco. And collect he did, continuously, from 1853 to 1855. Not all his collections were above reproach, however, and his managerial abilities were alleged to be questionable. The Secretary of the Treasury sent a 'secret agent' to investigate and, upon his recommendation,

Hammond was forced to resign.[3] He did so, but only after he took $24 000 (equivalent to about $500 000 in 2014) with him, claiming it to be interest against payments that he had made. The resulting lawsuit, which dragged on for several years, produced only 'equivocal results'.[4]

Influential within San Francisco's innermost circles, RP Hammond was surrounded by some of the most influential United States military men of the day, many of them veterans of the Mexican-American War. One, who had not been involved in the war, but who went on to play a central role in the Civil War (1861–1865) on the Union side was his business partner and family friend, William Tecumseh Sherman. Another notable military friend, although not resident on the West Coast, was the formidable Robert E Lee. Most of RP's friends were, however, out-and-out Southerners both by birth and political sympathies, and were locally resident. One of these was another veteran of the Mexican-American War and the commander of the US Army in California, General AS Johnston.

But the most significant of all RP's army acquaintances by far was a Tennessee-born man who had gone on to become a Texas Ranger before taking part in the Mexican-American War, the man whom RP's oldest son, John Hays Hammond, was named after: Colonel John 'Coffee' Hays.[5] Colonel Hays, elected as San Francisco's first Sheriff in 1851, was another of those who benefited from President Pierce's political patronage when, two years later, he was made Surveyor General of California. In 1854, Jack Hays hosted his sister, the widow Sarah E Lea, who was introduced to, and then married, RP Hammond.[6]

Having the state's Surveyor General as a brother-in-law did nothing to impede RP Hammond's real estate business. After a promising start as the port's Collector of Customs, RP's realtor business prospered for some time despite a few long-lived legal disputes. The Hammond family, waited on by Chinese servants, lived on fashionable Rincon Hill, and RP was elected as the first President of what became the city's prestigious Pacific Union Club as he moved in banking circles. He was also well connected to the companies building the transcontinental railway. Although unsuccessful as a congressional candidate for the Democratic Party, RP invested in Californian gold mines and, at the time of his death, in 1891, was said to have 'amassed considerable wealth'.[7] Hammond was a hustler and passed on his insatiable appetite for money to his oldest son.

But, if RP Hammond was only half the raconteur that his son later proved to be, then he and his important house guests passed on much more to the boy – and we know they did. In particular, they impressed upon the lad the fact that the successful accumulation of wealth rested unequivocally on a settled and predictable economic and political environment. Without law enforcement, the pursuit of riches was impossible, or, as Jack Hammond was to suggest much later in his life, 'Lack of law-enforcement is a far worse thing than lack of laws.'[8]

A frontier town, surrounded by rugged mountains and peering out over the Pacific Ocean, San Francisco was notoriously lawless. It was a port that, throughout the 1850s and for decades thereafter, used 'crimps' – the equivalent of 'press gangs' – to drug, kidnap and force men into becoming sailors. To be 'shanghaied' and sent to remote destinations without choice was solidly West Coast in its origins. But crimps were only part of the problem. In the early 1850s, San Francisco was overrun by Irish-Australians – the so-called Sydney Ducks – who were responsible for a good deal of the arson, assault, robbery, theft and murder in a town with many corrupt policemen and an ineffective judiciary.

The response from the town's frustrated citizens, merchants and others came in the form of a series of short-lived but famously successful vigilance committees.[9] Led by William T Coleman, a close friend of RP Hammond's, and assisted in many other ways by 'Coffee' Hays, members of the committees of 1851 and 1856 abducted or tracked down those thought to have escaped natural justice, or physically retrieved them through well-planned and executed raids on the prisons. Suspects were tried before relatively ordered, quasi-legal proceedings, and those found guilty were sentenced to fines, deportations or, in serious cases, public hanging.[10] Many of these dramas of swift, populist law enforcement were later relayed directly by Coleman and Hays to the admiring and wide-eyed young Jack Hammond, who never forgot them.

But there were other stories that the boy almost certainly would have been told but which he chose, understandably, *not* to record in his autobiography. Given their parents' background, young Jack Hammond and his male siblings were raised to consider themselves as 'Southerners, and my brothers and I had many a fist fight with the Yankees of our own age'.[11] Antebellum Southern attitudes, lore and practices, from duelling to everyday manners, were part of the house of Hammond. And a good part of that hidden history was the Southern tradition of filibustering.

The word 'filibuster', rooted in notions of piracy, entered the English language, via the Atlantic, from great clashes at sea between the trading powers of the 16th and 17th centuries. The original Dutch word *vribuiter*, or 'freebooter', mutated into the Spanish *filibustero* and from there into English, resonating strongly with experiences in the West Indies. In the United States of America, the word had a special, lingering meaning in the slave-owning Southern states.[12]

The plantation economy of the American South devoured black men, women, children and the environment with almost equal relish. The largest producers needed access to a steady supply not only of slave labour, but also of fertiliser or guano to replace soil nutrients depleted by cotton and sugar. They also aspired to new land in order to expand production. The Caribbean islands presented themselves as a potential source for the former and the weaker states and offshore islands of Central America as possible providers of the latter. The revolutionary climate of 1848 opened a few windows of opportunity for those anxious to ensure the long-term economic viability of the South.[13]

In 1851, after three earlier unsuccessful attempts to overthrow the Spanish in Cuba, Narciso López, a Venezuelan-born revolutionary operating out of Louisiana with Southern political backing, assembled a third force of several hundred freebooters in a further attempt to conquer the island. Among those recruited was a former US Army lieutenant who had acquitted himself well during the Mexican-American War, William L Crittenden. The new expedition, too, proved to be a failure and, amid great outrage in the United States, many of the captives were forced to labour in mines in Spain while yet others, including Crittenden, were executed. The Spanish consulate in New Orleans was sacked and, with Southern tempers raised and Northern resentment rife, the stage was set for another round of such military adventures.[14]

The man who stepped into the breach was a son of Tennessee, William Walker, lifelong champion of slavery and advocate of Southern causes. Educated at Edinburgh and Heidelberg amid the revolutionary fervour that led to the upheavals of 1848, Walker returned the US to practise medicine briefly in Philadelphia. In 1850, he moved to San Francisco, where one in three of the citizens were Southerners. Here, via his involvement with the Democratic Party, he got to know both RP Hammond and 'Coffee' Hays.[15]

In the summer of 1853, Walker recruited 50 layabouts in the harbour for the first of two attempts to establish and hold the cross-border republics of Lower California and Sonora, around the Gulf of California, in Mexico.[16] The US government, opposed to filibustering as an instrument of uncontrolled Southern expansionism, ordered the local authorities to thwart Walker's use of San Francisco's harbour as a base for his efforts to extend the reach of ambitious, frustrated slave states.[17]

In late 1853, Walker was involved with what looked like a clash with RP Hammond when the Collector of Customs seized the ship *Arrow*, which was carrying more recruits for a 'republic' founded in a sovereign state. Walker, undeterred, and backed by positive public opinion, brought a civil action against the port authorities, leaving Hammond senior in an ostensibly difficult situation that was resolved when Walker managed to slip out of the bay aboard yet another vessel.[18]

Walker later went on to invade Nicaragua successfully, becoming, for a time, its self-styled 'President'. He was eventually executed in Honduras, in 1860, when yet another filibustering expedition went wrong. Walker, a popular hero, was honoured with parades in New York City and San Francisco. RP Hammond and his boys had reason enough to remember not only Walker but also the Southern tradition of filibustering.[19]

But, as we shall explore later, in some detail, the most startling omission of all of Jack Hammond's childhood tales, as recorded in his autobiography, covers the year 1861, by when the seven-year-old boy's streams of consciousness were starting to flow more freely. From the moment that Abraham Lincoln was elected as President, several important Southern elements in San Francisco society, including a few who had been supporters of William Walker, were unhappy that Californian gold was going to support the Union and its army.[20] All that stood between these Southerners and the creation of a 'Pacific Republic' that would support the Confederacy was the western region's Kentucky-born military commander, General AS Johnston.[21] The resulting conspiracy to capture city and state alike failed, but the contours of the Californian conspiracy lived on in the mind of the young Hammond, who appears to have used several elements of it in his plans to capture a city and state during the Jameson Raid.[22]

There were, however, other good reasons for the pre-pubescent Hammond to recall the Civil War and the years immediately thereafter. And he did. Many Southerners, including Colonel 'Coffee' Hays, were arrested but then 'paroled after giving their word to the northern officers that they would not join the southern cause'. More disturbing to the lad, however, was the worryingly equivocal stance that his businessman-politician father adopted during the years of the great American divide.

RP Hammond sat squarely on the political fence, or, as his son diplomatically put it much later, 'he was a Unionist, in that he opposed dismemberment of the Union, while his natural sympathies were with the South'. But the youngster, still wholly approving of RP's single-minded pursuit of money, was starting to have doubts about his father's Democratic Party affiliation and other political loyalties. RP Hammond, in turn, felt that his son was becoming too 'parochial' for his liking. Then, in 1867, when Jack was just 12 and on the threshold of adolescence, his mother, Sarah, died.[23]

At this important juncture the lad was 'packed off' to a boarding school, in Oakland, where 'Coffee' Hays owned a huge ranch, thus leaving his father free to devote himself ever more fully to his professional interests. With a head already brimming with ideas about the real and imagined relationship between the acquiring of wealth on the one hand and law-and-order issues on the other, Jack Hammond was approaching the ideal moment at which to bridge the gap between theory and practice. In another age, and in an unambiguously urban setting, a lad lacking close parental supervision might well have drifted into anti-social adolescent gang activity. Instead, time and place conspired to push him and his brothers into the open arms of frustrated former Texas Rangers.

Each weekend, and during almost every school vacation, for the next few years, he walked the three miles to his uncle's ranch. There, under the expert tutelage of his uncle and a close friend, Captain JC Freaner, Jack and a younger brother were not only regaled with endless frontier tales about Indian fighting and the Mexican wars, but provided with expert instruction about every conceivable skill necessary for an active outdoor life and survival in the wild. Instruction at the ranch school, however, was never confined to either the ranch itself or to acquisition of mere technical expertise; it was also character-forming and personality-shaping.

'Bravery,' Jack Hammond later recalled, 'was one thing Captain John Freaner insisted upon.' To this end, the captain 'ingeniously devised various tests' – which had to be undertaken by day or by night in the most daunting of settings – 'which he never would permit us to flunk'. 'It would take all our physical courage' to complete them successfully, and they 'learned to live the life of a typical young cowboy'. More importantly, however, Freaner impressed upon his charges that the most contemptible of all failings was cowardice; cowboys did not cry and, no matter how formidable the challenge, or what the psychological cost, a real man never blinked and walked directly into the path of danger.[24]

The extraordinary personal cost that this approach to life exacted from the pistol-toting adult Jack Hammond will become more evident as we come to trace his life more fully in the Jameson Raid era. For the moment, however, it is sufficient to note that not only was there always a part of Hammond that saw himself as a cowboy, but also how he revelled in casting himself as such, as a man capable of manifesting all the bravery of a Bret Harte character. It was also his uncle's finishing school that left him with an enduring admiration of the real 'cowboys' he was later wont to employ, including the Texas cowboy-turned-Pinkerton agent, Charlie Siringo, and the legendary Wyatt Earp.[25]

Moreover, in his mind's eye, the adult Jack Hammond sometimes saw his behaviour, or that in partnership with one of his adopted heroes, as being inspired by cowboys in ways that will be all too readily understood by those familiar with the 20th-century film genre. In Hammond's head, High Noon may not have come every day but it was never distant. Amid one of the many crises in the Coeur d'Alene in the early 1890s, during which time he *did* display bravery at times, a rumour did the rounds in Wardner that he was afraid of stepping out into that mining town. John Freaner would have been proud of Hammond's response:

> I sent word that I would appear on a certain day, and at a certain hour I would walk the full length of the street, down one side and up the other. If anyone desired to attack me, he would then have his chance. No attack was made; I had called their bluff … evidence of personal cowardice was prejudicial not only to the interests one represented, but to one's safety as well.[26]

On another occasion, vivid in his own mind, but unfortunately not to be found in his cowboy hero Siringo's own extensive memoirs, Jack Hammond and the then Pinkerton agent were called upon to pass through a crowd of menacing miners to reach the railway station:

> We walked together down the middle of the road, each of us carrying two pistols in our side coat pockets. As he walked Siringo kept his hands in his pockets. The outline of his guns could clearly be seen as he swayed ominously from side to side. Every man knew the guns were cocked, and our fingers were on the triggers. Although from time to time [Siringo] challenged them with the term 'coward', a fighting word in the West, no one dared take the offensive.[27]

The reader need not be a literary scholar to notice how there is an easy slide from 'his' guns to 'our' fingers; the elision is all too evident.

That brings us to a related point. In order to bridge the gap that sometimes existed between the high standard of courage he set for himself and what had actually transpired, or what he thought had happened, Hammond occasionally erected some rather flimsy verbal scaffolding. Unlike many of the historians whom he was always keen to set on a path of his own choosing, not all of Mr Hammond's peers were equally convinced of the veracity of his claims or his prognostications.

Charles M Rolker, who acted as Hammond's travelling agent in the US, buying mining equipment in the two years leading up to the Jameson Raid, was unsparing of his principal. Confiding in an influential friend in New York City, he portrayed Hammond as being 'vain, loud mouthed and a blowhard'. Twelve months later, Rolker was still of the view that 'There must be a beastly vulgar vein in the man besides considerable wind'.[28] Thomas Mein, manager of the Robinson Mine and fellow Jameson Raid conspirator, knew Hammond well and told his son, William, all about him. Hammond's autobiography, the younger Mein suggested, decades later, 'incorporated into it what had actually happened to other engineers', and, since even Hammond acknowledged that old Tom Mein had been a raconteur without equal, the source of some of Hammond's tales was probably all too clear.[29]

Historians familiar with the American West have also been more critical of Jack Hammond's versions of events long past. Perhaps the best of them, Clark Spence, sees Hammond's account of events during the Coeur d'Alene troubles as being 'biased and distorted', while another, familiar with the history of Americans abroad, notes 'inflated' claims.[30] After the Jameson Raid, a few of Hammond's seniors in the Rand mining industry were equally unforgiving. Julius Wernher of the all-powerful firm of Wernher, Beit & Co dismissed him as a mere 'windbag'.[31] Cecil Rhodes himself, without mentioning Hammond by name, drew a distinction after the Jameson Raid between those who did and those who merely talked.

To return to Colonel Hays's ranch school. In 1871, RP Hammond, perhaps not fully at home with young Jack's emerging preference for adventure and the outdoor life, placed his son aboard the newly completed transcontinental railway and sent him 'out east' to complete his schooling in New Haven, Connecticut. After 'thrashing' a bully and successfully completing his final examination at the Hopkins Grammar School, Jack gained admission to the prestigious Sheffield Scientific School at Yale College, where, many years later, he was to get an appointment as a professor.

The three years at Yale, from 1873 to 1876, not only provided Hammond with an excellent academic preparation for the career he was embarking on, but also gave him easy access to the emerging American capitalist and political elite. It also pointed the way to certain fraternal secret societies in an age that revelled in such things. In class, the scientific foundations of engineering came easily and naturally to him but, perhaps not altogether surprisingly, given his family background in San Francisco, his greatest interest lay elsewhere – in 'questions of public policy'. It was the course taught by a specialist in 'political economy and history' that provided him with an enduring interest in the subjects.[32]

The boy who, during his vacation rambles in California, had done some panning for alluvial gold was well on his way to becoming a 'mining expert', but one who also had a keen eye for how societies had evolved, were shaped, and ordered. The discipline and habits required by engineers – men who acted upon the world rather than waiting for it to act upon them – could, through 'public policy', be extended to economy and society to facilitate the production and successful accumulation of wealth. The mental slippage that came from mastering the principles of engineering and then applying them to those of social engineering was as easy as it was dangerous. It gave rise to an explosive political concoction that Hammond was to sip from for much of his eventful life.

At Yale – as at Harvard, where he taught years later – Hammond found that the arteries of influence and power ran close to the surface, and that with a bit of skill, they were surprisingly easily tapped into. The place was a dream come true for would-be financial vampires, and he felt that a man

had to go consciously about the business of cultivating capitalist connections. He later instructed Fred Bradley, one of his mine managers, to make
sure to 'strengthen himself with the various cliques'.[33] Hammond deliberately courted the kings and kingpins, as well as the poets and politicians, in
the grand imperial age and was always confident and comfortable in their
presence. Membership of the 'Book & Snake' society at Yale, as well as the
Freemasons – the latter something that he came to share with Rhodes and
Jameson – helped facilitate elite interactions.[34] So, too, did his engagement
in athletics and amateur boxing. One of those he met during his stay in
New Haven was fellow 'Book & Snake' member, JL (Jim) Houghteling, a
scion of the powerful Chicago banking firm of Peabody, Houghteling &
Co, who was to become Hammond's lifelong friend and business partner.[35]
Yale added a few finishing touches to a man who would become a zealous
conspirator, a dedicated but unsuccessful social engineer and a self-styled
capitalist 'revolutionary'.

After graduating, in 1876, the 21-year-old Hammond and two classmates
set course for Europe, where they were enrolled at the famous Königlich-
Sächsische Bergakademie in Freiberg. He never completed the demanding
four-year course, but Hammond applied himself to his studies reasonably
assiduously, although he later claimed that 'I didn't learn anything of importance at Freiberg'.[36] The three years there, however, were hardly wasted.
Vacations and weekends were spent socialising with aristocrats and royalty.
Then, when all was looking good, it got even better.[37]

On a trip to Dresden he was introduced to General Nathaniel H Harris, a
Confederate veteran of the Battle of Gettysburg, who hailed from Natchez,
Mississippi. The General, like Jack's uncle, Colonel Hays, was a man worthy
of admiration. But, more than that, he was an entrepreneur and the mov-
ing force behind the Mississippi Valley and Ship Island Railroad Company.
Indeed, so competent a businessman and formidable a manager of men was
Nathaniel Harris that Hammond later placed him in charge of his most
difficult mining venture in the Coeur d'Alene. But, in truth it was not the
General who caught Jack Hammond's beady eye; it was his niece.[38]

Natalie Harris, from Vicksburg, Mississippi, retained most of the attitudes
and values associated with the Old South; indeed, she had been raised on
a plantation worked with slave labour.[39] She was also beautiful, intelligent
and talented. Her musical talents were sufficiently promising for her to have
been sent to New York City to round off her education and then, under the
chaperonage of her uncle, on to the cultural capital of Saxony to refine her
singing voice. Jack was made for her, and she for him. By the time he left
Freiberg to return to the United States, in 1879, 24-year-old Jack Hammond
had won the heart of the Southern belle and extracted a promise of a marriage from her.[40]

But old RP was not willing to lend either the emotional or financial backing for the early marriage of a bright but still penniless oldest son who had failed to complete the course at the Bergakademie. So he wrote to Natalie and told her that it was necessary for Jack 'to apply his training to practical life' – 'to win his spurs' – before he would allow him to marry, a decision that may not have drawn the two men closer.[41]

The chance for Jack to win his spurs – in the sense of acquiring a little exposure to engineering problems at some of the leading mines of the day – came out west. Jack and a classmate from Freiberg spent several months visiting mines in Grass Valley, California, where Hammond not only made his first contact with many of the engineers whom he was later to interact with on the Witwatersrand but also saw something of the champion 'hard-rock' miners of the 19th century. Cornish miners, often rugged individualists, might have lacked the type of theoretical education that Hammond had been privileged to receive, but their expertise at working and extracting minerals from quartzite was without rival, and they too were a grouping that he would encounter again, in Johannesburg.[42]

Hammond was contemptuous of the Rocky Mountain Cornish almost from the moment that he first encountered them. 'Cornish miners,' he went on to record many years later, constituted 'a class of surveyors whose code of morals was frequently as primitive in its conception of right and wrong as their technical knowledge was rudimentary.'[43] It was a costly prejudice for an engineer to entertain in the Western mining world at the time and a very limiting one for any aspirant social engineer.

Engineers and hard-rock men, however, were among the least interesting folk that Hammond and his companion encountered in the six months of their travels through the mining strongholds of the Wild West. By the time they were done, more than a year later, they had experienced most of the customary hardships of life on the road but had also witnessed a bar-room shoot-out and street gunfights, narrowly avoided an Apache raiding party and met Wyatt Earp in Tombstone, Arizona. It was frothy stuff and filled a young man's head with tales of the sort that many men, including Leander Starr Jameson, might later have enjoyed around a Matabeleland campfire.

Back in San Francisco, however, it was Gardner Williams, later of De Beers' diamond mines fame, who alerted Hammond – then working for George Hearst – to a new opportunity. The Director of the US Geological Survey needed a few young engineers to collect statistics on the mining industry out west. Over the next six months there were more Wild West encounters including witnessing a lynching and seeing how a vigilance committee had sprung into life. More importantly, Hammond got untrammelled access to all the economic and social data that he needed to see on the properties he visited. It helped sharpen the accounting skills of a man whose interest in the cash flows and financing of the mining industry were developing at least as quickly as were his engineering interests. He completed the survey in record time.[44]

There was reason for the haste. In late 1880, Hammond set out to travel back east so as to complete one contract and enter another. In Chicago, Jim Houghteling took him in hand and had him spruced up before dispatching him onward to Maryland. On 1 January 1881, he and Natalie Harris were married at Hancock, in the ancestral heartland of the Hammonds. If the wedding was a triumph, then the honeymoon, in Washington, DC, was even more so. General Sherman organised them a fine suite 'at army rates' in the very best hotel in the city. But the couple's social highlight was dinner at the White House with President Rutherford B Hayes, who only the previous year had been the guest of RP Hammond in California.[45]

Any remaining business for the US Geological Survey was swiftly settled, but it was the capital's new governance structures that intrigued a man fascinated by 'public policy' ever since his days at Yale. In 1874, Congress, irked by the fact that the District of Columbia had gone bankrupt under local government, had used new legislation to bring the capital city under direct rule. It was governance of a sort that any authoritarian technocrat might approve of and it was to last for a hundred years. The city was run by a three-man Board of Commissioners, two of whom were appointed with the approval of the Senate, with a third drawn from the US Army Corps of Engineers. Hammond was much taken with this new development, and it later provided him with another way of seeing the Witwatersrand.

A little socialising with rich bankers – a prerequisite for any aspirant mine owner – followed. In New York City, the couple were wined and dined by the legendary Darius Ogden Mills, a family friend, who had made his fortune back in Sacramento by financing early mine and railway developers.[46] The reality of the Hammonds' own unflattering financial position hit home once they got back to San Francisco. For the next six months Jack was often away from home, acting as a consulting engineer to companies in California, Nevada and Arizona. But his network of engineering contacts expanded steadily, and he acquired ever greater expertise in assessing the true cost of mining operations.

Always pushy, Hammond was frustrated by a lack of hands-on experience and the start-up capital needed to develop a project of his own, so when a daunting new offer came his way in April 1882 he accepted it, even though it would take him away from home for an indeterminate period. Louis Janin, Louisiana-born and a graduate from Yale-Freiberg a cohort or two earlier, had acquired the *Minas Nuevas* (New Mines), in Mexico's Sonora state, once the object of William Walker's dreams of conquest, and needed a manager.[47]

The dictatorial Mexican president, Porfirío Diaz Mori, was a man inspired by economic dreams of the sort that Hammond found appealing.[48] Having seized power in 1876, Diaz facilitated the development of the country's transport infrastructure and opened it up to foreign investment in industry, mines and plantations. The resulting boom benefited local elites but excluded the dispossessed and the poor. The result was that remote, marginalised regions such as Sonora, in the northwest, were overrun by 'Indians, revolutionists and bandits of every sort and description' who, in turn, were pursued by the Mexican army.[49]

Hammond left, knowing that he would be 'exposed to personal danger and physical discomfort', and on the way south he had to use his 'pistol as the most persuasive argument'. The mine's financial affairs and infrastructure, badly neglected by previous owners, were in a shambolic state and run by a mixed crew lacking skills. Most of the technical problems were set right over the months that followed, in spite of harassment from the Mexican Army and the threats of groups of bandits in search of silver.

The progress made in improving mining operations – a minor part of the problems facing the new manager – was greatly facilitated by a stroke of good fortune. One day, shortly after his arrival at Minas Nuevas, Hammond was approached by an effectively destitute young man in search of work. Victor M Clement was a recent engineering graduate from the University of California whose luck had run out in another of the new mining projects south of the border. Hammond was as pleased with the company that his new appointment provided as he was with his technical assistance. Clement turned out to be a pleasant companion and a surprisingly good assayer, so Hammond took him on, extending his expertise by offering him systematic instruction in the same body of theory and principles that he had studied at Freiberg.[50]

But, much as had happened at the ranch school years earlier, Hammond made certain that Minas Neuvas became more than a technical college for his protégé. Already a bit more like an army camp than a mining settlement, Clement assisted Hammond in strengthening the mine's defences and in providing arms training to selected Indian employees for a 15-strong corps of bodyguards that could protect the management or escort the mule trains that conveyed silver to the coast. Learning how to command and 'read' men in a paramilitary setting, gather intelligence about bandits, and operate on- and off-the-job surveillance all formed part of Victor Clement's course of instruction.

Hammond walked about the mine with a Colt six-shooter strapped to his side. 'Sanchez', a bandit-turned-labour recruiter for the mine, was just one of the employees in need of close observation. In order to control excessive drinking by miners outside of working hours, which unnecessarily

John 'Coffee' Hays PHOTO: LIBRARY OF CONGRESS

RP Hammond

PHOTO: *THE AUTOBIOGRAPHY OF JOHN HAYS HAMMOND, VOL 1*

General Nathaniel H Harris

PHOTO: LIBRARY OF VIRGINIA

Victor Clement PHOTO: *SAN FRANCISCO CALL*

jeopardised weekday operations, Hammond set up a canteen that sold alcohol at prices that undercut those of any off-site competitors. The miners' accommodation, too, was situated within the perimeters of the camp, which further extended the surveillance that workers were subjected to after work underground. Here then, intentionally or unintentionally, with and without reason, was the perfect elision of 'engineering' and 'social engineering' in a setting of near total control.[51]

There were, however, lessons to be learned as well as to be taught. One that Hammond would never forget, and was later to haul out on the Witwatersrand, was taught to him by Sanchez. Bands of armed revolutionaries in need of men to bolster their numbers, or silver to back their cause, were no novelty around Minas Nuevas. One morning, the commander of just such a band appeared at the mine and threatened to press Sanchez and the men he had recruited into the service of the revolutionaries. Hammond was stunned by the bandit's response. Sanchez told the *commandante* that if the workers were forced to join, 'the first shot he himself shot would be at his officers, while his men would fire into their own ranks'. This had the desired effect and the commander and his men left Hammond's team intact.[52]

What so regimented a system did to the lives and minds of the workers can only be imagined. In sociological terms, it was the cousin of what Erving Goffman termed a 'total institution' and, possibly, not even such a distant cousin of the slave plantations of the American South or the mine compounds of southern Africa. But what is of more interest to us is not what such a system did to the workers but what it did to the attitudes and mindset of the managers.

Hammond and Clement, in their first permanent positions as managers, running a system that bordered on complete control in a virtually unpoliced part of a foreign country, were undergoing the worst possible sort of training for running a mine in a constitutionally governed state where workers were citizens with rights as trade unionists. Theirs was a shared, satanic apprenticeship undertaken amid hardship in a partially self-created system that, if employed uncritically in the United States, would seriously limit their ability to run any large modern mine.

But they never saw it like that, not then, or ever – not even after it helped precipitate arguably the largest mining war in American history. At the time, in Mexico, Hammond was well pleased with the progress that he and his protégé were making. Clement easily mastered every engineering lesson he was given, both social and technical. For Hammond, it was like looking in a mirror; he had, in effect, successfully replicated himself. For 15 years thereafter the two men, baptised in a font of silver, were inseparable, with Clement constantly at his master's heels.

The pressures of working at Minas Neuvas took a greater toll on Hammond than they did on the younger, unmarried Clement. Letters from home took three weeks to arrive, leaving the men feeling cut off from wives, lovers, friends, children and family. Hammond later claimed that the time he spent on the mine, in what he liked to call 'Old Mexico', was a period of 'incessant nervous strain' and one that left his health 'in a seriously run down condition'. It was not the first time that it had happened. Amid some lesser personal trauma, back at Yale, he had once gone down with 'dysentery' that lasted fully two months. Living up to the standards of manliness taught at the old ranch school came at some personal cost.

At one point, again perhaps not without reason, Hammond believed that he was being followed by Sanchez, whom he had dismissed, and later still he and Clement were shot at by the former bandit. Hammond was in a state of 'constant apprehension of an attack from either Indians or bandits, since both usually took advantage of disturbed conditions to rob, pillage, and murder'.[53] And when things reached their lowest ebb, he did as he frequently did later in life: he sent for Natalie. His intrepid wife and oldest child duly joined him, and for several months he was buoyed up as the physical and psychological toll mounted. It was a pattern that was to repeat itself in Hammond's troubled life. He needed near total control to deliver him the career success and wealth he craved, but when he was thwarted or had to settle for less, he was inclined to collapse beneath the pressure.

It was not the ideal formula for a self-styled capitalist 'revolutionary', and it would twice cost him dearly, leaving the air heavy with accusations of 'cowardice' – the greatest sin of all in the cowboy code he had learnt back at the old ranch school. After 15 months, he 'realized that there was neither wealth nor fame to be had at Minas Nuevas'.[54] He had, however, learned how to manage almost every aspect of silver mining nearly single-handedly and would leave with a fair command of Spanish. He resigned, leaving the faithful Clement in charge, with a silent promise to rescue him at the first opportunity. By late 1883 he was back with his family in the comfort of San Francisco. Jack Hammond had completed his first big round-up more or less successfully, his health had recovered, and he was ready to make the big transition from cowboy to capitalist.

CHAPTER FOUR

Cowboy Capitalists, Part I

Trails in the Northern Rockies

1882–1892

For a decade and a half, from the moment they met at Minas Neuvas, in 1882, and until after the Jameson Raid of 1895, JH Hammond and Victor Clement made certain that when they were not actually in the same place, doing the same thing – which was fairly frequently – they remained in close contact. Hammond, whose political, economic and social aspirations knew no bounds, saw Clement as an 'ambitious' man – a meaningful compliment from a man who knew all about what it meant to push on.[1] From 1884, when Hammond returned to San Francisco, until the moment that the two men left for South Africa, in mid-1893, they were constantly on the lookout for the chance to make their fortunes or advance and protect the interests of one another.

There was good reason for them to be circumspect. The Gilded Age, filled with exciting opportunities for West Coast bankers, mine owners and railroad companies, was not without risk for those who, like Hammond and Clement, sought profitable new ventures. Leading banks were becoming insufficiently cautious in making loans to the railway companies, whose frenetic extensions did not always guarantee returns by way of either heightened freight charges or enhanced revenue from passenger traffic. In the Rockies, the over-production of silver by new entrants to the industry undermined both the stability of the metal's price and confidence in the dollar at a time when its value was underpinned by both gold and silver. The agricultural sector, in search of export markets, was in an equally problematic situation. Farmers in the Midwest and South, quick to employ the new agricultural equipment, discovered that overproduction resulted in deflation and indebtedness and were looking around for ways to settle huge debts.[2]

These uncertainties, already manifesting as tremors on the stock market in the 1880s, grew in intensity and significance as the decade unfolded. In 1890, there was a significant financial quake during which the price of silver fell from $1.16 per ounce to 69 cents by the year's end. The US government responded with the passage of the Sherman Silver Purchase Act, which provided silver mine owners with some respite when it guaranteed a monthly federal purchase of 4.5 million ounces. The cry for ever more silver dollars by farmers – an inflationary currency that was cheaper to settle debts in than gold, which had gained in value – gathered momentum with the rise of the agrarian-based, anti-monopolistic Populist Party.[3] Increased insecurity relayed itself into bond markets and the more cautious redeemed dollars against specie.

The failure of Baring Brothers bank, in England, in 1893, acting as international fuse-wire, fizzed and spluttered towards the New York Stock Exchange, which had long been stacked with explosive potential by banks, railway companies and the pushy silver mine owners of the western United States. The 'panic of 1893' saw the biggest sell-off ever in the history of the New York exchange. By late 1894 the price of silver had fallen to 60 cents an ounce and, on November 1893, the US stopped minting silver dollars entirely.[4] The 1890s was no time for the faint-hearted to dabble in a strained economy.

The relatively secure financial platform from which Hammond and Clement launched their search for a break was San Francisco. It was there that Hammond was surrounded by the founding elite of his father's generation, a place where he had known many of its leading members since boyhood. In 1884, Jack Hammond became consulting engineer to the Union Iron Works, a position that in addition to offering a handsome monthly retainer, allowed him to take on any additional contract work that came his way as a rising mining 'expert'.

The Union Works provided Hammond with an excellent vantage point from which to survey the large infrastructural developments up and down the West Coast, as well as a base from which to develop new contacts. Contracts with the Army and Navy allowed him to maintain his relationships within the military establishment, while the forging of heavy machinery for the mines kept him abreast of developments in the extractive industries of the interior.[5] As importantly, his position put him in touch with some of the most important magnates in the West Coast shipping industry, including Simeon G Reed.

In 1883, having sent his wife east to recover from her experience in Mexico, while he took on much-needed new work, Hammond resumed active outdoor commitments as he regained his mental and physical well-being. It helped, he said, *a propos* the bandit Sanchez, 'not to be serving as a target for someone lurking behind a cactus plant'. Mindful of his obligation to his lieutenant back in Sonora, in 1885 he got Clement appointed as manager of the prestigious Empire Mine in California's Grass Valley. Together, they undertook several frontier consulting excursions but it did not take Hammond very long to appreciate that while the West offered many opportunities, the big money to back such ventures was to be found back east, in New York City.

The fault lines between fame and money, so absent in Mexico, were more easily worked in the United States, as Hammond later explained: 'If I were successful in New York, I could establish a national reputation.' So, soon after his return to the West Coast he opened a branch office in New York, in 'the most impressive skyscraper of the day' owned by Darius Ogden Mills. Hammond had known Mills since boyhood, at a time when the banker was still assembling his fortune through shrewd investments in mines and railways.[6]

The New York office proved to be a boon. It led to several exciting and, above all, lucrative ventures in places previously unknown to Hammond, including Colombia and Guatemala. Yet another successful excursion, back into Mexico to expose a 'salted' mine, was 'attended by considerable personal danger' and required special precautions.

'I felt that it would be unwise to make the trip into Mexico alone,' Hammond later recalled, so 'through Dominick Borden, a cowboy I had known in Arizona, I secured a bodyguard of American cowboys.' 'Although only eight in number,' he wrote, 'they constituted an army'. The trip called for more Freaner-like tests to avoid any display of 'rank cowardice' when re-establishing control of the sometimes unruly cowboys. Spotting a cask of cheap alcohol strapped to a mule, 'I pulled out my pistol and the demijohn disappeared in a shower of glass.'[7]

Hammond believed that, in the countryside, authority flowed from the barrel of a gun, but he also knew that clients looking to develop newly acquired mining rights up and down the length of the Rockies would be more impressed by the capital he could raise from prospective backers in the East. His strategy, facilitated by old Yale contacts, made for a virtuous circle: '… the financial backing I established through my eastern clientele greatly enhanced my reputation in my native state, and enabled me to demand and obtain much higher fees than would have been the case had I confined my professional activities to California.'[8]

Hammond positioned himself perfectly, linking Eastern capital to Western enterprise in a way that could only increase his growing national reputation. In keeping with his dreams, he was building a name for himself and straddling a continent.

★ ★ ★

The first sniff of a big chance came in 1887, during a routine meeting between Hammond and Simeon G Reed. Reed embodied the spirit of West Coast entrepreneurship. The foundations of his fortune lay back in the 1860s, when he had founded the Oregon Steam Navigation Company, which, in 1880, had mutated into the even more successful Oregon Railway and Navigation Company. Always keen to establish integrated chains of value, Reed also aspired to producing steel for the tracks needed by his and other rapidly developing railroad companies. So, in 1882, he paired up with Darius Ogden Mills to turn a faltering local venture into the ambitious, more financially robust Oregon Iron & Steel Company.

But the new venture did not do as well as expected, so Reed remained open to the idea of further diversification. In 1887, he spent three-quarters of a million dollars to acquire a valuable silver-and-lead mining operation in the neighbouring Coeur d'Alene, part of the east-west panhandle in the territory of Idaho, which, along with five other frontier territories, had yet to be incorporated into the ever-expanding Union. Sensing the increasingly turbulent economic times, Reed felt that the Bunker Hill & Sullivan Mine and Concentrator Company (BHS Co), would need a good manager to keep a watch on costs so as not to jeopardise profit margins in what seemed like a volatile business. Hammond suggested a man for the job: Victor Clement.[9] Reed readily agreed.

Clement reported directly to Reed alone and at once set about placing BHS Co on a more secure footing. As vigilant as a scout in Apache territory, Clement monitored the ruling prices of lead and silver closely and constantly adjusted costs accordingly.[10] He also attempted to expand output by extending the capacity of the smelter and concentration processes so as to benefit from economies of scale. In 1889, when the property rights of BHS Co were challenged in court, Clement persuaded Reed to hire Hammond as an expert witness and the company easily won its case.[11] Reed was impressed and further comforted when, in 1890, the passage of the Sherman Silver Purchase Act slowed the slide in the price of silver.

But Reed, going on 60, was in poor health. The new financial, managerial and technical demands emanating from Clement during the first 36 months of acquiring the company, along with visits to BHS itself, proved increasingly burdensome. So, in 1890, he decided to sell the mine, giving Hammond and Clement the chance they had been positioning themselves for ever since their return from Mexico.

Hammond snatched at the opportunity. Reed offered to sell the mine for a million dollars, and his own share in it for an additional million and a half. With the Sherman Act providing insurance of a sort against a further deterioration in the price of silver, it was the right moment to tap into an extended network. At age 35, Hammond had contacts right across the country, and within hours was off on a transcontinental mission. In Chicago, Jim Houghteling, his 'Book and Snake' brother from Yale, brought Houghteling & Peabody and other banks on board, while in New York Darius Mills obliged by buying an enormous block of shares in the restructured BHS Co. Hammond himself raised money from friends and another family connection, the San Franciscan banker William Crocker. By late 1892, Hammond owned about 33 000 shares in the venture. Clement, too, eventually owned 36 000 shares in the company; when his widow sold them, in 1903, they were worth $900 000 or, in 2014 terms, well in excess of $23 million.[12]

Nor was the wider brotherhood of Californian engineers forgotten as shares in the new venture were touted around an inner circle, with a good number going to Hammond and Clement's friends. The net result was – somewhat unusually (the bankers' investments aside) – that mining engineers were disproportionately well represented among shareholders in the company. As one leading historian of Western mining puts it: 'Bunker Hill & Sullivan was an engineer-orientated concern, not only in terms of operation but also in terms of investment.'[13]

Not all the consequences of this banker-friendly, engineering-heavy, restructuring at BHS Co were obvious from day one. For a start, raising large amounts of capital from close friends and professional associates tended to heighten the personal obligation of the moving spirit behind the venture. On the one hand, it gave Hammond a freer hand in shaping the company's fortunes than might otherwise have been the case. But, on the other, it heightened the need for him to come up with a profitable return for those who had placed so much faith in him. The share market was impersonal, but BHS Co was anything but.

In July 1891, Hammond became President of BHS Co. In September that year, the financial headquarters of the firm moved from the Coeur d'Alene to San Francisco. Clement, who had long been set on restructuring that went well beyond the technical, stayed on as mine manager. More importantly, BHS Co's fortunes were now fully in the hands of the Minas Neuvas veterans, a dyad that was not inclined to dwell too heavily on the differences between engineering and social engineering. Hammond and Clement both believed that any well-run outfit was spanned by a single arch, with not a great deal in either quantitative or qualitative terms separating equipment and machinery at one end from manpower and miners at the other. In short, by 1891, the management and owners of BHS Co had reconstituted themselves as an irresistible force. And, from the moment that *he* had first appeared on the property as manager, in 1887, Victor Clement had, almost consciously, started fashioning an immovable object in the shape of the mine's expanding labour force.

The mass of that object derived, in part, from the way that the Rocky Mountains in that part of Idaho and neighbouring Montana squeezed the social contours of the communities that lay within the folds of Shoshone County. The well-forested Coeur d'Alene district, about thirty miles in extent from east to west, seldom broadens out beyond three or four miles. Streams entering from the east flow westward through various gorges and then join to form the Coeur d'Alene River, which eventually debouches into the lake of the same name. So constricted was entry and exit to the district that the railway had to worm its way along the banks of the streams in order to reach the mining properties and congested little wooden towns of the county. The principal mines were at Wardner, the site of BHS Co, at the western end of the district, and at nearby Wallace, Gem and Burke.[14]

Getting in or out of the district was not always quick or easy. In the northeast, an old mountain trail led from Mullan, just south of Burke, through the surrounding Bitterroot Mountains and across the state border to Thompson's Falls in Montana. There was also an old stagecoach road that ran west from Mullan to Spokane. But by the 1890s, the chief routes in and out were via the branch lines of the energetically expanding railway companies – east from Mullan to De Smet in Montana, north as far as the Mission on the Coeur d'Alene River or, via the more popular route west, to Spokane or Tekoa in Washington State.

In Shoshone County itself, the tightly knit mining communities were characterised by close bonds of friendship and kinship. Because of the difficulty of communication, Coeur d'Alene workers were unusually dependent on the mines, railway companies and storekeepers – not only for their immediate economic well-being but also for the underlying sense of social unity. Reasonably secure financially when left to their own devices, these small neighbourhoods – extended fingers of economic and social cohesion spread out along the valley floors – were as capable of manifesting mutual help and tolerance as many working-class communities elsewhere in the country.[15] But, when threatened economically, infiltrated by spies, or flooded with unfamiliar outside elements, the same fingers were capable of contracting to form a fist as hard as a granite boulder.

By the early 1890s, then, all the ingredients for an eruption of volcanic proportions were present in the Coeur d'Alene district generally, and at BHS Co, in Wardner, in particular. On the one side stood the interests of capital, closely interconnected and highly personalised in an economic and political environment that was slowly deteriorating and, on the other that of labour, less organised and more vulnerable, but backed by mining communities with the potential for demonstrating extraordinary solidarity. And,

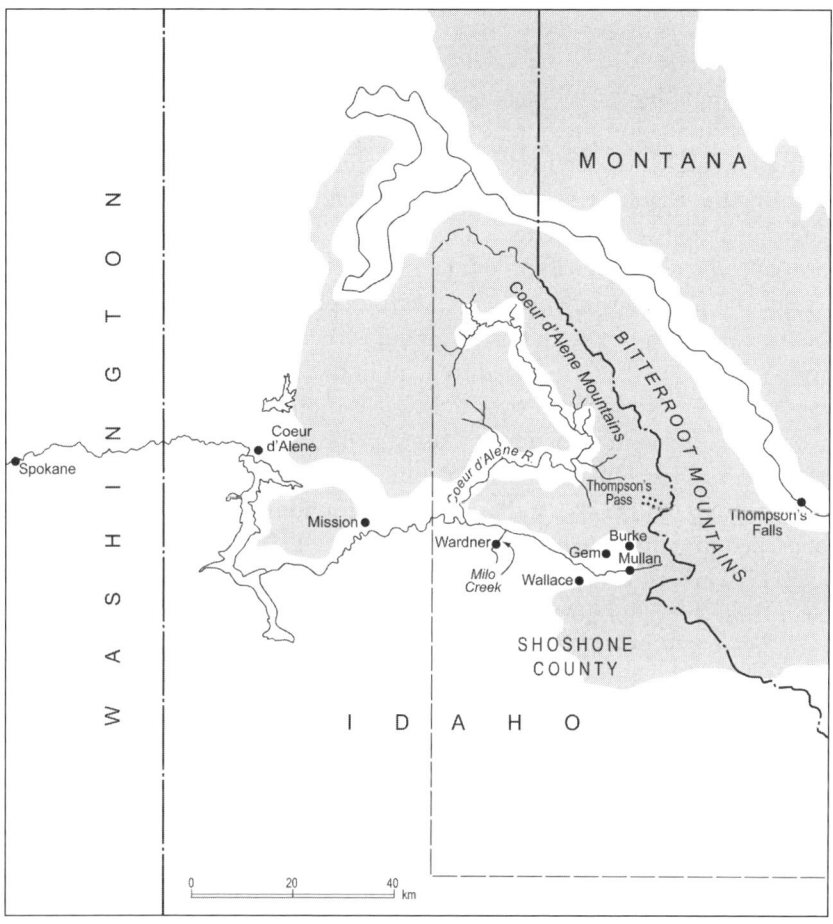

The Coeur d'Alene, Idaho, 1892–1893

between the two parties, with their social engineering projects to hand, were the men from Mexico: the Minas Neuvas twins.

★ ★ ★

When he arrived at BHS, in 1887, well before the company was restructured, Clement sought substantially more control over the workers than had been available to the mine management hitherto. Two Clement initiatives in particular stuck in the workers' craw and proved so profoundly objectionable that they fuelled the anger of organised labour for fully a decade. The manager, irked by the ways in which absenteeism and a lack of punctuality and reliability among certain workers impacted on the mine's productivity, decided to curtail access to the town's delights by erecting a company bunkhouse. It became mandatory for unmarried miners to live in the accommodation provided by the company at rates determined by the management. Moreover, in another move that smacked of debt peonage of the sort that characterised the post-slavery Deep South, all miners, married and unmarried alike, were forced to patronise the company store. That, too, proved to be an equally long-lasting grievance among the BHS miners.[16]

But the cost and inconvenience occasioned by these innovations paled beside the serious hardship that threatened when, in 1887, the miners' wages were cut as Clement responded to a fall in the price of lead – a trend that became more pronounced over the twelve months that followed.[17] As the workers recorded in a document later placed before the US Senate: 'In June 1887 the Bunker Hill & Sullivan Mining Company reduced miners' wages from $3.50 to $3 per day, and other underground men from $3.50 to $2.50, but failed to reduce their board which remained at $1 per day.'[18]

BHS workers, dissatisfied with wages that were now effectively lower than those prevailing on other mines in the Coeur d'Alene, or across the mountains in Montana, hit back. A strike forced Clement to back down, and the miners' wages reverted to the prevailing district rate of $3.50. Other underground workers, however, fared less well. Semi-skilled carmen and shovellers suddenly had to make do with wages cut from $3.50 to $2.50 for a longer, ten-hour, shift. This uneven outcome contained within it the seeds for yet further divisions and vulnerability in the face of arbitrary action from the company. In order to protect themselves, in November 1887, workers at BHS Co pledged their solidarity to the newly formed Wardner Miners' Union.[19] It was the first union in the Coeur d'Alene, a twitch in the fingers of labour.

An uneasy truce prevailed at BHS for twelve months thereafter. Clement enforced the unpopular company policy with regard to the bunkhouse and mine store while carmen and shovellers grew resentful that their wages were out of alignment with those paid to other underground workers for similar work on other mines in Shoshone County. The year 1889 saw a further and marked deterioration in the situation. Simeon Reed's property rights to the mine were successfully defended in court with the help of John Hays Hammond, but worker resentment at regional wage inequities mounted steadily. Clement, in consultation with his former mentor, decided that attack was the best form of defence.

In October 1889, he hired the first of many private detectives – Pinkerton agents no less – to infiltrate and spy on the union. From that moment a thin ideological mist began to roll down the hills and into the towns, spreading slowly over most of Shoshone County. Not long after the first spies started creeping about in the fog, Clement coerced, or persuaded, the editor of the local newspaper, the *Wardner News*, into allowing him to read the proofs of anything pertaining to BHS Co. In November, encouraged by Hammond, and anticipating more economic trouble as the industry lurched towards the crisis that culminated in the passing of the Sherman Act, Clement mooted the idea of a Coeur d'Alene-wide Mine Owners' Association. 'We will act in a body if necessary when dealing with Smelters and Railroads for incoming and outgoing freights,' he informed Simeon Reed, and we 'will also endeavor to regulate many abuses in the labor question etc.' (*sic*).[20]

In 1890, Idaho, a frontier state, slipped almost unnoticed into the Union with all the attendant advantages and disadvantages that came with oversight from Washington, DC. In the Coeur d'Alene itself, the mining industry hovered on the brink of a disaster that was only averted by the passing of the Sherman Act. At BHS, Clement, now in siege mode, pressed harder on the Wardner miners. The introduction of compressed-air drills at the mine produced new efficiencies but only at the cost of reducing yet more $3.50-a-day skilled miners to the status of $2.50-a-day carmen and shovellers. This time, the strike was successful and all underground workers were reinstated at the rate of $3.50 per day.[21]

Success at BHS by the Wardner Miners' Union did not pass unnoticed in the Coeur d'Alene. It emboldened other, hitherto more timid, souls. By the end of 1890 and another successful strike, at the Tiger Mine, three more unions had been ushered into life in Shoshone County – at Gem, Burke and Mullan. The fingers of labour were being drawn into a single nervous system and readied for more co-ordinated action. That stimulus to action came from the employers who, insisting on the use of company doctors at a monthly fee of $1 per employee, were slow to appreciate the need for establishing a hospital that might possibly provide better and cheaper medical care. All four of the unions then combined to form the Coeur d'Alene Miners' Union.[22]

The threat of a single union, one capable of shoving its fist in the face of *all* companies in the county, released more adrenaline into the system of Clement and the other managers and mine owners. But Clement was not demoralised; it was not all bad news. The sale of BHS was a promising development and he drew succour from the fact that, even from a distance, Hammond was becoming more involved in the running of the mine. Moreover, the union scare breathed new life into their long-cherished idea of creating a Mine Owners' Association.

There was nothing startling, or inherently sinister, in the notion of employers getting together to establish an association to enhance or protect their interests even though it may, arguably, have been the first such initiative in the United States. 'The avowed objectives of the association' were perfectly unobjectionable: 'co-operating in dealing with the railroads over freight rates, co-operation in effecting economies in the operation of mines and mills, and co-operation in dealing [with] the miners' unions'.[23] The Mine Owners' Protective Association, commonly known as the Mine Owners' Association (MOA) was neither college fraternity nor secret society, which makes it all the more puzzling why the moving spirits behind it – Hammond and Clement – behaved as if it were, or why they were at pains to keep its operations under wraps. Nobody knew for certain whether the MOA was established in 1890 or 1891 but, given the troubled history of BHS Co, the former rather than the latter seems the more likely date.[24] Not all owners in Shoshone County were members of the MOA, or eligible to become members. Membership was restricted to those owners who shipped the largest volumes of ore to smelters outside the district; those who ran small or speculative operations were 'barred' from the organisation. The dates, times or places at which the MOA met were never fully revealed and, as a semi-official organisation, it never published minutes of its meetings.[25]

Within weeks of Hammond's assuming the presidency of the recently restructured BHS Co, in July 1891, miners at BHS came out on strike on 8 August when the company refused to deduct a dollar a month from every worker's wages and pay it into a central fund that would help cover the cost of building a hospital at Wallace. Unwilling to lend credibility to the balled fist of the centralised Coeur d'Alene Miners' Union (CDAMU), and keen to retain control and surveillance of their own workers, Hammond and Clement offered instead to provide land and lumber for a hospital, provided it was erected at Wardner, or in nearby Milo. The union would have none of it. It took two weeks to 'settle' the dispute, the result a stalemate. BHS Co would no longer provide a doctor for workers, and the miners would be left free to dispose of monthly deductions as they saw fit.[26] Hammond, who had received no warning of an impending strike, was left fuming by his management's lack of intelligence and decided to extend the initiatives that Victor Clement had pioneered some two years earlier.

★ ★ ★

Within days of the resolution of the hospital dispute, Hammond, as President of the MOA, placed it and the BHS Co managerial team, comprising Clement, Fred W Bradley and Frank Jenkins, on a war footing. The aim was to implement a new round of wage reductions at BHS itself and, preferably, throughout the region. But the long-term – more ambitious – objective was, if not to destroy the CDAMU, then to render it wholly dysfunctional.[27] It was to be a war, a class war of a type familiar to many industrialising societies of the late 19th century, but especially so in the United States of America, a country born of revolution, blooded in civil war, filled with expansionist impulses and devoted to the unbridled pursuit of profit. As two historians of the state of Idaho note, in the mountains and valley regions of the Rockies at the time and elsewhere, across the sprawling United States, there was a disturbing tendency for 'representatives of capital and labor to equip themselves with private armies and to engage in open warfare'.[28]

Jack Hammond, a child of a US Army major and a schoolboy graduate of an informal school run by veterans of the war with Mexico, was part of a new generation of young men raised in states making the transition from actual warfare to class and industrial warfare. For Hammond and his ilk, guns were an integral part of imposing order, whether out on the frontier or within the emerging urban centres. The vocabulary of conflict and violence – 'guns', 'pistols' and 'rifles', 'battles', 'wars' – was part and parcel of his character and everyday conversation.

'Revolution', usually meaning an insurrection, but more especially an armed, urban uprising, was a word much favoured in the Hammond household. In the 1930s, looking back on a brawl that took place after a Yale-Harvard baseball game, Hammond placed himself at the centre of the fighting, claiming that it was his 'first revolution' and that it had been 'accidently started' – as opposed, no doubt, to those deliberately fomented.[29] The Jameson Raid, too, was described at the time, and later touted by Hammond, as a 'revolution'. His wife, Natalie, titled her book about her husband's misadventure on the Rand as *A Woman's Part in a Revolution*. Back in the Coeur d'Alene, in the 1890s, Hammond's preparations for what he may privately have seen as his 'second revolution' – one that he chose never to allude to in those terms and always avoided clear analysis of – were threefold, or more.[30]

The CDAMU claimed later that, in an effort to reduce wages across the board to $2.50 a day, the MOA made sure that 'every mine owner who belonged to the association paid 12% per annum on each ton of ore shipped from their respective mines, which went into a sinking fund, to be used by the association in reducing the miners' wages'.[31] Whatever the truth of the matter, what is certain is that in the contest that followed, the companies affiliated to the MOA appeared never to want for funds.

Clement had, ever since 1887, been served, albeit intermittently and without conspicuous success, by operatives drawn mostly from Thiel's Detective Agency in the neighbouring state of Washington. Hammond wanted much more from his spies. They would not only have to liase with BHS management about on-site issues but also help subvert branches of the union spread throughout the Coeur d'Alene. It was a daunting task, one requiring the finest professionals that money could buy, from an agency with an unparalleled reputation. In September 1891, the MOA, again following Clement, approached the Pinkerton Agency for help.[32]

The man Pinkerton's sent later that month to meet the President of the Mine Owners' Association and its Secretary, John Finch, could have come straight out of one of Jack Hammond's dreams. 'In his youth,' Hammond later recalled, the agent 'had been a cowboy and scout in Texas, Kansas, Indian Territory and New Mexico'.[33] Conservative and with ugly prejudices about recent American immigrants and 'money grubbing races', Charlie Siringo – half-Italian, half-Irish – did not have a cowardly hair on his head and packed a Colt .45 pistol. Unfortunately, despite all Hammond's later tales about his cowboy-detective hero, Siringo himself was left with less than clear memories about the MOA president, referring to him in his memoirs as 'Drummond'.[34]

With generous funding assured and a personalised intelligence system in place, Hammond was ready for an industrial war of a sort that his old ranch-school mentors would have understood all too readily. But believing that he was as fine a manipulator of man and the moment as he was of a mine and machinery, Hammond not only wanted to come out ahead on any body count, he also wanted to win hearts and minds. Again, Clement had shown the way years before. At some point in either late 1891 or the first quarter of 1892 – it is unclear which – Hammond, AM Esler and other mine owners began to pump money into the local newspapers at Wardner, the MOA fortress, and in Wallace, redoubt of the consolidated CDAMU.[35]

The *Wardner News* and the *Wallace Miner* were subsidised either wholly, or in part, by unknown new financiers. While the latter paper, perhaps in deference to the strength of the labour union in its hometown, retained its original name as the *Wallace Miner*, the *Wardner News* was transformed into the provocatively titled *Coeur d'Alene Barbarian*.[36] One of its new editors, another consulting engineer-turned-idea mechanic, Robert Edward Brown, promptly acquired an unflattering new sobriquet. While in Wardner, in the pay of the MOA, 'Barbarian' Brown remained loyal to the mine owners, but after the war of 1892, he had a change of heart and, thirty-six months later, when he saw Hammond embarking on another of his 'revolutions', opposed him.[37]

With so much of his capital and that of close friends at stake in a still weakening economic climate, Hammond felt the pressure mounting. Clement, like a bloodhound on the trail of an escaped convict, was all over the BHS property, sniffing at anything that could possibly contribute to reducing costs. Then, on 28 November 1891, Jack Hammond's father, RP Hammond, died.[38] The two men had not been close, but the death could not have come at a more demanding moment for a son who was always ready to defend his father's reputation.[39] Within weeks of the funeral, back in San Francisco, the BHS Co bloodhound began barking incessantly.

The union was not the problem; the owners were prepared for that. It was the Northern Pacific and Union Pacific railway companies. Squeezed by anxious bankers, the railways had been forced into raising freight charges.[40] Hammond and Clement were undeterred. The mark of a good general was the ability to turn adversity and weakness into advantage and strength. So, instead of waiting to confront their enemies one by one, the twins decided to launch a simultaneous, all-out attack on both the railway companies and the miners' union. It was the first genuinely radical, if not 'revolutionary', act in the dirty war that followed.

CHAPTER FIVE

Cowboy Capitalists, Part II

The Siege of Bunker Hill and Flight

1892–1893

O n Saturday night, 16 January 1892, the mine owners in the Coeur d'Alene used the rise in freight charges as the political battering ram with which to get the attention of those managing the railway companies. Their hope was that, by closing the mines, the Northern and Union Pacific companies would see reason and revert to the *status quo ante*. After that, the mine owners would push on and overrun another cost centre that needed to be brought into line – that of the labour union – and implement wage reductions for miners.[1] It was midwinter in one of the coldest parts of the United States and, although aimed primarily at the railway companies and therefore not officially a lockout, the closure of the mines had much the same effect on the hard-pressed miners. The Mine Owners' Association (MOA) was intent on using the lengthy stand-off with the railway companies to soften up the miners for a reduction in wages, which, by winter's end, they would be in no position to resist.

The rail companies did not budge for eight weeks, and the MOA and the union used the intervening period to prepare for the full-out war that they knew was coming. At the time of the restructuring of the BHS Co, 24 months earlier, Hammond had noted a 'particularly unfriendly' attitude towards Clement and his team. Later, he tried to sell the lie that, until 1891, 'There was not the slightest discontent among the miners at Bunker Hill & Sullivan.'[2] It was a bizarre claim to make of the birthplace of the union movement in the Coeur d'Alene and a mine that had already witnessed two strikes. Anticipating legal battles with the union, Hammond recruited his former adversary in the BHS rights dispute, the 'brilliant' WB Heyburn, as counsel for the MOA.[3]

Hammond had a healthy disrespect for small-town lawyers but it helped that Weldon Heyburn had qualified as an engineer before he ever practised law. But, what made Heyburn's appointment more appropriate, or more cynical, depending on your point of view, were the blatantly illegal actions that Hammond and the MOA engaged in during the opening weeks of 1892. Blooded in frontier Mexico, Hammond had scant respect for the law in a 'sage brush' state only recently admitted to the Union. So, disregarding a law that prohibited the importation of an armed force into Idaho, the MOA proceeded to hire guards from beyond the state's border who were supplied with – to use Hammond's own words – 'smuggled-in guns', to enforce order on the mines of Shoshone County.[4]

Here then was an arms smuggler, a distributor of rifles, an importer of a quasi-military mine security force who, while bemoaning the absence of law and order, was willing to violate state laws in the pursuit of profit. Reconciling such diametrically opposed ideas did not lend itself easily to public debate, or even to rational discussion. It was the stuff of bullies, secret societies and revolutionaries, or, as the union put it, of the 'polished plug-ugly who presided over the Bunker Hill & Sullivan Mine'.[5]

As hoped for by the MOA, the railway companies were the first to blink. By 18 March 1892, Northern Pacific and Union Pacific had both agreed to revert to their previous tariffs. It was an MOA victory that many miners and shopkeepers in the Coeur d'Alene applauded. There was a feeling that the mines had been hard done by the rail companies, and that the situation would soon revert to normal. Heartened by all this, the MOA pushed on, hoping to achieve a full-scale triumph by launching a head-on assault on the union and implementing across-the-board wage cuts that would reverse the gains the workers had secured in 1887 and 1890. 'AM Esler of the Frisco Mine and John Hays Hammond,' writes one historian, were known as 'bad losers' who had expressed their indignation in the press.[6]

On 28 March, the mine owners used one of their favoured outlets, the out-of-state *Spokane Review,* to launch the attack.[7] In a provocative 8 000-word statement that is judged to 'make unpleasant reading even today', it denounced the Coeur d'Alene Miners' Union (CDAMU) and its leadership, and announced that while miners would receive $3.50 a day, all carmen and shovellers, except for a few working in designated 'wet' areas, would be paid only $3.00 for a ten-hour shift. The response was unequivocal. On 29 March the union rejected the terms offered by the MOA, which then enforced a lockout.[8]

In mid-April, secure in the knowledge that Charlie Siringo could supply them with information from the heart of the union, Hammond and the mine owners poured reinforcements into MOA properties. Within days, 500 rifles were distributed to newly employed guards whom the Pinkerton and other agencies had recruited in Minnesota and neighbouring states. Once the insurgent paramilitary force had secured the perimeters of the largest mining properties, the MOA used the same conduits to start recruiting out-of-state 'scab' labour. An early skirmish occurred on 29 April, when an attempt was made to introduce four strikebreakers to the small Union Mine, but the striking miners persuaded two of the men to join the union and sent two others packing via the mountain trail to Thompson Falls.[9]

Hammond, noting that the litmus used at the Union Mine had turned red, realised that all similar small-scale tests were likely to give rise to the same result. So he reached for the antidote to what he saw as union poison, and stepped up the recruitment of scab labour. On 7 May, WB Heyburn, acting for the MOA, obtained a restraining order from the US District Court for the District of Idaho preventing the union from interfering with the operations of the mining companies or from taking on new workers.[10]

This success was the start of a trend that became more evident over the weeks that followed, and one that bedevilled attempts at legal resistance by the CDAMU. Whereas Shoshone County officials were often well disposed towards the miners and their union, Idaho state officials and those of the administration in Washington, DC, were not.[11] Within the Rockies folk tended to look after their own, but those beyond the mountains were less sympathetic to workers often seen as dangerous radicals.

For Hammond, whose public life was dominated by the need to display the plumage of 'fame or wealth', it was a matter of personal pride that the striking mineworkers not be allowed to claim the moral high ground in the war for the Coeur d'Alene. This was especially important politically at a time when the Populist Party, already making strides among farmers, was advocating the free coinage of silver and beginning to make progress among miners in Idaho and Montana even as their own union urged the Congress to abolish the tariff on lead-silver ores.[12]

Newspapers, including the Coeur d'Alene Barbarian and Spokane Review, were hard-pressed to hold the MOA standard high when, within weeks of the lockout, shopkeepers, starved of mineworkers' incomes, were forced out of business.[13] Hammond responded by trying to drive a wedge between the shopkeepers, cast as law-abiding citizens, and working-class miners who, unlike the strikebreakers, were presented as law-breakers.[14] And as the mining war of 1892 unfolded, 'Law and Order Leagues', the offspring of the San Francisco Vigilance Committees of 1851 and 1856 and bearing the unmistakable imprimatur of Hammond himself, sprang up all around the Coeur d'Alene. As Hammond boasted to a friend, in September 1892, when he thought that he had 'done up the union': 'All mines are working non-Union Miners − a Law & Order League composed of 400 of the best men (not Miners) − Merchants etc. − is having a good moral influence in our district.'[15]

After getting the injunction against the Union, Hammond and Clement turned the BHS Co offices and Wardner into the MOA stronghold.[16] The mine, as it was to be until the turn of the century, was a bastion for strike-breakers. Yet, all this came at a cost, as their spy, Siringo, knew only too well. The velvet glove of propaganda could not conceal the mailed fist of force. The MOA, a largely faceless organisation, was despised but it was the vehemence with which some of its members were regarded that was truly alarming. Death threats were sent to MOA office bearers from a group of workers who were not content to proceed at the slow, legal pace that the union initially advocated. Clement and Esler, the Pinkerton agent reported, were 'violently hated' by the unionists, as was 'Barbarian Brown' and Dr Simms of the MOA, 'who was later assassinated'.[17]

To his credit, Jack Hammond led his troops into a potentially hostile situation on at least one occasion. BHS Co had just acquired an expensive new mill and he and his team were determined to keep up production, maintain profits and declare the dividends that would enable them to keep friends and investors content. Early on in the war of 1892, Hammond personally recruited strikebreakers in San Francisco and escorted them north, into the Coeur d'Alene, by rail in a 'private car'. But here again, as with Sanchez in Mexico and three years later during the Jameson Raid, it is worth noting that, when the pressure became most intense, his wife, the intrepid Natalie, would suddenly appear at his side. Hammond, who prided himself on being a forceful leader of men, apparently found it impossible to talk the feisty lady around when it came to issues of personal safety. 'My wife insisted on accompanying me,' he recalled 'and although I had hoped to induce her to stop off at Portland, she would not do so.' 'If I was to be near danger, she insisted on being with me.' During the final stage of a high-speed train run to a stop outside Wardner from where strikebreakers bolted for the mine to avoid the approaching unionists, Natalie became stiff with fright. It was 'with difficulty', Hammond recorded, 'that I got her safely to the ground'.[18]

Throughout May 1892, the MOA imported 'scabs' by rail, who appeared in Shoshone County at the rate of around 15 a day until, it was estimated, there were in excess of a thousand at work in the Coeur d'Alene.[19] Significantly, spokesmen for the union referred to this formidable force of strikebreakers, some of whom were not averse to attacking striking miners, as 'Hammond's Brigade'. And, while many of the incoming strikebreakers were directed to the town of Gem and the mines closest to it – the Gem and Frisco – there is no doubt that Hammond had chosen BHS Co and Wardner as the main fortress from which to defy union members, who by then had been without wages for close on five months.[20] The result was largely predictable.

Bunker Hill became the focus of the most aggressive picketing while, throughout May, increasingly violent clashes between union members and

strikebreakers were seen at other sites. The CDAMU, hard-pressed to meet
the needs of its members, looked across the Bitterroot Mountains to the
waning Knights of Labor as well as the increasingly militant Butte Miners'
Union for assistance.[21] Support, in the shape of substantial financial aid as
well as a good deal of political and legal advice for a fraternal union in
Wallace, was readily forthcoming from Montana. Radicalised by a situation
in which they had, over several months, been placed on the back foot by
the MOA, and with a sense of foreboding about how things might end,
the CDAMU leadership did as Hammond had done and began importing
rifles.[22]

But, with Siringo embedded in the Gem Miners' Union, where he had
worked his way into the position of 'Recording Secretary', no secret could
be kept from the mine owners. Indeed, many of the union's best guarded
plans surfaced unexpectedly in RE Brown's *Coeur d'Alene Barbarian*. As
Hammond remembered it, 'Siringo's reports of union plottings he sent
secretly by mail to the Mine Owners' Association', and 'such was the accuracy of our foreknowledge of their plans that the unions finally began to
suspect the presence of a spy at their councils'. Among the more worrying
plots Siringo revealed to the President of the MOA was one 'to "do away
with" Clement and me'. It was Sanchez all over again. Another, more prosaic
plan was to sabotage underground workings at two of the mines.[23] But what
really got the wind up the leading mine owners, however, was gathering talk
among the strikers of a 'general uprising'.[24]

Having started what looked as if it could turn into a war, Hammond
began to suspect that not even the MOA's war chest could guarantee sufficient soldiers should it come to a shoot-out. Events, initially beyond his
control, then played into his hands and those of the other mine owners. In
late May there was a minor kerfuffle at Mullan when some union members
boarded a train in search of incoming strikebreakers. It became the subject of heated exchanges in the state press, and concern grew to the point
where even the Republican Governor of Idaho, Norman Willey, himself an
ex-mine superintendent, felt the need to be seen to be doing something
constructive.[25]

For four days, between 26 and 30 May, Willey and his party moved
between the MOA's de facto headquarters at Wardner and Wallace, where
the union's greatest strength lay, apprising themselves of the facts. The
Governor was careful not to take sides publicly while in the Coeur d'Alene.
But what really cheered the President of the MOA was what was happening in private. Willey's closest adviser, the man organising the state's National
Guard, was well known to Hammond and someone whom the MOA could
rely upon to help.

General James F Curtis was a man after Hammond's own heart. Indeed, the General had probably passed through RP Hammond's home on many occasions. Curtis was a founding member, indeed an executive member, of San Francisco's first and most powerful Vigilance Committee, that of 1851.[26] Better still, he had gone on to become the city's Police Commissioner and had reported directly to RP Hammond, President of the Board of Police Commissioners. Curtis did not disappoint the MOA. During the clashes that followed in Shoshone County, in 1892, writes one historian, 'he was even more sympathetic to the mine owners than Governor Willey had been'. He was their friend at court and 'continually encouraged the Governor to retain martial law'. The MOA was so grateful that, before the year was out, the owners donated $5 000 to the Idaho National Guard for the purchase of rifles.[27]

Sensing that the state was going to be more supportive of business than of labour, the MOA attempted to press home their advantage. On 1 June, Victor Clement, AM Esler and other leading mine owners forwarded a six-page letter to the Governor laying out their case against the union in considerable detail. Willey responded by stating that he would only declare martial law should violence break out in the Coeur d'Alene.[28]

It was, however, no longer a question of 'if' there would be bloodshed but where, when and at whose instigation it would occur. The unionists, realising that they were losing the political struggle, displayed their anger at the annual Fourth of July celebrations, when American flags were shot at and spat upon.[29] The miners had already lost an estimated $1 million in wages, but the conflict was no longer about restoring 50 cents per shift to the pay packets of underground workers impoverished by bunkhouse and company store policies.[30] Anger quickly spread through the valleys, and soon gave way to blind rage. One of the last things the unionists saw with any clarity was the outline of Hammond's cowboy-detective, Siringo.

On Saturday, 9 July, the Recording Secretary of the Gem Miners' Union, C Leon Allison aka Siringo, resigned from his position. Information leaked to the MOA's *Coeur d'Alene Barbarian* had effectively exposed him as an informer. Although vulnerable, Siringo lingered on in town. That evening there was a fist-fight at a local saloon after a few guards from the Frisco and Gem mines got involved in an exchange of words with some union men. Days earlier, a mine guard had shot dead a union member, which may have helped fire up the altercation. Hours later, Siringo heard about an imminent union-led attack on strikebreakers at the adjacent mines, where scabs were working under the protection of a phalanx of armed guards, backed by the presence of the National Guard. That night, the National Guard armoury was breached by unknown persons, presumably striking miners or men sympathetic to the union, and some rifles stolen.[31]

On Sunday 10 July, as darkness fell, well-armed unionists took up positions on the hillside above the Frisco Mine while, some distance below, mine guards monitored their movements from various small buildings. As always in such situations, nobody was sure who fired the first shot. Nor did it matter. The root of all such problems lies not with who shoots first, but with a willingness to resort to arms in the first place.

During the ensuing gunfire the union men realised that they were more exposed than were the company guards, and so a small detachment, armed with 'black powder', was dispatched to destroy the Esler-owned mill, valued at $200 000, towards the rear of the property. A parcel of gunpowder was tossed into the flume and the mill exploded, destroying an adjacent building and resulting in the death of a guard and the injury of several more. More shots were pumped into the guards' stronghold and, when a second of their number expired, at least 50 or more guards surrendered.[32] The strikers then marched the defeated guards down into town, where they were held prisoner in the union hall.

With the victory at Frisco assured, union members' attention reverted to what they saw as the MOA's agent of prime evil – the Pinkerton man, the agent who had infiltrated their communities. But Siringo, as physically courageous as he was innovative, had received advance warning of the approaching union men. He made his escape from the boarding house where he had been living through a hole he sawed through the wooden floor of his bedroom. He levered a trunk into place, lowered himself through the hole and crawled to safety beneath an adjoining boardwalk.[33] From there he fled into the nearby hills, waiting for an opportune moment to return to town.

General Curtis, who had for some days been aware that the situation was beyond the capacity of the National Guard, had already requested Governor Willey to appeal to Washington, DC, for the assistance of federal troops. President Benjamin Harrison, grandson of the president of the same name who had made RP Hammond one of the beneficiaries of his patronage – had campaigned vigorously for Idaho and other territories to be admitted to the Union.[34] But Curtis was the not the only man taken aback by the ugly turn of events in the Coeur d'Alene.

Clement, a man it will be remembered who Siringo had already noted as being hated almost as much as the provocative AM Esler, had seen the writing on the wall some days earlier.[35] Appreciating Hammond's habitually uncompromising line with unionists and knowing how heavily invested the company was in the new mill at BHS, he had already appealed to Governor Willey for additional armed protection. But to no immediate avail. When Esler's mill went up in smoke, Clement appealed directly to Hammond to activate his extensive Republican links to ensure that federal troops were at once dispatched to Shoshone County.[36]

Hammond was pushing against an open door. President Harrison's mind would have been concentrated on an event closer to home, one that had occurred four days before the Frisco Mine explosion and helped to lift the morale of militant unionists. On 6 July, locked-out steelworkers at Homestead, Pennsylvania, had opened fire on Pinkerton agents making their way to mills up the Monongahela River in barges. A day's fighting left three Pinkertons dead, a dozen wounded and the rest taken prisoner. Lines in the sand were being drawn, out east, and in the west.

In Gem itself, things were at least as bad as up at the Frisco Mine. At 6.00 am that Monday, 11 July, even before the dynamiting of the mill, a company guard at the Gem Mine had been shot by a union marksman, or a sharpshooter sympathetic to the strikers' cause. Company guards fearing the worst responded by setting up a barricade overlooking the main street near Bill Daxon's Saloon, a well-known union stronghold. In the ensuing gunfight, three union men were shot dead and half a dozen wounded before an uneasy truce was declared. Blood, the harbinger of logic, saw the appointment of a committee and an agreement of sorts was reached. All of the Gem company's strikebreakers who surrendered to union men would be disarmed and given safe passage to Wallace. There they would have 24 hours to collect any unpaid wages and leave the county.[37]

With the management of the Gem and Frisco mines defeated and the properties cleared of strikebreakers, the unionists set their sights on Fort MOA. That night, 11 July, over 500 armed unionists invaded *Barbarian* country, the source of their six-month-long travails, and took control of the hills around the barricaded and heavily guarded BHS Co. The property needed all the protection that could be mustered. The mine was worth about $2 million and, in the months prior to the strike, was paying profits said to amount to about half a million dollars a year.[38]

The union men, sensing that they were close to the heart of the beast, remained keen to maintain the moral high ground. The BHS Co was to be denied the opportunity of shooting even one union member and, amid discipline significantly tighter than had been evident earlier that day, the strikers set about trying to achieve their objective without bloodshed. Instead of attempting a head-on assault on the mine and its guards, they overran the thinly guarded concentrator on the outskirts of the property and proceeded to pack the building with the finest negotiator known to modern industrial man – over 4 000 lbs of dynamite.[39]

In the absence of federal troops, Clement's short-term thinking became wonderfully clear. At a meeting between mine owners and armed unionists in Wardner, on Tuesday, 12 July, Clement surrendered the BHS mine to union guards and agreed to the immediate dismissal of the strikebreakers, who would be given until the following morning to board a train to take them out of the county.[40] Making the best he could of the situation,

Clement sent Hammond a telegram outlining what, amid the planning of funerals elsewhere in the county, would have to pass as a triumph for investors in BHS Co. 'Not a cent's worth of damage has been done to our property,' he told the President.[41]

Knowing how strongly Hammond felt about the underlying economics of the situation, Clement was not about to betray his mentor by making any further concessions to the union. As with all agreements, it was not only what was *on* the paper that would determine the outcome of the conflict, but what was *not* on it. At the Wardner meeting he had deliberately not entered into discussions about re-employing strikebreakers, a possible resumption in production, other unpopular company policies or wage rates. In essence, Clement saw the Wardner agreement as a truce, sensing that the company's bargaining position would strengthen dramatically once the federal troops arrived.[42]

The following morning, having received the outstanding wages due to them, hundreds of strikebreakers at Bunker Hill, along with a few women and children, were escorted aboard trains destined for the landing at the Mission, on the Coeur d'Alene River. There, a steamer would collect them for onward travel to Washington State. But, while waiting for the steamer to arrive, eight to twelve mounted, shooting, yelling men descended on the passengers, scattering them in all directions, including into the river, before picking off the stragglers and robbing them of any cash or valued possessions. No passengers died but, in Spokane, the morning newspapers dubbed it a 'massacre' and, given the troubles in Shoshone County, wrongly attributed it to union men.[43]

Between the shootings at Gem on 11 July, and the half-hearted concessions made at Wardner on 12 July, and indeed for a full day thereafter, Clement put the Governor under constant pressure to expedite the arrival of federal troops. Heyburn, acting on Hammond's instructions as President of the MOA, did likewise and 'proved himself a master alarmist in the brief form of the telegram, magnifying the casualties and colouring his messages with picturesque and forceful language'.[44] Then, when the first few troops eventually *did* trickle into the county at the Mission, on the morning after the 'massacre', on 13 July, Victor Clement was not ready and had to slow down their arrival.

The union was still firmly in control of the company concentrator, and Clement had to wait until the last of the strikebreakers were clear of the property. The BHS management was, to all intents and purposes, in a state of siege. So, while US Army troops under Colonel WP Carlin prepared to link up with Curtis's Idaho National Guard, Clement looked around for short-term concessions. On 16 July 1892, he announced the repeal of BHS's much-hated policies in regard to the bunkhouse and company store – relief that workers at the mine in Wardner had been in search of for at least half a decade.[45]

But that, too, was a concession made under duress – by a company notorious for being led by 'bad losers'. Management at BHS continued to hanker after control of workers via the bunkhouse; in 1893, confronted with ongoing labour problems at the mine, Clement's successor, Fred Bradley, again contemplated the closure of the mine until such time as 'the community will be glad enough to see us start up, boarding house and all'.[46] While headed up by Hammond, BHS Co remained unwilling to take any steps towards reconciliation.

Hammond's anti-Cornish prejudices appear to have become entrenched at Bunker Hill. In early 1894, although the company employed men of a dozen different nationalities, not one of them was Cornish – in sharp contrast to other mining communities in Arizona, California, Idaho, Montana or Nevada.[47] Fred Bradley went even further when it came to manipulating class, ethnic and religious tensions in the valley. Believing Irish workers to be at the root of all labour problems at BHS, Bradley resolved to replace them with 'Americans'. To the same end he encouraged Protestant artisans and merchants in Wardner to establish a 120-strong branch of the anti-Catholic 'American Protective Association' (APA). Bradley saw the branch as a source of anti-Catholic agitation, a league for the 'best citizens' and as a 'secret society for the preservation of law and order' and, 'before long, the APA warned that it would lynch anyone who interfered with company business'.[48]

These developments may not have been initiated by Hammond, but they were undertaken with his full approval, and hint at the levels of aggression and fear that underpinned his discussions with Rhodes and Jameson, in 1894, on the need for a pre-emptive capitalist 'revolution' on the Witwatersrand.

With the proclamation of martial law on 13 July 1892 – which lasted four months – General Curtis and Colonel Carlin were ready to do the state's bidding, which coincided, to an extraordinary degree, with the wishes of Hammond and the MOA. Curtis oversaw the removal of the County Sheriff, a local sympathetic to the strikers, and replaced him with Dr WS Simms, the county coroner, a man notoriously close to the MOA. Charlie Siringo then emerged from his mountain retreat and helped Curtis to identify militant union leaders. In essence, Curtis and Simms moved in unison, acting as far as possible like regular county and state authorities and using Carlin's troops only as back-up to help enforce compliance with martial law.[49]

Governor Willey and the MOA's objective was to use the authority of the state to get the mines back to production as quickly as possible. To this end, they employed two tactics. First, they approved and oversaw the arrest of the strike leaders as well as the mass detention of union members. Commencing on 15 July, the core of about a dozen union leaders and hundreds of ordinary members were taken in and locked up. But, since the average number of detainees under martial law exceeded 300 a day, they easily exceeded the capacity of the local jails. The detainees were therefore herded into the infamous 'bull pens' of union folklore – abandoned or empty storage facilities and warehouses.[50]

Fourteen union leaders, including George Pettibone, supposedly responsible for blowing up the Frisco mill, were subsequently charged with conspiracy and a range of lesser offences and appeared in various courts in Idaho between August and September 1892. Clement and Siringo were prominent among witnesses for the prosecution, with Heyburn, too, taking a leading role in proceedings. But of John Hays Hammond himself, President of the MOA, there was no sign. On 28 September, Pettibone and three others were found guilty of conspiracy while ten other defendants were found not guilty. In early March 1893, however, the United States Supreme Court, presided over by Chief Justice MW Fuller himself, set aside the judgments of the Idaho court and the four prisoners were released to return to the Coeur d'Alene as folk heroes.[51]

By then, however, the price of silver was again in sharp decline. In the aftermath of the 'panic' of 1893, silver fell from around 85 cents an ounce, in 1892, to just 62 cents by June 1893.[52] During this deep depression, from January 1893 to June 1894, the Coeur d'Alene Miners' Union, whose origins derived in good measure from the actions of BHS Co and the MOA – and against expectations – continued to strengthen. In May 1893, the CDAMU became a founding member of the more radical Western Federation of Miners. In 1905, the Western Federation, in turn, affiliated itself to the Industrial Workers of the World (IWW), commonly known as the 'Wobblies' (IWW), which played a central role in the struggles of organised labour in the United Sates in the 20th century.[53]

The attempt by Curtis, Carlin and the MOA to deprive the union of leadership while the Coeur d'Alene was under martial law was thus, depending on one's timeframe and long-term vision, only partially successful. Their second offensive, to get the mines back up and running, enjoyed slightly better results – with one predictable exception. Under military protection, hundreds of strikebreakers were reintroduced to mines in Shoshone County. The industrial climate was further 'stabilised' when, in the latter part of 1892, many employers relented and reverted to the union rate of $3.50 a shift for miners, while many valued workers who were still union members, were re-employed by the mine owners.[54]

But, shot through this narrative, from 1887 to at least the turn of the century, if not a little beyond, were the bitter and intransigent influences of the cowboy capitalists, the old Minas Nuevas twins, Hammond and Clement.

Within 48 hours of the strikebreakers being escorted off BHS property, on 13 July 1892, Clement and his deputy, Fred Bradley, backed by Curtis and Carlin's troops, were supervising the return of the very same 'scabs' to the mine.[55] Just two weeks later, on 29 July, BHS resumed full production but, unlike any other employer up or down the Coeur d'Alene, the company stuck to its pre-strike wage structure and resolutely refused to concede the union rate even *before* the price of silver began its new slide, in 1893. In effect, the non-unionised miners at BHS, like those in Sonora, were working under the protection of federal troops paid for by the taxpayer.

It was not only the highly contested and frequently violent frontier setting of the Coeur d'Alene that eventually drove Hammond and Clement out of Shoshone County. The fact that they were so despised helped ensure that, within months of martial law being declared, the valleys were free of their physical presence. However, their investments in BHS Co ensured that they continued to exercise an indirect influence in Wardner through Fred Bradley, their hand-picked successor as mine manager. The real driver behind their withdrawal from Idaho was not 'The Call of Africa', as Hammond disingenuously asserted, but the comprehensive collapse of the hidden economic and political support mechanisms that had underpinned their ruthless operation in the Rockies over half a decade.

As Hammond admitted in his more honest moments, the real hammer-blow to his overweening ambition came with the presidential election in the first week of November 1892. The victorious Democratic candidate, Grover Cleveland, unlike his Republican rival, the incumbent Benjamin Harrison, wished the dollar to be backed by gold exclusively rather than by gold and silver. The defeat of a policy of bimetallism, along with President Cleveland's disapproval of high tariffs, heralded the rescinding of the Sherman Silver Purchase Act. Without the benefit of guaranteed purchases, the price of silver slumped and Western mining companies, such as BHS, were once again exposed to the vagaries of over-production and falling profits. For Hammond, his mood swinging wildly between the demands of fame and wealth, the election of Cleveland came as a personal blow. It was also a particularly serious professional one in view of his role as President of the Board of BHS Co and the fulcrum of its tight network of investors.

As the Cleveland election celebrations drew to a close in the District of Columbia, Republican lights in the Coeur d'Alene began to dim. On 19 November 1892, martial law ended in Shoshone County and in March, 1893, the United States Supreme Court set George Pettibone and other union leaders free. Governor Norman Willey continued to support the MOA to the best of his ability but was starting to feel the pinch as the People's or Populist Party, partly in response to the pounding that working men had been subjected to in the Bitterroot Mountains, began to make political headway in his state. 'The Populist legislature of 1893,' one of the troopers sent to the Coeur d'Alene in 1892, noted later, 'practically abolished the Idaho National Guard by withholding all appropriations for it.'[56] Over the five years that followed, Idaho sent a People's Party senator and two congressmen to Washington, DC, while trouble simmered in much of the Coeur d'Alene and Shoshone County, where, as ever, BHS Co was at the very forefront of discontent.

By the first quarter of 1893, the economic and political tide had retreated so far and so fast, that the arrival of the tsunami in the shape of the 'panic' on the New York Stock Exchange was only a matter of time. Once the market crashed and Cleveland set about implementing his new policies with regard to silver, Hammond had no more stomach for direct involvement in the ongoing industrial battles in the Coeur d'Alene, the MOA's steadily eroding position in Shoshone County or the social climate at Wardner, which had been unpleasant for as long as he could remember. As midyear approached, he knew that he had to find a man whom he could trust, a person bound to him by more than professional competence, someone with military experience and in whom the big investors had confidence. Only then could he resign as President of the board and withdraw the loyal but unpopular Clement as manager. Should such a brave and resolute man be found to fill the position of company chairman, then Bradley – the manager – could keep running the mine along exactly the same unyielding lines that he and Clement had pioneered at BHS. True, they would not be around on a day-to-day basis, but the union would soon discover that the more things changed, the more they stayed the same. Hammond knew exactly who to turn to.

Who better than Confederate General Nathaniel H Harris? His wife's uncle had been Hammond's business partner, in San Francisco, since 1890. The General was well suited to running a quasi-military mining operation in what Hammond saw as a state of 'semi-warfare' at a time when both the Democrats and Populist Party were pushing for labour reforms in Congress as well as the Idaho state legislature.[57] Depending on one's point of view, the appointment of Harris – President of the BHS Co board from 1893 to 1897 – was either part of a compact with the devil or an inspired choice, a man capable of reassuring family and other, closely connected, backers. On 15 June 1893, Hammond stepped down as President of the Board of the Bunker Hill & Sullivan Company and, at about the same time, Clement handed over his position as mine manager to Bradley.[58] The old commanding officers at besieged Fort BHS handed over to the new and the six-year-long war of attrition in Shoshone County resumed.

The battle lines in Shoshone County and Wardner, in 1893, were so familiar that the principal combatants could negotiate them blindfolded. On the one hand was the MOA, now led by Bradley but which, without Hammond in personal command, was softening at the core. On the other, the Coeur d'Alene Miners' Union, despite the deteriorating economic environment, had learned painful lessons and, in the face of Hammond's tactical retreat, was strengthening rather than weakening. The battle lines were recognisable but a waxing and waning in the strengths of the armies meant that things were slowly changing. The CDAMU renewed its demands for a minimum wage of $3.50 per shift for all underground workers in the Coeur d'Alene – and union recognition – but the company stood firm:

> The Bunker Hill and Sullivan remained intransigent and rebuffed all appeals for negotiation. Anticipating trouble, the company managers organized their non-union employees into militia companies: the Republican state administration supplied arms and ammunition and promised the imposition of martial law should violence erupt. While company officials, notably those of the Bunker Hill and Sullivan, imported non-union men and fired all union agitators they discovered on their payrolls, union militants demanded the dismissal of non-union labourers. Scabs and management sympathizers who refused to comply with requests to leave the district risked personal injury or death.[59]

The CDAMU had become as bloody-minded as any of the bosses.

Bradley, a graduate of the Hammond School of Business Management, took the fight to the union as well as to the railway companies whose freight charges ate into the company's profit margins. He hired Pinkerton and Thiel agents to do as Siringo had done before and infiltrate the union so as to improve intelligence. When the rail companies raised freight charges, in mid-1893, he refused to move BHS ore to smelters until they relented. But it was hardly plain sailing. On the resumption of full production, he was forced to pay all his underground workers $3.50 a day for several months or to cut back severely on the mine's output.[60]

As Chairman of the MOA, Bradley placed the rest of the Coeur d'Alene mine owners under renewed pressure for an across-the-board reduction of the old $3.50 rate. When war-weary mine owners would not agree he withdrew BHS Co from the association and told members that he would 'go it alone'. Faced with renewed wage cuts, the union brought out the Big Negotiator and the 'company's power house was dynamited'. The state and federal authorities responded as before and, in October, just weeks after the twins' departure, Bradley reported that 'a reign of terror exists here, and I hope that the US troops here will stay'.[61] And far away, in South Africa, Hammond – still a prisoner of the excessively personalised network of investors he had helped to create – wrote to William Crocker, the San Franciscan banker, growling his support for Bradley's uncompromising stand. 'If I could see my friends out of either hole,' Hammond snarled, 'I would gladly sacrifice my own holdings before letting those miserable scoundrels [the labour unionists] dictate terms to the Company.'[62] In Shoshone County, it was *plus ça change*.

Bradley won his battle. The wages of underground workers at BHS were reduced and the low-intensity war continued from 1893 right up to the turn of the century. And throughout that time Hammond, half a world away, lent his unqualified moral support to General Harris and Bradley. Hammond's appetite for cowboy-like, frontier adventurism and outright warfare remained undiminished. In November 1895, when he, Clement and a half-dozen of their California engineering cronies were already deeply embroiled in planning a coup d'état and only weeks away from the Jameson Raid, he again wrote to Bradley in encouraging tones: 'I congratulate you upon the success you are making with the Bunker Hill & Sullivan.'[63] For Hammond, war was peace, and there was hardly a year between 1890 and 1899 that he was not involved in making, preparing or responding to industrial war either personally or indirectly, via family and friends in the canyons and hills of the Coeur d'Alene. In his mind, Hammond was never far from the ranch school in Oakland.

In Shoshone County, the war came to a climax in 1899, shortly before Hammond felt that the dust had settled sufficiently in Johannesburg and Wardner for him to risk a return to the United States. In early April that year, the CDAMU planned yet another strike to pressurise BHS Co into paying union rates for all underground workers. Bradley's assistant, Fred Burbridge, who got to hear of the plan, responded by firing 17 union members and achieved a short-term success when he rode out a brief strike. By then however, the union leaders had lost all patience with BHS intransigence.

On 29 April 1899, mines up and down the Coeur d'Alene shut down as armed and masked union members boarded trains and made their way to Wardner. Burbridge asked Governor Frank Steunenberg for assistance and, once, again, federal troops were mobilised for a campaign in the Bitterroot Mountains. But, well before the troops got there, the Big Negotiator cleared his throat: 'At Wardner the rebellious miners dynamited and destroyed the Bunker Hill & Sullivan concentrator and burned the office and the boarding house.'[64] Burbridge abandoned the mine, fleeing to Spokane. Damage was estimated at $200 000 ($7 million in 2014 terms). As in 1892, union leaders were arrested and lives lost but, 'in the end, amidst great bitterness, the Coeur d'Alene unions were for all practical purposes destroyed for many years'.[65]

By the time this perversion of 'peace' settled in Shoshone County, two of the major antagonists had been in southern Africa for half a decade. Hammond and Clement may have been gone, but they were not forgotten. Members of the CDAMU, the Western Federation of Miners and progressive labour movements across the United States remembered them all too clearly. Unlike Rhodes and Jameson, who failed to do their homework on Hammond and Clement before entering into a conspiracy with them, or the four generations of American, British and South African historians who have ignored it since, organised labour in the United States was well aware of the link between the former president of the Coeur d'Alene Mine Owners' Association and one of the principal architects of the Jameson Raid. In 1900, shortly after the commencement of the Anglo-Boer War of 1899–1902, Thomas A Hickey, an activist in the American Socialist Labor Party and author of *The Story of the Bull Pen*, had no hesitation in drawing attention to the connection. 'Who may this John Hays Hammond be?' Hickey asked most pertinently:

> This Hammond is the gentleman who afterwards went to Africa, and together with the protégé of Cecil Rhodes and Joseph Chamberlain, the filibuster Dr Jameson, conspired a midnight raid upon the Boer Republic. Just as he smuggled rifles into Idaho in '92, so in '97 [*sic*] he showed his training by smuggling rifles in carloads of coke into the Transvaal. Oom Paul, however, pulled him up short, and ran the scoundrel out of the Transvaal.[66]

Looking back, then, it can be seen how, between them, in the 1890s, John Hays Hammond, General Nathaniel H Harris, Victor Clement and the two Freds – Bradley and Burbridge – played prominent, probably leading parts in the turmoil in the Coeur d'Alene. The seeds of trade unionism were sown in the Bitterroot Mountains, on the Bunker Hill & Sullivan property, in the late 1880s; from there they spread through the Coeur d'Alene and blew across the northern Rockies, joining those in Butte, Montana, the Western Federation of Miners and, ultimately, being distributed across the American plains in the form of the Industrial Workers of the World. In his ceaseless quest for fame or wealth, Hammond helped shape the greatest clashes between capital and labour in the Gilded Age. By the mid-1890s he was, as he hoped, becoming a figure of national importance in parts of the United States.

But, as the Dublin-born, well-travelled, Hickey noted, Hammond was destined to play a role on a stage that easily transcended the national. He was, in Hickey's terms, an 'international hireling of capital' and fated to influence events on a global scale. Had Hickey traced Hammond's career in southern Africa more carefully, he would have found much more to marvel

at. He would have understood how the American West, the Coeur d'Alene
and San Francisco – as embodied in the experiences and ideologies of John
Hays Hammond – not only shaped the planning of the ill-fated Jameson
Raid but also how the Raid itself helped poison southern African history
and plunged the British Empire into its greatest and mostly costly war ever.

Mining

CHAPTER SIX

Ghost Riders of the Coeur d'Alene

The Pursuit of Hammond, Johannesburg

1893–1894

Envisage a frontier territory in which invaders had conquered but never entirely subdued the indigenous peoples who far outnumbered them, and whose existence was predicated almost entirely on a seasonal hunting and subsistence farming economy. Furthermore, imagine a loosely cohering 'state', one without the rudiments of a standing army, served by a skeleton civil service, devoid of large urban markets or towns, and without an easily accessible or substantial tax base. Think of the same late 19th-century 'state' without navigable rivers, hundreds of miles from the nearest port, without anything approaching a national road, rail or telegraph system, and utterly dependent on coaches or ox-wagons for the transport of goods and passengers.

Contemplate, then, the bemused, conservative and poorly educated rulers of such a 'state' discovering that their tiny capital 'city' – a modest encrustation of churches, houses and stores – was less than 65 kilometres from the largest gold deposits on the planet and that it was the commodity that underwrote most of the world's trade and the international economy of what seemed like a distant universe. Then mentally activate the process of historical change. But, instead of running the tape past the mind's eye at normal pace, allowing for the normal, real-time, adjustments necessary for the emergence of a modern 19th-century state over a few decades, or a century or more, set your mind-machine to 'fast forward' mode. Note how the Afrikaner, Calvinist, nationalist, rural elite intent on holding on to its independence in a hinterland dominated by British imperialism struggles to develop economic policies that privilege agriculture even as 'their' republic is overrun by urban, modernising, capital-accumulating forces. These forces, led by non-resident mine owners, along with their agents and the editors of their newspapers, then choose to speak on behalf of tens of thousands of unenfranchised immigrants. The newcomers, whose numbers soon match, if they do not outnumber those of the incumbent power, demand: a proficient civil service, a liberal constitutional dispensation, corruption-free government, cheap African labour, an inclusive education policy, a free press, freedom from conscription, more appropriate police, prisons and legal systems, religious tolerance, modest customs duties, taxes and tariffs, an expanding transport infrastructure, a suitably progressive language policy, a supportive manufacturing sector, respect for property rights, racial segregation in towns, the suppression of African chieftaincies, protection against unfair trading practices by 'foreigners' of colour, and anything else they can think of that might be more in keeping with the emergence of a Euro-centric, industrialising state integrating into the wider world economy.

Such a system might come under some strain even if its ruling elite did make strategic advances and tactical concessions. That the elite might meet many of these demands and to a considerable degree, *without* being subjected to a coup d'état or all-out war for close on two decades may be attributed to anything from good fortune and tolerable governance to divine intervention and the truly miraculous. Of course, neither the Kruger government, nor the South African Republic, ever wanted for internal or external challenges between the retrocession of 1881 and the outbreak of the Anglo-Boer War in 1899. The early 1890s were characterised by large-scale African rebellions occasioned by increasing tax, territorial and labour demands from white farmers and the new mining industry. And more than once Irish bandits forced the government to refine and revise its planning for the policing of towns.

But the most obvious source of potential political resistance to the old order lay wholly in the new urban areas. The danger of this increased after 1890, once it became clearer that, unlike alluvial goldfields elsewhere, Johannesburg's wealth was predicated on the presence of continuous reef deposits, albeit of low grade, that ran to greater depths than anywhere else in the world. Once it was accepted that the Witwatersrand had a long-term future the idea of an attempt at a coup d'état, large-scale rioting or an urban insurrection, presented itself as an almost self-evident, logical, alternative to government, or misgovernment, by Pretoria's fragile elite. The birth of a notion of rebellion or revolt against Boer rule was thus not dependent on the emergence of deep-level mines or the 'Randlords' – although it obviously stood far more chance of success with their backing – it was built into the very architecture, the geopolitical structure of the South African Republic. Pretoria formally held political power but Johannesburg had the money.

In one sense, then, there was an underlying cognitive continuity to the idea that, one day, Johannesburg might be at the centre of an uprising, or a revolt, aimed either at coercing or dislodging the Kruger government or, more ambitiously still, of capturing the state in the South African Republic. Most of the largely futile ideological spadework behind such thinking, first in 1890 and later, just prior to Jameson's 'Raid', in 1895, was done by two Cape-trained advocates, the brothers Charles and James W Leonard. In 1890, as the recession on the Rand began to bite, JW Leonard launched the shadowy, but short-lived, Political Reform Association (PRA) of the South African Republic.[1] Publicly concerned to challenge concessions, the franchise laws and the rail and tax policies of the government, in private the 'inner circle' of the organisation had far more radical aspirations. The PRA's revolutionary aims, however, were blunted first, by Kruger's timely establishment of a Second Volksraad to represent immigrant interests, and secondly, by the speed of the economic recovery on the Witwatersrand after the discovery and the introduction of the MacArthur-Forrest process of gold recovery.

Significantly, it was an attorney, FW Bell, someone who moved in the professional circles frequented by the Leonard brothers and the founder of the legendary Johannesburg legal firm of Bell, Dewar and Hall, who, shortly after Jameson's Raid, reminded the curious about the much longer than suspected pedigree of revolutionary ideas on the Rand:

> Shortly after the time of the flag-pulling incident after President Kruger's disappointing visit to Johannesburg in 1890, a conspiracy was on foot to seize the artillery barracks and magazines at Pretoria as well as the public offices and members of the Executive Council. Plans were more fully mature than Mr [WT] Stead dreams of. But whatever revolutionary plans were on foot on different occasions long before the Raid, the clamour was persistent.[2]

In a frontier setting such as the Witwatersrand, where there was often significant two-way traffic between the criminal and the political, and vice versa – as evidenced by the Jameson Raid itself – not all radical ideas were doomed to a twilight existence in the minds of would-be revolutionaries. About 12 months after the apparent expiry of JW Leonard's Political Reform Association, an attempt was made to use a variant on the ideas outlined by Bell to challenge a key state institution.

In late 1891, in a surprise outcome to the trial of two highwaymen with links to the bandits-turned-gangsters of the 'Irish Brigade', the Chief Justice, JG Kotzé, sentenced Hugh McKeone and William Cooper to death for the attempted murder of two policemen. The idea of executing two murderous white men, whose real notoriety lay in the systematic robbing of black migrant workers making their way across the Highveld, deeply offended the moral sensibilities of many urban English-speakers along the Witwatersrand, as it did city dwellers throughout the rest of white southern Africa.

There followed a sophisticated, well-orchestrated oppositional campaign of public meetings and petitions that elicited the support of the King of Portugal, consuls, mayors of towns and thousands of citizens across the country. JW Leonard, in search of a mass political base, stepped forward and offered to defend the condemned men *pro Deo*.[3] When President Kruger seemed set on defending the decision of his Chief Justice, underworld elements in Johannesburg, with or without the knowledge of learned counsel, suddenly took matters into their own hands and put into action a plan designed to spring McKeone, Cooper and the leader of the Irish Brigade, Jack McLoughlin, from Pretoria's Visagie Street prison, close by the artillery barracks and the magazine.[4]

So seriously did the government take the threat posed by the Irish Brigade that all incoming stagecoaches into the capital were stopped and searched. Two armed detachments from the largely ceremonial State Artillery were deployed around the prison perimeter. When a half-hearted attempt was made to free the inmates by an unknown number of men, security was tightened further. Streets were barricaded, the prison was linked to the military headquarters by telephone, more State Artillery men were deployed and no less than 80 burghers were placed on standby.[5] The prison, if not Pretoria, was in a state of siege.

The attempted prison break, only months after the floating of the revolutionary ideas Bell had identified, shows that the concept of a putsch predated the Raid and Reform Committee, and ran along more or less predictable lines. The notion of a coup and the ways in which it might be executed therefore never depended entirely on the availability of Californian engineers in the Witwatersrand mining industry, or on the presence among them of one radical San Franciscan with close knowledge of the adventurism of filibusters like William Walker, Asbury Harpending's 'Committee of Thirty' or that city's Vigilance Committee.

But what Bell's reminder shows is that such experiences and ideas as Hammond *had* acquired – independently – back in California, Idaho and Mexico, resonated with the thinking of certain influential locals. These included Charles Leonard, whose imperialistic National Union was the successor to his brother's Political Reform Association, a few mine owners and many well-educated professionals, as well as Jameson himself. The origins of the events misleadingly termed the 'Jameson Raid' do not lie in either the American West or the Transvaal, but in *both*. John Hays Hammond was *not* the first to come up with the idea of a putsch in Pretoria, but he was the first willing to champion the idea of a coup who possessed both limited theoretical insight into, and a considerable practical experience of, what a revolution in a mining town might look like. He alone, as we shall see in due course, also entertained private notions about what form a stand-alone, American-inspired, constitutional dispensation for the Witwatersrand might take. All this, together with his privileged access to Rhodes – starting with the expedition through Matabeleland in late 1894 – made Jack Hammond *the* catalyst behind the events leading up to the Raid.

★ ★ ★

By 1893 southern Africa was already renowned for holding a treasure trove of gold and diamonds of unparalleled proportions. It figured in the imaginations of acquisitive men around the world and it would have taken nothing out of the ordinary for it to have come to Hammond's notice quite independently. But what seems more likely is that his introduction to the wealth of the subcontinent came via the San Francisco banking circles in which his father moved, and more especially the Pacific Union Club that he was chairman of.

In London, in the early 1880s, Lord Rothschild began taking a greater interest in the southern African diamond fields and looked about for a shrewd and trusted agent who might provide him with a critical assessment of the long-term future of the industry. His choice fell on Albert Gansl, a former agent of the San Francisco banking notables and a prominent member of the Pacific Union Club.[6]

Half a decade before Rhodes and Barnato set out to combine their interests and form what became the gigantic monopoly of De Beers, in 1888, Nathaniel Rothschild sent Gansl on a reconnaissance mission to Kimberley. It was Gansl who, in 1882, reported that the companies 'were ruining one another by over-production' and who 'argued strongly for amalgamation'.[7] It may well have been Gansl who also did some of the earliest thinking that led eventually to the formation of De Beers.

Gansl's ideas certainly helped ease the way to the Rothschild money that later underwrote the formation of De Beers. All this might help explain why Rhodes and Barnato held San Franciscans in high regard. It was Rhodes who, in 1885, appointed another Californian, Gardner Williams, General Manager of Kimberley Central. In small but significant ways, the pathways leading to the southern African diamond and gold mining industries both ran through San Francisco and the Pacific Union Club, and it would not be surprising if John Hays Hammond had not left the United States bearing a letter of introduction to Barney Barnato from Gansl.

As already noted, Hammond's lucrative six-month appointment with Barnato, starting in mid-1893, brought him a handsome income but failed to accommodate his insistence on being centre stage in whatever ambitious tasks he undertook, or to satisfy his need to expand his professional expertise. He resented Barnato's unwillingness to purchase the properties necessary to develop deep-level prospects and the fact that others in the gold mining industry had taken to referring to him as Barnato's 'white elephant'. Hammond also had a near irresistible urge to be, as he put it, close to the 'Big Man' – Rhodes – who snapped up his services towards the end of 1893.

It is worth noting how this seemingly innocuous move from one millionaire to another, from Barnato to Rhodes, also fitted in with Hammond's longer-term ambitions. Hammond never made a secret of the fact that he saw his southern African sojourn as a short-term career adjustment and that his long-term future, like that of most of his colleagues, lay in the United States. Looking back, then, it can be seen how, within a matter of 36 months, Hammond abandoned silver as the prospects for bi-metallism in the US dimmed with the exit of a Republican president, paused briefly around diamond mining interests, and then moved on to gold at a time when a Democrat president was ensuring that American trade and the dollar were underwritten by the gold standard. For those with great ambition, or those inclined to think in such terms, it was the ideal moment at which to think about nudging the South African Republic – a state with an almost reflexive loathing of British imperialism – more firmly into the orbit of the United States. After all, the ZAR was already experiencing a significant growth in bilateral trade with a country that was bound to become the region's economic powerhouse.

Experience gained on the Rand of gold mining, refining and sales in London would do Hammond no harm upon his return to the United States. He was capable of playing short term even when it was painful, as in Idaho, but seldom lost sight of the long game. He was willing to engage in 'revolutionary' activities, and more especially so when he was operating far from home, in Mexico or southern Africa, but he would never willingly jeopardise his chances of returning to the United States. In that sense his commitment to radicalism on the Witwatersrand differed from those of the Rhodes brothers – Cecil and Frank – Leander Starr Jameson, George Farrar or Lionel Phillips, all of whom were far more personally and politically committed to a future united southern Africa.

Hammond, like the rest of his American engineering cohort, then, was part of the profit-sharing locust elite, ready to devour as much as they could before moving on to new feeding grounds elsewhere. It was a technocratic elite, one invited in by other capitalists whose social universe rotated around

London's Park Lane. The Californians were unstinting when it came to giving of their professional expertise to better the long-term future of the mining industry, but there was no deep-seated affection for, or commitment to, the country they had invaded.

Frontier-like greed and opportunism were not always easy to reconcile with professions of radical zeal. Hammond was neither a coward nor a fool, but when problems that he had helped create became explosive or intractable, as they had in the Coeur d'Alene or Mexico, he was more than willing to withdraw and allow others to clean up his mess. Hammond had a tougher exterior than many of his fellow conspirators, and he talked a better revolution than most, but inside he was made of less stern stuff. One of his contemporaries who sensed this was the clear-eyed editor of the *Cape Times*, Edmund Garrett, who was also a confidant and friend of Rhodes. Garrett readily acknowledged – perhaps too readily because the source for much of his assessment may well have been the man himself – that Hammond had a 'background of American grit' and that he was possessed of a 'simple and attractive character'. Garrett's counterpart on the Rand, the editor of *The Star*, FH Hamilton, was even more fulsome in his praise of a fellow conspirator whom he saw as a 'forceful American' with a 'sincere and sterling character'.[8] Other journalists, including, as we will see, a former editor of the *Coeur d'Alene Barbarian*, had a less sanguine image of the man. But, be that as it may, Garrett also noted that Hammond's 'health and nerves were not made for stormy times'.[9]

When Hammond arrived on the Witwatersrand in mid-1893, he was quick to appreciate how capital-dependent the new deep-level mines already were, and how the need for an almost unlimited supply of cheap and unskilled black migrant labour was likely to expand. Unlike Kimberley, where his old Californian mentor, Gardner Williams, presided over a 'closed compound' system on the diamond mines, the gold mines on the Rand were still relatively 'open'. In Johannesburg, partly in deference to local white mercantile interests, black workers were given relatively easy access to trading stores on or near mining properties but could as easily visit the many illicit liquor outlets that left them inebriated.[10]

A marked lack of industrial discipline and drunkenness among members of this first generation of African workers, who were drawn from different cultural groupings and in the throes of being taxed off the land into the mines, gave rise to a great deal of inter-personal conflict and inter-tribal violence. For Hammond, who had no more respect for black workers on the Rand than he had shown for Indians on the Mexican mines, a twofold solution presented itself. In short, he sought as much control over his workers as possible at the point of production and place of residence:

> In order to ensure a permanent supply of efficient miners, I suggested
> to Rhodes that we establish native villages near the mines, where
> boys could live with their wives and families. The mining companies
> were to provide them with huts and small farms on which to raise
> chickens, hogs, cattle and the vegetables to help support themselves.
> I also thought it a good plan to attempt the civilizing of the wives so
> that their increasing wants would impose upon their husbands the
> necessity of continuous work, paralleling in that respect the duty of
> husbands in civilized communities. This scheme never met with the
> approval of the mine owners and has not been carried out.[11]

Thus, in the mid-1890s, Hammond came up with an innovative suggestion,
the folly or wisdom of which mine owners in South Africa still debate more
than a century later, without showing so much as a flicker of interest in
arriving at a mutually agreeable outcome with their workers.

Back in 1893, however, it was not so much the dismal lot of black workers
that commanded Hammond's attention as the emerging role and strength
of organised white labour in the South African Republic. This was a subject
of immediate and enduring interest not only to a consulting engineer and
profit-sharing employee of Barnato or Rhodes, but also to a psychologically
scarred American mine owner who was still involved in an ongoing war
with the Coeur d'Alene Miners' Union. When Hammond put the wind up
Rhodes and Jameson with tales about a possible uprising of white workers
in Johannesburg during the journey through Matabeleland, in 1894, it was
at least as much about a recurring Coeur d'Alene nightmare as it was about
what he saw on the Rand.[12]

In Hammond's autobiography, as is so often the case with his writings,
there is a remarkable silence about two aspects of skilled white labour on
the Witwatersrand, in the mid-1890s, that no 'mining expert', let alone
one of his standing, could have failed to notice. How was it possible for
Rhodes's leading engineer, one centrally involved in a conspiracy to overthrow the Kruger government via a popular uprising he helped organise,
to write several chapters covering his life in Johannesburg and the Jameson
Raid without once mentioning the name 'Witwatersrand Mine Employees'
and Mechanics' Union' or, more prosaically, the word 'Cornish'? Are these
chance omissions or, as seems more likely, are these gaps glaring precisely
because they point to a mine owner bitterly opposed to trade unions and
still engaged in a far-off struggle with them, as well as a mining engineer
with strong anti-Cornish prejudices? If the latter is true, then a few of his
personal failings, in late 1895, are easier to understand.

Founded in August 1892, the Witwatersrand miners' union was a threefold response to developments in the recession of 1889–1892: the transition

to deeper-level mining, the formation of an employers' organisation, in the shape of the Chamber of Mines, and the need to defend and entrench the privileges and wages of white workers. The union was not quite a year old when Hammond reached Johannesburg and heard how it had recently derailed an attempt by mine owners to have legislation passed that would help curtail the theft of gold. The idea behind the Gold Thefts Bill, sponsored by the Chamber of Mines, was that it 'would authorise espionage and the surveillance of employees by company agents'.[13] But, in February 1893, the miners staged a large street procession through central Johannesburg and lobbied members of the Volksraad with such success that the bill was promptly 'thrown out' and the union celebrated with yet another parade.

The union's triumph was a severe setback for the mine owners, who were sustaining significant losses through theft of amalgam and illicit sales of unwrought gold. It was not only the emergence of the union and the defeat of the Chamber of Mines that would have registered in Hammond's mind, but also the intense anger that the idea of using secret agents to spy on miners had aroused among workers. The defeat of the Gold Thefts Bill would have echoed strongly in the ears of the Coeur d'Alene mine owner and cowboy capitalist, a man who, barely 18 months earlier, had seen a war erupt largely as a result of his penchant for employing Pinkerton agents to disrupt and undermine the legitimate demands of miners.

It would be strange indeed if this doubly-reinforced fear of escalating working-class militancy – part Johannesburg and part Wardner – did not accompany Hammond on his trip into Matabeleland in 1894, and inform his campfire discussions with Rhodes and Jameson. If it did, however, it would have been largely incorrect. The union's 1893 anti-Gold Thefts Bill agitation was the high point in its pre-Raid achievements. So swift was the economic recovery in the months thereafter, culminating in the 'Kaffir Boom', that, by 1895, when a popular uprising was planned for Johannesburg, almost all union militancy had already drained away.

Hammond disliked Cornish miners, who were everywhere on the Rand. From the early 1890s they formed the single largest ethnic group of skilled 'hard rock' miners on the Witwatersrand, showing a preference for working on the mines to the east of Johannesburg, where complex faulting of the reef placed far greater demands on workers than it did on the West Rand. At the Chimes Mine, near Benoni, the first settlement was known as 'Little Cornwall', just as latter-day Alberton still boasts a suburb by the name of New Redruth. By the mid-1890s it was estimated that there were around 7 000 Cornishmen on the Rand.[14]

With a preference for working in small, tightly knit groups drawn from their villages back home and manifesting a 'sturdy independence' in keeping with their underlying Wesleyan Methodism, the Cornish hard-rock men had specialist skills when it came to shaft-sinking, an ability in ever greater demand as the deep-level mines were being developed.[15] Even Hammond and Clement – who had worked hard at keeping the Bunker Hill & Sullivan mine free of Cornishmen – could not get by without their help on the Witwatersrand. At the height of the 'Kaffir Boom' Hammond, who studiously refused to concede their ethnic identity in his correspondence or his later writings, was forced to go out and recruit 'hard rock' miners in the American West and pay them attractive bonuses to chase the reef at ever-greater depths.[16] But, even then, he could not quite escape the terminology that informed part of his self-perception as a cowboy. He wanted, he told Richard Parker, his American agent at the time, real 'rustlers' as foremen.[17] All the greater the irony, then, when it was a team of Cornish 'Cousin Jacks' that set the world shaft-sinking record under Clement's management at the Simmer & Jack Mine, in 1895, for Rhodes's Consolidated Gold Fields Company.[18]

Everybody who knew anything about the Rand was aware that, if there were to be a successful uprising of armed white miners in Johannesburg, it would be heavily dependent on the successful mobilisation of the Cornish, the labour elite of the day. Edmund Garrett, who told his story within 24 months of the abortive coup 'with the assistance of the leading actors in the drama', reported that it was thought that 'those old Celts', the Cornishmen, were 'the likeliest to prove ugly customers' when it came to fighting, and Jameson himself felt that an uprising, led by Hammond, would rely heavily 'on miners with Lee Metfords' once the shooting started.[19] John X Merriman, Treasurer General to the Cape government until Rhodes's questionable business ethics caused him to resign, in 1893, was another who knew that, without the active participation of leading working-class elements, an attempted coup d'état would probably fail. In a letter to Charles Leonard, on 27 December 1895, only hours before Jameson set out for Johannesburg on his ill-fated 'Raid', Merriman asked Leonard a razor-sharp question: 'Can you move the well-to-do working man? Until you do, the Boer will beat you. Revolutions are not made by those who live soft but require a backbone of men who have corns on their hands.'[20]

Nobody could accuse the Cornish of living soft. Indeed, it was precisely because they were escaping exceptionally hard times in the tin mines back home that they were so appreciative of their well-paid positions on the Rand. In Cornwall, the price of tin plummeted through the early 1890s, reaching 'rock bottom' at £64 a ton in 1894.[21] In Johannesburg, in 1895, Cornishmen earned in one day what they might earn in a week in Cornwall, and it underwrote their frequent trips home as long-distance migrant workers. Unlike African workers, however, they did not have to run a gauntlet of highwaymen to get back home safely.

Nor were the Cornish predisposed to socialism or trade unionism, given that they came from a mining tradition in which they offered their services on the basis of small-scale independent bargaining for the extraction of ore, or the development of mine workings – what they termed 'tribute' or 'tutwork' contracts.[22] Proud, clannish, independent-minded and possessed of their own language, the 'hard rock' men had a preference for staying within their own ethnic association, and for maintaining their cultural cohesion and self-reliance. All of this, together with an uptick in Cornish nationalism prompted by hard times in Cornwall, left the 'hard rock' men largely unmoved by the champions of British imperialism.[23]

After the Anglo-Boer War, many of the Cornishmen lent their support to a countryman, Tom Mathews, one of the country's great labour leaders. Mathews, who had immigrated to the United States in 1882, was one of the militant unionists in Butte, Montana, who had supported the Wardner miners in their struggle against Hammond and Clement during the war of 1892.[24] But, in 1893–1895 the Johannesburg Cornish were less radically inclined and less likely to be mobilised for a cause they did not see as their own. The miners' union was at low ebb in terms of activism and, even if it had not been, it would have been difficult for an Englishman to generate so much as a spark of revolutionary enthusiasm from Cornish nationalist granite. How much more difficult then would it have been for Hammond and Clement – American engineers and mine managers with no affection for Cornishmen – to mobilise them for an anti-Boer urban insurrection?

It cannot be 'proved', but one suspects that it was this underlying weakness on the part of the conspirators, an inability to get their revolutionary message through to Cornish and English miners with conspicuous success, that helps explain their belated recruitment of an East Rand mine owner to their cause in November 1895, just a few short weeks before Jameson triggered the Raid. George Farrar, although one of those later sentenced to death for his part in the conspiracy, was not an easy or a natural fit among the conspirators. Still in the throes of assembling his gold mining fortune, Farrar was hardly of the same financial stature of the main funders of the conspiracy, Cecil Rhodes and Alfred Beit.

But Farrar brought something other than money to the conspiracy, and that was a more common touch. A man with political ambitions of a conventional imperial type, he was, according to one of his daughters, 'impulsive' with a love of horse-racing. Farrar was born in Cambridge but raised in Bedford, where he attended a school favoured by military men in search of an education for their sons. After qualifying as a mechanical engineer and selling agricultural implements for a family firm in the eastern Cape for some time, he made his way to Johannesburg via Barberton. There, he concentrated his efforts at the far eastern end of the reef and, in 1893, helped found the East Rand Proprietary Mine, flagship of the ERPM mines.[25]

Farrar's most important mines, around Benoni and Boksburg, placed him closer to the heartland of Cornish miners than other mine owners, and the fact that his company was still developing, and of more modest size than many others, meant that there were fewer layers between him and his employees than was the case on some other properties. 'George Farrar,' one historian notes, was 'in closer touch with the mass of mineworkers than any of the other leaders.'[26] If there was anybody who could possibly offset a failure by Hammond, Clement and their fellow Californians to mobilise the white miners, it had to have been Farrar.

Looking back, however, it is clear that it was not only old Rocky Mountain ghosts that haunted Hammond after he had effectively been put in charge of Rhodes's belated charge to acquire deep-level prospects on the Rand. Hammond's earliest days working for the US Geological Survey, and his exposure to company accounts in Arizona and Nevada, had enhanced his awareness of the cost of mining operations. His experiences in dealing with railway companies and miners in the Bitterroot Mountains had sharpened this awareness. Such concerns were even more legitimate on the Witwatersrand, where the costs of mining constantly had to be offset against low grades of ore that required the milling of hundreds of tons of tough conglomerate in order to acquire a few ounces of gold.

But Johannesburg and Wardner were worlds apart when it came to controlling costs. In the American West, a robust and relative 'free' market economy, guaranteed by strong political and, if needed, military support, had allowed Hammond to attack or counterattack the railway companies and the unions by simply shutting off production when the profits of the Bunker Hill & Sullivan Co were threatened by increases in freight charges or demands for a hike in wages. In the South African Republic, however, the railways were state-owned and Kruger's policies, adapted to a less developed capitalist economy, kept afloat monopolies, such as that for the manufacture of dynamite.[27] On the Rand there was no way of circumventing suppliers of goods or services by halting production, finding alternative sources or bullying.

In San Francisco, Hammond had been forced to live with the problem of having to report to a highly personalised set of investors at the Bunker Hill & Sullivan mine. He had fought to maintain profitability, as he liked to put it, through engaging in 'semi-warfare'. On the Witwatersrand there was little room for open economic warfare of that sort, and an already nervous state was highly unlikely to come to the rescue of hostile foreign mine owners. On the Rand, once he had shifted his allegiance to the Big Man and encouraged Rhodes to divest himself of most of his existing properties and take a chance on developing deeper-level mines that would take time to come into production, there was renewed pressure. Hammond had to ensure a stream of promising dividends for an expectant stock market that was, to an unusual degree, underwritten by rapacious speculative elements.

It is against this background that one has to understand Hammond's desire to see world shaft-sinking records set on properties managed by Clement and other Californian cronies and his sudden willingness to tolerate the presence of Cornish miners. So acute was the pressure to contain costs that the issues of tariffs, taxation and other mining costs became absolutely central to his campfire discussions in Matabeleland and thereafter.[28] And, if the Boer state refused to create a genuinely 'free' market of the sort that, in the final analysis, is always buttressed by suitable political and military support, then what alternative was there to attempting a coup d'état and overthrowing a protectionist government?

CHAPTER SEVEN

Sheriff Bob Blinks and Cowboy Jack Steps Up

Johannesburg Sunlight, San Francisco Shadow

1894–1895

For reasons easily understood, neither Hammond nor Clement ever alluded publicly to the fact that they were embroiled in the ongoing Coeur d'Alene mining war. Indeed, it is not clear whether Rhodes and Jameson knew much about the twins' industrial war experiences, or of how well they stood up in battle when faced with a mill packed with dynamite. Had the imperialists probed the republican revolutionaries' credentials more carefully, they might have been less inclined to accord Hammond the central role in managing the urban insurrection that was meant to act as the real trigger for a Jameson-led invasion of the Rand.

A *soi-disant* cowboy, a 'windbag', with an obsessive dread of being cast as a coward, Hammond, right up to his death, remained keen to conceal his role as the principal aggressor in the Coeur d'Alene Mine Owners' Association (MOA) and the circumstances under which he and Clement had been forced to retreat from Bunker Hill. While in Johannesburg the thing that Hammond had more reason than most to fear, was the unexpected appearance of someone with first-hand knowledge of how his mind worked, of his love of conspiracy, of his social engineering proclivities and his Coeur d'Alene war secrets. Imagine, then, his horror on learning that his former chief of propaganda, his cutting-edge ideologist in Wardner, 'Barbarian' Brown, was in town.

Robert E Brown, it will be recalled, was the engineer who turned wordsmith when the MOA bought out the *Wardner News* and supported his appointment as co-editor of the revamped *Coeur d'Alene Barbarian*, in the early 1890s.[1] When exactly Brown left Idaho and arrived on the Witwatersrand is unknown, but it is likely to have been in the wake of the exposure of Siringo, the Pinkerton spy who had systematically leaked the plans of the mineworkers' union to the *Barbarian* at the height of the dirty war. In Johannesburg, Brown reverted to his original calling and took up the position of consulting engineer to the 'Research and Development Company' and, famously, attempted, but eventually failed, to develop mining interests of his own.[2]

At some point between his departure from the United States, where his life was threatened, and his arrival in the South African Republic, Brown had second thoughts about the role he had played in the war at Wardner. He also developed new reservations about the political and social damage that the mine owners had wrought in Coeur d'Alene communities, even though he retained some residual respect and loyalty for his former employer. During Hammond's trial, in early 1896, Brown made a point of calling on Mrs Hammond, in Cape Town, to warn her about the wrath of the Boers, and to urge her to persuade her husband to flee the country before the Kruger government took the opportunity of imposing the death penalty.[3]

But while Brown did not wish to see Hammond hanged, he could not find it within himself to sympathise with the locust elite that had invaded the goldfields. When the crisis in Johannesburg mounted during the closing days of 1895, Brown, as befitted a former editor, set out his sentiments in a letter to the *Standard & Diggers' News* with admirable clarity. The Boers, he suggested, were a 'brave people' and worthy of admiration for having 'won their liberty from a powerful foe'. He had respect for republics, including America and France, which 'owed their democracy to revolution' and would like to see 'the Transvaal governed by people who lived in it', and the franchise extended. But, argued Brown, the new immigrants 'already enjoy more wealth or at least the opportunity for wealth' than elsewhere. He was opposed to the Boers being overrun and 'the government given over to the control of a few venal conquerors'.[4]

For those living in a binary world, suspended forever between the need for fame or wealth, Brown's views were anathema. They were the more so when he chose to act on his convictions and sought to play a constructive, mediating role between the self-appointed American 'revolutionaries' he knew all too well and the Kruger government in the closing days of the Jameson Raid. Hammond, anxious and suspicious from the moment he first encountered Brown in Johannesburg, in early 1894, had a visceral hatred of his one-time political lapdog. In his contrived memoir, Hammond, himself an industrial spymaster of note, reserved his most vitriolic attacks for the unfortunate Brown, deeming him to be 'contemptible' because he was 'a paid spy of Kruger'.[5] Hammond despised Brown precisely because he was one of the few men capable of linking the would-be revolutionary's tawdry Coeur d'Alene past to the present.

On the Rand, Hammond and Brown sized each other up during the Kruger government's bumbling attempt to conscript immigrants for the military campaign against the African chief Malaboch, in May 1894. Although only four months into his new position under Rhodes at the Gold Fields Company, Hammond was casting himself as a leader of the American mining community, which, in engineering terms, he was. But, as ever with him, he was not content to lay down the labour law to his employees but determined to configure their political and military affiliations as well. The only stumbling block he could see was Brown.

'I called a meeting one night to which I invited the managers and other American officials of the mines under my management,' Hammond told a hand-picked, wide-eyed journalist some years later. 'The meeting was supposed to be a secret one, but we took care to have present an American whom we knew to be a paid spy of the Boer government.'[6] It was, however, unlikely that Brown, although probably already a government sympathiser and informer, was a 'paid spy' at that time. Not only was he actively pursuing his own career as a well-paid engineer with developing interests in mining, but Kruger's 'secret service' only assumed a full-scale professional dimension towards the end of 1894.[7]

The meeting, at which Brown was present, concluded on a note of personal triumph for Hammond. As he later told the journalist: 'It was through a little ruse on my part that his right to conscript Americans was never enforced' because, it was unanimously resolved that, 'we would resist all efforts of the Boers to send us to the front to fight the Kaffirs, and that if, in the face of our protests, we were drafted, our first shots would be fired at the Boer officers'. But the 'ruse', of course, was not Hammond's. It came straight out of the repertoire of his nemesis, Sanchez, who had first used it in Sonora to resist being drafted into a band of Mexican revolutionaries.[8] But it was good story.

Just as Sanchez had become part of the nightmare that eventually drove Hammond out of Mexico, so 'Barbarian' Brown came to contribute to a lapse in self-confidence during events leading up the Jameson Raid about eighteen months later. Whatever form they took – whether as an abstracted dislike of independent-minded Cornishmen, a dread of a potentially militant mineworkers' union, an inability to control deep-level mining costs without police and military support in a monopoly-ridden economy, or simply a person, such as 'secret agent' Brown – all these spectres from the past were in Hammond's mind many months *before* he went to Matabeleland with Rhodes and Jameson, in August 1894. Moreover, in the troubled Coeur d'Alene, 'the past was not even past'; he and Clement had abandoned their posts and left his wife's uncle, ex-Confederate General Harris, to hold the fort.

From within this powerful witch's brew of anxieties, fears and uncertainties

Hammond conjured up campfire-smoke images of a proto-revolutionary situation in Johannesburg so vivid that even Rhodes and Jameson felt that it demanded urgent intervention if the economic and political future of the Witwatersrand was to be ensured for the British Empire. The idea behind the 'Jameson Raid' and the planning necessary to effect it was *not* put together in the Matabeleland bush in 1894. What *was* planted there, however, were the seeds of an understanding that the situation in Johannesburg could not be allowed to continue and that a decisive intervention would be necessary sooner rather than later.

But once Hammond succeeded in achieving an underlying consensus on the need to link directly the capitalist cables running between Johannesburg's wealth and Pretoria's political power, he was unwilling to hand back the initiative to Rhodes, or to Jameson, who had been even more taken with his Idaho war-talk than had been the Big Man. Hammond saw himself as more of a leader than a follower, and Rhodes and Jameson both sensed it and understood the danger it might entail. At stake was the difference between an American/republican and a British/imperial intervention to bring the ZAR into the orbit of the great powers. It was precisely for that reason that, immediately after the Matabeleland safari, Rhodes went to Pretoria to bait the Kruger lion about railway tariffs and Jameson to Johannesburg to try to verify Hammond's prognostications about a potentially revolutionary situation on the Rand.

Jameson, as we will note in due course, was not only himself a successful man of action, but one with a profound admiration for American adventurers, frontiersmen and soldiers. Jameson went to Johannesburg having listened to a master raconteur's politically charged war stories. He *wanted* to hear a plea for intervention authenticated from other sources in a mining industry dominated by Californians of the same mind as Hammond. Jameson heard what he wanted to hear. For his part, Rhodes, imperial statesman and political philosopher, emerged from an ill-tempered, hastily organised meeting in Pretoria convinced that Kruger was intractably nationalist and republican in sentiment, and that he would never entertain the idea of gradual economic and political integration in a wider southern African dispensation.[9] Rhodes, more thoughtful than Jameson and the man with most to lose, got Hammond's prognosis reinforced from above. Jameson, newly recast as a populist-soldier and a 'hero' fresh from the Matabeleland war, got it from below.

Rhodes and Jameson sensed that the seed that Hammond had planted in their minds a few weeks earlier had begun to sprout. They were not the only ones to notice. Frederic Hamilton, the Rhodes appointed edi tor of the Johannesburg *Star* later recalled seeing an early sign of the seed swelling. Immediately after the Pretoria meeting, Rhodes went across to

Johannesburg and Hamilton 'formed the impression that a plan of intervention was already germinating in Rhodes' mind'.[10] The timing of this observation is important. Some weeks later, on a sea voyage to England, Rhodes and Jameson had the opportunity to discuss the matter in more depth. The Marquess of Winchester later insisted that 'the Raid was planned in the Burlington Hotel in London by Rhodes, Jameson, Maguire and others' in late 1894.[11] The accuracy of the detail aside, one thing stands out from this observation, that is, in the last quarter of 1894, Rhodes and Jameson felt they were in control of the idea of an intervention and that the initiative lay with them. But they were in London and Hammond was in Johannesburg.

★ ★ ★

Hammond returned from the Matabeleland mining safari, in 1894, charged with precisely the assignment that he had hoped for from the Big Man, the one that he had failed to persuade Barnato to buy into. His task was to sell off Rhodes's existing holdings in gold mines without causing panic in the market, and then systematically to reassemble a portfolio of properties capable of producing long-term dividends from the new, deeper-level properties. It was a project 'more commercial and financial than technical' that combined the need for personal and professional intrigue of exactly the sort that came naturally to him:

> Part of my task was to see that secrecy was maintained. Had even a whisper of our intentions been spread abroad, the price would have gone rocketing. Working independently through several brokers pledged to silence, I was able to secure most of the desirable land on favourable terms.[12]

It all helped ensure that 1895 was a year of spectacular success for Rhodes, Gold Fields and, of course, John Hays Hammond. Towards the end of the year, before the Raid, the engineer admitted to Ernest Rhodes that 'this has been an extraordinary year for money making'.[13]

It was during the covert switch from outcrop mines to deep-level properties, in late 1894, that Hammond was drawn into close contact with two men who were to play important parts not only in the immediate success of the Gold Fields project but also in the plotting of the Jameson Raid over the following year. One was Fred Hamilton, who he already knew as editor of *The Star* but who, by then, also suspected that Rhodes was bent on some sort of intervention on the Rand. The two not only shared Rhodes as an employer but also what was to become his biggest secret, and they worked together ever more closely. Significantly, Percy FitzPatrick later recorded that Hamilton 'was one of the first associated with the movement'.[14] Hammond easily captured Hamilton.[15]

Hammond's other new contact was Rowland Albemarle Bettington, one of the stockbrokers 'pledged to silence'. Looking back, it is hard to know whether Hammond was more taken with Bettington, or Bettington with Hammond, although one suspects the latter rather than the former. Bettington would have gravitated towards Hammond by personality type and profession just as surely as a river finds the ocean. The men and their families lived close by one another, on the Parktown ridge, and it seems significant that when Bettington had a house built for himself, in Princess Place, the residence was given the name 'Santa Clara', a small town that lay just 72 kilometres southeast of Hammond's hometown of San Francisco.

The son of an East India Company civil servant, Bettington was 12 years older than Hammond and had arrived in South Africa in 1872 as a 29-year-old filled with imperial fervour and soldierly ambition but insufficient funds to purchase a commission in the British Army. In the eastern Cape, where frontier wars were almost as regular as the seasons, Bettington for some time alternated between editing or owning small-town newspapers and pursuing a military career, notably during the Ninth Frontier War of 1877–1878. At that time, by his own admission, Captain Bettington was fully overcome by 'war fever'. In 1881, he made his way north, to Barberton, where he achieved some success as a broker.[16]

In Johannesburg, Bettington continued trading in shares, and in between kept his journalistic hand in by occasionally contributing articles to *The Critic* and other publications. Bettington's interest in journalism appealed to Hammond, whose pursuit of fame and the desire to influence public opinion made the courting of newspapermen and the press a lifelong passion. Bettington, was just one of several former editors, including Percy FitzPatrick, Lionel Phillips and Fred Hamilton, who came to play a prominent part in the Jameson Raid and its offshoot, the so-called Reform Committee. As a professional subset within the Reform Committee, journalists were trumped only by the even tighter networks of doctors and lawyers. Bettington, like Jack Hammond, was comfortable in all those circles.

Stockbroking and journalism were not, however, Bettington's only interests. Brave and possessed of a 'fiery' temperament, he was a thoroughgoing imperialist and particularly resentful of the victory that the Boers had achieved at Majuba in 1881, during their 'First War of Independence'. He served on the Executive of Charles Leonard's National Union and, by late 1894, was already active in the Rifle Club established by Lionel Phillips after the Pretoria upheavals that Sir Henry Loch had been called in to settle.[17] Hammond, an American republican, but also an Anglophile radical, found much to admire in Rowland Bettington. He was no John 'Coffee' Hays, but he clearly was a man one could rely on.

Partly by chance and partly by design, then, by the closing quarter of 1894 Hammond was being drawn into a small circle of radicals where the notion of armed rebellion or revolt, while not as clear-cut as it was to become later, was nevertheless already part of the group's conversation. Rhodes, Jameson and others might be sitting in the Burlington Hotel talking theory and the need for a decisive political intervention on the Witwatersrand, but back in Johannesburg Hammond was mixing with frustrated soldiers and men with a very practical interest in riflery.

Hammond, attuned to the needs of an industrial revolution literally and metaphorically, was in an environment where his darkest fears – already manifest before going to Matabeleland – were being fed continually. Among the mining elite there were sufficient mutterings about the inadequacies of the state for the Kruger government to start assembling a 'secret service' to provide it with a flow of counterintelligence about a possible urban insurrection.[18] But Hammond knew better than most that a 'revolution' would require careful planning. The main question was, what part was *he* to play in it?

Given his experience in the American West, Hammond felt that, just as he had provided Rhodes and Jameson with an early warning about simmering discontent in Johannesburg, so could he see other signs of social menace with a clarity not always shared by the circles in which he and Natalie moved. Organised crime was beginning to manifest itself in the town through the unregulated sale of alcohol to African miners – a problem he and Clement had grappled with back in Sonora.[19] Moreover, it was apparent that on the outskirts of the town and in its prison, black criminals were conducting a reign of terror among ordinary Africans even though no whites could, as yet, put a name to their organisation.[20] Not so with white gangsters, ex-bandits who specialised in gold thefts from the mines, with the connivance of the town's Chief Detective, Bob Ferguson, and whom English journalists, including the Lancastrian FR Statham, already knew as the 'Irish Brigade'.[21]

For Hammond, who took it as an article of faith that 'lack of law enforcement is a far worse thing than lack of laws', there was worse to follow.[22] In mid-October 1894, the Commandant of Police, DE Schutte, wrote an open letter to a Johannesburg newspaper, declaring, 'I acknowledge the rottenness of the entire police force, but decline to accept the disgrace attached thereto, having striven to reorganise the same, but failed through lack of support.'[23] The boom in mining stocks and a burgeoning criminal population was outstripping the state's capacity to enforce the law. These problems were compounded when, in December 1894, a resentful Ferguson was overlooked for promotion to the position of national Chief Detective.[24]

Ferguson's uncooperative attitude undermined policing in the town. By the New Year the law and order genie was not quite out of the bottle but the cork was under mounting pressure. Then, on Saturday evening, 26 January 1895, the cork popped and all hell was let loose upon the populace. 'One-Armed Jack' McLoughlin, leader of the Irish Brigade, executed a police informer in a shooting at the Red Lion Beer Hall, in Commissioner Street and, while making his escape, put another bullet through the head of a youth when he mistakenly thought that the young man was going to apprehend him. Two shootings, within minutes of one another, in the most densely settled part of town, sent shivers of fear through many underworld watering holes in downtown Johannesburg.

What could not be confined to the local dives, however, was what followed; it echoed through the press for days thereafter and up and down every important street in town. Having disposed of his informer-nemesis, 'One-Armed Jack' linked up with a pair of underworld associates, entered Rosenthal's Restaurant, in Commissioner Street, and there, in full view of members of the public, presided over a celebratory dinner lasting several hours. The dinner was still in progress when Ferguson got to hear of it but, fearing McLoughlin and resentful of his superior, Andrew Trimble, he declined to set out and arrest the suspect. McLoughlin finished his meal and then left, disappearing into the night.[25]

Fred Hamilton at *The Star* led the public charge against Ferguson, pinning the word 'coward' to the Chief Detective's already shady reputation. It was a label of dishonour, one that Hamilton's close associates considered to be the most serious any man could face. Two weeks later Ferguson resigned but, by then, three other white men had been murdered in Johannesburg without any arrests being made. A full-scale colonial 'panic' followed. Rumours circulated that black men were involved in sexual assaults on white women. A run on gun shops followed. Sheriff Bob had blinked and, as he did, Cowboy Jack stepped forward.

From that moment on, *The Star* began a mass-based campaign designed to channel public outrage in ways that consciously pointed to the history of San Francisco in the 1850s. The Californians in town – and there were many of them – would certainly have understood the parallel being drawn, but for the majority of working men, English and Cornish, the comparison would have been unfamiliar if not a touch strained. Despite that, the campaign was driven with a focus and urgency that suggested that the editor was being strongly influenced by someone with first-hand knowledge of San Franciscan history.

The campaign commenced on 5 March 1895, when Rowland Bettington wrote a letter to the editor, which started by drawing attention to a recent murder of a white worker. The letter then continued, as might be expected from one who was a leading office bearer in the National Union, to reproduce a litany of familiar complaints about the franchise and the language question, and so on. But what the author really wanted was a public meeting, to be held in the Stock Exchange building three nights later, and to set about establishing a 'Vigilance Committee'.[26]

Vigilance committees – more American than English – were, however, not part of the populist repertoire in Johannesburg despite the fact that one had sprung into life in 1888, as part of a response to the Irish Brigade.[27] Hamilton was left to educate the majority of his non-American readers in a blunt, didactic leader:

> Let anyone who wants to know what lawlessness means when it once gets a good grip on a big town read the history of the Vigilance Committee in San Francisco, or a half-dozen chapters of Mark Twain's 'Roughing It' and then let the reader ask himself why what took place in western America in the early fifties should not happen here?[28]

This simple nudge in the right direction was followed, on 12 March, by a remarkable, half-page article written by somebody who identified himself only as 'An American on the Rand'. The essay, 'Vigilance Committees – A Famous Association', was centred unambiguously on the early history of San Francisco. Not only did the author endorse militant populist action unsanctioned by the law as a way of controlling crime, but from the examples presented two other things stood out. The author bore some knowledge of American industrial history, and was also familiar with individuals in banking circles. He particularly admired the founder of the city's most famous Vigilance Committee, William T Coleman, whom he lauded for the way he succeeded in paying every last cent that he owed creditors long after a declaration of bankruptcy had freed him from that obligation.[29]

The article was almost certainly penned by a son of San Francisco. And the campaign to set up a vigilance committee in Johannesburg was probably being covertly influenced by the same man who had helped oversee the establishment of the Law and Order Leagues in the Coeur d'Alene 36 months earlier but who did not want to risk the danger of being identified by name, by 'Barbarian' Brown. The essay had Hammond's fingerprints all over it, and further evidence came from the great public meeting itself.

The gathering of the notables at the Stock Exchange on 8 March 1895, might as well have been compiled from a Who's Who of those who were later centrally involved in the Jameson Raid. The meeting was initiated in response to a letter by Bettington and then supported by the article on San

Francisco written by Hammond that appeared in a newspaper edited by Fred Hamilton and owned by Cecil Rhodes. Lionel Phillips was elected as Chairman of the committee and the main address was delivered by James Leonard, a 'great friend' of Kruger's new reform-minded State Attorney, Ewald Esselen. Leonard was commendably honest and left the audience in no doubt as to what lines the mine owners were already thinking along. 'We want above all things,' he said, 'the head of a department that shall be a police department,' and then added the rider, 'We want such a man to regard himself as the head of a quasi-military organisation and to feel proud of his own position ...'[30] The feedback from the deputation that subsequently went to petition Kruger as a result of this public meeting came from Abe Bailey. Ideological hardliners, warmongers, if you will, men such as Bettington, Hammond and the Leonard brothers, were setting the pace many months before the 'Jameson Raid' transpired.[31]

But, for the student of the Jameson Raid the long-term significance of the short-lived Vigilance Committee probably lay elsewhere. It was hardly a dry run for an urban insurrection yet to be planned in any meaningful way, but it nevertheless gave some of the local radicals – 'revolutionaries' if we use the term lightly, 'jingoists' if we wish to be pejorative – the opportunity to mobilise and test the nature and depth of public support for populist action directed against the government. The result was disappointing. It reminded those like Charles Leonard and Bettington that the fortunes of the National Union were not, to put it mildly, rapidly reaching a high point. If there ever was to be an urban insurrection the National Union, too, would be playing catch-up politics.

For Hammond, however, the outcome, while disappointing, was hardly a disaster. Through Bettington, a kindred spirit and fellow 'war fever' sufferer, he had gained some traction with an influential figure in the National Union and got the opportunity of working more closely with the Chairman of the Chamber of Mines, Lionel Phillips, and Fred Hamilton – men who were at the heart of political and economic intelligence on the Rand. He had the inside track, and that placed him at an advantage when discussing the possibilities of a 'revolution' with the always peripatetic Rhodes and Jameson. He was on site, they were not.

At some point between late 1894, and mid-1895, Hammond found himself virtually in total command of the strategic high ground that separated Phillips and the powerful Wernher, Beit group on the one hand, from that of Rhodes and the Gold Fields group on the other. After Loch's visit to Pretoria in June 1894, Phillips – who stood in relation to Beit as Hammond did to Rhodes insofar as he, too, was the man on the spot – was increasingly of the view that 'some form of revolutionary action' would be necessary 'to force concessions for the gold mining industry'.[32] To this end Phillips had moved closer to the National Union people but he, like them, was wary of letting the 'too-powerful' Rhodes into their midst because he would use any initiative to further his own, far more ambitious, political ends. It was Hammond who urged upon Phillips, in particular, that 'Rhodes was indispensable because he alone could secure British recognition and provide an armed force to come to their aid'.[33] It was the old Coeur d'Alene guarantee; if all else failed then call in the National Guard or, if necessary, federal troops.

With the close associates Beit and Rhodes seldom in town together, and Phillips wary of getting too directly involved in a revolutionary chat with Rhodes, Hammond was left in a privileged position when it came to further talk about planning an urban insurrection. As the principal purveyor of revolutionary talk in Matabeleland, in 1894, and conveniently free of any local naysayers, Hammond repeatedly used the argument with Rhodes that he should become more involved in the plotting or risk being left behind.[34]

Part of that argument, which can be deduced from statements made later by Rhodes, was that Phillips, Leonard and others were, in effect, forging an alliance with certain 'Progressive' elements in the Boer leadership. Among the names regularly mentioned were those of the Chief Justice, JG Kotzé, who like at least one other judge – de Korte – was in debt to the Corner House, Piet Joubert, the Vice President of the Republic and Commandant-General of its armed forces, and Joubert's son-in-law, Abraham Malan.[35] But the most interesting names by far were those of Ewald Esselen, and his friend, the mercurial editor of the anti-Kruger newspaper *Land en Volk*, Eugène Marais.[36] Esselen, a trusted acquaintance of Rhodes's, had resigned a judgeship in order to revert to private practice before Kruger made him State Attorney.[37]

Hammond's political intelligence further back-footed the out-of-town Rhodes. It placed Hammond back at centre stage when it came to talk about overcoming the Kruger government and took the political initiative away from Rhodes, philosopher-king, and Jameson, action-man hero, back to the Witwatersrand. Rhodes, as we know from his later confession to WT Stead, already entertained fears that the real impetus for radical change in the South African Republic was coming from Americans and, without naming him outright, probably from the mercurial Hammond himself. For Rhodes, a sickly man whose many wills testified to the fact that he knew time was against him, the situation in Johannesburg by mid-1895 was becoming intolerable. If there was to be an uprising it had to be imperial rather than republican.

At some point in July or early August 1895, the scales in Rhodes's mind, balanced between caution and pragmatism ever since Matableland, tipped away from conjecture and talk and came down lightly on the side of conspiracy and direct action. In a letter to Alfred Beit, he expressed his disappointment at the lack of leadership coming from London on questions of empire. 'I wonder,' he lamented, 'how the English Empire has held together. You might say, oh yes, wait – but as you know we will wait too long and with its marvellous wealth Johannesburg will make South Africa an independent Republic, which you and I do not want.' 'If Johannesburgers succeed without me,' he opined, 'it's all up for a South African Union. Now I fear those fellows may have a revolution and a successful revolution in spite of me.'[38]

Evidently, at that point in August, even though he still held private reservations about the role the Americans might play in an insurrection that could well swing in a republican direction, Rhodes was more fearful still of a 'cosmopolitan republic' that could 'gravitate to Europe and away from South Africa'. But the Big Man was not about to embrace despair. He, Jameson, his principal informant on the spot and others, including Alfred Beit, had accepted the need for overt intervention on the Rand. Rhodes thought that things were looking hopeful. 'Johannesburg is ready' for the big idea – an uprising – he wrote, 'which makes England dominant in Africa, in fact gives England the African continent' and 'Hammond is enthusiastic'.[39] Of course Hammond was 'enthusiastic'. Had not Cowboy Jack helped shape a 'revolution' in the Bitterroot Mountains and seen to it that the Coeur d'Alene was brought to heel?

CHAPTER EIGHT

Rivalries in the Camp

The Beit Boys and the Rhodes Boys

c 1890–1895

The extraordinary thing about the coup d'état or 'revolution' that some hoped for on the Witwatersrand in 1895 is not that it ended in failure, but that the conspiracy it was based on managed to achieve any sort of coherence in the first place. Consider planning and organising a set of interlocking, synchronised events culminating in a coup in which the principal political champion and main financiers are of European origin and seek, in the main, a British – imperial – outcome, but are thousands of kilometres away from the site of the proposed action.[1] Contemplate an urban insurrection – the trigger action for the 'revolution' proper – being loosely informed by republican thinking imported from the West Coast of the United States, two oceans away. Then imagine the fail-safe mechanism for the entire operation, the military guarantee for success, being under the direction of a Scottish medical doctor. He, upon assuming command of a force of 500 armed and mounted men, made up for the most part of rough frontiersmen-turned-soldiers, then assembles his would-be invaders more than 300 kilometres away from the insurrection.

Such a scheme might have prompted some doubts in the minds of the conspirators themselves, but, for the most part, these went unrecorded or surfaced only after the event. But for the social historian, one interested in patterns of conflict as well as cooperation, it prompts a host of questions about the would-be revolutionaries themselves. What personal experiences, if any, did the leading conspirators have of armed conflict, 'revolutionary' disturbances or insurrections? To what extent, and in what ways, did they share a political vision? Given that the conspirators were involved in a top-down plot, one that consciously eschewed socialist, trade-unionist or other forms of self-organised white working-class involvement, to what extent were they bound only by their business and professional relationships? And to what extent would such an unusually configured plot, one that aimed at a 'revolutionary' outcome and carried with it the threat of the death penalty, have to be cross-threaded by intimate friendships or, as likely, by ties of kinship?

In short, what was the political and social glue – the basis of trust – that held together first the small revolutionary core, and then, when it became clearer that the coup de main had to be aborted, the hastily constructed, larger 'Reform Committee'? The Reform Committee, as we will come to learn, was an afterthought of failed revolutionaries. It was positioned by word and deed to suggest that it was merely the public face of a deeper-rooted, longer-standing 'reform movement', one with a legitimate agenda for political change championed by otherwise loyal leaders of civil society.[2] It is this deliberate blurring – the downplaying of the original revolutionary plan propagated by the core conspirators as being merely a bungled attempt by over-zealous 'reformers' – that has taken in most historians and encouraged them to telescope what started out as an attempt at a coup d'état into the far more anodyne 'Jameson Raid'.

We need to look anew at the social origins of a failed urban insurrection and understand how, when placed under intense pressure, self-styled 'revolutionaries' drawn overwhelmingly from just four professions – engineering, the law, journalism and medicine – regressed into being mere 'reformers'. It was the always-perceptive CW de Kiewiet who, more than half a century ago, noted that the 'Jameson Raid' offered 'a classic illustration of an insensitive and arrogant attitude' and then explained that 'Of the agents of the new industrial age ushered in by gold and diamonds some were vulgar and arrogant men, with the illusion that their work as persons was equal to the great forces they commanded'.[3]

The three interlinked chapters that follow will be devoted to exploring how on the Witwatersrand in late 1895 a pride of hungry lions, within a matter of days, metamorphosed into a sizeable flock of bleating lambs.

★ ★ ★

Those entering the stage of global history for the first time do so listening to the echoes of a chorus sung by the generation that has just departed. Of the European-born mining magnates associated with the 'Jameson Raid', four – Alfred Beit (1853–1906), George Farrar (1859–1915), Lionel Phillips (1855–1936) and Cecil Rhodes (1853–1902) – were born within six years of one another. If one was being cavalier with the term 'magnate', one

Alfred Beit PHOTO: BEIT FOUNDATION

Lionel Phillips PHOTO: JOHANNESBURG ART GALLERY

George Farrar

Col Frank Rhodes

could add the name of Leander Starr Jameson (1853–1917) of the Chartered Company to that list. What faint echoes of global history might such a cohort have heard from those who had just left the stage?

None of them had personal experience of the popular upheavals that swept Europe in 1848. They could not, however, have avoided hearing about how serious a threat such revolutionary spasms posed to the state, or how difficult they were to suppress at a time of unprecedented urbanisation. Nor could they have been wholly unaware of the Paris Commune of 1871, and at least one of them – Jameson – actually witnessed the start of it. As 20-year-olds, three of the five – Beit, Phillips and Rhodes – were in Kimberley, in 1875, when Alfred Aylward's 'Black Flag' Rebellion was put down by colonial troops. The idea of an urban insurrection was therefore, albeit largely in the abstract, not entirely unfamiliar to those who encouraged an uprising on the Rand in 1895.

By the same token, all five would have been aware, from an early age, that their careers were coming to fruition at the same moment as the British Empire was reaching the zenith of its influence and power. What these forty-somethings were attempting to do, in 1895, was to link, in new and novel ways, the idea of an urban white immigrant – as opposed to a rural black – insurrection in an independent republic to that of imperial expansion. In retrospect, it seems an unlikely recipe for success. But, as evidenced by the case of Hammond, the highway of history is fed by any number of roads, tracks and footpaths. To track the route that each of the principal actors in the 'Jameson Raid' took in order to get to the South African Republic, in 1895, would require several volumes. Under the circumstances, perhaps the best we can do is to follow one or two of the major roads that members of the cohort followed to the Rand.

Cecil Rhodes knew a good deal about the British Empire and its armed forces. The Empire and its fortunes became something of an obsession with him, and he once described his younger self as a 'rabid jingo'. The army was central to the household of seven brothers and two sisters in which Rhodes grew up. He was the sickly fifth son of a vicar, and no less than four of his brothers – including a much-loved older brother, FW 'Frank' (1851–1905) – joined the army. Both Frank, a colonel, and another brother, Ernest, a captain, later joined Rhodes in southern Africa and, at one time or another, were employed by the Consolidated Gold Fields Company in its Johannesburg office before the 'Raid', where they worked closely with Hammond. In terms of personality and profession, there was little in the make-up of either Ernest or Frank to discourage their successful younger sibling from thinking about a military-like solution to the problem of neutralising and then incorporating Kruger's republic into a much wider economic – and ultimately political – federation.

Anyone operating along the expanding frontiers of southern Africa in the late 19th century would have been aware of the old adage about possession being nine-tenths of the law, and what could be achieved by means of a timely armed incursion. Rhodes certainly did, and well before the 'Jameson Raid'. The man was a habitual offender. In the early 1880s when he sensed that the Boer freebooter republics of Stellaland and Goshen threatened the coveted 'road to the north' he was instrumental in getting them dissolved. Stellaland was folded into the Cape Colony. And Rhodes was personally involved on behalf of the Cape when Goshen was overrun by a military expedition, under Sir Charles Warren, in 1885.[4] Goshen had collapsed only after Kruger, in a piece of brinkmanship of the sort he specialised in, was stared down.

And when the state would not do Rhodes's bidding, he was willing to act independently. Oral tradition has it that, in the late 1880s, he hired bandits, led by Scotty Smith, to raze 'Free Town' in the Orange Free State, when the hamlet emerged as a centre for illegal diamond buying that threatened the profitability of the De Beers Company.[5] The charter of the British South Africa Company, founded in 1889, made explicit provision for territorial expansion, and an armed 'Pioneer Column' occupied Mashonaland in 1890. And, within months of that occupation, militarised elements of the Chartered Company made concerted, albeit unsuccessful, attempts to acquire parts of Portuguese East Africa. For Rhodes and Jameson, the idea of armed occupation – the notion of imperial expansion, with or without approval – was part of the zeitgeist.

As might be expected, Jack Hammond did not always find it easy managing all the Rhodes brothers. The Big Man himself was no problem. Hammond had decided from early on that Cecil Rhodes was one of the finest men ever to have walked the face the earth. Nor was Ernest Rhodes any cause for concern, not least because, after 1894, most of his formal business with the Captain was conducted by letter and at a distance.[6] In personal terms Frank Rhodes, too, was largely beyond reproach. Everybody, including Hammond, thought of him as an 'officer and a gentleman' at a time when those terms were not used lightly. For Hammond, who knew his way around the English establishment, Colonel Rhodes was 'one of the noblest men I have ever met'.[7]

Nobility, however, did not go very far when it came to corporate intrigue and the hurly-burly of frontier gold mining. As Cecil Rhodes's immediate representative at Consolidated Gold Fields in the months leading up to the 'Raid', brother Frank may have been a touch short of the asking price. On 26 November 1895, at the height of the 'Raid' plotting, Hammond wrote to Sir John Willoughby, Jameson's leading military adviser: 'I am very busy initiating Colonel Rhodes into the intricacies of Rand financiering.

The Colonel does not impress me as having the broad grasp that Captain Rhodes had, but takes to work more kindly.'[8]

Frank Rhodes, then, was in no position to control Hammond either professionally or personally. A year or so later, in 1896, once the feeding frenzy that accompanied the 'Kaffir Boom' had subsided, the senior manager in Gold Fields' Johannesburg office, HL Sapte, felt that Hammond – first cousin to avarice – had been guilty of 'gross mismanagement and reckless expenditure'.[9] The self-important Hammond had been making bad market rather than engineering calls.[10]

Hammond's reservations about Frank Rhodes seem, however, to have extended beyond qualms about the Colonel's business acumen. In that he was not alone. As a soldier, Frank Rhodes had distinguished himself in the wars of empire, but his experience and skills were far from those required to deal with industrial conflict or urban insurrection. For all the Colonel's qualities, suggested FE Garrett, the editor of the *Cape Times*, Frank Rhodes was 'no revolutionary'.[11]

In Johannesburg, where as a co-conspirator and editor of the *The Star* he got to see the Colonel close up, Fred Hamilton, too, was unsparing in his criticism of Frank Rhodes. 'The promised leader was an even greater disappointment,' he wrote. The Colonel's skirt-chasing propensities and neglect of matters military worried even Jameson, and Hamilton felt that 'As a leader and main organiser of a conspiracy,' Frank Rhodes 'lacked every quality except courage and personal charm'.[12] Cecil Rhodes's authority and charisma could not simply be transferred to his brother.

If Frank Rhodes's deficiencies as a conspiratorial 'revolutionary' were manifest to the likes of Garrett and Hamilton, then they were even more so to Hammond, with his first-hand knowledge of industrial warfare in the Bitterroot Mountains and in Mexico. In terms of leadership, the conspiracy to overthrow the Kruger government was at risk from the moment the Colonel arrived on the Witwatersrand, in June or July 1895. The consequence was profound – indeed, it may have done more to determine the outcome of the events that have collectively become to be known as the 'Jameson Raid' than almost any other consideration. In effect Hammond, sensing the emerging leadership vacuum, drew on his considerable American experiences and, albeit belatedly, became the de facto conspirator-in-chief in planning the insurrection and the coup d'etat that was supposed to follow. And when *that* happened, the planned Johannesburg uprising, in theory always a British-inspired and British-led scheme to secure an outcome favourable to empire, mutated into something much looser, an American-inspired, American led initiative with a probable 'republican' twist to it.

Curiously enough, this tension between a possible imperial or republican outcome to the uprising – something Hammond failed to think through with any clarity during the plotting phase of the Raid but then actively responded to in opportunistic fashion once he started losing control of events – stayed dormant until the closing days of the Raid. By that time, however, the difference between a possible imperial and republican outcome had become marked for reasons that had more to do with impending failure than questions of political principle. Those differences, and the ways that possible consequences were to be greeted, however, could also be traced back to the principal funders of the 'Raid', Cecil Rhodes and Alfred Beit, and some of the professional rivalries between the Corner House group and Consolidated Gold Fields.

Alfred Beit (1853–1906) was born and raised in Hamburg and, at the age of 20, did a year's voluntary military service in the 2nd Hanseatic Infantry Regiment. His real talent, however, lay in assessing the value of diamonds and, after an apprenticeship in Amsterdam, he went to Kimberley in 1875. There, Beit, another confirmed bachelor, fell under the spell of Rhodes and his imperial dreams. Rhodes, in turn, was quick to detect in Beit an unusual financial genius that, over time, became central to the emergence of the giant De Beers Consolidated Mines.

After 1888, Beit based himself in London where, in 1890, he founded Wernher, Beit & Co. which soon became centrally involved in the development of the new Witwatersrand gold mining industry. The Johannesburg face of Wernher, Beit & Co, was H Eckstein & Co, which was managed by Lionel Phillips, and which, in turn, spawned Rand Mines, in 1893. Together, the three companies constituted the core of what, in colloquial terms, became known as the 'Corner House' group.[13]

Lionel Phillips was, in every sense of the word, the senior partner in H Eckstein & Co. Born of a Jewish family in London, he had obtained a sound if not excellent education and had qualified as a mechanical engineer before making his way to Kimberley and, from there, on to Johannesburg in 1889. Never short of political courage and with undoubted leadership qualities, Phillips was as ambitious as he was talented. On the Rand, he soon distinguished himself professionally and personally. By the mid-1890s, the powerful Corner House group accounted for about 40 per cent of the Witwatersrand's gold production, and from 1892 to 1895 Lionel Phillips was President of the Chamber of Mines – in effect, the Minister of Finance of a small, exceptionally profitable, industrial island in a huge feudal sea in a time of unprecedented wealth-creation.

But there was another, less attractive side to Phillips and to his wife, Florence. In the early 1890s Lionel Phillips was an important, if not the central, cog in the wheel of corruption that rolled back and forth between Johannesburg and Pretoria. Conspicuous consumption and a nouveau riche lifestyle expressed itself in the 'sumptuous residence', 'Hohenheim', that Phillips built on the Parktown ridge. Power and wealth, displayed so flagrantly attracted social lightning in the form of envy and resentment. Phillips was facetiously referred to as 'The King of Johannesburg' and his home was dismissed as 'Phillips' Folly'. According to his wife, Lionel Phillips was especially strongly disliked by the President, who may have sensed just how manipulative H Eckstein & Co could be with Kruger's close friend, AH Nellmapius.[14]

Phillips was neither a simple-minded imperialist nor a kneejerk jingo. He was wary of Rhodes's personal ambitions and sufficiently pragmatic to undertake some long-term political work within the republican framework, which may only have added to Kruger's hostility. By 1893, Wernher, Beit & Co were secretly funding *Land en Volk*, the most stridently anti-Kruger Afrikaans-Dutch newspaper in Pretoria.[15] Indeed, it was the Corner House group, rather than Rhodes's Consolidated Gold Fields, that was at the fore-front of attempts to co-opt a small group of Pretoria professionals into a possible Boer fifth column.

For all that, the idea that those concerned about the future of the South African Republic would probably have to choose between ruin or rev-olution came to Phillips even before it was more fully appreciated by Hammond, Jameson and Rhodes. After Kruger's botched Malaboch con-scription campaign, in May 1894, Sir Henry Loch's visit to Pretoria and the public humiliation of Kruger, Phillips's thinking took a more radical turn and, as we have already noted, he and frontier soldier Rowland Bettington became actively involved in the Witwatersrand rifle club.[16]

By early June 1894, as President of the Chamber of Mines, Phillips's overview of the industry's problems and possible long-term solutions was sufficiently sharp for him to test his ideas informally before a few well-placed insiders, including Hammond, at Consolidated Gold Fields. But Phillips and Hammond, the former accountable to Beit and the latter to Rhodes only, operating in a market characterised by increasing speculative activity, and by jockeying to acquire genuine long-term deep-level pros-pects, never enjoyed as full and trusting a relationship as did their principals, whose major interests saw them firmly locked into De Beers. Phillips could no more bring himself to acknowledge Hammond's undoubted abilities than Hammond was willing to acknowledge Phillips's formal standing in the mining industry or to sing his praises.[17] So, when Phillips wrote to Beit, in June 1894, outlining what he saw as the emerging choices on the Rand, he did so in broad brush strokes without bothering to indicate that his conversations almost certainly included Frank Rhodes and Hammond, and refusing to mention them by name:

The President [Kruger] is absolutely rabid; and many of his old
friends tell me that he has such an opinion of his actings being under
Divine direction that he is untractable [sic] and oblivious to all argument. If events fulfil appearances, it means ultimately a frightful loss
to the industry or revolution. Now of course our mission is to avoid
both. The Gold Fields people urged me to go down to Cape Town
and talk over matters with Rhodes. I felt inclined to do this, but
two considerations deter me … should I be wise to trust Rhodes'
advice?[18]

Rhodes and Beit may have been joined at the hip when it came to De Beers
and empire, but their chief lieutenants on the Rand were not.

There is other, albeit inconclusive and indirect, evidence that suggests
that there was little love lost between the Phillips and Hammond families.
In writing her *Recollections*, which looked back on the Raid and its sequel,
Florence Phillips found it difficult to be magnanimous when it came to the
issue of Jack Hammond and imprisonment of the Reformers in Pretoria.
'Lionel Phillips, George Farrar, Colonel Rhodes,' she wrote, 'were most
united and happy.' Hammond, she acknowledged, 'was not very well' with
the dysentery which, Hammond argued, was aggravated by stress. But, that
said, there is a poorly disguised tone of resentment in Florence Phillips's
description of Hammond. 'He remained away most of the time, and, except
toward the end, shared very little of the imprisonment of the others,' she
wrote. 'He had to thank his ill health, his clever wife, and the fact of his
being an American citizen for his immunity.'[19] Not much generosity there,
then.

What could have prompted such sharp comment from Mrs Phillips who,
as evident from her writings, was also capable of making more compassionate and well-rounded judgements? Was it possible that her husband's
manliness – the ultimate frontier virtue – had been questioned by the one
man among the Reformers who had an obsession with such matters? We
will never know for certain, but it seems as if it might.

In the stormy days leading up to the preparation for the Johannesburg
uprising, when Phillips was under considerable pressure, Florence was seriously ill back in London. What Phillips did next and the response that it
elicited from one of his close co-conspirators was unforgettable:

[Lionel] announced to his fellow Reformers that, as I was danger-
ously ill, he might possibly be obliged to leave at a moment's notice.
One of them (I will not mention his name) said to him, 'Phillips, you
cannot do it men will call you a coward. In fact, if you heard your
wife was dead, you dare not leave now.'[20]

Could the man who refused Phillips the moral right to visit his wife under potentially life-threatening circumstances be the very same person whose own health problems helped spirit him away to the coast for a protracted period once the Reformers were imprisoned?

Whatever the truth of the matter, within the ranks of the Randlords, the emerging industrial aristocracy, all was not well between the House of Beit and the House of Rhodes. At least some of this underlying, almost always well-concealed, friction centred on Hammond, the wild card in an otherwise more predictable pack. It will be recalled that Julius Wernher, by inclination more cautious and discreet than Beit, cast Hammond as a 'wind-bag'.[21] Percy FitzPatrick, in charge of intelligence for H Eckstein & Co from 1892, Secretary to the Reform Committee in 1895 and author of *Jock of the Bushveld*, does not appear to have held Hammond in especially high regard, if at all. It is noticeable how in FitzPatrick's account of events leading up to the 'Jameson Raid', *The Transvaal from Within* (1899), Hammond is almost entirely absent.[22] More telling still is that when Sir Percy toured California in 1920, he and Hammond, old Reform warhorses, somehow contrived not to meet.[23]

Lionel Phillips, as already noted, was circumspect when it came to dealing with Rhodes or his Johannesburg-based deputies. And, when it came to Hammond, Phillips had his own reservations reinforced, in-house, from an angle and at a depth that must have been painful for Rhodes's gold mining guru – from fellow Americans, Californians of sorts and engineers. 'Barbarian' Brown was not the only professional man in Johannesburg who bore some knowledge of Hammond's dangerous social engineering proclivities back in the Coeur d'Alene. There were at least two others and neither was willing to defer to Hammond whom many in town, including the man himself, saw as *the* leading light in the American mining community.[24]

James Hennen Jennings (1854–1920) and Henry Cleveland Perkins (1846–1926) were the most experienced, talented and highly esteemed engineers in the Corner House group in the early 1890s.[25] Phillips relied on the Harvard-educated Jennings as his chief consulting engineer, while Perkins, a New York-born, self-taught mining expert, was put in charge of Rand Mines in 1893. For FitzPatrick, they 'were men of the highest position and influence in the community' and, as part of the American locust elite passing through the Witwatersrand, both went on to become million-aires.[26] Both were conservative by inclination, tending to remain aloof from organised politics, confining themselves to their areas of technical exper-tise, and when pushed would take up conciliatory-reformist rather than radical-revolutionary positions.[27] Perkins, on hearing of those who had got embroiled in the Jameson Raid, was alleged to have said, 'bloody fools to take part in politics'.[28]

Between them, Perkins, Jennings and Phillips, even more so than the man Hammond characterised as 'Kruger's paid spy' – 'Barbarian' Brown – posed a formidable challenge to the authority Hammond derived from his position at Consolidated Gold Fields. More importantly, their inside knowledge of his propensity to bluster and import hare-brained schemes from real or imagined Wild West experiences allowed them to call his bluff as the acknowledged leader of the American community in Johannesburg. In late 1895, as first the urban insurrection, then Jameson's Raid and finally the hastily concocted Reform Committee began to falter, the trio of Brown, Jennings and Perkins left Hammond feeling exposed and vulnerable.

Rivalries and tensions – between the House of Rhodes and the House of Beit, and between Lionel Phillips and Hammond on the one hand and Jennings and Perkins on the other – mounted steadily throughout the six weeks preceding the Raid. In late November 1895, Hammond, sensing that he, Frank Rhodes and Consolidated Gold Fields were leaking authority and losing traction among the core conspirators, complained to Jameson about their problems. Jameson – faithful servant – personally conveyed the message to the Big Man during his last visit to Cape Town before he was overcome by Pitsani fever. Rhodes was no more inclined than Hammond to see the reform-minded Eckstein outfit steal their revolutionary thunder, so he wired Rutherfoord Harris, Secretary to the Chartered Company, in London: 'Dr Jameson back from Johannesburg. Everything right. My judgement is it [the uprising] is a certainty … A. Beit must not consult Phillips, who is all right but anxious to do everything himself and he *does not wish to play second fiddle*.'[29]

But, such were the pressures mounting in Johannesburg during the closing weeks of December 1895 that neither the ineffectual Beit nor the hard-pressed Phillips could control Jennings and Perkins. Indeed, as the planned revolutionary moment approached and then receded, the cachet of the two conservatives within the American mining community grew at the same rate that Hammond found himself haemorrhaging authority and prestige. So desperate did the position become that, a few weeks before the Raid, Hammond appealed to Rhodes to persuade Beit, by then back in Cape Town, to travel north and get Jennings and Perkins into line. But Beit, no less prone to a serious attack of nerves when in tight straits than was Hammond himself, was already feeling ill and unwilling to risk his personal safety.[30] The net result was that when the crisis was nearing its peak, Jennings and Perkins took matters into their own hands, leaving Hammond stranded high and dry.

More than 30 years later, in penning his often puffed-up *Autobiography*, Hammond could still not bring himself to spell out fully the pain and humiliation he felt at being effectively bypassed by his Corner House colleagues.

Kruger had barely reached his home when he was approached by a deputation of Americans [led by Jennings and Perkins] who had gone to Pretoria independently, without the sanction of the men in control of the Reform Movement. The group included those very men for whose disciplining we had desired Beit's presence.[31]

But, even as the clock struck midnight in Johannesburg and Jennings and Perkins saw through Hammond and his hoped-for American-style 'revolution', there was still one man out there who, until it was all hopelessly too late, had every confidence in Cowboy Jack and a huge posse of miners supposedly armed with Lee-Metford rifles. His name was Leander Starr Jameson and he was predisposed to believe just about every campfire tale he had ever been told about the Coeur d'Alene, Charlie Siringo, Mexicans, Wyatt Earp and the Wild West. For, as one historian has noted, although perhaps not understanding fully the pertinence of his observation, 'Dr Jim was partial to Americans.'[32]

CHAPTER NINE

Dr Jim's American Outriders and Medicine Men

C 1891–1895

The revolutionary winds of 1848 left few corners of continental Europe unshaken, and even the relatively sheltered British Isles did not escape the powerful gusts of liberalising populism. It was not surprising, then, that among well-educated Scots, some of the principal beneficiaries of the Enlightenment, fresh breezes promising freedom and political progress would be welcomed rather than shunned.

In Edinburgh, Robert Jameson – Leander Starr Jameson's father – and his wife, Christian Pringle, embraced the emerging ethos with gusto, at the expense of prudence and professional advancement. The pair eventually presided over a family of 11 children. Robert trained as a lawyer, abandoned law and, as a radical and free thinker, came to advocate a string of liberal causes, from anti-slavery and anti-corn law agitation to political reform, as well as being an admirer of the Irish nationalist Daniel O'Connell. In the same vein Leander Starr, in later life, became an admirer of William O'Brien, in effect, Parnell's chief lieutenant in the Irish Home Rule movement.[1]

Christian Pringle remained supportive of her husband as his ideas developed and he moved from Edinburgh and law to becoming an editor and newspaper proprietor in East Anglia, when Leander Starr was just 18 months old. She was close to her father, a major-general in the British Army and, intriguingly, had family in Charleston, South Carolina. It would seem that both parents had links to America. Leander Starr – 'Lanner' to his siblings – was named after an American friend and business associate of his father's.[2]

Leander Starr, born in 1853, entered a household sensitive to developments in radical European thought, as well as one with respect for American achievements and independence, albeit one with moral objections to slavery – something that may have loosened some of their ties with kin in South Carolina. These broadly formative influences, however, replete with contradictory elements about race and slavery, were later, albeit briefly and incompletely, refined by young Jameson himself. He was undoubtedly 'partial' to Americans but, as we shall see, not many of them were Yankees.

Robert Jameson may have been a slightly overbearing father; in later life, on at least one occasion, Leander expressed his disgust at unrestrained patriarchal power – and especially as exercised by Boers over their children, employees or servants.[3] The fact that most of Leander's brothers were 'high spirited, intelligent, red-blooded and, perchance, rather rough young fellows' may have helped shape the young boy's character. Small, courageous and physically active, he could, however, also manifest a 'brooding imagination' and, throughout his life, would retreat into an inner world of books, showing a preference for works of biography and history. It may also be significant that, of all his siblings, it was Middleton – 'Midge' – the artist whom he supported financially throughout most of his career, who was the most loved brother.[4] Indeed, it was while on a visit to Midge, then living in Paris, in 1871, that 16-year-old Leander glimpsed the first stirrings of the Commune.[5]

Jameson registered as a medical student at University College, in Gower Street, London, in 1870, from where he eventually graduated in 1877. During his time in London, several of his brothers had spread themselves around the globe; Julius and Sam made their way to southern Africa. Already developing his skills at playing cards and gambling, Leander was an excellent medical student and, had he stayed on in England, it was said, was destined for a career as a 'famous surgeon'. He was a good listener but had a brusque manner and, his biographers claimed, affected a cynical outlook on life. All of this, in turn, fed into a lifestyle that appears to have been characterised by alternating spells of frenetic activity and self-absorbed reflection.

In 1875–1876, before graduating, Jameson undertook the important, underdocumented transatlantic trip that, sadly, both his biographers neglected to probe more fully.[6] The outline of that mission is well known – he accompanied an 'opium eater' on a trip to the United States to help cure the patient of an addiction to morphine.[7] The knowledge he gained from treating an addict may have stood Jameson in good stead later in life. In the southern African bush, in 1892, he self-administered morphine nightly in order to help him fall asleep at a time when he was said to be suffering from a malaria-induced fever and unnamed 'other complications'.[8] He would have known very well what the risks were.

Jameson's choice of East Coast America as a destination for a working holiday was presumably not by chance. It may have allowed him to re-establish contact with members of the extended family in Charleston. We do not know exactly which cities he visited, although his Oxford-educated friend Seymour Fort later recorded that Jameson's reminiscences about the places he had visited were 'more Bohemian than historical' in nature.[9] It may also have afforded him the opportunity to explore the nature of his own sexuality. 'He flirted with men,' one African frontiersman claimed years later, 'like a woman.'[10] The trip may also have accelerated his appreciation for risk and spontaneity and contributed to a growing dislike of conventional ethics and procedures – something that he later came to share with his dearest friend, Rhodes.

But, in 1875–1876, America had more to offer Jameson than lessons in 'bohemianism'. The United States was celebrating a hundred years of independence, marked by an impressive exposition in Philadelphia, but, for someone with an interest in new frontiers and the expansion of the English-speaking world, there were other developments worth noting. Out west, Colorado was admitted as the 38th state and the trans-continental railway was completed. What might have struck Jameson more forcibly, however, was the Battle of the Little Bighorn, the Great Sioux War and the start of a campaign by the American army over the months that followed that ultimately crushed all armed Native American resistance.

Jameson's American experiences may also have heralded a developing propensity to bouts of restlessness, as manifested in ceaseless movement and long-distance travel, which, by preference, was usually undertaken alone.[11] This syndrome, clearly evident in the early 1890s after the Chartered Company's occupation of Mashonaland, reached near-pathological proportions in the months leading up to the Raid.[12] Back in 1878, however, a further stimulus came via his brother Julius, who sent him a diamond from Griqualand West. At the same time, Jameson chanced upon a letter from an American, Dr Prince, requesting that University College help him find a partner for his Kimberley practice.

The decade-old, male-dominated diamond fields provided Jameson with precisely the sort of frontier experience that he hankered after. He not only partnered the ageing Prince in private practice, but also commanded a position in the town's hospital that placed him in close contact with, and in some instances put him in charge of, leading medical men in town, including several who later surfaced in the Reform Committee. Among these contacts, the most important by far was Dr Henry Wolff, who became part of Jameson's trusted inner circle of Americans. The diamond fields also provided Jameson with ample opportunity to indulge his old passions for card-playing, gambling and, possibly, womanising.

But, crucially, it was in Kimberley that Jameson met and got to know Cecil Rhodes, the charismatic individual behind what in 1888 would eventually emerge as the De Beers Consolidated Mines and, in 1889, the British

South Africa Company that lay north of the Limpopo. In late 1886, Rhodes's first, much-loved young partner, Neville Pickering, died. Jameson, quick to console his friend, moved in to share a cottage with Rhodes, and the pair embarked on a phase of their friendship that was to become 'as strong as a marriage bond'.[13] Jameson thus grew closest to Rhodes at a time when the Big Man was, simultaneously, emotionally bereft *and* experiencing his most intense dreams of expanding the British Empire. Jameson fell in love with both the man and his extraordinary vision of an imperial Africa.

Once the Chartered Company occupied Mashonaland, in 1890 – the bridgehead of what was eventually to become Rhodesia – Jameson was set to become if not an imperial dictator, then the governor of a part of empire that was so far removed from any form of civilian rule that he could do much as he pleased.[14] Having invaded and occupied one country, what was there to stop an intemperate man from contemplating the acquisition of a second? In 1891, Rhodes's latest acquisition became Jameson's playground, but the couple only gained full possession of their prize after the defeat of Lobengula's powerful Ndebele regiments.

The 1893 'Matabele War', in which out of about 900 armed and mounted men, no fewer than 50 of whom were American, proved to be a personal triumph for Jameson.[15] His leadership qualities were displayed in a configuration he was comfortable with, that is, within fluid, semi-formal volunteer form, free from rigid military command structures and the set-pieces he was contemptuous of, yet backed by modern armaments, including the devastating firepower of the Maxim gun.[16] That frontier war helped shape Jameson's emerging leadership style. As one historian notes pertinently, after the war Bulawayo had an air of Dodge City, something that was evident when Jameson was called upon to formally inaugurate the town in June 1894:

> [H]e stood on a box opposite the uncompleted Maxim Hotel and announced impatiently, 'It is my job to declare the town open gentlemen. I don't think we want to talk about it. I make the declaration now. There is plenty of whisky and soda inside, so come in.[17]

It was during the 1893 'Matabele War', too, that Jameson's partiality for Americans, and more especially frontiersmen and Southerners – or those who, like John Hays Hammond, combined a bit of both – received a further important boost. By the time the Johannesburg uprising and the Raid came round fully two years later, Jameson's mindset – increasingly predisposed to act rather than yak, frontier-style – had been set to American rather than British voltage systems. For that there were several Americans, including Hammond, to thank, but there were two others, firmly based in Rhodesia, who stood out more clearly.

One was a man of extraordinary scouting, soldierly and survival skills of the sort that Jack Hammond could – and eventually did – come to drool over in personal as well as professional terms. His name was Frederick Russell Burnham, and he really was extraordinary.[18] Born on a Sioux reservation in Minnesota in 1861, by the age of 14 Burnham was earning a living in California where his scouting skills were honed by cowboys and frontiersmen. A few years later he distinguished himself as a tracker for the US Army in the Apache Wars and also became involved in some classic frontier feuding in remote Arizona.

Despairing of the American frontier, which by 1890 was closing, and craving new challenges, Burnham, his wife and a brother-in-law, Pete Ingram, a former Montana cowboy, took themselves off to southern Africa in 1893 so as to insert themselves into Rhodes's expansionist thrust north. Burnham and Ingram arrived just in time to take part in the war against the Ndebele. More pertinently, the two were involved in what became one of the ideological cornerstones in the founding of the new settler society – the ambush of Major Allan Wilson's ill-fated Shangani Patrol.[19] Wilson and more than 30 others, isolated from the main body of soldiers engaged in a brave, protracted, but ultimately futile attempt to see off the larger Ndebele regiment that had surrounded them.

The fate of the Shangani Patrol captured the imperial imagination but, for the small number of Americans involved in the war, and for Jameson who had been in the United States at the time of the great war with the Sioux, Wilson and his men might have evoked memories of other great North American tragedies such as the massacre at the Alamo and the Battle of the Little Bighorn. One of those in whom it might have evoked those comparisons was the second of Jameson's American intimates.

Captain – later Major – Maurice Heany, then approaching 40, trailed scents of culture, ethnicity and masculinity that Jameson found irresistible. Of Irish descent and a cousin of Edgar Allan Poe's but hailing from Virginia, only the bare outlines of Heany's early career are known. He had certainly been a member of the Bechuanaland Border Police and had obtained a concession to mine gold around Mazoe before the Pioneer Column entered what was to become Rhodesia in 1890. He was also a co-founding member of the famous trading firm of Johnson, Heany and Borrow.[20]

Some of the silence about his life before moving north in the 1880s may have been fashioned by Heany himself. An impulsive man given to making important, sometimes vital, decisions with unseemly haste, nobody seems to know for certain how he acquired the rank of captain although it was rumoured that he had attended and then absconded from West Point military academy under mysterious circumstances.[21] During the 'Matabele War' of 1893, Heany was active on the fringes of the Shangani Patrol and fulfilled his duty with sufficient courage and prominence to impress Jameson.[22] Later, in the weeks leading up to the Raid, Heany, along with three Englishmen – Captains HM Heyman and H Holden, of the British South Africa Company, and AL Lawley, who had helped construct the Beira railway – were hand-picked by Jameson and sent south to assist with the planning and training of white miners for the hoped-for urban uprising.

Hammond and Frank Rhodes alike were of the opinion that, in any crisis, it was the Virginian voice of Heany that was most likely to get through to the importunate Jameson. When the amateurish revolutionaries-turned-reformers realised that Jameson was going to jump the gun and invade the Republic without their say-so, it was Heany and Holden who were sent, via different routes, to Pitsani to try to persuade the Napoleon of the Bush to sit tight and wait on new orders from the Witwatersrand. But Hammond and Colonel Rhodes were poor judges of character. As one analyst noted, not long after the Raid, those intent on sending messages of peace should prefer doves over hawks.[23] And so tradition has it that Heany eventually reached Jameson and gave him the message forbidding him to set off without the explicit approval of Hammond, back in Johannesburg:

> Jameson walked up and down for some little time, and then said, 'I am going'.
> 'Thought you would,' said Heany.
> 'And what are you going to do?' said Jameson.
> 'Going with you,' said Heany.
> 'Thought you would,' said Jameson.[24]

With the benefit of hindsight then, it is perhaps predictable that those historians best disposed toward Jameson have sought to kill if not the messengers, then their reputations. Colvin, struggling to contain himself, writes: 'Captain Heany was not the most suitable man for such an errand,' while Jameson's friend, Seymour Fort, dismisses Heany and Captain Holden as 'two rather irresponsible messengers'.[25]

Perhaps so, but these judgements ignore Jameson's culpability in what happened, and here it is important to note just how receptive his ears had become to American ditties by the time that he received the message to back off from any invasion. Ever since their meeting in Matabeleland, in late 1894, Jameson had been persuaded by Hammond's revolutionary bravado, including, no doubt, tales about the supposed successes back in the Coeur d'Alene. Why else had he been allowed to take command of the planning for the uprising?

Moreover, for at least two weeks prior to the arrival of the two messengers Jameson had been working exceptionally closely with his American

counterpart, his informal intelligence officer and one-time Kimberley sub-
ordinate, Henry Wolff.[26] Dr Jim trusted Wolff implicitly even though a few
years later, once safely back in New York City, the latter made an unsuccessful attempt to distance himself from the Jameson Raid.[27] Not surprising,
then, that when Jameson got a milk-and-water instruction not to invade
from another of his favoured American insiders, he was not inclined to take
it as seriously as he might otherwise have done. Heany's impetuous response
was just another feather in the balance of a scale that had started to tip days
earlier.

By then the equipoise of Jameson's mind had long since been disturbed
and his judgement of Boer military prowess become hopelessly flawed. In
his view, as brave and gifted as Americans were as frontiersmen at home and
abroad, just so inadequate were the men of the South African Republic.
Jameson's contempt for the Afrikaner-Dutch, and his readiness to scoff at
their capabilities as fighters, pre-dated the 'Matabele War' and the latter-day
emergence of Jameson the conqueror.

In 1885, Sir Charles Warren's force, with the political backing of Jameson's
hero, Rhodes, had seen off one of Kruger's commandos in the contest to
determine the fate of the Afrikaner freebooter republic of Goshen. Then, in
June 1891, Jameson had personally headed off the proposed Adendorff trek
across the Limpopo into newly occupied Mashonaland.[28] The Boers, he
concluded, could either be stared down or brushed away. After his 'Matabele
War' success, Jameson began displaying signs of the onset of some grandiose
notions.

The public humiliation of Kruger during the Loch visit, in early 1894,
increased Jameson's sense of self-importance as he moved into one of his
phases of withdrawal and increasingly lost touch with urban life. Interestingly,
he sensed that he was no longer always on an even keel. On Christmas Eve
1893, he confided in brother Sam that '… by the end of the next dry season
I shall try to get off for a few months – as one gets a bit stale and uncivilised
after so long an interval on the veld'.[29] In another letter to Sam, in January
1894, he again picked up on the theme of a solitary, unmediated existence of profound introversion: 'Four years on the veld continuously become
monotonous, and the last six months with a High Commissioner to deal
with has been most trying to temper.'[30] By the time that Jameson linked
up with Rhodes and Hammond, in August 1894, he was ready for action,
and his little jokes about the supposed vulnerability of the Kruger state had
become steadily more inflated.

The story goes that, in May 1894, on hearing of the Boer rumblings that
followed the Loch visit, Jameson, immersed in a biography of Clive of India,
looked up and said: 'I have a jolly good mind to march straight down off
the plateau with the men I have here and settle this thing out of hand.'[31]

By October 1895, the logistics necessary to bring about a triumph may have been scaled down but his imperial-military personality loomed ever larger. He confided in Dr Hans Sauer, a former Kimberley colleague, that the Boers held no terrors for him. 'I could,' he claimed, 'drive them out of the Transvaal with five hundred men armed with *sjamboks* [leather whips].'[32] And, as Pitsani fever slowly enveloped Jameson's brain and his contempt for the Kruger state grew deeper, life gradually began to mimic the art of comedy. The men and weapons needed to overthrow the Boers shrank. 'Anyone could take the Transvaal with a half-dozen revolvers,' scoffed the would-be liberator.[33]

Jameson's demons pulled him back and forth between private withdrawal and public hyperactivity with alarming, unpredictable regularity. Modern medics might speculate about his suffering from a bipolar disorder and there was no shortage of men at the time who took the view that Jameson's most ill-considered actions during spells of hyperactivity were, not to put too fine a word on it, 'mad'. Years later, looking back on Jameson's reckless alienation of land immediately after the 'Matabele War', WH Milton, the Administrator of Mashonaland wrote: 'I think that Jameson must have been off his head for some time before the raid.'[34] Sir Graham Bower, Imperial Secretary to the High Commissioner, claimed that the ill-conceived attempt to stage a coup d'état might have been successfully halted but that 'Jameson went mad and ran amok'.[35] Joseph Chamberlain, Secretary of State for the Colonies and implicated in the Raid by Rhodes himself, was pleased to hear that the Big Man had repudiated Jameson, who, he concluded, 'must be mad'.[36] Even Charles Leonard of the National Union said, 'What a pity that the hand of a madman should have retarded the victory of our cause.'[37]

It is impossible to determine now what Hammond thought of 'Dr Jim' before their aborted 'revolution' fell apart. All of Hammond's writings post-dated the Raid, by which time Jameson's shortcomings had been laid bare, and their relationship, for a time, collapsed. Early on, Hammond found Rhodes's friend to be an 'engaging companion', but after things had fallen apart he felt that Jameson was capable of dishonesty, unwilling to stick to his word, impatient, nervous, lacking in judgement, and a man who was possessed of a 'military psychology'.[38] As is often the case, the bitterness of the separation after the Raid might point to the depth and strength of the relationship prior to it.[39]

At the height of the Raid, Jameson may have been manic but he was not stupid; the two are not coordinates. As noted, Jameson had sent a quartet of military men, including Heany, to represent him in Johannesburg while his most trusted American confidant of all, Hammond, supposedly prepared the Rand miners for the coming 'revolution'. But Jameson also kept in close contact with his brother Sam as an alternative source of intelligence. He

Charles Leonard

and Rhodes both took the precaution of making certain they had siblings present at the scene of the proposed action to protect their interests and to keep them fully informed of the progress of the planned uprising. Jameson, however, had an additional network to keep him abreast of political developments – that of the medical profession.

We have already met Sauer and Wolff, the ex-Kimberley doctors. Significantly, it was Wolff who played – by far – the most important role both in supporting Jameson personally and in the practical aspects of organising the invasion.[40] But, by the time the would-be revolutionaries' hidden sympathisers emerged from the shadows, a half-a-dozen more medics had been identified. Dr AP Hillier was another of Jameson's former confidants on the diamond fields, and the man that he chose to funnel funds to his artist brother, Midge.[41] The remainder of the list was made up of Drs WH Brodie, WTF Davies, DP Duirs and RT Mitchell – several of them leading figures in the professional medical association of the Witwatersrand.[42]

Not all these doctors were simply opportunistic followers of Rhodes and Jameson, nor were they reluctant 'British' imperialists. Hans Sauer, a South African, and Jameson's former partner in the practice at Kimberley, and Oscar Somershields, a Norwegian by birth, both manifested an aggressive, expansionist mindset long before Rhodes or Jameson ever did so. While out on a hunting expedition in Mozambique, in 1883, the two doctors, probably liquor-laced, seized Inhaca Island from a contingent of Portuguese soldiers and then annexed it in the name of the British Empire. It may have started out as prank at the expense of the despised Portuguese but the sequel was arduous and, as they discovered, not very funny.[43]

Profound class and ethnic prejudice was, of course, not confined to the significant numbers of journalists and doctors already noted. There were many others in the ranks of the multinational Reform Committee who viewed the Boer state and Kruger with contempt and, like Sauer and Somershields before them, seriously underestimated the consequences of what they did or said.[44] And, when it came to conceit and downright swagger there were a fair number in the legal profession on the Witwatersrand who played second fiddle to no man.

Charles Leonard, Chairman of the National Union, the weak-muscled political arm of immigrant agitation for the franchise on the Rand, and his brother, JW Leonard, were, as already noted, Johannesburg's leading advocates. Between them, the Leonards had a near monopoly on legal work coming from the powerful Chamber of Mines, and by the mid-1890s Charles Leonard was running one of the largest and most lucrative legal practices in the English-speaking world. Just as Halley's Comet lit up the night sky, so Leonard illuminated the heavens of justice and, trailing in his wake, came the lesser lights – the numerous attorneys – who briefed senior counsel.

The analogues were clear. Jack Hammond exercised power over many, but not all, of the Rand's mining engineers; Jameson, although largely absent, was *primus inter pares* among the doctors; while Charles Leonard wielded huge political and professional influence over the town's lawyers. And, just as in the case of the doctors, once plans for the urban insurrection began to go awry, the core of would-be revolutionaries, realising that they were about to be spotted walking naked down Main Street, grabbed as much reformist sheeting as they could find to cover their nakedness. Charles Leonard, who Colvin claimed 'lacked the more robust qualities of leadership' fled first to the Cape suffering from 'brain congestion' and then on to England once the 'revolution' spun out of control.[45] By then, however, the Reform Committee boasted a half-dozen attorneys: WHS Bell, DF Gilfillan, WE Hudson, W van Huylsteen, C Mullins and EP Solomon.

In similar vein, we might note that it was the legal profession, via Charles Leonard, who did most to provide the English, Johannesburg-based conspirators in the Jameson Raid with a bridgehead into Afrikaans-Dutch Pretoria that allowed them to cultivate a Boer fifth column. More specifically – and as we shall explore in more detail later – it was legal work coming from Lionel Phillips's Corner House, some of which Leonard passed on to Advocate Ewald Esselen, that helped grease the wheels of influence in Boer 'progressive' circles, which included Esselen's friend,

Eugène Marais. And Marais himself later went on to study law at the Inns of Court.[46]

But of all the professional groupings involved in the public face of the insurrection, none was more important than the mining engineers.[47] The engineers made up five members of the Reform Committee, just one less than the doctors and the lawyers. Those arrested were JH Hammond, VM Clement, JS Curtis, C Butters and T Mein, although another brother engineer, R Parker, avoided arrest by disguising himself as a priest before escaping to the Cape.[48] In reality, then, the engineers, too, numbered six. But the engineers differed in two respects from the other groupings. First, they were *all* Americans and, for the most part, initially dedicated to a wholly revolutionary rather than a reformist outcome for the uprising. Secondly, and as might be expected of practical men, they were overwhelmingly responsible for dealing with the logistics of the planned uprising.

Looking back on the 64 members of the Reform Committee who were arrested, and the far smaller and more ambitious core of those intent on overthrowing the state, one is struck by how graduate-laden and top-heavy was the leadership of both the secret and the public movement.[49] About one in three of the revolutionaries and reformists alike were ambitious, university-trained and wealthy men. Not only was the all-male movement without meaningful individual or collective representation from shopkeepers and tradesman, but it also lacked miners or any element drawn from the organised white working class.[50] If successful, the uprising would have been more of a small elitist putsch than a 'revolution' driven by popular support. Taken at face value, then, the revolutionaries and reformists alike were all head and no heart – men trained to think rather than thump. By the same token, it is understandable that, once placed under pressure, the 'revolutionaries' and reformists alike, very belatedly, prioritised thought and political principles over actions and logistics and, just as rapidly, drifted apart.

As a top-down attempt by learned professionals to conjure up an urban insurrection that was meant to precipitate a popular revolution, the 'Jameson Raid' was without a meaningful parallel in the history of the British Empire if not the modern world. A failure of such grand proportions prompts the historian to retrace the steps of the conspirators in order to understand where, when and how they went about planning the raid. Might not poor activists be good schemers?

CHAPTER TEN

Wisps and Curls Rising
above the Brew

A Chronological Outline of the Plot

c 1894–1895

Looking back on the Jameson Raid, 40 years later, one of the first to be drawn into the revolutionary conspiracy in Johannesburg, Fred Hamilton, editor of *The Star*, was 'amazed afresh at the sheer craziness of the adventure'. It seemed 'preposterous', he wrote, 'that grown men should have associated themselves with it, and incredible that they should have risked ruin and a sporting chance of the hangman's rope in order to further it'.[1] Critical from the outset, yet broadly supportive of the need for some sort of political intervention on the Witwatersrand, Hamilton was not the only newspaperman to see that elements of the 'plan' were if not daft then clearly imprudent. On reviewing a key component of the 'revolution' as advocated by, and presided over by John Hays Hammond, Edmund Garrett, editor of the *Cape Times*, saw it as being 'wild and hazardous'.[2]

In many ways, then, it is unhelpful to think of the proposed uprising in Johannesburg, in late 1895, supposedly the start of a 'revolution', as having been 'planned' in the conventional sense of the word. Almost all the events that played out in the South African Republic over the closing weeks of 1895 and first few days of 1896 were ad hoc and wholly unplanned. The arch-conspirators, having discovered that the supporting cast for Act Two had run out on stage even before the curtain went up on what was supposed to be a play about seizing revolutionary power, were forced to make hurried changes and entertain the audience as best they could with an unrehearsed song about reform.

Seeing the principal conspirators and the Jameson Raid as part of a frontier farce is, of course, neither new nor novel. It was an analogy that forced itself upon near-contemporary commentators as well. Seymour Fort, one of Jameson's two principal biographers and champions, later suggested that 'There was, in fact, so much play-acting and make-believe all round, that even to themselves the leading conspirators did not appear to admit the actual facts of the situation.'[3] But it was Violet Markham who made probably the most telling observation of all, just 48 months after the farce in the veld had ground to a halt. Back in 1900, she wrote:

> Judging from the facts at present before the public, the historian of the twenty-first century will probably criticise Dr Jameson's incursion as more amazing in the folly of its execution than criminal in its inception. Truly the principles on which the Johannesburg revolution of 1896 was conducted savour more of the conspiracy in a comic opera than the plots of capable men.[4]

But, even if the Raid and the uprising linked to it was 'comic opera', it was never the complete article. The 'revolution' was not sufficiently carefully thought through; it was something that was always in the making, a set of linked mutating events – more theatre workshop than command performance. And yet, for all that, by the time Dr Jim set off there *was* a recognisable plan in place – one replete with interlocking component parts that required careful synchronisation. It was Jameson's refusal to acknowledge that the 'movement' that was supposed to trigger his own incursion was failing, if it had not already failed, that caused him to set off in the hope that by reversing the agreed order of things – incursion first, uprising second – the 'revolution' might yet succeed. But the weakness of the linkages within the plan, together with the fact that the fireworks went off in the wrong sequence, only further exposed the weakness of the original plot.

The 'planning' of the 'Jameson Raid' and the uprising is thus better captured not by looking back at what the final blueprint looked like, but by trying to understand how an ad hoc, hastily put-together 'blueprint' allowed Jack Hammond to play a disproportionately large part in its conception and failure. In order to understand how the thinking behind the plot evolved over time, it is necessary, then, to recap the events of 1894–1895 and trace how the conspiracy gained the emotional, if not the logical, momentum to take it forward, and then promptly lost most of its ideological and political traction as it disintegrated in some confusion.

In May 1894, with the spectre of the Coeur d'Alene mining war still peering over his shoulder, and the Kruger government's willingness to mobilise foreigners, including Americans, for the Malaboch campaign, before him, Hammond began to make his presence felt in local politics. It will be recalled that it was at about this time that Hammond first suspected 'Barbarian' Brown, his former employee from Wardner, of being a 'spy' in the employ of the South African Republic. Then, a few months after the humiliation of the State President, at the time of Sir Henry Loch's visit to Pretoria, in June of the same year, Hammond began noting how Lionel Phillips, Chairman of the Chamber of Mines, and Rowland Bettington, the war-mongering stockbroker, were becoming ever more actively involved in promoting local rifle clubs.

But it was the August–September tour of Matabeleland that year, with Rhodes and Jameson, that did most to persuade Hammond that he had an important, probably even a vital, role to play in the future of the goldfields and all of southern Africa. Rhodes, who felt that his imperial ambitions for Africa were being thwarted by the timid British government, and Jameson, who was in need of stimulating company, were keen listeners when it came to what the future of the region might be. Although no details of the discussions ever emerged, there can be little doubt that not only did Hammond raise the idea of a possible uprising on the Rand, as he later admitted, but that he also embellished his own role in the Idaho mining war, including such aspects as the smuggling of arms, the infiltration of secret agents, putting down rebellious miners, managing public opinion and mobilising state and federal troops. Hammond might have been a braggart but there was no denying that, when it came to planning upheavals, he had some practical experience.

The result was that Hammond, either intentionally or, more likely, unintentionally, caught Rhodes and Jameson in something of an ideological pincer movement. On the one hand he offered them prophecies of doom about an imminent uprising led by working-class elements in Johannesburg and, on the other, hinted that his own experience of industrial warfare in Idaho held out some prospect of appropriating, or redirecting, a revolutionary upwelling in ways that might safeguard the economic or political future of the mining industry and the country. Tales of gloom, offset by occasional flashes of hope, fed into the underlying mood of despair of both Rhodes and Jameson, and offered Jameson a way not only of lifting his own flagging spirits, but of reigniting the aspiration of an imperial future for a united southern Africa in the heart of his sorely troubled master. There is little doubt that such war talk formed the very substance of the campfire discussions, and the validity of this analysis can be tested against what came in its wake.[5]

Rhodes and Jameson were aware that they had been corralled by the American. But, it will be recalled, they remained sufficiently cautious to go directly to the Witwatersrand where they tested the political waters independently in an effort to establish the accuracy of Hammond's gloomy prognostications. The results were affirmative, and the idea of an armed intervention began to bed down in the minds of Rhodes and Jameson.

Likewise, it will be recalled that, by December 1894, the imperialists were airing the outlines of such revolutionary thinking before the Marquess of Winchester within the comfort of their much-loved northern political fortress – the Burlington Hotel, in Cork Street, London.

The remainder of that English visit, in early 1895, was a triumph and further bolstered the partners' dream of first consolidating, and then spreading, imperial glory from the Cape to Cairo. Queen Victoria entertained Rhodes at Windsor Castle, and Jameson – already the 'Lion of London' as a result of his Matabeleland exploits – was made a Commander of the Bath. A banquet, in Jameson's honour, presided over by the Prince of Wales, was held at the Imperial Institute where he got the opportunity to air more of Rhodes's growing political ambitions.[6]

It was all heady metropolitan stuff, but the corrective came soon enough once they returned to southern Africa. In March 1895, on the way back to Mashonaland, Jameson stopped off in Johannesburg and received a sharp reminder that while he and the Big Man were away and dining with royalty, Hammond had got the bit between the teeth and begun to test how ready the town's inhabitants were to challenge the Kruger state if mobilised along populist lines. Jameson had walked straight into Hammond and his friends' efforts to launch a San Francisco-style Vigilance Committee in the wake of the scandal that had followed on Jack McLoughlin's staring down of Chief Detective Robert Ferguson after the shooting of George Stevenson at the Red Lion Beer Hall.[7]

A vigilance committee, by nature, constitutes an effort by a local community to opt out of the larger duly constituted legal entity – the state, which enjoys a monopoly over the legitimate exercise of force – and to take for itself the right to impose law and order without the approval of, or reference to, any external authority. In that sense, a vigilance committee that succeeds is a bit like a minor coup d'état in that it has rejected the vested authority of the constitutional state and appropriated the right to protect life, persons and property on its own terms. And, because the word of the sovereign is beyond question, vigilance committees are a more familiar part of the political repertoire in a republican dispensation than in any constitutionally governed monarchy.

Few understood the underlying realities of this better than did that child of the San Francisco Vigilance Committee and founder of Law and Order Leagues up down the Coeur d'Alene, John Hays Hammond. He knew what he was doing and watched how Bettington's original letter to *The Star*, on 5 March, calling for a public meeting as a precursor to the formation of a committee, was followed by others from a worried 'Citizen' and then, unsurprisingly, one from William Dodds, Chairman of the Mercantile Association, who first Jack Hammond, and then later his wife, Natalie, attempted, without success, to recruit for their Rand 'revolution'.[8]

Fred Hamilton, always more of an economic realist than a political dreamer, warned the warlike Bettington and others that trying to get the odd revolutionary spark to ignite a populist fire in good times was probably a fool's errand. It was advice he offered the first enthusiasts for change, back in January 1895, when their thinking was still very much in its formative stages, and then repeated, in June that year, when their half-baked notions showed little sign of leavening the plot in meaningful ways. In an editorial on 6 March, Hamilton, this time in his capacity as editor of *The Star*, did his best to put the bellows to the fire for a vigilance committee but his reservations were there for all to see:

> It is not a little difficult to arouse popular sentiment in Johannesburg at a moment when Modderfonteins stand at something over £11, and Glencairns at 84s; and some apology is perhaps needed for directing attention to the insecurity of life at a time when the share market continues to exhibit such phenomenal activity. Nevertheless, it is perhaps as well that even the subtle ecstacies [*sic*] of a boom should not wholly blind us to certain practical aspects of the homicidal epidemic which appears to be passing over Johannesburg.[9]

In the end a Vigilance Committee was formed, but it soon expired.

Jameson, who was only passing through town, was not around long enough to trace fully the arc of a flare sent up by what, in time, would become the core of the Rand conspirators. Instead, he departed with two impressions, both poorly refined and likely to be misleading if not checked constantly against local conditions. First, he was of the opinion that the 'murmur of approaching strife [was] growing louder'.[10] In that he was almost certainly mistaken. Hammond might by then have been humming a ditty more loudly than the miners, including the Cornish at the very mines Hamilton had identified, but the voices of most workers were muted. Not even Leonard's National Union took up so faint a tune.

Secondly, and more pertinently, Jameson sensed that, if left to its own devices, the initiative for political change in Johannesburg – one that he and Rhodes believed should take an imperial deflection – might be forfeited to Hammond and his American friends who were among the most prominent agitators on the Rand, some of a republican bent. That, the tenuous links developing between Hammond and Phillips around the issue of the Vigilance Committee and the thinking that it induced among those who were not out-and-out imperialists appears to have done most to catapult first the newly re-energised Jameson, and then Rhodes himself, into action.

The very idea of controlling, if not organising, a Johannesburg uprising had been planted in their minds by Hammond in Matabeleland, in 1894, and thereafter, as Rhodes himself later informed his friend WT Stead, he and Jameson were left largely playing catch-up politics.[11] The origins of the events that later became concatenated and seen largely as the Raid may have received a decisive boost from two ambitious and strategically placed British imperialists, but the *idea* of an uprising and having troops to support it was born in the mind of a frustrated American mine-owning capitalist whose insights derived from the far-off Bitterroot Mountains of Idaho.

Within days of his return to Mashonaland, in March 1895, the newly decorated Dr Jameson, now more than ever of a mind to storm down the plateau and take over the South African Republic for Queen and country, ordered so much new military hardware for a British South Africa Company 'expeditionary force' that it was commented on in London and then duly reported on in the *Pretoria News*.[12] Presumably Jameson went to Cape Town to personally report to Rhodes on the purchase of the new Maxim guns, artillery, ammunition, rifles, saddles and uniforms because within a week or two, in April, he was back in Johannesburg on his way back north to do some necessary political homework. It was all well within Jameson's dictum: act first think later.

Under the circumstances, Jameson appears to have been remarkably restrained, using private meetings with a dozen or more leading men – ranging from Ewald Esselen, the maverick State Attorney, to Lionel Phillips, George Farrar and the Leonard brothers – to sound them out about the political impetus for change and the mood of the miners rather than to signal his preparations for a possible armed invasion.

Significantly, Jameson also had 'frequent talks with Mr Hammond'. In his meetings with others, including sceptics such as Farrar, Jameson may have disclosed the extent of the arming of the 'expeditionary force' and relayed Rhodes's in-principle approval of a possible invasion.[13] Hammond would have emerged from his chats with Rhodes's chief lieutenant much heartened. He had, in effect, succeeded in selling his idea of a revolution to the Big Man, the man who, via Consolidated Gold Fields and the British South Africa Company, was his employer and the guarantor of his rapidly escalating personal fortune. It was the Mine Owners' Protective Association of Idaho all over again. Jameson nonetheless left town 'without settling upon any definite plan'.[14]

Thinking that he and Rhodes had reclaimed the idea of a 'revolution' from Hammond, and mindful of the fact that Phillips and the Vigilance Committee had made few inroads into popular consciousness, Jameson was left to stew over what their next move might be. The Rhodes people were on side, as was to be expected, but the cautious Corner House notables

– Beit and Phillips – would require more persuasion. No planning was possible until such time as they, and especially Phillips, the Chairman of the
Chamber of Mines, had been lined up. Between Rhodes and Jameson it
was decided that Jameson would tackle Phillips after Rhodes had had the
chance to draw in the more skittish Alfred Beit.

The month of May was largely lost in thought, but Jameson was back in
Johannesburg by June with what seemed like a handful of aces – approval
in principle from Rhodes *and* Beit, an armed 'expeditionary force' and, for
the first time, an agreed date for the invasion. The men, the moment and the
money were drawing into alignment even if there was still no evidence of a
proper 'plan'. Jameson's point of entry to Phillips came via the conduit that
Hammond had used to help set up the Vigilance Committee initiative – the
editor of *The Star*, and earliest of the emerging conspirators, the stubbornly
sceptical Frederic Hamilton.

Hamilton suspected that things were going to take a turn, probably for
the worse, when he was invited to a dinner at which only he, Jameson
and Phillips were present. He attempted to get out of it, but to no avail.
Hammond's absence meant that Phillips would not feel that he was outnumbered by Rhodes's agents and that the Doctor could focus his famed charm
directly on the Chairman of the Chamber of Mines. Hamilton watched and
then noted how Doctor Jim moved in on Phillips, who, in truth, had long
since been pushing in the same direction:

> After dinner Jameson opened out and outlined his plan, the essence
> of which was that Johannesburg was to arm, and that he and his
> troopers were to come to our assistance if required. The moment was
> timed for December. It would be financed, so far as the Rand end
> was concerned, by Wernher, Beit & Co., and at the Rhodesian end
> by Rhodes and the Chartered Company.[15]

Hamilton issued his usual warning about good wages being a poor spawn-
ing ground for warriors, but, on this occasion, went further and elaborated
on his misgivings. He could see 'no one in Johannesburg whom men would
follow in such an enterprise' and that it was hardly possible to 'organise
secretly a purely commercial town on a military basis'. But, by that time,
the smoke and mirrors had done their work and both Jameson and Phillips
dismissed his nay-saying.[16]

The boom, they felt, was so far advanced that a market correction was
imminent and that would concentrate the collective mind of the white
miners. There was, they also argued, 'a nucleus of good men in the town
who had experience of native warfare' – i.e. Bettington and other friends
such as Aubrey Wools-Sampson. Frank Rhodes, 'a soldier of experience

and ability', had been appointed Managing Director of Gold Fields and would appear shortly in Johannesburg where he would prove to be a 'capable and popular' leader. And to settle the issue, Jameson suddenly conjured up yet another ace: the scheme was not nearly as hastily 'improvised' as it might seem. Rhodes had been lobbying in London, and the Colonial Office 'would further it by all possible means'.[17]

By mid-1895, the idea of an urban uprising possibly supported by an armed invasion that would somehow give rise to local autonomy of a sort and/or precipitate a coup d'état in Pretoria was loosely in place in the minds of eminent and strategically placed men in four centres thousands of miles apart – Cape Town, Johannesburg, Salisbury and London. Given the logistical constraints this placed on any face-to-face meetings for planning purposes, and the need for secrecy, it is perhaps understandable that the closing months of the southern winter of 1895, July and August, saw no further developments in the thinking of the conspirators nor any notable political gains. All of this placed additional pressure on Jameson, a leading conspirator who, by his nature, was ready to act as a catalyst and travel vast distances in order to get things moving.[18] But Jameson was getting little practical assistance from Cecil and Frank Rhodes, who were content to ooze moral support.

The best that Cecil Rhodes, feet firmly in Table Mountain soils, could muster that August was, as we have already noted in passing, a letter to Beit filled with its imperial dream and nightmare sequences. 'I wonder,' he mused, 'how the English Empire is held together. You might say oh yes wait – but as you know we will wait too long and with its marvellous wealth Johannesburg will make South Africa an independent Republic, which you and I do not want.' Luckily, the matter appeared to be in hand: 'Johannesburg is ready [for] the big idea which makes England dominant in Africa, in fact gives England the African continent.' 'I hear Hammond is enthusiastic,' he added, and claimed that brother Frank, supposedly the mastermind behind the proposed urban insurrection, was bound for Johannesburg – an initiative that had been announced by Jameson fully two months *earlier*, at the dinner with Phillips.[19]

It was a big idea from the Big Man, one which, as formulated, implied that the Union Jack would soon be fluttering above Johannesburg and Pretoria. And, at the time of its writing, Hammond, who had already been briefed by Jameson, had few reservations about a possible imperial future for the Witwatersrand goldfields. But Jameson felt that things were drifting and so, in September, he called in at Johannesburg on his way to Cape Town to breathe more life into Cecil Rhodes. It was during a new round of meetings on the Rand, with the usual suspects, that he disclosed, for the first time, that he could mount a force of 1 500 fully equipped men, backed by

Maxim guns and some field artillery. He would also bring along with him 1 500 spare rifles and sufficient ammunition. The Johannesburg conspirators, who could probably already raise a thousand rifles from private sources, would be expected to back the insurrection with an additional 5 000 rifles, three Maxim guns and a million rounds of ammunition that would have to be smuggled into the country. 'Thus in the event of a junction of forces being effected,' Percy FitzPatrick noted, 'Johannesburg would be able to command about 9 000 armed men with a fair equipment of machine guns and cannon.'[20]

Within days of that meeting in early October, Phillips, Leonard and Hammond went to Cape Town to establish more precisely what military backing there might be for an armed uprising from the British High Commissioner should the need arise. Rhodes, assisted by older brother Frank, was all reassurance. The Chartered Company had just secured a strategically situated strip of land in the Bechuanaland Protectorate, from which Jameson might launch an invasion. If necessary, Rhodes himself would accompany the compliant High Commissioner, Sir Hercules Robinson, whose appointment he had helped effect, to assist with any negotiations that might follow between the 'rebels' and the obstinate Kruger government.[21] Interestingly, even at that stage, less than 12 weeks before the proposed uprising, the leading conspirators still saw events culminating in a 'rebellion' rather than a coup d' état, let alone a 'revolution'. It was to be an English-led insurrection, one in which Britain and Westminster might, if not call the shots, then shape the outcome.[22]

With the global politics supposedly in place, the meeting could, at last, address the more mundane aspects of planning the uprising. Leonard was drafted to draw up a manifesto of grievances and demands that would be used to justify the insurrection, while the uprising itself, and the logistics behind it, would be overseen by Frank Rhodes and Hammond. Once again Hammond, an American patriot who later claimed to be possessed of such profoundly republican sympathies that he could not possibly rally beneath the Union Jack, failed to demur in the face of what was manifestly an overtly, grandly geopolitical, imperial conspiracy.[23]

'British recognition would have to be obtained should the necessity arise,' Hammond recalled 30 years later, and 'we believed that once the lives and possessions of British citizens were in jeopardy, we could force the home government to support us'.[24] Not much hostility to empire in those sentiments. No, the fact of the matter was that Hammond was both comfortable and familiar with radical capitalist initiatives that, if or when they went wrong, could be guaranteed through military intervention. Was that not exactly what he had effected in the Coeur d'Alene, in 1892, when first state and then federal troops were called in to protect the Mine Owners' Association?

True to form, it was at about this time, too, that Rhodes, Jameson and Hammond held a meeting that *excluded* those who had only recently become embroiled in the evolving conspiracy. Two were veterans of recent wars that, in truth, had yet to run their full course – one back in the Rocky Mountains and the other in Matabeleland and Mashonaland which, just months later, in 1896–1897, were set to erupt in African uprisings in the wake of Jameson's Raid.

It was Hammond and Jameson, both captivated by Rhodes and inclined to the sort of radical acts that they thought might please the Big Man, who simultaneously attracted and repelled one another. True, all three men had a well-developed liking for conspiracies and secret societies and all three had questionable ethics, but it was the two that were most impetuous and given to rash decisions who had most to fear from each other. And, if Hammond is to be believed, which is a course not to be followed lightly, he suspected, quite early on, that the importunate Jameson might well take some unauthorised precipitate action. So, 'In the presence of Rhodes, Jameson and I shook hands as a solemn pledge that he would not cross the border until *I* gave him the signal.'[25] It was a point of honour among thieves intent on stealing a country.

Back in Johannesburg, in mid-October, with no commander-in-chief to report to and Frank Rhodes still coming to grips with running the office of Consolidated Gold Fields, Hammond took on the role of quartermaster as agreed to earlier with Jameson. Tasked with smuggling in sufficient rifles to supply an uprising, as well as enough food to withstand a possible siege by Boer forces, Hammond soon realised the enormity of the task he faced.[26] He immediately drew in Victor Clement, his old comrade, to help with the arms smuggling, and Jameson's old friend, Dr Henry Wolff, to acquire the more conventional supplies.[27]

Precisely because rifle-smuggling necessitated the greatest possible care, competence and secrecy, Hammond recruited only a trusted inner network of Americans, almost exclusively Californians – Charles Butters, Jack Curtis, Richard Parker and Thomas Mein – to help run the operation.[28] In addition, he received help in importing the guns from an unknown American mining engineer named Labram and from his old mentor, Gardner Williams, General Manager of De Beers. With the exception of Williams, all these men enjoyed ready access to mines that were within easy reach of downtown Johannesburg including the Robinson Deep, overseen by Captain Tom Mein, and Clements' Simmer & Jack.

Lee-Metford rifles, imported from Britain, were shipped to Cape Town or Port Elizabeth, from where they were forwarded to Kimberley. There, Gardner Williams and Henry Holden – the latter one of Jameson's military envoys – supervised the repacking and concealing of the guns in railway trucks consigned to Jack Hammond himself, in Johannesburg. One consignment was placed in specially modified Standard Oil barrels; if the spigots were opened to verify the contents, a small amount of oil would drain from the false bottoms.[29] Later on, rifles were buried beneath coke in open railway trucks destined for the gold mines.

But a lengthy supply chain, time-consuming and labour-intensive repacking and an unpredictable, unreliable schedule for freight trains all bedevilled operations, with the result that such limited quantities of rifles as there were arrived hopelessly late for the planned uprising.[30] A popular 'revolution' lacking sufficient firepower to challenge the force of the state was already halfway towards becoming a limp 'movement for reform'.

What was the business of many men became no-one's business, and the conspirators lost sight of many painful realities, including the fact that the Cornish and other white miners were far from the fire-and-smoke breathing insurrectionists required for a 'revolution'. The stark disjuncture between the real-world boom on the Witwatersrand and the dream world of a hoped-for uprising led by a few imperialists and mining capitalists – the very thing that Fred Hamilton had warned against – was growing larger. Even Hammond, who was never at liberty to disclose his part in the Bitterroot Mountain upheavals, half-sensed the problem. He noted: 'On many occasions I did go so far as to say that the law-abiding miners from England were enduring ill-treatment from the Kruger's government that the men I had known out West would never have tolerated.'[31]

In fairness to the conspirators, however, not all the incoming news was equally discouraging. As spring heralded the start of the closing quarter of 1895, there were two or three signs that the good times might be coming to an end and that the opportunity might yet present itself to prod the still sluggish white miners into action. The State President did what he could to help. In August, in an attempt to force importers to give preference to the state-owned Netherlands Railway that ran from Lourenço Marques to the Rand, rather than that linking Cape Town to the Witwatersrand, the government trebled the rates on the 64-kilometre section of track between the Vaal River and Johannesburg. When importers then unloaded their freight on the far side of the border and arranged for onward transportation across the river fords by ox-wagon, the government replied by closing the drifts, on 1 October. The resulting 'drifts crisis', another classic exercise in brinkmanship by President Kruger, ended when the British government, drawing on a clause in the London Convention, threatened the use of force to reopen the fords.[32]

But those like Fred Hamilton, hoping that a bout of financial sneezing might herald the onset of full-blown economic influenza, remained disappointed. The 'drifts crisis' did nothing to halt the onward and upward momentum of the supposed long-term value of deep-level mining stocks.[33] But the large-scale speculative machinations, that underpinned much of the 'Kaffir Boom' posed a far more serious threat. There was a huge market correction in share prices on the Paris Bourse, in October 1895, and this was followed by a lesser one on the local market on 'Black Saturday', 9 November.[34] Even then the setback was insufficient to completely undermine confidence in the longer-term prospects of the Witwatersrand gold-mining industry. Contrary to the expectations of Hamilton and others, the miners, like some workers on the morning after payday, snored on into the Sunday.

Some in the locust elite, transient conspirators, a few of whom were on their way to becoming dollar millionaires – looked to a setting economic sun as a portent of things to come, a day when the known order would be reversed and even greater profits would accrue to them. Yet others, looked towards Afrikaner-Dutch politics which, they believed, would give rise to a new dawn that might yet light up their insurrection. For the true believers among the latter, succour was to be drawn from within the ranks of the growing 'Progressive' opposition to Kruger's folksy, idiosyncratic and patriarchal style of government, or from the better-educated members of the Boer elite. Kruger's long-standing political opponents might soon be co-opted into a 'provisional government'.[35]

But it was not only within the confines of the Boer political elite that a crack or two was beginning to show. Afrikaner-Dutch ministers and their congregants, too, were being given a glimpse of, if not heaven itself, then of more secure and valuable property rights in the here and now. The resulting conflict about who owned what saw a serious rise in tension between members of the *Hervormde* and *Gereformeerde* Churches. But the Johannesburg conspirators failed to realise that disputes between the churches did not necessarily translate into divided loyalties when it came to such over-arching questions as nationalism and patriotism.[36] It was not, as we shall see, to be their only misreading of Afrikaner-Dutch religious life and practice. As the would-be revolutionaries were to discover, contempt founded on ethnic or racial difference eroded political and social insight.

Turning all these developments to the advantage of the conspirators would have presented those plotting a change of regime with a formidable challenge at the best of times. Trying to do so without the benefit of an undisputed leader, without a revolutionary core that was properly insulated from a second tier of Californian collaborators and a structure that lacked a clear-cut chain of command made it virtually impossible. This, together with the fact that two or three of the most important conspirators and financiers were thousands of miles apart and reliant on a commercial mining code for the most urgent telegraphic communication, meant that the months of August to October 1895 contributed virtually nothing to building a revolutionary momentum. In political and logistical terms, the conspiracy lacked everything it needed – leadership, pace, direction and the potential for mass support.

CHAPTER ELEVEN

Cowboy Jack's Secret Aspirations

Abducting the President and the District of Columbia Template

OCTOBER–DECEMBER 1895

John Hays Hammond was always reluctant to acknowledge, other than in grudging fashion, that the planning and execution of the coup was a failure from start to finish. So, while even Jameson later admitted freely to it all having been a 'bad blunder',[1] Hammond could only describe it in the most euphemistic of terms: 'There was no definite plan at first,' he conceded. He agreed that the movement 'was slow to gather momentum', without exploring why it should have been so. Like Jameson, keen to hide the extent of the Big Man's involvement, he would only say that 'certain of us gradually assumed leadership', before going on to name himself, Phillips, Frank Rhodes, Charles Leonard and George Farrar as the core conspirators.[2] In retrospect, however, it is clear why Hammond pussyfooted around the crucial issues involved in the planning of the 'revolution'. He did so for the same reasons that rendered his 'autobiographical account of the Coeur d'Alene troubles 'biased and distorted'.[3] Hammond dissembled, telling lies of commission and omission *because* he had played a definitive role in scandalously divisive events, events of national and international importance, motivated by his desire for fame underwritten by untrammelled greed.

It was not, as he claimed, 'certain of us' who 'gradually assumed leadership' when the absence of direction began to assume critical proportions in the months leading up to the uprising, it was Jack Hammond – Hammond with his knowledge of filibustering, Hammond the would-be cowboy and admirer of Wyatt Earp; Hammond the mining revolutionary and spymaster; Hammond with his personal dread of cowardice and dishonour; and Hammond the son of San Francisco, with a reflex-like respect for the popular, direct action of vigilance committees.

When Colonel Frank Rhodes failed to live up to expectations as military leader and Lionel Phillips, who had no personal experience of involvement in an insurrection, proved incapable of coming up with meaningful ideas for the planning of an urban-based revolution, it was Hammond who was forced to dig into his store of experience and historical knowledge and give shape and meaning to the Johannesburg 'uprising', which, upon *his* signal, would draw in Jameson to expand the British Empire for the political master they both adored, Cecil Rhodes. The Johannesburg insurrection and the 'Raid' that was to follow it was an Anglo-American initiative in conception and in its hoped-for outcome, but almost every aspect of its planning pointed to the hand of John Hays Hammond.

It was after Jameson's penultimate visit to Johannesburg, in September 1895, on his way to see Rhodes in the Cape, that Hammond began asserting himself more forcibly among the inner core of the conspirators, who by then included both George Farrar, to help with mobilising the miners, and, belatedly, Eckstein & Co's trusted 'chief of intelligence', Percy FitzPatrick, Lionel Phillips's colleague, who would help bolster the Beit Boys in a possible stand-off with the Rhodes Boys should serious political disputes arise.

In mid-October, once it was clearer that the importation of arms and ammunition was not going according to schedule, Hammond took steps to offset the logistical failure of his Californian engineering corps by modifying the original plot to meet any shortfall in the number of rifles and supply of ammunition.[4] Instead of relying only on the Johannesburg revolutionaries to come up with the necessary military equipment, the plan was altered to include a surprise raid on Pretoria and the seizing of the state arsenal, one of the walls of which was in such a state of disrepair that it would make for easy access.[5] It was estimated that it would require only 50 men to overrun the arsenal. The captured arms and ammunition could then be forwarded to Johannesburg by wagons and used to equip the thousands of white miners mobilised to that end.

The idea of seizing the state arsenal was almost certainly initiated by Hammond and probably first aired during early morning horse rides with Frank Rhodes. It was then taken to the other core revolutionaries – Phillips, Farrar and Leonard – for approval by 'the committee'. The 'committee' was, of course, the legalistic *ex post facto* term for the conspirators – a post-Raid rationalisation hinting at legitimacy. What is beyond doubt, however, is that, once the proposal had been agreed to, Hammond single-handedly took ownership of the foundational idea, radically extended it without referring it back to his co-conspirators, and then assumed control of all the contingent planning that went with it. Hammond was, in effect, hoping to run a revolution within a revolution.[6]

We know this because, after decades of silence about the matter, even when telling the story of 'Jameson's Raid' to the few carefully selected journalists in whom he had confided, Hammond confessed to it in his *Autobiography*, published shortly before his death in 1936:

> I did have one further idea about which I kept very quiet. It seemed
> to me that once the arsenal at Pretoria was captured it would be
> a relatively simple sequel to take Oom Paul [the State President]
> himself back to Johannesburg with us. I felt confident that, when
> subjected to this other environment, he would prove more receptive
> to our ideas.[7]

At work here was the mind of the revolutionary mining capitalist behind most of the planning of the hoped-for 1895 uprising in the South African Republic – egotistical, irresponsible and utterly lawless.

Sensing that, to all intents and purposes, Frank Rhodes was perfectly useless as a soldier when it came to conducting urban warfare, let alone a revolution, Hammond began to fold his new covert ambition – to abduct the State President – into the already approved plan to seize the arsenal. By that late stage, mid-October 1895, Lionel Phillips, too, had not come up with any ideas that a Coeur d'Alene veteran, or a man who had mobilised cowboys and Indians in Mexico, might put to good use. This gave rise to a few ironies that Jack Hammond, a leader of men and growing in self-importance with each passing day, would have relished.

In order to find a base from which a smallish band of trusted Americans might mount a strike against the arsenal, and then go on to capture Kruger, Hammond looked around for a suitably situated property that he could hire. A vacant farm at Irene, once owned by one of the State President's close friends, AH Nellmapius, but by then administered as part of a deceased estate by Phillips, though H Eckstein & Co, presented itself as a delectable choice. The Beit Boys, who themselves were never above a bit of bribery, would be helping to mount an attack on Kruger from a property that had been owned by one of the State President's own notoriously corrupt friends.

And, because the abduction of Kruger was Hammond's idea, this time round Cowboy Jack did not share his real intentions with even those Californian managers whom he had entrusted with smuggling rifles into Johannesburg. In Hammond's own words, as set out in his memoirs:

> I obtained a lease of property just outside Pretoria, ostensibly for
> prospecting purposes. There I assembled fifty hard-boiled Americans
> of an adventurous spirit who were supposedly prospecting for gold.
> They knew as well as I did that there was no gold in the vicinity, but
> were quite content to humour my whim so long as they were paid
> for it. Most of them had been discharged from companies under my

control for good and sufficient reasons, including drunk and disorderly conduct. The mine managers, totally unaware that anything out of the ordinary was intended, remonstrated against my giving employment to men they had dismissed. They said this was subversive of discipline. I told them not to worry; experience had taught me how to handle such men, and, indeed, I found them tractable and not altogether uncongenial.[8]

Had the revolution succeeded, Hammond would have proved himself a man among men twice over, *the* hero among many heroes. It was the sort of exploit that would have warmed the heart of Coffee Hays and John Freaner. Always an individualist, Jack Hammond's ego was, by now, showing signs of running amok.

But his secret scheme – the plot within the plot, one that drew on the 19th-century filibustering tradition of the Old South – did not end with the abduction of the State President. Hammond's personal ambitions went further, drawing inspiration from the American Constitution, in the hope that he might one day help bring about a new, politically independent dispensation for the Witwatersrand goldfields that would see it emerge as a virtual state within a state, leaving the Boers to carry on running their 'backward' agricultural republic much as they had always done. Here again, Hammond left a clear indication as to what the thinking was behind the 'ideas' that would have been put to Kruger after his capture.

In the latter half of May 1896, after the core conspirators and most members of the 'Reform Committee' had been tried and sentenced and Hammond was still in prison, his wife, Natalie, fell seriously ill. The Kruger government responded to a family crisis by granting Hammond compassionate leave and allowing him to take time off from prison so that he might return to Johannesburg and support his wife. It was during those few days at home, on 17 May, that Hammond took the opportunity to dictate some notes to his personal secretary, Arthur Kelsey, recording his thinking of how one day the goldfields could be best administered. The region, he suggested, 'might be governed by commissioners and a judiciary appointed by the President of the Republic almost precisely as the District of Columbia is governed'.[9]

Hammond, through his earlier association with the United States Geological Survey, knew a good deal about the city of Washington as the Mecca of federal power and, via influential political friends, how exactly the once exceedingly corrupt District of Columbia was governed. It was not just the fact that, after 1874, Congress had abandoned local government and opted for direct rule that Hammond approved of, it was the composition of the Board of Commissioners itself that was most appealing to him.

Two of its three commissioners were appointed by the President, with the approval of the Senate, but the third – a technocrat – had by law to be selected from the US Army Corps of Engineers.[10] Would it be too fanciful to suggest that, in Hammond's post-revolutionary dream world, a world in which Johannesburg stood in relation to the Witwatersrand goldfields as the city of Washington did to the District of Columbia, John Hays Hammond, the most talented mining engineer in the South African Republic, might be the chief commissioner?

And could it not have been that it was because the usually politically astute Cecil Rhodes had detected these American ambitions in Hammond, his chief mining lieutenant on the Witwatersrand, that the Big Man was pulled into the plotting for what became the 'Jameson Raid'? It certainly accords with the explanation that Rhodes later gave WT Stead for getting drawn into the conspiracy sooner rather than later. In the latter part of 1895, Rhodes was playing catch-up politics, lagging behind, not leading, the unfolding conspiracy on the Rand.[11]

As with most people, it was history and personal experience that informed Hammond's thinking, and his planning for the Rand revolution was no exception. In the case of the Raid, however, it would seem that the planning for the abduction of Kruger and seizing the arsenal was, in part, an opportunistic extension of an idea that had been around for some time. But it is only by going back and re-examining Hammond's earliest socialisation more carefully that we can appreciate fully how this part of the planning was shaped by both Rand and American experiences.

As noted earlier, there was nothing especially 'Californian' or novel in the notion of seizing the Pretoria arsenal and members of Kruger's executive. It was an idea that had been around in frontier Johannesburg ever since the Boer government threatened to hang two white highwaymen with 'Irish Brigade' connections in 1890. That said, the architecture of Hammond's 1895 scheme seems to have had a good deal in common with the foiled plot in San Francisco on the eve of the Civil War, in 1861. It was a conspiracy in which several of Hammond's father's friends had played a significant role.

It will be recalled that it was shortly after the war commenced, in 1861, that two California-based Southerners, Asbury Harpending and Ridgeley Greathouse, formed the clandestine 'Committee of Thirty', which, as with Hammond's 'Reform Committee', recruited individuals only on the say-so of the founding members. The objective of the Thirty was to seize control of San Francisco and then turn California and the neighbouring state of Oregon into a 'Pacific Republic'. As Harpending later remembered it:

> Our plans were to paralyse all organised resistance by simultaneous attack. The Federal Army was little more than a shadow. About two

hundred soldiers were at Fort Point, less than a hundred at Alcatraz and a handful at Mare Island and the arsenal at Benicia where a 30,000 stand of arms were stored. We proposed to carry these strong-holds by night attack and also seize the arsenal of the militia at San Francisco. With this military equipment we proposed to organise an army of Southern sympathisers, sufficient in number to beat down any armed resistance. All of which may sound chimerical at this late day, but then, take my word for it, was an opportunity within our grasp.[12]

The commander of the US Army in California, it will be recalled, General AS Johnston, would be 'taken by surprise and subdued with force'.

Behind Harpending and Greathouse's attempted seizure of power, however – as with the hoped-for Witwatersrand 'revolution' – lay other deep-seated political and economic objectives. In the case of California, the principal objective behind the attempted coup was thus to block off any gold shipments to the North. All supplies of the precious yellow metal would then be diverted to the South across the Arizona desert.[13]

It would be foolish to suggest that the plan for a coup in San Francisco, in 1861, was a template, matching in all important aspects the scheme hurriedly agreed upon by the Johannesburg conspirators in 1895. That is *not* the argu-ment that is being pursued here. What is being suggested, however, is that on the balance of probabilities, it is extremely unlikely that the American who had abrogated to himself the right to plan the contours of the Johannesburg uprising was unfamiliar with the broad pattern of thinking that informed the Harpending-Greathouse scheme.

As we have seen, Hammond was raised as a 'Southerner' in a family of Southerners living through the Civil War in San Francisco. Indeed, so concerned were authorities about the loyalties of some members of his extended family that the men were made to swear that they would not take up the Confederate call to arms. It is inconceivable that Hammond, who, unusually, chose to remain silent about the Harpending-Greathouse con-spiracy in his *Autobiography*, bore no knowledge about the 'Committee of Thirty' and its aspirations. Indeed, one suspects that Hammond chose *not* to raise the subject in his memoirs precisely because readers might be tempted to pursue some of the similarities between it and the structures that led to the formation of the 'Reform Committee' in Johannesburg. Nor is it likely that Hammond, a keen analyst of policy and a man with a profound inter-est in political economy, a mine owner who had himself lived through the American administration's shift from silver to bimetallism during his time in the Coeur d'Alene, would not be aware of the importance of gold in times of war and as an instrument for underwriting international trade.

Hammond was certainly aware of the explosive growth in trade between the United States and the South African Republic, if for no other reason than that he had personally been responsible for the importation of millions of dollars' worth of mining equipment. And, in the age of bimetallism, might not a man witnessing a significant shift in the pattern of international trade be interested in where gold might be marketed?

But all that is speculation. There is not a shred of evidence to suggest that Hammond, profoundly Anglophile right up to the moment when the political situation forced him into parading his American and republican sympathies, had any intention of facilitating a permanent shift in relations between Pretoria and Washington, DC, so as to fit with the changing economic circumstances of the mid-1890s. What is not in doubt, however, is that by October 1895 his ego was continuing to inflate at an alarming rate, and that, being pushed to make up for the deficiencies of Frank Rhodes, Lionel Phillips and George Farrar, he was drawing more heavily on his American experiences in the Coeur d'Alene, San Francisco and elsewhere to inform such little planning as there was for the Johannesburg uprising.

By late October 1895, then, the thinking behind the 'revolution' had been fleshed out only slightly more than at the start of that month. The idea was that, once the citizens of Johannesburg had been suitably mobilised and secretly armed, an ultimatum consisting of the demands contained in Charles Leonard's manifesto would be sent to the Kruger government. If, after three days, no positive response to their demands had been received, there would be a night assault on the arsenal at Pretoria and President Kruger would be abducted and removed to Johannesburg.[14] At that point, a 'provisional government', including a few Boer notables sympathetic to the need for reform, would be declared. When the Boer commandos attacked and laid siege to the town, which had sufficient food for two months, Jameson, based in Pitsani, would ride in with 1 500 armed men and additional military supplies to provide adequate policing and protection for the town's inhabitants. And, if all else failed, the High Commissioner would send in British troops.[15]

Although hard-pressed, Hammond was confident of his leadership qualities and ready to put the finishing touches to this master plan. He was, by then, as one historian puts it, 'the most significant conspirator in the reform group'.[16] Indeed he was, hands down. But, as ever, the pressure was beginning to get to him and he was caught in the scissors: between an overweening ambition to leave his mark on the coming revolution and an understandable, creeping fear of failure.

In early October, with the uprising two months away, Hammond told Pope Yeatman, one of his Californian engineering friends, that he had 'not been well'.[17] Mrs Hammond, his sharp-eyed confidante, must have been among the first to notice. As the tension mounted, he did as he usually did and let his wife into the secret of what was being planned. His instinct was to try to do the chivalrous thing and he arranged to send her away to Cape Town, in good time, well before the uprising started.

But Natalie Harris, drawn from genteel Southern society, was having none of it and vowed to stand by her man. And so, just three days after he had set in motion the arrangements for her seaside stay, he was forced to undo them. He wrote to their Cape Town agent telling him that 'my wife has changed her plans', and that he should 'go to the Vineyards Hotel and see if you can secure me four good rooms for the months of December, January, February and March'.[18] A 'revolution' was coming but it was to be an aristocratic affair, to be followed by a holiday at the seaside and then, in February, by a trip north through the Suez Canal and on to England where the family hoped to be 'permanently established' by the summer of 1896.[19] A man might help overthrow a state, but there was no need to linger.

The Hammonds may have been aristocrats-in-residence for the season's coming revolution but they were not the only members of the locust elite to see the 'revolution' as being a one-off diversion, a matter that demanded their attention for just long enough to snatch history back from the back-veld Boers who had dared to appropriate it, and then to put it back on track for what would be a glorious, industrialised, future.

When Jameson passed through town on his final visit to Johannesburg, just days later, Hammond told him about the projected trip to England, set for two months after the uprising, and invited Jameson to join him on the journey north. But Jameson, hasty and one step ahead, was keener to get to England in January – only days after a bright British future would have overtaken the dreary Boer past.[20] Undaunted, Hammond – then still a close friend of the Doctor's – 'tried to persuade him to wait until February'. When Jameson hesitated briefly, Hammond wrote to Sir John Willoughby, Jameson's military adviser, suggesting that, after the revolution, he too consider joining a probable East Coast exodus.[21]

With national business and pleasures private settled for the upcoming Christmas season and into the foreseeable future, Hammond decided to make one, final out-of-town trip. It was to be a journey that would not only help consolidate his rapidly deepening friendship with Jameson, but allow Natalie to become a little more involved in the planning for the days that lay ahead, days that would surely cement his role in history.

Early in November, the couple took the train to Kimberley, where Hammond updated Rhodes on preparations for the Johannesburg uprising.[22] As was so frequently the case, Rhodes left no record of the meeting. All the more the pity, because it was probably at this point in the plotting that Rhodes again got the strong impression that Hammond, Clement and the other Californians had assumed such a vital role in what was happening in Johannesburg that he and Jameson might be in danger of losing control of what they had hoped to be a British, imperial annexation of the ZAR to an American-manned republican revolution.[23]

Hammond, a fox contemplating the chicken run, may have been under the impression that he alone appreciated the full extent and nature of the American-inspired thinking that went into the planning of the Johannesburg uprising. But Rhodes was no fool even though, right until the closing moments of the planned uprising, Jameson continued to trust Hammond and the inner circle of Americans. Hammond and his wife left Kimberley unaware that Rhodes was becoming increasingly alarmed at the prospect of an intentional or unintentional American takeover of what he privately saw as a purely imperial project. But his fears may have been overblown because, at that time, Hammond was apparently still content to see an outcome to the uprising that might be favourable to Queen and country. And so, amid mounting misunderstandings and suspicions that were starting to prompt thoughts of betrayal and were only fully manifest once the 'revolution' had actually started, the Hammonds left Kimberley for Johannesburg, via Mafeking.

The Hammonds arrived in Mafeking at a propitious moment; just days after Jameson had dropped the last piece into the geopolitical puzzle that provided the filibusters with the base necessary for a possible military strike into the ZAR. Local African tribes, only recently locked in the Bechuanaland Protectorate, had, from the early 1880s and until the Warren expedition, in 1885, suffered various incursions at the hands of Boer adventurers and mercenaries. These African groupings were no less well disposed to the Kruger government than were the Witwatersrand conspirators. On 29 October 1895, exploiting pre-existing ambitions and rivalries among Barolong polities, Jameson had persuaded Chief Silas Molema to allow him to rent him a border farm for £300 per annum – payable in advance – and the promise of an additional farm elsewhere once matters with the Boers had been settled.[24]

It was on the farm Mabete, which comprised the Pitsani rail siding, that Jameson and his 500 troopers commenced their military drills. The collaboration of at least some local Africans in what eventually became the Jameson Raid did not end there. Indeed, when the filibusters eventually did set off from Pitsani, in late 1895, they were accompanied by a 'posse of Kafirs' and 'Cape Boys' ('Coloured' men) estimated to have been 70 strong, which did most of the necessary heavy lifting for an otherwise exclusively European expedition.[25] Sadly, in keeping with the times, neither the Boer victors nor the Brit losers bothered to record the now lost names of the black Jameson Raiders.

While in Mafeking, Hammond, in effect the 'director of intelligence for the Rand conspirators', hired a rugged little Cape cart and bought sufficient provisions for he and Natalie to undertake a comfortable, leisurely ride back to the Witwatersrand, where he would meet Jameson for the last time before the uprising, then scheduled for mid-December.[26] The purpose of the journey, however, was to study the topography of the western Transvaal and to plot 'the best route for Jameson to follow' for a ride into Johannesburg should the need arise. Even amid the bitterness that followed on the botched revolution, Hammond was proud of the fact that when the impatient Jameson did eventually did set off from Pitsani, he chose to follow the route laid out by the Hammonds rather than that mapped by Sir John Willoughby.[27]

Jameson resurfaced in Johannesburg, on 17 November, for a final set of briefings, fresh from discussions with Rhodes in Cape Town.[28] Closer to Rhodes than any other man on earth, Jameson had by then started to pick up on the Big Man's growing uneasiness at the vanguard role taken by the Americans in the planning of the revolution. But he and Rhodes were in a difficult position; in the presence of the Big Man himself, he – Jameson – had shaken Hammond's hand and given a solemn undertaking not to set off for the Witwatersrand until he had received Hammond's personal go-ahead.

As things stood, Rhodes and Beit had put up the money for an uprising that was supposed to lead to an intervention that would secure a British future for the goldfields, but he – Jameson – the man waiting in the wings with an armed force, could not move without an American's say-so. In political and military terms, Hammond and his Americans might, and could, veto an initiative that had been designed to expand the empire.

Under the circumstances Jameson's final mission in Johannesburg was clear. Somehow he had to wrest back the political initiative from the Americans, though without Hammond's feeling that he was reneging on a promise not to intervene militarily without his agreement. It was at this crucial late stage that Jameson suddenly introduced an insistent personal concern into his discussions with Hammond and the rest of the core conspirators. He was, he now claimed, concerned about how a purely military incursion under his command might be seen by the British South Africa Company's shareholders, and by people in Britain, if he could not provide proof that he had not undertaken an invasion on a personal whim. He needed to be able to show that the citizens of Johannesburg had called upon him at a time of great crisis.

What was needed, Jameson insisted, was what later became known as the 'letter of invitation'. It was a request that, if necessary, could be read to the men he had assembled at Pitsani in order to explain what exactly they would be volunteering for if they did set off for Johannesburg. It was

a document that might subsequently be shown to angry or puzzled shareholders of the Chartered Company should things go wrong.[29] At first glance
it might have seemed a not entirely unreasonable request. An incursion into
the Republic might indeed turn out to be a hazardous affair once the Boers
had mobilised, and the British South Africa Company had already acquired
a reputation for opportunistic and rapacious actions.

Upon closer examination, however, Jameson's request and reasoning
might have raised an eyebrow or two. He and Rhodes were both approaching the apex of their careers. Rhodes was a member of the Privy Council
and Jameson had only recently been made a Commander of the Order of
the Bath; their status and standing were plain for all to see. Rhodes was
almost beyond questioning as the Chairman of the Chartered Company,
which, as anybody who could read a newspaper knew, had, as far back as
March, bought so much military equipment for an 'expeditionary force'
that even the *Pretoria News* had reported on it. Moreover, after his military
exploits against the Ndebele Jameson was loved and respected as a leader
of men and hardly in need of being able to read from a letter in order to
motivate the troops under his command.

But what is interesting and possibly revealing about Jameson's sudden search
for written authorisation to assist in the capture of a president and the overthrow of a state was the personal gloss that he added to his appeals. He pleaded
that he needed the document so that his critics would not view him as a 'pirate'
should he and his forces have to enter the Republic.[30] It was a strange, seemingly inappropriate term to choose, but one that he returned to more than
once before and after the ill-considered 'Raid' had been set in motion.

Why would Jameson be anxious to avoid being cast as a 'pirate'? Surely a
more plausible fear would have been to be termed a 'brigand' or an 'outlaw'
– as he was during the Raid. Was the word 'pirate' not his euphemism for
another term then still in everyday use in American political discourse and
one that Hammond, in particular, would have understood perfectly clearly?
Despite a love of things American, Jameson did not want to be cast as a freebooter or, more accurately still, as a 'filibuster' and have to settle for a minor
part in what might become some Stars and Stripes production.[31] Indeed that
was precisely why he needed a letter – to help secure the outcome of any
revolution on the Rand for him, for Rhodes and for their Queen and country.

Hammond, believing that he still held the moral and political trump card
– in the form of Jameson's pledge not to invade without his personal say-
so – could see the point. He was not put out either by Jameson's plea for a
letter of invitation, or by its wording. Indeed, so comfortable was he with
the contents of the document and the sentiments contained in a letter that
he believed would never be used, that he later claimed, quite incorrectly, to
have been one of four conspirators to have drafted it.[32]

In fact, the letter was drafted by that arch-jingo and imperialist, the lawyer Charles Leonard, Chairman of the National Union. When Leonard told Fred Hamilton that five of the core conspirators had 'signed a letter of invitation to Jameson to cross the border' and to prevent him being seen as a 'pirate' should things go wrong, Hamilton exclaimed, 'Charlie are you mad?'[33] No madder than Jameson, some might have been tempted to say. Hamilton was not the only one to sense that it was not only irresponsible to hand a letter of that sort to a man of volatile temperament but, at his suggestion, to then leave it undated so that it could be appropriately doctored should the need arise. Percy FitzPatrick, the slightly more cautious 'secretary' to a 'committee' that was still not sure whether it was in the 'reform' or the 'revolutionary' business, refused to sign what amounted to a political blank cheque.[34]

Hamilton's questioning of Leonard's sanity prompted second thoughts in the lawyer's mind. But it was too late, the letter, signed by Hammond, Phillips, Frank Rhodes and Farrar, was supposedly beyond retrieval. As Edmund Garrett, who spoke to the leading conspirators immediately after the 'Raid', noted, Jameson 'regarded it as a great stroke having secured it'.[35] Indeed it was; with it the military initiative that might help clinch the revolution was back in the hands of the core imperialists. By signing the letter, Hammond had again proved himself a Rhodes man at heart, and, for all his half-baked ideas from the American West, would come out in support of an imperial push if and when the moment presented itself.

Jameson knew that the letter was filled with sentiments that made it clear that, above all else, it was England and Empire that was being put to the sword by an arrogant and oppressive Boer government. 'The position of thousands of Englishmen and others is rapidly becoming intolerable,' its signatories intoned. 'The state's every public act,' it continued, 'betrays the most positive hostility, not only to everything English, but to the neighbouring states.' The Kruger government was denying immigrants their 'public liberties', which 'violates the national sense of Englishmen at every turn'.[36] All these allegations had been happily endorsed by Hammond, whose republican sensitivities would resurface once the revolution began to sputter, to the degree that he personally organised the raising of the flag of the Zuid-Afrikaansche Republiek above the Consolidated Gold Fields building, Rhodes's Johannesburg stronghold.

Charles Leonard then attempted to do the impossible and reclaim the letter from Jameson. The lawyer told the Doctor that he had had second thoughts, that the invitation to invade was a mistake. But Jameson, well into a game of imperial poker that he believed he could win on his own, was not about to sacrifice his ace to a political tyro. And so he did as many a good poker player might and a man with questionable ethics would, and 'bluffed'

his way out of the problem. 'Awfully sorry, old man,' the Doctor was alleged
to have said, 'but it has gone down to Cape Town by the last train.'[37] A sceptic, however, might have felt that, having gone to so much time and trouble
to get the letter, and given what was at stake in political terms, it probably
nestled in Dr Jim's back pocket.

Despite the difficulties surrounding the signing of the letter, problems
that Hammond later found sufficiently embarrassing never to allude to ver-
bally or in writing, his relationship with Jameson, and Jameson's with him,
had never been stronger. The two took leave of each other with each believing, not without reason, that they were united in their loyalties to Rhodes
as well as being the strongest and most reliable of partners in a dangerous
conspiracy. The pledge and letter were linked; both spoke to revolutionary
solidarity, although the former had been sealed with a handshake and the
latter with a document. What could possibly go wrong? The clock was far
from striking midnight and time was probably still on their side. Hours later,
Jameson was off south to try to bolster the manpower for his Pitsani force,
which, like that of the Johannesburg conspirators, was woefully under-
strength. The planning of uprising in Johannesburg, he felt, was in the hands
of the Californian and on track,

Had 'Dr Jim' but known it, however, he was probably in greater need than
ever of a shot of morphine to help him sleep soundly on the Cape Town-
bound train that night than at any other time in his increasingly troubled
career. He and his fellow conspirators were up to their eyeballs in codes,
pledges and secrets but their basic objective and planning was about as well-
concealed and hidden from the view of curious outsiders as was the course
of the Nile as it flows through the Nubian desert.

A few days later, James Bryce, the noted liberal, constitutionalist and
recent British cabinet minister, checked into a Johannesburg hotel en route
to Cape Town. To his amazement Bryce almost at once picked up on whispers to the effect that rifles were being smuggled into mine properties, and
that the Kruger government was about to be confronted by a stern military
challenge. Few men of international eminence passed through Johannesburg
without dining at the Hammond home, and an invitation was swiftly forthcoming. Bryce decided that he could not let the opportunity pass without
probing Hammond about the rumour.

Bryce was brushed off, but he then began to pursue Hammond. 'I would
find him at my office when I came in in the morning,' Hammond complained, 'I would find him at my home when I arrived there at night.' But,
instead of taking his visitor's increasingly pointed questioning as a sign that
there had been serious breaches in the confidentiality and secrecy that was
supposed to hide the conspirators' planning from public view, Hammond,
'chief of intelligence' in the revolutionary movement, chose to dismiss it as

the insight of a single astute mind. 'He could not prove that anything out of the ordinary was going on,' Hammond later opined – as if that were the test – 'but no person of sensibility could fail to suspect that something was toward.' Not content with toying with his guest's curiosity, which, by then, had begun to reveal some 'pertinent or embarrassing questions', Hammond proceeded to patronise Bryce into silence: 'I finally told him that he possessed all the necessary attributes of a first-class American newspaper reporter.'[38]

Bryce, who went on to become an outstanding British ambassador to the United States, may or may not have been reassured by the suggestion that there were other career paths open to him, but it did not make the underlying problem go away. It was not just one 'person of sensibility' who knew something was afoot: two or three agents in the state's newly established secret service suspected that the mines were being used for the storing of arms and food; scores of men in the press, stock exchange and mining industry knew what was planned; and fully half the town had a fair idea of what was coming.[39] And, with the passing of each day and several delays in settling on the precise date for the start of the Revolution, the information available to the government grew more accurate and precise. On 22 December 1895, seven days before Jameson bolted, an unidentified Scot – who may have been the trade unionist JT Bain – wrote to Commandant-General Joubert, warning:

> The English parts of the population hereabouts intend to rise on the last day of this year to try and overturn the government. Rhodes is at the bottom of the whole business. Colonel Rhodes, his brother, is here to superintend the affair and Rhodes has a number of men on the Bechuanaland frontier ready to be sent in, also the Cape Mounted Rifles and Black Watch, under the pretence that English are being killed.[40]

But Piet Joubert and a few others in the fifth column in Pretoria may well have had reasons of their own for ignoring any such warnings.[41]

John Hays Hammond's hoped-for revolution, one in which he played a leading if not *the* pre-eminent part in conducting the intelligence and logistical planning of operations, had long since begun to fall apart. All that was left was for Hammond to begin unravelling. But he would not have to do so on his own. Jameson, feeling increasingly uncertain about what might reasonably be expected of the Johannesburg conspirators, was back at Pitsani and preparing himself privately for a daring action that might yet please Rhodes. Betrayal was in the air.

Blasting

CHAPTER TWELVE

Rangers and Rustlers

c OCTOBER–MID-DECEMBER, 1895

The first sign that it was going to be a turbulent political season came late in January 1895, in the wake of the sensational shootings at the Red Lion Beer Hall and the public disgrace of the town's Chief Detective, Bob Ferguson.[1] Amid the minor moral panic that fed into the agitation for a vigilance committee, it was Kruger's progressive-minded State Attorney, Ewald Esselen, who had appointed Andrew Trimble as the country's Acting Chief Detective, who became a target for recrimination.[2]

Trimble's appointment, too, was immediately seized upon and contested by those political and underworld elements who wished to see the reinstatement of Robert Ferguson. The situation became increasingly complicated during the months that followed, when conservative notables in Pretoria also objected to Esselen's public flirtation with reformist ideas, as advocated by Charles Leonard and the jingoistic National Union.[3]

The State President, aware of growing opposition in the Volksraad to his government by Progressive elements assuming the proportions of a fully-fledged political party, viewed the criticisms of Esselen and Trimble's credentials with mounting concern.[4] The appointment of both men, a move originally intended to co-opt oppositional elements and calm some of the intra-elite discontent, proved to be counterproductive. Once the mine owners' conspiracy on the goldfields assumed shape and Esselen's association with reformist criticism became public, Kruger felt that the situation was intolerable.[5] The government refused to confirm the appointment of the Chief Detective, suspecting that the rejection of Trimble would probably precipitate Esselen's resignation – which it did.[6]

From the state's point of view the downside to these developments was that they not only presented the Rand revolutionaries with new grounds for criticism of the Kruger administration, but that they also happened to free up Esselen and Trimble for possible co-option into the 'reform movement' at a later date – the one being a Boer notable touted as a possible member of a 'provisional government', and the other an officer who could be used to manage 'law and order' during an urban uprising.

The upside for the government was, however, that by November 1895, several weeks before the planned 'revolution', Kruger had managed to get rid of the leading political doubtful within his Executive Council – the man responsible for administering and overseeing the state's policing and the operations of the recently inaugurated secret service. More pertinently, as early as September 1895, the Republic's secret agents had become interested in the Robinson Deep as a possible destination for smuggled small arms. That may also have accounted for the fact that the mine's elderly manager, Captain Thomas Mein, was among the first of Hammond's Californian stalwarts to waver publicly when Jameson's intention to appropriate the uprising for an imperial rather than a republican end became clearer in the closing weeks of 1895.[7]

Mein was not the only American to be alarmed by what Hammond and his friends were up to. Back in the Bitterroot Mountains, Robert E Brown, editor of the *Coeur d'Alene Barbarian*, had helped Hammond and the Pinkerton agent, Charlie Siringo, shape the war against the miners at Wardner. But, by May 1894 Brown had reverted to his original calling as a mining engineer, become a popular Assistant Manager at the Primrose Mine and lost all his taste for armed conflict.

Although hardly the 'paid spy' that Hammond characterised him as in his memoirs, by late 1895 Brown was indeed strongly opposed to the idea of overthrowing the state by force. At a social gathering at the Simmer & Jack Mine, in early December 1895, and in the presence of Hammond, Brown openly warned the miners 'not to be made the tools of the clique of capitalists and the combination'. 'You dare not hope that the overthrow of the Government with the help of these [capitalists] will better your condition,' he declared.[8] Throughout the crisis of late 1895 Brown acted as a conduit, providing the government and seemingly the State President himself with flows of counterintelligence while seeking openly to influence the political choices of certain leading American mining engineers and their working-class compatriots.[9] In the Coeur d'Alene, Brown had started out as a reformist and been transformed into a 'barbarian' by Hammond and his mine-owning friends. On the Rand the roles were reversed; it was Brown and the Beit Boys, Jennings and Perkins, who forced a 'revolutionary' Hammond to become a 'reformer'.

Looking back, then, it can be seen that while the government was not fully apprised of what the Rand revolutionaries contemplated in the last quarter of 1895, and certainly knew nothing of Hammond's scheme-within-the-scheme to abduct the State President and effect a separate constitutional dispensation for the Witwatersrand, it was increasingly alert to the possibility of serious trouble erupting in Johannesburg.

However, it was the Beit rather than the Rhodes Boys who proved to be the least discreet. On 20 November, four days before Rhodes was moved to complain to Beit about him, an arrogant Lionel Phillips could contain himself no longer. Delivering an address in his capacity as the President of the Chamber of Mines, he made the familiar demands for 'reform' but then added a rider that was unmistakably 'revolutionary' in tone. Nothing was further from his heart – but perhaps not his head – Phillips said, 'than a desire to see an upheaval, which would be disastrous from every point of view, and which would probably end in the most horrible of endings – bloodshed'.[10]

With war talk becoming increasingly public, Kruger's agents began pushing back.[11] In addition to focusing on issues of class in the way that RE Brown had, they drew attention to Rhodes's well-known imperialist ambitions. Hammond got the point but probably overstated things when, years later, he told a journalist: 'The ingenious plan was followed of telling the American and other non-British immigrants that the whole affair was nothing but an English plot to induce us to spend our money and to shed our blood in order that the country should be brought under the British flag.'[12]

In terms of what Rhodes and Jameson, as opposed to what Hammond himself privately, hoped for, the 'ingenious plan' was not all that far off the mark. It was a cautionary tale that resonated with the 2 000-strong American contingent on the Rand, including Hennen Jennings and HC Perkins of the Corner House as well as many white mineworkers. Nobody knows exactly when the 50- to 80-strong 'American Working Men's Committee' was formed, under the leadership of JJ Taylor, but, by mid-December, it was sending messages of support directly to the State President, in Pretoria.[13]

But if pro-republican sentiments were beginning to make inroads into parts of the American elite, there was no indication during the closing weeks of November and early December that it was giving Hammond and his Californian engineers much reason for second thoughts. State counter-propaganda was a political problem that Phillips and FitzPatrick could be left to deal with, all the more so since some of it was coming from the Corner House notables.

Hammond and his Californians took working-class support for the uprising as read, expecting that it would be forthcoming when the great day arrived. For him and his engineers the major problems were technical rather than human or motivational. Their more immediate challenges lay elsewhere and were overwhelmingly logistical in nature – questions as to the where, when and how, rather than why, since that had long since been decided. Hammond's perspective was that of a positivist, of a scientific capitalist, even though he always fancied himself as something of a behavioural scientist. His values left him inclined to treat *all* factors of production as if they were inanimate. They were the views of a man whose gross and persistent misreading of working-class needs had, only months before, helped set the Coeur d'Alene alight.

This tendency on the part of the principal conspirator, to conflate scientific and social scientific analysis in ways that gave rise to questionable links and conclusions, contributed to problems that became ever more serious in the opening weeks of December. For one, the date for the insurrection had been tentatively set for 26 December. It was an extraordinary, inexplicable choice for the start of a 'revolution', given that the uprising would be dependent on the active support of white miners busy with the customary seasonal celebrations and accompanying excesses. Indeed, so gross a misreading of working-class behaviour was this on the part of the would-be 'revolutionists' that it was soon changed to 28 December.[14] But that date, too, was the choice of political and social illiterates. It fell on the Saturday that marked the high point of the summer season's horse racing, and so the crucial date had to be moved to 6 January.[15]

By early December one or two Fleet Street journalists and a couple of English war artists in-the-know had gathered in Johannesburg to witness the expected uprising and must have been puzzled by the blundering and excuses which, at face value, appeared simply laughable. And they were.[16] The real reason for the delay could be traced to a logistical failure in the supply line for imported arms as overseen by Hammond and the Californians.[17] At source, in Kimberley, Gardner Williams had simply been unable to pack, conceal and forward rifles to the Rand in anything like the quantities required. By mid-December, only 500 rifles of the 5 000 required for the proposed uprising had arrived in Johannesburg.

At first glance seemingly trivial, these excuses, and the manner in which they were dealt with by the principal players, contributed centrally to the disaster that was to follow. Hammond, for whatever reason, possibly out of hubris and an unwillingness to be seen to be letting down Rhodes and Jameson, was simply unwilling to admit that a logistical problem for which he bore great personal responsibility necessitated postponements of the date set for the revolution. Instead of acknowledging the lack of rifles as the primary cause for the delay, he and his co-conspirators sought refuge behind the secondary, socio-political reasons for the delays. There certainly were serious problems in mobilising the miners. Indeed, that was why George Farrar had been co-opted into the conspiracy.[18] But that was *not* the reason given for the delays – it was all about Boxing Day and horse races. Even that, however, might not have proved fatal had the uprising not been designated as the trigger event and had they been dealing with a phlegmatic co-conspirator in command of their supporting military force. But they were not; they were dealing with Leander Starr Jameson.

By then Jameson had, for several weeks, accepted and approved of Hammond as both the leading conspirator and chief organiser of the proposed Johannesburg uprising. Their earlier back-and-forth jostling as to who would assume the lead role in initiating and organising the revolution was largely a thing of the past. It was to be a Gold Fields, not a Corner House, revolution and it was fitting that Hammond should be in charge of operations on the Rand. Jameson had not only bought into many, if not all, of the American's claims of personal experience of armed conflict in Mexico and 'out West' – several of which had a basis in fact – but had also been persuaded by Hammond's presentation of himself as a sort of capitalist cowboy, as someone ready to take on all comers regardless of the odds or the possible outcomes.

What Jameson did *not* know about was Hammond's reliance on his wife for support during moments of conflict, of his propensity to collapse under pressure, and for his health to give way. Jameson saw Hammond only as a man who would not flinch when placed under enemy fire, a man who, like the Americans Burnham and Heany, could be relied upon. In short, for Jameson, Hammond was the key, the very embodiment, the driving force behind the long-projected uprising on the Witwatersrand.

Hammond, too, had set aside the contestation as to where the initiative for the revolution might derive from and, as the witching hour approached, he sought loyalty from Jameson. Jameson, in turn, believed that Hammond was unwavering in his commitment to staging the uprising even if he did not appreciate that it might pave the way for him to sweep in and snatch the South African Republic for Rhodes and the British Empire. The old see-saw, love-hate, relationship between Hammond and Jameson appeared to have been settled rather neatly.

Friends who believed they shared deeply held convictions, their commitments sealed with a handshake in the presence of Rhodes himself, were unlikely, when placed under pressure, to exchange trivia via telegrams, or by word of mouth through trusted messengers. Thus, or so reasoned Jameson, if Hammond *seemed* to be accepting piffling reasons and making excuses for delaying the start of the uprising, it could not be an accurate reflection of Hammond's personal convictions. They were far more likely to be a reflection of a collectively held position dominated by the more conservative elements among the core conspirators.[19] As a gambling man, Jameson was inclined to call the conspirators' bluff, ignore messages urging delay, and push on regardless, confident in the knowledge that, beneath the hogwash about hangovers and horse racing put out by the timid, stood one dependable, strong soul who, duty bound, would certainly rise in revolt: 'Jameson thought it a frivolous pretext to adjourn a revolution for a race-meeting.'[20]

This, then, was the rickety spinal column of interpersonal trust and loyalty that held the conspiracy together during the opening weeks of December 1895. Hammond's limitations and weaknesses probably ran a little deeper than did those of Jameson. But the good doctor, too, was not always given to carefully considered action or, for that matter, irreproachable honesty. Out in the bush at Pitsani he, too, was beginning to experience a few problems.

If Hammond failed to meet his target of 5 000 rifles then Jameson, too, fell well short of meeting his commitment to provide a column of 1 500 armed and mounted men. In the end, as we shall see, the doctor commanded just 500 men on his drive towards the Witwatersrand, although he may originally have assembled a few score more while still encamped at Pitsani.

The full force at Jameson's disposal, assembled by early December, comprised two parts. The first consisted of 120 men of the Bechuanaland Police, under the command of Major Raleigh Grey, based at Mafeking. The main body of men at Pitsani consisted of 470 policemen on the payroll of the Chartered Company, under the command of Sir John Willoughby. In theory, this constituted the most loyal and potent part of Jameson's strike force since it included a few members of the original 'Pioneer Column' of 1890 and other veterans of the 1893 Matabele War. And so it may have been since, whatever else their shortcomings might have been, neither Jameson personally, nor those under his command who surrendered at Doornkop on 2 January 1896, were ever accused of cowardice or lacking in military skill.

The problems lay elsewhere. At least 120 of the 470 men in the Chartered section of the force, about one in three, were neither pioneers nor veterans drawn from Rhodesia, let alone 'policemen'.[21] A few were indeed former soldiers with experience of colonial wars elsewhere in southern Africa, but, for the most part, they seem to have been recruited from the human flotsam and jetsam Jameson had found drifting around Cape Town and Kimberley during the hectic weeks leading up the Raid.[22] Drunks, confidence men, opportunists, petty criminals and the unemployed were hardly a novel feature of 19th-century armies; indeed, in the age of industrialisation they constituted a fair proportion of most armed forces. It was, however, one thing to control and discipline such men in barracks, garrison towns or ships for a fixed term and quite another to command their commitment, loyalty and respect in a bush camp, on an open frontier for a supposedly secret operation that was repeatedly delayed for reasons not fully disclosed.

Both Hammond and Jameson's preparations for their hoped-for 'revolution' fed, in small but important ways, off the massive social dislocations and underclasses generated by industrial revolutions under way in America, Britain and southern Africa. In Hammond's case he consciously selected ill-disciplined, 'hard-boiled' Americans rejected by his mine managers to serve in the strike force that would attack the Pretoria arsenal and then abduct the State President. Although Jameson had less choice and time at his disposal to select men, he, too, did not hesitate to take in what Marx termed 'lumpen-proletarians' to help first overthrow a state, and then, hopefully, act as 'policemen' controlling Johannesburg once the 'revolution' was under way. The difference was that Hammond's Americans were never called into action and stayed in town until supposedly needed, late in the day, while Jameson's more numerous wild men were out in the bush, fully mobilised for a project that was constantly being delayed. In order to appreciate more fully the nature of the problem that confronted Jameson – one that fed directly into his well-established reputation for gambling and impatience – it may help to pause and examine briefly the mindset of some of the men he commanded.

On 28 September a young Scot, based in Bulawayo, part of the 'expeditionary force' Jameson was then still actively recruiting, wrote to his mother, back home in Berwick-upon-Tweed:

> It is rumoured about that the volunteers here have been raised for some purpose; but it is not certain what it is. If it's fighting I am going to be in it. The pay is ten shillings a day, all found, and I expect loot as well. It is causing great excitement here, and everybody is on tiptoe of excitement.[23]

A second trooper, with the smaller of the forces – the Bechuanaland Police – also with a mother in Berwick-upon-Tweed, noted that the men Jameson recruited were 'a frightfully mixed crew'. It included, he noted, men from Lancashire. He had, he told his mother, met 'some of them, straight from Manchester', and 'these provincial men can lie'! On balance, however, he felt that he, personally, had probably made the right career choice. 'The [Bechuanaland] police seem to me preferable to the British South Africa [Chartered Company] police which is having all the scum of Cape Town, Kimberley and Johannesburg drained into it,' he wrote.[24]

Jameson's notoriously importunate behaviour and legendary impatience, something that historians have traditionally seen largely in relation to his terse communication with the other conspirators and his ill-advised dash from Pitsani into the Transvaal, cannot be so neatly divorced from the quotidian realities that he faced on the eve of the Raid. Jameson was not dealing with officers and men disciplined and trained by the British Army, even though most of his officers, and many of the men, had indeed once been regular soldiers. As even an embittered Hammond was to concede in his memoirs, Jameson's '… chief problem was to hold his forces, many of whom were volunteers owing him only nominal obedience'.[25]

Not surprisingly, as the days in desert-like Pitsani dragged on to no apparent end, volunteers began to desert and Jameson experienced increasing difficulty in keeping the rest focused and motivated.[26] Indeed, even some of the better-class, time-expired men in the Bechuanaland Police threatened to pack up and leave.[27] A fair number may have. Thus, at almost the same time that Hammond began to haemorrhage personal support in the shape of influential American engineers and miners, Jameson either already was, or felt that he was, in danger of losing a part of his rag-tag battalion. Hammond was losing support from the top down, Jameson from the bottom up.

And the more Jameson and Hammond sensed the earth beginning to move around them, the more they were inclined to cling to each other. The rise in political temperature occasioned by the approaching 'revolution' did in 30 days what months of planning never fully achieved – it eliminated most of the caution that had characterised their early face-to-face interactions, and seemed to weld them to a stronger, common purpose. Indeed, it may have been the very emotional affinity that they felt when placed under intense pressure that accounts for the depth of the anger and resentment that was felt in the wake of the Raid and for years thereafter. A sense of 'betrayal' is, after all, at least as much a measure of the depth of love and prior commitment as it is of subsequent disdain and loss.[28]

After the Raid, Rhodes, as might be expected, remained remarkably true to Jameson and, to no lesser degree, to Hammond when he refused to hand over certain incriminating telegrams that had passed between his two lieutenants. The details of those missing, presumably coded communications will forever remain unknown. But the tone and nature of their contents can probably be broadly inferred from one or two of the telegrams that passed between the two march hares in the increasingly frenetic days leading up to the Raid and that were somehow preserved.

On 7 December, Jameson received a telegram from Colonel Frank Rhodes telling him that the uprising, planned for 23 December, would have to be postponed. Unhappy with the news, Jameson, who had been in close consultations with Dr Henry Wolff, responded in terms that became increasingly agitated.[29] On 12 December, frustrated by the endless procrastination and timid responses that could be traced back to a few Corner House engineers, Jameson instructed Frank Rhodes to place matters in the hands of the veteran of the Coeur d'Alene mining wars. He could rely on the no-nonsense American to push things along: 'Let JH Hammond inform weak partners [Beit and Phillips's men] the more delay the more the danger. Dr Wolff will explain fully reasons to anticipate rather than postpone action.'[30]

Word of the encampment at Pitsani was beginning to spread among the local Boers, and one or two of Jameson's officers were, as he put, it 'blabbing', while the rest of the men were wondering what the plan was.[31] But Hammond, long accepted as *the* pre-eminent leader of the large contingent of American engineers on the Rand, found his authority being challenged. Questioning of the need for a full-blown 'revolution' to effect meaningful change in the fortunes of the mining industry was no longer emanating only from the familiar senior quarters in the Corner House; some of it was starting to come from a different Californian source, and from a mine manager with impeccable credentials and a significant following.

Captain Thomas Mein, was, strictly speaking, neither American nor a captain yet he was both of those and more.[32] Already in his mid-fifties at the time of the Raid and more readily known among miners as 'Poppa Mein' for reasons that spoke well of him, the title of 'Captain' had been bestowed as a mark of affection and respect by neighbours back in California. Mein, the son of a tenant farmer, was born on the banks of the Tweed, in the Scottish Borders, in 1841, and, when young Tom was three, his family had emigrated to the northeastern United States. In 1859, aged 21, he had moved out west to earn his fortune on the mines. Largely self-taught, he became a successful mine manager and, showing qualities of leadership, was elected as a California Assemblyman.

In the late 1860s, Mein met and married Mary Swift, an immigrant from County Fermanagh, a woman whose popularity among working people was rivalled only by that of her husband. Together, the couple moved about the Western mining world, based first at the famous El Callao mine, in Venezuela, and then, in the late 1880s, at a mine in Alaska which, with the help of Henning Jennings and Henry C Perkins, had been purchased by the expanding Wernher, Beit & Co. This association continued when Jennings invited Mein to come to Johannesburg and manage the Robinson Deep Mine in 1891. It was not by chance that, in the early 1890s, most Scottish and Irish miners found their way to mines immediately to the southwest of the town just as surely as the Cornish gravitated to the southeast of Johannesburg.

For most of the final quarter of 1895, Tom Mein was content to identify closely with Jack Hammond and those American engineers intent on mounting a radical challenge to the Kruger government.[33] That loyalty, to the underlying economic cause and fellow Californians, remained largely intact throughout the crisis month of December. Indeed, Mein, who was suffering from silicosis, was among those on the Reform Committee who were prosecuted and fined for their part in the Raid. But, for reasons that can only be guessed at — possibly the lack of sufficient arms and ammunition — somewhere along the line, in mid-December, Mein began to doubt that an armed uprising was either desirable or possible. There may, however, have been more deep-seated personal and political reasons for his increasingly active challenge to Hammond's leadership. It was one of Tom Mein's sons who years later dismissed Hammond's *Autobiography* as being 'filled with lies' – a sentiment doubtless informed by tales that he had once heard from his father.[34]

Mein was Hammond's senior by 15 years, and had acquired his trade almost entirely through hands-on experience. His primary affiliations lay with Perkins, whom he had worked under at El Callao, and Jennings, who had brought him to southern Africa. He was, when all was said and done, a Corner House man. The Meins could turn on the managerial style when necessary, but were nevertheless cut from rather different cloth than the Hammonds. They could empathise with working men and women while Natalie Hammond, a classic Southern belle, was, like her husband, more at home in the company of eminent people.

With the notable exception of Alfred Beit himself, several of the Beit Boys, including Lionel Phillips, had long been wary of Rhodes and Jameson's imperialist ambitions.[35] They had, however, been mollified by the presence and role of Hammond who, like most of the core conspirators, appeared to be more interested in reforming the mining industry than in overthrowing the state for the greater glory of Queen Victoria and the British Empire. In that sense, too, Tom Mein had always been more of a 'reformer' than he had been a 'revolutionary'. But then, in mid-December, Mein heard of two troubling developments that, over the days that followed, caused him to gradually distance himself from the 'revolutionary' Anglophile and turn him into a 'reformer'.

First, Britain had, for many years, laid claim to certain tracts of disputed territory which it saw as part of British Guiana but which Venezuela considered to rightfully belong to it. The United States, in line with the Monroe Doctrine, was opposed to further direct or indirect European colonisation in either North or South America and viewed the British claims and attendant pressures with mounting concern. American cautionary statements and British diplomatic and naval bravado escalated, and on 17 December President Grover Cleveland addressed the United States Congress, invoking the Monroe Doctrine – a development which many informed observers read as a possible prelude to armed conflict.[36]

News of growling across the Atlantic by Great Britain and the United States did not go down well with many of the Americans on the Witwatersrand.[37] It sat poorly with mining engineers such as Jennings and Perkins not only because they were American nationals but because they had first-hand knowledge of Venezuela. And it sat particularly poorly with Tom Mein, a Celtic-American, whose political reservations about the English would have been aroused twice over.

The day after President Cleveland's address to Congress, Abe Bailey, a Rhodes supporter to the point where he named his sons Cecil and John, and Aubrey Wools-Sampson returned to the Witwatersrand after a visit to England. On the homeward leg of their sea voyage, they had been accompanied by Dr Rutherfoord Harris, Secretary to the British South Africa Company.[38] At ease in each other's company, Dr Harris had confided to his fellow Englishmen that Rhodes and Jameson were committed to seeing the Union Jack flying above Johannesburg as soon as the uprising and the invasion had run their course.[39] This news could not have come as a shock to Hammond since, as we have already noted, he had long been allied to the Rhodes and Jameson cause. Moreover, he had only recently appended his signature to the infamous 'letter of invitation' – a document filled with special pleading about the needs of 'Englishmen' who were being wronged by the Boers.

It is unlikely therefore that the Bailey–Union Jack enthusiasm would, of its own accord, have given Hammond cause for second thoughts as to the wisdom of the 'revolution'. As one historian correctly observes: 'The flag question was in fact only an outward manifestation of a host of flaws and weaknesses in the conspiracy.'[40] What the information did do, however, was to feed into Hammond's personal concerns about the shortfall in smuggled rifles for the uprising and the likelihood of his hand-picked team's inadequacies being exposed. But for some of the Beit Boys, influential men such as Jennings, Perkins and Mein, the news only confirmed what had long been suspected. Rhodes and Jameson were more set on effecting an imperialist coup than in getting the Kruger government to undertake necessary reforms in the mining industry.

For several Americans in the Corner House, the deeply Anglophile Hammond either could not see, or would not see, what was really at stake. The locust elite – like Hammond himself – would, if forced, put money before monarch. As Louis Cohen, the journalist, put it some years later, Tom Mein 'neither cared for fair political treatment nor fleas, Boers or British'.[41] Within days of Abe Bailey's public revelations, Mein was heard to say, 'If this is a case of England gobbling up this country, I am not in it; otherwise I am up to my neck in it.'[42]

Edmund Garrett notes that it was these developments – the Venezuelan crisis and fear of a full-scale English takeover of the state rather than an armed uprising leading to reform – that, on 17 and 18 December, began to tip the scales against Hammond's leadership of the American community, which now increasingly took its cue from Mein and his fellow Reformers, many drawn from the House of Beit. 'It is out of this atmosphere,' Garrett suggests with considerable understatement, 'that Mr Hammond as an American citizen, eventually came to emerge as a doughty champion of the "*vier kleur*".[43] But Mr Hammond was not yet quite done. He may not have had formal experience as a politician in the Californian House of Assembly, as had his rival, Tom Mein, but he had learned a trick or two of his own in the Coeur d'Alene.

If the absence of white miners was one important ingredient missing from the class alliance driving the supposedly broad-based reform process, then another was William Dodds and the local Mercantile Association. The conflict in the Bitterroot Mountains had taught Hammond just how anxious shopowners could become if their goods and property were exposed to civil disorder, and he and Clement had rapidly co-opted them into the 'Law and Order Leagues' that duly became the backbone of reaction. Johannesburg was no different; the next step necessary was clear.[44]

Within hours of the Bailey–Union Jack news surfacing, Hammond and the core conspirators attempted to reassure larger shopowners. Should it become necessary, Dr Jameson's troopers would ensure the safety of commercial property in the town. But the revolutionaries, men of business, appreciated the need for interim measures and saw to it that appropriate structures were put in place. The conspirators looked for a man to lead an ad hoc police force and made the inspired decision to offer the position to the Irishman, Andrew Trimble.[45] Not only had Trimble been a victim of Kruger's purge to rid the police of Progressive sympathisers but, as a former soldier, he possessed the military experience necessary to enforce the law-and-order issue so close to Hammond's heart. Trimble, the ex-detective from Kimberley, was duly recruited and, as one of the 'fiery spirits' identified by Colvin – the other being Rowland Bettington – and was one of few to emerge from the uprising with reputation intact, if not enhanced. However, not even Trimble's appointment as police chief could persuade Dodds or the Mercantile Association to enter the conspiracy as 'reformers'.[46]

In passing it is interesting to note, yet again, that Hammond could find little room in his autobiography for either Trimble or Bettington. Indeed, Trimble, who emerges with honour in other accounts of the Raid, does not warrant a mention in Hammond's memoirs, while Bettington, who *did* attempt to link up with Jameson, also gets short shrift. Would it be stretching things to suggest that those two were ignored by Hammond precisely because he sensed that they had offered examples of the honour and duty that he felt had been required of him?[47]

Looking back, then, it is clear that, around mid-December 1895, Hammond's position as leader of the American community and the Johannesburg uprising was increasingly insecure – as, for different reasons, was Jameson's as commander-in-chief at Pitsani. But the two responded to their deteriorating positions in markedly different ways. The more

Hammond's nerve dimmed, fearing that Jameson might jump the gun, the brighter Jameson's glowed, in the belief that all that was necessary was for him to demonstrate courage and determination. Intense pressure tends to seek out the fault lines of personality long before it finds out weaknesses in logic.

By Christmas Day Hammond, still with insufficient arms to meet his side of the bargain and worried about Jameson's mounting frustration, was beginning to buckle beneath the pressures. He went to an emergency meeting at Frank Rhodes's residence, Saratoga House, to discuss the 'flag question', which, by then, was a mask hiding many uglier facets of imminent failure.[48] It was decided once again to delay the uprising, until 4 January, and to inform Rhodes about the lack of preparedness and the need to hold Jameson in position until he got the call.[49] The stream of telegrams between and around Hammond and Jameson at this juncture reveal, in the starkest terms possible, how as Hammond continued to falter, Jameson became increasingly resolute. The die was cast for disaster; the 'Raid' would occur well *before* the uprising.

On Friday 27 December, on the eve of the date originally set for the uprising (termed 'the floatation' in conspiracy talk), Jameson, incandescent with suppressed rage, sent Rutherfoord Harris, in Cape Town, a telegram dripping with menace:

> They [the faltering Johannesburg revolutionaries] have two days for floatation. If they do not, we will make our own floatation with help of letter which I will publish. Inform John Hays Hammond, Dr Wolff, AL Lawley [one of Jameson's several on-site emissaries on the Witwatersrand], whom you may rely upon to co-operate.[50]

For Jameson, the backbone of the revolution, as ever, was still solidly American and led by Hammond. On the same day, just hours later, he telegraphed his brother Sam: 'Dr Wolff will understand. Distant cutting Bechuanaland Police have already gone forward. Guarantee already given. Therefore let JH Hammond telegraph instantly all right.'[51]

But Hammond, deeply alarmed by what he was hearing and reading, responded instantly: 'Wire just received. Experts' reports decidedly adverse. I absolutely condemn further developments at present.'[52]

Out in the bush, however, Jameson was still seeing Stars and Stripes by day and by night. Just hours before setting off on Sunday 29 December, he sent a final telegram to Wolff – by then back in Johannesburg among the faint-hearted revolutionaries – with the clearest message yet to his friend, the Champion of the Coeur d' Alene. Seeking guidance as to whether he should be making for Pretoria or Johannesburg, he concluded by reminding all that [I]: 'Have great faith in JH Hammond, AL Lawley and miners with Lee–Metford rifles.'[53]

Never was a man's belief more misplaced. And it was not only faith that was about to take a beating; so, too, were hope and charity.

CHAPTER THIRTEEN

Cowboy Jack Talks Fast and Fires Blanks

From Revolutionary Imperialist to
Republican Constitutionalist in Four Days

28 DECEMBER 1895 TO 2 JANUARY 1896

By mid-December 1895 parts of the Kruger state were on the semi-alert for an imminent uprising on the goldfields. Indeed, almost everybody on the Rand itself knew that trouble was brewing and the strain was beginning to take its toll. Hitherto seemingly commonly held positions cutting across ethnic and national identities began to fray as suspicions about objectives – other than those usually heard about the need for political and economic reform – began to mount. And, as ever sharper questions chipped away at what had once seemed like solid foundations, the courage, insight and integrity of the core conspirators was subjected to growing criticism.

Caught between an incoming veld fire started by Jameson threatening to overwhelm them from without, and the urban conflagration he had helped stoke from within, John Hays Hammond was left with ever less room in which to manoeuvre. Not certain whether to look to his left or right, he decided to push on straight ahead. On Friday 27 December, his unruly squad of armed Americans were dispatched to take up their position on Nellmapius's estate at Irene, outside Pretoria, await the signal to attack the arsenal in the capital and then abduct the President.

It is difficult to imagine that this development went unobserved in greater Johannesburg, let alone within the American mining community itself. Indeed, it may well have sounded the alarm among long discontented elements within the Beit Boys, for it was at that point that Lionel Phillips seemed to lose the last of what little control he had ever exercised over rogue elements in the Corner House group. Hennen Jennings and Henry Perkins, backed by a few other unaffiliated Americans such as RE 'Barbarian' Brown and Tom Mein, sensed that the latest delay in the date set for the uprising – 6 January – might afford 'reformists' the opportunity to head off the 'revolutionaries' led by Hammond and Clement – both Gold Fields and Rhodes men. Jennings and Perkins got together early on Saturday 28 December and, pointedly excluding the most prominent American in town, set up a meeting in which they took the lead in what, in effect, was a series of political manoeuvres to sideline Hammond and subvert the coming 'revolution'. From then on Cowboy Jack's position as the American revolutionary leader unravelled.

When President Kruger returned to Pretoria from his annual tour of country towns, on 28 December – the day before Jameson invaded the country – a few well-informed Boer supporters again warned him about escalating rumours of an armed uprising. Kruger responded with his now famous reply that anyone wishing to kill a tortoise was best advised to wait for it to stick its neck out before striking. No sooner was Kruger back home, however, than he was approached by Jennings and Perkins requesting that he grant them a private audience. The President did so knowing that it almost certainly was not the tortoise he wanted.

Four decades later, the humiliation of having been bypassed by brother engineers and members of his Californian cohort was still all too apparent. That impromptu approach to Kruger, Hammond recalled, was made by 'a delegation of Americans who had gone to Pretoria independently, *without the sanction of the men in control* of the Reform Movement. The group included those very men for whose disciplining we had desired Beit's presence.'[1]

By then, however, Alfred Beit's health had already given way. He was the first of at least a half dozen conspirators – including Charles Leonard and Hammond – who imploded beneath mounting pressures.

Jennings and Perkins told the President that they harboured no ill feelings towards him or his people. They wished to see bloodshed avoided because that might '… prepare the way for outside troops to enter the Transvaal', and that would mean 'the subjugation of the Republic and the elevation of a foreign ensign'. They urged Kruger to consider seriously the reformist demands being pressed upon him and the need to make some strategic concessions. But Kruger, a veteran of anti-imperialist struggles, was less concerned about an uprising in Johannesburg than he was about a British threat coming via his long-standing enemy, Rhodes. Kruger said that 'a storm was coming' and that it was a moment for 'people to obey the laws'. The State President then asked, most pertinently, whether the Americans would line up behind or against the government if it came down to a rebellion, and they informed him that, if forced to choose, they would have to side with the Uitlanders. Kruger, eyes firmly fixed on his oldest enemy of all, responded: 'You are all alike. All tarred with the same brush. You are British in your hearts.'[2]

But the 'foreign ensign' question, shorthand for more complex, deep-seated differences, simply would not go away. Journalist Edmund Garrett, who tracked the course of Jameson's Raid and the failed uprising just weeks after the fiasco, reported that the question as to which flag to raise – the Union Jack, the Stars and Stripes or the *Vierkleur* – was still being debated by the revolutionaries-turned-reformers on 31 December 1895.[3] The fact that the raising of the Stars and Stripes was still being mooted as a possibility at that late stage of proceedings was a tribute, if that be the word, to one radical American capitalist – Jack Hammond.

In the hours before that debate, the Scottish-American Tom Mein was again among those objecting to the imposition of an imperial dispensation on the South African Republic. But, in truth, the die had been cast weeks earlier when reservations about the shortfall in smuggled arms and the confirmation of a Rhodes-Jameson imperial agenda became more widely known. And the one Californian who was by then most firmly caught in the ever-tightening logic of events, ideology and personal pride was, once again, Cowboy Jack. It was not as if he had not foreseen the problem or failed to try to avert it. Amid all the other telegrams exchanged in the days leading up to Jameson's departure from Pitsani, none was more powerfully worded than Hammond's: 'I absolutely condemn further developments at present.'

As Hammond put it later: 'However, incredible it might seem that Jameson should actually plan to start without receiving word from the Reform Committee and *from me personally*, even that remote possibility had to be guarded against.'[4] Well, if truth be told, the 'Reform Committee' had not yet been formed and events then were still being dictated by a tiny conspiratorial core and Jameson was not about to be thwarted by words from even the most trustworthy of his American allies. As the disappointed Jameson complained in a telegram to Cape Town, on the same day that Jennings and Perkins had gone to see the State President: 'First delay was races, which did not exist; second policies – already arranged. All mean fear.'[5] Imputations of cowardice were deeply resented among Johannesburg's 'revolutionaries' and 'reformers' alike.

By that Saturday Jameson had lost faith in the Rand's revolutionary core and was unwilling to entertain pleas for more delay, even when it came from the mouths of two specially selected messengers, including one of his trusted American insiders, Maurice Heany. Neither Major Heany, who arrived cross-country by horse, nor Captain Henry Holden who disembarked from the train, at Mafeking, could persuade Jameson about the degree of unpreparedness in Johannesburg. By then words of caution were entering Jameson's head via one ear and exiting from the other without encountering any intervening hindrance. With spirits up and eyes fixed east, Jameson's British South Africa Police and Grey's Bechuanaland Border Police set off on Sunday night, 29 December 1895, joining forces at Malmani. The unified column headed for the goldfields, slicing across the Highveld, inflicting a gaping wound in the body of white southern African politics.

The Saturday before Jameson set off – the day originally set for the uprising – proved to be a singularly disconcerting for Hammond. The unofficial American deputation to President Kruger was not the only bad news emanating from the capital that day. Pretoria, he learned, was full of Boers who had trekked into the capital from remote country districts for communion services – *nachtmaal*. Not only were there an unusual number of farmers in town but, given the nature of the journeys they had undertaken, they were also well-armed. Hammond had overlooked the vital fact that the Afrikaner-Dutch were a profoundly religious people and had neglected to determine the *nachtmaal* cycle.[6]

Given what was happening out at Pitsani, Sunday 29 December was, by comparison, a reasonably calm day in Johannesburg. It would, of course, have been decidedly less so had the conspirators known that Jameson had tired of their procrastination and was preparing to move. The rump of the revolutionary core on the Rand – Frank Rhodes, Hammond, Phillips and Farrar – again met at Saratoga House.[7] There, despite the fact that they had by then drawn scores of other well-placed citizens into their conspiracy, they continued to act as a self-appointed executive committee, a secretive cabal, accountable to nobody but themselves and their financiers in the Cape – Rhodes and Beit. It was the last time they would do so. The unfolding events were about to downsize them from a militant 'revolutionary' vanguard to mere hopeful 'reformers'.

The agenda at the Saratoga House meeting appears to have focused on the number of smuggled rifles. The conspirators appear not to have been unduly put out by the Jennings-Perkins initiative and resolved to push on and start distributing such arms as they did have to white miners via Victor Clement, at the Simmer & Jack Mine. The elite strike force was in place at Irene, and the uprising was not far off.

Monday 30 December started reasonably well but then descended into the worst day imaginable for the core conspirators, and for Hammond in particular. Clement commenced supervising the unpacking of a few Maxim guns and several hundred rifles at the Simmer & Jack Mine, from where they were forwarded to various encampments around the town or to the Gold Fields building to await redistribution.[8] At the height of the crisis, a few days later, two out of the five redoubts on the town's outskirts boasting artillery were manned by Americans.[9] But all the activity around the Simmer & Jack exacerbated an unexpected outcome.

The warning signs had been there for several days. One or two unnamed mine managers, possibly led by Victor Clement, had started pressuring the miners – not excluding reluctant Americans – to take up arms in support of the uprising. Captain Knight and a small party of miners under his control fled Johannesburg. Upon their return to the United States, they complained: 'Many miners were forced into taking up arms by the officials, who shut up all the boarding houses and bought all the available provisions and literally starved the men into accepting their terms. The Michigan men say that John Hays Hammond deserves no sympathy.'[10]

If Captain Knight was correct and the mines concerned did fall under the control of Hammond and Clement, then it was a tactic that reeked of the labour war in the Coeur d'Alene. But the problem went deeper than that.

As far back as Christmas Day, Cornish miners, alarmed at the prospect of being drawn into an armed conflict not of their making, had started abandoning the mines, town and country.[11] They made their way to the railway station in their hundreds and, when they could not force their way into the crowded carriages bound for the coast, were willing to take up standing positions in open trucks. Their suspicions were compounded when, on Boxing Day and the day after, George Farrar and various mine managers along the East Rand spent hours attempting – unsuccessfully – to mobilise them for what was portrayed as an imminent urban uprising.[12] In the event, all that the unpacking of rifles at Simmer & Jack did was to confirm the Celtic miners' worst nightmares.

As part of an ethnic 'labour aristocracy' remitting close on a £1 million a year to England's southwestern margin, the Cornish had everything to lose and nothing to gain from an imperialist plot, and they told anyone who would listen that what was happening was merely a 'capitalist trick', and that they – working men – would end up paying for the adventure.[13] Kruger's effort at stemming the tide by getting trade union allies, such as JT Bain, or mine managers such as RE Brown, to point out the class dynamics informing the planned uprising had not been entirely in vain.[14] It was not only the 'Boer commandos' that thwarted the Jameson Raid; it was also, albeit in smaller part, some excellent counterpropaganda.

For Hammond, the mass departure of the Cornish miners may have played into a long-standing prejudice that harked back to his earliest days on Californian mines.[15] It was not by chance that his private secretary, Arthur Kelsey, took time out to note that 'The Cornish miners began their exodus, and it is no exaggeration to say that 75% of this nationality left.'[16] But the Celts by then had more to contend with than the opinion of one man as word spread rapidly among the local English and then across the mining communities worldwide that the famed 'hard rock' men were 'cowards'. At stations on the way down to the coast Cornishmen were assaulted or handed the dreaded 'white feather'. The Raid was not just about politics, it was about extreme, gendered politics.

In Durban, the authorities were so concerned about the possibility of a hostile reception for the miners that the train was not allowed to enter the main railway station and had to be diverted to a distant siding in order to allow the 'Cousin Jacks' to disembark in safety.[17] As Jameson entered the country, so the Republic's finest white miners were exiting it and the planned uprising lost most of its working-class muscle. A combination of arrogant expectation on the part of the conspirators and the neglect of steady political work left the revolution short of manpower.

Predictably, the insults and taunts directed at the Cornishmen left Hammond cold. But what it did do was to serve as a warning of what might come the way of those conspirators who tried to back out of their revolutionary schemes or were less than wholehearted in their public support of Jameson. Mass political mobilisation, even incomplete and largely ineffectual warmongering, was not a tap that could just be turned on or off. And the 'revolution' was not going at all well.

At lunch Hammond was served a second slice of humble pie when he attended another meeting of Americans that was neither authorised, nor convened by him, to hear Jennings and Perkins report back on their audience with the State President two days earlier. The list of those attending read like a who's who of mining engineers. The mood of the meeting could be gauged from the fact that it was JS Curtis, the true pioneer of the Witwatersrand's deep-level stratigraphy, rather than Jack Hammond, the brash pretender, who was elected as chairman. So reformist in inclination were those present that not even Tom Mein, who refused to distance himself publicly from Hammond, was considered to reflect the mood of the meeting accurately. It was resolved to send a second delegation, comprised exclusively of moderate Americans, to approach Kruger the next day, and the choice of delegates must have horrified Hammond: JS Curtis, RE Brown and timber merchant FR Lingham.[18]

In his autobiography Hammond deals in characteristically disingenuous fashion with this awkward moment in his political regression from aspirant 'revolutionary' to reluctant 'reformer'. The 'I' – always so prominent in his writings – suddenly fades from view and all that he recalls is that '*We* appointed a committee of three to go to Pretoria on Tuesday and once more lay *our* demands before the president.' It was as if he had agreed and been party to the original Jennings-Perkins initiative, and without any mention of the 'spy' Brown![19]

In truth, Hammond left that lunchtime meeting still hopeful; his arsenal-attackers and the would-be abductors of the President were waiting at Irene and, when the great day eventually dawned, he might yet emerge as Hero of the Revolution. He returned to his office and was speaking privately to one of Kruger's trusted economic advisers, the industrialist Samuel Marks, when

a clerk entered the room and passed him a slip of paper on which was written, 'Jameson has crossed the Border'. 'I was thunderstruck!' he claimed.[20]

Just how closely Hammond's ego and the original idea of the 'revolution'
were linked to the Irene project became clear when, shortly thereafter, one
of Jameson's deployed 'Rhodesians', AL Lawley,

> ... rushed into headquarters waving a telegram and shouting; 'It's
> all up boys, Listen to this! The contractor has started the earthworks
> with seven hundred boys; hope to reach terminus on Wednesday.'
> And so [wrote a chastened Hammond] vanished our designs for tak-
> ing the Pretoria arsenal. All we could now do was to revamp the plan
> to fit the altered circumstances.[21]

The attack on the arsenal may, by that time, have genuinely become, in
Hammond's mind, uncoupled from his plan to abduct Kruger, but, even by
his account, the twinned initiative had originated with him alone, months
earlier. Even then, the attack-abduction scheme did not simply 'vanish' in a
puff of blinding insight or smart thinking, as implied in Hammond's autobiography. It was, in larger part, dismantled later that day by some Boer
informants.

Late that afternoon, the conspirators learned that government agents
had been alerted to the unusually large number of 'prospectors' that had
congregated on the Nellmapius estate near Pretoria, and the 'revolutionaries' in Johannesburg correctly assumed that more rigorous examination
would follow in the morning. The Irene strike force, composed of American
adventurers who had at the last moment been provided with an officer or
two who spoke Afrikaans-Dutch, had been rumbled and would have to be
evacuated under cover of darkness. But the conspirators had a trick hidden
up their sleeves. By the time that Abraham Malan, part of a Boer fifth column and the son-in-law of General Piet Joubert, got around to investigating
what was going on at Irene, the following afternoon, the birds had flown.[22]

By nightfall on 30 December, the conspirators had lost the military initiative and now, instead of planning on how to *attack* the Pretoria arsenal
and abduct the State President, Hammond had to worry about how best to
defend Johannesburg against a possible Boer invasion. 'Before eight o'clock
that evening,' Hammond recalled, 'we had organised an emergency Reform
Committee.' 'Emergency' indeed.[23] Caught short militarily and politically,
the core conspirators, until only hours before the enthusiastic self-appointed
advocates of a 'revolution', but by now vulnerable to charges of treason,
hastily erected the pseudo-democratic structure of a 'Reform Committee',
broadening the base of the town's representatives in ways that helped per-
petuate the propagandistic myth that the new umbrella structure was merely

the most visible part of a much wider-still 'reform movement'. But there *was* no broad-based 'reform movement', only an inchoate set of hoped-for interlocking and synchronised military moves conceived of by an avaricious American cowboy-capitalist.

The Reform Committee, as noted earlier, was for the most part a hastily cobbled-together formal structure for Johannesburg's professional elite or, more accurately, that part of the professional elite that was most directly or indirectly dependent on the goodwill and patronage of the mine owners and their agents. About a third of the committee, and certainly its most articulate and persuasive component, consisted of university-educated men. Of the 64 members of the Reform Committee subsequently arrested, three were former newspaper editors, six were Californian-based mining engineers (in truth more mine owners than 'engineers'), another half-dozen were medical doctors and no less than seven were drawn from the town's legal profession.[24]

Absent from this Reform Committee, it will be recalled, were small-scale traders, merchants or shopkeepers, boarding-house keepers, cab owners or drivers, or any of the hundreds of canteen-keepers and publicans. Nor were the town's skilled artisans – builders, boiler makers, carpenters, electricians, printers, plumbers and a host of others – represented on the committee. Nor were the town's legions of clerks, cooks, shop assistants, waiters or barmen represented. Trade unionists were notable for their absence, as were representatives of the bulk of the town's white working-class men – the miners – let alone other minorities such as Africans or women. Suggesting that it was a Reform Committee was one thing, having the temerity to refer to it as a broad-based 'reform movement' was utterly risible.[25]

Given the Reform Committee's elitist nature, it is not surprising that Hammond – writing in the mid-1930s, when Europe was again heading towards war – could suggest, without a hint of irony, political embarrassment or even a modicum of self-insight, that 'The Reform Movement as a whole was Fascist rather than Bolshevik in nature. Direct action was finally undertaken by a group of hard-headed successful conservative men of affairs, not by hot-headed irresponsible radicals. It was the moneyed element that finally assumed the leadership.'[26]

The Reform Committee was thus mercifully free of irresponsible radical elements. At about that time the committee – which met in 'perpetual session' – assumed responsibility for safeguarding the town's inhabitants and property, the word 'revolution' suddenly disappeared from the private and public lexicon of the conspiratorial core, only to reappear in their memoirs many years later. But even after their 'revolution' was no more, they somehow forgot to put out the ideological trash. The Reform Committee, in a fit of absent-mindedness or misplaced arrogance, slipped into referring to itself as the once hoped-for, long-plotted 'provisional government'![27] Amid a very hasty retreat from a 'revolutionary' position, the new 'reformers' had failed to clear the site of all their ideological detritus.

Hammond went to bed on Sunday 29 December a 'revolutionary'; on Monday evening, 30 December, he slumbered as a 'reformer'; and by the third night, Tuesday 31 December, his metamorphosis was complete and he laid his head to rest as a republican constitutionalist. He was no longer a 'revolutionary' or a reformer, but that rare and most wonderful of things, a *Vierkleur*-respecting man. Truly, in an age filled with engineering and other miracles his was probably the most profound transformation of all. Clearly, Tuesday 31 December had been another extraordinary day in the life of slippery Jack.

With the mines closed and the town centre filling up with men who had been discharged, lost their positions or never had any to start with, questions about the town's security and 'law and order' became of primary concern to the 'provisional government'.[28] On the mines, and around Rhodes's Gold Fields building, scores of trusted miners were armed with smuggled rifles, but hundreds of unemployed males and thousands more white miners, although unarmed, were becoming agitated. At a loose end, they were starting to mill about the town.

Mobilising a strike force capable of engaging or threatening mounted Boer commandos, should the need arise, became an immediate priority. Rowland Bettington, the most vociferous warrior among the early conspirators, a man with considerable experience of colonial frontier conflict and soon promoted to the rank of colonel, was an obvious choice to lead what became 'Bettington's Horse'. Two troops, each 60 strong, were provided with horses procured from the Robinson, Simmer & Jack and Langlaagte mines under the direction of Gold Fields and Hammond loyalists, including Clement and Mein.[29]

The mounted force, it was resolved, should as soon as was practicable be supplemented with armed and well-drilled brigades organised along national lines that could help protect the town in case of a Boer attack. In this way, the town was eventually served by American, Australian, 'Afrikander' (that is, those African born), Irish and Scottish brigades, as well as a notably modest Cornish brigade.[30]

The military forces, outward-facing, were complemented by an ad hoc police force of about 300 men swiftly organised by Andrew Trimble when the Kruger government withdrew the republican police, the 'Zarps', from the town that Tuesday morning.[31] Trimble, cunning and courageous in equal measure, demonstrated another quality all too rare among the 'reformers' – genuine insight into the populist nature of the Victorian cult of masculinity that dominated white male working-class culture. A former dragoon-turned-detective, Trimble made certain that the officer corps he selected and placed in charge of rough and ready constables (not excluding many former criminal elements) included several of the town's most prominent professional boxers. The latter included the former world champion, JR Couper, Arthur Tully and other well-known local pugilists.[32]

With some redoubts in place to protect the town's fringes, the Reform Committee believed mistakenly that it was still setting the agenda rather than reacting to events unfolding elsewhere. It put in place additional mechanisms to protect vulnerable sections of the population, which did not include African workers who, by then, were as stranded as were many white workers. An ambulance corps was formed, volunteer nurses were recruited, and a Relief Fund set up. The first corporate subscribers to the fund included H Eckstein & Co, Consolidated Gold Fields and leading timber importers to the mines such as Karri Davies and Fred Lingham. A few of the original core conspirators, including Lionel Phillips and George Farrar, acting in their personal capacities, contributed generously to the Relief Fund.

The one name conspicuously absent from the list of early contributors, however, was that of the hidden architect of the 'revolution', the world's best paid engineer who, by his own smug admission, earned more than did the American President of the day – John Hays Hammond. But then so, too, were the names of almost every other member of the unloved locust elite that had invaded Johannesburg.[33]

Hammond had more to worry about than the destitution that he and his fellow conspirators had helped create. He needed to wrest the initiative away from the Beit Boys and their allies who, that same evening, were due to report back to the American mining community on the second deputation that had waited on the State President. Humiliated by having been sidelined at earlier meetings, Cowboy Jack was determined not to be seen supplicating yet again before the likes of Brown, Jennings or any of their 'undisciplined' allies. He needed to recapture his position as leader of the American engineers and the planned uprising no matter what the price. But, in order to do that, he would have to be more proactive and rely on two Californian stalwarts, Victor Clement and the already conflicted Tom Mein.

It is not known where or when Hammond met privately with Clement and Mein prior to the meeting that evening to hear what Curtis, Brown and Lingham had to say. What was discussed can, however, be inferred partially from what later transpired at the mass meeting. First, Hammond had to bend the knee to Mein and accept that most Americans were against the idea of the uprising being hijacked by Jameson or anyone else keen to raise the Union Jack as a sign of imperial triumph. They were all, it seemed, in favour of 'reform' taking place within a republican framework.

Hammond would have to out-Beit the Beit Boys in his enthusiasm for 'reform' if he were somehow to regain control over the wider American community. Second, the managers would have to ensure that the meeting was packed with Consolidated Gold Fields men, miners who owed their jobs to Hammond, Clement or Mein. That would help ensure that the meeting would be chaired by Mein.

By the same token, it may be safely assumed that Curtis and his team, as well as Jennings and Perkins, retained most of their suspicions about Hammond – that he was an out-and-out Rhodes man, and that, in the final analysis, he would go along with Jameson and, if necessary, live with an imperial solution. But this old Corner House-inspired perception, backed by Brown (who by then most probably *was* a government agent), was, as we have already had occasion to note, only partially correct. Cowboy Jack, eager to safeguard what was left of his reputation, was genuinely on the move and more than ready to swim with the republican tide.

What happened at the mass meeting that evening is best rendered in Hammond's own words. But here again, as with his account of his interactions with Charlie Siringo in the Coeur d'Alene, his version of his real or imagined role in the proceedings is best understood against the backdrop of his fixation on the American West. More particularly, it is worth remembering that Hammond's memoirs were penned in the mid-1930s, at a time of enormous popular appetite for Western movies. The themes of such movies often revolved around codes of personal courage, honour and masculinity and would have resonated perfectly with Hammond's own adolescent experiences at the ranch school in Oakland.

Hammond's writings about the Jameson Raid, which often read like film scripts, are hardly fiction but they are as glossed and romanticised as are memories of the American West. Historians and lay readers need to be sensitive to the way in which Jack Hammond's mind could float freely across the ill-defined frontiers of 'fact'. The ways in which memories are encoded are often influenced by imagined audiences.

Hammond's version of the meeting held on Tuesday evening, 31 December, reads as follows:

> Over five hundred Americans, including mine managers, mechanics, foremen, and carpenters, attended. Captain Thomas Mein, manager of the Robinson mine, was in the chair. Brown reported for the deputation. Although he was pro-Kruger in his sordid sympathy, he was forced to admit that Kruger had given them no satisfaction and it was his own opinion that nothing further could be done.
>
> Mein announced from the platform that the meeting had been called to decide whether the Americans would give their support to

the revolution then brewing against the Boer oligarchy. This was as far as he got.

Brown and his fellows decided to break up the meeting by making it impossible for anybody to speak. So loud was the uproar that, just as I made my somewhat belated entrance to the hall, Captain Mein was about to adjourn the meeting in despair.[34]

Enter the hero of the hour:

Perceiving that that situation was practically out of hand, I walked rapidly down the aisle, mounted the platform, and raised my hand for a hearing.

'What's going on?' I demanded. 'Sit down everybody … Brown, I consider that the report you have brought back from Kruger is an insult. We don't want any Kruger men in this hall. Whatever talking is going to be done in this room is going to come from the platform.'

The hubbub gradually subsided, particularly as threatening gestures from the American miners under my management lent authority to my words.[35]

At that juncture, Hammond goes on to suggest, he 'respectfully requested' anyone present who was not American to leave the room. He then proceeded to deliver a short homily on the American Declaration of Independence and the right of oppressed men everywhere to 'throw off a despotic government': '"That is all there is to it," I explained. "You won't find anything in the Declaration of Independence that limits this principle to latitude or longitude."' 'It's a clear cut issue,' he said, 'to be faced by us Americans here and now.' It is a theme that we shall have occasion to revisit later in this work.[36]

And then, intent on displaying all his anti-imperialist and 'revolutionary' finery, so as not to compromise his newly-discovered republican sensitivities, he thundered:

You know as well as I do that we won't stand for having a British flag hoisted over Johannesburg. All we want is justice from Kruger and his grafters. You can rely on me that I'll shoot any man who hoists any flag but the Boer flag.

The assemblage applauded vigorously. The vote was immediately taken and, out of the more than five hundred present, all but five voted to take up arms against Kruger. The George Washington Corps of one hundred and fifty members was at once organized for active service, and pledged its support to the revolutionary cause.[37]

Such, then, were the self-satisfied musings of a man of 80, looking back on his conduct and career in a moment of extremis.[38] By his account, having been previously marginalised by the odious Corner House men and their allies, he had recaptured his leadership of the American mining community, refocused the political attention of his followers, mobilised them for action and set them on the right path.

But it was a filmic fiction, one so redolent with contradiction, irony, paradox and interpersonal conflict that to analyse it fully would require a work all of its own.[39] In his version, Hammond managed to square the circle and, while supporting the Republic's *Vierkleur*, succeeded in getting the Americans to subscribe to his 'revolutionary cause'.

That may, of course, have been precisely the confused political outcome that he sought in order to buy more time, but it came at the cost of personal credibility. From that moment on, Hammond's legitimacy among the American mining community and his standing as a leader became even more questionable. And so he lost caste among the inner core of the conspirators. But there was no going back; he was for the four-colour flag.

As soon as the meeting ended, Hammond rushed to the Gold Fields offices where the Reform Committee was discussing a proposal supposedly emanating from the Boer government for the citizens of Johannesburg to lay down their arms.[40] In truth, however – and as we shall later explore in some detail – it was a small, self-appointed delegation consisting of Eugène Marais, editor of *Land en Volk*, and the same Abraham Malan who had been sent to 'investigate' what was happening at Irene, that is, fifth column elements in Pretoria who were by then as desperate to get themselves out of a fix as was Hammond.[41] The wily Kruger, who chose never to challenge the credentials of Marais or Malan publicly, was more intent on monitoring whether the men were among those who might be co-opted into a 'provisional government'.

Hammond and Phillips on the one hand, and Marais and Malan on the other, now found themselves in a difficult position. In truth, it was a case of two core 'revolutionaries' talking to two of their chosen Boer collaborators, but the discussion had to take place in a way that suggested that the one lot were members of the Reform Committee and the other delegates of the Kruger administration – which they clearly were not. The result was that both parties were called upon to accommodate their apparent principals; it was bluff and double-bluff.[42]

Hammond and Phillips therefore had to play along with the majority on the dummy organisation they had hastily constructed and had to continue leading – the Reform Committee. They cast the two Boer emissaries as an 'olive branch' delegation, dismissing them as a sign of Kruger's weakness at a time when Jameson had yet to be checked by the commandos. All the

Reformers were willing to do was agree to send yet another deputation to Pretoria to wait on the State President.

To his credit, whether out of fear or insight, Hammond was starting to see the writing on the wall more clearly than many of his closest comrades in arms. They, in turn, like those who had attended the mass meeting of Americans, continued to lose confidence in him as a leader not only because of his manifest inability to arm the uprising – a crippling, ongoing problem – but also because of his increasingly nimble political footwork that did more to safeguard his personal position than that of the 'revolution'. Their growing reservations would have been compounded the following morning, Wednesday 1 January 1896.

Shortly after dawn, Hammond entered the Gold Fields building, where the purposely bloated Reform Committee was meeting, determined to take out additional, forward political cover by getting it to formally adopt the position that he had advanced at the previous evening's mass meeting. Some days later, Jack Hammond's loyal personal secretary, Arthur Kelsey, recorded what then transpired:

> For an American to assist in the overthrowing of a Republic in order to aggrandize a monarchy would be to forfeit all respect from his countrymen. There is not the slightest evidence that any of the Americans on the committee either contemplated such a crime or welcomed the situation thrust upon them. Mr John Hays Hammond, the only American among the leaders took the appropriate step as soon as possible after daylight. He hoisted the Transvaal flag and he both demanded and obtained an oath of allegiance to it from the some eighty-in-all members of the Reform Committee. No one demurred.[43]

And with that act, symbolising at once retreat and submission, Cowboy Jack made what, in effect, was his final public intervention as a 'leader' of what had once been an attempt at a revolutionary putsch. After that, as he noted, 'the Boer flag that I had procured', fluttered above 'our headquarters, where it remained throughout the crisis'.[44] From that moment on, Hammond, whose nerves 'were not made for stormy times' became ever less visible in the uprising on the Rand.[45]

Even as Jameson and his men galloped towards a phalanx of phantom miners supposedly armed with rifles smuggled in via De Beers, the more astute members of the Reform Committee realised that henceforth their business would change. It would focus heavily on the logistics and politics of crowd control, inter-elite negotiations with the Boers and the demobilisation of a half-dozen or more brigades. The committee decided that it would send 'a representative', rather than a 'personally powerful' delegation led by Lionel Phillips, to meet President Kruger.[46] That, too, was a sign of things to come. As Hammond faded into obscurity, Phillips became the 'movement's' most prominent leader.

The situation had become utterly farcical. The Phillips delegation made its way to Pretoria in order to negotiate a 'reformist' end to a deadlock with the State President of a Republic to which it had pledged its loyalty. Yet, on the same day, other messengers dispatched by the Reform Committee set out for the western fringes of the Witwatersrand to link up with the invaders. Jameson – the leader of a faction hoping to effect an imperial coup – received poorly crafted notes from the old conspiratorial core, including Phillips and Frank Rhodes, but *not* Hammond, that bore lingering traces of 'revolutionary' fervour.[47] These confusing signals emanating from Johannesburg left Jameson believing that he was not yet fighting for a lost cause and, with the notorious 'letter of invitation' still in his back pocket, he drew ill-founded consolation from the correspondence. Aware that his push on behalf of Cecil Rhodes had already been repudiated by imperial authorities ready to throw them to the wolves when they sensed misadventure, he resolved to fight on. But, more anxious than ever to avoid being dismissed as a mere 'pirate', he welcomed an offer to be met and escorted into town by the rebels.[48]

The widening gulf in understanding between the core conspirators, not to mention that between Jameson and Hammond which became unbridgeable the minute the invasion got under way, was not the only, or even the most serious, problem now facing a dummy Reform Committee presided over by erstwhile revolutionaries. Having stoked the political fire to accommodate an insurrection that was said to be imminent, the 'reform movement' leaders now had to manage the growing crowds – or 'mobs', as Hammond now preferred to see them – who had got wind of Jameson's proximity and were raring to participate in an uprising led by the Hero of Matabeleland.

By New Year's Day 1896, slots for crowing before midnight were at such a premium that cocks were queuing spontaneously.[49] Joseph Chamberlain, Rhodes's silent partner in the British cabinet, abandoned Jameson and his invading troops to the mercy of Sir Hercules Robinson, the ineffectual High Commissioner for Southern Africa.[50] The Reform Committee grabbed as many slots as it could find. In two telegrams to Sir Hercules, in Cape Town – one of them signed by Hammond – it twice repudiated Jameson, their would-be saviour, inviting the High Commissioner to travel north and come to their aid by intervening with the State President to help bring about a settlement.[51]

In Pretoria, the crafty Kruger sucked yet more of his 'Progressive' political opponents into the process of dealing with the delegation from

Johannesburg. So messy a problem did it present that the State President refused to see the delegation personally and, instead, got them to put their case to the Chief Justice, JG Kotzé, and two others.[52] But Phillips and his colleagues, who later that day celebrated getting 'all they wanted', had been outsmarted by the man they cast as a yokel.

The government agreed to an armistice; it would initiate no hostile steps against those in Johannesburg, provided that the forces gathered in the town, in turn, agreed to take no action against the state or its officials. As a further sign of good faith, the Chief Justice requested that a list of names of those on the Reform Committee be forwarded to the government.[53] Phillips and his delegates agreed to do so and, out of sight, an old crocodile, seemingly asleep, flicked open an eyelid and slowly raised its body.

The betrayals of confidence and misunderstandings marking the hoped-for revolution had reached the high-water mark. Jameson, sensing political weakness and a lack of will on the part of the co-conspirators in Johannesburg, had ignored the agreement with Hammond and set off for the Rand uninvited, carrying with him the letter of invitation. Hammond, Clement and the Californians had failed to import the rifles necessary to support a popular armed uprising and Phillips had, in effect, just guaranteed that Jameson, who was being trailed by Boer commandos preparing to close in on him, would not be supported militarily from beyond or within the town. It would take a brave man or a fool, or a liar, perhaps all three, to explain it all to the Reform Committee, let alone a crowd of miners with imperial loyalties.

The Phillips delegation got back to Johannesburg at around eleven and, before the clock could strike midnight, reported back to the crowd gathered outside the Consolidated Gold Fields building. Hammond, once *the* moving spirit in the American vanguard, who felt it incumbent on him to help keep the Beit Boys with their 'reformist' tendencies in check, was content to watch from the wings while Phillips told the crowd that Jameson 'must have made a mistake' when he set off from Pitsani, and that the State President had declined their offer to be held hostage in return for Jameson's safety. Matters were in hand, however, because Sir Hercules Robinson was going to Pretoria to act as a mediator, an armistice was in place and a list of the names of those serving on the Reform Committee had been handed to the Kruger government. The joy of the Reform Committee members must have been unconfined, but some in the crowd, eyes on the clock and sensing the approach of midnight, were less content:

> The crowd kept interrupting Phillips with cries of 'How about Jameson? … What are you going to do about Jameson?' Phillips knew how to handle the mob. 'We intend to stand by Jameson. Let's

have three cheers for Dr Jim.' The response was hearty and the crowd slowly dispersed.[54]

What the Reform Committee intended doing about Jameson was indeed the burning question, but the original revolutionaries were by then in such disarray that they failed to caucus a coherent response.

At some point between six and seven the following morning, Thursday 2 January, a messenger from the embattled Jameson appeared at a time when the disintegrating Reform Committee had not yet convened. The trooper reiterated what Jameson had put in writing the previous day – he would welcome some men being sent out to help him during the final push into Johannesburg. Colonel Rhodes interpreted this as a request for assistance from a brother soldier rather than a cosmetic-political plea to avoid being seen as 'filibuster' or a 'pirate', in the face of an explicit instruction, from Sir Hercules Robinson, to abandon an invasion of a friendly state and return to Pitsani. Jameson had touched a vital nerve.

Acting without reference to the other core conspirators, Frank Rhodes did what any military man would have done under the circumstances and dispatched some mounted men under the command of Rowland Bettington to ride out towards Jameson. But Colonel Rhodes knew as little about politics as he did about urban insurrection. He simply did not have the necessary authority or charisma, and was as exposed as was the architect of the revolution and champion of the Coeur d'Alene.

Bettington's small, hastily assembled force was barely beyond the town's outskirts when the Reform Committee convened. Originally put together as a 'get out of jail' initiative to help manage the shift from Union Jack-led fervour to Vierkleur-supporting temperance, the Reform Committee was beginning to believe in itself. Intent on following its 'reformist' mandate, a huge outcry went up when it was learned that Betttington had gone to Jameson's assistance. It amounted to a breach of the armistice agreement reached earlier with the government. Within 20 minutes of Bettington's having set out, his orders were countermanded by the Reform Committee.[55] One moment there was a flash of 'revolution', the next only the thunder of 'reform'.

Andrew Trimble, once a corporal in the Inniskilling Dragoons, by then a full-blown 'Lieutenant-Colonel in command of a foot regiment 500 strong', also felt that the right thing to do was to go to the Doctor's aid.[56] Trimble was also Cecil Rhodes's own secret agent within the wider conspiracy and a man who, more than most, would have felt a personal loyalty to his old friend Jameson.[57] What was needed, Trimble argued, was a surprise attack on the Boer commandos massed around Krugersdorp, where Jameson's force was by then on its last legs. Three times he asked the already chastened Frank

Rhodes for permission to allow him to lead a few men into battle, and was repeatedly refused permission.[58]

Jameson, whose disregard for the critical pledge – not to set off for the Rand without Hammond's explicit say-so – had triggered the entire fiasco, found his fortunes sinking even faster than his expectations of help from Johannesburg were rising. He had left Pitsani thinking that it was only fear among those around Hammond that was preventing them from signalling the start of the miners' insurrection, and that once they heard that the invasion was under way, they would all take heart and the revolution would commence. But the time had arrived for monstrous insult to be added to great personal injury, and it came in the form of yet another message from his erstwhile colleagues informing him not only that he should not expect help from them, but also reminding him that he was under an imperial instruction to abandon his misadventure:[59] 'The High Commissioner's proclamation was handed to the Doctor by Mr Godfrey Lys, Manager of the Crown Reef Mine, whereupon Jameson cursed the men of Johannesburg for a lot of cowards.'[60] The white flag of surrender was hoisted, although not by Jameson himself, at Doornkop, at about 9.15 am on the morning of Thursday 2 January 1896. Dr Jameson's American-inspired filibustering adventure was over.

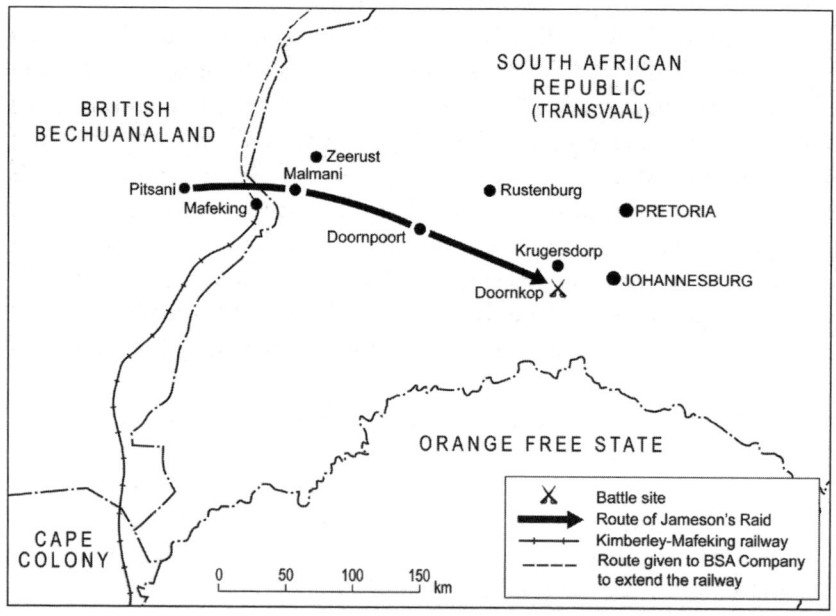

The Jameson Raid, 1895–1896

The accusation of cowardice – in effect, the second such accusation lev-elled against the Johannesburg co-conspirators by Jameson – was made public and circulated widely in southern Africa, England and the United States. Jameson's denunciation questioned the conduct and pride of vari-ous Victorian gentlemen on the Rand. But the knife twisted most deeply in the heart of Hammond, an unusually self-centred man, because it called into question all his Southern values of personal honour and manliness. The accusations would have been difficult for most men to fend off at the best of times. But for Hammond, who had failed to carry his American cohort with him while leading a 'revolution' that had to be aborted because of *his* logistical and political failures, it was utterly devastating. He spent the next 30 years of a long life trying to come to terms with the charge and to repu-diate Jameson's claim.[61]

Kruger's commandos, at home in the countryside, rounded up Jameson and his men without too much difficulty. All the boasts about needing only a half-dozen men with revolvers, or 500 men with *sjamboks*, to take over the Boer state must have seemed a little hollow that morning at Doornkop. For President Kruger, the question was how, where and when to round up the members of the Reform Committee. Having a list of names supplied by the revolutionaries themselves made for a good start. But the Reform Committee, too, had a little rounding-up of its own to do. The town was full of stray political bulls who, believing that Jameson had been betrayed by the self-appointed and -styled Reform Committee, were starting to see red.

CHAPTER FOURTEEN

The Big Roundup

A Weak Agrarian State Corrals
Ascendant Mining Capitalists

3–9 JANUARY 1896

The Jameson Raid – shorthand for the quasi-revolutionary spasm that engulfed part of the Highveld in late 1895 and early 1896 – was part of an indeterminate contest, a dangerous short-circuiting between the limitations of an agricultural state centred on Pretoria and the rapidly gathering strength of industrial capital located in Johannesburg. Looking back, it can be seen that the Raid was merely the precursor to the more significant, globalised struggle for control of the country's mineral wealth that was to take place between 1899 and 1902. It took the Anglo-Boer War and the British Army to prepare southern Africa more fully for the emergence of a stronger state, one capable of accommodating the interests of both 'gold and maize' in an economy underpinned by cheap black labour in ways that helped secure the long-term future of both the Rand mining industry and the Boer farmers.[1]

Even with Jameson's backing, however, the contestation between gold and maize was more evenly poised and the outcome far less certain back in 1895. Indeed, Hammond, who had relied on federal troops to ensure dominance in the infant state of Idaho in his war of 1892, was aware that it might take external intervention to secure the revolution that he and his co-conspirators had initially hoped for. But Jameson's precipitate action ensured that there could be no British military intervention to secure the immediate future of the mining industry.

The result was that, even after Jameson had surrendered at Doornkop, the Kruger government and the 'provisional government' remained locked in a tense stand-off. The State President and his commandos could not be certain that imperial forces would not be summoned to aid a Reform Committee backed by an unknown number of probably well-armed white miners, and were reluctant to violate the armistice. The 'provisional government', for its part, feared that the Boers might, at any moment, invade the town. Having failed to start the armed urban uprising that would have invited Jameson's intervention, the conspiratorial core instead found itself having to find ways of winding down an unarmed male populace that it had mobilised politically – albeit imperfectly – to foment a 'revolution'. It was almost as difficult to halt a half-botched insurrection as to start one.

On the morning that Jameson surrendered, Thursday 2 January, Hammond was – by his own account – still in revolutionary mode. The Reform Committee had, he recalled, decided that the Johannesburg fort, manned by a contingent of Boers, who were 'well provided with guns sent from Pretoria', should be secured. And who better to lead so dangerous an operation than a San Franciscan who knew all about Asbury Harpending's plan to seize Alcatraz during the Civil War? Some were not yet willing to attack, but not Hammond: 'I felt that this should be delayed no longer; if Jameson was such a short distance away his arrival might be the signal for a Boer bombardment.' So, with the help of a 'well-known American saloon owner' – almost certainly Sam Height – and a few others, Hammond convened a small group to carry out their plans.[2] It is significant that Cowboy Jack, who could no longer rely on the support of Californian mining friends, was reduced to leading and mobilising such American strays as he could find around Height's Hotel.

But, to Hammond's dismay, he met with resistance from an unexpected quarter:

> One of our fellow conspirators who previously had been an ardent advocate of the scheme, now began to suggest difficulties. Since this did not correspond with his earlier enthusiasm, I said: 'There isn't going to be any monkey business about this. You're going into the fort first, and I'll be right behind you. If I see the slightest sign of anything wrong, I'll shoot you.'[3]

For the second time within days, Cowboy Jack had threatened to train his revolver on men drawn from his own side. But, as with the cock-crowing business, things came in threes. It was always the person to cross him next who was in the greatest danger. In Hammond's eyes the situation was fraught, but he was not going to tolerate any further hesitation. And, as importantly for a man recording his memoirs in the 1930s and intent on underlining his manly qualities, had he not provided a potentially fine script for a cowboy movie?

But no sooner had Cowboy Jack uttered his threat than there was an unexpected knock on the door and they were passed a note – 'Jameson has surrendered at Doornkop'. That seemed to change everything. Shortly thereafter they learned that 'a considerable Boer force had gone to the fort after Jameson's capture'. As Hammond explained later, that 'compelled us to abandon our plans for seizing the fort'. It had been another close shave for the faint-hearted around him.[4]

Indeed, Jameson's surrender that Thursday, 2 January, was the signal for a general splitting of the herd of workers still milling about in the streets of Johannesburg. Having been pushed around for weeks while waiting on the arrival of their champion, Jameson, whom they now suspected of having been betrayed, they were ready to turn on those who had led them into an uncomfortable political space. And, nearby, mounted Boers were getting ready to ride into town.

By the time that Hammond got back to his office, the Gold Fields building was surrounded by a crowd several thousand strong. By then, Trimble and his pugilistic officers had locked up about 600 others who were deemed to be a risk to public safety.[5] Even so, there were still more than enough miners left to generate a distinct sense of menace.

'Ugly as had been the mood of the mob the previous night,' Hammond remembered, 'this one was in noticeably worse temper.' There was 'a horrible appearance of cowardice in the air' and members of the Reform Committee were, in effect, left in a state of siege. There were constant taunts of 'What about Jameson now' or 'Judas', and shouts suggesting that 'the building be blown up with us in it' – a threat that resonated strongly with anyone familiar with the mining war in the Coeur d'Alene. Phillips and Leonard, but once again neither Hammond nor Rhodes, were sent out to the balcony to address the crowd. But they were both shouted down as the few revolutionaries-turned-reformers atop tried to maintain control of the throng of reformers-turning-revolutionary below.[6]

An unnamed firebrand in the crowd promptly led a breakaway section, numbering close on 500 men, towards the nearby post office, threatening to put it to the torch. It was the last thing the already badly compromised Reform Committee needed, and its members were saved only by the timely intervention of the disillusioned and embittered Bettington, who did not spare the would-be arsonists:

> When one of them proposed a march of 10 000 miners on Pretoria, [Bettington] replied with taunts. When they were really wanted, he said, all they would do was wear a bunch of ribbons in their button-holes, and now that it was too late they shouted for trouble. The first man who broke the law he would hang on a lamp-post! And so with bluff, bluster, shouts, and curses, the mob sullenly dispersed.[7]

Inside the building, the born-again Reformers found the going at least as hard, as members of the Australian and Scottish corps, under 'Karri' Davies and Tom Mein, threatened to march out and rescue the raiders, who by then were on their way to Pretoria. It took an order of the committee to dissuade them.

But the main body of the crowd, still outside the building and very angry, refused to disperse. Eventually it was decided that Jameson's sickly older brother, Sam, would be pushed forward to quell the fury, and he did: 'I beg you, for my brother's sake,' he said, 'to maintain a spirit of calm restraint. We have done everything in our powers for him, and used our very best judgment. In the face of the complicated circumstances, no other course could have been taken.'[8]

To the relief of Hammond and the key 'reformers', the crowd then 'melted away' but the cloud of cowardice remained above the building.

By the time members of the Reform Committee awoke the following morning, Friday 3 January, the populace was more convinced than ever that their 'Dr Jim' had been abandoned by a set of self-appointed 'leaders' operating with agendas they had never been party to setting. Indeed, even some of the members of the Committee were beginning to ask why they had suddenly received a call to do public service in a structure that was not of their own design for an end that was uncertain. 'The plight of the Reformers,' Hammond later recalled, 'was pitiable', none perhaps more so than his own. He clung to the idea of what might have been, knowing that, amid charges of cowardice and his own failures as a leader, it was all degenerating into utter confusion. 'The revolutionary atmosphere was a combination of Armageddon and a psychopathic ward,' he wrote, but then, never one to shy away from the big lie when badly needed, continued: 'Our aspiration for reform had not abated, but untoward facts confronted us.'[9] By Hammond's account the 'reformers' were Jameson's victims and, depending on where one chose to start or stop the whole sorry tale, in some limited sense, they were.

But having felt the political heat coming from the crowds below, the born-again 'reformers' were about to be exposed to a chilly blast of diplomacy directed at them from Whitehall, by Joseph Chamberlain. The Secretary of State for the Colonies, as Cecil Rhodes was discovering, was a man who stood second to none when it came to cock-crowing.[10] All the Queen's horses and all the Queen's men were getting ready to put Humpty together again – well, at least until preparations could be made to wage a decisive imperial war.

Until such time, however, the original conspirators had to cope as best they could with the menace that the unarmed, but deeply disillusioned and disgruntled populace posed for the 'Reform Committee'. Jameson had 'received popular canonisation', and, outside the Gold Fields building, a smaller but arguably more militant section of the crowd was slowly edging its way towards a more genuinely 'revolutionary' position:

> A demagogue or two mounted a cab and addressed the crowd, denouncing the Reform Committee, and declaring the time had come to depose them and elect a People's Committee. There could be no mistaking the fact that a strong feeling existed against the Reform Committee for consenting to an armistice that did not include Jameson.[11]

Alarmed by the increasingly militant noises emanating from would-be street revolutionaries, yesterday's mining-house revolutionaries and their recently recruited allies in the Reform Committee scrambled to secure their assets in a town threatening to return to something approaching normality as the weekend approached. With the help of Trimble's thousand-strong force, all offices were shut, merchants and storekeepers ceased trading, the number of guards protecting business premises was increased and the holiest of holies – the stock exchange – went into recess. Faced with the prospect of an uprising, the erstwhile revolutionaries who had planned on fomenting an urban insurrection were now desperately trying to ward one off. Johannesburg was in lockdown.[12]

With the town – as opposed to the mines – under direct threat from without and from within, a few of the hastily drafted members of the Reform Committee began to realise that their interests and personal positions might have less in common with those of the core conspirators than they had originally imagined. The situation at ground level had mutated with unexpected rapidity and, as it had done so, the political climate on the upper floor of the Gold Fields building, too, had changed.

In effect, the majority on the Reform Committee began to deride some of the decisions reached and positions advocated by old core conspirators, the leaders of 'the movement'. The children of the revolution were threatening to devour their parents. Hammond was one of those who must have read the proceedings of the Committee with particular concern. Feeling it incumbent upon them to explain the hopeless position confronting the town, the Reformers found a few scapegoats. 'We blame the paralysing intervention of the High Commissioner,' who had repudiated Jameson and then, with a deal less clarity, 'for the departure from all implied by the original resolution to raise the Transvaal flag.'[13]

The Kruger government, which had yet to put a foot wrong throughout the entire debacle, sensed that things had reached a tipping point. With Jameson behind bars, the Reformers trying to put out fires started by themselves, and a back-footed High Commissioner on the way to Pretoria, the State President was in a position that, short of a direct imperial military intervention, was almost unassailable. For the British and the supporters of empire the situation was humiliating and was neither forgotten, nor forgiven, until that fateful day in Vereeniging, in 1902.

On the Saturday after Jameson's surrender, 4 January, about 500 armed and mounted Boers entered and occupied central Johannesburg as a prelude to the government reassuming control. Like victorious lions, the commandos could not resist marking out reclaimed territory. They appropriated various items of clothing from the guild of Zulu washermen that had been given permission to remain in the town and deal with the soiled garments of an all-white 'revolution', commandeered meat at the abbatoir and threatened to seize a herd of cattle found at the Robinson Mine – a much-hated centre of conspiracy.[14]

By the following morning the mood in town was so downhearted, and rumours so rife, that the Reform Committee deigned to issue a public statement claiming that negotiations were formally under way in Pretoria: 'It was the first occasion that the Committee had shown any disposition to take the public into their confidence.'[15] When the planned uprising had failed to materialise, the self-styled 'revolutionaries' had taken the Reform Committee and a slew of the town's professionals into their confidence, and when the rickety Reform Committee eventually also faltered it took the public into its confidence. That then was the topsy-turvy world of the champions of a democratic order, of would-be 'reformers' bent on securing the franchise for white miners. But no problem; the Queen's envoy was on his way to help clean up the mess.

The High Commissioner, Sir Hercules Robinson, left Cape Town on the day Jameson surrendered but only got to see the President, in Pretoria, on Monday 6 January. Robinson, Hammond complained, did nothing to ascertain the state of affairs in Johannesburg over that weekend, and by the time the High Commissioner met him the President's hand had strengthened immeasurably. Kruger, who knew that Robinson had already issued a proclamation ordering Jameson to abandon his botched intervention, was not inclined to compromise. He told the High Commissioner that peace could be restored only if the Reformers laid down their arms, a suggestion that was instantly agreed to by Robinson and Chamberlain – men once both well within Cecil Rhodes's inner circle.

The High Commissioner conveyed Kruger's terms to two intermediaries entrusted with the awkward business of persuading the Reform Committee to accept the ultimatum: Sir Sidney Shippard, a former imperial official whom the Reformers had sent to put their case to Robinson, and Sir Jacobus de Wet, the British Agent in Pretoria.

The residual danger now lay in how, and what, precisely Shippard and de Wet told the beleaguered members of an already splintering Reform Committee. Their main message was as clear as it was unambiguous and was faithfully conveyed to the committee members on the morning of Tuesday 7 January. The injunction to lay down their arms was, however, not well received by revolutionaries-turned-reformers attempting, at the last possible moment, to cultivate a notion of public accountability.

Sir Sidney and Sir Jacobus, more gentlemen than officers, understood the problem. They sensed the need to find a way of exercising additional pressure on the Reformers in order to get them to accept the ultimatum. Whether born out of a genuinely mistaken shared conviction or 'bluff', the two baronets conveyed the impression that Jameson's life and those of his troops were at risk if the Reform Committee's brigades did not lay down their arms. Sir Sidney, however, feeling the need for an added, positive incentive, stated – without the slightest authority to do so – that, if the ultimatum were complied with, 'not a hair on the heads' of those behind the entire repertoire of treasonous acts would be harmed. Trimble was one of those who did not believe Shippard and reminded him that his Tswana name, *Morena Maka*, meant the 'Father of Lies'.[16]

Shortly afterwards, members of the Reform Committee instructed the Secretary, Percy FitzPatrick, to issue a rare public notice:

THE REFORM COMMITTEE,
Notify hereby that
ALL RIFLES ISSUED FOR THE DEFENCE OF LIFE
AND PROPERTY,
IN TOWN AND ON THE MINES,
Are to be returned
AT ONCE TO THE CENTRAL OFFICE,

In order to enable the Committee to carry out the agreement with the Government, upon the faithful observance of which so much is dependent.[17]

By order of the Committee

But the brigade members were, almost by definition, those who had been most imbued with notions of bravery, honour and masculinity during the days of crisis and had, as we have noted, in some cases only been prevented from attempting to march to Jameson's assistance by 'order of the Committee'. Bleeding authority and leached of legitimacy, yesterday's 'provisional government' had to find some other way of persuading its troops to lay down their arms and, what better way to do so than to get the bearers of the bad news to make the case for doing so?

Gone for good were any ideas of addressing crowds beneath a fluttering *Vierkleur* from the balcony of the Gold Fields building, the erstwhile revolutionary redoubt of Frank Rhodes and John Hays Hammond. The business of empire was, for the moment at least, no longer the empire's business. It was time to put the interest of the monarch before money and what better place to do so than in the Rand Club which, with its fine line in anti-Semitism, was in any case better suited to accommodate the two knights than the jumped-up 'King of Johannesburg', Lionel Phillips?

'This crowd' (the men from the monarchy were notable for attracting 'crowds' rather than mere 'mobs') 'proved very intolerant of anything like impartiality in references to Jameson, the Government and the Reform Committee.'[18] The baronets found that they had to adopt an almost pleading tone as they supplicated for mass support of the ultimatum. Sir Jacobus, whose name gave him away as being colonial-born, soon got into roiled waters and was later rebuked by Chamberlain for his trouble. Sir Sidney, an Oxford man, struck the right note with a crowd composed largely of Englishmen. Hammond, having only recently shed his revolutionary-republican skin, had by then reverted to his Anglophile, aristocracy-loving self and was most relieved to hear the terms that were being extended not only to Jameson but, more importantly, to members of what he could only bring himself to refer to as the 'movement'. As he later recalled: 'Shippard made a particularly good speech again promising that, if the arms were given up, Jameson and the Reform leaders would be saved.'[19] A glimpse of the hangman's rope concentrates a man's mind.

Shippard's pleas eventually succeeded and disarming took place in line with FitzPatrick's earlier, futile 'order'. That same night, as if to drive home the terms of an abject surrender, an unauthorised party of about 30 gloating, armed and mounted Boers under the command of Lieutenant Eloff of Krugersdorp, rode through the centre of town, firing blanks. The republic's cowboys, from its own wild west, were giving advance warning of the roundup to follow.[20]

By the following morning, Wednesday 8 January, most of the 'brigades' had been fully disarmed. The rank and file were paid between 15 shillings and one pound for each day they had been away from work on inactive service and told that they 'should resume their normal avocations without delay'.[21] The revolt of the professionals was over and the members of the working class should return to their stations. Somewhere out on the open Atlantic, several thousand Cornishmen might have been forgiven for indulging in a smile.

The Kruger government, which had for some time been courting trade union and working-class support, was ready to drive home its advantage. In yet another shrewd move, the State President swiftly granted a pardon to 'all who took up arms against the Republic in Johannesburg with the exception of the leaders, the members of the Reform Committee, and captains of troops and drill instructors, and all engaged in the training of men'.[22] With one surgical slice, the Kruger government had isolated the brains and brawn behind the revolt from the mass of men and women living in the mining town.

A proclamation made it clear that the government intended ferreting out all 'the principal criminals, leaders, instigators or perpetrators of the trouble at Johannesburg'. To that end the town was sealed off and a pass system introduced, with the only legitimate exit being via the railway station, on production of a return ticket. A few who attempted to flee by road quickly learned the lesson when they were shot at as they transgressed the three-mile cordon thrown around the town. And, for just a few, extraordinary hours, the mine owners, storekeepers and ordinary inhabitants of a 'white' mining town, who bayed continuously for an effectively controlled, state-run regime to govern every movement of black Africans, got to know what it was like to live with a 'pass system'.[23]

With the political heat threatening to exceed midsummer temperatures and nowhere to run to, the Reform Committee began to melt away:

> Members resigned, discovering that they had never been acquainted with the real nature of the business in hand, and that the first intimation they had of armed force was the distribution of rifles and the parading of Maxims from which they now thought well to disassociate themselves.[24]

But a few who adopted disguises managed to get through the net. Richard Parker, a Jack Hammond faithful, transformed himself into a priest and travelled to Cape Town. Andrew Trimble, using his mastery of Afrikaans-Dutch, a few cosmetic touches and a false beard so as to pass himself off as an elderly Boer, also managed to escape the Johannesburg dragnet.[25]

Hammond, unlike the worldly-wise Trimble, who refused to believe the assurances offered by the Queen's men, saw little reason to try to escape. By Hammond's own telling, it was not as if escape was entirely out of the question. Indeed, he and three other core conspirators were offered, but declined, the use of four strong horses to carry them to the Natal border. Nor, to his considerable credit, would it be the last time that the devil pushed inducements to escape to within his and his wife's reach, only for them to reject temptation. As an admirer of aristocracy, kings, castles and later Kipling, as a man with a son at Eton, Hammond simply refused to believe that knights of the realm might play them false. So, when Natalie Harris expressed her anxieties about the possibility of his arrest, 'I assured my wife, that Great Britain would not allow this after having made promises of protection.'[26] Trimble, the Irishman, had an instinctive understanding of Perfidious Albion. Hammond, an American romantic with a twist of madness, had clearly not grasped it.

As Hammond put it, after he cast himself as a victim of the deceitful and irresponsible Jameson rather than the prime instigator behind the conspiracy: 'Up to the last moment I believed we were in no danger.'[27]

The Californian was, however, just about to experience another rude awakening in the kingdom of political dreams. Unfortunately, his immediate problem lay not with the British, in whom he had so much confidence, but with the Boers, whom he despised.

'On the Thursday evening, January 9th, after the Boers were finally convinced they had secured all the guns, they began to round us up.' It was almost unthinkable: sundry detectives, policemen and members of the State Artillery, the agents of a supposedly weak agrarian state, went about their business arresting American and British nationals, some of the most powerful men behind the richest mining industry in the world.

Cowboy Jack, however, could not bring himself to record it that way. He had failed to bring about the imperial-guaranteed structural change that would have helped to ensure the even greater financial returns that he, the Rhodes brothers, Beit, Phillips, Leonard and a clutch of other local professionals wished to bring about through revolution during an unprecedented boom in gold shares. But charting the trajectories of greed and power were unbecoming of an American elder statesman, so, when writing his memoirs, he chose instead to cast it in the personalised terms that might again lend itself to a movie script:

> I was in Heath's Hotel when, at a quarter to nine in the evening, Lieutenant Pietersen sent up his card. I knew what this meant. I scribbled on the back of the card: 'If you promise that I will not be handcuffed or submitted to any indignity, I'll come down. I'll blow the brains out of the first man who lays hands on me.'
>
> He sent back word that, on his honour as a gentleman, he would observe these conditions.
>
> With my gun in my pocket, I descended to the lobby. Tossing it on the bar, I said, as debonairly as I could under the circumstances 'Let's have a drink together, Lieutenant, it may be the last one I'll get for a long time.'[28]

It was his third threat to shoot someone in as many days. Despite having merely talked fast and fired blanks, Hammond left the famous long bar at the American saloon with his notions of honour intact. But, as had happened once before, when he had run into unexpectedly tough times as a younger man at Yale, he could feel that his bowels were in an extremely sensitive condition. He sensed that Colonel Coffee Hays and his other Texas Ranger mentor, John Freaner, like most other men in Johannesburg, would have seen him and the Reform Committee as 'cowards', and for that, Hammond felt, they only had Jameson to blame.

Hammond's co-conspirators were taken in that same day. Like him, they were held overnight in the cells at Doornfontein to await transportation to Pretoria the following morning. On Friday 10 January the handful of mining magnates and the rest of the Reform Committee were carted off to Pretoria, leaving behind their clerks and secretaries to tidy up the business end of what they had once hoped would be a fully-fledged capitalist revolution. Fittingly, it was those quill-men who had the last word. Shortly before midday a notice was put up in full public view:

REFORM COMMITTEE
All accounts against the Commissariat must be filed immediately, as all affairs are being wound up. The temporary offices are in Tattersall's Buildings.[29]

What had been conjured out of campfire smoke in Matableland, in late 1894, as a set of American-inspired dreams and nightmares about a possible industrial future for the gold-rich South African Republic, had turned into an imperialist military misadventure and political disaster, only to end its life as an accounting exercise close by a Johannesburg betting shop, in 1896. Out of it all, Cowboy Jack, a gambler of note, had enhanced his personal fortune to the point where he boasted of becoming a millionaire, but had lost much of his reputation. He had never wanted fame or money; he had always wanted both. It would take some serious, very public repositioning before he could ever walk the streets of a Californian town again with his head held high. He was, however, a very well-connected man and, as ever when disaster threatened, his wife would venture to his assistance. Natalie's uncle, General Nathaniel Harris, would understand the pickle that he had got himself into, but it was yet another kinsman – Uncle Sam – who could now do most to help them survive the Boer onslaught.

Undermining

CHAPTER FIFTEEN

Intelligence and Counterintelligence Networks in Johannesburg and Pretoria

C 1890–1895

The criminal-political notion of overthrowing the elected government of the Zuid-Afrikaansche Republiek (ZAR) by force of arms
and installing a 'provisional government' that might be acceptable to many
Boers, while simultaneously being more accommodating of mining interests on the Witwatersrand, predated the 'Jameson Raid' by more than five
years. The roots of this hybrid stretched back to 1887–1888, but the first
unmistakably 'political' bloom on the plant, nurtured through its transition
by the brothers Charles and James Leonard, appeared during the 1889–1892
depression precipitated by a brief crisis in the gold-recovery process on the
Witwatersrand.[1]

Born in the Cape Colony, the Leonards, imperialists and leading players
in the theatres of political conspiracy as practised by ambitious advocates,
formed part of an unbroken thread running from the late 1880s, when they
represented rebellious Irish 'social bandits', to the Jameson Raid in 1895.
Not only were the jingoistic brothers consistent in their desire to bring
about the forcible overthrow of the Kruger administration, but they were
also remarkably steadfast in their choice of possible Boer collaborators who
might constitute the core of a 'provisional government' in a longed-for new
order.

The Leonards were centrally involved in the secretive, short-lived Political
Reform Association (PRA), formed in Johannesburg in late 1889, just as the
recession began to bite. Their hope then was that after the overthrow of the
Kruger administration the republic would, for a time, be run by a triumvirate – a form of government the Boers were comfortable with – consisting
of Commandant-General Piet Joubert, the Pretoria-based advocate Ewald

Esselen and James Leonard himself. The PRA, although seemingly generous in its accommodation of Afrikaner-Dutch interests, nevertheless raised
eyebrows in the capital and caused Kruger's Executive Council to toy more
seriously with the idea of using secret agents to monitor seditious or suspicious political activities.[2]

In August 1892, just a few months before the ZAR presidential election – contested by Joubert with the backing of Esselen as his campaign
manager – and partially in response to the formation of the Witwatersrand
Mine Employees and Mechanics' Union, Charles Leonard helped launch
the Transvaal National Union (TNU). The TNU would work closely with
the mine owners and seek to offset any influence of the trade union in
Pretoria by agitating for the extension of the franchise to all immigrants.
Having sacrificed the notion of rule by triumvirate, the TNU nevertheless again hoped to appeal to progressively inclined Boers serving in the
Volksraad, including Joubert and Esselen.

But in practice the National Union proved to be more of an attraction
for a small core of British imperialists keen on military solutions to the
political problems in the Transvaal than it was for most of the Rand's disen-
franchised white mineworkers. One such member on its executive and later
a close associate of Hammond's was the Johannesburg stockbroker Rowland
Bettington, who, by his own admission, suffered from 'war fever' and who
attracted the attention of an alert state undercover agent long before the
plot of 1895 had crystallised.[3]

While the National Union spluttered along in its attempts to publicly
mobilise resistance against the Kruger government through agitation around
the franchise issue on the Rand between 1892 and 1895, at least one of the
larger mining companies that made extensive use of the legal services of the
Leonards and Esselen was beginning to develop a more insidious, long-term
plan to influence politics in Pretoria itself.

The Corner House group, comprised of H Eckstein & Co along with the
diversified and emerging giant of the Witwatersrand goldfields, Wernher,
Beit & Co, was well attuned to the ways in which cash loans and hidden
investments could either corrode or help bring around the attitudes of those
already questioning Kruger's seemingly inflexible republican beliefs. Under
the leadership of first Lionel Phillips, and later with the assistance of Percy
FitzPatrick, the Corner House companies put up the money for personal
loans to High Court judges, bought a controlling interest in an Afrikaans-
Dutch newspaper and, via Esselen, subsidised Joubert's presidential election
campaign.[4]

The Corner House not only ran a branch office in the capital but also
made sure that some of its officials spoke Afrikaans-Dutch – *die taal* – and
that members of the firm drawn from both cities were active in the Pretoria

Club where the members were, if not bilingual, then comfortable with those speaking a second language. Like the Rand Club, in Johannesburg, the Pretoria Club was the conduit *par excellence* for the exchange of intra-elite information about matters economic, professional, political and social. The difference was that whereas the cigar smoke in the former smelt of finance, in the latter it reeked of politics.[5]

But even as the Corner House men extended their political influence via ethically questionable means in Pretoria in the early to mid-1890s, the leading mine owners in Johannesburg always remained personally and professionally close to those, such as Bettington and the Leonard brothers in the National Union, who flirted with the idea of mounting a military challenge to the Kruger government. For Lionel Phillips and others in the Corner House group, it was never simply a question of furthering change by constitutional means in the capital, or by insurrection on the Witwatersrand; the answer was always *both* with now one and then the other tendency holding sway. In the final analysis, it was the arrival of Hammond in late 1893 and his influence after 1894 that forced the hand of Beit and the Corner House men into giving priority to revolutionary activity.[6]

After the Kruger administration botched efforts to conscript immigrants into a military campaign against the African chief Malaboch in May 1894, Phillips, never far from the bellicose Leonard brothers or Ewald Esselen (by then co-opted into the Kruger government as State Attorney), took a renewed interest in the possibilities that armed revolt might one day offer in order to effect a change of government.[7] By late 1894, Phillips, although still not holding out much hope for an imminent rebellion, began providing financial support for the formation of rifle associations in Johannesburg and Pretoria.[8] What is clear is that secret agents appointed by Esselen, in his capacity as State Attorney, informed him of this provocative, unsettling development.[9]

The existence of a few radicalised if not wholly 'revolutionary' networks devoted to economical mining in Johannesburg and political undermining in Pretoria, including a few leading Boer collaborators, predated Hammond's appearance on the Witwatersrand by at least eighteen months, probably longer. This left Hammond, the architect and major activist behind the events that unfolded in 1895, at an initial disadvantage. Until he spent a few weeks in prison in Pretoria, in 1896, the Boer capital was part of an opaque world for Hammond. There is no surviving record of his ever having visited Pretoria between 1893 and 1895. Unlike his wife, who prided herself on the ability to follow the outlines of Afrikaans-Dutch, Hammond neither spoke nor read *die taal*. And, unlike several Corner House notables, or Rhodes himself, Hammond – otherwise almost always a 'club man' – did not join the Pretoria Club.

The result was that, between 1892 and 1893, the Corner House men often had far better political information than did Hammond and Consolidated Gold Fields. So, when the revolutionary conspiracy on the Rand deepened in 1894–1895 and Hammond started taking control of the flow of intelligence, he had to rely on English-speaking sources previously aligned with the Corner House group, thereby contributing further to the rivalries between the Beit and Rhodes factions among the Reformers, and between Hammond and Percy FitzPatrick in particular.[10]

Hammond, with a near insatiable desire to be present at any historical juncture where armed intervention, big capital, conspiracy, secret agents and political power met, was born to involvement in the intelligence set-up leading up to the 'Jameson Raid'.[11] By the mid-1890s, approaching the age of 40, he was a veteran when it came to assuming the hard or soft roles necessary for the entrenchment of mining capitalism – mounting armed struggles, employing Pinkerton agents, smuggling guns across state lines, controlling editors, lobbying politicians or getting public opinion massaged into place.

But for eighteen months, from the moment that he effectively came to head Consolidated Gold Fields on the Rand, in mid-1894, until that fateful trip through Matabeleland with Rhodes and Jameson later that year, during which the prospects for a 'revolution' were first debated with greater clarity and purpose, Hammond devoted almost all his time to acquiring and developing deep-level mines for Rhodes's company.[12] Pretoria and the politics of the Boers remained of secondary importance, while Johannesburg demanded all of his attention and energy as the most sought-after mining engineer on the Witwatersrand.

There were other factors, including social Darwinist notions, that contributed to Hammond's early indifference to Boer politics. His oft-paraded 'Anglo-Saxon' pride placed him above most Afrikaner-Dutch, whom he held in contempt. He was always unable to either 'feel' or 'read' the depth and subtlety of Pretoria's politics as Kruger battled purposefully to manage the transition from a previously exclusively agrarian economy to one that was significantly more industrialised. Inbuilt disdain made Hammond partial to the company only of those Boers who were Joubert supporters and who had become disaffected after what they saw as the rigged election in 1893, or those who willingly recast themselves as part of a 'Progressive' opposition that often grossly underestimated President Kruger.

When Hammond, with all his 'revolutionary' zeal, *did* eventually set out to cultivate an intelligence network of his own – somewhat belatedly in 1894–1895 – his agents in the capital had to travel to Johannesburg to see him there rather than him go to Pretoria to debrief them on site. His collaborators and informants were either Afrikaners already on the Corner House payroll and/or Boers with visions of the state that went wider than mining on the Witwatersrand. All of them, however, had a healthy respect for Boer military prowess and a deep-seated, anti-imperialist desire to retain their independence from Britain.

Even on the eve of the planned 'revolution' in Johannesburg, whenever there was talk of Boer involvement in a 'provisional government' in circles frequented by the Leonards and others, it was always the same names that came to the fore.[13] But it is at least as significant that Hammond himself later had virtually nothing of substance to say about Joubert, and that he made no mention at all of Esselen in an autobiography notable for its strategic silences and self-aggrandising content.[14] What Hammond could not achieve entirely, however – for the simple reason that the public record would not allow him to do so – was to eliminate entirely from his account the role of Joubert, Esselen and their closest lieutenants. Hammond had, by 1895, it would appear, drawn into his circle both Joubert's son-in-law, Abraham Malan, and Esselen's close protégé, Eugène Marais.

Given these significantly overlapping agendas, loyalties, personnel, skills and visions for the future, let alone differences in personality and temperament, it can be seen that there was plenty of room for confusion or a parting of the ways among those in the various intelligence-gathering networks operating in the ZAR in the early to mid-1890s. In order to appreciate these imbrications and the consequences that they held for Hammond's on/off Johannesburg 'revolution' and the Raid of 1895, it is necessary to tease out the differences in more detail.

Progressive Boers and the Politics of Disillusionment: the Triumph of Conservatism in the Presidential Election of 1893

The presidential election of 1888, like that of 1882, had resulted in a decisive victory for the forceful President SJP (Paul) Kruger over General PJ (Piet) Joubert, a cautious, pietistic and reflexive opponent. Coming in the wake of the discovery of the Rand goldfields and the opening of new urban markets for Boer farmers, the 1888 election had taken place during a period of unprecedented economic progress.

By contrast, the 1893 election fell squarely between economic cycles: the recession of 1889–1892 was barely over, and the boom of 1893–1895 not yet fully born. The effects of the recent slump, however, ensured that a rather shaky present weighed more heavily on the electorate than did the prospects of an uncertain future. Concerns hinging on import duties, the national bank and an inability to raise a state loan on competitive terms cut across many constituencies. In the urban centres, as few in number as they were modest in size, there were questions about corruption that could be traced back to the government's concessions policy, which, it was argued, translated into monopolies that benefited only the President's friends. And, as ever with ethnic nationalists in uncertain economic times, many of the problems were allegedly attributable to foreigners. 'The Jews' were said to be in the forefront of those profiting from the emerging economy, while senior posts in the civil service were dominated by the arguably even less popular 'Hollanders' that Kruger had recruited.[15]

The centre of this political dissent lay over the nation's capital.[16] In Pretoria, perhaps not the best place from which to test the electorate's vision, a few republican professionals, of the sort that frequented smoke-filled rooms, were of the view that the need for revitalisation was widespread. The majority of voters, they felt, were ready to accept change, elect a new leader and push for modern, progressive policies that might be better aligned to the needs of a faltering economy and urban markets. They were further heartened by the fact that a few Volksraad members, too, were often at odds with the President's policies.

They were not unduly concerned by the lack of a charismatic or outstanding leader capable of championing the policies necessary to smooth the change from a rural economy to one increasingly dominated by mining and urban immigrants. For Pretoria-based Progressives, the anti-Kruger sentiment among rural conservatives seemed so pronounced that it would trump any misgivings that voters might have about the qualities of their modernising candidate. It was not that the Progressives' glass was half-full, but that Kruger's was so obviously half-empty. This time round, the Progressives believed, not even a candidate who had been defeated twice before by Kruger could lose to an incumbent who had bled so much of his popularity. Nor were they much put out by the appearance of a third candidate, the politically ambitious Chief Justice, JG Kotzé.

There is little doubt that Joubert wanted to be the State President in 1893 and probably for several years thereafter. Respected as an entrepreneur, wealthy farmer and landowner, the General enjoyed all the outward trappings of success. Joubert's earthly success, however, was tempered by his belief that access to the highest office in the land was wholly dependent on, first, the will of God and, second, on that of the people. He genuflected in the presence of both; while God may have been approving of the posture, the people were less convinced of his ability to offer firm leadership other than in times of war against African tribes. Reticence, at times of almost mystical proportions, meant that the General had to be pushed to stand for election, and then led from behind. Unable to keep up with the liberal views of his campaign manager on the franchise question, Joubert was forced to belatedly and publicly distance himself from his fired-up election committee.[17]

PJ Joubert PHOTO: PERRY CASTAÑEDA LIBRARY, UNIVERSITY OF TEXAS AT AUSTIN

Commandant Abraham Malan

Eugène Nielen Marais

The presidential election of 1893, during which the General had to be coaxed into presenting a distinctive profile before an electorate composed almost exclusively of brother Boers, offered a clear illustration of Joubert's political limitations. Indeed, the eventually close outcome reflected the energy of the General's campaign committee more than it did that of their candidate. The closeness of the result also accounted for the bitterness it engendered among his most ardent supporters.

Joubert's campaign committee was chaired by the charming 34-year-old Ewald Esselen, who, in 1890, had resigned from his poorly paid position as a judge in the High Court to practise as an advocate in Pretoria, and had become a club creature of note even in an age dominated by club life. As affable as he was articulate, the young Esselen started his career by studying medicine in Edinburgh but had then married a Scotch lass and changed direction radically to study law in London.[18]

Returning to his native Cape Colony, Esselen practised briefly as an advocate but never hid his political ambition. In 1885, he was selected to represent the Richmond constituency in the Cape Legislative Assembly as a member of the Afrikaner Bond. There, he met and was soon on good terms with Rhodes. The following year, the restless 28-year-old Esselen accepted the position of judge, in the criminal court in Pretoria. So trusted was Esselen by Rhodes that when Rhodes, Charles Rudd and Hans Sauer set out to examine the potential of new gold discoveries in the South African Republic, in 1886, they were, rather surprisingly, joined by the young judge. Ewald Esselen was present when, on 4 August 1886, the Rhodes agents 'chipped some pieces from the Main Reef and leaders on the farm at Turffontein'.[19] Rhodes had a friend at court in the republic right from the birth of the Witwatersrand.

A few months later, when Esselen found himself cash-shy in Pretoria, in June 1887, he did not hesitate to touch Cecil Rhodes for a personal loan of undisclosed proportions. The diamond magnate, who was passing through the Witwatersrand, was happy to oblige, replying, 'My Dear Esselen, I enclose a cheque. Kindly send promissory note to myself at the Club, Kimberley,' before going on to ask for some of the political gossip in the capital.[20]

By then, of course, Esselen had settled into his poorly paid position on the High Court having, after some wrangling, earned the approval of Chief Justice Kotzé and President Kruger. Just beneath Esselen's benign exterior, however, lay a formidable intellect, great ambition and a complex political identity. Two well-informed contemporary Pretoria insiders above the fray of intra-elite Boer politics captured some of Esselen's impatience, and his reck-lessness, when they characterised him as a 'brilliant political adventurer'.[21]

Esselen was a man capable of making radical, unpredictable shifts not only in the career paths he followed but also in political choices that smacked of opportunism. Lionel Phillips, in his dual role as mine owner and President of the Chamber of Mines, did more than most to persuade Esselen to buy into the Randlords' vision of a state in which industry took precedence over agriculture rather than the other way round. But even Phillips, who went out of his way to cultivate Esselen's support for reformist projects designed to improve the fortunes of the mining industry, considered him to be 'impulsive and lacking in discretion'.[22] Nor, with exception of his support for the weak-willed Piet Joubert, was Esselen a man given to notable personal loyalties.

Indeed, within twenty-four months of his arrival in Pretoria, in 1886, he and Kruger fell out when Esselen got involved in some questionable scheming to further his own ambition at cabinet level at a time when he was a judge and not yet quite 30.[23] Esselen made little attempt to conceal his desire to command the destiny of his adopted homeland at the very highest level. In 1895, just three weeks before Jameson attempted to invade the Witwatersrand, it was noted as far afield as Westminster that Esselen was a man 'subject to whims' who 'cannot control his tongue', someone who 'had designs on the Presidency of the South African Republic, and evidently counts on the Uitlander for support'.[24] Ambition and opportunism, the very stuff of politics, do not equate to treason or treachery, but can serve to fuel it.

One of the sharpest observers of the 1890s, Olive Schreiner, was just one of those who could never quite establish the essence of the inner man. Shortly before the outbreak of the Anglo-Boer War, she penned a hasty note to her brother, WP, then Premier of the Cape Colony, so as to cover up one of Esselen's indiscretions. 'Destroy Esselen's note I sent you yesterday,' she asked, 'and of course show it to no one.' 'Yes, Esselen is a dear loveable fellow,' she continued, 'yet there is something I've not got at in him.'[25] He was an enigma, with one adversary venturing to suggest that he was mentally unstable.[26]

As a student in Edinburgh and later in London, Esselen had embraced the causes of anti-imperialism, nationalism and Transvaal independence and become a vicarious patriot. Indeed, in 1880, he abandoned his medical studies to do volunteer work during the First Anglo-Boer War and then went on, in 1881 and 1884, to serve as Kruger's unofficial secretary during complex constitutional negotiations. As Charles Cowen, editor of the imperialist mouthpiece *Zingari* and a bitter critic of Esselen's, pointed out, this meant that, by as early as 1881, the always ambitious and impatient young Esselen had already chosen to go against 'the established law of the country of his birth and the adopted home of his parents'.[27]

Esselen's Progressive sentiments were not, however, the by-products of spontaneous nationalist eruptions spurred on by a Celtic wife, although that might have played a small part. What seems more likely is that his attitudes were partly shaped in Edinburgh, and later in London, by the radical Scot,

A cartoon depicting Advocate Ewald Esselen THE SCHRÖDER ART MEMENTO, 1894

Dr Gavin B Clark, who, in turn, was taken with the anti-imperialism of Irish nationalists.

It was not by chance that, shortly after Esselen returned to Pretoria, in 1886, he was the moving spirit behind the founding of a reformist-inclined, nationalist youth league: *Jong Zuid-Afrika*. Its members, some conservative Afrikaners believed, shared revolutionary impulses of the sort that character-ised the *Carbonari* in early 19th-century Italy. But, in truth, Jong Zuid-Afrika was more likely to have been inspired by Young Ireland, a group of radical-ised post-1848 anti-imperialist nationalists that Clark certainly, and Esselen probably, were familiar with.[28]

Clark, a graduate of three British universities, was 12 years Esselen's senior. By the early 1870s he was sufficiently impressed by Marx's analysis of capi-talism for him to have joined the International Working Men's Association in London. From there on he developed notions that embraced all forms of progressive, anti-imperialist, constitutional nationalism. As a member of the Fabian Society and the Scottish Home Rule Association, the doctor was also sympathetically disposed to Kruger. It was even rumoured that he had been present, on the Boer side, at Majuba. Clark certainly assisted Kruger during talks leading to the London Convention of 1884, and he later became the South African Republic's agent-general in London. He too, as we shall note, was not beyond political recklessness.

Esselen would have drawn succour from the fact that, shortly before returning to southern Africa, Dr Clark – one of his mentors – was elected to Westminster as the independent member for Caithness. In parliament, Clark associated himself with the political causes of that set of radicals who many later saw as heralding the coming of the modern Labour Party.[29] Clark's career suggested that avant-garde politics and radical thinking alike could find a place in even the most venerable institutions.

Clark championed the independence of the Zuid-Afrikaansche Republiek. In early 1900, by which time Esselen had long since tried to dis-tance himself from the events leading up to the Jameson Raid but retained a stake in casting Rhodes as the chief culprit behind the uprising, Dr Clark was still sufficiently strongly involved in anti-imperialist and anti-war prop-aganda to become involved in some messy politics that harked back to 1895. A clerk, working in the offices of Bourchier Hawksley, solicitor to the British South Africa Company, stole a set of letters that, it was said, proved Joseph Chamberlain's complicity in the plot, and sold them to Clark, who was then roundly condemned in the House of Commons. It made for a serious scandal at the time, was widely reported on, and helped ensure that Clark lost his seat in the general election that followed.[30]

If there was anyone of a constitutionalist-nationalist bent with a decided taste for intrigue in Pretoria, in 1892, who would have understood the

economic changes that the South African Republic was undergoing and
known about Karl Marx, industrial development, class conflict and a few
theories of revolution, it was likely to have been Esselen.[31] Not surprising, then, that Esselen's lieutenant in the Joubert campaign, a precocious
22-year-old full of ideas but still lacking in political experience or a full
tertiary education, was impressed by the leadership and insight provided
by the campaign chairman, whom he viewed as a man of great potential,
perhaps even a president.

Eugène Nielen Marais, all raw gunpowder, required very careful packing.
His ideological fireworks often had to be angled away from targets before
they could be ignited; preferably under adult supervision. Despite his name
and later fame as an Afrikaner literary giant, Marais thought and wrote in
English. In the early 1890s, only twenty-four months out of his teens, he
began to take an interest in political intrigue and most things secret, including agents, codes, oaths and 'special branches'.[32]

In a flash of self-insight that went to his romantic delusions and naivety,
Marais later told a colleague that, at the time he was dealing with Hammond
and the Reform Committee, he was essentially still a 'boy'.[33] And it was true;
there was always something of the child and the world of magic about him.[34]
A Freemason and member of the Pretoria Club, this young, blue-eyed Dr
Jekyll confided in Jong Zuid-Afrika members that he had been conducting
a few experiments with morphine, to which he eventually became seriously
addicted.

Outwardly as charismatic and charming as Esselen, who had problems
of his own with alcohol, Dr Jekyll's personal proclivities, including a willingness to dispense with the truth when pushed hard, remained fairly well
hidden for most of his adult life.[35] It was, however, Mr Hyde, young and
wild, that frightened members of the public by proving that he was impossible to manage. That he was an anti-Semite, filled with nationalist fervour,
moral rectitude and a reform agenda might not have set Marais apart from
many of his compatriots, but that he was a journalist and newspaper editor
certainly did.[36]

Having started out as an attorney's clerk, Marais decided to turn his linguistic talent and writing ability to better account and took up journalism,
even though Esselen always remained keen on his furthering his legal studies. By age 20, Marais was working on the *Transvaal Observer* and also writing
– in Dutch – in the then still insignificant *Land en Volk* that he became
editor of in October 1890. Ambition and depression economics, not always
the closest of companions, were kind to him. In July 1891, he and a friend
bought *Land en Volk* for £500, with Esselen, standing surety at the bank,
financing the deal.[37]

Two things helped Marais transform *Land en Volk* into a significant mouthpiece in the capital, albeit one that was never a financial success. First, shying away from the stiffer and more formal Dutch, he began to present his readers with stories written in the vernacular, in the Afrikaans-Dutch of everyday usage.[38] Second, he and the newspaper, swimming with the underlying economic currents, eased into the 'Progressive' trend in politics. It was within the latter context that he first met Abraham Hugo Malan.

Malan, a tall bearded Boer ten years older than Marais, was presumably part of the Malans of Doornpoort in the Rustenburg district, where many clansmen had long been disproportionately well represented. Although not particularly well-off financially, Malan was no yokel. Articulate, bilingual, literate and with interests in 'Progressive' politics and intrigue that fed into his military and organisational skills, Malan was as at home in the Pretoria Club as the next man. More importantly, he was a son-in-law of Piet Joubert and as deeply devoted and loyal to his parents-in-law as they were loving and supportive of him.[39]

Immediately after Joubert was nominated as a presidential candidate, in late 1892, Esselen convened a 'congress' of his supporters which his conservative opponents criticised as an unnecessarily 'Americanised' development.[40] While Malan was active and visible at the congress he was not elected to the campaign committee. After that he played a shadowy role in the run-up to the election, although it seems self-evident that he, Marais and Esselen not only involved themselves in organisational matters but also ensured that *Land en Volk* remained solidly behind Joubert. Indeed, so close did Malan and Marais become politically that, in 1897 – after Marais had followed Jack Hammond and was living in London – Marais was briefly willing to entrust Malan with the editorship of the paper.[41]

Throughout the election campaign of 1892–1893 all public pronouncements and the thinking of those associated with the Joubert committee remained steadfastly constitutionalist. Even though their candidate was a military man, the Commandant-General of the Boer forces, it was accepted that the election would be free and fair, that the outcome would reflect the political preference of the people in a way that would be beyond dispute, and that there would be no need to resort to arms.

But when Kruger was eventually declared the winner of the election, by the slender margin of 745 votes in a three-way contest after complex political manoeuvres, serious disputation and a hastily convened official commission of inquiry, some in opposition circles began to flirt with more radical possibilities.[42] The idea of unseating Kruger by military means, no matter how sloppily conceived or filled with wishful thinking, was never confined to the Leonards or restricted to Rand Club members.

It is impossible to know now where these treasonous thoughts emanated from, or by whom and where they were discussed. Nor were they necessarily exogenous. In this rough-hewn rural republic, Boer leadership contests on horseback and under arms, rather than via the ballot box and newspaper editorials, were not unknown. Yet, this time it was different. First, those advocating extreme forms of contestation were in the capital itself rather than in the countryside. Second, the chairman of the opposing campaign committee, Esselen, and his chief whip, Marais, were articulate, modernising young nationalists of the Jong Zuid-Afrika ilk whom Kruger sympathisers had cast as harbouring unhealthy, possibly even revolutionary, impulses. Third, the defeated candidate was a respected general with a primary constituency that drew on the commando system over which he presided.

At *Land en Volk*, in 1893, Marais either echoed or, just as likely, channelled bellicose talk about the protest or unspecified 'violence' that might follow if a recount of the votes cast in the presidential election were not granted. Thirty-six months later Marais advocated the need for armed resistance against a Kruger government intent on making changes to the Executive Council, which, in Marais's opinion and perhaps that of his long-time legal friend, Esselen, were probably all unconstitutional.[43]

For his part, Kruger was under no illusion as to what it was that was being threatened. Writing to the pro-government *Volksstem* in 1893, he demanded that 'there must be no more talk of armed revolt against the result of the election'. Joubert, sensing that he was being back-footed, weighed in with a letter calling for 'calm and restraint', which was slightly odd given that he also claimed there was 'no danger of civil disturbance'.[44]

For all that, it would seem that the General and his supporters, led by Esselen, who had lost his own parliamentary seat during the 1892 elections, were left deeply disillusioned by the election outcome and, one might speculate, by the fact that all the talk about armed protest or resistance remained just that – talk. The leading historian of the election refers repeatedly to Joubert and his leading backers as being 'embittered' over the months that followed, while Marais's biographers are of the view that his unhappiness persisted right up to the Jameson Raid.[45]

Once opportunistic war-talk had blown over, Esselen, along with Marais and Malan, resumed what seemed like the long haul along their preferred path of constitutionalism as prescribed by the law. Within months of the election, in late 1893, Esselen launched and was elected Chairman of the *Volksvereeniging*, the pro-Joubert 'People's Union', and this time Malan was elected to serve as an executive member.[46]

In retrospect, then, it is clear that younger Afrikaner nationalists, led by Esselen, had pinned their hopes for political change on the outcome of an election held towards the end of a period of economic recession. Their disappointment with the outcome was palpable and some, including Marais and possibly Malan, flirted with the idea of mounting an armed challenge to the result. But whatever their underlying proclivities for revolutionary activity, it would seem that, by 1892, and certainly after 1893, there was a small group of Pretoria-based Afrikaners who were sufficiently disillusioned with conventional political processes in the republic to constitute a potential catchment pool for those in Johannesburg whose own thoughts were turning to revolution. No wonder that some on Kruger's Executive Council, more especially Dr WJ Leyds, felt a growing need to beef up state security.[47]

The problem for would-be revolutionaries on the Rand, however, was that not all those identified as potential Boer radicals were of a piece. Joubert, although a man with a national profile around which many people might be mobilised, was a no-hoper, and would always have to be prodded into action from the rear. Esselen, by training and temperament more given to formalistic legal processes, would be harder to draw into a conspiracy, but his two Young Turks, Marais and Malan, were perhaps more inclined to proactive interventions.

The Corner House: Rand Money and Politics in the Capital

Few, if any, in the South African Republic in the early 1890s, had a better understanding of how gold and silver might corrode, if not corrupt, a man's will than the senior office bearers in the Corner House. Given Wernher, Beit & Co's large and diversified portfolio of mining and land interests, the group was quick to appreciate the importance that politics in Pretoria held for long-term success and more than willing to play a waiting game. Stated crudely, the Corner House had been injecting slow-acting poison into the veins of the Kruger administration for some years before Rhodes, Hammond and Consolidated Gold Fields, manifesting American-style industrial haste, could wait no longer and advocated a single, lethal dose.

Kruger strongly disliked Lionel Phillips of the Corner House, whom some bent the knee to as the 'King of Johannesburg'.[48] There were ample grounds for Kruger's distaste that had nothing to do with anti-Semitism. As early as 1890, in the opening months of the depression, Phillips used insider business dealing and loans to exert influence over Kruger's close friend and influential informal economic adviser, AH Nellmapius.[49]

Not content with being able to reach inside Kruger's kitchen cabinet when necessary, the mining companies, including those of the Corner House, were also adept at exerting influence over members of the Executive Council and the Volksraad. Wernher, Beit & Co contributed generously to Joubert's 1892–1893 election costs.[50] Moreover, and as already noted, by the mid-1890s, Phillips himself had at least one impecunious judge in the republic in his thrall by providing him with cash and a loan.[51]

Interestingly, Eugène Marais, foremost critic of the day when it came to pointing out corruption in presidential circles, and an otherwise fearless editor who, backed by Esselen, seldom feared libel action, appears not to have ever named the Corner House or any of its office bearers in his protestations. There may have been good reasons why the dog chose not to bark.

Cheered by the narrow margin of the Progressive defeat in the presidential election, and by the gathering momentum of an upturn in the mining industry, it took Wernher, Beit & Co little more than two months to regroup and redouble efforts at increasing their traction in Pretoria. In August 1893, the company set up a secret fund designed to continue shaping Boer public opinion and increasing the number of Progressives in the Volksraad.[52]

Esselen and Marais, disheartened by Joubert's defeat, formed an obvious focal point in manoeuvrings to keep open the path to eventual constitutional change in the republic. The politically adventurous Esselen had already nailed his colours to the mast when, in late 1892 and at considerable cost to Joubert's campaign, he had openly attended a meeting of the National Union, the mine owners' front organisation, in Johannesburg, advocating the granting of the franchise to immigrant workers.[53]

As a member of the Pretoria Club and a leading lawyer in the capital, Esselen now had unrivalled access to political news and gossip from within Kruger's Executive Council and the Volksraad. What Joubert did not impart directly to Esselen he picked up from Abraham Malan or other sympathetically disposed members of the Volksraad. Wernher, Beit & Co had good reasons for making sure that the talented Esselen, like the Leonards, always got a fair share of the firm's legal work.[54]

What the Corner House men and their allies were really in search of, however, was a way of ensuring that club talk and political scandal might be leveraged to public advantage in their struggle against the Kruger administration. They did not have to look far. Eugène Marais and *Land en Volk* had been performing that function, free of charge and exceedingly well, over several years. All that was needed was to make sure that Werhner, Beit & Co got first sight of any sensitive information, and that the editor of the paper gradually became more beholden to them, in Johannesburg, than he already was to Joubert and his allies in Pretoria. And, when it came to re-channelling power, money was sometimes a great facilitator.

Marais, however, was seldom motivated by money alone or the prospect of wealth and enjoyed a modest – often frugal – lifestyle. By late 1893, however, he had a bank loan to service and a growing need for morphine, even though his habit was still comparatively well under control. It was the silky-tongued Charles Leonard, he of the National Union and the professional and political confidant of Marais's idol, Esselen, who was asked to ease Marais into the wider orbit of the Corner House group.

Backed by the company's secret fund and acting on behalf of a nameless 'consortium', Leonard approached Marais with an offer to purchase *Land en Volk* while retaining his services at a handsome salary for two years, and allowing him to continue exercising independent editorial control of the paper. It was an easy decision. The fly had barely touched the water when the trout struck. The consortium bought *Land en Volk* for £2 500, Marais got a salary of £50 a month, and when the time came in 1895 the full purchase price would be handed over to young Marais in exchange for his share in the venture.[55]

Leonard, true to form, used the opportunity provided by the negotiations around the acquisition of the paper to sound Marias out as to whether or not he thought that an armed revolt might dislodge the Kruger administration. Marais, although not opposed to the use of force as a matter of principle, was sufficient of a realist to tell Leonard that any such confrontation would probably end in triumph for the Boer republican forces.[56]

From late 1893, and unknown to anyone other than those in Marais's inner circle, *Land en Volk* was owned by the Corner House even though, on the street, it still appeared as if Marais were both the editor and sole proprietor. The depression of 1889–1892 had paved the way for a part of domestic politics in Pretoria to become increasingly radicalised, just as surely as, after 1893, the 'Kaffir Boom' was to stimulate even greater economic greed among the deep-level mine owners in Johannesburg. Two hitherto fairly well-separated forces were, through a combination of chance and design, being brought into closer alignment, releasing new and ominous possibilities.

In this rapidly changing environment, intelligence and counterintelligence networks assumed increasingly important roles. Marais and Malan, advocates of Progressive Afrikaner nationalist politics in which 'revolution' was but a pipe dream on the margins of rural society, were beginning to collaborate with insurgent European financiers who believed that an urban 'revolution' might be the key to ensuring the future of industrial capitalism. The parties were edging closer, albeit not always consciously or easily. The one party could no longer do entirely without the other, and both awaited the birth of a new, better-integrated political economy that was never ever fully defined.

Marais, disillusioned by the patriarchal and venal politics of the Kruger administration, and vulnerable to both political attack and physical assault, was looking around for ways of better protecting his personal and professional life.[57] Assurances of confidentiality and secrecy, along with a more secure personal financial situation, helped him ease his way into these new and treacherous overlapping fields of political gravity. His already formidable political connections to the Progressives, who were growing in influence within the Volksraad and which, via Malan, could reach into the highest echelons of the government, provided him with a stream of sensitive information that he was quick to relay to the paper's new owners back in Johannesburg.

In October 1893, the manager of Wernher, Beit & Co's Pretoria office, C Marquardt, decided that, in future, all Marais's confidences would be conveyed to the Corner House under cover of the company's 'general code'.[58] The following year, long before leading figures in the Corner House and Consolidated Gold Fields groups bought into Hammond's idea of a fully-fledged urban revolution Marais began reporting to Percy FitzPatrick, who headed the 'Intelligence Department' at the Corner House. It was slightly unusual nomenclature – terminology of a sort more suited to a war office than a mining finance house.[59]

By May 1894 Marais was plumbed into the 'intelligence' division of Wernher, Beit & Co but was still moving slowly along the constitutional path advocated by Esselen, when the State President – invariably cast by his opponents as being inflexible and myopic – made a bold, calculated and imaginative move. Sensing that his opponents in Pretoria were steadily gaining ground in the Volksraad, and intent on undercutting them and perhaps influencing the bonds developing between them and industrial capitalists in Johannesburg, Kruger offered Esselen, one of his foremost Afrikaner critics, the position of State Attorney in his cabinet.

Significantly, the President's decision to attempt to co-opt Esselen politically came immediately after Kruger had met with a deputation from the Chamber of Mines to discuss the prevalence of gold theft on the Witwatersrand, and had agreed to undertake some reorganisation of the police on the Rand. Kruger was far from being implacably opposed to the industry, and the appointment of Esselen, who was comfortable with Johannesburg's upper crust, would reassure the Chamber of the President's seriousness.[60]

It is difficult to know fully the reasoning behind Esselen's unexpected decision to accept Kruger's offer. The maverick's unexpected transformation from arch-critic to comfortable insider came at some personal and public cost. General Joubert was, for some weeks, reportedly unhappy and perplexed. In the middle ranks of progressive Afrikaners the criticism could be more personal and cut deeper. Newspapers out to defend the new appointment found it necessary to fend off repeated accusations that Esselen was either a 'turncoat' or, worse still, a 'wild revolutionary'.[61] Esselen did not, however, waver in loyalty to General Joubert, which endured right up to the Anglo-Boer War. His ambition upon assuming office, in May 1894, appeared to have been moderately reformist insofar as he insisted only on being given a free hand in reconfiguring the state's rickety detective and police services.[62] But his hankering after high office and his love of intrigue had clearly not disappeared.

By then, however, Esselen may already have been outgrowing his political boots. Within four months of his appointment as State Attorney, some of the State President's conservative supporters expressed the opinion that Esselen's ambitions ran far deeper than overseeing the reform of the police. Six months later, in October 1894, the solidly pro-Kruger *De Volksstem*, while critical of Esselen's supporters, conceded that he had 'a right to desire to be State Secretary or even State President one day'.[63]

If the *Volksstem* editorialist was correct in entertaining such suspicions, then Esselen openly yearned for a far bigger say in the affairs of state, including foreign relations and the geopolitical future of southern Africa. It was a vision that could readily accommodate General Joubert's own long-dormant vision of a 'much diluted form of republicanism', one that 'actually favoured a South African confederacy under English protection with self-rule for the constituent colonies'.[64]

No one appears to have noted it publicly, but conservatives may by then have had one more reason to be wary of the new State Attorney. In September 1894, Esselen's older brother, Daniël Johannes Esselen, a career diplomat who had served the Kruger administration for half a decade, was recalled from Swaziland and appointed Under-Secretary of State. Fluent in three languages, a law agent and someone who a few years later showed an aptitude and taste for covert operations, DJ appears to have got on well with his brother. This meant that, by the final quarter of 1894, Ewald Esselen was not only formally in control of the South African Republic's detective, police and security forces but also that, should he ever need it, he had additional eyes and ears deployed in the heart of State Secretary Dr W Leyds's Department of Foreign Affairs.[65]

When Ewald Esselen's personal aspirations were lined up beside Joubert's vision for southern Africa in this way, they not only complemented one another; they were also not that far removed from Rhodes's expressed desire to see an economic federation in the region as a precursor to a political union. When Esselen became State Attorney, in 1894, the idea of a united South Africa seemed, for some, to be less dream-like.

The mining industry approved of Esselen's modernising police initiative to the point where the Chamber of Mines helped underwrite the cost of the salaries of at least three Pretoria-based operatives – seemingly members of the same family with anglicised names, Charles, Freddy and William Ueckermann – whose task, among others, was to combat the illicit sale of alcohol to black mineworkers on the Rand. Carl Ueckermann – to give him what seems far more likely to have been his real name – appears to have been related to Marais, while Fred Ueckermann worked from within Esselen's government office.[66]

But the Ueckermanns' pedigree aside, in his search for new undercover agents Esselen was fishing in waters that Marais, had been trawling in for months. In late 1893, and presumably with the financial backing and certainly with the knowledge of Charles Leonard and his new masters in the Corner House, the editor of *Land en Volk* had hired a team of private detectives to investigate cases of corruption involving some of Kruger's close political allies. Heading up the Marais's team of sleuths was JP de la Court Schröder, a German-trained spy who had previously served as a policeman in Johannesburg.[67]

It is difficult to imagine that Esselen and Marais, who were as thick as thieves in the weeks before the Jameson Raid and then again immediately thereafter, did not exchange notes about the detectives that they had hired to investigate criminal offences targeting the Chamber of Mines or the government. Moreover, by the same token it is fairly unlikely that between 1893 and mid-1894, when they were dealing almost exclusively with largely criminal investigations, that they did not share with their closest political allies – General Joubert and his son-in-law, Malan – the fact that they were both hiring secret agents.

At some point during the latter half of 1895, as the plot underlying the Jameson Raid took shape, Ewald Esselen, Joubert, Marais and Malan – acting singly or collectively – had access to information obtained from secret agents about a political conspiracy to overthrow the state. Through various acts of commission and omission, they appear to have tolerated Hammond's planned urban revolution, the attempt to capture the Pretoria arsenal and abduct the President and, if necessary, to assist Jameson's filibustering force.

How the principal ingredient in this slow, thickening soup of agents and intelligence-gathering changed from being one initially focused on crime to one more overtly political in character after Hammond assumed command of the conspiracy during the latter part of 1895, can be traced via Esselen's own, growing interest in running undercover operatives. As already noted, it came at the same time that Marais was making use of private detectives to uncover political scandal that could be fed into *Land en Volk*'s stridently Progressive agenda. Once again, one can only speculate that Esselen, playing second fiddle to the ineffectual Joubert, may have been hoping that one day the presidency might fall to him in a reformist dispensation.

What is undeniable is that, after the election of 1892, and more especially so after May 1894, a few leading Progressive elements in Pretoria, who started out with a domestic political agenda of their own, were slowly becoming aligned with other disillusioned elements in the mining industry, in Johannesburg. But the wily State President, having facilitated Esselen's move into the position of State Attorney, sensed the emerging danger and, having second thoughts, began to back-pedal.

CHAPTER SIXTEEN

State Attorney versus State President

1894–1895

When, in May 1894, Kruger appointed Esselen to his cabinet, with the discretionary option of his attending such meetings of the full Executive Council as the State President might determine, it was on the clear understanding that the State Attorney would have a free hand when it came to reforming the detective service and the police force.[1] From the very outset, however, the President and Esselen may have had a few different, as well as several overlapping, personal priorities.

Paradoxically, it may have been Kruger who at first had the greater interest in political intelligence. The appointment of Esselen coincided with the commandeering crisis of May 1894, when the government had botched its attempt at the enforced mobilisation of immigrants for the war against Malaboch so badly that it had precipitated a visit to Pretoria from the British High Commissioner for South Africa, Sir Henry Loch. It was Loch's pointed questions to British residents about their access to arms and military skills that later prompted the formation of the rifle associations in Johannesburg and Pretoria, which received financial backing and political support from the Corner House. It was an alarming development that clearly needed monitoring.

Esselen, while intrigued by the unfolding events, was more interested in justifying his unexpected move into the Kruger government by paying careful attention to the mounting economic grievances of his powerful friends in the mining industry. Paramount among these complaints was the theft of amalgam from the mines and the burgeoning trade in illicit gold buying. In June 1894, the State Attorney appointed a man with a shady past, JW Howcroft, as a 'special detective' in Pretoria. Although Howcroft

attended local meetings of the Rifle Association and Uitlander organisations, and compiled reports containing the names of Rowland Bettington,
Charles Leonard and others, he was more focused on theft of gold amalgam
and jewellery than on politics. It may have been for that reason that, after
six months, Esselen agreed to Howcroft's moving across to Johannesburg.[2]

There Howcroft joined the excellent George W Taylor, who had been
recruited as a fully undercover member of the 'secret service' four weeks
after Howcroft, in July 1894. In 1894, the mix of Taylor's work mirrored that
of Howcroft's. But it was only a matter of weeks before he too came up
with the name of Bettington as a 'mischievous and dangerous person'. By
late 1895, Taylor was fully abreast of ongoing gun-smuggling operations in
Johannesburg and, even though he never mentioned Hammond by name,
he kept Esselen fully informed about unmistakable, proto-revolutionary
activities. If Esselen did not see the coming of the revolt in Johannesburg
then he was either incompetent or stupid – but he was neither.[3]

Howcroft and Taylor were forerunners of a fully-fledged 'secret service'
that was established after the 'Jameson Raid' and was roundly detested in
British imperialist circles.[4] But Esselen's creative reforms in the overlapping
detective, police and 'secret service' functions were hampered by problems
with personnel, who often had shady backgrounds, were corrupt or disloyal
and routinely spied on or undermined each other.[5]

On occasion these machinations extended as far as the State Attorney
himself. When Esselen got wind of the fact that a once trusted confidant
in Pretoria, Detective William Ueckermann, was gossiping about the State
Attorney's heavy drinking, he swiftly transferred him to Johannesburg.
There, demoted and without meaningful work, Ueckermann became a
strong Esselen opponent within the ranks of the local police force.[6]

Esselen and Trimble: the Trojan Horse

Although the chaos that reigned in the state's various security agencies in
1894–1895 cried out for reform, it could, at times, also play directly into
the State Attorney's hands. It meant that, for most of his short tenure in
the cabinet, Esselen alone was capable of understanding fully and directing
the incoming and outgoing flows of intelligence within the new 'secret
service'.[7]

This was a reasonable arrangement during the first months of Esselen's
appointment, when criminal work took precedence over the political. But
once the situation was reversed and the conspiracy to overthrow the government began to eclipse the more mundane problems of illegal alcohol

President SJP Kruger
PHOTO: PROVINCIAL ARCHIVES OF THE FREE STATE, COLLECTION OF
DR HENDRIK MULLER

Advocate Ewald Esselen
PHOTO: *DIE HUISGENOOT*

sales and illicit gold buying on the Witwatersrand, the State Attorney had need of the assistance of a man whose integrity and loyalty was beyond question. Esselen was then on the lookout for someone who understood his awkward position and might sympathise with the aspirations of those 'Progressive' elements being drawn into the orbit of the conspiring mine owners – all that, while helping him to manage the ongoing criminal work on the Rand.

The person who came to fill that role, and whose appointment and retention on the Republic's payroll eventually became a career-ending issue for Esselen, was one Andrew Trimble. Everything that went before in Trimble's career, everything about the timing, positioning and conditions attached to his recruitment, everything about his role as Chief Detective in the South African Republic, everything that he did before and during the days of the urban revolution, and everything that Trimble did thereafter, point to his bravery, loyalty and trustworthiness as a conspirator and to his being an agent of Cecil Rhodes, Ewald Esselen and the Rand mine owners.[8] And, as always with Hammond – who later was at pains to conceal the innermost workings of those behind the Raid – there is a stunning silence around Trimble in the American conspirator's autobiography.

It will be recalled that the barest outline of a plot for a coup in the Zuid-Afrikaansche Republiek – if it should prove necessary – was first fleshed out by Rhodes, Jameson and Hammond during their mining safari through Matabeleland in September 1894. This was followed by the extremely unpleasant and unsuccessful meeting between Rhodes and the State President in Pretoria, on 2 October 1894, after which the mining magnate and Prime Minister of the Cape Colony abandoned all hope of bringing Kruger around to his way of thinking about the need for an economic federation of southern African states. For Rhodes it appears to have been the last straw. As Trimble's daughter, Edith, noted years later in a well-researched but unpublished biography, in 1894: 'Important officials of the Republic, including significantly Mr Ewald Esselen, called on Mr Rhodes during his visit.'[9]

Now, as we know, history proceeds by both chance and design, but, shortly after the camel's back gave way, seemingly antithetical forces began to interact in ways that, in retrospect, are so remarkable as to force us to explore possible links not only between those prominent members of the Pretoria Club – Esselen and Rhodes – but also between them and Andrew Trimble.

Esselen assumed office in May 1894, with a brief to reform the police services and, more especially, to clamp down on the theft and sale of gold amalgam and the illicit sale of alcohol to black miners. Part of the State Attorney's problem, however, lay in ridding the town of its allegedly corrupt Chief Detective, Robert Ferguson, a staunch supporter of the State President whom Kruger cultivated as both an official and a private source of intelligence.

In June 1894, four weeks after taking office, Esselen set an undercover operation in motion when he deployed Detective LB Donovan to monitor Ferguson's shady dealings and to lay the groundwork for his dismissal.[10] At first, Esselen may have been intent only on cleaning up criminal activity within the police, but as this drawn-out morale-sapping exercise unfolded and the mine owners' priorities shifted towards staging a full-scale coup d'état, so too may those of the new State Attorney.

Esselen would have heard of the unsuccessful outcome of the meeting between Rhodes and the President via members of the Executive Council, and if not through them, then via his brother, DJ Esselen, who had just taken up his position as Under-Secretary of State under the influential Dr Leyds, the State Secretary. Either way, it could not have come as news to State Attorney Esselen, who, as we have seen, had already met privately with Rhodes and with whom he had a long-standing relationship of trust.[11]

What exactly transpired at the Rhodes-Esselen meeting in the first week of October 1894 is unknown, but it was one of the most important meetings in the history of southern Africa because, immediately thereafter, the State Attorney manifested the greatest urgency possible in acquiring the services of a new Chief Detective, who would be responsible not only for Johannesburg, where Kruger stalwart Robert Ferguson had long been in control, but for the entire Zuid-Afrikaansche Republiek. All indications point to Rhodes's having told Esselen that the Kruger government would have to be overthrown at a point yet to be determined. The details might have been fuzzy but the intention was clear enough for even Edith Trimble to draw the correct, albeit overstated, inference many years later: Trimble's appointment was pivotal to the conspiracy. 'My father's appointment the following month, in November,' she recorded, 'caused the conspirators to postpone the decision' [to proceed with an immediate attempt at staging a coup d'état].[12]

It is true that the State Attorney may have undertaken the project to find a Chief Detective in good faith, attempting only to accelerate the delivery of better policing for his reform-minded friends in the Chamber of Mines. But, given how he later turned a blind eye to reports from his own secret agents about the rifle clubs and gun-smuggling, it is more likely that he already knew that Rhodes and Hammond were intent on fomenting an urban 'revolution'. Esselen was set on finding how best to position himself in relation to the mine owners, deepen trust and facilitate an outcome that would accommodate Joubert and other 'Progressives' in the long-touted 'provisional government'. If Esselen was doing so, he would not have been on his own. His and Joubert's protégés, Eugène Marais and Abraham Malan, were already aligned in that way.

It was not only the *timing* of Esselen's initiative that was interesting, however, but also where and to whom the State Attorney turned in his accelerated quest to find a Chief Detective. That Esselen turned to the Cape Colony was predictable; it was always the first port of call when trying to finding experienced talent in southern Africa. As a former supporter of the Afrikaner Bond and Member of the Legislative Assembly, Esselen was well-connected in the south. Nor, by the same token, should we be taken aback to learn that he looked first to a brother lawyer, a judge in the Cape Supreme Court, a noted Afrikaner sympathiser and a former Cape premier, Sir Thomas Upington, for assistance. It was Upington, an Irishman from Cork and an advocate who had seen Trimble at work during court proceedings in Kimberley, who facilitated the hasty secondment of the Ulsterman, Trimble, from the Cape Colony's detective force to the Boer republic.[13]

Thomas Upington was a man familiar with Rhodes's ambitions as they related to the encirclement of the Boer states. Indeed, it was Upington, as Prime Minister of the Cape, who authorised the Warren expedition to clear Stellaland and Goshen of Boer filibusters in 1884. It was an initiative that Rhodes was so keen to see brought to a satisfactory conclusion that he made sure that he was personally present. It was also an expedition in which Trimble had served as an intelligence officer attached to the quartermaster's store. Indeed, it was during the Warren expedition that Rhodes first became

acquainted with Trimble. But, curiously, there is no surviving correspondence recording Esselen's original approach to a judge who still enjoyed easy
access to Rhodes.[14]

Esselen used a back channel, rather than a direct approach, to his opposite
number in the Cape ministry. Upington then directed the State Attorney,
again in a way that appears to have avoided any official channels, to obtain
a recommendation from a man possibly of Irish descent, the colonial-born
McLeod B Robinson, by then the Police Commissioner at Kimberley.[15]

Here again Esselen left no paper trail, later noting simply that he had
been in contact with Robinson, who had put two names to him: Detectives
Easton and Trimble. It was only after all the preliminary hard work had been
done via confidential 'Irish' back channels with men all familiar with, and
known to, Rhodes, that the State Attorney was ready to make an official
move that he was willing to leave on record. On 23 October 1894, Esselen
wrote to his opposite number in Cape Town, WP Schreiner, a new member
in the Rhodes ministry, requesting his assistance in the seconding of a man
suitable to assist him in the reorganisation of the Republic's police force.[16]

Here, too, Esselen would have known that he was pushing against an
open door. Schreiner and he were close friends and trusting confidants who
sometimes used nicknames when corresponding informally on important
matters.[17] Schreiner, like Esselen, was the colonial-born son of a German
missionary, a product of the English legal system and a Freemason. They
knew each other from time spent at the South African College prior to
going abroad to further their studies, and both had been admitted to the Bar
in Cape Town before taking up positions either in, or closely linked to, the
Cape Legislative Assembly.

The two also had a great deal in common politically. In the autumn of
1893, Esselen, then a full-time 'Progressive' devoted to unseating Kruger in
the upcoming presidential election, had gone south for private discussions
with certain high-placed Cape Colony officials about the possible future
leadership of the Boer republics.[18] It was during this visit that Esselen and
Schreiner met at the City Club for what became a significant personal
marker for both men.[19]

Confiding in one another, they confessed to having ambitions for the
region that would see inter-state economic agreements on rail tariffs, leading to an economic and then possibly a political federation. There was
nothing unusual in Esselen's taking such a stance; indeed, it reflected a position he shared with the leader of his party, Piet Joubert.[20] More pertinently,
as Schreiner later reminded Esselen, in an anguished letter just after the
Raid, they seemed to agree that Rhodes was the man best placed to further
their 'higher aspirations' for a greater southern Africa, and that Jameson's
folly had left them in a 'bitter position'.[21] It is clear that Esselen, intensely

desirous of holding very high political office, was an admirer of Rhodes before he left the Cape for the north, in 1887, and throughout the months leading up to the Raid.

So when Esselen wrote to Schreiner inquiring about a possible second-ment from Kimberley, in October 1894, Schreiner *knew* what was coming because he had already been informed of McLeod Robinson's recommen-dations to Esselen via the Secretary to the Law Department, JJ Graham. It was at about this point, and in the most senior echelons of a Rhodes minis-try, that the shortlist was reduced to just one name – Trimble.[22]

It is possible but highly improbable that the premier of the Cape, Rhodes, did not know about Trimble's imminent departure from the diamond fields. Perhaps unsurprisingly, given what followed in 1895, no documentary evi-dence of any high-level exchanges around the secondment appears to have survived. And, as significantly, in the 1950s, when Edith Trimble set out to recover a record of her father's service – that of a one-time pensionable employee in the Cape colonial civil service – there was simply no trace of it. The normally fulsome Cape administration archives were, and are, inex-plicably bare.[23]

Matters then proceeded at a pace that, when measured against the pre-vailing tempo of official inter-colonial exchanges, was positively blistering. In less than three weeks – by 18 November – the details of the secondment were hammered out by Robinson in a mining town where Cecil Rhodes was the uncrowned king and Trimble the Chief Detective responsible for curtailing all illegal diamond-buying (IDB) operations.

Esselen, who knew Rhodes and Jameson and had secretly supported their geopolitical goal by thwarting the Adendorff trek into territory nominally controlled by the British South Africa Company, in 1891, was at pains to keep the influential Cape network that he had used to secure Trimble's secondment – no mean feat in its own right, albeit one with a precedent – as secret as possible at the Pretoria end.[24] The detective's appointment, as well as the conditions of service attached to the 'secondment', stank to high heaven, and Trimble, as aware of it as was Esselen, did his best to conceal it by dissembling and lying about it *before* the final planning of the uprising was in place.[25]

In May 1895, Trimble told a commission of inquiry that 'I know nothing about whose influence secured my appointment. I believe I was selected from the whole of the Cape Colony to come here.' He continued: 'As far as I am aware my appointment was the result of a conference' between Mr McLeod Robinson, Commissioner of Police at Kimberley and the State Attorney (Esselen).[26] Could that really have been so? Could Esselen, a cabinet minister in an independent Boer republic, successfully negotiate the secondment of an Acting Chief Detective from the most important industrial centre of a British colony after a nationwide search, without securing the written approval of his ministerial counterpart in one of Her Majesty's governments?[27]

It had to have been Trimble himself who, some decades later, told Colvin, Jameson's biographer, that it had actually been Sir Thomas Upington who had initially facilitated the secondment. Upington, one assumes, was acting at Rhodes's behest in order to accommodate Esselen's request to get a Cape official to be released for duty in the South African Republic. And, if that is so, it would help explain several things relating to Upington, Jameson and Trimble and the sequel on the Rand, which, at face value, are equally puzzling for those of an inquiring mind.

First, it was apparently just by chance that Sir Thomas Upington was visiting Johannesburg on 27 December 1895, when he heard it openly stated that Jameson and 800 men were on the border waiting to invade the Republic. He attributed his source to a Free State 'Dutchman', but it would be surprising if, at the time, he had not obtained at least some of his information from his nominee, Trimble. It is as remarkable that in the subsequent Cape Colony's Select Committee of Inquiry into the Jameson Raid, chaired by Sir Thomas, neither he nor WP Schreiner saw fit to disclose that they had both been actively involved in the secondment of Mr Trimble to the South African Republic.[28]

Hammond later portrayed the Cape Select Committee as being dominated by an 'anti-Rhodes faction' rather than by a few former disillusioned supporters, some of whom were indirectly, albeit possibly even unwittingly, involved in setting up the Esselen-Trimble collaboration.[29] But the whiff of a cover-up gets stronger when one learns that Sir Thomas Upington – then as the newly installed Attorney General in a Gordon Sprigg ministry – was also the Chairman of the Select Committee. Again, this is explicable only if one assumes that the Cape government was officially unaware of Upington's role in Trimble's secondment.

But what is less easily explained is why the carefully worded minority report to the findings of the Committee, which sought to exonerate Rhodes and the Chartered Company of *any* responsibility for the Raid, was penned by none other than Sir Thomas Upington.[30] Such sentiments, badly out of keeping with those of the majority and from someone known to be sympathetic to the Boers – including, no doubt, Esselen – fit with those of a man who was himself indirectly involved in the build-up to the Jameson Raid, and might not have wanted his own role in the Trimble affair fully exposed.

Nor did Attorney General Upington's concealed interest in mitigating the consequences of the Jameson Raid for those in Kimberley end there. In the aftermath of the Raid, Gardner Williams, the General Manager of De Beers and the American consul in the city, was charged for his role as

Hammond's arms smuggler-in-chief, but received only a nominal fine. So slight was the rap across Williams' knuckles that the US government failed to relieve him of his position as consul.[31]

But, to return to Trimble, it is also worth noting just how fuzzy his conditions of service were upon leaving Kimberley and taking up his new position under Esselen. Both Cape Town and Pretoria appear to have been unusually lax in terms of setting out the conditions under which he would be seconded from a British colony to a Boer republic – an unusual, if not a unique, arrangement. Trimble, a man eligible for early retirement if he so wished, received his offer of an appointment from Esselen, by telegram only, and replied, also by telegram, the following day, on 18 or 19 November 1894.[32]

He was 'still in the service of the Cape government', Trimble told members of the commission in Johannesburg some months later, and it paid him 'a nominal shilling a day' for service that was pensionable. By then some insiders in the Kruger administration already suspected that he may have been a 'British agent', and that he was being funded secretly by the Cape government under Rhodes.[33] In the same hearing he told the commissioners that, as of 18 May 1895, he had 'leave of absence for three months more', that is, until mid-August 1895. But when that period expired he was reappointed by Esselen at the specific request of the Chamber of Mines, headed by none other than an arch-conspirator, Lionel Phillips.[34]

Trimble went on to tell the commission that 'if there was a war between England and this country, and I was in the service here, I would fight for this country'.[35] Strange that, because, as things turned out, while admittedly not 'in service' at the time of the Hammond-planned uprising, Trimble chose to become actively involved as a rifle distributor and a would-be cavalryman willing to ride to the rescue of Jameson. Likewise, it is interesting to note who stepped forward – again, months *before* the uprising – to act as 'character witnesses' when Trimble's fitness to hold office was being probed: HEO Green and G Richards.[36] True, both men were originally from Kimberley, which suited Trimble's needs, but, by May 1895, Green was Assistant Secretary at the Chamber of Mines, where Phillips held sway, while Richards, Manager of Consolidated Gold Fields, was drawn, quite literally, from Hammond's office.

But what precisely was it that made Trimble so acceptable as a man who, even with or without the knowledge of an Upington or an Esselen, might be able to infiltrate the security agencies of the ZAR on behalf of Rhodes, Hammond and all the other Jameson Raid conspirators?[37] How did they – if not Esselen – *know* that Trimble would prove to be a trustworthy ally in any uprising? The answer was that Rhodes bore personal knowledge of him and had seen him operating at close quarters while 'in service'.

As a young man Trimble joined the 6th Inniskilling Dragoons in County Fermanagh and was part of the regiment when it was mobilised for the Anglo-Boer War of 1881. But the war ended before the Dragoons could be deployed and Trimble, along with others, such as Rowland Bettington, was humiliated by the defeat of the British at Majuba. After the war, Trimble rose through the ranks of the police force in Durban but resigned as a sergeant when he was offered the position of third-class detective in Kimberley, around 1883.[38]

But it was during the Warren expedition of 1884–1885 that Trimble caught the eye of higher-ups such as Rhodes. They were clearly impressed, because it was directly after the Warren expedition that Trimble's career as a detective in Kimberley took off. Not only were his political instincts solidly anti-Boer, but he could be trusted with gems worth thousands of pounds while conducting frequent undercover operations aimed at curbing illicit diamond buying.[39]

But both Rhodes's and Dr Jameson's acquaintance with Trimble went beyond professional duties. Both notables visited the home of the Chief Detective sufficiently frequently for some in the family to form strong opinions about them. Jameson, who was rumoured to have led an interesting life among the ladies of Kimberley after dark, or so the family tradition had it, once benefited from a Trimble favour when the Chief Detective had a woman deported who, it was thought, was in danger of ruining the Doctor's reputation.[40]

According to his daughter, Edith, Andrew Trimble 'admired Rhodes' and, even though he had some reservations about the magnate's scruples, 'was able to discuss anything at all with Rhodes'. Rhodes confided in the IDB detective about the fortunes of the diamond industry and, over time, Trimble became familiar with 'Rhodes' schemes, dreams, plans, big ideas, "visions", call them what you will'. Being blessed with a cool head, so Edith claimed, allowed her father to have a 'calming influence' on Rhodes.[41] Andrew Trimble himself was as clear as he could be without ever revealing his role as Rhodes's secret agent in the conspiracy. 'I had the honour,' he later recorded, 'of carrying out the most confidential work for Mr Rhodes, both in connection with Imperial matters as well as other matters connected with recovering stolen diamonds ...'[42]

There was good reason for Rhodes to trust Trimble with his life – indeed, on one occasion he had apparently done so quite literally. In 1891, drawing their inspiration from the radical American organisation bearing the same name, economically marginalised white diggers in Kimberley had formed a chapter of the Knights of Labor. Strongly opposed to all manifestations of monopoly capitalism, the Knights were soon active across the diamond fields and suspected of having been behind the dynamiting of the De Beers head office. More pertinently, Trimble had hidden in the ceiling of a hotel where he heard a leading Knight take an oath to assassinate Rhodes – a plot that the Chief Detective then managed to foil.[43]

Mr Rhodes had good reason to befriend Trimble and to call on him. Mrs Trimble, however, was no admirer of either Rhodes or Jameson, which must have made for some awkwardness. As Edith recalled conversations with her mother decades later:

> Modest, lovely, reserved she had not liked Cecil Rhodes with his curious way of speaking when he had visited them in Kimberley. How could she have liked Dr Jameson their family doctor for having told her husband to slap her face hard when she showed signs of hysteria?[44]

As Gilbert and Sullivan would have agreed, the lot of an IDB detective's or of a secret agent's wife was not a happy one.

Be that as it may, in the South African Republic, in the mid-1890s, Esselen and the mining companies had need of a man who could deal with the theft, smuggling or sale of hundreds of ounces of illicitly acquired gold amalgam on the Rand. What is revealing, however, is that it was not only Trimble who moved north after his hasty and puzzling secondment. Within weeks of his arrival in Johannesburg, Trimble put pressure on the State Attorney to appoint additional detectives to assist him in his work. Despite a short and not wholly convincing campaign to try to recruit the sons of Boer farmers, he soon settled on four or five men, *all* of whom he knew from Kimberley. Trimble's supposedly temporary move was thus backed up by other, permanent appointments, approved of by Esselen, who, at the time of the former's secondment hinted that Trimble's own appointment would, in all probability, also become permanent.[45]

The net effect was that as the uprising on the Rand approached during the last quarter of 1895 – and even *after* Esselen had resigned his position and his former Chief Detective had been dismissed – Trimble remained in informal contact with a set of agents, detectives if you will, who had privileged access to extremely sensitive political information in Pretoria and in Johannesburg. Some of this, one may speculate, might even have been fed to him by Eugène Marais – who, like Hammond, was a Freemason – or Abraham Malan.[46] As Colvin recorded, throughout the Jameson Raid, Trimble, using 'certain secret societies with which he was acquainted', organised 'a secret service, which penetrated even into the Department of State and kept a close watch on the government in Pretoria'. Thus it was that, via an intercepted telegram sent from Zeerust to Kruger, Trimble got to hear of Jameson's unexpected, 'mad' invasion fully 24 hours before even Hammond and other leading Reformers were informed of it![47]

It is interesting to reflect, in passing, on how Trimble operated during the high days of the Rand upheavals. We need to ask from which of the core conspirators, other than Colonel Frank Rhodes, the senior army officer he respected most of all, the former Acting Chief Detective might have been taking instructions and receiving his funding in late 1895.

After Trimble had effectively been dismissed by Kruger's Executive Council, in mid-November 1895, he insisted on staying on in Johannesburg. At short notice, without capital of his own to back so ambitious a venture, he immediately set up a private detective agency that employed several ex-Kimberley detectives, all of whom had previously been recruited and deployed by him with Esselen's explicit approval.

As a man familiar with intelligence, secret service and undercover protocols from his experiences in Durban, Kimberley and the Warren expedition, not to mention a brief exposure to Scotland Yard in London, in 1891, Trimble had a wealth of British and colonial experience to draw on as he sought a template for the new agency. It is curious, then, that of all models available to him he chose to construct it and run it along the lines of the 'Pinkerton Agency', an outfit that he, personally, bore no knowledge of, and that subsequently he and all the detectives he had engaged 'became the employees of the Reform Committee'.[48]

There was only one man among the key conspirators who admired Pinkerton agents, knew how they operated, had hired and worked with them, and who subsequently cast himself as having been the man in charge of intelligence during the Jameson Raid. That man was, of course, the veteran of the Coeur d'Alene mining wars, John Hays Hammond.

Trimble was the ultimate professional. 'Neither the fact that he was attached to the Intelligence Service,' Edith Trimble later recalled, 'nor that he was in the Secret Service was ever disclosed by him.' She had to work it out for herself years later. She accepted that he had been involved in 'Secret Service' but somehow could not bring herself to believe that he had been a Rhodes-Esselen agent from the moment of his recruitment, in November 1894, right up until the moment that he eluded and then escaped from the Kruger forces in early January 1896.[49]

Whether Esselen was fully aware or not of what he had done and of all its implications, he had, over 12 months, between November 1894 and 1895, allowed a Rhodes-Hammond agent in the shape of Trimble to penetrate the South African Republic's overlapping state security agencies and link up with the mining house conspirators. But the State Attorney had made another error in assuming that he alone was aware of the worrying circumstances in which Trimble and his team of Kimberley imports had materialised. With the Johannesburg uprising drawing ever closer, by the closing weeks of 1895 Esselen was scrambling for a reason to resign. So badly had Trimble's recruitment been handled that the State President and others in the government had long since begun to entertain the suspicion that maybe Esselen, but certainly Trimble, was trying to advance Rhodes's imperialist objectives.[50]

Indeed, Kruger had reached the conclusion that both Esselen and Trimble had to go by late May 1895, fully six months *before* Trimble was sidelined and Esselen resigned.[51] In order to appreciate how the State President got his insight into what was happening within the State Attorney's portfolio, and why he allowed Esselen to jump before he could be pushed, we need to understand Kruger's political instincts and tactical sense.

The Bush Telegraph and the People's President: Boer intelligence and the coming of the Jameson Raid

It was not only the British imperialists spread around southern Africa in the mid-1890s that underestimated President Kruger's political ability, capacity for statesmanship or his popularity with the broad mass of his people. Afrikaner-Dutch nationalists, educated townsfolk and various professionals in Jong Zuid-Afrika often forget that they were easily outnumbered by farmers. The Boers were a God-fearing, semi-literate Christian people who placed a premium on face-to-face meetings, honesty and plain speaking, and they stood second to none when it came to bravery, cunning born of rural hardship or a love of republicanism. It was these same 'backward' people that elected Kruger as their president four times between 1881 and 1898.

It was precisely *because* the President understood the frailties and strengths of small communities steeped in Old Testament beliefs and people who wanted to *talk* rather than write to him, that Kruger made certain that he remained personally accessible. In Pretoria, where he often spent part of the day sitting on the front stoep of his house, Kruger was as famously approachable as he was out on the streets. More importantly, he made a point of travelling through the rural districts each year, chatting to his male voters and their wives.

Personal interactions within his wider constituency kept the State President informed about the latest economic, political and social prattle. But, in a state in which some of the borders were still subject to disputation by African tribes and British imperialists contesting Boer claims, there was also a good deal of talk about the Boer commando system and the preparedness of the Commandant-General Joubert for military or security operations. During Jameson's invasion, Kruger often learned about the latest developments well before Piet Joubert did.[52]

Just two examples will remind us of how adept Kruger was at keeping the lines of communication open. First, as early as May 1894, at the time of the conscription crisis, he was already being informed privately about developments in American and other Uitlander circles by Hammond's nemesis – R E 'Barbarian' Brown. It was a private channel that remained open to, and that was used by, the President right into the critical days of the Raid.[53]

Second, as early as August 1894, just 12 weeks after Esselen had assumed office and some months before the planning for the Jameson Raid took shape, the President had met privately with the politically adroit Police Commandant DE Schutte and the man who was then still Johannesburg's Chief Detective, Robert Ferguson – both Kruger loyalists. At that meeting, attended by an unnamed third party but with the State Attorney noticeably absent, they had a discussion about the Maxim gun – the weapon that Jameson had used to such devastating effect against Ndebele tribesmen in 'Rhodesia', in 1893, and thought he would use to defeat the Boers when the filibusters invaded. Ferguson claimed that it was immediately after *that* meeting that Esselen redoubled his efforts to have him entrapped.[54]

Likewise, it is significant that after Ferguson had been forced to resign for reasons that had as much to do with his questionable effectiveness as a criminal investigator as it had to do with his political loyalties to the State President, he continued to be active in the Fordsburg Vigilance Committee, a civic structure dominated by Kruger loyalists intent on getting rid of both Esselen and Trimble. In this way, when Trimble's appointment was finally vetoed by the Executive Council on the grounds that he was not a naturalised citizen, in 1895, Ferguson was ready to once again become Johannesburg's Chief Detective.[55]

Nor was the State President content to confine his intelligence-gathering to the capital and countryside; he was equally interested in political developments taking place among his cabinet members and the mine owners.[56] In that regard it was often the State Secretary, WJ Leyds, who urged upon Kruger the necessity of employing secret agents or other trusted confidants to become involved in deep undercover work.[57] The President's ability to deal with the personalities and the inter-personal politics of members of the Executive Council was, of course, not immune to some counter-manipulation. That became increasingly apparent during the months leading up to the Johannesburg uprising and Jameson's ill-disciplined charge across the Highveld. At that time the interaction between Kruger, Esselen, Joubert and EJP Jorissen – born and educated in Holland – become a subject of real interest.

Jorissen, an independent-minded, unlovable man who in his later years suffered mental health problems, had drifted in and out of Kruger's favour over many years. By training a theologian with liberal views, he had, upon emigrating, re-tooled himself as a lawyer, earning the displeasure of a profession priding itself on keeping numbers low and fees high. Having earlier served as State Attorney in a Kruger cabinet, Jorissen was later made a Judge of the Supreme Court in 1890.[58]

The State President approved of Jorissen's fiercely supportive stance on the question of Boer independence and often put his legal skills to good use when it came to constitutional matters. But, perhaps as importantly, Kruger also drew succour from Jorissen's dislike of, and reservations about, his own long-standing rival, General Joubert. Jorissen and Piet Joubert had clashed on various issues over many years. But, in the latter half of 1895, as the conspiracy to overthrow the government deepened, two developments centred on Jorissen appear to have pricked Ewald Esselen's interest. Not only was Kruger once again drawing Jorissen – who craved recognition – closer to him, but the Judge was showing an unhealthy interest in the doings of not only Piet Joubert but also of his son-in-law, Abraham Malan.

It was at this testing juncture, in August and September 1895, just weeks before Esselen resigned from his position, that he enlisted Jorissen's services and had him, and a second agent, sent to the far northeast of the republic. By sending a Judge of the Supreme Court to Vendaland in the guise of a game hunter to investigate possible arms smuggling from Portuguese East Africa on the eve of the mine owners' 'revolution', Esselen was trying to kill two birds with one stone. He was not only isolating Jorissen from Joubert and Malan but also trying to keep him clear of political developments in Pretoria and Johannesburg. But, as we shall see in due course, the secret mission did nothing to curb Jorissen's interest in Joubert and Malan, or in the Raid. On the contrary, it only heightened his interest in political intrigue and reinforced his desire to provide Kruger with inside information.[59]

As noted, long before Jorissen ever went to Vendaland Kruger had started doubting the wisdom of his having tried to fend off 'Progressive' criticism by appointing Esselen and allowing him a free hand in running the detectives, police force and secret agents. Then, as now, the State President was portrayed as being too conservative, cautious and slow in responding to challenges to his authority or that of his government. It was a view not entirely devoid of merit when applied to some of his policies as they related to Johannesburg or the mining industry. But what many critics misunderstood was just how well Kruger had mastered the element of timing in the art of the possible.

Kruger had a remarkable ability to test the depth and strength of an opponent's political resolve through the exercise of brinkmanship. It was a quality much in evidence during the Warren expedition, as well as in the 'drifts crisis' shortly before Jameson invaded the country. Likewise, the State President was adept at allowing events or people to take their course until the moment arrived to take decisive action. Allow the fruit to ripen and fall before rushing in to collect the prize was a maxim that Kruger followed, sometimes almost to a fault.

The same quality was on display during the run-up to Jameson's invasion, when Kruger was said to have remarked that, in order to kill a tortoise, you had to wait for it to extend its head before cutting it off. The mistake that many contemporary analysts and observers made, however, was to think that Kruger was willing to use that tactic only when dealing with other states, in the field of foreign relations. The fact is that he was equally adept at using it in domestic politics, and he employed it brilliantly in dealing with Esselen and Trimble.

In the wake of a series of dramatic murders, in Johannesburg, during the opening months of 1895, Hammond, drawing on a repertoire of political tricks inspired by San Franciscan history, had persuaded Rowland Bettington, Lionel Phillips and others to test the political waters by setting up a Vigilance Committee demanding reform of the detective division and police force.[60]

Unfortunately for the conspirators, however, their short-lived Vigilance Committee spawned an unusual suburban offshoot. In Fordsburg, the Afrikaner-Dutch citizens suddenly took at least as much interest in the composition of the detective division and the police force as did their more numerous English-speaking counterparts, because the agencies were among the few employers willing to take on burghers and their sons. Stephanus Lombaard and Izak de Vries, conservatives wary of the State Attorney and unsettled by the arrival of Trimble and his Kimberley posse, drafted a petition demanding his dismissal and requesting an urgent audience with the State President.[61]

Kruger responded by calling a meeting of his full Executive Council, thus forcing Esselen to acknowledge that Trimble's appointment had never been formally sanctioned and that the State Attorney had only 'spoken privately to the President about the matter'. Kruger then interjected, saying that he had expressed his dissatisfaction with the appointment at the time, implying that it was not only the process followed during Trimble's mysterious appointment, which, in truth, *was* broadly in line with the 'free hand' that he had given Esselen, but also that he had developed serious reservations about the detective himself. With the rabbit flushed, Kruger let loose the dogs, ordering a commission of inquiry to examine the legality and operations of the entire detective division in Johannesburg.

The President had long since sized Trimble up, during several face-to-face meetings, as being a secret agent. Trimble might have unwittingly reinforced Kruger's suspicions by telling him, to his face, that unless he undertook serious police reforms being urged upon him, 'You will have British troops within five years.'[62] That was merely a variation on what Rhodes had said to Kruger in October 1894.

The 'Detective Inquiry' sat early in May 1895, and the commissioners – Kruger stalwarts – used the excuse of an apparently irregular acquisition of horses in Kimberley by Trimble to probe his appointment and the structure and function of the Johannesburg detective division. But it was less of a forensic inquiry about horses than a political ploy about courses by the State President, and it succeeded in exposing how problematic Trimble's appointment had been, as well as the role that Esselen had played in it. It was classic Kruger; the commission adjourned, *sine die*, making no real findings at all.

It was only *after* the State Attorney and Acting Chief Detective had been publicly exposed, during the course of hearings that were widely reported on in the Witwatersrand press, that Kruger privately arrived at the conclusion that Esselen and Trimble both had to lose their positions.[63] And still the President chose not to act, being content to play the waiting game by going so far as to suggest, in a formal letter to Esselen, written on 29 May 1895, that he still enjoyed Kruger's confidence.[64] It was only when Trimble was refused naturalisation and lost his position, in November 1895, that Esselen got an excuse to resign and the tortoise lost its head.

After his hasty resignation Esselen, accompanied by his former Secretary, Charles Rorke, left for the Cape Colony for a month at some point in the first week of December 1895. He did so only after having publicly reaffirmed his commitment to the former Acting Chief Detective and other Johannesburg-based detectives who had also been dismissed for not being naturalised citizens. He did so in fulsome fashion at a farewell dinner for Trimble that was attended almost exclusively by his own ex-Kimberley loyalists. Trimble, by then running his own Pinkerton-like outfit, in turn heaped praise on Ewald Esselen.[65]

By the end of the first week of December 1895, in the midst of a deep conspiracy to overthrow the Kruger government, Esselen was already in the Cape where, should he have wanted to do so, he or his trusted assistant, Rorke, would have had ample opportunity to meet with Rhodes or his agents or, if necessary, with members of the Reform Committee visiting the great man.

Trimble, however, remained in Johannesburg even though he had lost his position and was ostensibly still a serving officer in the Cape Colony, a man who berated Kruger and praised Esselen. He intended staying on, he said, with his 'reformist' sympathies out in the open and increasingly on public display.[66]

But the links between Esselen, Trimble, Rhodes, Hammond and conspirators in the mining industry had not given way; they had merely become a bit less visible. The remaining threads connecting the Afrikaner-Dutch collaborators to the planned urban uprising and a 'provisional government' held firm, and when Jameson jumped the gun and headed for the Witwatersrand the Boer fifth column was left with the unenviable task of extricating itself from a treasonous conspiracy. We will now examine in greater detail how exactly the fifth column behaved during the days of the Raid itself, to determine precisely how involved the Boer collaborators were.

CHAPTER SEVENTEEN

Mobilisation and Manoeuvring

1895–1896

The fifth column – Piet Joubert, Ewald Esselen, Eugène Marais and Abraham Malan – like John Hays Hammond, never envisaged the overthrow of the South African Republic. Nor did they or Hammond – republicans to a man – wish to see the republic incorporated immediately, or ever, into the British Empire as a mere colony, even if that was the secret ambition of Cecil Rhodes. And the last thing that they or Hammond wanted was for Jameson to set out on some madcap invasion, thereby unleashing international military and political forces that would prove impossible for them to control and limit possibilities for a more realistically aligned political economy.

Rather, what the Boer collaborators and many of the mine owners appear to have looked to was an armed uprising in Johannesburg that might see a military stand-off, which, in turn, would pave the way for the collapse of the Kruger government. Hammond, however, had private misgivings about the stand-off strategy that he never revealed fully to his co-conspirators. Drawing on incidents in Californian history, as was his wont, he hoped to guarantee the outcome of the uprising by raiding the state arsenal in Pretoria and abducting the State President for a forced 'negotiation' back on the Witwatersrand. And, as with Asbury Harpending, in San Francisco, in 1861, 'Our plans were to paralyse all organised resistance by simultaneous attack.'[1]

With Kruger staring down the barrel of a gun, the mine owners would usher in the progressively inclined 'provisional government' in which Joubert or Esselen – or both – would play leading roles.[2] That, in turn, could lead to public endorsement via an expanded electorate in which Uitlanders on the goldfields would not only enjoy the franchise but also wield greater influence. For Hammond, drawing on American experiences and hoping privately for a slightly modified outcome, the new government would usher in a separate, regional, constitutional dispensation for the Witwatersrand. The District of Columbia might serve as a model that would not do violence to the overall architecture of a modern Boer republic.[3]

In Hammond's hoped-for regime, the Boers would remain in control of the republic, thereby retaining significant control of the supply of cheap black labour for their farms. Enfranchised Uitlanders would, however, guarantee the untrammelled development of the mining industry, helping to create an expanding market for farmers who, in turn, would prosper from an ever-expanding urban sector that would supposedly ensure better balanced economic growth.

In short, what most of the mine owners wanted was a new dispensation in terms of political economy – a shift from the dominant, existing 'maize and gold' alignment to a reprioritised 'gold and maize' dispensation or, at worst, a more equitable system of power-sharing approximating a genuine partnership. The Boer collaborators, for the most part, wished to see an end to the corruption that flowed from Kruger's concessions policy, which seemed to privilege foreigners and 'Jews', and a civil service with more educated Afrikaners in the upper echelons instead of the detested Hollanders.[4]

All of those dreams, along with any that Rhodes and Jameson might have entertained privately, died somewhere out in the scrub around Pitsani on the night that the Doctor, much taken with the exploits of Clive of India and a few frontier tales from America, mounted his horse and suddenly felt six feet tall. In that same instant, 320 kilometres away, Hammond's huge ego suddenly shrank, causing him to switch from advocating a full-blooded armed revolution to a mere paper-waving exercise demanding reform. And the four ambitious, resentful Boer collaborators, intent on lowering the State President into the political grave they had been digging for him since 1891, realised instantly, and to their horror, that Kruger's corpse was up and a-twitching. For a week or more, dreams and nightmares swapped partners regularly, dancing their way through the long night into the dawn of a new reality.

Ewald Esselen

Of the four collaborators who left fingerprints of a sort on the documents relating to the Jameson Raid, few are as badly smudged or as difficult to read as those of Ewald Esselen. Those of a charitable disposition will point to the fact that he did not compromise or embarrass the State President by resigning from his position as State Attorney, in public fashion, before Kruger had to fire him. Likewise, defenders will point to the fact that, once the Raid got under way, Esselen rushed to assure the President of his loyalty to the republic.[5] Moreover, there can be little doubt that it was the folly of Jameson's Raid that turned Esselen back into a strong anti-imperialist supporter of the republican government – his dominant political reflex – even though thereafter he continued to remain a close admirer of, and adviser to, an ever more out-of-favour General Joubert.

Esselen's was not an unusual political position for avant-garde Afrikaner nationalists to adopt *after* the Raid.[6] JC Smuts and his trusted lieutenant, Mostyn Cleaver, another member of Jong Zuid-Afrika, also switched and became notable Kruger and republican loyalists after 1895. One modernising strand of 'Progressive' Afrikaner-Dutch nationalism lay buried beneath the political rubble of the Jameson Raid. Thereafter, most Afrikaner 'intellectuals' were left stranded in the face of populist republicans with agendas ever more ethnic and racist.[7] As Smuts warned Esselen, a loose cannon albeit a brother advocate, in 1899: 'It is a time for us to work *silently*.'[8]

But no apologia can dispel fully the notion that Esselen bore foreknowledge of the mine owners' plans for the coming of an armed urban uprising that might culminate in a military stand-off, even if he did not initially know about their additional hope for an attack on the state arsenal or Hammond's secret plan to abduct the State President. Through Esselen's acts of omission, and those of commission by Marais and Malan, he was indirectly, if not directly, implicated in the mine owners' conspiracy for an uprising and a subsequent change of regime. Nor were his behaviour and words in the weeks leading up to Jameson's unexpected invasion, or in the days immediately thereafter, either by date or deed such to suggest that he was not aware of his role in a conspiracy gone badly wrong.

Esselen probably first met Rhodes around 1885 when, as a member of the recently formed Afrikaner Bond, he briefly represented the constituency of Richmond in the Legislative Assembly of the Cape Colony. It may have been love at first sight. Charismatic and outcome-driven, both men had hopes of political success that easily transcended the confines of the colony. Esselen, a confidant and friend of President Kruger's, saw his immediate future in law, north of the Vaal, where between 1886 and 1890, he served as a criminal court judge. It was not long after this, in 1887, that he approached Rhodes to assist him with that personal loan for an undisclosed amount. Rhodes's geopolitical imperial aspirations were already becoming limitless, and by 1890 he had cemented his political relationship with Cape Afrikaner nationalists such as Esselen.[9]

Whether Esselen's decision to resign from his position on the bench and become actively involved in politics postdated Rhodes's 1890 visit to Pretoria is not clear. But, whatever the reason, the two were good, some said great, friends, and Esselen's return to political life was bound to have been discussed when Rhodes, brimming with long-term imperial visions for southern Africa visited the capital. It may also have been at this juncture that Esselen saw, not for the first time, the possibility of reaching a variant on the *modus vivendi* that Rhodes and the Bond had pioneered in the Cape. The medium-term political needs of nationalists and imperialists could – seemingly – be reconciled.

While in Pretoria, Rhodes attempted – unsuccessfully – to get Esselen to secure for him an interview with Kruger in the hope of selling the idea of a loose economic federation of states to the State President. Esselen, described by one close contemporary at the time as a 'political adventurer', would act as interpreter for the two great political powerhouses of the era. But Kruger was not going to be steamrollered into a meeting, and in the end Rhodes left, allegedly muttering to Esselen, 'The old devil! I meant to work with him, but I'm not going on my knees to him. I've got my concession [the royal charter for the British South Africa Company] and he can do nothing.'[10]

Kruger did not want the landlocked Zuid-Afrikaansche Republiek (ZAR) to be encircled by British imperialists or forced into a federation without putting up a fight. So, for some months in early 1891, with the country mired in an economic downturn, he did not intervene actively when a number of disgruntled Boers in the north of the republic began thinking that the grass was greener on the far side of the Limpopo, in Chartered Company territory. Things came to a head when the leader of the dissidents, Louis Adendorff, allegedly obtained a concession from African chiefs to establish a Boer settlement that might come to enjoy access to the east coast via southeastern Mashonaland. The prospect of Boers, Kruger sympathisers, 'invading' territory under the control of the British South Africa Company, rather than the Chartered Company's police invading the Transvaal, as happened in 1895, alarmed Rhodes and his friend and confidant Jameson.

In May 1891, Rhodes sent several intermediaries, including Jameson, to meet with Kruger in an effort to get the State President to dissuade Adendorff from trekking into what was eventually to become Rhodesia. The conduit Jameson and his political lieutenants used to set up discussions was a close friend of Esselen and Eugène Marais – Jim Taylor – a man who both spoke *die taal* and enjoyed easy access to Kruger.[11]

Kruger, an exponent of brinkmanship, gradually changed his position on the wisdom of a Boer move north, and it was his personal disapproval, along with a government proclamation, that did most to undermine the legitimacy of the proposed exodus. In the end, however, it took an armed stand-off on the banks of the Limpopo between Jameson and his company police and the trekkers to put a stop to what seemed like a Boer 'invasion'.[12] Adendorff's retreat fed into Jameson's growing contempt for Boer fighting prowess and ended in his and the company policemen's humiliation at Doornkop in January 1896.

But the real question was who, or what, caused Kruger to move from tolerating, perhaps even encouraging, the trek north to active opposition? It most certainly was not Jameson. The covert intervention, it seems, may have come indirectly, via Joubert, who was being advised by someone who not only had insight into constitutional and geopolitical problems, but might also have been working on behalf of Rhodes and his new interest.

By late 1891 there was at least one person, perhaps more, in Pretoria who had a shrewd idea as to who was the moving force behind the scenes. It seems likely that he or she may have been a journalist. This unknown observer regularly clipped items of biographical interest from the *Weekly Press*, a local newspaper. The printed extracts were then pasted onto sheets of plain white paper, to which handwritten comments were added, and posted to Flora Shaw, in London. Shaw, who was the colonial editor at *The Times*, later acted as intermediary between Joseph Chamberlain and Rhodes, and was made to testify at the inquiry into the events that led up to the Jameson Raid.

In late 1891, shortly before Shaw set out on a trip to South Africa, her secret informant in Pretoria posted her another short biography, this time of Esselen. Under the heading 'Private Notes', Shaw's correspondent wrote:

> Mr Esselen is a great friend of Mr Cecil Rhodes. He had the notoriety of being the British South Africa's [*sic*] secret agent at Pretoria during the trek troubles in June 1891 and was looked upon with suspicion by burghers and govt. He is a clever advocate, but unprincipled and very ambitious. Leader of the General Joubert faction, and would be State Secretary should Joubert ever become State President.[13]

It was also around mid-1891 that Esselen, acting as a surety at the bank, put up the money for Marais and partner to buy the newspaper *Land en Volk*, which soon became the oppositional mouthpiece *par excellence* for those opposed to 'Krugerism'.[14]

Because he did not then occupy an official position, Esselen had been unable to insert himself as interpreter when Kruger met Jameson in 1891; the role that day fell to the State Secretary, Dr Leyds. Esselen, like his older brother Daniël, who later worked under Leyds, was, however, always comfortable playing the role of intermediary. Interpreting was a role that provided Ewald Esselen with privileged access to the private conversations of powerful men during negotiations of historic importance. In 1881–1883, he twice assisted Kruger in the constitutional talks with statesmen and advisers that culminated in the London Convention of 1884.[15] True, he had missed out when Jameson came to consult Kruger, in 1891, but, some three years later, he got another chance when, as State Attorney, he was summoned to interpret, in Pretoria, on 2 October 1894. It seemed to vindicate Esselen's earlier decision to try and squeeze a little nationalist milk from an imperialistic cow growing steadily fatter.

Rhodes, having completed the grand conspiratorial safari through Matabeleland with John Hays Hammond and Leander Starr Jameson, again requested, and this time was granted, an interview with Kruger. By then, Esselen had been State Attorney for six months. It was a very scratchy meeting between an ambitious imperialist and a dyed-in-the-wool nationalist, in the course of which Esselen got possibly the first inkling of the revolutionary agenda of the Witwatersrand mine owners. It may also have given him more insight into what the future of the republic might look like if Jong Zuid-Afrikaners of his and Marais's ilk positioned themselves intelligently and strategically. It was just days after that historic Rhodes-Kruger exchange that Esselen moved to secure the secondment of Andrew Trimble.

It was probably Esselen and/or Marais who later briefed their friend, the journalist John Scoble, about what transpired during that fiery exchange between Rhodes and Kruger in 1894: 'Mr Rhodes informed [Kruger] *that he would lose his country* unless he changed his mode of government and his strictures were so severe that the interpreter was almost afraid to translate them literally.'[16] Not long thereafter, Esselen may have caught another glint of revolution in the eyes of a Rhodes messenger.

In early March 1895, Rhodes sent an unknown emissary north to try and obtain backing from the Boer republics in an attempt to set up a customs union that might eventually further regional political integration. The emissary, clearly on intimate terms with the great man, met GA Middelberg, Resident Director of the Netherlands Railway Company, and Daniël Esselen, by then Under-Secretary of State in the Pretoria administration, at some undisclosed venue. The telegram that followed from the Rhodes man was sent from the border village of Viljoensdrift.

In a lengthy telegram, the Cape premier's representative relayed how he had discussed railway matters with the two ZAR men, whom he attempted, initially unsuccessfully, to agree to go south for a face-to-face meeting with Rhodes. He had found Middelberg 'intractable'. But, referring to the Under-Secretary in friendlier terms as 'Swazi Esselen', after the satisfactory settlement that had been reached around the Swaziland issues during the previous year, implied that Daniël Esselen was much more supportive of the new mission. The emissary then concluded the telegram to Rhodes in altogether puzzling fashion, telling him that 'I have only to add that you must remain [in Cape Town] and postpone the parental desire to see your poor children'.[17] Who exactly Rhodes's 'poor children' might have been remains unknown, but only weeks later Daniël Esselen accompanied Middelberg to the railway conference in Cape Town.[18] By early 1895, both the Esselen brothers were well placed to offer valuable assistance to anyone intent on facilitating Rhodes's geopolitical ambitions.

In April 1895, Leander Starr Jameson, then actively seeking land in the Bechuanaland Protectorate from which he might launch a military expedition to the Rand if necessary, called in at Johannesburg on his way back north, having concluded negotiations with Rhodes in the Cape. Jameson took the opportunity of having one-on-one discussions that already hinted at 'military plans' 'with all the leading people' in the town, including Hammond and Ewald Esselen.[19] With the sole exception of Ewald Esselen, every one of those 'leading people' subsequently became centrally involved in the unfolding revolutionary conspiracy. And it was about this time, too, that the State President's concerns about the State Attorney's loyalty began mounting more rapidly.

There is thus a thin surviving paper trail that links the Esselen brothers, chronologically and geographically, to Rhodes, the Viljoensdrift emissary and then Jameson himself, stretching all the way from October 1894 to April 1895, that is, precisely at the time that the foundational thinking behind, first, the Johannesburg Vigilance Committee and, second, the proposed coup d'état was taking shape. But it is not only the Esselens' *entry* into a nexus of a conspiracy that suggests Ewald's involvement in developments right up the moment that Jameson invaded the South African Republic, but the timing and nature of their *exits* from elevated public office.

The first to go was Daniël Esselen, who, after serving the Kruger administration for five years, resigned as Under-Secretary of State in June 1895.[20] He then moved a few blocks away, joining the Pretoria firm of De Jongh & I Stegmann as an attorney. There, even though he remained a confidant of Dr Leyds's, he was also within easy reach of Ewald's network of young 'Progressives'. So it was that, in August–September 1895, though without an official position in the state administration, Daniël Esselen was still able to play an important role during the 'drifts crisis', yet another pre-Raid development that intersected with Rhodes's regional ambitions.[21]

But it is the timing of brother Ewald's resignation that arouses the most deep-seated suspicion. Almost from the moment of his appointment, in May 1894, Ewald Esselen *knew*, from reports of his agents Howcroft and Taylor, that the mine owners' backing of the rifle associations pointed to a possible armed challenge to the Kruger government on the Rand. Notwithstanding, Esselen went ahead with the contentious recruitment and appointment of Trimble that year, and by May 1895 the State President arrived at the conclusion that, in principle, things were so untoward in the security agencies under Esselen's control that both the State Attorney and Acting Chief Detective would have to relinquish their posts. And, by the closing months of 1895 it had to have been clear to Esselen that if not the planning for a coup, then the actual smuggling-in of arms and the logistical support for a mooted uprising in Johannesburg was accelerating steadily.[22]

Throughout the latter part of 1895, Kruger and his supporters in the Executive Council pushed to make the State Attorney's position politically untenable. Yet despite encountering ever more substantial headwinds within his portfolio, including some that surfaced around the 'Detective Inquiry', Esselen chose *not* to go, but to brazen things out, eventually resigning only on Friday 15 November 1895, just six weeks before the date first mooted for the coming 'revolution'.[23]

Esselen's delayed resignation contributed to rising political tensions on the Rand, and at least one foreign observer later went so far as to suggest that it was, in its own right, one of the factors that had contributed directly to the Raid.[24] More intriguingly, at some point between his shock resignation and the final week of December 1895, Esselen, well aware that his beloved adopted state was being threatened by an urban uprising if not an armed invasion, suddenly embarked upon several puzzling journeys.

In the last week of November 1895, Esselen appeared at a formal dinner in Johannesburg held in honour of Andrew Trimble, an occasion characterised by mutual praise-singing.[25] Trimble, once of Durban and an active undercover Rhodes agent, was well placed to provide his former boss with important contacts in that city.[26] But the spy might not have been Esselen's only source of information for introductions in the British colony. Daniël Esselen, Ewald's brother, was a well-connected veteran when it came to politics on either side of the Tugela.[27]

What exactly the purpose of Ewald Esselen's trip to Natal was at a time of mounting tension in the ZAR remains unknown, but by Friday 13 December he was in Durban and moving about in influential circles with a plausible cover story. He and the leader of the 'Progressives', General Piet Joubert – then still officially on holiday in Natal – were set to attend 'Dingaan's Day', the commemoration of the massacre at Blood River, in the Weenen district, on Monday 16 December.

Joubert, the main Boer speaker at an event so sacrosanct to nationalists that his presence there would be beyond the reach of even the most ardent conservative critics in Pretoria, arrived in good time to attend a church service that Sunday morning. Esselen, however, was to have no formal part in events and managed to keep so low a profile that his presence eluded almost all of the republican press, which was under the impression that he was in the Cape Colony. On that same Sunday morning, 15 December, Esselen boarded a 'special train' reserved for Natal VIPs, calling at Pietermaritzburg and later disgorging its passengers at Estcourt, from where the esteemed guests were transported to nearby Weenen by 'government mule train'.[28] Why Fred Hamilton, editor of *The Star* and another prominent Jameson Raid conspirator, seems *not* to have reported on Esselen's movements in a neighbouring colony – something that was later picked up on in London – raises more questions.[29]

Among Esselen's fellow passengers on the 'special train' were Sir John Robinson, the premier of Natal and Harry Escombe, the Attorney General. Clearly, in the eyes of the Natal government, Kruger's former State Attorney had lost little, if any, of his standing or status and was treated much like any of the other honoured guests. The train and the mule train, let alone the lull between events the following day, afforded Esselen ample opportunity for informal talks with the leaders of the British colony closest to the ZAR in geographic terms.

As importantly, the commemoration at Blood River gave Esselen the chance to speak to General Joubert, whom he had last seen in Pretoria two weeks earlier, and to update him on recent developments on the Rand. It was immediately after their rendezvous at Weenen that Joubert abandoned his idea of holidaying in Natal and, instead, returned immediately to his farm in the eastern part of the republic. The General's retreat to Wakkerstroom marked the start of the idiosyncratic behaviour that characterised his actions and movements in the lead-up to and throughout the crisis.[30] Indeed, it was from the farm, shortly after Christmas, that he was asked to return to Pretoria urgently but insisted that his return to the capital be kept 'secret' – at a time when one would have expected his appearance in public might have helped to inhibit conspirators and reassure nervous patriots.[31]

What the informal discussions in Weenen revolved around that day will probably forever remain unknown. But, might it not be that, in addition to briefing the General, Esselen had set out to inform and reassure Robinson and Escombe that matters on the Rand were in hand and that both the Secretary for the Colonies in Whitehall, Joseph Chamberlain, and the premier of the Cape, Cecil Rhodes, knew of what was about to transpire?

It would seem that, just as few knew that Esselen was off to Natal, so almost no one realised that he did not return to his Boer republic base, by then under threat, but almost immediately set off directly for another British stronghold – the Cape Colony. This meant that he not only had to forego spending the festive season with his family, in Pretoria, but that he would be out of the country when the date originally mooted for the Johannesburg uprising, 28 December 1895, came round.

In the Cape, as in Natal, Esselen kept an exceedingly low profile but he

did travel with a private secretary, suggesting that he was a busy man attending to confidential, undisclosed matters of a semi–official nature. Charles
Rorke, who had previously served as his secretary in the State Attorney's
office, in Pretoria had, like Esselen, resigned from his position immediately
after Trimble was denied naturalisation, thereby further impairing the 'institutional memory' of the secret service.

Given what Esselen knew from agent Taylor, however, the move south
was a decision born either of ignorance or as an attempt to place some distance between him and conspirators. The closing days of the year found him
in Cape Town, within easy reach of Charles Leonard, Rutherfoord Harris
and Cecil Rhodes himself.

Nobody now knows how, or where, Esselen spent Monday 30 December
1895, the day that news of Jameson's Sunday-night invasion began to circulate in official circles in the Cape. He was simply silent and out of sight that
day, although on the following day, Tuesday 31 December, he sent Kruger a
long, wordy telegram expressing his outrage at Jameson's action and assuring the State President of his loyalty and intention to return to the capital as
soon as was possible. From what happened over the next few days, it would
seem that Esselen, quite understandably, was in something of a panic.[32]

Significantly, Esselen was not the only man to go missing in Cape Town
that fateful Monday. No lesser a person than the Prime Minister of the
Cape Colony, the Hon. Cecil John Rhodes, also disappeared from view
until night fell, while an international crisis, one that he had helped precipitate, mounted rapidly. As the premier's famous supporter, Edmund Garrett
later recorded: 'On Monday, the 30th December, 1895, those who sought
Mr Rhodes in Cape Town learnt that he was at Groote Schuur, and those
who sought him at Groote Schuur were told that he was riding the slopes
of Table Mountain.'[33] The premier may have gone horse riding for the day
but only a novice would discount the possibility that he spent some of that
day consulting top legal advisers, including Charles Leonard and perhaps
Esselen.

Leonard had already seen Rhodes by the time WP Schreiner called in
to see the premier at Groote Schuur late in the afternoon of Sunday 29
December. Schreiner noted rather coyly that, at that time, Rhodes had a
house guest, and that on the following morning, 30 December, 'Rhodes was
out riding with another gentleman whom I [Schreiner] need not name'.[34]
The name of the 'other gentleman' the Cape Attorney General insisted on
keeping confidential may never be known, but it is reasonable to assume
that it was that of a close friend and a trusted political ally of both Rhodes
and Schreiner.

As a brother advocate, a former Bondsman, a secret supporter of Rhodes's
southern African federation project and, until recently, a member of the

Kruger cabinet, as well as being the man who had requested Schreiner to second Chief Detective Andrew Trimble, Esselen's name fits the bill of the 'other gentleman' almost perfectly. Moreover, within days Esselen and Schreiner were corresponding on the most confidential and intimate terms possible about their love of Rhodes, and about the political problems arising from the Jameson Raid debacle.[35]

Esselen scurried back north as soon as possible after his telegram to Kruger of 31 December. Although the exact date of his return is unknown, he would have travelled via Johannesburg. As we shall see shortly, it was within a day or two that he met Kruger, who then gave him a dressing-down for having once appointed Trimble, who was, even as they spoke, busy distributing arms to the Uitlanders in Johannesburg. But who might Esselen have met in Johannesburg before his brief, unhappy return to Pretoria?

The answer is again indeterminate but it would seem that there was a strong possibility that Esselen had a meeting with Andrew Trimble. It is Trimble's daughter, Edith, who in her biography of her father points in this direction.

It was a person, wrote Edith Trimble, who went by the alias of 'Stringer' and whose real name was known to the Secretary of the Reform Committee, Percy FitzPatrick, but which he refused to reveal, and who had a meeting with Andrew Trimble in late December 1895.[36] 'Stringer' was a man 'who did not see eye to eye with the Reformers in everything' but 'who had become very friendly with Jameson', presumably during the course of 1895, at meetings held in Johannesburg. 'Stringer' was no fighter and 'had no liking for armed rebellion'. He was more of a politician – 'organising and presenting petitions to get results'.[37] A former campaign manager perhaps?

'On his arrival from Cape Town' – on a date that is unclear but which clearly was *after* the invasion – 'Stringer' 'took the misery of his soul first thing to Trimble because he, too, was not actually a member of the [Reform] Committee'.[38] Taken on its own, this fragment suggests but hardly 'proves' that it was Kruger's former State Attorney who met Trimble. Indeed, Trimble's daughter thought that it might have been a relatively obscure local estate agent. But, what happened thereafter once again hints at, even if it does not fully point to, Esselen.

At some point between Saturday 4 January and Sunday 5 January 1896, realising that all was lost, Andrew Trimble, behaving like the secret agent he really was, donned his disguise as an elderly Boer and boarded a train, not for Kimberley or the Cape Colony, which had an extradition treaty with the ZAR but for the greater safety offered by Britain's nearest coastal colony.[39]

Esselen by then had his own idea of how to stand by his President in the latter's hour of need. Within five days of his return he spoke to the correspondent of the *Natal Mercury*, a source not known for its support of Kruger.

He may have been following-up on the informal discussions that he had had with leading politicians in Natal three weeks earlier. The essence of the interview was relayed to *The Times*, in London, which carried it on Monday 6 January. For the benefit of English readers, Esselen reiterated his belief in the growth of the Progressives' franchise policy and hinted at its eventual adoption by the State President. Just why Esselen chose to toss the imperial dog a bone shortly after his return to the republic is far from clear.[40]

That, however, was not the only sign of divided loyalties to be detected in Esselen's behaviour after his return from the Cape Colony. The date of Esselen's return to Pretoria is unknown but, shortly thereafter, the one man who knew 'Stringer's' identity, Percy FitzPatrick of the Corner House, went into hiding in a room in Johannesburg, hoping to avoid arrest for his modest part in the failed uprising.

FitzPatrick, latterly Secretary to the Reform Committee, took the precaution of burning all documents that could implicate Wernher, Beit & Co in the disaster. He then wrote to his wife saying that he was waiting to hear from someone in Pretoria as to whether or not the conspirators were going to be granted bail before he would give himself up.[41] It was the same problem, at roughly the same time, that so exercised Charles Leonard's mind in Cape Town until it prompted him to send Esselen the indiscreet telegram that caused them such great anguish.[42]

On Saturday 18 January 1896, FitzPatrick decided to hand himself over to the republican authorities. The following morning, he slipped into Pretoria and checked into the Pretoria Club, presumably as a prelude to surrendering the next day. While still there, however, he learned that Jameson and a few of his men were being escorted to the Pretoria railway station for the journey to Natal that would eventually see them shipped to Britain to stand trial. FitzPatrick was part of the crowd at the station that bid the unhappy filibusters farewell.

During FitzPatrick's brief absence, however, Esselen called in at the Pretoria Club, hoping to have a discussion with the erstwhile Secretary to the Reform Committee who, to all intents and purposes, was still a fugitive from justice. Why Esselen, by then allegedly a Kruger stalwart, wanted to see FitzPatrick is unknown. But as one sharp-eyed historian observes, it is interesting to note that Esselen *knew* where to find FitzPatrick, who had decided only the previous day to travel to Pretoria.[43]

What it was that was so important or urgent that Esselen was willing to be seen meeting an enemy of the state will never be known. But what we *do* know is that, in the run-up to the unforeseen invasion, Esselen and FitzPatrick had been Eugène Marais's principal financial and political mentors, and that Marais and Malan, acting as the self-appointed 'Olive Branch' delegation, had done all that they could to try and get the Reformers out of the resulting political pickle. And, Esselen was clearly involved in the cover-up after the Raid. With the benefit of hindsight, then, it is equally difficult to see the timing of Esselen's resignation as Kruger's State Attorney, in mid-November 1895, as being purely coincidental, and, as we will again note in due course, it becomes almost impossible to see it as wholly fortuitous when considered in parallel with the movements of the other conspirators and those of his chief ally, Commandant-General Joubert, who, just two weeks after Esselen's resignation, also decided to take extended leave.

Looking back, everything points to the State Attorney's clinging to office through most of 1895 for reasons related to the coming and the timing of the planned uprising. First, he and Joubert probably needed to get distance and time between themselves and the uprising before taking up promised positions in the 'provisional government'. Second, Esselen wanted to remain in control of the state intelligence agencies for as long as possible not only so that he, personally, could keep abreast of developments relating to the scheduling of the 'revolution' but also in order to regulate the pace and content of the intelligence he dribbled into the system. By delaying his departure, the State Attorney was providing Hammond – behind schedule in his arms-smuggling operations – more time for the importation of rifles and, at the same time, keeping the government in the dark for as long as possible. If that was indeed his objective, Esselen appears to have succeeded remarkably well. The Kruger government was caught largely off-guard by the various developments that played out in late December 1895.

Third, by lingering in office, the State Attorney provided Andrew Trimble and his small posse of Kimberley detectives with political protection for as long as possible. It allowed the Acting Chief Detective space and time to consolidate and develop his relationship with Hammond and other mine owners – something Trimble put to good use once the Reform Committee took control of Johannesburg. More importantly, it enabled Trimble to embed his ex-Cape detectives in the law-enforcement agencies and to develop a counterintelligence capacity before and during the Raid.[44] Here again, and as we shall note later, the timing of Trimble's movements in the weeks leading up to the invasion, like those of Esselen and Joubert, do little to allay suspicions. On the contrary, they deepen them.

Lastly, when the State Attorney's resignation *did* eventually come, it, like the Jameson Raid, caught Kruger and almost all of his cabinet by surprise. The cat and the mouse had been eyeing each other from close quarters over many months, with each waiting for the other to make the first move. Esselen's decision to leave, notes a leading historian of the ZAR's security services, was 'sudden and unexpected', further contributing to what already amounted to disorganisation, and it led directly to a 'tragic' collapse of the services on the very eve of the Raid.[45]

Here, then, lies a problem. How could the State Attorney, a former judge and advocate with legendary organisational gifts, a patriot to the bottom of his socks, who, just weeks later, assured the State President of his undying loyalty to the republic, not have foreseen the consequences of so hasty a retreat from office? Here, if ever, there was a case for placing country above personal circumstance, yet Mr Esselen baulked.

But the problems around Esselen's departure do not end there. At the same time as the State Attorney was scurrying from office, a file or two went missing that could not be located by his successor, Dr Herman Coster. It was bad luck, the sort of thing that could happen to anyone in a hurry, except for the fact that the mislaid files contained the reports of one of Esselen's secret agents – information that would have been closely guarded. Sadly, too, they were the reports of his very best agent – the Johannesburg-based, George Taylor – replete with his account of the arms-smuggling operations on the Rand!

Taylor, suggests one analyst, was an agent whose loyalty to Esselen was beyond question. Given that, Taylor's movements, at a time of acute political tension, prompt awkward questions. On 23 December 1895, he, too, suddenly put in a request for five days' leave, which, even though it fell within the season of celebration nevertheless raised an official eyebrow.[46] Where the agent went during that break is unknown but it could not have been far away. The missing file was causing problems.

The Acting State Attorney, Coster, asked Taylor to provide him with handwritten copies of all earlier reports to Esselen, at a time when intelligence was at a premium.[47] Taylor must have known that his many reports were a source of potential embarrassment for Esselen because, as early as mid-August 1895, he had told the then State Attorney about an 'association' in Johannesburg that did not rule out the possibility of a 'revolution' if its political demands were not met promptly.[48] Such reports could only raise questions about his former boss's competence or, more worrying still, about his political loyalties.

Esselen was supposedly a model professional, the man who had founded and chaired Joubert's 1893 election committee. He was also the State President's personal choice for reorganising and modernising the republic's ragged intelligence and law-enforcement agencies. Yet he actually left his portfolio in total disorder after 18 months in office. The more one looks at Esselen's hurried departure and its consequences – things out of character and which he must have been able to foresee at least in part – the more troubling the exit becomes.

The real question thus becomes: where, when, why and by whom was Esselen given the signal to abandon his position so hastily? Perhaps the first thing to notice in this regard is the rather unusual manner in which the

State Attorney took leave of the State President and the Executive Council. It was calculated to make absolutely certain that there would be no questioning of his decision and no delay in his departure. As noted in *Land en Volk*, almost certainly by Marais himself, Esselen chose to walk right into the lion's den when he opted to deliver his resignation at a meeting of the Executive Council that was attended only by the State President and two of his diehard conservative allies – Kock and Wolmarans – 'the other members coincidentally being absent'. The result was that the State Attorney's resignation was 'accepted immediately'.[49]

General Joubert's absence from what in retrospect turned out to be a most important meeting was, *Land en Volk* would have us believe, mere chance, a 'coincidence'. It may have been so. But it should be remembered that Joubert was also a great practitioner of the art of the strategic absence when it came to potentially awkward or incriminating political decisions. It was, notes the foremost historian of the 'Progressive movement', 'a favourite gambit' of General Joubert's to claim – usually truthfully but not invariably so – that he had not been present at an Executive Council meeting when matters that later turned out to be politically explosive had been discussed.[50]

In the matter of Esselen's departure, it meant that Joubert was never called upon formally either to endorse or to reject the resignation of the State Attorney, a man who was not only a close friend but also his supporter-in-chief. It seems reasonable to assume that Esselen would have canvassed his intention to resign with Joubert and possibly even Marais before acting on it. As things stand, however, it would seem that the advocate acted somewhat precipitously.

Equally noteworthy is the fact that Esselen's resignation, while clearly the subject of some regret in Johannesburg, did not unleash howls of anger and protest from the Chamber of Mines or the mine owners. That was strange, given that Esselen had long been the darling of the mining industry. It was almost as if neither Esselen nor his political allies wanted to make too much of the resignation at the time. He was intent on making a low-key departure, one in keeping with a pronouncement made back in 1894, after the hurtful outcome of the 1893 election, in which he lost his seat, that he wished to withdraw from all public political platforms.[51]

But most interesting of all to note, however, is in whom the arch-conspirators on the Rand were confiding during the hours immediately preceding Esselen's resignation. On 7 November 1895, the last strip of land in the Bechuanaland Protectorate required to launch an invasion into the republic was transferred to the British South Africa Company. Moreover, writes Colvin, 'On Thursday November 14 Dr Jameson left Cape Town for Johannesburg. The pretext for the visit was the illness of his brother, Sam; but the real reason was to complete his arrangements with the Reformers.'[52]

It was within hours of Jameson's arrival in Johannesburg, on Friday 15 November, that, after months of unsuccessful goading by Kruger and his allies, the State Attorney finally tendered his 'sudden and unexpected' resignation. Historians may thus not know from whom, or where and when, exactly Esselen got the nod to vacate his office immediately and steer clear of all public politics for a time, but they do know where to focus their search.

Finally, it is unlikely but does remain a faint possibility that Rhodes had played Esselen for the fool, allowing him to draw in Andrew Trimble, only for the State Attorney to discover later on that the Acting Chief Detective was an imperialist agent, someone more interested in serving the conspirators and furthering his own career than he was in 'fighting for the country', as he had put it during the May 1895 hearings.

But if Esselen *did* entertain any such suspicions, his sense of patriotism would have prompted him to clean out the nest of Kimberley detectives *before* he left office and, once the Reform Committee seized control in Johannesburg, to hurry across to tell the State President that their ranks had been infiltrated by Trimble, a double agent, and that they had been betrayed. Instead, it was Kruger who, upon learning that the former Acting Chief Detective was working for the conspirators and was helping to arm the rebels, sent for Esselen and gave him a lecture on 'English' treachery lasting a full 15 minutes. Waiting for the tortoise's head to emerge could be a costly business.[53]

Marais and Malan

Esselen and Joubert's political commissars for the 'Progressive' movement, the young men who provided the collaborators-in-chief with crucial intelligence as well as a personal link to the conspirators, did not have a good war. Eugène Marais and Abraham Malan were also beneficiaries of the State President's tortoise philosophy when he failed to question openly the credentials of the two self-appointed peace emissaries shuttling between the ZAR's capital and Johannesburg's self-styled 'reformers'.[54]

Marais and Malan's political manoeuvrings and movements during December 1895 all point to Joubert, even though it is impossible to pinpoint the time and place of their meetings. It would seem that, during the extended crisis proper, Joubert was keen to keep his meetings with them as discreet as possible. Joubert, in turn, appears to have been kept on a need-to-know basis by Marais and Malan, and, given their frantic shuttle diplomacy he was left playing catch-up politics.

Joubert, as we shall see, got himself into hot water with the State President during the crisis. Esselen, Joubert's long-standing legal adviser and greatest political supporter, did or said nothing to distance himself publicly or privately from Joubert, Marais or Malan during the Raid, which was understandable since he was in Cape Town for most of the time. Nor did Esselen do so in the immediate aftermath of the crisis even though he had rushed to assure the State President of his loyalty, and it has been claimed that there *was* contact between the principal collaborators during the crisis.[55]

It is from within this nexus of conspiracy and collaboration that Marais and Malan's behaviour during the December 1895 crisis has to be distilled. *That*, in turn, requires tracing the outline of the relationship that the editor of *Land en Volk* developed with Mr and Mrs Hammond in the mid-1890s. The intermediary in that relationship was likely to have come from within the Corner House group – probably via Percy FitzPatrick or Jim Taylor.[56]

Marais could have been introduced to the Hammonds late in 1894, that is, shortly after Jack Hammond returned to the Rand from Matabeleland and the conspiracy-defining mining safari with Rhodes and Jameson. But, what seems more likely is that it was after the plot began to thicken – in the last third of 1895.

In mid-1895 Marais lost his wife, who died tragically just after the birth of their only child. It was against this backdrop and his increasingly heavy use of morphine that he was first drawn into the Hammonds' social circle. By the time that Hammond played godfather to the hastily christened Reform Committee, in December 1895, he and other conspirators were sufficiently comfortable in Marais and Malan's company to describe them as 'personal friends'.[57] And, within a year of the crisis being formally resolved, Marais voluntarily followed the Hammonds into exile, and found himself accommodation about a half-hour's walk from the couple's new home, in London.[58]

Natalie Harris, an aspirant author more concerned about class, demeanour and manners than her engineer husband, who often had to rough it with lesser mortals, was especially taken with the charismatic, good-looking, urbane Marais, a man of letters. In later years she confided to a South African ambassador that Marais was 'the finest flower of civilisation of any man she'd known'.[59] It was an exceptional compliment, one befitting a man who, as will become apparent, may have done more than many others to spare her husband from the hangman's rope.

Mrs Hammond may have been less taken with the tall, bearded, less dapper Abraham Malan, who lacked Marais's obvious qualities and vulnerability even though in truth, and as we shall see shortly, the Hammonds owed him at least as much by way of gratitude. In her account of the crisis, *A Woman's Part in a Revolution*, Natalie Harris was slightly contemptuous of Malan's

father-in-law. Indeed, she almost certainly hinted at Piet Joubert's conspicuous lack of political courage and his strategic absences before and after the
failed revolution – and possibly his appearance and habits – when, after the
commutation of her husband's and the other principal conspirators' death
sentences, in May 1895, she recorded in her diary (subsequently published)
that 'General Joubert is sent off with a ten days' leave of absence to take his
annual bath'.[60]

Marais warmed to the Hammonds' company in a year as emotionally
fraught as it was professionally taxing. Esselen's drinking was starting to
attract unwanted attention around the same time that Marais's dependence
on morphine was deepening. Marais was forced to take leave twice that year.
On the first occasion, after his wife's death, he went to a brother's farm, at
Boshof. The second time, he and a friend sailed off to Mauritius and Marais
made the first of many attempts throughout his life to shake off his lifelong
drug dependence.[61]

During Marais's absence, in September 1895, and while the plot around
the uprising was still thickening, an old friend who within a year also
became of the co-owner of the newspaper, Charles Falconer, moved across
to Pretoria to manage the business affairs of *Land en Volk*. Falconer, a Scot
and an ardent imperialist, had previously been the manager of the printing
works at *The Star*, in Johannesburg, where the editor, Fred Hamilton, was
one of the first to join the Hammond conspiracy. Marais and Falconer's
friendship seems to have run deep enough for Falconer to read some letters
addressed to Marais personally.[62]

The timing of Falconer's arrival, his increasing involvement in the management of the newspaper and his eventual acquisition of a share in the
business may well all have been above board and fortuitous. It would, however, be a touch naive to think that it did not also enable the conspirators in
Johannesburg and the paper's real owners to keep a closer watch on Marais
and keep him on track in the weeks leading up to their planned uprising.

In precisely the same way, and for the same reasons, contingent though
they may have been, it is striking that it was soon after Marais returned from
Mauritius, and just weeks before the coming of the revolution, that Marais
became a stringer for Rhodes's *Cape Times*. It was a political and financial
gift that lay within easy reach of Consolidated Gold Fields and John Hays
Hammond – a man with a long history when it came to manipulating news,
and his fellow conspirator, Fred Hamilton.[63] The conspirators were thread-
ing Marais into the plot for an uprising in ways that Esselen, Joubert and
Malan were not. He, unlike the other three, was ever more directly in their
pay, and having to go far more public in his support of the mine owners.

Marais now began to speak with a forked tongue – professionally at
least. At home, in Pretoria, he championed independent-minded patriotism

aligned with 'Progressive' causes, while abroad, in the Cape, he was the source of biting copy about the Kruger government of a type that might sate the appetite of imperialists. Between these two positions lay the hoped-for urban uprising and the coming of a 'provisional government'. But the difference between the two positions was so marked that, by November 1895, the pro-Kruger *De Volksstem* could no longer resist casting *Land en Volk* as a Rhodes organ working for unnamed external interests. Marais responded with a libel suit, seeking £5 000 in damages (eventually settling for a mere £50 in 1896).[64]

By December 1895, then, Marais was in the emotional, financial, political and professional thrall of the Johannesburg conspirators in general and the Hammonds in particular. But John Hays Hammond, too, was by then irrevocably involved with the four Boer collaborators, and with Marais in particular. Their interdependence, in its conscious and subliminal aspects alike, was supported by the often rickety interpersonal structures that transcend the nature of 'trust' in treason-centred conspiracies. But when the little man, Leander Starr Jameson, had an attack of grandiosity, on the night of 29 December, and invaded the Republic, Marais and Hammond were linked by a bridge that had to be as strong as that which spanned the Firth of Forth.

Standing at either end of the Johannesburg-Pretoria divide, Marais and Hammond had to anchor one another, but, in truth, as time passed, it was Hammond who began to need Marais more than Marais had ever needed him. There were sound reasons for this fundamental shift in gravitational forces. While the conspiracy was still in the hatching and the future open-ended, it was the Pretoria-based Marais who had to supplicate for crumbs of financial support at the mine owner's table in Johannesburg. But once Jameson put paid to the idea of a successful uprising on the Rand preceding an invited invasion, Hammond was instantly compromised. The balance of power shifted back to Pretoria and it was Hammond, trapped in Johannesburg, who needed political help in the capital.

The precise details are impossible to retrieve now because they were sheathed in lies at the time and thereafter, but over the weekend of Saturday 28 and Sunday 29 December – and possibly even some days before that – Marais and Malan – travelling singly, more probably collectively, were both in Johannesburg at least a day *before* news of Jameson's invasion broke. In Marais's case this can be verified twice over – once directly, and more indirectly, by his own telling.

It is certain that Marais met Charles Leonard and, in all probability, Hammond on Sunday 29 December, because the following morning's edition of *Land en Volk* echoed the voices of both conspirators – the one loud and proud, the other whispered and manipulative. The National Union

manifesto of Uitlander demands, as authored by Leonard days earlier, was
there for all in the nation's capital to read in a specially translated Dutch
version.[65] But in the same issue Marais told his readers that there was nothing but war-talk on the streets of Johannesburg and that a 'reliable source'
had informed him that there were no less than 24 Maxim machine guns
and over 30 000 Lee-Metford rifles on the Witwatersrand. Marais's 'reliable
source' for this was, almost certainly, the town's smuggler-in-chief of small
arms, the self-proclaimed dissembler and spreader of disinformation about
all issues relating to the uprising and its weapons – Hammond.[66]

By that same Monday afternoon, 30 December, Marais and Malan, moving in lockstep and needing to report back to General Piet Joubert, were
back in Johannesburg. They still believed that they would witness an act of
defiance, backed by a show of force that might herald the coming of the
'provisional government'.[67] It was to be a momentous day, a day second in
importance only to the day of Jameson's invasion, which, unbeknown to
them, had been set in motion 14 hours earlier.[68] And if, as Marais lamented
later, he went there as but a 'boy', then he emerged as a man who had
seen, close up, how Hammond and the other mine owners made hercu-
lean efforts to stem the 'revolutionary' political tidal wave that they had
threatened to unleash across the country and to reduce the surge to a mere
reformist trickle in Johannesburg.[69]

Marais and Malan later asserted that they had gone to Johannesburg at
the behest of General Joubert in order to assess the crisis on the goldfields.
The unstated implication, one they were happy to leave untested, was that
the request was directed at them by the General acting in his *official* capacity. The fact is, however, that there is no surviving documentation to back
their claim or the even less likely variant thereon offered by Marais some
decades later – that he went there on the instructions of Kruger's Executive
Council! What is far more likely is that they went to Johannesburg at the
behest of Joubert to gain badly needed first-hand intelligence.[70]

What they heard during two meetings that afternoon shook them to the
core. At the first meeting, with Abe Bailey and James Leonard, Marais and
Malan were told the bad news about the mounting tensions around the
question of the 'flag', or, put in its decoded form, the fact that Rhodes and
Jameson were privately intent on seeing the republic incorporated into the
British Empire. Bailey, of course, was well placed to tell that tale. He had
heard it first-hand from the Secretary of the British South Africa Company,
Rutherfoord Harris, on board the ship that brought them back to Cape
Town only days earlier.[71]

The spectre of an imperial sword concealed behind the reformist shield
that Marais and Malan and their principals had hitherto believed would be
used only to force open a path to a 'provisional government' may have come

as a shock to the Boer collaborators but it was part of an existing, familiar repertoire of republican nightmares. Was it not the very child-monster that Kruger and many burghers foresaw as the only outcome possible from the unholy Esselen-Trimble marriage?

More pertinently, if what Bailey had told the Boer collaborators was true, then it probably meant that not only was an invasion by Jameson no longer merely part of a fallback position for the conspirators should the uprising fail; it might well be part of a two-pronged imperialist push with an uprising on the Rand backed by a simultaneous invasion from the far west. If that were true, it was a development that neither Hammond nor Marais and Malan would have been party to, even in plot form.

Moreover, if some sort of imperialist denouement were now on the cards then Malan, and via him his father-in-law, albeit with diminished responsibility, were in potentially serious trouble. Abraham Malan, who appears to have hailed from outside the republic and was therefore not an enfranchised burgher at the time, must have been familiar with the farm Doornpoort, near Koster, in the Rustenburg district, not least because the property and surrounding farms were thickly settled by members of the extended Malan family. It was also the district in which Kruger, too, owned a farm – at Boekenhoutfontein.[72]

Malan may or may not have been aware of the fact that, at Doornpoort, a part of the estate belonging to JH Malan, the Volksraad member for Rustenburg, had been hired by an American doctor as a staging post for hundreds of remounts, supposedly to serve a stagecoach line to Mafeking that was soon to be inaugurated. But even if Marais and Malan were *not*, at that stage, aware that Dr Henry Wolff was a former sidekick of Dr Jameson's in Kimberley and hand in glove with the Johannesburg conspirators, Malan – himself a military man – must have started to rethink what the real purpose of the hundreds of horses grazing out at Doornpoort might well be.[73]

But at the time all that Marais and Malan could do was to sit tight and monitor developments. The 'flag question' was still being contested, and Hammond and his Americans were not likely to be party to handing the Witwatersrand goldfields over to their old enemy, the British. And, even if the Boer collaborators did *not* know about Jameson being at Pitsani and the real purpose of the remounts at Doornpoort, Hammond did. He knew that Jameson was in a holding position waiting on his personal go-ahead, only to be issued if the uprising had started and was in danger of failing. True, the situation in Johannesburg was extremely fluid and troubling indeed, but it was hardly fatal.

CHAPTER EIGHTEEN

Managing the Aftermath

1895–1896

Hammond, Marais and Malan

Sometimes, in midsummer afternoons on the Highveld, the first rum-blings of political thunder are followed by bolts of lightning swift and powerful. So it was on the afternoon of Monday 30 December 1895 and the strike was so powerful that it destroyed almost the entire central nervous system of the original, fifteen-month-old conspiracy. Shortly after four o'clock that afternoon, Hammond, after meeting with American miners, was back in his office, in the Consolidated Gold Fields building, when he received the shattering news that Jameson had ignored his explicit, personal instruction to the contrary and summarily invaded the South African Republic.

If many of the conspirators believed that their armed 'revolution' would play itself out in large measure as bluff, and that a show of force in itself would be sufficient to earn them the reforms that lay at the centre of their grievances via a provisional government's challenge to Kruger, that possibility evaporated the moment that Dr Jameson crossed the border. Armed foreigners on horseback went earlier to talk about a revolution rather than to reform, and it would now require a huge effort for the conspirators to present themselves as mere reformers.

For Hammond, in particular, the position was extremely grave. Unlike some – probably most – of his co-conspirators he had always genuinely wanted a full-scale coup d'état, not a mere political stunt that would give rise to reforms. He wanted to rid the country of Kruger and its corrupt insiders and set up a provisional, power-sharing government. He envisaged a separate constitutional dispensation for the Witwatersrand, run along the lines of the District of Columbia but which might be located within the republic. It was a vision that his inner core of Boer collaborators could probably live with. Jameson's invasion, however, meant that instead of Hammond being in control as agreed, thus ensuring his personal goal of a republican denouement, events now turned on what would be seen as a 'British' incursion in search of an imperialist outcome. Instead of the dog wagging the tail, the tail was now wagging the dog.

Hammond was also compromised in other ways that few of his fellow British co-conspirators were. The modest quantity of small arms he had smuggled into Johannesburg could have been used in either a situation of political bluff or, if necessary, as part of the revolution that he personally wanted – the urban uprising. But his problems hardly ended there. His 50 Americans, in position at Irene, were waiting on instructions to engage in special operations within Pretoria that were clearly revolutionary rather than reformist in intent.

The first, purely military objective of that special force Hammond had been forced to share with Lionel Phillips and his co-conspirators for the simple reason that the Americans were encamped on the estate of the deceased Alois Nellmapius – a property administered from the Corner House. It was common knowledge that it was the men at Irene who would invade the capital and seek to capture the arsenal and, by so doing, help ease the shortfall of arms and ammunition in Johannesburg.[1]

But on that Monday morning, 30 December, *before* news of Jameson's invasion broke in Johannesburg, Hammond and his co-conspirators had, unintentionally, caused the situation at Irene to deteriorate markedly, leaving him even more vulnerable than he already was. Hammond, already badly over-extended, had suddenly started to doubt the ability of his American strike force to seize the arsenal and abduct Kruger without the assistance of locals to help them navigate the unfamiliar linguistic terrain.

In order to cope with this problem, 'the conspirators', but almost certainly Hammond himself, asked the 'son of a well-known ex-commandant of Colonial forces' (probably Aubrey Wools-Sampson) to mobilise a 'couple of men of the farming class who could speak the *taal* and give the time of day to any Boer they might encounter'. Neither the hastily appointed commander of the supplementary force nor the undisclosed number of Afrikaner-Dutch who accompanied him out to Irene were informed about the ultimate objective of the expedition.[2] Instead, they were told that they were taking stores for a 'trading' venture based on the Nellmapius estate, and put in charge of a 'couple of well-laden "buck wagons" drawn by oxen'. The provisions had been taken to Irene via the main road and been speedily unpacked.[3]

If things had run according to plan, Hammond would, at the right moment, and as with Jameson, have personally given the signal for the attack on the arsenal to commence and for the President's abduction. But Jameson's unforeseen invasion had changed all. Hammond was now confronted with a situation where there were untested Boers wandering around Irene talking to various undisciplined American cowboy types who already knew of his plan to attack the arsenal, and one or two who might even have been in on his secret to abduct the President.

Information about the secondary objective, the capture of Kruger, was so sensitive that Hammond had probably shared it with only his most trusted soul mates in Johannesburg – his lieutenant in all Idahoan and Mexican conflicts, Victor Clement, and his wife, Natalie Harris.[4] His secret was almost certainly safe with them, but the Americans and the Boer 'traders' were now quite probably the weakest link in his personal political armour.[5] Any loose talk by the cowboys and/or the taal-speakers and he would be a dead man walking. His fears, as we shall come to see, proved to be well-founded.

By late afternoon on Monday 30 December, Hammond and the mine owners had two important objectives that had to be secured with all possible haste. First, they had to make ever more energetic efforts to get Jameson to pull back across the border so as to help dispel the notion that the invasion was part of a Rhodes-imperialist filibuster seeking to capture the Rand's rich goldfields. Second, the Americans at Irene needed to be withdrawn at once and pulled back under the cover of darkness. In the end, the latter objective was easily achieved; the first never. Within hours of news of Jameson's invasion, Hammond ordered the strike force at the Nellmapius estate to withdraw stealthily to Johannesburg, a mission that was accomplished by midnight.[6]

But with the outrageous example of Jameson's ill-discipline haunting him more insistently with the passing of each hour, Hammond grew increasingly concerned that, despite the conspirators' pre-emptive withdrawal of the Americans from the Irene estate, his deepest secret – the plan to abduct Kruger – might have been blown. It would have taken only one 'cowboy' to have spoken out of turn to one of the Afrikaner-Dutch 'traders' for a rumour about the plot to capture the President to get back to Pretoria. If that happened, it might have the gravest consequences not only for him, personally, but also for Eugène Marais, for Abraham Malan and for Malan's father-in-law, Commandant-General Joubert. He had to take Eugène Marais and Malan into his confidence, and try to head off the possibility of any loose talk surfacing in the capital.

Less than two weeks later, caught unprepared and pushed into making a sworn statement before State Attorney Herman Coster, Marais was forced to dissemble and lie about what happened next. He had gone to Johannesburg that Monday afternoon, he suggested, at the behest only of General Joubert but made no mention of the simultaneous presence of his partner, Malan. There, Marais had 'met a person whose name he promised not to divulge' who had taken him first to the Goldfields Hotel and confirmed that the 'reformers' were in a position to arm and mobilise 2 000 men. The mystery man had then taken him to a nearby location where, much like the 'reliable source' quoted in that very morning's edition of *Land en Volk*, he had confirmed the extent of the weapons at the disposal of the would-be rebels.[7]

Some weeks later, during the preliminary examination of the accused 'reformers', Marais offered a modified account of all that had transpired on that Monday afternoon, 30 December. In the latter version, he acknowledged Malan's presence, confirmed other meetings that they had had with various 'reformers', but pointedly made no further mention of the unnamed man.[8] For whatever reason, the State Attorney chose not to probe the discrepancies in either of Marais's statements or those of Malan, who had also offered two different accounts of events that day.

Marais's behaviour and statements, the logic of the situation and subsequent developments, however, all suggest a different version of what happened next. At some point after five o'clock that afternoon, Marais went not to the 'Gold Field's Hotel [*sic*]' but to the Consolidated Gold Fields building, where some of the smuggled weapons were being kept. It was just bluster to suggest otherwise; if Marais's mystery man was so concerned about keeping his identity hidden, why would he have agreed to be seen with Marais at a popular hotel? At the Rhodes headquarters Marais had then spoken to the man whose name he had promised not to reveal – Hammond – who had just returned from a mass meeting of extremely agitated American miners.

It was almost certainly at that juncture, too, that Hammond told Marais about the base at Irene that was about to be evacuated, and about his original intention to abduct Kruger. Now *that* was information sufficiently explosive for a man not to want to have his identity revealed and for Marais, in turn, to have to promise that he would never disclose his source. It was also likely to have been at that meeting that Hammond would have told Marais to take Malan into his confidence and to make certain that General Joubert got to hear, via a back channel, through their intercession only, about the Americans and Boer 'traders' on the Nellmapius estate.

The two Boer collaborators rushed back to Pretoria, where Malan presumably lost no time at all in finding and briefing his father-in-law – at whose request the pair had gone to Johannesburg in the first place. Within hours of the news of Jameson's having invaded the Republic reaching Cape Town, Ewald Esselen made the move that, in effect, put distance between himself, Marais, Malan and, in its remotest aspect, Joubert. Esselen, by far the sharpest mind among the collaborating 'Progressives', had his secretary,

Rorke, send two telegrams to the State President. 'All Afrikaners,' Esselen suggested were 'shocked and outraged' by Jameson's 'treasonous and irresponsible' invasion and they would be returning to Pretoria at once to assist him in efforts to 'ensure our independence'.[9]

The sincerity of Esselen's protestations about Jameson's invasion, easily the most fortuitous aspect of a conspiracy that was meant to usher in a 'provisional government', but within a republican framework, is not at issue. After all, even John Hays Hammond was outraged by the unauthorised filibustering.

Why Esselen felt it necessary to reassure Kruger twice, in writing, of his loyalty while out of town, may have had something to do with the terms on which they had parted at the time of his resignation. But, what is equally interesting to note is that thereafter there is no record of the State President making use of Esselen's undoubted legal talents, either upon his return to Pretoria or over the extremely taxing months that followed.

Joubert, Jorissen and Malan

The problem for Joubert and the young collaborators was that their movements between Pretoria and Johannesburg over the weekend of 28 and 29 December had already attracted the attention of a few Kruger stalwarts. One in particular, Judge EJP Jorissen was a member of the iron guard of hated 'Hollanders' that the State President chose to surround himself with. Indeed, Jorissen had shown such hostility to Joubert and the inner core of the 'Progressives' over the last quarter of 1895 that, as we have seen, Esselen had found it convenient to send him out of town on a mission as a 'secret agent' to investigate gun-running in the distant northeastern reaches of the republic.[10]

Long convinced of his calling as a conservative, pro-Kruger bloodhound, keen to reclaim his position in the State President's inner circle and revitalised by his recent role as an intelligence operative, the news of Jameson's invasion left Jorissen with a surge of adrenaline. He could not resist rushing into battle and engaging at close quarters. On Monday 30 December, the same day that Marais and Malan were in Johannesburg, Jorissen waited for General Joubert to make his presentation to the Executive Council as to what his plans were for dealing with Jameson, allowed him to return to his office, and then pounced.

Supported by the in-favour Chief Justice, JG Kotzé, Jorissen collared the State President before he could leave the chamber and poured out his suspicions. Kruger, grappling with the invasion problem, was in no mood for tortoise-watching and had Joubert summoned from his office. It was a decision that he later regretted because what followed tore the ruling Afrikaner-Dutch elite so far apart that it could be offset only by the even greater menace of British expansionism during the years leading up to the Anglo-Boer War. As Joubert re-entered the chamber, Jorissen erupted, shouting: 'Do you know that your son-in-law is connected to the Johannesburg rebels?' 'What's this?' the General asked. 'It's high treason,' yelled Jorissen, and 'you must resign from your position – I demand it of you.'[11]

If ever there was a moment for the State President or General Joubert to hint at, or to state categorically, that Marais and Malan were acting in an official or semi-official capacity on behalf of the Pretoria government by talking to the mine owners in Johannesburg, then surely this would have been it? Yet both men chose to remain silent about the status of the young Boer lions.

Sensing, however, they had been party to the detonation of a huge explosion, Kotzé and Kruger rushed in to try and douse the resulting fire. But instead of calming the situation they only made it worse. 'Brother Jorissen is too hasty,' Chief Justice Kotzé opined wisely. 'Yes,' intoned the State President, 'he is too hasty and should apologise.' But Joubert could tell a firefighter from a flock of sheep and got the underlying message. It was not that Jorissen was misinformed or wrong – merely that he had chosen to intervene prematurely. It was tortoise time yet again. This time, however, it was Joubert who needed to sit it out, so, still furious, he turned on his heels and stormed out.[12]

Monday 30 December, had started badly for the General and the two young collaborators but it got steadily worse. That same night, upon their return from Johannesburg, Malan or Marais, or both, informed Joubert about what was happening out at Irene.[13] The only good news was that, even as they spoke, the American 'prospectors' and the Boer 'traders' were withdrawing to Johannesburg under cover of darkness.

The General found the news only partly reassuring. Over the previous 48 hours, the activity at the Nellmapius estate had attracted the attention of the stationmaster at the local rail siding. On Sunday 29 December, a train of 20 trucks from Mashonaland had arrived at Irene, carrying a large number of horses, together with harness and saddles. The stationmaster, his suspicions aroused, had telegraphed the Commissioner of Police (and ex-Stellaland filibuster), JG van Niekerk, requesting that detectives be sent to investigate and report on so unusual a consignment. At the same time, other informants noticed that a large number of horses recently purchased around Halfway House had suddenly been moved westward.[14]

Given this, and what he had been told by his son-in-law, the General could no longer afford to be seen as quiescent, so on Tuesday morning,

31 December, he acted. He ordered the State Artillery to prepare to move west and join Boer commandos intent on intercepting Jameson's Raiders. But the moment Kruger heard of Joubert's order, he countermanded it. Van Niekerk, acting privately, had presumably alerted the State President to an unusual build-up of men and horses at Irene, which hinted at an attack on the capital. The General then had either to disclose to the President that he already knew that the Nellmapius estate no longer constituted a clear and imminent threat – and reveal his sources – or be content with being countered and pretend to be dealing with the problem.[15]

Not being able to send out the heavier firepower necessary to see off Jameson's Maxims did huge damage to Joubert's rapidly waning reputation as a military man. There had already been complaints about his slow response to the invasion, and were it not for one telegraph line that, quite fortuitously, had not been cut by the invaders Jameson's force would have reached the outskirts of Johannesburg undetected. Moreover, Boer commandos were already complaining bitterly about a lack of ammunition and sufficient rifles. It was Tuesday; he was still in the capital and the situation nearby needed urgent tidying-up.[16]

Part one of what might be termed 'Operation Conceal' was easily achieved and with considerable panache, part two even more readily so, with security ensured in a manner that could not be surpassed.[17] It was not without reason that Joubert had earned the sobriquet '*Slim Piet*' – 'Smart Pete' – and that which had not come to him naturally was often supplemented by input from his formidable adviser, Esselen.

The General threw a cordon, consisting of members of the State Artillery and a few of van Niekerk's detectives, around the Irene estate. The security forces of the Kruger state were now effectively sealing off the site of Hammond's San Franciscan-inspired folly from any outside investigation. But Joubert's *pièce de résistance* came with his second move when he sent in Malan and a few men to establish whether there was any remaining threat on the Nellmapius estate. He could only have got the answer from his son-in-law that he knew would be forthcoming.[18]

As expected, Malan found no Americans at Irene. But what is interesting is that we *know* – from Hammond himself – that his 50-strong 'cowboy' contingent *had* been camped there for several days prior to the search. Malan might have found no Americans there but there must have been plenty of evidence, ranging from ash to wagon tracks, showing that they had been there for some time and then departed hastily. Why, then, is it that in Afrikaner-Dutch folklore, otherwise so rich in tales about the Jameson Raid, there is such a deathly silence about the fact that Hammond's 'cowboys' had indeed been encamped there? It would seem that neither Joubert nor Malan ever breathed a word of what had been found at Irene.

Joubert's cover-up countermanoeuvre helped Hammond conceal the plot to abduct the State President for another 20 years, until he chose to tell 'The True Story of the Jameson Raid' to Alleyne Ireland, in 1918, but probably also helped earn him some of the lenient treatment afforded him by the Boer authorities after his arrest and during his imprisonment. Hammond's debt to 'Slim Piet', Esselen and their two lieutenants, Abraham Malan and Eugène Marais, was great.

Joubert's problems were by then, however, not only military in nature but also deeply political. Not surprisingly, once the immediate crisis was over, he had to be *seen* to be taking a far tougher line with Jameson and the conspirators in order to allay suspicions among Kruger's close advisers.[19] But so hard-pressed was Joubert that Tuesday that, ignoring Jorissen's accusation about treasonous behaviour within his family's ranks, he was forced to send his son in law back to Johannesburg directly after the search of the Irene estate. The Boer collaborators were as desperate as Hammond.

Just how politically troubled Joubert had become by that Tuesday, 31 December, was noted by none other than his friend, Chief Justice JG Kotzé. So well-disposed was Kotzé to Joubert that, years later, Kotzé failed to mention that only 24 hours earlier he, personally, had witnessed a brother judge demand the Commandant-General's resignation! The Chief Justice was more forthcoming about several other events that day.

Late in the afternoon, he and Judge Ameshoff had gone on a coach ride into the countryside and, on their return, heard rumours that wagons carrying field guns had been seen moving along the road between Johannesburg and Pretoria. This alarmist talk almost certainly stemmed from the previous day's excitement at Irene. Later that same evening Kotzé walked across to the Commandant-General's home to get 'the latest report' on the unfolding position in and around the capital:[20]

> I found the General [Joubert] walking up and down his *stoep* in rather agitated manner. He was disturbed in mind at the idea of his probably having to attack Johannesburg and the consequences thereof in the event of Dr Jameson slipping through with his armed band. I assured him that there was not ground for anticipating anything of the kind, as within the next twenty-four hours, Jameson and his men would be surrounded and forced to surrender.[21]

The General and Kotzé were then joined by JG van Niekerk and the military situation was debated and discussed anew until Joubert's visitors eventually took their leave and set off in the direction of the Commissioner of Police's home in Church Street, which lay close by that of the State President. Along the way, for reasons that could only have grown directly out of their discussions with Joubert, Kotzé and van Niekerk again wrestled with the rumour about wagon movements along the Johannesburg-Pretoria road. Van Niekerk suddenly ventured a startling new opinion, one that had escaped the notice of the canny Commandant-General of the Boer forces himself, that 'they were a mere ruse to cover some other secret movement'.[22]

But not even van Niekerk, that experienced old western Transvaal free-booter, could take that line of thinking any further. Apparently, it was left to the Chief Justice, the least military of men, a man trained to listen to and interpret nuanced discussion, to make the penny drop. It was a coin, one suspects, that Kotzé might first have caught a glimpse of amid all Joubert's stoep-fretting about the Johannesburg uprising.

'Who knows,' the Chief Justice suddenly exclaimed, 'that a rush might not be contemplated after all on Pretoria, but from another quarter of town, in order to capture the President!'[23] Inspired stuff but, one suspects, an idea derived more from Joubert's anguishing than the war experiences of a judge. But, whatever the origins of the thought, Kotzé and van Niekerk were so seized by this notion that they went directly to the State President and roused him from bed in order to alert him and discuss the implications of so dastardly a plot.

Kruger, who had heard of the wagon movements, was not unduly per-turbed. When van Niekerk put it to him that he might be abducted the State President was 'rather amused', and said that 'the scouts who were out would give him timely warning of any hostile approach'.[24] What is strik-ing about all this, however, is that by Tuesday evening, 31 December, the Commandant General had clearly made no provision to protect the State President's home against such a raid, even though he must have known – via Malan and Marais – that it was a real possibility. Indeed, it was only *after* the Kotzé-van Niekerk visit that Joubert placed armed guards around the State President's house and had a horse made ready for Kruger, who had not rid-den in years, to flee on.[25]

Even after the clean-up operation at Irene had been completed that Tuesday afternoon, the Commandant-General remained mired in military and political problems. Eight weeks later, *De Volksstem* was still of the view that his attitude throughout the Jameson Raid debacle had been 'inexplicable' and 'secretive'.[26] And it often was. How else do we account for the fact that on 1 January 1896 it was a junior member of Joubert's civilian staff, Daniel Bouwer – rather than a soldier – who was told to link up with JJ Lace of the Reform Committee and make one more – futile – effort to get Jameson to turn back?[27] That would be the same Lace who was 'a personal friend' of Hammond's.[28] Fully two years later, Joubert was still trying to explain his strange role during the Raid to a sceptical public, and to defend his reputa-tion and that of his son-in-law, but without long-term political success.

Abraham Malan's loyalty to his father-in-law knew no bounds, even though Jorissen had accused him of treason. So, on that Tuesday afternoon, 31 December, he scurried off back to Johannesburg to link up with his partner in crimes against the state. Eugène Marais was already there, helping Hammond iron out wrinkles in a huge mantle of constitutional reform that he was now intent on draping over what he and others had previously been willing to cast as a 'revolution'. It was within this same fraught context that, as Marais pointed out later, boys might become men almost overnight.[29]

The Night of the Long Lies and the State President

Hammond had manufactured the raw cloth for his ploy the previous evening, after Marais and Malan had hurried back to Pretoria. He had persuaded the core conspirators, yesterday's revolutionaries, to broaden their support base and increase public credibility by weaving that larger and more protective political fabric in which the mine owners might best wrap themselves. It was crafted so as to make for seamless ideological continuity, and it worked. The so-called Reform Committee, a description adopted uncritically by imperialists at the time and by many historians later, should, as Hammond only once let slip in an otherwise carefully worded autobiography, be more correctly designated as the '*emergency* Reform Committee' – the illegitimate political offspring of the original, 'revolutionary' conspirators. It was a bastard child, hurriedly conceived on Monday evening, and first wheeled out on Tuesday morning, 31 December.[30]

But the few government officials on duty in Johannesburg, still in telegraphic communication with the capital, were not fooled, and refused to recognise the Reform Committee as a legitimate or representative body. This tends to underscore the interpretation that, when Marais and Malan met the full Reform Committee later that night they were unlikely to have been there in an official capacity.[31] Why the State President would empower an ideological arch-enemy such as Marais, or Malan, who hours earlier had been accused of treason in his presence by a Judge of the Supreme Court, is a mystery only to those blinkered by notions of nationalist purity, and has formed a bone of contention that has since been chewed to the marrow.[32]

The initial lack of recognition of the Reform Committee was a huge blow to Hammond and the conspirators. So, by the time Marais and Malan met with the full Reform Committee that night they were better prepared, and the first thing that Hammond and the one-time revolutionaries did was to push their collaborators into pretending that they were an accredited deputation sent by Kruger.[33] The truth of the matter was that Hammond and the conspirators on the one hand, and Joubert and his emissaries on the other, were by then both in desperate need of political salvation, of a resolution that would be forthcoming *only* if they could lay claim to a status that neither of the parties had. And so they dissembled, embroidered and, when necessary, simply lied. So, ignoring the earlier ruling of government officials locally, Marais and Malan recognised the Reform Committee and presented Joubert's personal approval of their private mission as if it had been officially endorsed by the entire Executive Council, including by Kruger, and that they were therefore legitimately representing 'the government'.[34]

Hammond and Marais were both good at 'bluffing', or deceit, to be precise. Indeed, Hammond considered 'bluffing' to be a necessary part of an American politician's repertoire.[35] In order to make the proceedings that followed more palatable to a few of the gung-ho hotheads, such as Bettington and Trimble, who were keen to rush to Jameson's rescue, Hammond dubbed the Marais-Malan initiative the 'Olive Branch delegation'. It was nomenclature designed to convey the impression that the centre, Johannesburg, was holding firm, and that it was the periphery, Pretoria, that was crumbling, when in fact it was the other way round.[36]

Marais and Malan played their part to a tee. They told the Reformers that the Executive Council was ready to entertain their legitimate grievances. At 11.55 pm, after the meeting ended, they sent a telegram to Joubert, telling him that they had met with the Reform Committee and that they had told its members that 'the government' would appoint a 'commission' to meet with a delegation from the Commitee the following day. 'We wish respectfully to suggest,' the telegram continued, 'that General Joubert, Chief Justice Kotzé and Mr Johann Rissik (the respected Surveyor General and close friend of Ewald Esselen's) be nominated as the commission.'[37] Respectfully? Marais and Malan's audacity was predicated on their assessment of two things – Joubert's now desperate need to push Kruger as far as he could politically, and the State President's naturally hesitant nature.

The General's response to the telegram has not survived but, as we shall see, there clearly had to have been one. Joubert *must* have agreed to Marais and Malan's suggestions immediately because, minutes later, the same telegram was sent to the State President bearing the new date, 1 January 1896.[38] All now depended on Joubert persuading Kruger to proceed along the lines suggested. And, as Marais and Malan had banked upon, Kruger was not about to alienate the General any further with the military situation still unclear.

The State President's response was, as so often was the case, subtle and nuanced. Keen on keeping Joubert and Malan within the broader Boer family at a moment when Jameson and his filibusters were closing in on the republic's economic heartland, Kruger agreed to the setting up of a three-man commission to hear out the Reformers, but it could only serve as the eyes and ears of his Executive Council. The committee would relay any messages received, but could not commit the government to taking action. Nor was Kruger about to be told whom exactly should represent the state when he had only just overruled his Commandant-General as to how the State Artillery should be deployed.

Kruger thus agreed to go along with the Malan–Marais proposal that JG Kotzé, who had proved his loyalty, be part of an eyes-and-ears commission. Kotzé would, however, have to be supplemented by a brother judge, HA Ameshoff, who would not only appear to be 'neutral', replacing Johann Rissik, but would also, in all likelihood, also not get too far out of line from his Chief Justice. If, however, there was to be an out-and-out political appointment on the government delegation, it would have to be a Kruger loyalist rather than the feckless Joubert, and preferably one opposed to Joubert, Malan and Marais. That third man – Jan Kock, of the Executive Council – fitted the State President's needs as if he were the offspring of Clio.[39]

The first meeting of the two sets of deputies, one led by Kotzé, the other by Lionel Phillips, took place in late morning.[40] The Chief Justice heard them out and then told the Reformers that he could not make a statement but would report back to the Executive Council, and that, if it proved necessary, they would meet again later the same afternoon.

When the two delegations reconvened, the Chief Justice gave the Reformers precisely nothing, telling them only that the High Commissioner, Sir Hercules Robinson, was on his way north and that their 'grievances would be earnestly considered'. For reasons unknown – but which may have had something to do with imperialist fantasies or the venue at which they chose to report back to their followers – the jingoes then lost the plot: 'At the Pretoria Club a crowd of sympathetic Pretorians was assured, by Mr Abe Bailey and the others, "We have got *all* we wanted".'[41] The journey back to Johannesburg may have been a sobering one but, if not, the news on the following morning must have done the trick.

At 9.15 am on Thursday 2 January 1896, Jameson surrendered to Boer forces under the command of General Piet Cronjé at Doornkop, outside Krugersdorp. The military collapse of the invaders was the anvil on which Kruger hammered out every political advantage that his government enjoyed from that moment on. Of the Boer fifth column, however, there was, unsurprisingly, almost no sight at all.

CHAPTER NINETEEN

Agents, Conspirators and Collaborators

Buying Time, Saving Face

1895–1896

Joubert – Missing in Action

On Thursday 2 January 1896, Commandant-General Piet Joubert was back in the capital, ostensibly directing overall military rather than political operations and taking precautions to prevent the abduction of the State President or a surprise attack on the state arsenal as planned by Hammond. Ewald Esselen, who just four years later would accompany Joubert into battle during the Anglo-Boer War as a legal adviser, was also on his way back to Pretoria, from Cape Town, having assured Kruger of his loyalty.[1] As we have seen, what Esselen's business there was, or who he consulted with, during the momentous upheavals up north is not easily established. Of Abraham Malan, so recently a supposedly fully authorised government deputy negotiating at the highest possible level with rebel leaders in Johannesburg, there was now no sign, and his partner, Eugène Marais, too, was back at his editorial last.

Given what transpired at Doornkop and the fact that the Boer collaborators, like Hammond, were by then in full-scale retreat and intent only on dissembling in ways that might minimise the charges of treason, the absence of the four notables was potentially all the more embarrassing. Marais, the storyteller, sensed the problem and attempted to deal with it by spinning another of those yarns that he liked weaving into his history, later claiming falsely to be one of ten guards who accompanied a broken Dr Jameson to prison in Pretoria.[2]

Marais's effort to limit reputational damage, however, paled beside the needs of Commandant-General Joubert. The Jameson Raid was the undoing of the General both in the eyes of the State President and in those of the Boer electorate. Shortly after the Raid, Kruger clipped Joubert's political wings, handing the position he had previously held as Superintendent of Native Affairs to Piet Cronjé, Jameson's nemesis. And, in 1898, in another three-way contest for the presidency, Kruger garnered over 12 000 votes while Joubert limped home in third place with under 2 000 votes.

The General may have been Hammond and the other conspirators' first choice to head a Boer-led 'provisional government' because he was an aggressive entrepreneur, a man of precisely the type necessary to forge a new marriage between 'gold and maize'.[3] But, sadly, Joubert was also an inept politician.

Joubert resisted expulsion from Kruger's inner circle – as we shall see shortly – but his problems were so deep-seated that they could not be successfully overcome in the public domain. There can be little doubt that the seeds of Joubert's downfall derived from the fact that Marais and his friend, Esselen, had drawn young Malan into the mine owners' orbit.

Joubert's difficulties could, in part, be traced back to poor timing – a problem he shared with his adviser Esselen, and as manifested by the latter's unfortunate appearance at a National Union meeting during the General's presidential election campaign in 1893. Through September and October 1895, Esselen's secret agents warned him repeatedly about an alarming build-up of smuggled arms and the rustling of political leaves in Johannesburg and Pretoria. Esselen may have chosen to ignore these signals for undisclosed reasons of his own, but it is difficult to imagine him not sharing such information with his political soul-mates, Joubert and Marais.

Then, in mid-November 1895, just as Jameson was passing through Johannesburg and with the projected date for the urban 'revolution' just weeks away – something Esselen may or may not have known about – he chose to resign as State Attorney, adducing the non-appointment of Trimble as a reason. He then scurried from office with such haste and attendant disorganisation as to raise the eyebrows of any half-conscious observer, let alone that of a close friend and long-standing political ally. Yet amid all this gathering political turbulence in Pretoria and unrest in Johannesburg, Joubert, the man in charge of the South African Republic's armed forces and the commando system – like the three monkeys – saw, heard or spoke no evil. It was extraordinary.

Yet, more wondrous still was what happened next. On 1 December 1895 – 15 days after his own political adviser had scarpered from office – the Commandant-General announced that he was going on holiday, to Natal, and for two months! Two closely connected politicians, the two most talked-about Boer members of a possible 'provisional government', chose suddenly to become invisible and eschew all public life on the eve of a proposed urban revolt.[4]

What Joubert's request for leave at such a critical time said of his relationship with the State President, or of Kruger's assessment of his General's competence, is impossible to tell. But, yet again, it smacks of a tortoise tale – of the State President's political instinct to wait and watch before striking.

Joubert's absence at this critical juncture, notes one otherwise careful analyst of the ZAR security forces, was 'unfortunate'.⁵ Perhaps so, but even when one makes allowances for the fact that Joubert himself was an orphan, what it brings to mind is Oscar Wilde's tart observation: 'To lose one parent may be regarded as a misfortune; to lose both looks like carelessness.' Joubert was summoned to Pretoria, by telegram, from his farm at Wakkerstroom on 26 December, just three days before Jameson invaded. Moreover, at a time when the republic was under threat General Joubert, for reasons that are difficult to understand fully, wanted his return to the capital kept secret.⁶ And when all the 'coincidences' linking the four Boer collaborators are stacked atop Marais's secret meeting in the Consolidated Gold Fields building, Joubert's scrambling around Irene and Esselen's departure, the camel's back will hold no longer.

Judge Jorissen, Judge Kotzé and Kruger clearly thought so. It is significant that, during that famous falling-out in the Executive Council chamber, it was *Joubert's* head that Jorissen demanded rather than that of his son-in-law, who, the Judge – correctly – saw as but a messenger boy, someone who had had a 'connection' with the 'rebels'. But, perhaps at least as telling as that fatal political exchange, on Monday 30 December 1895, was Joubert's subsequent behaviour. Once the stress began to tell, he started behaving in ways that were completely out of character and totally unexpected. Joubert the great conflict-avoider, Joubert the sage, Joubert the Progressive and Joubert the reasonable all disappeared as he fought to save his career.

Late in January 1896, just as the conspiratorial faithful forsook the Rand Club to resume regular worship 'between the chains', General Joubert – on his knees over Christmas, as befitted a pious man – stood up to challenge the State President. The situation had returned to 'normal'; in Johannesburg, money and mining were once again in the ascendant, while in Pretoria political power and intrigue were assuming their rightful place in the natural order of things. Everywhere, 'reform' trumped 'revolution'.

On 27 January a bullish Joubert wrote a letter to the Acting State Secretary demanding 'redress' from the State President and his government for Jorissen's outburst. Four days later, he received a red rag by way of reply. It was, the Acting State Secretary suggested, a 'private matter' that had taken place under 'privileged' circumstances of confidentiality and, given the unsettled political climate, was best resolved amicably between the warring parties. Within a week Joubert was back at them, insisting upon an urgent, in-depth inquiry into Jorissen's demand that he resign and, when no response was immediately forthcoming, threatening to hand over the cor-respondence to the press.[7]

Marais was an obvious outlet for any such publicity, but it was a risky strategy, one that might backfire. So, instead of going to the press, Joubert sought legal advice from an advocate or two, which, although unrecorded, would most likely have included Ewald Esselen. On 8 May 1896, Jorissen was summonsed to appear before a magistrate as defendant on a charge of libel. It was the start of a lengthy series of court skirmishes and appeals to the High Court that hinged on whether or not the Jorissen eruption had taken place under 'privileged' circumstances within the Executive Council.[8]

The play was supposedly about the law, but the plot was all political. What was really happening was that the Commandant-General was putting the State President's feet to the fire and steadily applying the heat. Kruger was being made to pay for having sided with Jorissen and Piet Cronjé, and for some months Joubert had the upper hand. Midway through, he told the State President he was no longer able to serve the same state as Jorissen, and that Kruger needed to choose between them. But, as we have seen, Kruger was a grand master when it came to close combat and patience. The President knew that he could not be seen publicly to side with a 'Hollander' against the General, and so Jorissen suddenly left town on six months' leave-of-absence spent in Europe. By year's end all that remained was a pending High Court action in which Jorissen was being sued for £5 000 for having allegedly defamed Joubert.[9]

But, at that late juncture, Joubert did as he probably always intended doing, or was advised to do, and on 23 November 1896 the case was with-drawn without explanation. Given what the four Boer collaborators had got up to during the Raid, it was simply too risky to proceed with an action that would have necessitated hearing awkward evidence that might have substantiated Jorissen's accusation of treason.[10]

But for close observers of Pretoria politics there had been a straw in the wind even before the case was withdrawn. In mid-November, a rumour did the rounds that, on Esselen's advice, Marais was about to depart for England where he would embark on legal studies. What nobody at the time knew, however, was that, in effect, Marais was going into self-imposed exile of the sort that his mentors, the Hammonds, had embarked upon only weeks earlier. Marais left Cape Town, by ship, on 12 December 1896. Once in London, a prime Boer collaborator and the arch-conspirator behind the Johannesburg uprising became further entangled socially, enjoying much-needed cooling-off periods before they could return to America and South Africa, respectively.[11]

Throughout the difficult months following the Raid, Joubert contin-ued his lurch to the political right in an attempt to regain lost ground and demonstrate that, when it came to nationalism and patriotism, he stood second to no man — and that included the State President. Joubert was forced to face widespread allegations and rumours of everything from incompetence, as evidenced by the unpreparedness of the state to counter Jameson militarily, to behaviour so unresponsive that it bordered on treason.[12] And, as one suspects in the matter of the proposed libel action, it was left to Esselen to try and calm the General down with some sage advice. But it was an uphill struggle and did not always work.

Throughout the trial of the Reformers and the sentencing process, Joubert adopted an inflexible, hard-line approach tailored to populist politics at a time when Kruger was playing the statesman on the world stage to great acclaim. In the Executive Council, the General was in a minority, insisting that the death penalty needed to be enforced on Hammond and the other conspirators. So adamant was he in his stance that Esselen eventually had to drop Joubert a note, reminding him of the political advantages of granting clemency.[13]

The General behaved as if he were seeking to atone for sins past, and perhaps those of his son-in-law, and was wholly out of kilter with most members of the Executive Council when it came to the question of suitable punishment for the Reformers. So bizarre and out of line was Joubert's response that it has puzzled historians. 'If we take into consideration his all-round reputation for benevolence,' writes one of Joubert's biographers, 'then his unforgiving attitude in regard to the "Reformers" is almost incomprehensible.'[14] That is, unless you begin to question the General's real motives and start thinking the unthinkable.

Esselen — One Step Forward, Two Steps Back

Esselen's advice to Joubert about the need to manifest compassion when it came to the condemned mine owners was born, in the first instance, of his own liberal convictions, but, as he made clear, there were also political advantages to be gained from adopting such a position. Indeed, questions as to how principles and politics might best be reconciled remained at the top of Esselen's own agenda through the first half of 1896 as he continued to take out insurance against his own exposed position during the Raid.

One of Esselen's difficulties was that, in December 1895, Charles Leonard, the public political face *par excellence* of those behind the aborted urban uprising, had fled south, where he suffered from 'brain congestion'. But, as we have seen, Esselen, too, had been in Cape Town during the height of the invasion crisis. Would those two, brother advocates and both National Union sympathisers of note in the same city, not have spoken to one another let alone to their confidant and friend Rhodes? Then, on 13 January 1896, Leonard got his wife, also in Cape Town, to contact Esselen in the Republic, via telegram, suggesting that he was about to return to Johannesburg and requesting that Esselen use his influence to try and delay his possible arrest, presumably so that he could tidy up a few messy loose ends.

But, as Leonard realised soon enough thereafter, it was hardly the action of someone who had lost contact with a man who had resigned as State Attorney only eight weeks earlier. Given what had transpired in the interim, it was more like a plea from one friend to another who, without spelling it out, could still rely on his partner to come to his assistance precisely *because* they were both still partially ensnared in the aftermath of what had been a treasonous conspiracy.

Esselen scribbled a hurried note to JH ('Onze Jan') Hofmeyr of the Afrikaner Bond, asking after Leonard. Three days later, on 20 January, Hofmeyr, who might not have known all of what was at stake, replied. He had, he said, not seen Leonard since he had slipped into Cape Town aboard a down 'special train' and then hurried off to Sea Point, where he was still holed up. A doctor claimed that Leonard was genuinely ill, suffering what some would have called a 'nervous breakdown', but a friend was of the opinion that he was merely in a 'funk', depressed by the sad turn in events.[15]

Unfortunately for Esselen, however, the prosecution in Pretoria learned of Leonard's approach. As the preliminary examination of the conspirators gathered momentum during February 1896, so the former State Attorney's anxieties steadily mounted. Any reasonable man might conclude from the January telegram that he and Leonard were intimately connected, possibly even co-conspirators. Esselen let Leonard, by then in England, know how unenviable his own position had become.

On 17 March 1896, in the Grand Hotel, London, Leonard sat down and wrote to Esselen, trying to set matters right. It was one advocate writing to another, not so much for personal reassurance – which was the author's inclination – but for the record. It was an impossible task. How would one conspirator and fugitive, in the presence of an unseen third party, intimate to a second, an erstwhile collaborator magically reconfigured as a patriot, that their relationship – hopelessly compromised and contaminated by time, place and historical momentum – had *nothing* to do with a plot so treasonous that one could not even speak its name? Leonard tried, but the answers he offered only conjured up more urgent questions:

Dear Sir,

    I desire to say that I am extremely grieved that you should have been placed in such a [the word 'sad' is deleted in the original] difficult position (as I now learn has been the case) by sending you a telegram from Sea Point to say that I was returning to the Transvaal. I was ill in bed at the time and acted on impulse. It was the merest accident that I thought of your name, but I now see how it might have led to the assumption that you were in some way connected with me in the events which were then affecting men's minds so strongly. I wish to state emphatically again that you had nothing to do with me or all those events; that it was blind chance which made me hit on your name, and that I profoundly regret that you should have suffered in any way from my action.[16]

Here, then, was a letter between friends who had known each other since their college days in Cape Town back in the 1870s that started, rather formally, with 'Dear Sir' and ended personally: 'Such amends as it is possible for me to make I now make sorrowfully.' But then Leonard suddenly remembered that there was supposedly no intimate connection between them, and that it was all just business as usual. So he concluded, 'Use [the amends] as you think fit.' And Esselen did. He forwarded the letter to the State Secretary, who asked for a copy so that it might be used in evidence should the state get round to prosecuting Leonard, and Esselen obliged.[17] So much for honour among advocates, if not thieves, intent on stealing a country.

    But, by then, Leonard's missives were not the only political winds buffeting the former State Attorney and not all could be confined to the hidden corridors of power in Pretoria; some were painfully public. That very same month, Piet Viljoen, Mining Commissioner for the Heidelberg district, wrote a strongly worded letter to the editor of *Ons Volk* alleging that Esselen had been complicit in much of Trimble's manifest treachery. The increasingly beleaguered one-time State Attorney's response was almost predictable. He huffed and he puffed mightily, but could not blow the house of Viljoen down.[18]

    As in the earlier matter of the Commandant-General's dispute with Judge Jorissen, Ewald Esselen responded by threatening to sue the author and the editor for libel. But, as with Joubert, the threat came to nothing. Before Esselen could have his day in court, the charges were suddenly withdrawn. For reasons that Esselen and Joubert alone knew fully, two of the men suspected of being leading figures in the Boer fifth column during the Jameson Raid were unwilling to test the allegations of conspiracy or treason levelled against them in open court. As the scribe John Scoble noted later, after the Jameson Raid, Ewald Esselen 'cut a very sad figure' in Pretoria.[19] So quiet was the normally ebullient Esselen that when he did eventually take a first tentative political step, nearly two years later, Francis Dormer, editor of *The Star*, dropped him an encouraging note saying, 'I am so pleased to find that you have found your voice again.'[20] In truth, it was more whisper than voice.

Andrew Trimble

Trimble, it will be recalled, was dismissed from his position as Acting Chief Detective early in November 1895. He did not linger in Johannesburg but soon set off for the Cape Colony where, so he later claimed, he attempted to settle a few issues pertaining to civil service benefits for a post that he had by then relinquished and for which no record has survived. He, Colvin wrote years later, travelled to Kimberley to 'claim his pension', 'knowing up to that time nothing of the plot that was brewing' back on the Witwatersrand.[21]

This was part of a dissembling narrative that Trimble's daughter snatched at eagerly. 'If my father had known anything about the Reformers' plot,' wrote Edith Trimble, 'he would have passed on his information to the Commissioner of Police and or Attorney General'.[22] How, when or why Trimble would have got around to telling Attorney General, WP Schreiner, or Commissioner of Police McLeod, that their premier was implicated in a conspiracy to overthrow the government of a neighbouring state is hard to know. Both officials had cooperated fully with Esselen to get Trimble seconded to the Witwatersrand in the first place. Moreover, once the plot had failed, one or more very senior men – in all probability of cabinet rank – must have either ordered or sanctioned the removal from the Cape archives of all records relating to Trimble's secondment. The truth may have been more mundane.

Given what happened subsequently, it seems far more likely that Trimble hurried south to be debriefed and then received new instructions as to how best to support the conspirators. His return to Kimberley that November took place at almost the same time that Jameson was passing through the diamond city on his way to Mafeking and Pitsani. He would also have been well placed to interact with Gardner Williams at De Beers, who was then attempting to accelerate the delivery of smuggled arms to Hammond in Johannesburg. Trimble, along with George Farrar, figured prominently in the unpacking of concealed rifles on the Rand.[23]

While in Kimberley, suggests Colvin, Trimble 'was invited to visit Johannesburg' by the core conspirators and he hurried back. On 3 December, the republic's former Acting Chief Detective was the guest of honour at a farewell dinner attended by his former boss, Ewald Esselen, and a half-dozen of the ex-Kimberley loyalist detectives. It was then that Trimble chose to reveal that he would be opening a private detective agency modelled on that of Allan Pinkerton – an American-style outfit, one specialising in covert operations for major industrialists.[24]

The costs of Trimble's 'detective agency', manned exclusively by ex-Kimberley detectives who, like their boss, had been dismissed by the Kruger government because they were not naturalised citizens, were met from funds controlled by the conspirators.[25] Trimble later told Colvin that it was only on 18 December, after he had been ushered into the offices of *The Star*, presided over by Fred Hamilton, that he met Frank Rhodes, George Farrar, Lionel Phillips and John Hays Hammond and heard, for the first time, about the conspiracy. The following day, or so Trimble claimed, he returned and took 'a solemn oath to obey Colonel Rhodes in all things until he should be released by him'.[26] But it was so much hogwash, a false timeline designed to cover up the fact that he had been in secret service for Cecil Rhodes, almost certainly, and Hammond, probably, from the moment he was recruited so hurriedly by Esselen in November 1894.

Even Edith Trimble, who conceded readily that her father was in 'secret service' of some sort, but was unwilling to entertain the idea that he had been undercover before he swore his allegiance not only to the core conspirators but also to Frank Rhodes in person, knew that there was something wrong about the timeline that Andrew Trimble had suggested to Colvin. She knew because, in the course of conducting her research, in the 1950s, she had come across both oral and written evidence suggesting that her father *knew* what was afoot weeks before the meeting with Colonel Frank Rhodes.

AC Duff, once an employee at the National Bank and a close friend of her father's, told her that Andrew Trimble had told him about the plot as early as November 1895, and that it would be supported by a simultaneous cross-border incursion by Jameson.[27] Edith Trimble dismissed Duff's contention as a 'mistake', which it may have been. But then, rummaging through her father's papers, she came upon yet more evidence that she was eventually also to dismiss as 'a mistake' but which, in fact, pointed directly to Cecil Rhodes.

On Monday 6 January 1896, by which time the core conspirators were under immense personal pressure, Trimble was forced to think about fleeing Johannesburg. Knowing that he risked being arrested by the Boers, Trimble asked the man he considered to be his commanding officer for a note effectively releasing him from duty to the 'reformers' and, at least as importantly, the Rhodes family itself. Frank Rhodes was happy to oblige and hastily penned as innocuous a note as possible to his younger brother – in effect to his own 'commanding officer'. Trimble, it seems, was entitled to expect special treatment from the great man:

Dear Cecil,

This is to say that A Trimble has rendered us all good service during the last month. If you can do anything for him I will be glad.

Yours ever,

Francis Rhodes.[28]

Trimble never used the note because, fearing extradition from the Cape, he
fled instead to Natal where it was not until 12 months later that he got to
meet Rhodes face-to-face.

As a former dragoon, Trimble's loyalty to Frank Rhodes came via the
unwritten codes that bound British officers in peace and war. But that to
Cecil Rhodes was informed by other connections, from a secret society
replete with its own codes and oaths. At least three of the men in *The
Star*'s office on the day that Trimble pledged himself to the cause of the
Reformers – Frank Rhodes, Lionel Phillips and John Hays Hammond –
were Masons. Hammond had joined the Goldfields Masonic Lodge No 2478
when he first took up his post in Johannesburg, in 1893. George Richards
of Consolidated Gold Fields head office was another Mason. Indeed, he
was the Grand Master of the District North, and even though most deeply
involved in the activities of the Reform Committee at the time, was never
charged. That would be the same Richards who had popped up out of
nowhere as a 'character witness' for Trimble at the 'Detective Inquiry', back
in May 1895, when the detective was on Esselen's payroll.[29]

As previously noted, Trimble used his Masonic connections during the
Johannesburg uprising to penetrate 'into even the departments of state',
and he 'kept a close watch on the government'. At one point he succeeded in intercepting a telegraphic message from the Boer commander at
Krugersdorp to the State Secretary, in Pretoria, pleading for more ammunition – a development that triggered the dynamiting of the railway line at
Langlaagte.[30] But, in order to gather intelligence in the capital itself, Trimble
required the help of Boer insiders, agents who spoke Afrikaans-Dutch, and
men who could be trusted in moments of great duress.

Nobody knows who Trimble's informants in the capital were, but, from
first principles, there is one outstanding candidate. Eugène Marais was not
only an out-and-out Hammond collaborator throughout the crisis but was
also well-connected. Marais was a man with a great interest in codes, dissembling, private detectives, political intrigue, spies and undercover agents,
and a newspaperman known to telegraph operators. Moreover, like Andrew
Trimble, Marais was a Freemason.[31]

But, if Trimble was relying in some small measure on Marais's loyalty as a
Mason during the days of crisis, what might it tell us of the wider network
of Masons that he had access to from much earlier on – during the months

that he was Acting Chief Detective and working for a senior government official who was also a Freemason, State Attorney Esselen?[32]

It is unlikely that Esselen did not know that Trimble was a brother Mason when he had him headhunted. Indeed it may well have been a further inducement to recruit so unlikely a candidate into the republic's police force. Certainly, after the 'Detective Inquiry', at which Masonic Grand Master George Richards – who reported directly to John Hays Hammond – appeared on Trimble's behalf, the State Attorney must have known that his Acting Chief Detective was also a brother Freemason.

It can therefore be taken as read that Esselen, Trimble, Marais, Hammond and Marais all knew that they were Freemasons in the months leading up to the Raid. None of them *needed* to be Masons in order to perform either their official or unofficial covert functions prior to the uprising, but what they did all need, if they were not to be discovered and exposed, was discretion, secrecy and trust – things that Freemasonary and oath-taking would have further facilitated.

It is against this additional background that we need to deepen and further refine our understanding of the actions and behaviour of the conspirators before, during and after the Raid. It is not what some *did* for each other that enabled them to be arms smugglers or state security agents, but what they did *not* do. They never acknowledged each other's roles and they never revealed what they did know.

Esselen and Marais did not betray Hammond or Trimble to the Kruger government, even though they had to have known about the arms smuggling. Hammond and Trimble, in turn, never betrayed Esselen or Marais. Years later, Trimble was still at pains to tell Colvin that he had first learned of the Johannesburg conspiracy only after he returned to Johannesburg, in mid-December 1895. Trimble *had* to lie about this because, had he not done so, he would have revealed a network of Boer collaborators that stretched from Marais and Malan back to Esselen himself and then, possibly, to Joubert.

Trimble's importance, however, easily transcended that of the Freemasonary that helped grease the wheels of the failed revolution on the Witwatersrand. The fact that Trimble was the personal agent of Rhodes and had, with the assistance of first the Cape Attorney General, WP Schreiner, and then State Attorney Esselen, penetrated the Kruger government and its security agencies as far back as 1894 lay at the very heart of the conspiracy in the South African Republic. If the Rhodes-Esselen-Trimble link were ever exposed it would have been the Premier of the Cape Colony, not just Jameson, who would have gone on trial in London, with devastating political consequences for several senior politicians in Cape Town as well as in Westminster.

Here again, Trimble's movements after he escaped from Johannesburg in January 1896 and made his way to Natal reveal just how thoroughly the southern African regional political establishment were keen to protect him and, via him, the standing of his spy boss. It was Jameson, not Rhodes, who would be the fall guy.

On reaching Durban, Trimble, having disposed of his Boer and false-beard disguise, made his way to the main police station. There, with the help of a trusted friend as intermediary, he re-established contact with the officer who has taken him on as a constable a decade earlier, Superintendent RC Alexander. Alexander, who had a telegraphic request to arrest Trimble – wanted 'dead or alive' in Johannesburg in exchange for a reward of £100 – acted as if he lacked the authority to take him in.[33]

Instead, Alexander, the intermediary – Willie Daugherty, 'Inspector of Nuisances' in the borough – and Trimble decided on a course of action that would keep the agent's identity secret. They also took steps to ensure that his presence in the colony would not be detected by any British authorities keen to get at the southern African conspirators rather than Joseph Chamberlain in Whitehall, and make certain that Trimble would not be extradited to the Kruger republic. Their next port of call was the offices of advocates Harry Escombe, the Attorney General of Natal and his partner, the London-trained Henry R Bousfield.

But Escombe, who, like his premier, Sir John Robinson, had shared a coach with Esselen in the 'special train' at Weenen only weeks earlier, could not afford to be seen to be so close to a wanted man. He therefore got Bousfield to provide Trimble with a written opinion recording that there was no 'Extradition Law or Treaty' between the colony and the South African Republic.

The absence of a formal extradition agreement meant, as Advocate Bousfield spelt out in a document designed to be read by senior members of the Natal ministry or any senior judge in a local court of law, and dated 4 February 1896, that:

> The only fear at present is the interference of England in regarding the offence as having been committed in a country over which her Suzerainity extends. Mr Trimble is as safe and probably safer in Natal than in any other country in South Africa, but though he is safe here from arrest and extradition now it is impossible to advise him how far this will apply to the future. In the Cape he would apparently be liable to arrest under the Act in force there.[34]

But the Rand revolutionaries' precautions against Trimble, their principal undercover agent, being taken and then extradited to either Britain or the Transvaal and then revealing the central roles of Rhodes and Esselen, went

*'Secret Agent' and Acting Chief Detective
Andrew Trimble.* PHOTO: KILLIE CAMPBELL LIBRARY

Police Commissioner McLeod Robinson
PHOTO: SOL PLAATJE AFRICANA RESEARCH LIBRARY

Sir Thomas Upington PHOTO: HET VOLKSBLAD

WP Schreiner PHOTO:AFRICANA MUSEUM JOHANNESBURG

beyond getting sound legal advice. Those conspirators with most to lose had a plan B. As Edith Trimble recorded:

> As soon as the American Consul [at Durban] learned of the fugitive's arrival he took immediate steps to notify my father that a United States vessel was in harbour and about to leave and ready to take him to the States to prevent his arrest should the legal decision resolve that he must be extradited to the Transvaal to deal for the rebellion.[35]

It requires little historical imagination to figure out who on the Rand might have been behind the American Consul's offer.

Armed with the reassuring legal opinion of senior counsel and a new, unknown identity Trimble was now a wanted man in two British colonies. But Escombe was taking no chances and so Trimble was summoned to Pietermaritzburg for an interview with none other than the Governor of Natal, Sir Walter Hely-Hutchinson.[36] So, just as Trimble's entry into the Rand conspiracy had been facilitated by the Premier of the Cape Colony and his Attorney General, Schreiner, so Trimble's exit from the Witwatersrand was safeguarded by the Governor of Natal, its Premier, Sir John Robinson, and his Attorney General, Harry Escombe. The failed Johannesburg revolution may have been conceived of by an American in the shape of John Hays Hammond, but its trajectory involved the active and passive assistance of two British colonies.

Dr Jameson's trial, in London, ran for eight days, between 20 and 28 July, when he was found guilty and sentenced to 15 months' imprisonment without hard labour. Through almost all of this period, from January to around June, Andrew Trimble was near invisible, living under an assumed name and probably receiving financial support from the Durban Agent of the Chartered Company, the Hon. R Jameson, a man unrelated to the by-then-heroic, notorious Doctor. As a curious Australian news correspondent speculated late in May 1896: 'At the collapse of the movement Trimble discreetly disappeared, and he is probably now in England.'[37]

But he was not. He was living in Durban, and upon the outbreak of the African revolt in Rhodesia, in March 1896, Trimble quietly began recruiting Natal volunteers for the war north of the Limpopo. By the time the date was set for Jameson's trial, he had a new and public role as an auctioneer in the port city. Even then, however, the prime conspirators took care to check that he remained loyal and on-side. Immediately after his release from prison and banishment from the ZAR in June 1896, Lionel Phillips went to Durban, where he sought out and discussed undisclosed business with Trimble. Likewise, when Rhodes passed through Durban, in December 1896, on his way to Cape Town and London, there were more confidential discussions between Rhodes and his former superspy.[38]

Hammond

The Republican government, however, had never been fooled by the peripheral movements in and around the so-called reform movement. It knew that Hammond was the brains behind the uprising on the Rand, and the state unerringly prosecuted and then had him and the other core conspirators – Phillips, Farrar and Frank Rhodes – sentenced to death for treason. Of the conspirators of the second rank, as we have already noted, few were as important as Trimble, but the reward of £100 for him being apprehended dead or alive was never claimed, and he and Rhodes remained in contact.[39] Charles Leonard, arguably the other most wanted man, was never extradited.

In retrospect, John Hays Hammond, like Theodore Roosevelt an admirer of 'manly virtues and practical politics', and a man who later missed becoming the Vice President of the United States of America by a narrow margin, achieved two extraordinary personal outcomes.

First, by playing a brilliant political endgame Hammond succeeded in selling to the world the fiction that the mine owners had never been intent on fomenting a revolution, but that they wished merely to usher in an era of accelerated reforms. Second, with the odds heavily stacked against him and them, he managed to conceal, tolerably well, the identity and number of Boer collaborators out to assist him effect political change within a largely republican framework.

It is one of the great ironies, then, that Hammond's American-inspired uprising and Jameson's botched British-imperialist Raid gave rise to ever greater Afrikaner political cohesion and ethnic unity, in turn setting the stage for the outcome that he and the Boer collaborators had hoped to avoid – a bloody war, the loss of the republic and the triumph of hegemonic British imperialism in southern Africa. Gold eventually triumphed over maize, but not in the way envisaged by one Californian mining engineer born in the great period of United States expansionism and with a deep love of conspiracy and covert action. And the Anglo-Boer War, in turn, laid the foundation for 100 years of bitter ethnic, racial and nationalist strife in southern Africa.

Milling

CHAPTER TWENTY

Organising a Rescue Party for Cowboy Jack

The Old South Reaches out to Washington, DC

1896

Despite being born in 1859, only months before the outbreak of the Civil War, Natalie Hammond (née Harris) bore many traces of the antebellum South.[1] But, as her adoring husband knew, she had moved on with considerable success and was, by the 1890s, the embodiment of the 'New Woman' being feted back in the United States.[2] Attractive and articulate, courageous and innovative, she could hold her own in any company, with a decided preference for those at the upper end of the social scale. Despite having had a modest education, she was well-travelled, could provide an intelligent reading of most political situations and was a shrewd judge of character. Proudly Christian, a great friend, caring mother and loyal wife, she was a pillar of strength both within her family and later, that slice of upper-crust Washington society that aspired to, or had, aristocratic forebears.[3]

She shared her Southern roots with Jack Hammond who, as we have seen, despite being Californian by birth, was raised as a 'Southerner'. Like her husband, Natalie Harris placed great store on what she considered to be the quintessentially Southern value of 'honour', which included elements of courage, loyalty and manliness. When, at the height of their post-Raid travails it was put to her fraught husband – already ill and probably facing the death sentence – that he should flee the country she retorted: 'He is the father of my sons, and I'd rather see him dead than dishonoured.'[4]

There was, however, another less attractive side to Natalie Harris's personality. Like her husband, she could, on occasion, be manipulative, opportunistic and snobbish. As will be recalled, she also had a sharp tongue that could inflict racially tinged sarcasm. 'General Piet Joubert,' she confided to her diary, was sent off on 'ten days leave of absence to take his annual bath'.[5] Like many in her cohort, Mrs Hammond had views on race and racial purity that accorded easily with notions of social Darwinism. The lady was long out of the South but the Old South had never fully left the 'New Woman'.

She was born on a modest-sized cotton plantation, 'Avenel', worked by a few slaves and owned by her father, James Harris.[6] The estate appears to have taken its name from the orphan heroine, Mary Avenel, in Sir Walter Scott's 1820 historical romance, *The Monastery*. Mr Harris was a lawyer and later a highly regarded judge in Vicksburg, Mississippi. He and one of two younger brothers – Nathaniel – hailed from Natchez, and both had a sound legal education – the one at Amherst College, the other at the University of Louisiana. Judge Harris and his wife, Mary, had three daughters, but Nathaniel – a partner in his brother's legal practice – never married and lived at Avenel until at least the coming of the Civil War.[7]

All three Harris brothers served the Confederacy faithfully during the Civil War. The Judge, turned auditor, was deployed in the post office, at Richmond, while the younger brothers joined the army and served with great distinction. Nathaniel Harris attained the rank of brigadier general, having fought at the battles of Second Bull Run, Chancellorsville, Gettysburg and Spotsylvania. Before the siege of Vicksburg, in 1863, however, Mary Harris and the three girls moved to Eufaula, in Alabama, where they stayed until the entire family was reunited on their Warren County plantation, in 1865, at the end of the war. The brothers resumed their legal practice for a time and Nathaniel, a beneficiary of the Gilded Age, eventually became President of the Mississippi Valley and Ship Island Railroad Company in the 1870s. The Judge and his family, however, moved on to New York City where, after her mother died during childbirth in 1871, the young Natalie completed her schooling and trained as a singer.[8]

Raised with Mississippi mud between her toes by a father and mother who were both held in high repute and, with a noted Confederate war veteran as an uncle, Natalie Harris had powerful ties to the Old South as well as its peculiar Democratic elite. When Nathaniel Harris was made President of the Bunker Hill Company upon Jack Hammond's departure for southern Africa, in mid-1893, the General gained ready access to the Republican elite that dominated San Francisco's banking and mining circles, further strengthening the family's political connections.

But this cross-party network of influence on the Harris side of the family, formidable on its own terms, paled beside that which Jack Hammond could command in his own right. Muscular tentacles of influence and power, developed over two decades on both the East and West coasts, some via his father, allowed him, whenever necessary, to put the squeeze on Capitol Hill and, on occasion, to reach into the White House itself. This ability to lobby decision-makers in Washington, DC, derived from at least three formidable, often overlapping, sources of power cultivated by the family over many years.[9]

First, it will be recalled that Jack Hammond himself came from a family with extensive military connections via his father, Major RP Hammond and a favourite uncle, the Texas Ranger, Colonel John 'Coffee' Hays – both of whose political careers were underpinned by strong interests in San Francisco's local economy. Prior to his death, in 1888, RP Hammond had been a member of the prestigious Aztec and Pacific Union Clubs, which, between them, had conduits leading back into the upper echelons of the military establishment on the East and West coasts. Jack Hammond, a 'club-bable' raconteur, had followed his father into these and other elitist, solidly male institutions.[10]

Second, and at least as important – no, probably more so – Jack Hammond was an Ivy League graduate, and his Yale cohort, then in its prime, had representatives in almost every institution of note in the United States. Within a day or two of Hammond's arrest, Charles W Truslow, a wealthy Manhattan lawyer, and Hammond's college friend, the Chicago banker James T Houghteling, laid plans for a political campaign to ensure that Hammond and his American friends received a fair crack of the whip from the Kruger government. General Nathaniel Harris moved in to pick up the tab for Truslow whenever the lawyer checked into the fashionable Shoreham Hotel, in Washington, where he pushed against many open doors. It was another Yale man, Assistant Attorney General Edward B Whitney, who paved the way for Truslow to see the Secretary of State, Richard Olney, who in turn primed American diplomatic staff in Cape Town and Pretoria to make crucial representations in what became known as the 'Hammond Affair'.

Third, as a noted mining engineer, Jack Hammond was extraordinarily well in with the United States banking, financing and railroad elites – again on both coasts – a link that he had painstakingly constructed early in his career. In addition, and by virtue of his many successes, he enjoyed the highest possible standing in the leading professional bodies in his field, such as the American Institute of Mining Engineers, which had 2 500 members by 1896. Hammond's San Francisco offices were in a building owned by the banker William H Crocker, a Yale graduate and son of Charles Crocker who was one of the big four investors in the Central Pacific Railroad. In New York, his office was in the prestigious Mills Building, owned by yet another famous banker and financier, Darius Ogden Mills.[11]

In short, once Natalie Harris realised the possible consequences of her husband's arrest, she drew solace from the fact that the couple enjoyed unparalleled access to every military, social, political and economic network of note in the United States, a web of influence that extended across party political lines. What she might not have appreciated as readily, however, was that there were other factors favouring a campaign to minimise the risks her husband was exposed to. Intra-elite politics are created by design, but it is chance and historical circumstance that allows for them to be activated most effectively. And there were several reasons why 1896 was a propitious year for a vulnerable but influential American stranded in remote southern Africa.

Foremost was the fact that 1896 was an election year. President Grover Cleveland, a Democrat, had presided over three years of economic recession caused, in part, by his unwavering support for a gold, rather than a silver, standard, which, in turn, had tended to affect the money supply negatively.[12] The country's political elite were engaged in a vigorous debate as to which of the precious metals should underpin the monetary system. It was a good moment to concentrate the public's mind about the plight of a half dozen of its leading engineers who were in trouble in a part of the world that was growing in economic importance with the passing of each year. The South African Republic was the world's largest gold producer, and the value of its imports, including a significant proportion from the United States, had risen from $11 million, in 1891, to over $47 million by 1895. Along the Potomac, Pretoria was no longer an unknown entity.[13]

Moreover, both President Cleveland and his Secretary of State, Richard Olney, may have overreached themselves during the dispute with Britain over the Venezuelan border, in December 1895. Both countries were looking for ways to ease diplomatic tensions between them. The Jameson Raid, in which the well-being of prominent citizens drawn from both countries was at stake in a region where British imperial interests were paramount, offered an opportunity for renewed Anglo-American cooperation. If the Americans supplicated to the British in their efforts to get Whitehall to help safeguard the rights of US prisoners, a positive response from London was almost guaranteed.[14]

Jameson's importunate incursion into the South African Republic late in December 1895 did not pass unnoticed in the American South, with its tradition of filibustering. So, even before it became clear that American citizens were heavily involved in attempting to foment a revolution on the Witwatersrand, Senator JT Morgan of Alabama was preparing to cock a snook at British imperialists. Indeed, on 10 January 1896, the morning after Hammond was arrested, but without knowing what was happening in Johannesburg, Morgan got the Senate to approve a motion that congratulated those in Pretoria and other capitals on their 'success in establishing free representative government, republican in form, and in opposition to any foreign power that denies to them the full enjoyment of these rightful liberties' and that, by so doing, 'commerce' might benefit.[15]

Such largely reflexive anti-British attitudes, however, mutated rapidly during the weeks that followed as the American press and elites across the country were forced to think their way through the nature and implications of the Raid and revolution, and how best to protect the interests of the United States and those of its citizens who had helped precipitate a still-unfolding debacle. What at first glance looked merely like a pre-emptive capitalist strike gone wrong assumed more serious proportions once it became clear that one of the 'ringleaders' behind the plot was a prominent American facing charges of high treason and the possibility of the death sentence. The resulting shift in 'public' opinion and the tone of political discourse was the result of several slick, privately organised, powerfully motivated interventions.[16]

News of American involvement in the Jameson Raid reached the United States, via cable, on Saturday 11 January 1896, little more than 48 hours after the police had picked up Hammond and several of his Californian cronies on the Rand. It was just hours before the news of the arrest of United States citizens had spread from coast to coast and into the deepest recesses of political power in Washington.

Few had a better appreciation of the power of the press and journalists than did John Hays Hammond, his family or their well-educated friends. In later years Jack Hammond, who successfully cultivated several hand-picked journalists, who became close friends and helped to repair such reputational damage as he had undergone as a result of the Raid, was an active member of the National Press Club in Washington. Upon his death, in the mid-1930s, Hammond's much-loved collection of autographed photographs of the rich and famous of the day was deposited in the club's archives, where it resides to this day.

First out of the starting blocks on Hammond's behalf was his well-heeled Manhattan attorney, Charles W Truslow. On Sunday 12 January, the day after the news broke, he and a fellow Yale graduate, Richard Smith Jnr, were on an early train from New York City and heading for Washington. By 11 am, having used Smith as a key to gain access to the establishment, they were in Olney's office persuading the Secretary of State to gee-up the American diplomatic and consular services to protect the interests of Hammond and his colleagues.[17]

Olney, sensing that the Raid could provide the United States with a way of reopening diplomatic channels still clogged with Venezuelan sludge, embraced the 'Hammond Affair' with enthusiasm, even though he could not persuade Grover Cleveland to take a more direct – presidential – interest in the matter.[18] Immediately after the meeting with Truslow, Olney got the American Ambassador in London, Thomas F Bayard, to persuade Lord Salisbury to ensure that the British agent in Pretoria, Sir Jacobus de Wet, would take care of Hammond's interests. He also instructed the American consular official in Johannesburg, JC Manion, to 'take instant measures to secure John Hays Hammond's protection and fair play'.[19] Truslow and Smith returned to Manhattan, content in the knowledge that, within hours of Hammond's arrest on the Rand, the American's interests were in good hands on Capitol Hill and, across the Atlantic, in Whitehall.

Not wanting to find himself out of pocket in a profession known for its unparalleled ability to reconcile high principle with even higher fees, the attorney immediately contacted Nathaniel Harris to help lay the foundations for supplementary political campaigns in the South and on the West Coast.[20] General Harris did Truslow, his nephew and his niece proud; he was indefatigable. After a meeting to plot strategy, on 19 January, things swung into motion and accelerated a few days later when Hammond was denied bail in Pretoria. A slew of congressmen and senators, including some from the mountain states as well from Southern strongholds such as Alabama, Mississippi and Tennessee were asked to add their weight to mounting pressure on Washington.[21]

San Francisco went into an altogether predictable political spasm. The California Manufacturers and Producers' Association and the Presidents of the Chamber of Commerce and the Gold Mining Exchange were all in broad sympathy with the sentiments expressed in one of the petitions sent to the government, namely, that Hammond 'was illegally restrained of his liberty in prison in South Africa'. Governor Budd of California sent a telegram of support to President Cleveland while other civic bodies added to the enthusiasm for the causes manifested by California's two senators – GC Perkins and SW White – the one a Democrat and the other Republican. By the closing weeks of January, most of the Southern and West Coast political elite were united, singing lustily from the same sheet.[22]

In the north and northeast, James Houghteling lobbied in financial and other investment circles to garner support for his old friend. Houghteling got the so-called Meat King of America, the millionaire Philip D Armour, to join the clamour for sustained diplomatic action from Washington.[23] But anything that the Book & Snake or other Yale alumni could do was easily matched by the extraordinary efforts of Jack Hammond's formidable wife, who, thousands of miles away, was working her own brand of feminine magic.

Despite experiencing the first tell-tale physical symptoms of her third pregnancy, Natalie Harris was as mentally alert as ever. From the moment Jack was arrested, she made a point of either seeking out or staying in touch with Hammond's professional colleagues or employees in Pretoria and Johannesburg. While appreciating the central role that Jack had played in planning the failed revolution, and his consequent vulnerability as a 'ringleader', they would remain loyal and lend active, unqualified support to her efforts to free him. Some of those contacts were entirely predictable – old friends such as Victor Clement, Joseph S Curtis and Ernest Wiltsee, with the latter two, in particular, being notably active in mobilising support in the United States. But there were others that were more surprising, such as RE 'Barbarian' Brown, the Coeur d'Alene sceptic who had started out as a government supporter but again switched sides once the urban 'revolution' unravelled.[24]

Concerned about the debilitating and sometimes humiliating physical frailty that her husband tended to display when placed under intense psychological pressure, Natalie Harris started her campaign to free her spouse even before he appeared at the preliminary examination. There was little need for her to cultivate the American Consul, since he was already well known to her as one of Jack Hammond's many suppliers of mining machinery, and Manion did not fail them. Indeed, he proved to be loyal and supportive throughout the family's tribulations, even though, back in Washington, his professionalism was sometimes questioned.[25]

As importantly, Natalie Harris decided to take a more intimate approach, and focused her letter-writing campaign on those senior American politicians who were either friends of the extended family or whom they knew personally. Their Coeur d'Alene mining war allies were as good a place as any to start at, and so, on 19 January, she dropped a note to the pro-silver, Mormon-disenfranchising, Republican and Yale alumnus Senator FT Dubois of Idaho, pleading support for his old friend. Likewise, it was easy for her to direct a personal plea to Senator TC Catchings of Mississippi, once a private in the Confederate army, later a leading lawyer in Vicksburg and a close family friend of the Harrises.[26]

But Mrs Hammond's foray into quiet diplomacy faltered a little later that month, once her husband was refused bail and his health began to fail. Operating under mounting physical and psychological stresses of her own, Natalie Harris's earlier distinction between private and public initiatives began to give way, giving rise to an unforeseen consequence. On 30 January, without Jack's prior approval or knowledge, she sent a long and intemperately worded telegram, bearing her husband's name, to Senator JP Jones of Nevada, while at the same time releasing the contents to sensationalist newspapers belonging to the Hearst group. Unwittingly, this initiative, which publicly questioned the nature and effectiveness of Anglo-American cooperation, complicated the developing bilateral diplomatic momentum.[27]

Amid all these developments, the subject of most of the concern – John Hays Hammond, a man whose name was nearly always singled out for special mention in the American press while those of his accused compatriots were often ignored – was languishing in jail, in Pretoria. But, as we will

John T Morgan
PHOTO: BRADY–HANDY COLLECTION, LIBRARY OF CONGRESS

Richard Olney
PHOTO: LIBRARY OF CONGRESS

Senator George Clement Perkins

Thomas C Catchings

recall, Florence Phillips noted, with a measure of accuracy and irritation, that it was Natalie Harris who ensured that his status mutated from prisoner to patient guaranteeing that, 'except towards the end, [Hammond] shared very little of the imprisonment of the others'.[28]

Hammond *was* genuinely ill. The fact that he was diagnosed as having 'dysentery' was never in doubt; the deterioration in his condition was there for all to see, including the many doctors who attended him and the prison authorities. What was at issue was the cause of his illness and whether it, and the debilitating symptoms that he manifested, were exclusively determined by amoeba or bacteria, or whether, as he himself hinted at, they were more psychological in nature. With the benefit of hindsight, it would seem that, because the most severe symptoms displayed correlated almost perfectly with the waxing and waning of the enormous stresses that he was under, his illness may well have been psychologically-induced rather than physical in nature.[29]

Conditions in the Pretoria jail, unusually crowded in high summer, were not conducive to either the mental or physical health of the inmates, let alone those of elitist capitalists. Jameson and his lieutenants were, until they were shipped out via Natal on 19 January to stand trial in England, held briefly in a small self-contained block soon christened 'Jameson's Cottage'. But, until the 'cottage' was vacated Hammond – ill since shortly before his arrest – along with Lionel Phillips, George Farrar and Frank Rhodes were kept in one small cell, well apart from rank-and-file Reformers.

The thoughts of the four chief conspirators turned almost immediately to what the British imperial machinery in general, and Sir Hercules Robinson in particular, might deliver them by way of immediate relief. The answer was very little indeed and nothing tangible. Yesterday's revolutionaries, convinced that they should now be viewed primarily as either Her Majesty's loyal subjects or close allies, were outraged by a 'betrayal of trust' on the part of the High Commissioner who had caused them to lay down their arms. The best excuse they could come up with in his defence was that he was ill and losing his 'mental vigour'. Hammond, a great admirer of the British aristocracy, later found it 'ironical in high degree that, for his eminent services Sir Hercules should shortly after have become Lord Rosmead'.[30]

But, whatever the inadequacies of Her Majesty's government, the quotidian concerns of the four were, from day one, mired in the real and imagined failings of the prisons department of a republic founded, as a matter of principle, on the basis of a racial inequality – one which, even when they were plotting revolutionary changes, it had not once crossed their minds to question. Hammond, accustomed to having his culinary needs attended to by a former Rothschild cook, found it difficult to accept that his prison 'diet was the same as that provided for the Kaffirs' and that the four's taste for the disgusting local maize-meal porridge 'was not sharpened by encountering Kaffir hairs in the food'.[31] His self-esteem might have been approaching an all-time low but, even three decades later, his contempt for black Africans remained palpable.

As Hammond and his mining industry friends soon discovered, however, there was not much beyond their reach when it came to everyday needs. Men who for some years had not been beyond the corruption of state officials when it came to enhancing their business interests on the Rand, and who were long-time champions of good government in Pretoria, found that 'bribery of one kind or another usually produced amelioration of some particularly abhorrent regulation'.[32]

However, the conspirators quickly grasped the fact that money might not guarantee either their freedom or even their lives. Indeed, their plight was exacerbated when they learned that the state had also attached their fixed property. It was an unhappy development, one that further undermined the four's well-being, and was a consideration that, in the case of Hammond and the Americans, surfaced almost instantly in the ongoing lobbying and submissions around the Capitol.[33]

In short, despite having a small army of concerned American civic and political leaders fighting on his behalf back in America, Cowboy Jack's prospects seemed exceedingly dim. His Southern notions of courage and honour were being called into question and it was not clear that he would ever be able to return to the United States with head held high. His wife and children were at risk in a strange land, and his life and liberty were about to be publicly probed and weighed against a charge of high treason. His professionalism had been compromised and the security of his financial assets and property was under threat. Moreover, he and Jameson were at daggers drawn, and it was anybody's guess as to which of them Cecil Rhodes would defend. But, if forced to choose, chances were that the great man would look to rescue his dearest friend.

With privacy at a premium in a shared cell and his collywobbles increasingly difficult to control, Hammond leaked self-respect, ate less, lost weight and grew weaker. The manifest deterioration in his condition did little to assist Natalie Harris, who was entering the second trimester of what proved to be a troublesome pregnancy.[34] Her political instincts, however, did not desert her. With the campaign to free her husband already well advanced back in America, before the preliminary examination of the conspirators got under way in Pretoria, she looked around for ways of ramping up the pressure much closer to home.

CHAPTER TWENTY-ONE

The Kruger Government in the Saddle

and Uncle Sam Has a Word with Oom Paul

1896

The Hammonds needed a way of personalising Jack's case so that, once the force of the diplomatic and political pressures emanating from Washington reached Pretoria, a face could be put to the name of a man who, throughout the agitation leading up to the failed revolution, had never formed part of the deputations that appeared before the State President. Unusually for a person who loved few things more than interacting with the rich or the famous, and unlike, say, Lionel Phillips, Hammond had, up to that time, never met Kruger face to face. His image had to be managed in a way that allowed his profile to be distinctive, set apart, from that of his British co-conspirators. And what better way to underscore all that than to point to the fact that he was an American, a citizen of a sister republic and a committed Christian? The Hammonds worked at getting distance between themselves and others. Not surprising that when, four years later, Florence Phillips commented briefly on the relationships between the various women trapped within the Reform 'movement', she displayed little affection for Natalie Harris, noting only that 'Friendships of years were broken, and much bitterness of spirit aroused, in many cases these sores have never been healed'.[1]

With the assistance of Hammond's business associate, the industrialist and mine owner Sammy Marks, Natalie Harris was granted an audience with the deeply religious State President hoping that, at the same time she might get to have a word, in private, with the equally devout Mrs Kruger. Mrs Hammond thanked the State President for the magnanimity that he had displayed in dealing with those embroiled in the revolt and respectfully asked that he continue to show the same spirit of clemency in future. She underscored Hammond's status as a citizen of the great republic but it went down less well than she had anticipated when Kruger expressed 'disappoint-ment that the Americans went against him'. Undaunted, Mrs Hammond told him that, once the troubles were settled, he should 'come to America' to 'see how *we* manage matters'. And, on being shown out without having seen the President's wife, she pointedly asked that Mrs Kruger be informed that she – Mrs Hammond – would be 'praying to the same God that peace might come'. The observation was relayed to the President and was said to have left a favourable impression.[2]

As rapidly as the date set for the preliminary examination of the conspir-ators-turned-reformers approached, just as swiftly did Hammond's health falter. On 3 February, he attended the opening day of an extended inquiry that would last until 8 April, in order to determine whether or not the accused would be formally committed to trial.[3] The presiding officer, Mr Zeiler, had little difficulty in separating the wheat from the chaff. All the members of the dummy Reform Committee were released on payment of a bail of $10 000 each.[4] It was the first and last occasion that Hammond presented himself at the examination. By the second day, he was so palpably incapacitated that the prison authorities decided that he was not fit enough to attend the hearings. When Natalie Harris clapped eyes on her despond-ent spouse she was so alarmed that she told him, straight out, 'Jack, I am going to dig you out of this jail.'[5]

And she did – that very day. Using the Californian, Tom Mein, as her go-between she soon found a vacant cottage in the town that the owner was pleased to allow them make use of. As Hammond recalled it:

> … by the end the day, I had been moved into a small cottage in Pretoria. My wife, her maid, and my sister Betty were permitted to be with me. Captain de Korte, a Dutch officer serving with the Boers, lived with us in the house. Thirteen men formed the exterior guard.[6]

Having made themselves known to Mr Kruger had done them no harm.

But, to Natalie Harris's dismay, the move to the cottage did nothing to improve the condition of her husband, who felt that an infection picked up on a trip to Rhodesia 'had been aggravated by distressing experiences in the jail'. What precisely those experiences were he chose not to elaborate on. Hammond – Natalie now believed – also had a 'feeble pulse and a heart which murmured when it beat'. All in all, circumstances demanded that she place her husband in even more congenial surroundings to facilitate his recovery. With the assistance of the lawyers, she lodged a new appeal that Jack be allowed to move to their home, in Johannesburg. She was convinced that her husband's life was in danger, a view shared, though to a lesser extent, by Dr Murray, their physician.[7]

The lawyers, sensing that high-level diplomatic interventions were beginning to lower the political temperature in the Boer capital, decided that, if they were to make representations on Hammond's behalf, they might as well request that similar concessions be considered in regard to Lionel Phillips, Frank Rhodes and George Farrar. To everyone's surprise, their request was granted on condition that the conspirators posted bail of $50000 each. All four would then be allowed to move into private accommodation – Hammond into his home in Parktown and the other three in a cottage at Sunnyside, Pretoria. With Hammond's local assets frozen, it was left to his first employer and friend in South Africa, Barney Barnato, to stump up the required cash.[8]

By 18 February, the day of the infamous Braamfontein dynamite explosion, the entire Hammond ménage was back in its luxurious home on the ridge overlooking Johannesburg. Mrs Hammond noticed that her husband's health showed 'a decided change for the better' but, after a week or so, it once again began to deteriorate. Fully apprised of the political support they had garnered in Washington, and as determined as ever, Natalie decided to up the stakes and requested that her husband be allowed to recover his health by the seaside, in far-off Cape Town.

The Hammonds' request was granted on condition that an additional $50 000 was lodged as bail and, once more, the ever-helpful Barnato came to the family's rescue. But so concerned was Mrs Hammond that the authorities might change their minds that she bundled her husband and son onto the overnight train, fully two days before she and her loyal maid scarpered to the coast.[9]

Never before, or since, in the history of the country, perhaps the world, had a prisoner being held on charges of high treason been afforded such generous, pre-trial consideration on the grounds of dysentery alone. In Cape Town the Hammonds lived briefly in Rhodes's cottage on the False Bay coast and then, for two months, just down the road, in a fine hotel at Muizenberg.[10]

Over the weeks that followed, Hammond's health improved so markedly that he could soon walk about reasonably freely. During this time he and his wife heard news of the fate of the other Reformers or saw one or two others who had collapsed in the face of the storm on the Highveld. Charles Leonard, whose levels of anxiety were matched only by those of Hammond himself, had collapsed in Cape Town suffering from 'brain congestion' before fleeing to England. Richard Parker, Victor Clement's successor as manager at the flagship Simmer & Jack Mine and who had escaped from the Rand dressed as a priest, was advised by Hammond to flee to America. RWM Schumacher from the House of Beit, who had been so recalcitrant a witness at the preliminary examination that he was locked up for contempt of court, was another at the coast 'for building up'. But probably the saddest case of all was their fellow American, JS Curtis, who had suffered a stroke that had paralysed one side of his face and whose mental condition had deteriorated to such an extent that some went so far as to describe him as 'deranged'. So poorly was Curtis that the state first postponed, and then dropped, all charges against him.[11]

The Hammonds, however, were never so hard-pressed that they could not find the time to do a little political work when the opportunity presented itself. Hammond had visits from several high-ranking officials, including Rhodes's successor as Prime Minister of the Cape Colony, Sir Gordon Sprigg, whose railway tariff problems Jack promptly attempted to leverage to the advantage of Rand interests. Natalie Harris became a close friend of Jessie Rose-Innes, wife of James Rose-Innes, the eminent Cape lawyer whom the British government had briefed to keep a watch on the proceedings relating to the trial of the Reformers.[12]

Hammond's health, although still precarious, held up reasonably well as the date for the Reformers' trial – set for 24 April – slowly came into view. The couple's nerves were set further on edge when, a few days before Hammond was due to return to Pretoria, JC Manion, the American consular agent, and 'Barbarian' Brown – feeling increasingly guilty about his earlier roles as a Boer sympathiser and informer – arranged a private meeting with Natalie Harris of which Hammond apparently bore no knowledge.

News from the north was not good. Manion and Brown were of the opinion that Hammond would almost certainly face the death penalty if he returned to stand trial. Even more alarming were rumours that he could be 'assassinated' on the way back or – the ultimate horror for anyone raised in Mississippi – that he might be 'lynched' by the Boers.[13] So terrifying were these prospects that the normally unflinching Natalie Harris lost her composure and all sense of perspective. Without waiting for her husband to reappear from a doctor's appointment, she commanded their coachman to rush her to the nearest person of influence she knew. 'Dear Mr. Rose-Innes,' she pleaded, 'I am in need of a friend; my distress is so great that I can no longer distinguish right from wrong.' She had, she claimed, toyed seriously with the idea of rendering her husband unconscious with chloroform and getting him placed on a ship back to the United States rather than lose him, but could not contemplate the dishonour. Rose-Innes reassured her that her husband would be doing the right thing by returning to stand trial, and that he would have given his own brother that same sage advice.[14]

Amid all these distressing developments, Hammond's health underwent another sudden deterioration. 'Just before my scheduled departure,' he recalled in his memoirs, 'I became so ill that my friends petitioned the

Boer government for a stay.' But this time the Kruger government was having none of it and he was ordered to be present when the High Court in Pretoria convened at ten o'clock, Friday 24 April. Hammond reached the capital, but not the court, at the last possible moment. His health was such that he was unable to attend the first day of the hearing, and by then Advocate JW Wessels, counsel for the defence, had already reached an understanding with the state's prosecutor, Dr Herman Coster.[15]

As 'far as the leaders were concerned', Hammond recalled, 'we were of one mind to accept whatever punishment might be decreed for us in order to exculpate as far as possible the other Reformers, many of whom had been induced to enter the revolution by our example'. To lend effect to this outcome, three of the core conspirators had already agreed to plead guilty to a charge of high treason, working on the assumption that they would be tried in terms of the existing South African Republic's statutes, rather than Roman-Dutch law, which prescribed the most dire penalty possible for so serious a crime against the state. Hammond belatedly agreed and then duly appended his own signature to the plea of guilty.[16]

The trial, however, took several unexpected turns. First, given that several judges of the Transvaal High Court, some of whom also owed the mining companies money, had either been involved in prior negotiations with the Reform Committee during the crisis or one or other of the processes leading up to the trial proper, the state had appointed a new judge, Justice R Gregorowski, a man with a much-feared reputation, to hear the case. Second, counsel for the defence was shocked when the prosecutor produced the notorious 'letter of invitation', signed by the four core conspirators, that Dr Jameson had used as his principal reason for invading the republic, and which had resulted directly in lives being lost. The raiders had neglected to destroy all their correspondence and dispatches prior to surrendering at Doornkop. Third, once the gravity of the case against the accused had been demonstrated beyond reasonable doubt, the State Attorney asked for the death penalty to be imposed, as prescribed by Roman-Dutch law.[17]

But Judge Gregorowski must have been aware of the fact that, barely five years earlier, the Kruger government had responded to widespread international diplomatic and popular protests at the death sentence being imposed on two Irish highwaymen. Their sentences had been commuted to lengthy periods of imprisonment at the last moment and the judge probably knew that he would not have the final say in the matter before him as regarded the core conspirators.[18] On Tuesday 28 April he therefore did as Roman-Dutch law commanded him and handed down the death sentence to Hammond and the three other accused, but, in passing judgment on Lionel Phillips, pointed out that the gift of mercy rested with the State President and the members of his executive.

As sentence was passed, Hammond was 'angered by Boer treachery to the point where' he felt that 'fear could play no part'.[19] Natalie Harris observed that 'Although pale and weak from protracted illness' her husband responded to the registrar's question 'in a firm voice' and, like his co-conspirators, accepted his sentence 'without showing any outward sign of emotion'. The remaining members of the Reform Committee, minus JS Curtis, were sentenced to two years' imprisonment and a fine of $10 000 each. Natalie Harris, beyond grief – 'I had no tears to shed' – saw the trial as 'a mockery of justice and a travesty upon civilisation'.[20]

The absence of more dramatic responses on the part of the *soi-disant* revolutionaries upon learning that they would be sent to the gallows may have been born only out of an intentional display of bravery; it was certainly reported on in that way by members of the press. Hammond, by his own account, was beyond fear at that point and Frank Rhodes was said to have winked at his co-conspirators as he left the dock to take his seat. But, the pluck of the revolutionaries may also have been underwritten a little earlier by a few comforting words in private coming from their extremely competent counsel for the defence.

Advocate Wessels, like the judge, would have been aware of the fact that the case of the Irish highwaymen, in 1891, had demonstrated that, when it came to hanging white men in the South African Republic, the reach of the law was limited. It was inconceivable that Wessels, and his clients, did *not* know about the precedent of a death sentence for white men being commuted – not least of all because none other than Charles Leonard's brother, James Leonard, had been one of those representing the highwaymen during their appeals for clemency.[21] The predations of the Irish Brigade in the early 1890s had demonstrated how vulnerable towns in the republic were open to occupation by criminal-political invaders – a lesson that was not lost on those who planned the revolt on the Rand and the 'Jameson Raid'. But the fate of Irish Brigade members sentenced to death in 1891 had also taught the revolutionaries in Johannesburg – political criminals – that it was extremely unlikely that the state would ever execute four white men. President Kruger and his executive, too, knew the rules of the game.

In short, no matter how shocking the news of the imposition of the death penalty on Hammond, Phillips, Farrar and Frank Rhodes might have been for those in court, for the public at large, or indeed for newspaper readers throughout the Western world, it was part of a set piece. The subsequent scenes in Pretoria were drawn from a drama first staged in Pretoria in 1891, one in which the judge, the State President, his executive and the condemned men alike were only too aware what the likely denouement would be. That did not mean that the sentence was not harrowing for the Hammonds or the others involved. A likely outcome was not a guaranteed outcome, and things could certainly go wrong – but the situation was hardly as bleak as it was made out to be.

President Kruger, who had not put a diplomatic or political foot wrong throughout the half-cocked revolt in Johannesburg that was meant to trigger Jameson's invasion, played his part perfectly. Within hours of Gregorowski having donned the black cap, the President met with his executive and, after some debate, it was decided to commute the death sentences to 15 years' imprisonment. The Boers had succeeded in turning a potentially disastrous threat to the republic into an international diplomatic triumph. But, in politics, timing is everything. Kruger was not about to reveal his trump card to the press or to release the pressure on the self-styled revolutionaries until his government could extract maximum advantage from the situation. The four conspirators went to bed that Tuesday night to the sound of carpenters erecting the gallows, and still uncertain as to whether or not they were going to be executed.[22]

After a sleepless night, the condemned men arose on Wednesday 29 April to swop a few notes, but before they could settle into a fully-fledged discussion, the door to their cell was opened and they were confronted by Kruger's widely disliked State Secretary, Dr Willem Leyds. For reasons that are unclear but may have been part of the political play, but which Hammond attributed to pure malice, Leyds told the conspirators that their sentences had been commuted to life imprisonment. It was only days later that the commutation, to 15 years, was confirmed.[23]

This news had a near-miraculous effect on the dysentery that had plagued Hammond since the implosion of the revolution six months earlier. 'As if I had reached the nadir of human misery,' he recorded in his memoirs, 'my health began to mend from almost the moment I received the death sentence.'[24] For all that his influential supporters back in America and elsewhere knew, however, Hammond was still not only a sick man, but one facing the executioner.

Within hours of Gregorowski handing down the judgment, a Republican Senator from Nevada, WM Stewart, a lawyer devoted to furthering mining interests and passionately pro-silver, mobilised members of the US Congress to come out in support of a petition to President Kruger to have Hammond unconditionally pardoned. Vice President Adlai Stevenson and no less than 251 Congressmen and Senators supported a plea that was promptly forwarded to Pretoria by telegraph through Richard Olney at the State Department.[25] It was precisely the sort of international recognition and respect that President Kruger relied on to justify his earlier intervention in the 'Hammond Affair'.

In Pretoria, somebody in the know, possibly Sammy Marks, gave Mrs Hammond the tip that it might be an opportune moment for her to

renew her attempts to secure her husband's release. Already a beneficiary of
Kruger's benevolence several times over, the indefatigable and still-pregnant
Natalie Harris once again set out for the capital. But the Hammonds were
in danger of overplaying their hand. The President's decision not to hang
the conspirators was not one that enjoyed universal support among his Boer
voters. 'The interview,' Mrs Hammond noted, 'lasted five minutes and was
perfectly meaningless.' But just days later she was back at it, along with the
wives of other Reformers who, without an appointment to see the State
President, waylaid him in the street on his way home from a funeral. Kruger,
patient to a fault, told them: 'Wait, don't hurry me. I must go slowly or my
burghers will get out of hand.'[26]

For much of that May, Hammond and his co-conspirators, along with
the erstwhile members of the Reform Committee, were left to amuse and
fend for themselves as best possible. Cowboy Jack, free of the collywobbles, smoked smuggled cigars, 'played marbles' and took a closer interest
in his surroundings. He also heard about the exploits of some of the more
notorious inmates who had passed through the jail, later spinning them
into unlikely personalised yarns fit for chatter over drinks at the club, or to
be incorporated into his memoirs. It was precisely the sort of thing that, as
already noted, later allowed some of Hammond's critics to dismiss his autobiography as being 'full of lies', and to suggest that he took the experiences
of others to present as his own.[27]

Then, towards the end of the month, Mrs Hammond fell seriously ill.
Once again the Pretoria authorities proved to be accommodating and
understanding in equal measures, allowing Hammond to return to the family home in Johannesburg to take care of his wife without having to post
bail or remain under guard. He was, for the most part, out on his own recog-
nisance, in a relationship of trust. At about the same time other Reformers,
too, were granted weekend privileges on terms that were equally relaxed.
Once his wife was out of danger, Jack Hammond returned to prison under
his own steam. Recalling these events a few months later, his wife was at
pains to underscore for her readers how well Hammond's behaviour – then
still under question in some quarters for not having gone to the aid of
Jameson – accorded with the Southern norms they adhered to. 'No point
in my husband's career,' wrote Natalie Harris, 'has ever given me so entire a
sense of gratification as the confidence in his *honour* thus manifested by the
Boer government.'[28]

Back in the United States, however, news of Mrs Hammond's illness
only compounded the belief in certain quarters that Jack Hammond's own
health was still in a most precarious state. In early June, General Harris
prompted Senator Catchings of Mississippi and the family's New York
attorney, Charles Truslow, to mobilise the Yale old boy network and make

one last determined push to try and spring Cowboy Jack from prison in Pretoria. Assistant Attorney General Whitney, with the help of the Secretary of State, would try to persuade President Cleveland to send a 'personal cable to Kruger asking clemency for Hammond because of Hammond's poor health'. But Richard Olney, who had already gone about as far as he could with Grover Cleveland in foregrounding the 'Hammond Affair', would not budge. 'The President,' he told consular officials, 'would not feel justified in making any personal appeals to the President of the South African Republic on behalf of Mr Hammond.'[29]

The President of the South African Republic, however, content in the knowledge that Jameson was about to stand trial in London was, quite independently, readying himself to tidy up any of the remaining problems relating to the revolutionaries and the choir of Reformers. The Kruger government displayed customary adroitness in handling the matter. It sent up a kite on 30 May when, with the exception of Aubrey Wools-Sampson and Karri Davies, who refused to agree to the terms offered, it released all the members of the Reform Committee who paid a fine of $10 000 and, in lieu of banishment, made 'a promise to keep out of Transvaal politics for three years'.[30] It was precisely the signal that the four core conspirators had longed for; the endgame was about to be played in their strongest suit – money. Inevitably, an auction followed.

Advocate Wessels wrote to the Executive Council bidding $40 000 each for the release of four revolutionary leaders – money that Hammond, gaining rapidly in self-confidence, began referring to as 'ransom' money. The counterbid from the Kruger government came in at $250 000, a sum that Hammond, a man whose wallet opened only with the greatest difficulty when called upon to pay, felt was 'too high' for him, although in his view his 'fellow prisoners could have paid the sum without feeling its loss'. The figure eventually settled at $125 000 dollars each, on the proviso that any payment was accompanied by a statement of gratitude. Back on the path they hoped might allow them to recover lost dignity, the conspirators sent back a message telling Kruger that they would 'rot in prison before we would both pay him *and* thank him for accepting our money'. This created a temporary impasse, Hammond noted later, 'that lengthened our period of detention by several days'.[31]

On 11 June, a delegation of about 150 mayors from southern African towns arrived in the capital to petition, in person, for the release of the conspirators – a development with yet another faint echo of the campaign five years earlier that had led to a reprieve for Cooper and McKeone, the condemned Irishmen. The State President, having squeezed the last drops from what was starting to become a political lemon, relented and the deal was sealed at $125 000 without any expression of gratitude but on the explicit understanding that the four revolutionaries would refrain from any political engagement in the state for a period of three years on pain of banishment. Frank Rhodes, unwilling to accept the rider, was released on payment of his fine and put across the border in Rhodesia, where he helped his brother fight the resurgent Ndebele and Shona tribesmen. Lionel Phillips and George Farrar both agreed to the terms, but Phillips broke them when, not long thereafter, he authored an article in a London journal about the Raid. Hammond, however, was loath to be cut off from the Rand and the goose that laid the golden egg. He, too, agreed to steer clear of any formal involvement in local politics and his fine was paid by Cecil Rhodes, part of an advance on profits due to him from the operations of Consolidated Gold Fields.[32]

The Hammonds could not get out of Johannesburg fast enough. They had long planned to take up residence in London at some point in the first quarter of 1896. The original intention had been for Natalie to base herself in Cape Town, at the Vineyards Hotel, until after the revolution of the Rand's professional classes, and for the couple then to make their way to England in good time for the birth of their third child. True, the revolution from above had failed dismally, but it was still possible for the baby to be delivered in leafy London, though they needed to make a very speedy exit.

On 20 June, the same day that Jameson's trial in London commenced, the engineering staff at Consolidated Gold Fields took leave of their chief at a function where Hammond was handed a formal letter of thanks signed by some of the men who had reported to him before the troubles. The letter, carefully crafted, was predictably strong on sentiment and made no mention of the storms that had been visited upon the company by Cecil Rhodes and Hammond. 'Our respect for you as a man, our admiration for you as an Engineer and our affection for you as a friend,' the letter read, 'is most strong.' Hammond treasured a letter written to him by loyal stalwarts at a time when he was filled with self-doubt and plagued by reputational uncertainties that would follow him to London.

But stripped of the names of old friends – Victor Clements and Pope Yeatman – the letter had been signed by only a dozen of the more than 20 engineers Hammond had once commanded along the Reef.[33] There was no note from Rhodes, away fighting the new war in Rhodesia, or anybody else of substance in the company. Jack Hammond's future in the profession, well, in Johannesburg at least, was far from certain. No wonder he preserved that letter; it was a fig leaf of respectability handed to him at one of the most vulnerable moments in a long career.

In Cape Town, Hammond and his wife had a day or two more to contemplate their losses before boarding the steamer for Plymouth. Natalie Harris noted ruefully that 'Revolutions are expensive games to play'. Hammond himself, however, was deeply distressed about that which money – of which they already had plenty – could *not* buy. In particular, he fretted about those values that he had been taught as a boy by Coffee Hays and John Freaner, back at the ranch school in California. Through extraordinarily persistent efforts at lobbying in the United States, two other Southerners – Natalie and Nathaniel Harris – had, as it were, conjured up a writ of *habeas corpus* amid all his troubles. Hammond's body, thankfully restored to full health, was there for all to see, ready to travel anywhere in the world that his call-ing might take him. But what of the ways in which others now assessed his inner qualities after the debacle in Johannesburg? What were his peers back home in America making of him as a man? He already knew that serious questions were being asked in many quarters around the world about the courage, honour and manliness that the Reformers had displayed when they became aware of Jameson's plight at Doornkop. It would take much seri-ous thinking and a great deal of careful planning if he were to recover his self-image as a cowboy-knight and the respect of gentlemen in the clubs of London, Johannesburg and San Francisco. And how could they succeed if he could not become politically involved?

CHAPTER TWENTY-TWO

Smoking the Peace Pipe without Inhaling

Hammond and Jameson

c 1895–1896

Long before Leander Starr Jameson set off on his impetuous dash for the Witwatersrand, Jack and Natalie Hammond had decided that their third child would be born in England, and that when the time was right they would push on and return to America. It was a decision that had been made from a position of strength, but the debacle on the Rand had transformed it into one of necessity and weakness. With both his personal and professional reputation tarnished, Hammond needed time to demonstrate continuity in his career and to find ways of repairing the damage to his image as a man of courage and honour prior to returning to a sceptical United States.[1] These formidable tasks were made significantly worse by the messy denouement to the Raid, which had further complicated the always skewed interpersonal relations between himself, Rhodes and Jameson.

Cecil Rhodes was the key to the puzzle. In theory, the fiasco had left Rhodes – seen by most as the evil wizard behind it all – with an awkward choice. Given that the Raid had been triggered by Jameson's wilful disregard of Hammond's instruction not to set off until the conspirators had started the revolution, and by the Reformers' subsequent inability and/or refusal to go to the invaders' rescue, any choice made public would leave one of his two lieutenants stranded morally. Jameson might have been in the wrong on the day but his action was born of bravery and loyalty to a friend and the imperial cause. Hammond, for all his inaction, had provided them with a template for a revolution, even if he had failed to deliver the logistical support necessary for staging a successful coup d'état. The one was a long-standing intimate and personal physician, the other, also a good friend, was, arguably, the world's finest mining engineer, with unparalleled expertise in developing deposits of precious metals.

In practice, of course, Rhodes was not about to choose between the man closest to his heart and the man stuffing his wallet. Like most politicians, he saw no reason to be forced into making contrived choices and, instead, supported both friends in public and in private; there was always a third way.[2] But, while this tactic did much to ease the tension in his own corner of an awkward triangular relationship, it did nothing to relieve the hostility between Jameson and Hammond. That ugly wound never healed fully.[3]

It was Rhodes, partly out of self-interest, since his gold mines were by then financially more lucrative than his diamond holdings, who threw Hammond the lifeline that safeguarded his career in the short term. Indeed, by Hammond's telling, it was 'at Rhodes's special request' that 'I renewed my engagement with Consolidated Gold Fields'.[4] Either way, remaining on as consulting engineer, for the old firm, not only allowed Hammond to return to southern Africa every year but also paid handsomely.

It was January 1897, close on a year after the capitulation at Doornkop and the surrender in Johannesburg, before Rhodes got to see either Hammond or Jameson face to face. It was a lapse in time that, even making allowance for the Big Man's involvement in putting down the extended African rising in Rhodesia, excited some adverse comment. In the intervening 12 months, however, the unhappiness between Hammond and Jameson had continued to fester.[5]

For any man who outlives his cohort and documents his memoirs, death is a friend; it silences most contrary witnesses. Hammond, who lived 20 years longer than did Jameson, despite the two having been born within just three years of one another, could never bring himself to forgive Jameson for his folly. Out there, in the land of the pot and the kettle, as in love and war, the spoils went to the last man standing. In his autobiography Hammond condemned Jameson for manifesting 'the psychology of a military man', for having 'personal motives' and for being possessed of 'overweening ambition'. Hammond might as well have been writing about himself; perhaps he was. Long after Jameson's death Hammond continued to pick away at the scabs. The four 'leaders of the Reform Committee', Hammond alleged, were 'deeply incensed against Jameson for what we justly regarded as his betrayal of us'.[6]

Jameson, who belatedly acknowledged that he had been wrong to set off from Pitsani in defiance of the wishes of his co-conspirators, nevertheless felt let down by the lack of revolutionary spirit and zeal displayed by Hammond and his co-conspirators at the time.[7] Hardly surprising then that, during their brief overlap in prison in Pretoria, 'resentful glances' had been exchanged between the various aggrieved parties, that after the surrender 'Jameson was exceedingly bitter against the Reform Committee', and that, while in London, Jameson did not respond to letters from Hammond and others.[8]

What angered and frustrated Hammond most about this undeclared war, particularly during 1896, when he and Jameson were both in London and within easy reach of the world's press, was Jameson's studied refusal to refute publicly the accusation of cowardice that had been levelled at Hammond and the rest of the Reformers for not effecting a rescue attempt in the hours leading up to the humiliating surrender at Doornkop. A charge of cowardice was damaging to a Southerner's reputation at any time, but it was mortifying at the moment when the sun was shining so brightly on Britain and its empire.[9] Moreover, Britain was planning the celebrations that would mark Queen Victoria's Diamond Jubilee in mid-1897 − an occasion to parade heroes and victories and spurn the vanquished and the weak.

The accusation also came at a time when, as the western frontier in America was closing, there was an outburst of aggressive masculinity that would feed into the imperialistic expansion of the United States into Cuba, Hawaii and the Philippines, in 1898.[10] It was hardly the moment for a man intent on occupying a leading role on the stage of world affairs to be cast as a coward, or to be seen as faint-hearted.[11]

For the Anglophile Hammond, the charge of cowardice was doubly hurtful. It called into question his credentials as a member of the brave 'Anglo-Saxon race', a cause that he, an admirer of the British aristocracy, and his wife, who flirted with the notion of eugenics, were greatly attached to.[12] But, more importantly, it chewed away at his self-respect, at the notion of himself as a man − or, to use Owen Wister's characterisation of the noble male raised on the western frontier of the United States − as a 'cowboy-knight'.[13] And the humiliation was felt all the more deeply because Hammond came from an extended family that, on both sides, was immersed in the American military tradition.

Any feelings of humiliation or vulnerability experienced by the Hammonds in England were aggravated by a surge in interest in notions of bravery and chivalry as expressed through popular literature of the time. In 1898, Charles Major's novel, *When Knighthood was in Flower*, set in Tudor England, became a best-seller. It was followed by a slew of other successful historical romances about knights errant that presented 'a cognitive and libidinal map of US geopolitics during the shift from continental conquest to overseas empire'. For Hammond, a man with political ambitions, this 'redefining national power as disembodied − that is, divorced from contiguous territorial expansion', meant that both the Jameson Raid and his questionable role in it remained under scrutiny.[14]

As long as the charges of dishonour directed at the Reformers lingered, they not only made for a certain hushed embarrassment when the Hammonds were negotiating London's most elevated social circles, they also effectively barred the couple from making a dignified re-entry into the United States of America. Thus, between 1896 and 1899, when the coming of the Anglo-Boer War began throwing up a smokescreen that seemed retrospectively to justify Jameson's unfortunate raid, Mr and Mrs Hammond had to contend with the side-effects of a psychological and physical exile from the country in the worlds that mattered most to them.

The fact that he was not yet ready to return to America – ostensibly solely on the grounds of work commitments – was a recurrent theme in Hammond's private correspondence in the closing quarter of 1896.[15] But the real cause of the couple's delayed return to the United Sates almost certainly derived from the social stigma associated with the accusation of cowardice. For the Hammonds, the one raised as a 'Southerner' in San Francisco, and the other in Vicksburg, Mississippi, the manly code of honour, as exemplified by General Nathaniel Harris, remained of the utmost importance.[16] Jack Hammond found the imputation of dishonour, all of which he traced back to Jameson's impulsivity in December 1895, almost unbearable.

Public hostility to the chastened Reformers dated back to almost the moment that Jameson surrendered at Doornkop. Within hours of the diminutive Doctor's capture, 'a song dedicated to the "Hero of the Hour"', Jameson, was on sale in Johannesburg.[17] But, whereas praise – even such misguided praise – tends to surface almost instantly, the spread of criticism can be slow but deadly. It was not very long before the venom directed at the ousted Reformers began to do its work.

In March 1896, eight weeks after the collapse of the revolution, a three-act skit entitled *A Slump in Heroes: A Transvaal War Drama without Warriors*, started doing the rounds on the Witwatersrand. That the satire, which was unsparing of Rowland Bettington, the stockbroker who commanded the only military strike force at the disposal of the Reformers during the revolt, should circulate freely in Johannesburg was one thing. But that the same work was then published in London and New York was another. It was a low blow, one threatening the careers of those members of the locust elite who calibrated their economic and social success against American and English yardsticks.

Hammond emerged unscathed from *A Slump in Heroes*, although two others in his American inner circle – Fred Lingham, the timber merchant, and Charlie Butters, the engineer – were not spared. Nor were a few of the more prominent Englishmen, such as Abe Bailey or Fred Hamilton. The extraordinary silence around Jack Hammond, however, hinted at other difficulties with the *Slump*, which, after only a few weeks and in the face of a threatened libel action, disappeared from the bookshops in Johannesburg almost as quickly as it had appeared.[18]

Taken as a whole, it was striking how lightly the American conspirators, and more especially *the* chief conspirator, got off in the *Slump* – a silence that may have something to do with the fact that the author, Harold Bolce, who made enough money from the satire for him and his wife to undertake an extensive tour around the Mediterranean, was himself Californian. Trained at the University of California as a theologian, Bolce had gone on to become a journalist in Spokane, Washington, where he had a close-up view of the depth and strength of Hammond's connections and influence during the Coeur d'Alene mining war.[19] After his travels, Bolce again settled in San Francisco, where he eventually established the 'Cosmopolitan Church'. Could it be that it was fear of Hammond and the likes of Clement, Gardner Williams and Captain Mein that explains both American absences and the far greater prominence of Englishmen such as Bettington and Bailey in the skit?

Hammond, a champion of the 'free press' that embraced his causes and an enthusiastic underwriter of the printed media generally, was not beyond attempting to silence the voice of newspaper critics. Indeed, during the crisis on the Rand he had tried – unsuccessfully – to have a journalist at the pro-Kruger *Standard & Diggers' News* dismissed.[20] But the *Slump* was not the only problem the Reformers faced, and London was no mining town. It was impossible for Hammond or the Reformers to obtain insurance against the legendary English wit, and he found the derision draining. 'We had been selected as scapegoats,' he complained, 'and were being ridiculed in journalistic lampoons and music hall skits.' Then followed the painful rider: 'The opprobrium was undeserved and I could not understand why Jameson had so long been silent.'[21]

Any hope Hammond entertained that Jameson's trial, in late July 1896, might be the occasion at which the record might be set straight, was dashed when Jameson failed to clarify the issue surrounding the Reformers' alleged lack of courage in his hour of greatest need. Over the weeks that followed, Hammond became increasingly distraught about his public image and the whiff of dishonour that clung to him like the smell of wet dog. It became a prominent subject in his personal correspondence with fellow Americans. By early September, in the wake of yet another letter about the 'Raid' in the *Times*, he felt it necessary to beard the lion by writing to Bourchier Hawksley, the solicitor representing Rhodes, Jameson and the Chartered Company.

The letter to Hawksley was, by implication, a plea for him to exert pressure on Jameson to come out and exonerate the Reformers from charges of lack of loyalty and manliness. He found it 'extremely painful', Hammond informed Hawksley, 'to make a proper representation of my relation with Dr Jameson'. His main complaint was that

... the newspapers have persistently adhered to the opinion that after having invited Jameson to Johannesburg and having promised him aid, we deserted him, and these papers and the public generally have in consequence charged us with cowardice ... While I know Dr Jameson personally would not give public expression to such sentiments he has taken no steps to refute these misrepresentations ... Under the circumstances, Dr Jameson's silence has been a disappointment, perhaps an additional detriment to us.[22]

It was suitably understood, very English and designed to effect an outcome in England. The problem was, of course, that even if Jameson had issued a palliative statement, it would have done little to ease the Hammonds' passage back into the place that mattered most of all – the United States of America.

What Hawksley, Rhodes and Jameson might not have appreciated, however, was that the Hammonds were not inclined to wait on history to come to their rescue. Active and outcome-driven, they were always reluctant victims and not content to supplicate to Jameson via his solicitor. Kowtowing to Rhodes and freeing him or Joseph Chamberlain of any of the blame for the fiasco on the veld came easily to the Hammonds, who always had a special relationship with power or wealth, but they refused to bend the knee to Rhodes's lieutenant of choice, who, for the moment at least, possessed neither.[23]

Indeed, by the time Hawksley received the complaint about Jameson's silence Hammond had, for some weeks, been thinking how, without reneging on his deal with the Kruger government to steer clear of Transvaal politics for a time, he could mount a campaign in the United States centred on the written word that might vindicate his role in the failed Raid. Self-consciously 'Anglo-Saxon', he had access to a transatlantic culture that emphasised good government and honour – classic virtues that were part-English and part-American.[24]

But given the target audience, his campaign would have to be driven by those capable of identifying the attitudes, beliefs and values of contemporary readers in the United States, and of addressing audiences ranging from engineering professionals to the ordinary man or woman in the Pullman car. The authors who lent themselves to such a project were drawn, first, from within the ranks of the family and then, with some foresight and a little luck, one of the foremost journalists in the United States.

Nobody had better, longer or more widespread experience of riding to Hammond's aid than the redoubtable Natalie Harris. During the latter half of 1896, when not rocking new baby Richard's cradle out in the English countryside, or entertaining her husband's many guests, Natalie was studiously editing the diary that she had kept during the family's travails on the Witwatersrand only months earlier. Mrs John Hays Hammond's *A Woman's Part in a Revolution* was published, simultaneously, in London and New York City, in February 1897. The political context of the work was there for all to see, in the preface:

> To the American Public, whose sympathy was my chief support through the days of bitter trial, this book is gratefully dedicated. My personal experience forms the subject of my story. The causes of the Revolt in Johannesburg, and the ensuing political questions, are but lightly touched upon, in deference to the silence enforced upon my husband as one of the terms of his liberation by the Boer Government.[25]

The message was clear: John Hays Hammond was an honourable man but one who for the moment was not allowed to defend himself.

But was he? Or was the loyal Mrs Hammond – in part at least – being used as a cat's-paw, clearing the way for other sympathetic works that would defend her husband's role in events that, having only recently been recast as a legitimate attempt at reform, were now, post-trial, once again being proffered as a failed attempt at a revolution?

Bits of Natalie Harris's diary certainly do not read as if they are based purely on 'personal experience' recorded in the heat of battle; they seem more like a deliberate attempt to set the record straight about Jameson's indiscretions. Thus, at the time, Jack told her that 'the Reform Committee were greatly surprised when they received the report from Mr Lace, as Jameson had no right to expect aid and succour from Johannesburg for the following reasons'. Then followed, in point form and quasi-legalistic language, several reasons to show how deaf Dr Jameson had been to instructions from Johannesburg.[26] It was not the spontaneous flow of prose to be expected of a diary entry.

A few pages later, Mrs Hammond described how the notorious 'letter of invitation' calling for Jameson's assistance and signed by five of the core conspirators fell into Boer hands: 'It was picked up on the battlefield, in a leather pouch, supposed to be Dr Jameson's saddle bag. Why in the name of all that is discreet and honourable didn't he eat it'![27] The Doctor's reputation did not emerge unscathed from the account of Natalie Harris's 'personal' experiences. The book was favourably reviewed by James Bryce, who had seen the coming of the upheavals on the Rand while visiting the Hammonds. Jack Hammond, architect of the onslaught against the workers in the Coeur d'Alene, as well as the aborted 'revolt' in Johannesburg, was of the view that it 'did much to allay prejudice against the Reformers'.[28]

The appearance and reception of his wife's book must have brought Hammond some relief because, over the previous six months he had made repeated, mostly unsuccessful, attempts, to frame the ways that editors of some of America's largest mass-circulation magazines portrayed the Raid and its aftermath. Here again, his primary objective was to portray Jameson as the sole villain of the piece and to free the Reformers of all charges of 'cowardice'.

When Hammond learned that Poultney Bigelow, an American author and foreign correspondent with a decided interest in muscular imperialism, had passed through Pretoria and interviewed President Kruger, he immediately sat down and wrote his fellow Yale alumnus a three-page, typewritten letter.[29] What he did not know was that Poultney, a man who later in life briefly admired Hitler and Mussolini, had only a passing interest in the Jameson Raid, and that he was preparing a more broadly focused work entitled *White Man's Africa*.

But Hammond, deeply concerned about his image in America, was taking no chances. So, in order to be helpful and informative, he took the liberty of offering Bigelow his own, unsolicited version of the Raid:

> I attribute the failure of the movement to the fact that Dr Jameson, against our express wishes, left before we had received our guns and had completed our organisation. We would have had a very different story to tell had Jameson obeyed our orders. One of the most galling accusations is that of the cowardice of the Johannesburgers in having invited Jameson to their rescue and then having deserted when he was not more than 16 miles from Johannesburg.[30]

Hammond's intervention, however, bore little, if any, fruit. When *White Man's Africa* appeared, in late 1897, the *Chicago Tribune* was full of praise for the author's portrayal of Kruger's many manly attributes but felt that 'Mr Bigelow's rehash of the Jameson episode adds little that is new'.[31] Most Americans, not least of all those holding progressive Republican values, remained deeply sceptical of the Rand Reformers.

In many instances, Hammond could only play catch-up politics by trying to cast doubt on others' reading of the failed revolution. When his former chief at the US Geological Survey, Dr GF Becker, undertook a professional visit to the Rand soon after the Raid, he visited Hammond in prison. Becker then approached Kruger with a message from his former employee to the effect that, while Hammond fully expected to be punished for his role in the failed revolution, his health would prevent him from spending any prolonged period in jail.[32]

Upon his return to the United States, however, George Becker made the mistake of presenting a paper on the subject of the 'Revolt of the Uitlanders' that did not accord with Hammond's interpretation of events. The response was instant and, given the two men's prior relationship, brutal. Hammond wrote a letter to the editor of the *Engineering and Mining Journal* dismissing his colleague's view as mistaken in fact and emanating from preconceived, prejudiced ideas.[33]

When the New York-based *Cosmopolitan* magazine approached Hammond about the possibility of his authoring an article on the Raid, he saw the chance to get his own view across with the sort of conviction matched only by the writings of his wife. He briefed William H Hall the former State Engineer of California, providing him with precisely the interpretation that would assist in the resurrection of his reputation and that of the Reformers.

Then, on 31 December 1896, he re-approached Miss Bushford in the editorial department at *Cosmopolitan* with what looked like an exciting alternative proposition. 'I have not seen a truthful account as of yet in any of the American papers about "the Johannesburg revolution",' he complained, but 'a friend of mine who has had exceptional facilities of getting "inside information" is writing an article to be sent to one of the American papers.' William Hall, he explained, had heard the story of the Raid from 'those who figured prominently in the affair, but who were unable themselves to make any statement owing to their pledge to the Transvaal Government' who had granted them their freedom. A nod was as good as a wink. Mr Hall, Hammond went on to confide, had informed him that he would be forwarding his article to Mr Charles W Truslow of the Mills Building in New York, from where it could be retrieved by any interested editor.[34]

Then, three days later, Hammond wrote to Truslow, his attorney in New York and the man who had done as much as any to lobby US Secretary of State Richard Olney during Hammond's short spell in prison in Pretoria, telling him that he was sending him an article written by William H Hall. Hall was not only the President of the Society of Hydraulic Engineers, he said, but 'very well known to the leading capitalists of the United States' as well. As Hammond saw it:

> The *Cosmopolitan Magazine* will probably send a representative to consider the question of its publication, if you can make reasonable terms with them, for of course Hall should be compensated [*sic*]. You are fully at liberty to dispose of it.[35]

Hall, a man as motivated by money as the man who had effectively commissioned an article to present his own views of Jameson and the Raid, was going to be 'compensated' so, not surprisingly, Hammond requested that his attorney 'treat the letter as confidential'. In retrospect, there was no need; the article, alas, was never published.

The *Cosmopolitan* initiative, however, not only illustrated just how desperate Hammond had become to salvage his reputation by late 1896, but also how his love of conspiracy and manipulation could, on occasion, compromise ethics that, in his view, intersected only tangentially with questions of 'honour'. Getting Hall to author the article – if he really was going to be the author and not Hammond himself – was a questionable way of circumventing his 'pledge' to the Kruger government. His paying Hall to circulate his own views raised yet other issues. But what was most damning of all about the episode was Hammond's failure to disclose, either to Miss Bushford or even to Truslow who his supposed 'friend', Mr WH Hall, really was.

'Mr Hall' was, to give him his full name, William Hammond Hall. He was John Hays Hammond's cousin and he hailed from Hagerstown, Maryland, as did many others in their extended family. Hall, like Hammond, was an avaricious man with deep insecurities. Like Hammond's father, when the latter was still Collector of Customs in San Francisco, William Hall had sometimes found it difficult to distinguish between the public and private purse in California. After a while he 'gave up engineering for land speculation, a pursuit he had followed ardently even as state engineer'.[36] As a speculator, Hall soon realised that cities such as San Francisco would become abnormally water-dependent and he later got involved in some dubious business schemes, at least one of which, the Sierra Ditch and Water Company, Hammond secretly funded in the hope of sharing in windfall profits.[37]

But Hammond was not only readying himself to use Hall in an attempt to regain lost personal prestige. He was, with the help of Rhodes and other capitalists, positioning his cousin to advise the mining industry on how best to secure a reliable supply of water for the Witwatersrand.[38] More importantly still, while in southern Africa, Hall gave evidence to the Kruger government's 1897 Industrial Commission – the state's own attempt at post-Raid reform. Hall's evidence to the commission mirrored many of Hammond's own views on the optimal arrangement between the state and capital, and how to further modernise the republic's still-booming mining industry.[39]

In this indirect way, then, Hammond used a family connection to make certain that his own influence and that of Consolidated Gold Fields continued to be exercised during his time in 'exile'. Moreover, it further facilitated ways in which capital raised on the Witwatersrand by Hammond and his engineering peers contributed, albeit in modest fashion, to the development of California's own gold-mining and hydroelectricity projects between 1895 and 1914.[40] All the more the pity, then, that a 'family row' between Hammond and the cantankerous Hall ended in a libel suit before the US District Court in New York, in 1913.[41]

But just when the setbacks with Becker, Bigelow and Hall threatened to push Hammond into a state of despondency about the decline in his standing in the United States, the Gods of Yale commanded that he be sent the help that might help restore his reputation in a manner befitting the elite. The decisive nudge towards the restoration of his reputation came via one of Hammond's former classmates, the influential and well-connected George C Webb.[42] The scion of a powerful, military family, Webb pushed one of the rising journalistic stars in the American firmament in Hammond's direction in 1896.[43] The man who tipped the scales in Hammond's favour was Richard Harding Davis.

Smelting

CHAPTER TWENTY-THREE

Aligning Fact and Fiction

Regaining a Reputation Lost

C 1895–1899

Richard Harding Davis was 32 years old when he met Hammond, who played his part in inspiring an ambitious young man to new journalistic and literary heights at a crucial moment in his career. Editor of the New York-based and widely circulating *Harper's Weekly*, Davis was also a correspondent for several newspapers given to sensationalist accounts that did not distinguish carefully between fact and fiction, a phenomenon then dismissed as 'yellow journalism'.[1]

Davis really shot to fame, however, about 18 months after meeting Hammond, at the height of the American imperialist push that manifested itself most clearly in the Spanish-American War of 1898. It was Davis's accounts that, in large part, helped transform Theodore Roosevelt into a national hero. But it was in the immediate prelude to the American invasion of Cuba and the Philippines that Davis and Hammond became firm friends, and collaborated on three projects that did much to enhance the profiles of both men in the United States.

By his own telling, Davis and George Webb were both at London's Savoy Hotel on the day that Jameson was sentenced, 27 July 1896. On learning that Hammond, too, was in the hotel, Davis spiked their conversation with the observation that 'if I had to choose, I would rather be in Holloway [prison] with Jameson than in the Savoy with Hammond'. Webb immediately suggested that such an opinion was ill-founded and, without informing Hammond of Davis's views, arranged for the two to meet and exchange notes over dinner at the Savoy.[2]

Hammond realised at once what was in the offing. Davis's 'influence on the press at the time was great', and his 'attitude was therefore important';

in short, it was an opportunity not to be missed. Hammond plied the news-paperman with his interpretation of the debacle at Doornkop, stressing Jameson's personal culpability. But the young man was only half-convinced. Hammond suggested that Davis verify his account of Jameson's flagrant disregard of instructions by speaking to Henry Holden, an intimate friend of the Doctor's, and one of the two messengers sent by the 'Reformers' to dissuade Jameson from setting off for the Rand before the revolution was set in motion.[3]

That did the trick. When next he saw Davis, about a month later, the journalist had been fully persuaded of Jameson's folly and, sensing a new angle to what was becoming an old story, was ready to come to the defence of what he saw as the much-maligned Reformers. 'Since [Davis] was first and foremost a newspaperman,' Hammond recalled, 'he composed a feature story and cabled it to the American newspapers.' He continued: 'He did the Reformers a great service.'[4] Indeed he did. But it was one Reformer in particular who benefited from an extremely timely intervention in the United States.

On 6 September 1896, the *San Francisco Call* ran Davis's lengthy account of Jameson's shortcomings beneath the bold – linked – headlines of 'Justifies the Raid' and 'Heroism of the Leaders Portrayed'. There was even a por-trait of the source of Davis's inspiration: 'John Hays Hammond, the Noted California Mining Engineer, Whose Heroism in the Transvaal is Set Forth in a New Light by Richard Harding Davis'.[5]

This small explosion of positive coverage could not have been better placed or timed; the article sealed the budding friendship between Hammond and Davis. A cowboy-knight, mocked for his 'cowardice' in Johannesburg and London, was, in fact, readying himself to ride back to California and the old West as a 'hero'. The ghosts of the Texas Rangers, Coffee Hays and John Freaner, could smile again.

After this West Coast vindication, and amid Hammond's unsuccessful conniving with other editors of popular American magazines, Davis became a frequent guest at the Hammond's first English home, in Bickley, Kent.[6] It was, however, not only Cowboy Jack who was delighted with the first meaningful steps taken to resurrect the Reformers' honour but also the author himself. Davis felt that, with a little effort, the article could be trans-formed into if not a short book that would be commercially viable, then a pamphlet that would circulate even more widely. That was the genesis of the 56-page *Dr Jameson's Raiders vs the Johannesburg Reformers*, published by Russell, in New York, in 1897.

The aim of *Raiders* was twofold, and its objectives could not have been laid out more clearly. It was, in the first instance, a direct assault on Jameson, underscoring the misguided foolishness of the Raid and consequences of his silence about the opprobrium that had been heaped on the revolution-aries-turned-reformers. More importantly, it was an intervention focused on Hammond and designed to erase the stains of cowardice from his sullied reputation.

Raiders opened with a grudging acknowledgement that Jameson had 'paid for his adventures like a man'. But, after that, it was open season on the Doctor:

> As he has had his turn, it seems only right now that he [Jameson] should give place in the public eye to those who have suffered as well as himself, and through his action, whose plans he spoiled and whose purposes his conduct entirely misrepresented to the world. For these other men of the Reform Committee have lain, owing to him, in a far worse jail than Holloway and some still lie there, some have been sentenced to death, while others have been fined fortunes, and, more than any else besides, they have had to bear the odium of having been believed, both in the United States and England, to have shown the white feather in deserting a comrade, and of failing to keep their promise of help they had held out to him.[7]

The counterattack against the charge of cowardice is sustained, with Jack Hammond emerging as *the* standard bearer for the Reformers. But, unlike the newspaper article that preceded it, the emphasis in *Raiders* shifts to the broader issue of 'conscience', something that embraced 'moral as well as physical courage'. In the closing paragraph of the work, Jameson and Hammond are pitted against one another in a contest that the brave cowboy-knight was destined to win:

> When people accuse the Reform Committee of cowardice, and of being men who failed to keep their word they should put before them these two pictures – the one of Jameson, surrounded by his 500 troopers, saying: 'Those men at Johannesburg are funking it and I am going to stir them up' and three days later raising the white flag; and the other of the American, Hammond, when still shaken with fever, he returned to serve out his sentence, and stood alone at midnight knocking for admittance at the gate of the Praetoria [*sic*] jail.[8]

The fictionalised parts of Davis's tale about Hammond appealed to readers and reviewers almost as much as did sections that offered a more factually accurate account of the Raid. But Hammond had, of course, been highly selective not only in what he had told Davis but also, more importantly, in what he had withheld. Hammond could tell lies of commission when

it suited his purpose, but his speciality was the untruth of omission. So, in
Raiders, the emphasis fell squarely on Hammond as a would-be law-abiding
Reformer, a reluctant revolutionary, with no mention of his planned attack
on the arsenal at Pretoria, the plot to abduct President Kruger, or his desire
to inflict constitutional changes on the South African Republic that would
benefit the mining houses.

All of this was largely of a piece with what Hammond later told another
journalist over a series of two articles, in 1918, that first appeared in the
North American Review and were then promptly republished in book form, in
Boston, as *The Truth about the Jameson Raid by John Hays Hammond as Related
to Alleyne Ireland*.[9] What that title implied about the earlier, Davis version is
another question.

The Ireland version, told at the tail end of the First World War, allowed
Hammond to develop one or two new fictions tailored to the times and
the preoccupations and prejudices of new readers. Thus, the revolt on the
Rand played out against a 'Kaiser-Kruger Plot' to foil British ambitions, and
Hammond's own attempts to mobilise workers for the revolution had to
take place in the face of counterpropaganda spread by President Kruger's
secret service, among whom there were 'many German agents'.[10] That was,
of course, so much hogwash. Hammond's fancies could be made to float
as easily in a John Buchan spy novel, such as *The Thirty-Nine Steps*, as they
could in a Charlie Siringo tale about the old West or the script of an early
cowboy movie.

None of that mattered a great deal. Davis's *Raiders* was picked up on with
almost as much enthusiasm as was his earlier newspaper article. Once again,
the work greased the rails that allowed Hammond to slide back into the
United States as a 'hero' by the time that the Anglo-Boer War broke out two
years later. A favourable review in the *Chicago Tribune*, for example, was heralded with the headlines, 'The Filibustering Doctor was too Eager for Glory
and only Spoiled the Plans of his Friends' and, predictably, 'Hammond's
Moral Courage'.[11]

The need for Hammond to separate fact and fiction more precisely – a
temptation that he often did his best to avoid – was lessened through continued interactions with his new chum during the latter part of 1896. Davis
was not only already a much-admired journalist but was also becoming a
novelist of note. For him, having direct personal access to an accomplished
engineer such as Hammond, a man of action who was as intelligent as he
was well-travelled, was a godsend.

'In the evenings at Bickley,' Hammond recalled in his memoirs, he, Davis
and Natalie Harris 'would sit and talk for hours.' In fact, so impressive were
the tales that the host told that Davis began to see in Hammond the experiences and qualities that might be woven into the character of the hero

Natalie Harris PHOTO: LIBRARY OF CONGRESS

Theodore Roosevelt PHOTO: LIBRARY OF CONGRESS

Richard Harding Davis

in a novel that was taking shape in his head. That work, *Soldiers of Fortune*, became a best-seller, was turned into a play and was twice filmed – before and shortly after the First World War.[12]

What appears to have eluded historians of both American and South African literature, however, is how the novel's hero, Robert Clay, was in good measure based on John Hays Hammond.[13] Moreover, by failing to recognise Hammond in the experiences and make-up of Clay – despite a nudge in the right direction by the man himself – analysts have also failed to detect a ghostly outline of the Jameson Raid in a novel about a failed coup d'état set in a South American republic.[14]

There is just no mistaking the Clay-Hammond link. Clay, who has the 'spirit of a soldier', comes from a military family; indeed his father was a filibuster in Cuba.[15] As a boy who lost his mother early, Clay considers a 'ranch in Colorado' as 'home' even though speculators have since 'cut it up into town lots'.[16] The young Clay is a widely admired 'cowboy' before qualifying as an engineer and, after obtaining a little experience on the Kimberley diamond fields, aspires to become an 'engineering expert'.[17] And the young lady whom Clay successfully woos in the novel clearly shares many of the attributes that Davis would have seen close up in Natalie Harris.[18]

'Olacho', the fictional Latin American coastal republic in which the drama unfolds, differs radically from the landlocked Transvaal, which, fortunately for President Kruger, was isolated from the threat of naval bombardment in an age of gathering American imperialism underwritten by an ever-expanding fleet.[19] Nor was the attempted coup in Olacho led by an American mining engineer, although the successful countercoup by an indigenous opposition, supported by trusted American workers, is directed by Clay and his faithful.[20] Yet, for all that, if the ears are strained but slightly, faint echoes of the Jameson Raid can be heard. So, there is a background border dispute between Ecuador and Venezuela, telegraph wires are cut at critical moments, cartridges are packed in tubs of lard and rifles are concealed in 'piano cases'.[21]

Soldiers of Fortune was a huge success for Davis, and, for those in the know about American politics and the elite of the engineering profession, it was not difficult to spot John Hays Hammond in the guise of Robert Clay. Hammond knew this and 'accepted the compliment', and he and Davis remained friends until the latter's death in 1915.[22] Between them, *A Woman's Part in a Revolution*, *Dr Jameson's Raiders* and *Soldiers of Fortune* acted as icebreakers, opening a narrow passage back to the United States, where Hammond's reputation nevertheless still lay largely frozen in a sea of suspicion.

This emerging transatlantic opening did nothing, however, to induce a thaw in relations between Hammond and the unfortunate Jameson. Indeed, most of the icebreakers' work had come at the expense of the Doctor's own reputation. Jameson was in poor shape physically and mentally. He had been released early from Holloway Prison, by royal command, late in 1896, after having undergone surgery for gallstones, and was living in Down Street, Mayfair. When Cecil Rhodes eventually appeared, in January 1897, he received confirmation that the relationship between Jameson and Hammond had broken down. The situation was intolerable; the one he needed personally, as a friend-physician, the other professionally, as Midas-engineer. Moreover, they would have to work together in the Matabeleland mining industry once the African risings were suppressed. It was left to Rhodes, the alchemist, to mix Hammond's oil of contempt with Jameson's water of forgiveness. It was an initiative that the former friends could not shun.

Even then, the reunion was not easily effected and the mixture barely cohered until Jameson's death, in 1917. Rhodes used Maurice Gifford, a Rhodesian veteran who had lost an arm in combat, as the principal intermediary to try to establish a *modus vivendi* between the warring lieutenants. Hammond, who by his own admission was still deeply resentful, was the more difficult of the two to persuade about the need for reconciliation. In order to avoid any scab-picking, both parties agreed to avoid, as far as was possible, discussing events leading up to the Raid.[23]

This arrangement worked tolerably well for several months, until Jameson returned to Rhodesia to resume his duties. Sensing how important the reconciliation was to Rhodes, both men did their best to keep their feelings under control. In order to isolate the detonator from the dynamite, Hammond took Frank Rhodes along whenever visiting the Doctor. Jameson, ill but keen to see the thing through, relayed only good news to brother Sam, back in Johannesburg: 'Hammond and Frank Rhodes have been to see me several times – very friendly but on the basis of no discussion of past events,' and then, 'Frank and Hammond come frequently, and I am on most affectionate terms with them.' But the marked absence of the more intimate form of address – Jack – probably told another, more painful story.[24]

The re-establishment of cordial relations between the Raider and the Revolutionary cleared the way for a professional relationship when the men were dealing with Chartered Company business, and reduced the chance of embarrassing exchanges whenever Hammond was called upon to travel to southern Africa. Nevertheless it is interesting to note that, more especially so in 1897, it was his cousin, WH Hall, who spent more time with Rhodes and Jameson than did Hammond himself. With the political heat in the country still abating, Hammond seemed content to allow Hall, who was contracted to Consolidated Gold Fields, to do most of the new consulting work for the company.[25]

It was not until another visit, in 1899, that Hammond again got to meet

Jameson face to face in Rhodesia. It was also during this visit that Hammond re-established contact with some unnamed politically 'Progressive' Boers – the comprador force that he had once hoped would help usher in a new era of capitalist development on the Witwatersrand. He also took the opportunity provided by his wife's acquaintance with the President to arrange for a meeting with Kruger himself. He then proceeded to advise the President as how best to go about negotiating the issues of reform with the Uitlanders if he was to avoid going to war with Britain – a war to which the Jameson Raid and the Johannesburg revolution had made an enormous contribution.[26]

Back in London, and after 1897, Hammond's sense of self-worth gradually reasserted itself, assuming proportions last seen in his Johannesburg hey-day, in 1895 – when, he and Natalie claimed, they had enjoyed a social life without parallel anywhere in the world. Davis and the publicity gains made back in the United States no doubt helped, as did the truce with Jameson as the edge came off the old saw about cowardice. The Hammonds moved from Bickley to nearby Chislehurst, where a rail connection placed them within easy reach of Charing Cross station, only ten miles away, allowing the Hammonds to entertain the great and the good in large numbers.[27]

One of the Hammonds' visitors there was Eugène Marais, who, in addition to studying law in London at the suggestion of Ewald Esselen, was, like the American couple, serving out time in exile before returning to the country of his birth. Elements of the old nexus linking members of the Boer fifth column to the Rand mine owners were clearly still intact. Having already told a few lies in order to gain admission to law school, Marais got Rhodes's former private secretary and later Secretary to Consolidated Gold Fields, in Johannesburg, Henry Currey, to propose him as a man of integrity and good standing in order for him to be accepted as a member of the Inner Temple.[28]

With the return of their former social buoyancy, the Hammonds found it easier to navigate London's aristocratic, artistic and political circles. The noisy celebrations of imperial glory, as marked by Queen Victoria's Diamond Jubilee, helped drown out many of the whispers of cynicism up and down the Thames. Amid public celebrations of imperial expansion and personal achievements, perhaps even those who had tried, but failed, were given a bit more leeway than usual as the century began to draw to a welcome close. As Hammond was happy to recall many years later:

> Of an evening in London one would find oneself in the midst of a thoroughly cosmopolitan assemblage. Under the same roof one might meet Viscount Grey, the statesman, Lecky the historian, Kipling, the writer, and Lady Elizabeth Cust's son, Sir Lionel, head of the National Portrait Gallery, the Duke of Argyll, and Sir Edward Elgar, the composer and conductor.[29]

These foundational interactions with the elite appealed greatly to both Hammonds and provided them with the sort of social currency that was invaluable once they were back in America and Washington.

Amid an embarrassment of social riches, it was the arch-imperialist, Rudyard Kipling, who perhaps got the closest view of the already much weakened triangular relationship that had once existed between Rhodes, Hammond and Jameson. It was Hammond, the first among the three to meet the poet, who was quick to introduce Kipling to Rhodes.[30] They became friends and Kipling then migrated south to spend a few northern winters on Rhodes's estate in Cape Town. But, of the three would-be musketeers it was Jameson that Kipling chose to immortalise.

So inspired was Kipling by Jameson's 'triumphs and disasters' that it moved him to pen 'If—', his famous ode to Victorian stoicism. Hammond forgot to point to the connection in his autobiography.[31] It was understandable. The opening lines of the first stanza might not have been to Hammond's taste: 'If you can keep your head when all about you / are losing theirs and blaming it on you, / If you can trust yourself when all men doubt you, / But make allowance for their doubting too; ...'

At the end of the day, however, it was not only the light and noise around the celebration of British imperialism that provided Hammond with some of the cover necessary for the gradual rehabilitation of his reputation. The closing years of his London exile witnessed the extraordinary surge in American imperialism. For some decades the United States had been content to make foreign conquests informally, through commerce and trade. But from the mid-1890s onwards, the United States began to use its growing navy to secure its long-term strategic interests in more direct fashion. The annexation of Hawaii, the outbreak of the Spanish-American War and the occupation of Cuba, in 1898, all bore testimony to an era of unashamed American territorial expansion.

From his home in Chislehurst, Hammond followed the Spanish-American War with interest and patriotic fervour. His new young friend, Harding Davis, was posted to Cuba where he served as war correspondent for the sensationalist Hearst newspapers. But, as importantly, Hammond went out of his way to cultivate the friendship of the eminent US Ambassador to the Court of St James's, John Hay.[32] Unlike in the rest of Europe, where political sympathies lay with Spain, in London the British – having rediscovered their diplomatic affinity with the Americans after their tangle in Venezuela – were solidly in support of the United States. This change, to a geopolitical climate in which military adventurism was viewed less critically than it might have been in mid-century, gave Hammond yet more political space. In retrospect, American involvement in the Jameson Raid seemed less out of step with the times and the evolution of American foreign policy.

Men like Hammond and his friends found themselves judged a bit more sympathetically.

Across the Atlantic, these shifts in the political current did not free Hammond fully from Republican disapproval of his role in the debacle on the Witwatersrand. But, as with the Harding Davis intervention, it did provide him with slightly more wiggle room when he eventually did return to the United States. But the old hostility among some Republicans was slow to die. It was Tom Reed, a former Speaker of the House of Representatives, who, at a banquet held for Hammond after the publication of *The Truth about the Jameson Raid*, stated: 'I was for hanging you, until I heard your story and now I am here to honor you.'[33]

But the acerbic Reed had long since become part of a minority. In late 1899, the Hammonds, keen to see their oldest son, Harris, into college, returned to the United States after an absence of six years. In New York, they were met by a clutch of reporters and several Yale alumni. Hammond was back, rehabilitated and ready to engage the constituency that he and Natalie were born into – the American elite.

CHAPTER TWENTY-FOUR

Back in a Country Fit for Cowboy Heroes

Hammond's American Success Renewed

1899–1906

As Jack Hammond knew, his party political affiliation was at odds with that of his father, siblings and others in the family. Although raised a Southerner, with Southern attitudes and values, his sojourn at Yale in the 1870s helped confirm him as a Republican, while the rest of his kin remained loyal to the old Democratic Party. It made for political and personal tensions that could, at times, be troublesome.[1] Likewise, he cherished a romanticised attachment to the idea that the Hammonds derived from Anglo-Saxon stock and were thus entitled to a privileged position in the world. In American eyes, his British imperial sympathies, infatuation with English aristocracy, loyalty to Rhodes and involvement in the Jameson Raid all hinted at a man some steps away from the bedrock political and social values enshrined in the United States Constitution.

Leading members of the Republican political elite had taken a dim view of the Jameson Raid. Massachusetts senator Henry Cabot Lodge saw the Jameson Raid as a 'sordid speculation'. Theodore Roosevelt who, like Hammond, was partly in debt to the writings of Richard Harding Davis for his rising star, was of the opinion that the messy sequel to the Raid showed that the British were 'beginning to shirk the burden of empire'.[2] Davis's well-primed intervention, in 1896, had done much to help offset the reservations that many of his countrymen held about Hammond's politics. But the outbreak of the Anglo-Boer War, just weeks before the arrival of the Hammond family in New York harbour, in November 1899, brought with it new challenges about Hammond's views in regard to British imperialism and the Boer republics. Questions about his credentials *within* the American elite might be deflected fairly easily. His public views on British foreign policy, the expansion of empire and the virtues of republicanism would, however, prove more difficult to finesse.

Sensing there was no way around the problems that the Anglo-Boer War posed for them on home turf, Hammond and wife Natalie decided to champion the British cause and lost no time in attacking the Kruger government. Happy in the knowledge that John Hay, the American ambassador whom Hammond had cultivated with due diligence in London, was back in Washington, DC, and priming President McKinley from within the administration about 'the true situation in South Africa', the couple stepped into the fray knowing that they were not without hidden allies.[3] A following wind, generated by the recent Spanish-American War and the United States' imperialist thrust, also eased them forward.

In a series of interviews widely reported on in local and national newspapers during late 1899 and 1900, Hammond, a prime mover behind the filibustering raid that had paved the way for the conflict in southern Africa, claimed that 'England was carrying on a just war and that the Boers were wholly to blame for the current difficulty'.[4] Alert to the fact that the political elite respected the rapier more than the ramrod, he took the time to refine an address he delivered on the 'Transvaal Trouble' as a pamphlet, published at his own expense in New York City.[5] This was complemented by a carefully researched lecture on 'The Boers and the Uitlanders', delivered by Natalie Harris at the Century Club, in San Francisco, in January 1901. That, too, was published privately.[6] While the overt purpose of these and similar interventions was to provide local sceptics with a rationale for the Anglo-Boer War, they also helped to justify events leading up to the Raid.

Not everybody was convinced by Hammond's arguments, nor was his role in the Raid so easily forgotten or forgiven. Out on the West Coast, where locals had long had the opportunity to see the Hammond family operate at close quarters, there were some brutal counterattacks. In a letter from East Oakland, Henry Weeks told the editor of the *San Francisco Call* that the 'American people need no assistance from this convicted buccaneer to form an intelligent opinion of the war'. In another letter, to the *Los Angeles Herald*, a former 'Boer' complained that 'people of the Hammond type' were 'professional robbers' and 'trespassers' who 'sought to cover their own crimes under the charges made in this purported interview'.[7] Other editors and journalists did not need prompting from readers to see where Hammond had come from or what he was trying to effect. The *Chicago Tribune* simply refused to buy into the argument that there were elements of a 'race war' to be detected in the Anglo-Boer conflict. It considered the war to be a solely capitalist and financier-driven initiative, noting that Rhodes and the mine owners controlled the South African press and that this allowed them and Hammond great leeway in shaping public opinion.[8]

The Raid and its sequel was, however, hardly an unmitigated disaster for Hammond. Indeed, in slightly fortuitous fashion, it provided him with a few new, albeit circumscribed, ways of regaining some of the financial and professional momentum needed to resume his career. For a start, the outbreak of the war occasioned the flight from southern Africa of his older cousin, William Hammond Hall – the noted hydraulic expert and former State Engineer – and Hall's reappearance on the West Coast. Nobody knew more about the courses, drainage patterns and potential water reserves of California's parched valleys than did Hall.[9]

Hammond, still charting success by the stars of fame and wealth, saw in Hall's return a way of using his financial contacts on either side of the Atlantic to mobilise vast amounts of capital and unlock new sources of profit. Hall's unparalleled knowledge of the state's natural assets was a formidable source of intellectual capital in its own right, but when dropped into the context of the extended family it became priceless. Jack Hammond's own engineering skills were further supplemented by drawing in his two younger brothers into promising new ventures. The one, Richard, had already demonstrated his interest in irrigating the dry San Joaquin Valley so as to increase land values. The other, William, was the State Surveyor General and had inside knowledge about patterns of development, land ownership and the value of real estate.[10]

For obvious reasons, members of the family who were heavily involved in various hydroelectric and irrigation projects between the late 1890s and early 1920s were never formally linked or legally recognised via a privately or publicly floated corporation. Instead, as one historian rightly points out, the family acted more as 'a mutual aid society', with members engaging in a series of highly profitable ad hoc deals.[11] Thus, before the parting of their ways, in a libel suit, in 1913, and an allegation that Hammond had failed to meet his financial commitments, the cousins had agreed upon an annual settlement for money or services exchanged. William Hall, embittered, felt cheated by his more worldly-wise cousin.[12]

There was, of course, nothing particularly new about the family harnessing information gained in public office for private gain; it was a practice that stretched back to Major RP Hammond, who had been Collector of Customs in San Francisco, and John 'Coffee' Hays, who had been Sheriff of San Francisco, and then US Surveyor General for California.

Ventures such as the Mount Whitney Power Company, the Pitt River hydroelectric project and the Yosemite Power Company facilitated Hammond's profitable re-entry into the new American business. These endeavours were later supplemented with related investments, such as the purchase of Lake Eleanor, bought in 1908 and eventually incorporated into the great Hetch-Hetchy project, which helped ensure San Francisco's expanding population with a permanent supply of water.[13]

None of this signalled Hammond's abandonment of his primary calling as 'mining expert'.[14] Here, too, the efflux of American engineering talent after the Jameson Raid and just before the outbreak of the Anglo-Boer War played into his hands. Some, such as Victor Clement, had been closely involved in planning the coup on the Witwatersrand; yet others, such as Henry A Butters – brother of Charles – Ernest Wiltsee and Pope Yeatman, had never been directly implicated in the failed revolution in Johannesburg.

But, regardless of their previous actions and views, experienced troopers who had earned their spurs in southern Africa remained friends and were soon involved in several new professional initiatives with the omnipresent Hammond.[15] He himself was constantly on the move, sniffing out profitable mining opportunities not only in familiar haunts such as California, Colorado and Utah but also in Mexico, the scene of his first assignment as a young mine manager, at Alamos, in Sonora.

He was barely back in the United States when, in 1900, via an invitation procured with the help of John Hay, he and Henry Butters were negotiating with the modernising Mexican dictator, Porfirío Díaz, for the construction of an electric tramway system in Mexico City. Hammond and Butters had worked together on a similar project in Cape Town, and now raised the necessary finance for the new project from Wernher, Beit & Co.[16] As noted earlier, this was but one of several instances in which capital mobilised via the Witwatersrand mining industry helped underwrite development projects on the North American continent.[17]

There were yet other things linking Hammond's southern African experiences and ongoing investment in the Rand gold mines to his race prejudices and public pronouncements once he was back in the United States. When the Witwatersrand mines experienced an acute shortage of cheap black labour in the aftermath of the Anglo-Boer War, Hammond came up with a solution that even contemporary white South African mine owners would have found startling. In a lunch-time address to members of the California Club, in Los Angeles, in late 1903, he advocated the 'enslavement of Kaffirs', which 'would also lead to a betterment of their condition'.[18]

In 1906, similar anachronistic and deeply reactionary views saw Hammond become a partner of Belgium's King Leopold II in one of the great scandals of the age – the utter degradation and slave-like exploitation of African labour in the Congo. Via his new mentor, Daniel Guggenheim, Hammond and his friend, Harry Payne Whitney, acquired shares in the American Congo Company, which sought to exploit minerals and rubber at a time when Leopold's horrific practices in tropical Africa were already widely known in concerned and informed public circles.[19]

Given his unethical views on civilised progress and the search for profits, it came as little surprise when, in 1908, Hammond confided in his newest friend,

the recently inaugurated President William Taft, that his [Hammond's] 'southern heritage made him sympathetic with the Southerner's attitude towards
the Negro politically and socially'.[20] A history of slavery made it easier for
some leading members of the American political elite to accept Hammond's
starkly 19th-century views on racial oppression and personal gain.

Not all Hammond's enterprises bearing the scent, if not the substance, of
southern Africa proved profitable, however, let alone trouble-free. When it
came to extractive industries Hammond might, as was often asserted, have
been born with the 'Midas touch', but in other instances he proved to be
as fallible as any other investor. His involvement with Mark Twain and the
strangely unedifying Plasmon business offered a case in point.[21]

Samuel Clemens, battling chronic digestive problems, first met Hammond
when he visited the Reformer in the Pretoria jail and found the engineer
suffering from 'dysentery'.[22] It was presumably at that time that Clemens first
recommended the use of Plasmon – a derivative of milk – to Hammond.
Whether Hammond tried and benefited from the product, or whether it
was merely the desire to continue sailing in the wake of another great man,
he, like Clemens, was convinced that Plasmon had all the makings of a transatlantic commercial success.[23]

By 1901, with Plasmon sales booming in belly-plagued England, Twain
– neither a gifted businessman nor a man born with a head for figures –
was ready to extend his operations to the United States. Who better to
help raise the necessary capital than his new friend, John Hays Hammond?
Hammond became the principal investor and persuaded Henry Butters and
Butters's son-in-law, to buy stock in the new venture. But the business,
poorly administered by a succession of dishonest and incompetent managers, turned out to be a disaster.[24]

By 1904, Hammond had lost patience with Clemens and yet another
odious manager, RW Ashcroft, who had insinuated himself into the
great writer's affairs. Plasmon was becoming a pain at the remote end of
Hammond's digestive tract. With a flourish worthy of old Charlie Siringo,
Hammond dispatched a lawyer and an armed guard to occupy the Plasmon
offices while simultaneously executing a series of legal manoeuvres that
would enable him to gain control of the company. It did not work and set
in motion a long-running sequel that culminated in Hammond successfully
defending a libel suit brought against him by Ashcroft in early 1910.[25]

Hammond was out of Africa but his southern African experiences shaped
his behaviour for a decade after his return to America, perhaps longer. Much
of the period 1900–1908 was spent readjusting to an America changed from
the one he had fled back in 1893. Old fantasies and emotional reflexes, however, including that of the cowboy-knight, continued to lurk, just waiting
for the opportunity to manifest. In his mid-forties and subject to attacks of

malaria, Hammond was mindful of his health and the need to show his body more respect.

'The winters of 1900 and 1901 were spent at Del Monte, California' where 'one of our chief pleasures was to get up at five in the morning and ride with the cowboys in the roundups'.[26] The fact that automobiles – the new mode of private transport for the wealthy – were displacing horses, only added to this rural romance. So, too, did the Hammonds' expanding interest in questions relating to conservation, the natural environment and national parks, issues that he and Natalie Harris – all set to lecture on the topic – raised pertinently when President McKinley and John Hay dined with them at Del Monte.[27]

Although it now seems paradoxical, this ongoing fascination with cowboys, the closing of the frontier and the eclipse of the Wild West did not leave the Hammonds at risk of becoming anachronistic. On the contrary, the formative years that Jack had spent as an adolescent on Coffee Hays's ranch back at Oakland preparing him for a manly life in the great outdoors suddenly rendered him a person *ahead*, rather than behind, the times. Just as his involvement in the Jameson Raid *pre-dated* the spurt in American imperialism that came with the formal annexation of Hawaii and the outbreak of the Spanish-American War, so his interest in frontier heroism, issues of masculinity and race, and a desire to expand the United States' trade and influence in markets across the globe, had been running in advance rather than behind those of the elite. The Hammonds had no difficulty in relating to enduring issues that, dressed in new clothing as questions about conservation and eugenics, figured ever more prominently in the national debate.[28]

The assassination of William McKinley by an anarchist, in Buffalo, New York, on 14 September 1901, saw Vice President Theodore Roosevelt become the 26th President of the United States. Roosevelt's occupation of the residence that he swiftly christened the 'White House' marked the zenith of certain romanticised ideological discourses that had been in the making of American public life since at least the 1870s. Press-friendly and self-promoting in ways Hammond could relate to, Roosevelt was the epitome of the successful cowboy soldier-turned-national politician.[29]

Roosevelt entered the New York state assembly in 1881 while still in his early twenties, and had published what was to become a classic of its sort on naval warfare in the following year, but began a gradual withdrawal from more active public life when he purchased a ranch in the Dakota Badlands in 1883. After a compounded personal tragedy, in 1884, he retreated to the ranch and reconstructed himself, ideologically, psychologically and physically in ways that allowed for the more credible adoption of progressive policies on issues relating from conservation and hunting to imperialism, masculinity and Manifest Destiny. This dramatic refashioning of the inner persona paved the way for Roosevelt's re-engagement with public life in the 1890s as the President of the Board of Police Commissioners in New York City (1895–1897) and then as Assistant Secretary of the Navy (1897).

But it was the outbreak of the Spanish-American War, in 1898, and his military triumph at San Juan Hill, in Cuba, publicised by the writings of Harding Davis, that propelled Colonel Roosevelt and his Rough Riders – volunteers, replete with cowboys – to national fame. After being elected Governor of New York (1899–1900), the roads to the vice presidency and then, by chance, to the White House, opened up for Roosevelt.

When Jack Hammond had left America, in 1893, his personal and political stars were not fully aligned with those in the national political firmament. By the time of his return, however, and more especially so after the catapulting of Roosevelt into the presidency, he found himself moving in an environment that was far less disposed to be critical of some of his earlier flaws and possible shortcomings. Instead of having to work at aligning his fortunes with the stars, it was as if, in his absence, the heavens themselves had moved and he suddenly found himself orbiting in a universe that was more in accordance with his ambition and style.

After 1898, the political environment was also more tolerant of Hammond's swashbuckling mode and more indulgent of the racial views of Southern elites.[30] The new setting allowed for a more forgiving attitude to be displayed towards early American adventurers, such as William Walker. When Harding Davis slipped out of fictional mode, in 1906, to pen another big seller, *Soldiers of Fortune*, he found it easy enough to endorse Gardner Williams, Major Fred Burnham – nemesis of the *Mlimo* in the African uprisings in Rhodesia – and Jack Hammond as 'real ambassadors of their country' and as part of a select band of men that Americans could be truly 'proud of'. They were also men of a stamp that Roosevelt was quite happy to be associated with.[31]

But, as a man of Dutch extraction, Roosevelt's admiration was not confined to those who could, by and large, be seen as having come out on the winning side of the Anglo-Boer War of 1899–1902. Like many of his countrymen, Roosevelt held Afrikaners, the Boer commandos and the marksmen who had withstood the might of the British Empire for close on three years in high regard.[32] And, just as the war had nudged a few of Hammond's former Rand-based mining colleagues into seeking him out as they sought to re-establish themselves in the United States, President Roosevelt suddenly found himself being appealed to by what, at first glance, seemed like an unlikely set of refugees from the Anglo-Boer War. Foremost among these was the charismatic but chronically impecunious Boer general, Benjamin Johannes Viljoen.

Born into a poor Afrikaner family, in a cave on the eastern frontier of the Cape Colony, as a young man Ben Viljoen had made his way north to Kruger's republic, where he served as a policeman for some years. First in cosmopolitan Johannesburg and later in Krugersdorp, Viljoen was in the vanguard of the first generation of urbanising, proletarianised Afrikaners on the Highveld and thus without the customary easy access to appropriated or conquered land for farming.[33]

Cosmopolitan mining towns not only familiarised him with the nature of urban crime and the underworld, but also with the English language and the requirements of primary industry, giving his politics a decidedly 'modern' twist. In the early 1890s, Viljoen was known as an anti-Kruger Progressive and one of the founding members of a ginger group within the broader family of Boer nationalists known as the 'Young Afrikaners' – in short, precisely the type of man that Hammond and, later, the Reformers admired and cultivated as a counterweight to Kruger and his rural constituents. But, as with other progressive Afrikaners, the Jameson Raid turned Viljoen into a militant republican and he had gone on to fight with distinction in the Anglo-Boer War before being captured and sent to the island of Saint Helena as a prisoner of war.[34]

After the war, unable to be reconciled to the idea of British rule, the cash-strapped and property-less general undertook a lecture tour of Britain, hawking memories of a bitter and bloody war. But the British political and military establishment remained fearful of his reputation for duplicity and as a man consumed by lingering, radical republican sympathies. All that the stay in England did therefore was to bring home to Viljoen how out of place he would continue to feel if he returned to imperial southern Africa and so, always adventurous, he sought the counsel of none other than Joseph Chamberlain, the Secretary for the Colonies. A nod was as good as a wink and Chamberlain, married to an American, advised the general to make a new home for himself and other disaffected Boers in the United States, among other colonials who had, famously, defeated the imperialists.[35]

Roosevelt, however, was alert to the problems that the arrival of Boer settlers in the United States might give rise to in Whitehall. When Viljoen called upon Roosevelt – in 1902–1903 – the American President, despite his underlying sympathies, proved reluctant to be seen to be providing succour to some of Britain's recent, still recalcitrant enemies. So, instead of giving the general and a few of his followers a place in the American sun, Roosevelt offered to use his good offices with the Porfirio Díaz regime to give them access to farming land, on reasonable terms, in neighbouring Mexico. The unstated assumption was that, if the deal did eventually turn sour, the Boers and their families could re-cross the border and, along with millions of other American immigrants, take their chances and settle as farmers in the arid southwestern United States.[36]

Díaz, however, saw in Ben Viljoen and his followers the opportunity of furthering his own agenda, and offered them access to land in the Yaqui Valley, in the northwestern state of Sonora. But the fertile, well-watered valley was as menacing as it was promising. Two decades earlier, the Mexican dictator had attempted to clear the area of most of the warlike Yaquis – an indigenous people akin to the Apaches of the American Southwest – and either conscripted many of the defeated Indians into his army, or had them sold off into slavery on the plantations of the Yucátan Peninsula.[37] The Boers would form a modernising agricultural elite on conquered land and provide Díaz with a useful buffer against resentful Yaqui tribesmen prone to ongoing armed resistance.

But it was an offer that even poverty-stricken refugees cast adrift half a world away from their homeland could afford to turn down, and it did not leave the freedom-loving, restless Viljoen particularly well-disposed to the cynical dictator once he had been to see all that the offer entailed. A compromise was reached when, instead, the Boers were granted access to riverside property, on what soon proved to be an onerous contractual basis, at Santa Rosalía, in the northern border state of Chihuahua.[38]

Even before the new project could get under way, however, Viljoen, was off to participate in the Anglo-Boer War military spectacle that came to form one of the highlights of the St Louis World's Fair of 1904, planned to celebrate the centenary of the Louisiana Purchase. There, under the direction of the noted impresario, Frank Fillis, he was joined not only by scores of other Boers, but also by a cast of several hundred others – black and white – who re-enacted scenes of triumph and disaster on a grand scale. But, for Viljoen, St Louis delivered unexpected personal bounty when he found and then bigamously married his second wife, Myrtle Dickason, a widow, who accompanied him back to Mexico once the exposition concluded.[39]

However, Viljoen, his new American wife and a good number of Boer families soon discovered that the 200000-hectare settlement at Santa Rosalía was not fully to their liking. Problems in obtaining title deeds from the Díaz regime, uncontrolled flooding and the unfamiliarity of a peasant culture rooted in a different language and religious beliefs all contributed to a sense of growing disillusionment. When, in 1905, the general heard of yet more southern African Boers about to seek refuge in Texas or other parts of the Southwest, he, members of his family and many – but not all – of his followers were all prepared to quit Mexico.[40]

Although happy enough to turn his back on Díaz, who had always had reservations of his own about the Boer settlers, Viljoen did not leave Mexico without friends. One of those he had impressed and who was less pleased to see him and his camp followers depart for United States, was Francisco Madero, son of a wealthy landowning family in the northern state

of Coahuila, a notable with mounting misgivings about the nature of Díaz
and his ageing dictatorial regime.[41]

The Anglo-Boer War refugees moved to the hamlet of Chamberino, near
La Mesa, in the irrigated Mesilla Valley that pointed towards the Rio Grande
and lay northwest of El Paso, close to where the borders of Mexico, New
Mexico and Texas meet. It was difficult to conceive of a more promising
strategic location in the arid but rapidly developing American Southwest. El
Paso offered the financially straitened Viljoen and his stragglers the prospect
of American citizenship, access to California and Los Angeles to the west,
or Colorado further north, a ready market for their livestock and produce,
and, should the need ever arise, a convenient back door to their Mexican
contacts south of the border.[42]

But history had contrived to do far more than settle Ben Viljoen, for-
merly of Krugersdorp, halfway around the world in surroundings that, to
him and his followers, were so reminiscent of parts of southern Africa. It
had dropped the feckless Boer general in El Paso, at the very gateway of
the principal route into Mexico that was being increasingly used by the
American architect of the failed revolution in Johannesburg, the Californian
precipitator-in-chief of the Jameson Raid – John Hays Hammond.

Ben Viljoen spent most of his life searching for the funds that would allow
him, his extended family and followers to lead the secure, settled lives they
wanted, while Hammond's engineering genius and financial acumen meant
that he almost always had more capital than he knew what to do with. But
for those crucial differences, Viljoen and Hammond might well have been
just two peas in a pod. Both were born frontiersmen, adventurous, peripatetic,
self-confident and extroverted, men much taken with the army, military men
and modern weaponry. Fiercely republican, but hardly immune to some of
the delights that came from imperial recognition or respect, both men were,
when necessary, willing to ingratiate themselves with the powerful, the rich or
both. Strong advocates of law and order in public, both men were, in private,
willing to circumvent the law when they felt thwarted by its strictures.

Acutely aware of the power of the press in the age of cheap, mass-
circulating newspapers, both Viljoen and Hammond were boastful, egotistic,
narcissistic men, craving public exposure and publicity. Although nominally
Christian, neither was particularly religious and both were frequently willing
to bend broader truths to narrower instrumental purposes. They also shared
a love of conspiracy, intrigue and plotting and, both being Freemasons, had
an affinity for male secret societies.[43]

Active in Witwatersrand political circles throughout the 1890s, Viljoen
almost certainly first met Hammond in Johannesburg, at some point in
1894 or 1895. When they first became reacquainted, in the United States,
is unknown, but both were prominently involved in the St Louis World's

Fair in 1904, and, given a common South African background, their fame and personal proclivities for name-dropping, it is unlikely that they did not meet. But, what is perhaps even more interesting is that, although it is clearly documented that they met frequently after 1908 – for purposes that we will speculate about a little later – neither of them chose to mention such meetings in their memoirs. For the moment, however, all that needs to be noted is that, first by chance and then later by design, Viljoen and Hammond were fated to interact in not one but two revolutionary settings – first, in Johannesburg, in 1895, and then again, after 1910, during the Mexican Revolution. In order to understand why that should be, and what the nature of their business might have been between 1909 to 1917, we will have to let Viljoen be for the moment and rejoin John Hays Hammond.

After 1901, Hammond, moving in the shadows of a larger-than-life President, found much to admire in Roosevelt. True, the new President was a Harvard rather than a Yale man, and he may have shown bad judgement by entertaining a 'Negro politician', Booker T Washington, in the White House shortly after his inauguration, but he was, after all, a Republican and they shared an interest in Anglo-Saxons, conservation, elitist white male organisations and the workings of the press. Roosevelt, in turn, was sufficiently impressed with Hammond's credentials as man and kindred spirit to see to it that he was drawn into his – by-invitation-only – 'Boone and Crockett Club', where they rubbed shoulders with, among others, Henry Cabot Lodge, Gifford Pinchot, Thomas B Reed and Owen Wister, author of the iconic novel *The Virginian* (1902) and the voice behind the idea of the cowboy-knight.[44]

By 1907, it was Hammond's turn to hold up the mirror to an often self-admiring, self-sustaining and largely Republican elite that spanned the continent. As the only ever Chairman of the New York City-based Rocky Mountain Club – an 'Eastern Home for Western Men' – Hammond was delighted to be able to draw Roosevelt into the ranks of his club in the critical months leading up to the selection of a new Republican presidential candidate.[45] Many decades later, upon Hammond reaching the age of 71, the Rocky Mountain Club organised 11 celebratory dinners in ten venues across the world – from Manhattan to Manila – ensuring that the Chairman's portrait got pride of place on the cover of *Time* magazine.[46] By then the club had served its purpose fully, and two years later it was disbanded.

When it came to government policy, Hammond was more conservatively inclined than was Roosevelt. While broadly supportive of the President, Hammond frequently felt a touch uncomfortable with some of the progressive and reforming ideals that underpinned Roosevelt's determination to see that everyone got a 'square deal'. Yes, the President was a supporter of the gold standard and high tariffs and the building of the Panama Canal.[47] But to Hammond it seemed that Roosevelt's support for organised labour was not always well informed. In 1903, a mine in which Hammond had a sizeable stake, at Cripple Creek, Colorado, ground to a halt during a strike organised by the Western Federation of Miners – the radical union sired during the Coeur d'Alene mining war more than a decade earlier.

True to form, Hammond not only demanded that Governor James Peabody send in state troops to help rout the unionists but, in an echo of his earlier Idaho experiences, was pushed into an unguarded comment criticising Roosevelt for his reluctance to send in federal troops to crush the strike. It resulted in a sharp personal exchange between Roosevelt and Hammond, which Hammond then made Peabody pay for politically. Hammond and the President, however, remained on good terms and the press was comfortable in referring to them as 'friends'.[48]

As ever, Hammond's easy access to, and ability to communicate directly with, the American President of the day came not so much from his political insights, which appear to have been limited, fairly pragmatic and often self-serving, but from his legendary economic muscle, the ability to finance electoral campaigns and raise funds.[49] Indeed, the fact that his political profile was becoming ever more prominent could be traced back to his successful re-entry to the United States as a mining 'expert'. It had taken barely 36 months for him to become an economic force of note.

His natural port of entry into the mainstream of the economy lay on the West Coast, in his hometown of San Francisco. In early 1903, Hammond resumed his position as consulting engineer to the Union Pacific and Southern Pacific railway companies.[50] But the really big deal, the one that restored Hammond to his coveted former position as the most highly remunerated salaried man in the world, came a few weeks later. Between 1903 and the time of Hammond's resignation in 1907, allegedly on grounds of ill health, Daniel Guggenheim and the family's mineral Exploration Company took on the part that Rhodes and Consolidated Gold Fields had played in his life between 1894 and 1899. His salary was half a million dollars a year and, with an interest in shared profits, his annual income was said to be in excess of $1 million. Combining the art of modesty and science of measurement in unequal proportions, he publicly valued his time at around five dollars a minute.[51]

At some point around 1905–1906, at age 50, this heady mixture of gathering fame and fortune caused Hammond – probably not for the first time in his life – to give serious thought to the possibility of his running for high office without having first to experience the tedium of climbing the party political ladder. Most of his life up to that point proved that, in a robust democracy and capitalist economy, power and wealth could be short-circuited in a host of interesting ways. And, as far back as 1902, he had got his first glimpse of what a future American President might look like and positioned himself accordingly.

CHAPTER TWENTY-FIVE

The Phantom Vice President

Greasing the Squeaky Wheels of Big Business

C 1906–1913

Hammond's rediscovery and wooing of William Taft, then serving as Governor of the newly acquired Philippines and back briefly in New York City, he later claimed, was 'informal' and 'almost accidental'. Well, not quite. Hammond knew how to work the angles, or, as he preferred to put it: 'Trifles often help turn acquaintance into friendship.' Back in London, having just met John Hay, pre-eminent American ambassador of the day, Hammond chanced upon information that Hay was ill: 'Stopping at a florist shop, I selected some flowers, and wrote a card, "From John Hays Hammond". This pleased the fancy of the genial diplomat, and after that we saw a great deal of each other.'[1]

William Taft had been Hammond's junior at Yale by two years and was a friend of Hammond's brother William long before Hammond became acquainted with the President-to-be. As Taft recalled it, he was lunching at the University Club, in New York, when 'a waiter brought a card from a gentleman who was also taking luncheon, which was followed by the owner of the card, and he proved to be my old college friend, John Hays Hammond. He had been out of college 26 years, and I had been out of college 24, and we had not met since I graduated.'[2] Some friendship! The gap, however, proved no barrier to the development of a real intimacy that commenced, two years later, in 1904, after Theodore Roosevelt had recalled Taft to Washington, DC, to become his Secretary for War.

Taft, a considered man whose heart lay closer to the certainties of the law and precedent than it did to the unpredictability and improvisation of political life eventually – and uniquely in American history – went on to become both President of the United States (1909–1913) and the Chief

Justice of the Supreme Court (1921–1930). President Roosevelt for some time held Taft in the highest regard, as a man with not only the requisite political values expected of a modern and progressive Republican with a decided gift for administration, but also as one whose real ambition was, hopefully, to hold the highest legal office in the country.

When Taft was recalled to America the relationship between him and Hammond strengthened. Hammond, predatory and widely travelled, was the consummate insider with an ingrained love of intrigue, conspiracy and powerful men in every corner of the Atlantic world. Taft, a touch awkward and sleep-deprived, a consequence in part of his corpulence, was inclined to be more sedentary and studious, although they both shared a liking for golf – a competitive, individualistic form of recreation well suited to swapping gossip and news.[3] Later, once Taft was President, he was said to run a 'golf' rather than a 'kitchen' cabinet – one in which his brother, Charles P Taft, and Hammond, who became business partners, were most closely involved.[4] Hammond and Taft got on exceptionally well, and their wives, neither of whom were averse to reaping the social spoils of high office, got on equally well. The Tafts and Hammonds became the closest of friends.[5]

In 1906, the couples were together, celebrating the Hammonds' silver wedding anniversary, when Taft, as Secretary of War, received a phone call from Roosevelt offering him a position as a judge on the Supreme Court. Taft, by Hammond's telling, 'was inclined to accept'. But by then the Hammonds and Mrs Taft had a very good idea that, should Roosevelt relinquish his hold on the White House, in 1908, William Taft was likely to obtain his blessing as the next – likely – Republican president. Both Hammonds and Mrs Taft therefore urged Taft to turn down the offer since he 'could be virtually certain of an appointment to the Supreme Court if such a vacancy occurred during any ensuing Republican administration', but that the chance of contesting the presidency might come his way once only.[6] Taft declined the offer, and it turned out to be a wise choice. It also happened to be one that did Hammond no harm.

Between 1906 and 1908, in an interlude marked by an economic recession that reached a low-water mark with a 'panic' on the stock market, in 1907, Hammond, whom one historian describes as having a 'lust for publicity', puffed out his financial plumage, portraying himself as every inch the millionaire.[7] He kept a 200-foot yacht, manned by a crew of 20, at the ready at the Battery to glide him to the port of Gloucester, in Massachusetts, where he had a home, and maintained a large fleet of 'speedy automobiles, each of a price to buy a home for the usual wage earner'.[8] Most folk would have got the point.

Throughout the 24 months of manoeuvring leading up to the Republican National Convention in Chicago, in June 1908, Taft was careful to keep

William Taft (left) with John Hays Hammond
PHOTO: *THE AUTOBIOGRAPHY OF JOHN HAYS HAMMOND, VOL 2*

his views on domestic and foreign policy aligned with those of Roosevelt. Hammond, who may have been slow to disclose the full extent of his own ambitions to Taft, or may have not done so until late in the day, did like-wise. The two of them were all for retaining the high tariffs that protected American industries, but were concerned about monopolies or 'trusts' and keen to ensure that the common man got a 'square deal'.[9] Even Roosevelt's anti-trust instincts, however, had to be tempered by the times. Hammond, a major proponent of big business, was happy to support the President when Roosevelt allowed US Steel to purchase the Tennessee Coal & Iron Company in 1907. He was, however, equally content to see Taft reverse the decision, in 1911, thereby contributing to the famous falling-out between Roosevelt and Taft.[10]

Shortly after Taft's return from the Philippines to become Secretary for War, Hammond began taking a public interest in questions relating to the navy and the need to secure the long-term trading interests of the United States in the Far East.[11] Here too, he and Taft were following the lead not only of Roosevelt, who had a special interest in both issues, but also of the leading naval strategist of the day, the imperialist Captain Alfred T Mahan.[12] On such questions there was perhaps even more need for caution. The

Republicans, fretting about the financial burden of empire, were becoming keen to grant the Philippines independence.[13]

When Roosevelt decided that he would not seek a third term in office and that he was going to endorse Taft as his successor, Hammond's next move was clear.[14] In November 1907, citing 'poor health' as his reason, Hammond resigned from his position as a major-time employee at the Guggenheim Exploration Company but continued to provide the family with professional advice as and when required.[15] Hammond's health recovered almost from the moment he resigned and he continued to lead an active life for more than a decade thereafter. In the six months following his resignation, he spent much of his time lining up potential support for Taft's candidature while, simultaneously, assessing carefully what a Taft presidency could potentially bring to the house of Hammond.

Quite a lot, it seemed. Encouraged by Taft, a Midwesterner from Ohio, Hammond based himself in California. With a nod and a wink from Roosevelt's chosen one, Hammond not only successfully garnered West Coast support for Taft's candidature in big business circles, but also began to sound out rich and influential Republicans about his *own* prospects as a possible running mate for Taft. He did so not because he was 'seeking personal advancement', he claimed later, but because he was trying to spike the chances of two other possible vice presidential candidates with whom Taft was not enamoured.[16] Either way, it was most unusual and could not be easily reconciled with what transpired thereafter. The truth of the matter was perhaps best captured by one analyst, who noted:

> Perhaps the most interesting thing about it all is that Mr Hammond proceeded to make a campaign for the nomination. As a rule the vice presidential nomination is thrust upon some modest citizen who pretends that he does not want it. Mr Hammond is otherwise. He wanted it and was not ashamed to say so.[17]

The critic, who perhaps had a better understanding of Hammond's limitations than most, also noted that 'his friends are hinting that Mr Hammond has his eye on the presidential plum four years hence'.[18]

Hammond was encouraged by what he heard in elite circles in San Francisco and Los Angeles. Leading members of the Republican Party were fulsome in their support for Taft and inclined not to alienate or dismiss a rich and influential sidekick seen to be lobbying on his behalf. Hammond was greatly cheered when the man who would lead the Californian delegation at the national convention, the unlovable local newspaper baron, Michael de Young, indicated his support for a possible Taft-Hammond ticket.[19] The danger in such heavily top-down politics, however, lay in taking for granted the support from lower down. A few weeks before the Republicans were scheduled to meet for their national convention, at the Coliseum, in Chicago, from 16 to 19 June 1908, the Hammonds moved back to their home in Lakewood, New Jersey. Seemingly secure in the knowledge that they had the backing of the Californian delegation for a Taft-Hammond ticket, Jack travelled north, to his palatial residence in Gloucester, to do some final lobbying among the Republicans of his second 'home state'.

The visit did not go as well as it might have done. There were minor problems around registration but by 8 June he was back at his Lakewood home. It soon emerged that Hammond was not only campaigning on behalf of Taft but that he had also set his sights on securing the Republican nomination for the vice presidency for himself. In order to ensure maximum flexibility, he would not be an official delegate but would move around, without hindrance, to use his 'influence wherever it would be most useful to Taft'. Although without a formally designated constituency, he would be accompanied to Chicago by Natalie Harris, also unelected, who would act as his 'principal assistant'; between them, they would try to ensure that the Tafts and the Hammonds ran for the two highest offices in the land. It was again made clear to the press that Hammond was his own man and that he had long since severed his ties to the Guggenheims, who operated the hated 'smelter trust'.[20]

But it was not plain sailing on the way to, or in, Chicago. That many Democrats should be suspicious of Hammond and his ties to the political elite was understandable but many 'progressive' Republicans, too, could not see him as an anti-trust man, as a true believer in a 'square deal'. The *Chicago Tribune* characterised Guggenheim as 'the head of the most oppressive trust which bears upon the interest of the miners, the prospectors and working men of the great west', and Hammond as a 'Trust Servant'.[21] Others questioned Hammond's devotion to republican and democratic values. 'Mr Hammond,' someone with a memory that stretched back a decade or more informed the editor of the *New York Times*, is 'a wrecker of republics, the instigator of conspiracy and war, the aider and abetter of raids, and the henchman of the Rand plutocracy'.[22] Although far away in the Cape Colony, Dr Jameson figured, albeit indirectly, in convention discussions.

But any reservations about Taft's running mate rooted in southern Africa's history were like being tormented by a feather when compared to the kick in the groin Hammond received on the eve of the convention. Having counted on de Young to deliver him a half-dozen hog-tied delegates for a Taft-Hammond ticket, Hammond got de Young to invite the Californian delegation to join them for a private dinner on the eve of the opening. The delegates, however, decided to kick over the traces.

Rank-and-file Californians were all for Taft, but wanted nothing to do

with Hammond. Not one of the six delegates accepted the invitation. When
Hammond persisted and asked GA Knight privately whether he might still
be willing to nominate him for a position on the ticket, the reply was reportedly savage: 'Knight told Hammond to stick to the mining business, which
he understood, and leave the vice presidency, which he did not understand,
alone.' In the same revealing account it was reported that de Young, elitist to
the core, was 'thoroughly disgusted by the *un-clublike* manner in which the
California delegation has treated him and his candidate for the vice presidency, John Hays Hammond'.[23]

Understandably Hammond's account of the convention in his autobiography fails to mention, let alone dwell on, the events that effectively put
paid to his chances as a candidate for the vice presidency. A man who was
unable to carry his true home state was unlikely to garner significant support elsewhere. Instead, he underscored how some complications had arisen
with the New York delegation and how, in the interests of national unity, he
eventually withdrew in favour of the man who became President Taft's Vice
President – Congressman James S 'Sunny Jim' Sherman.[24]

William Taft's election as 27th President of the United States and
Hammond's failure to secure significant popular support left Republican
notables with an awkward problem. How was the President's close friend, a
man of great ambition and a party stalwart with deep pockets, to be accom-
modated in the wake of so personal a setback? Nor was Hammond the only
person that needed special consideration; in order to ensure some continuity
in the administration or repay various political debts, Taft needed to accommodate Richard A Ballinger and one or two Teddy Roosevelt stalwarts
such as the conservationist Gifford Pinchot.[25] To his credit, Taft instantly
and generously offered Hammond a position in his cabinet as Secretary of
the Navy.[26] It was a position that, in recent memory, had been occupied by
Roosevelt and, coming as it did in the wake of America's expansionist thrust
and what John Hay had famously characterised as 'a splendid little war', it
was not an offer to be sniffed at.

But the President may have badly underestimated the ambitions of his 'old
college friend' because Hammond, following the advice that he had once
proffered Taft, declined the offer in the hope that something better might
present itself in the fullness of time. The problem, however, simply refused to
go away. Throughout his term of office, with one noteworthy exception, Taft
found it nigh impossible to come up with a position in his administration, as
opposed to within the party, that Hammond found acceptable. Regardless
of what the President eased his friend's way, whether it was Secretary of the
Navy, a minister to China or even an ambassadorship in any one of several
western European capitals, Hammond found them all unacceptable.[27] It was
Roosevelt who, in the wake of the convention, successfully prevailed upon

Hammond to become the President of the League of Republican Clubs. It was a long-term responsibility but one not without serious tensions.[28]

Hammond could not abide the thought of a life without easy access to the most powerful leaders in industry and in political life, of exchanging views with them, influencing them, or simply observing them in action. But, as his pursuit of the vice presidency revealed, he seldom wanted real power – to assume full, open, sole or ultimate responsibility for tough decisions that went beyond his narrow expertise as a mining 'expert'. His almost clandestine role in the shadowy mine owners' association, back in the Coeur d'Alene in the early 1890s, spoke to the same lack of underlying confidence, as did his willingness to give way to Lionel Phillips once the Jameson Raid went awry. His business and engineering prowess, too, often tail-gated those of others rather than led the way. On the Rand he built on the lead that had been given to him by others when it came to developing deep-level mines, and in California he belatedly developed interests in hydroelectricity.

The cat-and-mouse game between Taft and Hammond did little to damage their friendship. Hammond simply made certain that he and Natalie remained extremely close to the President and his wife, and in 1909 it was at the Tafts' suggestion that the Hammonds moved house, to Washington, DC. There the Hammonds eventually occupied three different homes – each one more prestigious than the last. The capital was handy for the East Coast political and business clubs that a man of affairs needed to frequent, while Hammond kept up his old West Coast ties via a newly established Sierra Madre Club. For her part, Natalie Harris engaged effortlessly with the cream of Washington society.[29]

With the channel to formal political office clogged by his personal insecurities, and allegedly semi-retired on grounds of 'poor health', Hammond was understandably reluctant to isolate himself fully from the flow of funds emanating from the world of business. The Hammonds did not want for cash but their elevated lifestyle and the desire to continue wielding influence in New York, San Francisco and Washington came at a price. Such was Hammond's reputation for creating wealth, however, that there was no need for him to go out and find new business opportunities since – as with Mark Twain and Plasmon – they found him, one or two dragging their distinctive African tails behind them.

The legendary Fred Burnham, once Jameson's chief scout in Rhodesia, possessed the personal credentials that appealed to Cowboy Jack from first principles although he did not, as yet, know him well.[30] Early in 1909, Burnham returned from a trip to the Yaqui River Valley, in the northwestern Mexican state of Sonora, north of Alamos, where Hammond had managed his first mine, with what looked like an attractive proposition.[31] It was, however, far from unproblematic. The potentially rich farming land Burnham had identified was located squarely within the same, brutally conquered Indian territory that the Mexican government had first directed General Ben Viljoen and his followers to some years earlier. After careful consideration, the cautious Boers had decided that the valley was not yet suitable for settlement.[32]

Burnham had acquired the water rights to the valley from WE Richardson, a successful, Los Angeles-based mine manager and entrepreneur in Sonora, who had obtained a concession from the Mexican government and gone on to found the Compañía Constructora Richardson. But raiding by resentful Yaquis, contesting the appropriation of their land and forcible removals conducted during 1903 and 1908, had rendered the Richardson Construction Company's Mexican interests increasingly vulnerable and in urgent need of capital if the firm was to avoid bankruptcy.[33] Burnham had noted that the valley 'had soil sixty feet deep', and that there was 'not a pebble in it', and correctly concluded that, 'once irrigated, it would be one of the garden spots of the world'. Given several similar Californian success stories, in which he and other family members were involved, Hammond was immediately interested.[34]

Northwestern Mexico and the American Southwest, c 1910

The proposed project – in broadly the same domain where William Walker had once presided over his short-lived 'Republic of Lower California', in 1853–1854 – had elements that Hammond instinctively found alluring. Yes, it promised substantial long-term profits, but it was also situated sufficiently close to the international border to afford it protection from the United States, and it was a scheme that could attract a good number of settler-farmers. Moreover, the enterprise could rely on many of the existing skills and resources in the extended Hammond family network – an ability to raise capital globally, excellent connections with the governing elite on both sides of the border and an unsurpassed knowledge of hydraulic engineering in desert valleys. The only potential downside was the long-term political future of Mexico where, in early 1908, the dictator Porfirío Díaz had told an American journalist that he might be ready to make way for a democratic order.

Unlike Hammond's interest in another venture during the Taft tenure that ended in an acrimonious libel suit – the National Cotton Improvement Company – Burnham's prognosis proved accurate. With the support of Richardson and a partner, HA Sibbett, the project was successfully launched as the Yaqui Delta Land and Water Company.[35] By late 1908 the company was attracting interest among land-hungry settlers up and down the West Coast, and hundreds bought into the scheme. The company was eventually sold to the Mexican government, in 1930, at a price that Hammond did not complain about.[36]

The Yaqui Delta Company was, however, neither Hammond's nor the Guggenheims' only interest in Sonora. During 1905–1906, before the stock market crash of 1907, they had started reopening and developing the Aduana mines in the Alamos district, which Hammond was intimately acquainted with from his earliest years in Mexico. The Minas Neuvas and Promontorio mines were provided with state-of-the-art mining equipment and a smelter was constructed near Navajoa, which, along with the town of Alamos, were connected by rail between 1907 and 1908.

Once the Taft administration put down deeper roots, around 1910, and it became clearer that Hammond would not become formally involved in government, he became more active in his position as 'consulting engineer' to the Guggenheims. The corporate vehicle chosen for a more aggressive drive into Mexico, under the advice and guidance of Jack Hammond, was the American Smelting and Refining Company (ASARCO), which owned extensive assets, including the richest gold mine in the country, the Esperanza.[37]

Moreover, it was during the same short overlapping period, between the dying days of the Díaz regime and advent of the Taft administration, that Hammond's friends expanded their investments in oil and petroleum in

Major Fred Burnham PHOTO: BURNHAM FAMILY COLLECTION

Daniel Guggenheim PHOTO: LIBRARY OF CONGRESS

General Ben Viljoen

Mexico. Here their most important interest was acquired in the Tampico region, on Mexico's east coast, in 1910. Working through the well-connected RA Mestres of the old regime, Hammond acquired 60 000 hectares between the Pánuco River and Tuxpam and then sold off 4 000 hectares to Rhodes's old company, Consolidated Gold Fields, in order to help raise the necessary capital. Mestres was given to Transcontinental Oil to oversee and develop, while Hammond directed the new International Petroleum Company.[38] The net effect of all of this was that, while Hammond was playing an important, shadowy role on Taft's watch between 1909 and 1913, he was simultaneously keeping his economic muscles in excellent trim by becoming ever more active in the wider political economy of Mexico and in the province of Sonora in particular, at precisely the same moment that revolutionary politics were beginning to threaten Díaz's rule.

Now, Díaz was no Kruger, nor did conditions in Mexico, in 1910, bear an overwhelming resemblance to those in the South African Republic in 1895. Yet, for all that, the two historical brews did share a few basic ingredients beyond the presence of John Hays Hammond. In both cases, governments presided over entrenched agricultural economies that were having to make space for new industrial dispensations in settings scrutinised by a powerful, imperialist neighbour. Students of comparative international history, sniffing the aroma, might therefore be forgiven a little nostril-twitching even if they are to be denied the satisfaction of a full meal. Despite the obvious limitations, it is nevertheless worthwhile to track the Taft-Hammond interactions between 1909 and 1912.

Following a sharp recession and the alarming 'panic' on the stock market in 1907, the Taft administration was understandably preoccupied with economic issues. Looking back, Hammond was probably correct in recalling that Taft left his mark as President by driving banking reforms and laying the legal foundations and thinking for the coming of a badly needed United States Federal Reserve Bank.[39] Far less successful, however, was Taft's foray into the vexed terrain of tariff reform. In 1908, departing from the path of Roosevelt and that of almost all his Republican predecessors, Taft had campaigned for tariff reform, and once in office immediately set about trying to implement his election promise. The 1909 Payne-Aldrich Act, however, turned out be the sort of compromise that satisfied few. It lowered the overall tariff rate by a paltry five per cent and, to the delight of the likes of the Guggenheims, Hammond and others in the 'smelter trust', raised rates on certain strategic resources such as coal and iron.[40]

Feeling the need to defend the tariff compromise Taft, as befitting a man more conservative-progressive than progressive-conservative by nature, went on a nationwide speaking tour in September 1909. Hammond, a radical conservative if ever there was one, joined the presidential party for the latter half of the tour, having been sent ahead to persuade the Chief Forester, Gifford Pinchot, a staunch Roosevelt loyalist, not to resign because of his differences with RA Ballinger, Taft's Secretary of the Interior. First Hammond and then Taft failed to persuade Gifford to withdraw his resignation, thereby fuelling the interpersonal rivalries that later contributed to a notoriously bitter parting of the ways between the cautious and conservative Taft and the progressive Roosevelt in 1912.[41]

By January 1909 Hammond saw himself as Taft's primary unofficial 'fixer', as the man who, to all intents and purposes, was the incoming administration's informal Vice President. That month – weeks before Taft's inauguration – Hammond gave a dinner for 'the governors attending [a] White House meeting', even though he claimed that he was never able to shape the President's opinion. That did not, however, prevent Hammond from getting the President's personal secretary, CD Norton, fired 'for assuming unusual authority and pretending to have a greater degree of influence over the administration than he actually possessed'. Norton, of course, might well have confronted Hammond with a similar indictment.[42]

But perhaps the clearest indication that Hammond had insinuated himself into the role of *éminence grise*, in a presidency not notable for its intellectual depth or sparkle, came when he joined Taft for the latter part of the 1909 tour. The presidential party headed south to Texas and the border towns of El Paso and Ciudad Juárez, for a series of unprecedented cross-border meetings with Mexico's ageing President Porfirío Díaz, then 79. Faced with mounting political instability and popular discontent at home, Díaz needed the high-profile exchanges to shore up his credibility in the run-up to an election that would herald an eighth term in office. Taft, in turn, was responding to the needs of American investors who, having poured millions of dollars into the Mexican economy, were becoming anxious about growing political instability south of the border.[43] But, with the Americans having recently lost a president to an assassin's bullet, and many Mexicans disenchanted with their erstwhile political messiah, the security of the two heads of state was a matter of primary concern.

Hammond, who during his earliest days at Alamos had been tracked by a purported assassin in the shape of the bandit Sánchez, admired Díaz greatly as, much later, he did Benito Mussolini. Mussolini provided Hammond with a much-prized, signed photograph for his collection and also decorated his son, John Jnr, for providing the radio equipment necessary for a push into Africa to acquire an Italian colony.[44] As for the millions of ordinary Mexicans, those too marginal to help secure Hammond's private or public fortunes directly, he held them in contempt. They were, he alleged, characterised by 'general ignorance', had an 'excitable temperament' and cursed by a 'tremendous inertia of chronic racial weaknesses'.[45] None of this bode well for ensuring Díaz's safety during the summit. But neither was the safety of the recently elected William Taft fully assured.

The exchanges between the two presidents were, in Cowboy Jack's view, taking place along a frontier pregnant with territorial claims that had yet to be settled, and one replete with all the attendant dangers. Frontier situations required frontier-like precautions and timely preparations of a sort that were beyond the ken of an embryonic Secret Service. And who better to ensure the safety of a president than a man who had himself once planned the abduction of a president in a far-off southern republic?

Four thousand Mexican and United States troops and an undisclosed number of Secret Service agents, Texas Rangers and US Marshals were called upon to undertake the more orthodox aspects of protecting the two heads of state. But the most daunting task of all – protecting Taft's huge frame from an attempt at assassination at close range – was left to a 250-strong private security detail organised and paid for by the hidden hand in the Coeur d'Alene mining wars of 1892 and the man behind the master plan for the failed Witwatersrand revolution of 1895.

As ever, Hammond was unwilling to assume direct, personal control of the force he established or to assume direct responsibility for the under-cover detail. That he left – or so he claimed later – to 'Major Burnham, my old friend of South African days', who was also his new partner in the Yaqui Land venture. In fact, at the time, as Hammond later acknowledged, Burnham was hardly 'an old friend'. Hammond, as was the case when he was based in Johannesburg in the 1890s, was at least as interested in the informal expansion of the zone of American influence via finance, com-merce and trade as he was in the formal annexation of countries via war or the threat of war. Making use of his extensive American contacts, Major Burnham assembled what, in essence, was a private capitalist army recruited from 'scouts, cattlemen and customs guards' and then 'had them sworn in as peace officers'.[46]

Burnham may not have been the only 'old friend' that Hammond mobi-lised. It was at this same critical chronological, geographical and historical juncture, at El Paso in 1909, that Hammond helped ensure that his new business partner, Burnham, was introduced to another military man and scout who might not only be useful in finding men to guard President Taft but who also, in the longer term, might prove to be an extremely useful ally when it came to protecting their interests in the new Yaqui Delta Company.

General Viljoen, as will be recalled, was acquainted with both sides of the border, increasing well-connected in northern Mexico and precisely the type of frontiersman that Hammond and his partners might need to protect the Yaqui estate, because it was already clear that Díaz's hold on power was waning.[47] In the Coeur d'Alene mines, Hammond had used the cowboy,

Pinkerton agent and spy – Charlie Siringo – to provide mine owners with inside information about militant unionists. In the case of the Mexicans and the Yaquis, it would seem, from what transpired later, that Hammond and Burnham may have been assisted by Ben Viljoen. And, by the same token, it was probably necessary for Hammond and Viljoen – both slippery customers when it came to intelligence gathering or arms smuggling – to forget their border meeting when recalling their personal histories. Hammond, of course, had other, even more pressing, business at hand.

Never before in the history of the United States – and never since – had one man – a person not holding elected public office – so successfully marshalled a large, exclusive, armed plain-clothes unit and folded it into presidential security forces to facilitate a summit between two heads of state. It was a meeting at which, among other things, the security of American investments, not excluding those of the convenors of the President's private army, featured prominently.

Burnham's deployment was vindicated and became cause for some private celebration when, towards the end of the summit, he helped detect and disarm a would-be Taft assassin.[48] In a way, the entire summit could be seen as a personal triumph for cowboy-knight Hammond. By 1910, Hammond's reputation in America, as a man in good standing with a respectable political pedigree and great wealth and influence, had been fully and publicly reinstated. All that was left for the self-styled Southerner's triumph to be complete was for him to reappear in London, and to be acknowledged, in England, as a knight-cowboy.

Refining

CHAPTER TWENTY-SIX

From the Court of St James's to the Mexican Revolution

Diplomacy and the Dark Arts

C 1910–1914

In 1935, looking back over John Hays Hammond's extraordinary life, then in its 80th year, a New York evening newspaper, once edited by the great Walt Whitman, assumed a typically benign view of the ageing notable. Hammond had lost neither his love of publicity, nor his ability to spin the press or others with self-serving yarns. 'At heart,' the interviewer concluded, he 'was a good American imperialist' even though knowing that imperialism had fallen on hard times. What a bad imperialist might look like was also made clear. Hammond, the journalist suggested, was 'not of the breed to run whimpering to a United States Consul the moment the natives caught him in the act of trying to take something away from them'.[1] Thus the passage of time easily blunts the truth and, if worked upon steadily, can help destroy it almost completely.

Jack Hammond's remarkable career epitomises that of a manipulative, rapacious, self-serving imperialist. His tracks were to be found all over Mexico during the opening decades of the 20th century. And it was precisely *because* the scent of American capitalists in Mexico was so pervasive by the time Taft's Republican administration left office in 1913 that the Democratic administration of Woodrow Wilson (1913–1917, and 1917–1921) was so suspicious of their activities.[2]

Even as Presidents Taft and Díaz met for their border summit, in late 1909, unrest was mounting across Mexico, a country where over 25 per cent of the land, 50 per cent of the oilfields and 75 per cent of the mines were American-owned – and a goodly portion of that by the Guggenheim, Hearst and Rockefeller families, not to mention Hammond.[3] But by hinting at retirement, in 1908, Porfirio Díaz had committed a cardinal error. The suggestion that a repressive era is drawing to a close and that reform, or even more radical transformation of economy and society is a possibility, sometimes lets the genie of expectation out of the bottle, thereby accelerating the emergence of ever more radical expectations.

In 1908, Francisco Madero demanded, in *The Presidential Succession in 1910*, an honest election and a single term of office for the next Mexican leader. Madero became the people's candidate, was briefly jailed, and, when Díaz was declared re-elected, sought refuge in the United States. In the north of his country Pascual Orozco and the 'cattle-rustler-turned-revolutionary', Pancho Villa, began to actively oppose the Díaz regime, as did another rebel, Emiliano Zapata, in the south. In May 1911, Díaz's forces were finally routed and the old dictator fled to Paris.[4]

Hammond, whose admiration for Díaz was matched only by his racist dismissal of ordinary Mexicans, was deeply disturbed by the dictator's departure. The political upheavals and lack of public order in Mexico marked the start of a revolution that, in one form of another, was to last fully a decade. Nor was his mind set at ease by the ascent to power of Madero, whom he dismissed as a 'sincere idealist' – a slur straight out of industrial America, where the 'practical' man, above all, was the hero of the age.[5]

As early as March 1911, President Taft dispatched 30 000 troops to the Mexican border to impress upon the revolutionaries that American lives, investments and property would, if necessary, be protected by force.[6] Only days later, Hammond, who had met Woodrow Wilson a few years earlier while on holiday in Bermuda and, like others, saw him as being someone made of 'presidential timber', had occasion to share a train ride into Washington, DC, with the newly inaugurated Governor of New Jersey.[7]

Wilson, identifying Hammond as one of the principal architects of the administration's belligerent Mexican policy, requested a private discussion during which he expressed reservations about the wisdom of deploying troops along the border. Hammond, of course, was a veteran when it came to having troops assemble on neighbouring borders so as to safeguard lives and property; it was his own story of the Jameson Raid. And, when the Governor questioned how Taft's decision had been reached, Hammond responded with the classic defence of those devoted to intrigue and the desire to avoid accounting publicly. But, said Hammond, 'suppose the President has certain information which you have not?' 'For instance,' he went on, 'there may be serious trouble down there in which American lives will be endangered, as well as the lives of foreigners who, under the implication of the Monroe Doctrine, look to the United States for protection.'[8] A sceptical Wilson remained unconvinced.

Suspicions as to precisely whose interests were being protected by the United States Army went beyond Governor Wilson of New Jersey and were freely articulated by a few of the more insightful analysts. One correspondent informed readers that 'there [was] a shorter cut to the truth' when looking around for an answer as to why American troops were being deployed along the Mexican border. Pointing to the Guggenheims and Hammond as being close to Taft, he noted that both capitalists had 'heavy interests in north-western Mexico' – an area that in the latter case included mines and the Yaqui Delta Company. 'So the assumption is both fair and fairly accurate,' argued the analyst, to state that 'the Guggenheims and Hammond were instrumental in having a great portion of our standing army sent to the Mexican frontier'.[9]

Threatening border manoeuvres by federal troops lay well within the historic province of Hammond's lived-experience; had not the state and army come to his and other mine owners' aid in 1892, back in the Coeur d'Alene? By 1911, however, Hammond was in his mid-fifties, powerful, rich, a self-appointed director of a secret service that protected the head of state, as well as being the most prominent member of President Taft's 'golf cabinet'. He could hardly be dismissed as a *soi-disant* cowboy with a Midas touch when he happened to command an important part of the Republican Party's electoral machinery.[10] Instead, John Hays Hammond saw himself, and, more importantly, was perceived by many of the country's notable leaders, as a mature, wise man derived from ancient noble Anglo-Saxon stock – more of a knight-cowboy.

The President and the First Lady, Helen Taft, had no doubt that John Hays Hammond and Natalie Harris had the class, 'English' pedigree and other qualifications necessary to represent the United States at the Court of St James's during the coronation of George V, in 1911. Thus, just as Jack Hammond the unelected cowboy-politician was beginning to toy seriously with idea of military intervention, this time in Mexico, Hammond the knight-statesman was appointed as America's 'Special Ambassador' to the coronation by the President of the United States. Like God, power and wealth often worked in less than mysterious ways.[11]

After four years of exile in London, during the late 1890s – when the social and political upheavals around the Jameson Raid had yet to settle fully – the return of the Hammonds to Westminster and Whitehall was a dream come true.[12] While still a young girl, the Hammonds' daughter, Natalie, had composed a tale about the 'Adventures of Sir John Hammond' and their oldest son, it will be recalled, went on to build himself a medieval-style castle in Gloucester, Massachusetts. In their minds, the Hammonds had never been far from the Court of St James's. Old Southern saws about aristocratic English roots being successfully transplanted into the Big House on the plantation in Mississippi were about to be given real flesh and muscle, and the American public simply loved it.[13] Members of the press across the nation, only slightly less than the Hammonds themselves, were hugely taken with almost every aspect of the arrangements covering the Special Ambassador and his wife's attendance at the coronation. Everything from Natalie Harris's gown and formidable collection of antique royal jewellery to the nature and location of the Hammonds' residence in London came under scrutiny.[14]

During the coronation celebrations, spread over several days, His Excellency, Ambassador John Hays Hammond, once a proudly self-proclaimed revolutionary, was civil in the company of his nemesis, Sir Leander Starr Jameson, but positively basked in the company of other newly elevated Reform Committee baronets – Sir Abe Bailey and Sir George Farrar. Much taken with his new, albeit temporary status, Hammond was of the opinion that even the 1 000-strong contingent of ordinary South Africans lining the procession route, 'who knew of my connection with the Jameson Raid', now saw him as no less than a hero: 'As our carriage passed they raised a loud cheer, which both Boers and Englishmen joined.' When Crown Prince Rupprecht of Bavaria ignored the order of precedence for seating, the Special Ambassador quickly put him in his place, because 'too often England and Continental Europe had patronized us in this respect'.[15]

Upon his return to Washington, Hammond resumed his shadowy role as one of America's foremost investors in Mexico, and as unseen economic-cum-military adviser to President Taft. But all was not well. Theodore Roosevelt was becoming increasingly irritated by Taft and some of his golfing friends. He felt that, between them, they were beginning to betray some of the progressive causes and people that Republicans had previously been devoted to.[16]

In Mexico, despite upheavals occasioned by the unfolding revolution, the Richardson-owned, Hammond-financed, Yaqui Delta Land and Water Company was making significant progress albeit at the expense of the indigenous Indian population. Of the 300 000 acres acquired in late 1908, 250 000 had been carved up into smaller irrigated plots acquired by hundreds of settlers drawn largely from Los Angeles and surrounds.[17]

Hammond and his partners also toyed with the idea of creating a winter holiday resort for the American ultra-rich in an area that Díaz's army had, within living memory, largely swept clean of its Yaqui inhabitants. The plan was a variant on ideas drawn from the repertoire of San Franciscan moguls that Hammond admired, and a scheme that presaged later American initiatives of the same type in Cuba.[18]

But unfortunately for Hammond and his partners, Francisco Madero was marginally more sensitive to the injustice done to the Indians of Sonora, who had been there for over 300 years, and now did not want anything that was 'not just and fair to the Yaquis'.[19] Such sentiments only heightened

Indian resentment which, in turn, fed into the discontent spreading across the border regions of northern Mexico. It also did nothing for the confidence of American investors. President Taft, alarmed by the cost of keeping federal troops mobilised, turned for help to the Governor of Texas, who, during the closing quarter of 1911, ordered Texas Rangers to patrol the unruly Mexican border.[20]

By then, however, Taft's ability to undertake a new military initiative was, like that of his administration, losing steam at almost the same pace that Roosevelt's disillusionment with his chosen one's stance on anti-trust legislation, conservation, machine 'bossism' and tariff reform was gathering momentum.[21] In mid-November 1911, with the party convention to nominate a candidate for the 1912 presidential election barely seven months away, the tensions in Republican ranks burst into the open.

Roosevelt 'came out in open warfare against Taft', Hammond later bemoaned, and formed a new independent party, the Progressive Party – the so-called Bull Moose movement.[22] Although privately fearing the worst possible outcome in the 1912 election, Hammond remained loyal to Taft. He publicly criticised Roosevelt for having 'selfish' ambitions and used his position in the League of Republican Clubs to protect Taft's interest.[23] Taft, in turn, remained true to his friend, golf partner and radical-conservative adviser by making Hammond – whose interest in foreign affairs continued to burgeon – president of the commission to organise the celebrations to mark the completion of the Panama Canal.[24] This 'quasi-diplomatic' appointment allowed for yet more meetings with leading politicians and statesmen in European capitals. It did no damage to Hammond's inflated ego, and some in the ever-vigilant press corps began speculating anew about his ambition to be Vice President.[25]

Torn between 'a wish to serve California' in some undisclosed capacity and the 'desire to take the stump for Taft's nomination', Hammond took the latter course. Briefly relinquishing his role as champion of the Panama-Pacific Exposition before the commission completed its European tour, he rushed home to attend a Republican convention that would do more to determine his future and the fate of the companies in which he was interested than the canal ever would.[26] Unwilling to assume the role of delegate bound by the discipline that flows from a mandate, he again cast himself as a 'free agent' – as a 'master of my own time' – who could 'use my influence wherever it seemed to me most advantageous'.[27] What his role was, or how effective he was in helping secure Taft's nomination over Roosevelt is unclear, but the convention machinery was said to have been manipulated to extremely good effect.

Taft won the nomination but lost Roosevelt's friendship and support for the better part of a decade, the party was hopelessly split, and the door left wide open for the election of a Democrat in 1912.[28] For Hammond, the consummate inside operator, the election of Woodrow Wilson, a former President of Princeton, was a disaster at every level – personal, political and professional. His disappointment was palpable. As he recalled in his memoirs, 'With the election of Wilson I lost interest in politics for the time being. I left Washington for New York, and did not return to the capital until 1917, and then I bought a home there.'[29]

★ ★ ★

In truth, however, Hammond had *never* had an interest in politics for its own sake. What he *did* have was an enduring and profound interest in political economy and the ways that it could be bent to money-making for the powerful corporations in which he had large stakes.[30] It was not Woodrow Wilson's politics that he couldn't cope with – he could live with most men's politics, including those of a Mexican dictator – it was the president's 'academic calm' and reservations about armed conflict, big business, imperialism and militarism that Hammond could not abide. As Hammond noted, the world that he – Hammond – was born into 'was one where driving power and physical energy were essential to survival. Frontiers were being extended on every hand,' and 'on many of these I lived and encountered adventure. This seemed but part of the day's work.'[31] It was not the *politics* of America that separated Hammond from Wilson, but the profound *economic* uncertainties of Mexico during an extended revolution that dragged on from 1910 until 1920.

The transition between the closing 24 months of Taft's presidency in 1911–1912, and the advent of the first Wilson administration, in March 1913, proved to be an especially torrid time for most American capitalists and corporations with financial interests in Mexico. A few, including the de Young, Hearst, Otis, Mills and Rockefeller families, had strong economic ties to California, and particularly San Francisco, where Hammond easily negotiated the tight, intra-elite politics in a city that operated on a scale and in ways rivalled only by Chicago, New York and Washington.[32]

Both Hammond and Daniel Guggenheim were comfortable operating on the East and West coasts and equally heavily invested in a future that depended, in good measure, on political stability in Mexico. But, regardless of who they were, or where exactly they were based, almost none of the pre-eminent capitalists of the era got satisfaction from the Wilson administration when it came to United States policy on Mexico.

In Hammond's case, the net effect was that, as in Idaho in the early 1890s, and on the Witwatersrand in 1895–1896, he once again became deeply imbricated in fighting a capitalist war in Mexico between 1910 and 1917. And, just as he had drawn a lieutenant or two from the mine-owners' war in the Coeur d'Alene into his abortive uprising in Johannesburg, so, for close on a decade, in Sonora, he occasionally relied on military men from southern Africa – Major Fred Burnham of 'Rhodesia' and General Ben Viljoen of the Zuid-Afrikaansche Republiek – in a struggle to protect the value of his investment in the troubled Yaqui Delta Land and Water Company.[33]

Burnham's experiences of Mexico, however, long predated his southern African exploits. As a young man he was once based in Tombstone, Arizona, from where, among other things, he undertook errands for those smuggling guns into Sonora.[34] He was a man out of Hammond's dream world. The closing of the American frontier and rise of imperialism saw Hammond's affections, ambitions and action-man fantasies evolve from a fixation on cowboys and Pinkerton agents securing capitalism on the home front to armies and military men operating in foreign countries.

Hammond's real contributions to the Mine Owners' Association during the Coeur d'Alene mining war of 1892 were so well concealed in his autobiography that they have avoided being analysed convincingly and are now largely forgotten. Most historians have also failed to pick up on the continuities and similarities between the roles he played in that theatre of industrial war and the part that he assumed for himself in the Johannesburg uprising barely 36 months later, when, in 1895, his actions were so manifestly treasonous that he was sentenced to death. Indeed, it is probably precisely *because* of that narrow escape and his notorious role in the Jameson Raid that he was at even greater pains to conceal his covert operations in the Mexican Revolution of 1910–1920.

Almost no hard evidence of the secret war that Hammond was part of, in Sonora and elsewhere in Mexico, during the revolutionary era has survived.[35] It was another of those subjects studiously avoided in his autobiography because it involved Americans and Mexicans whom he could ill afford to identify by name. And, as with all wars fought largely behind enemy lines, it was an effort that relied on undisclosed allies and allegiances, agents, bribery, corruption, conspiracy, gun-running, the manipulation of office bearers and proxies and forms of pragmatism that rendered all objectives – other than that of protecting capital – irrelevant.

What follows is, in large part, a speculative account of John Hays Hammond's Third Capitalist War – for him, a frustrating conflict, one in which he was confined to playing an indirect role in a country in which he was not resident, but a frequent visitor. It is a version in which the historian who has traced Hammond's role in his First and Second wars in considerable detail is forced to take note of fragments of evidence that point – coincidentally or serendipitously – to recognisable, well-established patterns of behaviour on the part of the subject, and of movements over time and in places that hint at some covert operations.

The removal of Porfirío Díaz and the election of Francisco Madero as President of Mexico, in November 1911, came at a challenging moment for many of the leading American financiers, including Hammond. Madero's accession, initially strongly supported in the turbulent northern and north-western parts of the country, followed a period of heavy US investment in Mexico and in the mid-term of Taft's presidency. Taft and his 'golf cabinet' friends had to contend not only with a new president south of the border, who was intent on partly checking, if not reversing, the capitalist excesses of the old regime, but also with the need to think through the consequences of their actions and policies on a possible second term for Taft, at a time of deepening Republican divisions.[36]

The unfolding revolutionary momentum south of the border was, as in most such cases, ill-suited to a policy informed by principle alone, and Hammond, opportunistic and pragmatic to a fault, had sensed the direction that the wind was coming from and was well prepared. His adaptation to the demise of the Díaz regime and the advent of the Madero government, as well as his movements along the border between Mexico and the United States, were impressively proactive.

In 1909, just weeks after the historic, stage-managed, Díaz–Taft border conference – which failed conspicuously to bolster the Mexican dictator's ailing public image – Hammond sought influence over an important bor-der post. El Paso was not only on the major route leading to the mines at Alamos and to the Yaqui delta, but was also a vital channel for intelligence and a conduit through which counterrevolutionaries could smuggle arms into northern Mexico and Sonora.[37]

Having already introduced a junior partner in the Yaqui Land project, Fred Burnham, to Ben Viljoen at the border conference, Hammond sensed the benefits that might accrue from having military men in positions that could help protect his and the Guggenheims' interests in Sonora. Major Burnham would, if necessary, help defend the assets of the Yaqui Delta Company, on site, while General Viljoen and his Boers, who farmed at Chamberino, out-side El Paso, might help monitor the border.[38]

Like many others in the region struggling to make ends meet in an econ-omy emerging from a recession, Viljoen had for some time been looking for public office to provide him with a regular income. In 1908, he ran, unsuccessfully, in an election for a position in the Land Office at Las Cruces. Uncertain as to just how strong his network of political patrons was, he had already decided to run for the position of Collector of Customs at El Paso when Hammond, for reasons of his own, suddenly started taking an interest in the upcoming appointment.[39]

In November 1909, Hammond, President of the National League of Republican Clubs, got the party organisation in New Mexico to endorse his backing of the General's candidature for the position of Collector of Customs. For Viljoen, whose patronage bets were already hedged, the additional support was welcome but not crucial. Viljoen's opposition came from a local, AL Sharpe, who enjoyed the support of Hammond's long-standing rival for influence in Republican circles, the Chairman of the Republican National Committee and Postmaster General, Frank H Hitchcock.[40] The struggle between these two giants – Hammond and Hitchcock – as mediated through local Republican political structures raged on well into 1910 and ended in a triumph for Frank Hitchcock when Sharpe was elected. Significantly, Hammond, whose memoirs make no mention of either the El Paso contest or of Viljoen, reserved his contempt for the Postmaster General.[41]

But all was not lost. Hammond saw to it that he stayed close to Viljoen and, more importantly, to the most influential Mexicans, including the constitutionalist Madero who, in November 1911, eventually became President, with the intermittent backing of revolutionaries such as Orozco, Villa and Zapata. It was during these tumultuous times that Hammond, who later did 'not want to go into personal matters', disclosed that he had shown Viljoen 'many acts of friendship'.[42] What form these took is impossible to know, but might be imagined.[43]

By mid-1911, the Boer general, although still based on the border around El Paso, but having seen action at Ciudad Juárez a few months earlier, was already acting as a 'military adviser' to Madero, then technically still a 'rebel'. How or on whose recommendation this appointment was made is also unknown, but it is unlikely that it would have taken place without Hammond having been sounded out first, albeit indirectly. What is certain, however, is that Hammond would both have known about, and approved of, Madero's decision to get Viljoen to lead between 200 and 500 volunteers to confront militant socialist opposition in Baja, northwestern Mexico.[44]

The Baja revolutionaries, based on the west coast of the Gulf of California, were led by the brothers Ricardo and Enrique Magón of the *Partido Liberal Mexicano* (PLM), whose members were therefore referred to as 'Magonistas'. The brothers, from Los Angeles, were easily incorporated into Hammond's oldest and worst nightmare, one dating back to the Coeur d'Alene. Enjoying strong support from the Industrial Workers of the World – the Wobblies, who in turn had links to the radical Western Federation of Miners – socialists and other trade unionists in the port cities of southern California, the Magonistas advocated a genuinely revolutionary programme. Not only did they hope to expel all American capitalists, whom they cast as 'imperialists', from their state, but they also believed the land should revert to its original

Indian owners. It was a project that would have held a particular terror for the owners of the Yaqui Delta Company, just across the Gulf, where, at its narrowest point, the port of Guaymas was within easy reach of Baja.[45]

Unsurprisingly, then, the Taft administration, backed by a few US West Coast interests and supported by the President's brother, Charles, and Hammond – members of the notorious 'golf cabinet' – proceeded to grant Viljoen and his troops permission to pass through United States territory unhindered on their way west into Baja to help crush the Magonista occupation of Tijuana.[46] General Viljoen himself had previously been vocal in advising the Mexican government's 'War Department' that 'the United States is becoming tired of the shooting and other acts of anarchists on the California-Mexico border,' and that measures were urgently needed to put a stop to such incidents.[47]

Hammond's most pressing concern was not with Baja itself, but with the revolutionary contamination that might spread across the Gulf of California, into Sonora and then among the disgruntled Yaqui, whose plight Madero himself had outlined so vividly in his 1908 book on Mexican politics. But here, too, a set of developments took place that some might ascribe to chance but which others would be hard-pressed to consider entirely serendipitous.

Shortly after taking office, in November 1911, Madero, the newly elected President, received a delegation of Indians in Mexico City, who made Yaqui dissatisfaction about current and historic injustices in Sonora and the greater delta region abundantly clear to him.[48] Madero indicated that he would implement a programme of land reform to address their grievances, and then, perhaps realising what was ultimately at stake, appointed General Viljoen, already his military adviser, as Commissioner to the Yaqui, charged with overseeing the proposed resettlement deal.[49]

But when Viljoen, his secretary and a Boer supporter, W Malan, arrived at Empalme, near Guaymas, some days later, he found the 900 Indian tribesmen assembled there to be most unhappy. Most were under the impression that they were going to receive ancient, now irrigated land 'privately owned by American and Mexican settlers' – for which read properties bonded to Hammond and his partners' Yaqui Delta Company. Viljoen was of the opinion that there were 'bad influences at work' and that 'outsiders' were 'interfering and giving advice continually against a peaceful settlement'. His attempts to 'calm their concerns', which in effect meant protecting the interests of Hammond, Richardson and Sibbett, were poorly received.[50]

The frustrated Yaqui assembled a second delegation to wait on Madero, in Mexico City, but returned with little to cheer about. True, they ensured that about 500 of their brothers who had been sold into slavery, by Díaz, would be allowed to return to their homeland from the remote Yucatán Peninsula, but they learned anew, from the highest sources in the land, that the Yaqui Delta Company's property would never revert to either individual or collective Indian ownership. All that Madero and Viljoen had succeeded in doing, in trying to protect American capitalist interests, was to import yet more landless discontent into a province already awash with Baja-like ideas about revolutionary restitution of their indigenous land rights.[51]

Viljoen found himself in a very difficult position, having to balance the interests of Madero, the Yaqui Delta Company and the Yaqui, for whom he was supposedly responsible. Not surprisingly, when he returned to Guaymas to address Yaqui chiefs not long thereafter, he was 'once again unable to negotiate to the satisfaction of all concerned'.[52] It was shortly after this breakdown in talks that Viljoen and Hammond – both egotistical by nature – had a brief but bitter public spat, in an El Paso newspaper. The General took umbrage at disparaging remarks about the late President Kruger made by Hammond, during a speech at an elite men's club in Boston, while Hammond was offended by Viljoen's upstart ingratitude.[53]

The differences of 1911 may have lingered precisely because neither Hammond nor Viljoen were in a strong enough position to drive home their advantages. South of the border, they needed one another. And, as we shall see shortly, the General may have turned a blind eye when Burnham, running well ahead of two of the senior partners in the Yaqui Delta Company, but perhaps not Hammond, created a private army to see off the revolutionary Yaqui. But it is significant that it was also at around this time that Viljoen, a slippery customer, was becoming increasingly sickly and vulnerable to political attacks from leading Magonistas.

Rumours began to circulate that the well-connected Boer General was hoping to become a Mexican citizen, a development that was congruent with his appointment as Mexican Consul in Breslau, Germany, in the last quarter of 1912 but one that the often duplicitous Viljoen later denied vigorously.[54] The General left for Europe in August 1912, and received extensive treatment for his asthmatic condition before returning to his ranch, 'Hopeful Harvest', near El Paso, in mid-1913. Before sailing for Germany, however, he may well have had one more opportunity to assist the still beleaguered Americans holding out in southern Sonora.

Having failed to get the Madero government to defuse the rage of the Yaqui Indians and secure the property of the Yaqui Delta Company by purely political means, Hammond, without the support of his two senior partners, Richardson and Sibbett, may have flirted with a Plan B – using force if necessary to protect company assets. Assembling a small private army under revolutionary circumstances was no task for novices, but neither Burnham nor Hammond wanted for relevant experience. Both were 'filibusters' and 'soldiers' not only by temperament and training but also as unashamedly militant, vanguard capitalists intent on protecting investments and profits abroad.

Throughout early 1912, Fred Burnham built up an armed strike force to guard 'the mining and other property in Mexico owned by John Hays Hammond, JP Morgan, the Guggenheims and others', until there were '500 fully armed and equipped men on the banks of the Yaqui River' who were 'ready for any emergency'. So as not to 'excite the suspicion of the Mexicans, federals or rebels', the recruits had collected at the Yaqui River 'in twos and threes' and 'their ammunition, guns and machine guns, it was stated, had been smuggled across the boundary in the vicinity of El Paso' – terrain difficult to negotiate without the connivance of US forces and, probably, without Ben Viljoen knowing about it.[55]

But whether or not Viljoen, the Commissioner to the Yaqui, knew what Burnham was up, the fact of the matter was that Hammond had all but given up on Madero and was by then operating as a full-blown counter-revolutionary agent both in official and clandestine Mexican politics and militarily, on the ground, in southern Sonora. Hammond may have fooled the 'idealistic' Madero, but genuine revolutionaries, such as Orozco, Villa and Zapata, were far less easily taken in by the gringos.

Hammond was active deep within Mexico and all along the northern border. Not all of his movements or his counterrevolutionary intentions were secret. In February 1912, friends reported that Hammond had gone missing briefly in the southern state of Morales, where 'His project is in the heart of the revolutionary districts' controlled by Zapata.[56] On his return to the District of Columbia, the *Washington Herald* noted that Hammond was advising Taft directly, and that 'It is understood that the visit of Mr John Hays Hammond to Mexico had a great deal to do with the sudden activities of the War Department and the White House.'[57]

Hammond was by now also acting as the President's informal adviser on issues of national security, insofar as they related to protecting the interests of American big business in Mexico. And there, to all intents and purposes, he was serving as its full-time capitalist agent, hoping to assist a politically beleaguered Francisco Madero in his efforts to see off the wrath of more radical revolutionaries.

The situation across northern Mexico deteriorated markedly in early 1912, after Orozco turned against Madero. By early May, despite the presence of Burnham's private army, rebellious Indians were attacking American colonists in the delta, and, towards the end of that month, the nephew of the Governor of Sonora, Jesus Maytoreno, was killed on his plantation by Yaqui militants under circumstances that are unclear.[58] The position of the Americans was secured only after Pancho Villa responded to a request from the Governor. But later that year, Yaqui rebels were again active, launching attacks on bridges and railways all the way from Nogales to Hermosillo and Guaymas.[59]

On 20 September 1912, President Taft and an unnamed official in the State Department warned Madero that, unless the lives and property of Americans – and more particularly the assets of the Southern Pacific Railroad – were adequately secured within 30 days, he would be asked to resign from office and run the risk of external intervention in his country.[60] And on the obverse side of that document those of a cynical nature might have thought that they saw the ghostly outline of the fingerprints of the Southern Pacific's Consulting Engineer. His name was John Hays Hammond. Taft earned himself a sharp rejoinder.

Within hours, Juan Pedro Didapp, once a respected member of the Mexican diplomatic corps, but by now sympathetic to the revolutionary factions, publicly denounced the insidious role he thought American capitalists were playing in Mexico.[61] Didapp argued that Díaz, who had been followed by Francisco de la Barra as interim president, had not really been ousted by Madero, even though the latter's *Plan de San Luis* had, for some time, informed the revolutionary expectations of the peasants and peons. But Madero, instead of building on a positive start, had betrayed the cause by holding a largely unconstitutional presidential election while the states of 'Lower California and Morales were [still] under arms'. 'And, as always happened in great national crises,' suggested Didapp, the 'victory fell into the hands of the crooks. Madero, backed up by American crooks could be nothing else but one of them.' Madero, who had appointed many family members to office, ran a nepotistic state, had 'expelled all the people that overthrew the Díaz regime', and then had become personally indebted to 'Wall Street interests'. Señor Didapp named all the usual suspects but made it clear that those he held in the greatest contempt were 'John Hays Hammond and Charles Taft, the president's brother', who had both been paid 'with huge concessions in land and mining fields'.[62]

With less than six months left in office, William Taft knew that his time was running out and that his friend, Hammond, was becoming very nervous. In Mexico City, Madero was under political siege from revolutionaries, and in Washington the face of Woodrow Wilson was looming larger.

With approximately 1 500 well-armed hilltop Yaquis staging ever more raids into the valley from bases in the nearby Sierra Madre, Hammond sensed that the Yaqui Delta Company risked losing everything. With Ben Viljoen in Europe, he not only lacked easy official access to the valley itself but also, more importantly, to President Madero himself. The impasse demanded a dramatic public gesture to try to secure the company's assets and reassure big New York investors, such as the Knickerbocker Bank and HP Whitney. Always more follower than leader, Hammond, encouraged by Burnham, reached into his bag of African tricks and pulled out something

Cecil Rhodes had used when negotiating with Ndebele *indunas*, in the Matopos, back in 1896.[63]

In January 1913, with the Taft administration left with only about ten weeks in office, Hammond eased himself into the presidential slipstream for the last time and wrote to the Mexican Ambassador in Washington, making certain that the contents of his letter were republished in newspapers across the country. If Madero would only give Hammond permission, he, Hammond, accompanied by Burnham and an interpreter, would go 'unarmed' into the Indians' Sierra Madre stronghold and personally present an offer to them that might help 'pacify the turbulent tribe'. In short, he would attempt to split the Yaqui resistance by providing those who agreed to the deal access to a limited amount of irrigated land in the valley. The Yaqui would, in turn, get to provide wage labour to the Delta Land Company and its settlers.[64]

Southern Africa provided the British Empire with 'models' for the economic development of farms, mines and plantations of far-flung outposts, but clearly the lessons behind the creation and control of supplies of cheap, indigenous labour were never confined to British territories. During the age of American imperialism, the settler heroes and colonial practices of southern Africa clearly suggested themselves as models for those advancing capitalist interests in the mines and on the plantations of North America. Indeed, in the case of Sonora and the Yaqui it was not only the crude template, largely inspired by Rhodes himself, that was useful, but also some of the very actors who had been present in its formative years, including an American mining engineer, a Boer General and Jameson's scout in the war that led up to the founding of 'Rhodesia'.

Unfortunately for Hammond, the great initiative came to nothing. Hammond probably knew that it would, but sensed that it might help burnish the image that he had so carefully cultivated after the Jameson Raid as a man never lacking in courage.

Not everybody, however, was taken in. In San Francisco, the truth-telling editor of the *Evening Bulletin*, Fremont Older, drove his pen into the heart of the matter when he suggested that 'John Hays Hammond has announced that he proposes to settle the long pending Yaqui war, single-handed and alone'. 'This is appropriate,' Older suggested, 'inasmuch the gentleman representing the big interests in the United States and America was the cause of starting it.' The editor recapped the sordid history of the scheme, noting that, having been dispossessed, 'the Yaquis were assigned to the mountain tops and coyote ranges' which was the prelude to a war that had never ceased. Nor was he deceived by Hammond's offer of reoccupation of ancient Yaqui land: 'That means, under usual conditions of labor in Mexico, to become the slaves of himself and his associates'; it was just 'cold-blooded pillage'.[65]

Reality, however, had a far greater shock in store for Hammond. Just four weeks before Taft – and Hammond – left the White House, in mid-Feburary 1913, President Madero was assassinated in Mexico City by forces loyal to Victoriano Huerta. With the connivance of the American Ambassador in Mexico City, Henry Lane Wilson, Huerta – 'The Jackal' – had exploited divisions between revolutionary leaders to seize control of the capital over 'ten tragic days', *La Decena Trágica*. Mexico had a new dictator.[66]

Hammond claimed later that when Taft left office, in mid-March 1913, he 'lost interest in politics for the time being'. More accurately stated, his network for protecting US investors in Mexican projects, consisting of two presidents, with bit parts for Viljoen and Burnham, had ceased to exist in meaningful form. The cowboy-knight had fallen on hard times, times that Woodrow Wilson would endeavour to make even more difficult. It was enough to test a man's patriotism and sense of fair play.

CHAPTER TWENTY-SEVEN

Hammond, Mexico and Transnational Capitalism

C 1909–1917

Hammond's exceptional ability as a West Coast mining engineer and his impeccable East Coast banking connections laid the foundations for his financial successes in America in the early 1890s. His political mis-adventure in southern Africa, half a decade later, may have dented his political reputation but it failed to halt the gathering economic momentum of his career. A spell of self-imposed exile in the City of London allowed him to refurbish his tarnished image as a man of honour and as a professional engineer with enduring gifts, thereby paving the way for his successful re-entry to the United States, with the help of the Guggenheim family, between 1900 and 1908. It was, however, the ascent of his Yale friend, William Taft, to the American presidency that did most to bring Hammond's expanding wealth and political influence into near-perfect alignment in the world's most powerful capitalist democracy between 1909 and 1913. And, by the same token, it was the divisions within the Republican Party and its failure to reinsure Taft's re-election for a second term, in 1912, that did most to erode that handy arrangement.

The better part of the decade that followed, one bridged by the First World War, fell to two Democratic administrations under Woodrow Wilson, between 1913 and 1921, and could not have come at a worse time in Mr and Mrs Hammond's otherwise stellar careers. Jack, aged 60 in 1915, and the multi-talented Natalie Harris were both set to reach the apex of their economic, political and social trajectories when Theodore Roosevelt's charging Bull Moose movement split the Republican herd, allowing Wilson, more openly driven by principle, to capture the middle ground.

The dawning of a Democratic dispensation at 1600 Pennsylvania Avenue ended Hammond's untrammelled personal access to the President, such as he had routinely enjoyed under Taft. Wilson's public triumph was a private disaster for Hammond, a noted 'hero worshipper' with a long-standing preference for cultivating men of power and influence.[1] Summarily locked out of the White House and left without a way of getting at the sausages on the kitchen table, the old dog howled outside the back door until, many months later, he found a new route to breach the presidential redoubt.

Predictably, the barking was most pronounced during the opening months of the first Wilson administration. The root cause was the president's reservations about the operations of exploitative American concessionaries south of the Rio Grande and a reluctance to be dragged into Mexican politics by transfrontier entrepreneurs who had prospered under the Díaz dictatorship.[2] In Hammond's case, however, it was not only the huge profits that he garnered on behalf of the Guggenheims and others that were of concern. Foreign-owned extractive industries that employed relatively small numbers of skilled Americans on site were troublesome enough in their own right, but the Yaqui Delta Land and Water Company was different.[3]

The Yaqui Delta Company derived its income from irrigating and rendering the land productive through the raising of crops and the selling of land. It was an enterprise that extracted a higher emotional and symbolic price from a marginalised population dependent on agriculture than did mineral extraction, and all the more so since the enormous land holdings in question – around 3 000 square kilometres, the size of Rhode Island – had been acquired through the forcible dispossession of the original indigenous owners by the discredited Díaz regime.[4] Moreover, unlike mines and oil wells, whose life cycle was finite, the Yaqui Delta Company was a project that manifestly aimed at 'colonisation', one driven by American and Mexican 'settlers' intent on carving out a future within the country and from the soil.

The economic, political and social differences between long-term commercial farming by settlers on the one hand, and shorter-lived extractive industries on the other, meant that the Yaqui Delta Company occupied a position of unique importance in Hammond's extensive portfolio of transfrontier investments as well as in his mind, not to mention the minds of the governments of Mexico and the United States. While profits and property were always important considerations when it came to protecting American interests at home or abroad, in the case of the Yaqui Delta Company things were a bit more complex; it was a case of having to protect the *lives* as well as the property of settlers. That alone meant that there was always a marginally greater onus on the part of the President of the United States and his administration to safeguard estates belonging to Hammond and his partners in Lower Sonora than there was to defend other American-owned mines and oilfields. Hammond knew this and thought that it greatly increased the moral and political pressure he could exercise over Wilson and the State Department. But when that protection was not instantly forthcoming, it only caused the beast to howl louder and longer.

Hammond was dismayed when, in 1913, just months after Wilson had assumed office, militant 'Bronco' Yaquis launched a series of attacks in Lower Sonora. When a quiet word with well-placed officials failed to get President Wilson, Secretary of State William Jennings Bryan or the Secretary of the Navy, Josephus Daniels, to draw a line in the sand for all to see, Hammond lost his composure. In a rare public attack on the administration, he vowed not to invest another cent in Mexico while Bryan was responsible for foreign policy below the Rio Grande and then, harking back to the high-water mark of American imperialism and masculinity in the late 1890s, muttered: 'A nation that does not protect its citizens and investors is unworthy of the name of a nation.'[5]

Aware that public gouging militated against the ability to yield influence in private, Hammond found Wilson's policy of 'watchful waiting' in regard to Mexico difficult to stomach, but he resisted the temptation of open criticism. Instead, he took some comfort when, in an address delivered at the Commonwealth Club of his home state of California, in late 1915, Taft brutally mauled the government's policies as applied in Mexico and the Philippines.[6] But after yet another challenging year in the Yaqui delta, one in which he, his influential partners in the company and their paid and unpaid agents had again failed to secure American military intervention to protect the settler colony in Sonora, he could no longer keep his peace. In the annual address to his beloved Rocky Mountain Club, held in Baltimore, in February 1916, Hammond characterised the Wilson administration's foreign policy on Mexico as being largely 'fatuous'.[7]

Self-serving public criticism of Wilson ensured that Hammond and those 'Captains of Industry' inclined to question the prevailing policies on Mexico were occasionally rewarded with a few short, sharp, smacks from Democrat-aligned sections of the press.[8] But such was Hammond's standing and influence in the country that, for the most part, he and his partners got off extremely lightly when indulging in such petulant outbursts. In Hammond's case some of his powder-puff treatment at the hands of the Fourth Estate could be traced back to a second, parallel, image of him that he had cultivated with some care ever since he had renewed his friendship with William Taft back in 1904.

If it was Cecil Rhodes who had helped round off Hammond's education as a financier with exceptional engineering skills, then it was Taft, a lawyer, who brought home to Cowboy Jack how border conflicts and disputes could be handled not only within the state but *between* states. It was Taft who taught Hammond that the sword beyond the frontier could be supplemented by the shield at home, and Hammond, sharp and pragmatic, engaged the new United States moneyed elite wielding both.

Taft hoped, one day, to be the country's Chief Justice at least as much, if not more, than he ever wanted to be President. In the end he became both. Hammond, a good and loyal friend, respected and supported Taft's deeper ambition even as their respective careers in politics came to complement one another ever more closely between 1909 and 1913.

The continuities in this mutually beneficial relationship, however, both pre- and post-dated Taft's term in the White House. Hammond was Taft's political 'fixer', while the President, in turn, encouraged his action-orientated friend to think about other, legal ways of resolving transfrontier conflicts and disputes. Hammond geed-up Taft politically, while Taft calmed Hammond down by suggesting that he follow more diplomatic and legal channels in trying to effect desirable outcomes. It was a peculiar partnership that worked well for more than two decades.

The second international peace conference, convened in The Hague, in 1907, at the suggestion of Theodore Roosevelt, built on the progress made in the first conference, held in 1899. For ambitious up-and-coming Republicans, including Hammond and Taft, the Hague conference underscored the need for new and more progressive ways of pursuing international peace. It also helped inject a more moral tone to political debate in a nominally Christian country, avoided messy city politics and underscored the need for statesmanship.

Shortly before, or shortly after, Taft entered the White House, Hammond began to take an interest in the socially prestigious and venerable New York Peace Society.[9] What precisely inspired this enthusiasm in a man of his pedigree is difficult to know, but he would probably have been spurred on by the new President. But what *is* clear is that it was Taft who encouraged his friend in another venture, driven by another of Hammond's many East Coast friends, the publicist Theodore Marburg.[10]

Marburg was a man after Hammond's own heart – refined, well-educated and wealthy, someone whose progressive interests slipped readily between high-level politics and low-level social theory in ways capable of distinguishing admired Anglo-Saxons from the 'lower races', as identified by the social Darwinists.[11] At a dinner in Baltimore, in February 1910, Marburg floated the idea of an American Society for the Judicial Settlement of International Disputes, with William Taft as its president.[12] It was a tentative step towards establishing a permanent tribunal devoted to the judicial settlement of international disputes – a world court. Taft was pleased with concept and man alike. As in the case of Hammond, when he was sent to London as a Special Ambassador in 1911, Marburg was made Envoy Extraordinary and Minister Plenipotentiary to Belgium in 1912.

Confident that his countrymen were now on a viable path to political progress, Hammond attended the American Peace Society's Congress, in Baltimore, in 1911, to deliver a lecture on 'A Businessman's Interest in Peace'. He offered an unapologetically capitalist perspective, advocating an extension of the Open Door policy, suggesting that China be 'neutralised' in 'the fashion of Belgium and Switzerland' so as to ensure that all nations enjoyed access to one of the world's great markets.[13]

The outbreak of the First World War, three years later, foregrounded questions about the pursuit of international peace and, as Vice President of the new Society for Judicial Settlements, Hammond sensed an opportunity to reposition Marburg's idea and sharpen the focus. In December 1914, he advocated the establishment of a 'Pan-American International Court of Business Arbitration' – a project more finely tuned to his needs and to those who had invested heavily in Central and South America. Nothing came of the venture but it did leave a clue as to his thinking.[14]

A few weeks later, in January 1915, with President Woodrow Wilson already seeing himself in a role as a possible peacemaker in Europe, Hammond, irritated by the Society for Judicial Settlements' 'unwieldy title' and 'academic and intellectual tone', set about recasting Marburg's original organisation. Rejigged as the 'World Court League', the new body emerged with Hammond as its first President and his old friend William Taft as Honorary President. An unsuccessful effort to draw Wilson into the League project weeks later met with disappointment.[15]

By then, however, the indefatigable Marburg had already launched another initiative, the League for Peace, which, after the sinking of the *Lusitania* became the 'League to Enforce Peace' and a forerunner of the League of Nations.[16] Here, too, Hammond and Taft played leading roles and this time, with Hammond working with the active assistance of a sympathetic insider on the White House staff, succeeded in getting Woodrow Wilson to come out in public support.[17]

Looking back, then, it can be seen how Hammond and Taft – the one a recent convert to the need for international law, the other a lifelong lover of jurisprudence who hoped to become Chief Justice – became committed to the pursuit of international peace in propitious times. The first push in that direction took place before Taft's election as president and gained momentum during his term in office (1909–1913). But the real drive forward from this committed Republican duo came during Woodrow Wilson's Democratic administrations and the First World War.

Focused on Europe and domestic politics, and then, after April 1917, on America's role in the war, members of the Fourth Estate had little if any recall of Hammond's problematic record as colonialist and imperialist. It was the advent of the Taft administration that had helped him make the transition from mere politics to diplomacy, and once Wilson was in office, it was the efforts to make organisations devoted to international peace work that caught the eye. During the First World War, but more especially towards the end of the second Wilson administration, in 1921 and thereafter, some in the press were wont to present Hammond as a grand old man, someone of good temper, sound judgement and great wisdom.

As early as 1908, a reporter from the *New York Times*, showing appropriate deference, had pointed in the new direction when he characterised Hammond as 'a very courteous, modest, sincere type of man'. A 100-strong committee planning a conference to promote the idea of a World Court to be held in Cleveland, in 1916, unanimously elected Hammond as its chairman, so it was claimed, because 'of his practical business sense, his diplomatic temperament and personal acquaintance with most of the rulers of the world'.[18] An extreme version of such uncritical treatment could be found in a report penned by a close family friend of Taft's for the *Brooklyn Daily Eagle* in 1925, the year in which the president's friend turned 70. 'John Hays Hammond,' gushed Louise Boardman Proctor, 'is a genial-mannered, kindly and humorous man with an eye that twinkles and a heart that responds to the best desires and needs of the "other man".' He was a modest man who had 'declined ambassadorships and cabinet portfolios under Presidents Taft, Harding and Coolidge' and, most recently, a Commissionership in the District of Columbia – a position of both national and local importance.[19]

Although many such reports were sepia-tinted, it was not as if they were devoid of substance. Age, respect and wealth had indeed, as is the case with most men, tempered Hammond over the intervening decades. He and Natalie Hammond had devoted much time and effort to their work in the National Civic Federation at the most senior levels of that organisation. Jack was especially committed to the Boys' Club Federation, where he served as Vice President. In motivational talks to the young he generally ended his addresses with a 'quotation from the plucky cowboy', reminding his listeners that success in life was not about starting out with a good hand, but in playing a poor hand markedly well.[20]

Much of the background colouring to this more favourable press portrait of Hammond had been laid down in an earlier era. It was, in largest part, a by-product of his well-publicised work in the peace movement between 1913 and 1921, when just about everybody – bar President Wilson himself – had either abandoned most of their critical faculties or undergone some inexplicable, near-total loss of memory when it came to arriving at a more rounded assessment of Hammond's career.

Looking back, it is utterly amazing to note how Hammond managed to successfully position himself as a leading champion of world peace. In 1896, as a self-styled revolutionary, he was convicted of treason and sentenced to

death for his role in an abortive attempt by mining capitalists to overthrow
the government of the South African Republic. In 1903, decades after the
American Civil War, but in the immediate wake of a war in South Africa
which many believed was precipitated by the Jameson Raid, he openly
advocated the enslavement of Africans in order to satisfy the need for cheap
labour in the Witwatersrand mines.

Just five years later, and closer to home, Hammond had acquired extensive concessionary land and water rights for a 'colonisation scheme' for
American 'settlers' over a huge part of Sonora notorious for the forcible
dispossession and exile of its indigenous Indians. In 1912, while Hammond
was publicly advocating the need for the 'judicial settlement of disputes', he
and his associate Burnham were assembling a force of mercenaries in the
besieged Yaqui delta to confront revolutionaries that included some of the
very same landless Indians. For Hammond, the barrel of the gun preceded
peace.

Again, in 1914, Hammond and other capitalists lived with 'bandit'-driven
violence south of the Rio Grande because, as the biographer of Pancho Villa
has noted, 'John Hays Hammond openly stated that their aim was to annex
the northern part of Mexico to the United States.'[21] Sustained disorder in
border states would invite American annexation, assuring the long-term
safety of the delta. Business had an interest in peace – usually after, rather
than before, war.

Nor could the leopard change its spots. As the war in Europe ended,
Hammond saw a new era of expansion for American trade beckoning, as
did others. But in terms of his own objectives and the tone that he chose to
adopt, it was the same old underlying argument about a world characterised
by a racial hierarchy and the need for firmness of purpose.

In an address to the American Academy of Political and Social Sciences,
in 1919, Hammond argued that: 'Anyone who is familiar with the condition in Latin America, in Africa, in the West Indies, for example, knows that
whatever measure of prosperity and civilization exists among the natives
has been developed by the activities of foreign capital in those regions.'
The guidelines of an 'ideal foreign policy' for the United States were therefore crystal clear. They would have to ensure that America had 'the greatest
degree of commercial independence' as well as '*compel* the greatest dependence from the rest of the world'.[22] Lenin could not have stated a formula for
global imperialism more crisply. Two years later, in 1921, Hammond became
one of the founding members of the enduring, highly influential, American
Council on Foreign Relations.

In fairness, it should be noted that, while many commentators and
observers at the time were so taken with Hammond's carrot of 'world peace'
that they failed to notice the barely concealed stick of financial self-interest,

modern analysts have proved to be a bit harder to hoodwink. 'Other prominent business members of the New York Peace Society' – a grouping that
included Hammond and banker JP Morgan, one cautious scholar notes –
'might have been influenced to take a narrowly self-interested concern in
peace.'[23]

Another historian is even less generous and more pointed in his opinion:

> It was not the visionary or spiritual pacifism which brought
> Hammond, industrialist Andrew Carnegie, or George Perkins of
> United States Steel to the forefront of the American Peace move-
> ment in the early twentieth century. Rather it might be said that
> such a movement was more Pacific than pacific in its orientation;
> more concerned with successfully securing the business aims of the
> Open Door [American policy on China] than in faithfully following
> the tenets of a warless society.[24]

But no one-dimensional juxtaposition of the emergence of the American
peace movement on the one hand and the underlying capitalist self-interest
on the other, can of its own accord reveal fully just how capable of instrumental and multifaceted action Hammond was at a time when Woodrow
Wilson was attempting to ensure that the interests of big business in Mexico
remained subservient to those of a Democratic administration. In order to
appreciate the larger picture in all its fullness, we need to consider anew
the fortunes of the Yaqui Delta Land and Water Company and Hammond's
expanding interests in Mexican oil.[25]

Hammond's major partner in the Yaqui Delta Land and Water Company
and its principal financial backer was HP Whitney, son of a former Secretary
of the Navy in the Cleveland administration. A good deal younger than
Hammond but also a Yale graduate, Harry Payne Whitney had inherited
$24 million, in 1904, having a decade earlier also married into the wealthy
Vanderbilt family. Besides the original owners of the concession, the brothers D and WE Richardson of Los Angeles and company manager HA
Sibbett, other noteworthy investors included Fred Burnham, Leigh Hunt,
Thomas Rogan, the Knickerbocker Bank & Trust of New York City and
several Californians who, for reasons unknown, wished to remain 'anonymous'. The complex legal affairs of the Yaqui Delta Company were handled
by FN Watriss, a Yale-educated attorney who, with Hammond's son, Harris,
became involved with the family's interests in the Tampico oilfields of
Mexico.[26]

Assured first of private and then public financial backing that ran into
tens of millions of dollars, as well as the support of the Southern Pacific
Railroad, which, by 1908, was providing it with links to urban markets in

Mexico and the United States, the Yaqui Delta Company opened new roads and developed facilities at ports along the Gulf of California.[27]

Consciously designated a colonisation scheme, with about 700 American and Mexican settlers by 1912, the estates, overseen by WW Mackie, once a state agricultural expert in California, commanded more than 320 kilometres of canals and 28 000 hectares of irrigated land, along with thousands more hectares of pasturage devoted to cattle raising and dairy products. The settlers, using the labour of the most economically vulnerable elements of the Indian population were soon producing an impressive array of agricultural commodities, ranging from alfalfa, beans, cotton, citrus and rice on the one hand, to all manner of tropical fruit and vegetable crops on the other. The gigantic Yaqui property was hardly a privately owned ranch of the type that Cowboy Jack could easily afford in his own right, but his attachment to the scheme suggested that it occupied a special place in his heart.[28]

As already noted, however, the ethical foundations of this new Eden were far from sound. The gardens rested on land that, to all intents and purposes, had been stolen from the indigenous Indians by the Díaz regime. Moreover, as seen from their hilltop mountain retreats in the Sierra Madre, by the 'Bronco', or armed and therefore 'wild', Indians, the land lost remained approachable from several different directions. Nor were other native Mexicans much taken with the idea of a colony of gringos in their midst.

It was not by chance, then, that the project was under almost constant surveillance by a few ex-United States Army officers during the early part of the Mexican revolution. It is not known how many of the American settlers had military experience, but the number is unlikely to have been insignificant. Captain Risher Thornberry, later a jujitsu instructor in the US Army, had seen service in Cuba, in the navy in the Philippines during the Spanish-American War and had lived through the Boxer Rebellion and Russo-Japanese War before settling for a time in Nagasaki. Based in the Yaqui Valley between 1909 and 1912, it is easy to see how his presence would have appealed to the owners of the Delta Company. It is equally noteworthy how, during the crucial years from 1913 to 1917, it was Major Fred Burnham who often put in an appearance on-site.[29]

Located in flat, low-lying country, most settler properties, each close on 280 hectares in extent and rectangular in shape, were locked into a larger grid defined by irrigation canals and roads. This left the lots vulnerable to enemy invasion. In order to bolster defences, Mackie's agricultural experiment station near the company 'headquarters', at Esperanza, was overlooked by a 21-metre watchtower suitably manned during times of crisis.[30] The private army of 500 'armed and fully equipped men' that the company assembled on the estate under Major Burnham, in 1912, would never have been wholly exposed or compromised. The set-up was of a piece with the quasi-military mode of production that Hammond had favoured through his early career – at Alamos in the 1880s, in the Coeur d'Alene in the early 1890s and on the Witwatersrand goldfields. On the Rand, African miners were housed in fort-like structures with single points of entry and exit manned by uniformed, whip-wielding guards known locally as 'compound policemen'.

The architecture, personnel, sociology and language employed in such endeavours, not excluding that in the Yaqui delta, frequently spoke to frontier enclaves, of industrial or plantation labour located if not on foreign soil, then on land whose ownership was debatable or disputed, as well as a military mindset that expected, nay, almost demanded, that assets and occupants be fully secured, or rescued in moments of crisis.

In its primary manifestations, capitalism in various forms, colonialism in various guises and imperialism in all its armed splendour is not a figment of leftist imaginations. Its coercive, contested and exploitative nature is there for all to see as progress for the privileged entrenches itself at the expense of the dispossessed, the vulnerable or the weak. In Hammond's case, long before Taft ever occupied the White House, federal forces, local police, state troopers and filibusters such as those commanded by Dr Jameson had sought to support him in his hour of need, with varying degrees of success. The difficulties posed by the Yaqui Delta Company might thus have been exceptional for an American administration such as Woodrow Wilson's, or even for a Mexican president such as Venustiano Carranza (May 1917 to May 1920), but for John Hays Hammond it was the stock-in-trade of an industrial pioneer.

Mobilising and operationalising forces of last resort for frontier or transfrontier duty, however, required privileged access to the innermost workings of the state and the White House. Nobody knew that better than Hammond. He had an excellent appreciation of how political power was formally constituted in America, and an unrivalled understanding of how its inner workings could be short-circuited to produce outcomes that benefited investors in the domestic or foreign ventures that he helped steer. He and Taft had formed a formidable political duo and, within weeks of Taft's presidency ending, in March 1913, Hammond looked round to see who, if anyone, was going to take up his old role within the new Wilson administration.

The search was neither arduous nor long, and, as with his rediscovery of 'his' old friendship with William Taft, in 1904, the road to success ran through Hammond's brother Bill and the Hopkins Grammar School of New Haven, Connecticut. Bill Hammond and Colonel Edward M House had been classmates at Hopkins long before House became an extremely successful 'fixer' in Democratic state politics, in Texas, or his subsequent move to Washington, DC. House was not a military man, and had been afforded the courtesy title of 'Colonel' in recognition of his many abilities in an era that celebrated American muscularity, even though, personally, he was devoted to the pursuit of international peace.

The Colonel had been among the first in Washington to appreciate that the Governor of New Jersey had the makings of a president and Wilson had rewarded him by making him an adviser so trusted that he was, for a time, allocated living quarters within the White House itself. Although Hammond had long known that House owned a holiday home at Cape Ann, only a few miles from his own in Gloucester, he had not engaged with the Colonel socially during Taft's presidency. Nor, for whatever reason, did they encounter one another at Wilson's inauguration. But, by spring 1913, Hammond felt the need to renew his acquaintance with his brother's classmate.[31]

'I believe that Colonel House can be and would be of great assistance to us,' Hammond later wrote to Taft, 'if we take the trouble to enlist his cooperation' in the search for international peace.[32] But, by then, Hammond had long since moved to secure Colonel House's friendship for purposes that presumably had far more to do with big business and national politics than they did with the League of Nations or the World Court – causes that lay much closer to the hearts of House and Wilson.

During the summer vacation of 1913, Hammond invited House to dine at Gloucester. 'At that meeting,' Hammond later recalled, House told him 'that he was called "the John Hays Hammond of the Wilson administration"'. And, in a way, he was. House was another who, without holding elected office, enjoyed easy access to the President when it came to formulating policy. Hammond, realising the dangers inherent in such a position, had a variant on his standard reply at the ready for Colonel House: 'I hope that you will have more influence with President Wilson than I had with President Taft.' 'I failed to use such influence that perhaps I should have exerted,' he claimed.[33] It was a quintessentially dissembling remark from a man who had only recently helped to ensure that the US Army and Texas Rangers were deployed along the Mexican border.

Most people found the Colonel to be an enigmatic, private person. Even Hammond, who scoffed at that notion, obviously could not fully conceal his own puzzlement and, in a few paradoxical sentences that revealed more about his own mode of assessment and hidden values, set out his position. 'House has often been called "the man of mystery",' he noted in his autobiography, but 'There is nothing peculiar about him'. Then, in the very next sentence, he added: 'He is a man without the usual pecuniary interests in life.' It was an unusual juxtaposition. According to Hammond, House was both ordinary and yet different. One thing, however, was certain: the Colonel was beyond the reach of money.[34]

Almost all of Hammond's efforts to enlist Colonel House in shifting Woodrow Wilson's foreign policies before 1917 came to nothing. It was not as if the President did little in regard to Mexico during its revolutionary upheavals; it was just that he remained deeply suspicious of both American big business interests south of the Rio Grande and the danger of war, and was willing to act only to protect what he considered to be the best interests of the United States as a whole.

Thus, in 1914, American forces occupied the port city of Veracruz for a period after a series of miscalculations that, in the final analysis centred on issues of diplomacy and protocol in Tampico. In his capacity as Commander-in-Chief, Wilson also sent the US Army, under General John J Pershing, on a 'Punitive Expedition' into Mexico, in 1916–1917, in what turned out to be a futile attempt to capture Pancho Villa after the 'bandit' had attacked the town of Columbus, New Mexico.[35] But that was as close as 'intervention-ists' among American big businessmen got to their longed-for ambition to secure the annexation of northern Mexico.[36]

Hammond was, however, slightly more successful in getting House to serve as a conduit for a few Republican messages to the President after 1917, or when it came to soliciting White House support for his and Taft's peace initiatives.[37] This marginal increase in traction occurred, in part, because Wilson's second wife, Edith, managed to place some distance between her husband and House, whom she disliked. The President grew even more disenchanted when House later counselled him to consider working with Republicans, such as Henry Cabot Lodge, to ensure that Congress would support Wilson's doomed attempts to get the United States to join the League of Nations. By late 1919, the Colonel and the President were thus no longer on speaking terms, and, perhaps predictably, Hammond and House's friendship grew firmer.[38]

The net result of all this was that, more especially so between 1913 and 1917, and then again between 1919 and 1921, once Wilson's second term in office was drawing to a close, Hammond and the big investors in agriculture, mining and oil in Mexico had to find other ways of burrowing their way into the innards of the State Department. In this regard they were assisted by the fact that, during most of the Wilson years, there were men either on, or very close to, the Mexico desk in the State Department who disagreed with his and House's cautious policies. Just how closely Hammond, Watriss and Whitney worked with these near openly-subversive elements in the State Department in an attempt to get American armed forces to invade and occupy the Yaqui delta, is best illustrated by tracing the unfolding crisis in Lower Sonora, in 1915.[39]

CHAPTER TWENTY-EIGHT

A Uniform of Greed

Sword of Colonialism, Shield of Law

C 1913–1920

By the first quarter of 1915, the menace and uncertainty arising from the drawn-out revolution had sapped both the Yaqui delta settlers and their large agricultural holdings of most of their earlier promise and vitality. Unending political differences, occasionally playing out as regional conflicts between leading elements in the revolution, including Carranza, Obregón, Orozco, Villa and Zapata, had seen the number of colonists dwindle from around 700 in 1912 to about 300, made up for the most part by Americans and a lesser number of Germans and Mexicans. And, at the core of the 300 were about a hundred diehards – those who had possibly invested most heavily and stood to lose all.[1]

1915 may well have been the tipping point insofar as the immediate financial fortunes of the Yaqui Delta Company were concerned. With bond repayments sharply down and likely to decline further with the passing of each year, both the company and remaining settlers were determined to protect livestock, standing crops and the upcoming spring harvest, with the last-mentioned alone estimated at being worth around half a million dollars.[2]

For the militant 'Bronco' Indians of the Sierra Madre, however, the out-look was, arguably, better than it had been for some time. The hired guns of Burnham's 1912 private army had long since disbanded amid internal disagreements among leading shareholders, and many of the Mexican revolutionaries were at odds with one another and the state. A few Yaquis aspired to establishing a republic of their own but many more were willing to settle for less; either way, the time was ripe for an attack on the colony.[3]

Several thousand Indians, not all of them Yaqui, were mobilised in late

April. In mid-May 1915, a force of about 500 men launched the first of a dozen attacks across the wider delta region. Although these early attacks did not entail the loss of many settler lives the onslaught was sufficiently serious for the Yaqui Delta Company to suspend its operations. It was, however, not only the company and the dwindling number of settlers in the colony who were distressed by what was happening. Mexican revolutionaries and state officials alike sensed that Yaqui predations might inflame American public opinion and succeed in prodding even the reluctant Wilson administration to take action. If Lower Sonora was occupied to form what Pancho Villa once characterised as a 'Yanqui Protectorate' it could be the prelude to a full-scale annexation of Mexico's border states, just as Hammond and other American investors advocated and longed for.[4]

But nothing could have been further from Woodrow Wilson's mind. Not only was he deeply suspicious of those American concessionaires commanding extensive estates in Mexico, he was also sympathetically disposed towards those who had been left indebted and poverty stricken through the entrenchment of such landholdings. He was, he said, 'more interested in the fortunes of the oppressed men and pitiful women, than in any property rights whatsoever'.[5] Wilson's problems, however, lay not in his own instinct for decency or fair play, but with the officials in the State Department responsible for implementing US foreign policy.

The President's most immediate difficulty stemmed from the sinking of the liner *Lusitania*, torpedoed by a German U-boat off the coast of Ireland on 7 May 1915, with the loss of numerous American lives. Wilson's response to the incident was so threatening that it caused his pacifist Secretary of State, William Jennings Bryan, to resign. This meant that most, but not all, of the crisis in the Yaqui delta unfolded on the watch of the new Secretary of State, Robert Lansing, a man who, along with several others in the State Department, was far more inclined to protect the interests of US capital and colonists abroad. Lansing, however, made certain that there was not too much distance between him and Wilson's right-hand man. A popular joke in Washington went: 'Question, how do you spell Lansing? Answer: H-O-U-S-E.'[6]

Lansing's two Assistant Secretaries of State – William Phillips and Frank Polk – were well known to Hammond, HA Sibbett, FN Watriss and others on the board of the Yaqui Delta Company. The Harvard Law School-trained Phillips had been in attendance throughout Hammond's spell in London as Special Ambassador, in 1911. Like Phillips, Watriss was a product of Harvard Law School, and he and Phillips would refer to one another, in writing, as 'brother'. Polk was a Yale man, but even more comfortable in Watriss's company since the two had once been partners in the same law firm in New York City.[7]

President Woodrow Wilson
PHOTO: HARRIS & EWING COLLECTION, LIBRARY OF CONGRESS

Edward M House
PHOTO: LIBRARY OF CONGRESS

John Hays Hammond and his daughter Natalie

Lower down the pecking order, in the Latin American section, the position for those seeking to influence the direction of foreign policy coming out of Washington was possibly even more promising. The head of the Mexican desk, Leon J Canova, was a former journalist, ambitious, adventurous to the point of being reckless, conservative and well-disposed to the interests of big business. He was, in short, the type of man that Hammond and Richard Harding Davis would have approved of and he dominated his portfolio.[8]

From the moment the Yaquis launched their spring initiative in 1915, Wilson, preoccupied with the *Lusitania* crisis, was on the back foot insofar as developments in Lower Sonora were concerned. Bryan, anxious to avoid armed conflict and to ensure that the US did not get embroiled in the Mexican revolution, settled on a variant of the administration's usual policy of 'watchful waiting'. The cruiser *Raleigh* with a contingent of marines aboard, was dispatched to the Gulf of California and instructed to lie at anchor off the coast of Sonora. If necessary, Admiral Thomas B Howard would supervise the evacuation of settlers from the estates, but there was to be no forcible occupation of the delta region.[9]

The deployment of the *Raleigh* was a minimalist response by the American administration; even so, it excited Mexican anxieties, for reasons easily understood. The Yaqui Delta Company and the settlers saw it as a job only half-done, and, as the Indian incursions continued, they upped the asking price of Washington. Building on the underlying logic of a 'colony', the settlers now petitioned for 'the establishment of a permanent American garrison at Esperanza', further hiking the concerns of Mexican revolutionaries.[10]

Indeed, it may be significant that, by 1915, Pancho Villa, who had firsthand experience and knowledge of Lower Sonora and the Yaqui Delta Company as a result of his incursions there, was becoming adamant that, once the revolution was over, American investment might continue but that foreign ownership of land would never be countenanced. In northwestern Mexico, informal colonisation via land concessions might be the forerunner of armed conflict and followed by outright annexation. In this way, then, Jack Hammond may well have helped shape Mexican policies on land ownership as they evolved over the next two years.[11]

As soon as the *Raleigh* was dispatched to the Gulf, the Yaqui Delta Company moved to ensure that the State Department was constantly reminded of the need for armed intervention in the delta. Early in June, HA Sibbett, the company manager, was sent to Washington where he joined forces with Fred Watriss, as they sought to exert pressure on Leon Canova and up the chain of command to Secretary of State Lansing. Their attempts were not characterised by an excess of subtlety. Watriss reminded 'Brother

Phillips' of Harry Payne Whitney's pedigree. 'In view of the services, material and otherwise which Whitney and his father had always rendered the Democratic Party,' wrote Watriss, 'the Department' might be inclined to 'further effort' when it came to protecting the company's interests in Lower Sonora. None of this, however, was drawn directly to the President's attention.[12]

Thus it was that, at almost the same moment that Hammond and 108 other leading American businessmen were publicly supporting the floatation of the 'League for Peace', a forerunner of the League of Nations, Hammond's own agents were privately encouraging the government to intervene in the Yaqui delta in the hope that it might bolster attempts to see the northern parts of the country annexed to the United States or, at the very least, force the hand of the Mexican authorities and get them to provide armed protection for the beleaguered settlers.[13]

On 12 June, the Yaquis unintentionally added fuel to the flickering flames of intervention when they launched another attack in the delta region, threatening, Lansing argued, 'to wipe out' the entire American colony. The President, persuaded by the Secretary of State of the gravity of the situation, agreed to send two additional cruisers to the Gulf but, again, on the explicit proviso that Admiral Howard was not to intervene, other than by way of evacuation, unless 'absolutely necessary'. Company officials and Canova considered the deployment of two more cruisers and 1 100 marines as almost a personal triumph.[14]

The arrival of additional American firepower in the Gulf of California persuaded Governor Maytorena of Sonora state to send General Leyva and 1 000 Mexican troops into the Yaqui Valley. Their twofold objective was interlinked: first, to protect the settlers from yet more Indian attacks and, second, by so doing, to deny the American marines an excuse for attempting an evacuation or a pretext for occupation.[15]

The three-way stand-off between the American forces, the Mexican army and the colonists of the Yaqui Valley escalated existing tensions to a new and more menacing level. The settlers, sensing that the presence of the *Raleigh* constituted a form of insurance, refused to consider evacuation as a possibility, 'barricaded their homes and prepared for a lengthy siege' – a development that, in effect, militated against Admiral Howard being able to execute his original brief. Frustrated by this new and unforeseen twist, Howard drew the only conclusion available to him, changed his position, and called for an 'occupation of the settlements'.[16]

At that point, Hammond, a veteran when it came to mobilising frontier-like armed forces or military interventions by the state in order to protect and secure private enterprise, was once again within an ace of securing the outcome that he and his colleagues in the Yaqui Delta Company desired – occupation as a prelude to annexation. This time, however, he was up against Woodrow Wilson.

The President vetoed Howard's plan for occupation. Aware that Mexican fears of annexation were not without foundation, and realising that they were in large measure a by-product of agitation by certain American investors, Wilson remained willing to countenance only the evacuation of the settlers. In the end, not even that proved necessary and the President's analysis and actions alike were vindicated. As the principal historian of the 1915 crisis in Lower Sonora notes, Woodrow Wilson was unwilling 'to employ American troops to secure the property of the likes of Hammond, Watriss and Whitney' – 'archetypes, in his mind, of the avaricious and exploitative concessionaries that he had denounced from the earliest days of his administration'.[17] The President, however, probably knew that he was far from free of colonialist ambitions at home.

In January 1916, men loyal to Pancho Villa, their leader increasingly frustrated that American support had shifted to his rival, Venustiano Carranza, attacked a train near Santa Isabel, in the northern state of Chihuahua. Sixteen employees of the Guggenheim-owned American Smelting and Refining Company (ASARCO), were pulled from the train, stripped and executed. Eight weeks later, Villa sacked the small town of Columbus, New Mexico, forcing Woodrow Wilson to dispatch the Pershing expedition in a futile attempt to capture his erstwhile ally.

For the second time within 12 months, unnamed American investors, but which almost certainly included Hammond and Whitney, sensed that turbulence in the northern border regions and the presence of American armed forces might yet deliver them their longed-for occupation and annexation of northern Mexico. The President responded with an extraordinary statement that, set within the wider context of his ongoing duty to assess German wartime ambitions for Mexico, went close to suggesting the existence of a capitalist fifth column within the United States.

In March 1916, Wilson publicly warned American patriots not to give credence to 'rumours of the most sensational and disturbing sort' emanating from 'sinister and unscrupulous influences' whose activities were centred along the border regions: 'The object of this traffic in falsehoods is obvious. It is to create intolerable friction between the Government of the United States and the *de facto* Government of Mexico for the purpose of bringing about an intervention in the interests of certain American owners of Mexican properties.'[18] The President made no mention of the Yaqui Delta Land and Water Company, nor did his press statement hint that there was a Trojan horse in his administration – the State Department.

By the end of 1916 the estates of the Yaqui Delta Company, as well as those of many others, including Mexican landlords, were falling into decay and disuse across Sonora. Hammond and his partners, who had invested tens of millions of dollars in the company, found themselves effectively reduced to owning title deeds – mere paper in a country being consumed by the flames of revolution.[19] Within months the situation deteriorated further when Mexico's rulers were pushed into addressing the land question far more directly than before. As Hammond, master of the half-truth, later noted:

> The final blow fell in 1917 when President Carranza passed the agrarian laws prohibiting the sale of land to foreigners. From that moment the colonization plan became inoperative. We carried the property until 1930, when it was finally sold to the Mexican government.[20]

But the truth was more complex. The final blow did not fall until 1919, and in the intervening years Hammond, his Republican allies in the Senate and other businessmen heavily invested in land, but more especially in oil, never once let up in their efforts to secure the long-term protection of their assets by getting the Wilson administration to intervene militarily in Mexico. But, since Hammond's efforts unfolded at precisely the same moment that he and Taft were publicly proclaiming the virtues of dispute settlement among states through a world court or a League of Nations, he remained careful to act only through agents. It was a familiar scenario – variations on a theme that those interested in the origins and events leading up to the Jameson Raid will recognise.

The man central to the plot that gradually evolved between 1916 and 1919 to force Woodrow Wilson to authorise a full-scale military invasion of Mexico, and to protect US assets and citizens there, was Albert Bacon Fall. Fall, who Hammond later had the temerity to describe to Calvin Coolidge as a 'scoundrel', after Fall had been found guilty of bribery and made to resign from his position as Secretary of the Interior in 1923, was a man with views that Hammond considered worth supporting financially.[21]

A Southerner, born in Kentucky in 1861, Fall was a lawyer from Las Cruces, New Mexico, who had risen to the rank of captain during the Spanish-American War and was an out-and-out frontiersman and imperialist. First active in Republican politics in lesser offices, Fall went on to serve in the US Senate from 1912 to 1921 before being elevated to the cabinet of the scandal-ridden administration of President Warren G Harding. Fall was later forced to resign for having taken bribes from oil men during the so-called Teapot Dome scandal (1921–1922). In 1916, at a conference held in Cleveland devoted to the cause of 'peace and an international court instead of international conflict', Fall, Hammond, Taft and Harding were happy to share a platform.[22]

Woodrow Wilson embodied almost everything that Fall was not. Within months of being elected to the Senate, Fall made a point of targeting the President in ways familiar to some shady small-town lawyers. Claiming Mexican foreign policy as his speciality, Fall was frustrated by Wilson's refusal to intervene militarily south of the Rio Grande. And within a couple of years Fall had persuaded other senior Republicans, including the influential Henry Cabot Lodge and Elihu Root, to support his pleas for more aggressive policies to protect American lives and property in Mexico. Wilson's failure to intervene decisively in the 1915 Sonora crisis added to Fall's frustration.[23]

By March 1916, Fall – like Lodge and Root, a dove of peace capable of flying anywhere on the continent except south of the Rio Grande – was appealing to the administration to raise an army of half a million men that would be responsible for 'the policing of Mexico or for the invasion of that country to protect our citizens if necessary'.[24] Such loose talk seemed less crazy after Pancho Villa's raid on Columbus. The Senator rushed to the border region, from where he issued more alarmist reports, which Wilson countered with his famous statement about 'sinister and unscrupulous forces'. It was open season, and Fall began a war of disinformation and propaganda, blaming the President for the 'disorder and destruction in Mexico', hoping that it would undermine Wilson's chances of re-election in 1916.[25]

It didn't and the usual suspects in the State Department continued to white-ant Wilson's cautious policies on Mexico. The President, mindful of the lessons of the history of the United States, remained unwilling to deny oppressed Mexicans the right to stage their own revolution.[26] At the Mexico desk, by January 1917, Leon Canova was advocating full-scale war as the only way of restoring order south of the border, when Hammond and others became demoralised by a new constitution which effectively allowed Carranza's government to nationalise all foreign-owned land.[27]

The closing years of the First World War also witnessed a diplomatic struggle between Great Britain and the United States as to how Mexican oil supplies might best be protected and secured. Here again, Carranza's new constitution contributed to the climate of instability. Around Tampico, on the Gulf of Mexico, where the major companies controlled by Hammond operated, a local bandit-warlord, Paláez, extracted protection money from producers as he engaged in armed conflict with forces loyal to the Mexican president. Hammond, along with several other American oil notables, remained pragmatic enough to support whatever big man was in power locally, regionally or nationally in Mexico and willingly handed over the monthly royalty destined for government coffers to the bandit.[28]

By 1918, having established himself as the leading critic in the Republican-dominated Senate of the Wilson administration's policies on

Mexico, Senator Fall was ready to squeeze additional benefits from the large American investors on whose behalf he spoke. Up for re-election that year, he made it known that he was unwilling to spend a dollar of his own money while campaigning in his home state. Unwilling to risk losing an influential insider who might be able to help in the struggle to hold on to the title deeds of the Yaqui Delta Company, Hammond, champion of international peace at home, stepped out of the shadows briefly and 'offered to pay a large portion of Fall's expenses'.[29]

Fall's re-election and the end of the war emboldened and encouraged those Americans heavily invested in land and oil in Mexico, as well as many in the Senate, along with Robert Lansing, and the white-ants in the State Department, to redouble their efforts and refocus their attempts to secure US intervention south of the border. Here again, Hammond's personal input is almost impossible to detect, even though, as a close friend of most of the most senior Republicans in the Senate and President of the National League of Republican Clubs, he could hardly claim ignorance about what was transpiring. As always, it was a subject not broached in his autobiography. Intent on burnishing his image as an elder statesman who had outgrown his reputation as an adventurous hero who had once recklessly pioneered the interests of big business in strange places, Hammond was careful to ensure that it was his agents and friends rather than he, personally, who contributed to the gathering momentum of the re-crystallising interventionist movement.

For all that, a faint trace of Hammond's fingerprints – testifying to an ongoing commitment to, and preference for, his and Harry Payne Whitney's 'colonization plan' in Sonora – is again to be detected. In December 1918, a broad-front organisation to advance the interests of American investors in Mexico and undermine the Carranza government and the new constitution was launched in New York City. The new organisation, designed to have a political reach beyond that of the existing Association of Petroleum Producers in Mexico (APPM), was the National Association for the Protection of American Rights in Mexico (NAPARM), under the executive directorship of Charles H Boynton. Among the founding companies that contributed to NAPARM's monthly budget of $20 000 was the Yaqui Delta Land and Water Company, and, serving on its executive committee was none other than the omnipresent Watriss, who in addition to serving on other boards with Hammond was a close personal friend of Harry Payne Whitney.[30]

Although at some personal distance from the day-to-day operations of NAPARM, Jack Hammond was clearly comfortable with the architecture of the organisation, its composition and its overt and covert operations – the Yaqui Delta Company's endorsement testified to that. True, NAPARM was not the hastily cobbled-together Reform Committee but it was of the same agitating, conspiring and subverting frontier family.

The officers of NAPARM were particularly active over the summer of 1919, expending much energy while the hard-pressed Woodrow Wilson was abroad attending to international post-war peace initiatives. The association published and distributed sensational anti-*Carrancista* materials, underscored disorder and chaos in that country and branded its government as pro-German and its constitution as 'Bolshevistic'. It also began compiling a 'Murder Map of Mexico', recording the number and sites of some 500 American deaths during the revolution.[31]

Drawing freely on NAPARM, APPM and another informally consti-tuted set of Mexican investors – the Murray Hill Group – for support, Fall, backed by senior Republicans, including Henry Cabot Lodge, thought through a novel initiative to corner the elusive Wilson in a pincer move-ment. An ostensibly bipartisan Senate subcommittee on Foreign Relations, chaired by Fall himself, would preside over extensive hearings and then compile a set of recommendations on Mexican policy for the President. At the same time, lobbyists would exercise relentless pressure on the already largely open door within the State Department.

The initiative came together during autumn and early winter 1919. Watriss conferred with Frank Polk and others in the State Department on a weekly basis.[32] Lansing and many others needed little persuading to push for a much firmer line from the White House. On Capitol Hill, Chairman Fall's subcommittee collected factual and sensationalist testimony from State Department officials and outside bodies and individuals with equal enthusiasm. And, as had happened once before with Villa and the raid on Columbus, events in Mexico played into the hands of Senator Fall when the American Consul in Pueblo, WO Jenkins, was kidnapped and held to ransom by bandits in late October.

Lansing, now floating freely through space that appeared to negate any of the laws of presidential gravity, sent Carranza a note so stiff that it brought the governments closer to war. The Secretary of State also appeared before the Senate subcommittee, where he characterised previous administration policies on Mexico as 'supine' or 'vacillating'.[33] It was all grist to the mill of Senator Fall, who ground out a draft motion for the full Committee on Foreign Relations that would recommend severing diplomatic relations with the unyielding Carranza government.

But the canny Wilson had long seen the forces closing in on him and was ready to do battle on all fronts and to live with any collateral politi-cal damage. As soon as the first reports from the Fall subcommittee started appearing, the President began sending signals showing that he was not about to be caught in an ambush. He noted that there were many 'liars' about when it came to tales about Mexico and repeated his opposition to 'imperialism' and the acquisition of any foreign territory.[34]

When Fall arrived at the White House to brief the sickly President about his draft motion on 5 December 1919, Wilson drew him in, suggesting that he provide him with a memorandum contextualising his proposed actions. Wilson then struck back – hard. He took personal charge of all American-Mexican negotiations, ordered an investigation into how the Jenkins matter had been handled by the State Department and wrote to Fall informing him that the Constitution made it clear that the executive alone had authority to break off relations with a foreign government.[35]

With the US Ambassador to Mexico an earlier casualty in a low-intensity war between the State Department and the White House, Wilson waited a further two months before confronting Lansing. In early February, 1920, the President wrote Lansing a letter so accusatory in tone that the Secretary of State proffered his resignation.[36] Wilson, who had seen off the first inter-ventionist movement constructed around the crisis in Sonora and the Yaqui Delta Company, in 1915, had checked an even more determined effort to ensure United States military engagement in Mexico in 1919. And, while it was true that Jack Hammond was not directly involved in either the 1915 or the 1919 campaigns, there is little doubt that both benefited indirectly from his financial and political support.

Despite these setbacks Hammond spent ten more years defending his and Whitney's investment in the Yaqui Delta Company and attempting to claw back as much as possible of their investment in the colonisation scheme. Those efforts, too, were characterised by his capacity to ingratiate himself within anyone commanding real power, complete pragmatism and a form of rank opportunism that left him ethically and morally blind to the conse-quences of his financially self-centred actions.

The first glimmerings of an opening came when Carranza, roundly dis-liked by American capitalists invested in Mexico, was assassinated during a revolt orchestrated by his successor, Alvaro Obregón, in May 1920. It is unknown when Hammond first met the Sonoran-born General Obregón but it could have been as early as 1916, during a visit by the latter to New York City. But regardless of when exactly it was, there can be little doubt that it was followed by further, close personal interactions between the two who shared a passion for the Yaqui Valley, which the Indians, betrayed by all, continued to fight for right up to 1929.

Hammond used Obregón's period in office, from 1920 to 1924 – a period of relative stability – to cultivate a personal relationship with the Mexican president. It proved to be mutually beneficial although it did not initially involve Yaqui Delta Company business, but focused more on difficulties facing Hammond's vast east coast oil ventures. When Mexican Seaboard

Oil was menaced by bandits under one 'El Diablo', in 1921, Hammond and his son approached Obregón and got permission to arm the company's employees. But, true to form, Hammond was not content to be confined by a defensive capacity; with Obregón's approval, he 'procured the services of seventeen men who had spent years with the Texas Rangers and similar bodies in hunting down criminals. They had been trained to act on the command, "Get your man alive or dead".'[37] It was back to old-style frontier business-as-usual, replete with cowboys and crooks.

When Obregón was confronted by a rebellion two years later, Hammond was in a position to return the favour. He not only provided the Mexican head of state with bridging finance but also persuaded President Coolidge to lift an arms embargo so as to ensure that Obregón's armed forces were supplied with the aircraft and other military hardware necessary to put down the revolt.[38] The two men got on well, but such reciprocities did not solve Hammond's long-standing problem along the Yaqui River, where the 1917 constitution still prevented the sale of the Yaqui Delta Company's land-holdings to anyone other than Mexican nationals.

Hammond, however, was willing to play the long game. He never lost contact with Obregón. 1926 saw the penultimate rising of the Indian 'Broncos', and the Mexican government responded by sending in General Francesco Manzo and 12 000 troops, supported by 20 aircraft, to bomb Luis Matos and 2 500 Indians out of their Sierra Madre strongholds. A 'war of extermination', one American reporter noted, was being fought against the 'bloody Yaquis'.[39]

The campaign against Matos, however, was making the world a safer place for big men, for those with capital, a desire for peace and an industrial world. Nobody knew that better than Hammond and Obregón. By the time Obregon prepared to stand for re-election as President, in 1927, negotiations between him and Hammond for the acquisition of the Yaqui estate and the irrigation works, which Hammond and Whitney owned personally, were well advanced.[40] Obregón, who already owned a nearby 'model farm', acquired the holdings and decided to divide it into 'two parts, one for himself and the other for agrarian disbursements'.[41]

All seemed well, and the moment Obregón was re-elected as President, in 1928, Hammond dispatched a telegram of congratulations, which was replied to instantly, signed 'affectionately' and deliberately passed on to the press so as to encourage new American investments in Mexico.[42]

The site of the one-time colonisation scheme, however, appeared to be both bloodstained and cursed. In July 1928, Obregón, like several others before him, was assassinated, and Hammond, Whitney and their partners had to start anew in their attempts to find a Mexican buyer. In the end, the owners of the Yaqui Delta Land and Water Company, marooned in the midst of the Great Depression, accepted three cents on the dollar for their assets, or a mere $9 million, from the Mexican government for a development that may well have cost two and a half times that amount over a period of nearly four decades.[43]

In 1935, Hammond, a man who tended to note only his successes, was forced to cut adrift from his Sonoran experiences, saying: 'Although we were much disappointed at being prevented from carrying out an enterprise of such inestimable value, we wish the present Mexican government every success which is about to start development of the Yaqui Valley along the original plans.'[44] Hammond, who in his time had used the sword of colonialism and attempted to employ the shield of international law in the hope of defending his assets in the Yaqui Valley, had been defeated. But Cowboy Jack was unwilling to leave a stain on his reputation, so he rearranged his memories, picked up a pen and prepared to ride shotgun into history, vigorously defending his career.

CHAPTER TWENTY-NINE

Riding Shotgun into History

The Old West Negotiates the 20th Century

C 1914–1936

In 1907, aged 52, just months before making his play to become the Republican Party's vice-presidential candidate on the Taft ticket the following year, John Hays Hammond resigned from his position at the Guggenheim Exploration Company, citing 'poor health' as his reason. His health, however, improved as soon as his new friend was elected President and he remained active in America and Mexico not only during the Taft administration, but also through the two Wilson administrations that followed.

Although by then in his mid-sixties, Hammond's appetite for financial gain from mineral exploration and extractive industries was undiminished, as was his desire to maintain contact with the frontier heroes of the Old West who had shaped his behaviour and self-image since his adolescent apprenticeship under Jack 'Coffee' Hays, his Texas Ranger uncle. Hammond cherished the connection he had established with Charlie Siringo, the one-time Texas cowboy and Pinkerton agent, during the Coeur d'Alene mining war in 1892. In 1925, while preparing his autobiography, Hammond also coaxed a rare letter out of Wyatt Earp, whom he had worked with during his early mining career out west, and who was once a friend of Charlie Siringo's.[1]

One of Hammond's prized friendships in the new age of mass communication was with a part-Cherokee former cowboy, Will Rogers, an actor, humorist and social commentator, who, from his base in Beverly Hills, became a national institution in the 1920s and 1930s. Rogers not only had a store of ranch experiences to draw on that Hammond was in awe of but also, more importantly, bore first-hand knowledge of South Africa.

As a youngster, having failed to secure a career in Argentina as a gaucho, Rogers had made his way to South Africa towards the end of the Anglo-Boer War. There he met and was employed by Texas Jack Junior, the adopted son of another American legend, Texas Jack Omohundro, legendary cowboy, frontier scout and Wild West showman. The young Texas Jack, a roughrider and sharpshooter who once played the role of Fred Burnham, moved his own 'Grand Wild West Entertainment' around South Africa before he died in Kroonstad in 1905.

When out west on business, Hammond would call in on Rogers in Los Angeles where, as the actor told it, they would talk about South Africa and the Jameson Raid. Hammond was 'mixed up in it', Rogers recalled, 'and it was what started the Boer War.' It was the closest that Hammond, the cowboy-capitalist, got to admitting the consequences of his own involvement in Wild West-style history. On one occasion Hammond brought Burnham along with him and the three enjoyed a chat about southern Africa while Rogers got the chance, up close and personal, to see the man that his one-time mentor, Texas Jack, had had been called upon to play in their dramatic productions. Rogers, a noted political commentator and wit, was clearly impressed by Hammond who, he suggested, 'by somebody's oversight, never became President'.[2]

But it was Major Fred Burnham, the famous scout whom Hammond had hired to protect President Taft during his visit to the Mexican border in 1909, that, of all his former frontier friends, the septuagenarian chose to stay closest to during the 1920s and 1930s. A friendship that had started with the founding of the ill-fated Yaqui Delta Company was re-cemented, in 1919, when Jack Hammond and his eldest son, Harris, invested in what became the hugely successful Burnham Exploration Company, which uncovered extensive oilfields in the Los Angeles basin.

From the first year of its operation, in 1923, until 1933, at which point it was still extracting oil from the same fields, the Burnham Company paid out $1 million in preferred stock, with bonuses, and yielded dividends in excess of $10 million.[3] In 1926, the two men and their spouses undertook an extended celebratory cruise through the Mediterranean. But if the Burnham Company helped turn Hammond, already an exceedingly rich man, into a fabulously rich one, it seems to have done little to change his underlying attitude to the accumulation of great personal wealth in an age otherwise noted for its philanthropy.

Hammond's calibration of success, measured exclusively in terms of acquiring personal fame or wealth, was laid bare in a remarkable interview with the journalist JP Glass in 1930. Looking back over the 19th century, the authoritarian and Anglophile Hammond suggested that democracy had forced American millionaires to use their wealth for mere 'social aggrandisement'. Then, probably reflecting on his beloved Anglo-Saxon origins, he added that 'Abroad their wealth would have gained them admission, in time, to the nobility. Here such a possession brought them only criticism and often indeed obloquy.'[4] The Hammonds' ostentatious public displays of expensive cars, houses, jewellery and yachts had clearly not been without a measure of private pain.

But 20th-century American millionaires, too, had perhaps not used their wealth to best effect or, if they had, had set an awkward if not downright alarming precedent. Andrew Carnegie and John D Rockefeller had, Hammond conceded, probably done well to use 'large portions of their money for the benefit of the people'. But he went on to note that the same millionaires had also 'set a fashion for philanthropy which has since gained the authority of a custom'.[5] It had become an irritating 'custom', one that he seems to have had no intention of following.[6]

Secure in his long-standing role as a powerful businessman and elder statesman within the Republican Party machine, Hammond, as already noted, managed to negotiate the Democratic administration of Woodrow Wilson with some difficulty. His ability to influence presidential power came via Colonel EM House, until the latter fell out of favour with Wilson towards the end of the First World War.[7]

Focused on the shield of international law that Hammond brandished with public pride during the Wilson years, the press failed to spot his sword of colonialism in Mexico and remained convinced of the benefits that two unelected advisers embedded within the White House bestowed upon the nation. 'The new idea that Hammond and House have injected' into Democratic and Republican administrations alike, the *Boston Post* reflected, in 1920, 'is that of controlling – or influencing – politics merely for what they conceive to be the good of the country.'[8] It was precisely the view that the two friends would have wanted taken of their roles.

Hammond and House remained close friends, but the return of two Republican Presidents – first Warren Harding (1921–1923) and then Calvin Coolidge (1923–1929) – meant that Hammond could once again find his way through the front door at 1600 Pennsylvania Avenue.[9] Ironically, it was probably organised labour that did more to keep Hammond in personal touch with successive White House incumbents in the 1920s than did big business.

The United States Coal Commission, legislated into life in September 1922, was conceived of almost exclusively as a fact-finding body offering a much-needed overview of the industry. President Harding appointed Hammond, whose reputation as an elder statesman was by now secure, as chairman of the commission. A series of damaging, well-organised strikes in the coal industry, starting in 1922, however, meant that, in theory at least, the commission had the opportunity of assuming a more important role in regulating conflicting class interests than had been originally intended.

But Hammond, the one-time capitalist-revolutionary, was content merely to play the Wise Old Man. It was a part in keeping with that of William Taft, who had been appointed Chief Justice of the Supreme Court the previous year, and Hammond, still the class warrior in Mexico, now advocated the cooperation of capital and labour in the United States. This approach fell within the spirit of the book that he and Yale economics professor Jeremiah Jenks published, in 1923, under the carefully managed title of *Great American Issues, Political, Social, Economic – A Constructive Study*.[10] The result was that when the commission did eventually issue its report, in 1925, it managed to disappoint government, big business and organised labour alike.[11]

Notwithstanding, Hammond's position on the commission, his lingering influence in the Republican Party gave him a fine vantage point from which to deliver his views on every president from William Taft to Herbert Hoover. Taft's virtues and Wilson's vices – viewed largely through the lens of Hammond's own financial interests in revolutionary Mexico – have already been traced, but it is probably his take on their successors that is more interesting.

In 1923, President Warren Harding offered Hammond the longed-for position of Ambassador to the Court of James's, but he was forced to decline because of concerns about the health of his wife, Natalie Harris. Harding's courting of Hammond as chairman of the Coal Commission helped earn him the approval of a man with an insatiable appetite for affirmation. Harding gained the engineer's blessing even though, as an insider in the oil industry, Hammond suspected that the President and some in his cabinet must have known about the corruption of Senator Albert Fall in what later became known as the Teapot Dome scandal.[12]

Calvin Coolidge, a man with a sleep disorder, notoriously private, had been a member of Harding's cabinet before becoming President, but he too denied any knowledge of Fall and his doings. Other than when conducting state business for the Coal Commission, Coolidge tried to keep Hammond at a distance. Hammond, for his part, tried his best to establish a deeper relationship. Drawing on a variant of the old trick he had employed to cultivate Ambassador John Hay in London – 'trifles often help to turn acquaintance into friendship' – Hammond sent Cooldige a box of 'particularly fine' cigars. But the President remained distant. 'Despite the fact that I saw a great deal of him,' Hammond lamented, 'I never felt close to him.' The result was that Hammond 'found it difficult to estimate either the man or his work'.[13]

Coolidge may, however, have had more insight into Jack and Natalie Hammond's underlying political beliefs than they had into his. The couple had long been admirers of things Italian – hers arising in part from a long-standing interest in culture and eugenics, and his out of admiration for Benito Mussolini, who had decorated their son, John Hays Hammond Jnr, with the 'Grand Officer of the Crown' for helping to keep the Italian government in radio communication with its colonial officers in North Africa.[14] Coolidge, who once suggested that no man should do for himself anything that could be done for him by someone else, sensed the makings of a good appointment. In the late 1920s, he offered Hammond the position of Ambassador to Rome – an offer which was again reluctantly declined, because of problems with Natalie's health.[15] That offer, the fact that Coolidge presided over the last of the good times before the market crashed in 1929, and the President's popularity out west, all helped save him from far tougher judgement by Hammond. Not all presidents, however, had the luck of the somnolent Coolidge.

Coolidge's successor, Herbert Hoover (1929–1933), had the misfortune of being modern America's most famous mining engineer, a graduate of Stanford University and therefore a man with a laudable West Coast pedigree and, to boot, a Republican with a wealth of international mining experience, including some in southern Africa. Of all American presidents, he had the least need of Hammond's advice or services.

Hoover had achieved what Hammond had always secretly desired, and the green-eyed monster duly put in a cameo appearance. Hammond, elderly and egocentric, calibrated the success or failure of all American presidents by the amount of personal access that he enjoyed to the White House. He and Edward House had manufactured advisory roles for themselves in the Taft and Wilson administrations and those presidents who scorned these precedents were, in his view, obviously the poorer for it. Hammond's judgement was again predictably unsparing.

'I did not enjoy the intimacy with Hoover that I had enjoyed with his predecessors,' Hammond complained. It followed, therefore, that in his eyes the President 'was, in many ways, a lonely man'. Hammond, presenting the left hand as decoy, suggested that Hoover 'possessed executive ability to an exceptional degree', but then delivered a telling blow with the right, claiming that he 'lacked the qualities of leadership'. This for a President who had the unenviable duty of dealing with the onset of the Great Depression – a formidable task he appears to have undertaken reasonably well. But, just in case anybody had missed the knockout blow, just 24 months after the President vacated office Hammond crowed that Hoover reminded him of Ovid's observation: 'An army of stags led by a lion would be more formidable than one of lions led by a stag.'[16]

Throughout these two decades, from Taft to Hoover, Natalie Harris Hammond, a remarkably capable leader of public opinion and charitable endeavours in her own right, remained rock-solid beside her husband in the social world of Washington, DC. Jack Hammond's enduring success as a White House insider was, in part, attributable to the grace, charm and energy of his talented wife.

Focused, politically astute and smarter than many a presidential wife, Natalie Harris presided over some of the most prestigious social events in the capital, and was almost always among the most prominent of guests reported on whenever the couple were abroad. Her movements during the coronation of King George V were followed with considerable enthusiasm and, if one is to judge from popular interest back home, left many within the American elite feeling the poorer for want of an aristocratic order of the type that the Hammonds loved.[17] When she and Helen Nelson, wife of the Panama-Pacific Exposition Commissioner Edward Morris, appeared at a ball in Rome, in 1914, they sported jewellery worth over £400 000. All this was breathlessly reported on not only back home, but as far away as New Zealand.[18]

Raised on a plantation in Mississippi during the closing years of slavery, Natalie Harris had most of the attributes associated with the Southern belle, including a few attitudes and beliefs with alarming Confederate undertones. But she adapted many of these in ways that allowed her to emerge as a quintessentially modern woman. She did this from a position of social strength; as many analysts know, it is when men are away fighting wars – usually in far-off places – that women's capacity for leadership is allowed to flourish, often in more defined 'female' fields such as caring, nurturing or the promotion of patriotic welfare works.

Natalie Harris was a distinguished and successful political lobbyist on behalf of her incarcerated capitalist-revolutionary husband while he was under sentence of death in the South African Republic, and went on to author a book that was published commercially on both sides of the Atlantic in the mid-1890s – during the Hammonds' period of political rehabilitation in England, after the Jameson Raid. While in London she became a founder member of the Women's Institute.

Her most active involvement with progressive women's organisations in the United States came later, when she supported certain of the causes for international peace being championed by her husband.[19] Even before Taft became President she was a leading member of the National Civic Federation focusing on the sad lot of underprivileged urban working-class women.

In 1912, Natalie Harris was guest of honour at a West Coast meeting of the Daughters of the American Revolution (DAR) – an organisation established in 1890 to promote patriotism.[20] By then she was already the Honorary President of the Women's Republican Association and, by 1916, although Washington-based, was also the First Vice-President of the New

York City chapter of the DAR. She was also an early advocate of female suffrage, a cause that her husband duly adopted. In that same year she also presided over the biennial convention of the General Federation of the Women's Clubs, held in New York City.[21]

Unlike husband Jack, who was not only content to play second fiddle but sometimes consciously courted the role, Natalie Harris was made of sterner stuff. In at least one instance we know of, she was more than willing to make public her disagreement about the leadership of an organisation close to her heart. In 1916, true to the military traditions of the Harris and Hammond families, she founded the 'Militia of Mercy' even though she was already active in several other wartime voluntary associations. The twin objectives of the Militia were to raise funds for ambulances and other equipment in the fight against infantile paralysis and, where necessary, to provide relief for those families of American soldiers abroad who were left in distress.[22]

As President of the awkwardly-named Militia of Mercy, Natalie Harris's impeccable Southern credentials helped to attract the support of the Daughters of the Confederacy, who joined the Militia in their thousands. But, within months, there were signs of tension in the New York City-dominated leadership, even though the root of the problem did not come from its Southern members. At a gathering held in the city, in May 1917, Natalie Harris chaired the first part of the meeting but the second part was presided over by Mrs William Grant Brown. It might not have been an unheard-of arrangement, but it was unusual.[23]

It was, however, a straw in the wind. Before the year was out, and to the great surprise of notables up and down the East Coast, Natalie Harris resigned as President of the organisation that she had founded. When a few concerned New York City women put it about that she might have resigned because she found the journey from Washington to the city too taxing, she was quick to issue a denial via the press. Her social secretary made it known that none of the reasons being offered publicly accounted for Harris's with-drawal from the Militia, and that 'she prefers not to say anything more ... about her resignation'. In high society, too, a nod was often as good as a wink.[24]

But it was not always what was happening at the apex of American soci-ety that concerned the elitist, class and race-conscious Hammonds, but what was happening among the lower orders of an economy founded historically on indentured workers, slavery and cheap immigrant labour, a society that was without the supposed benefits of a hereditary aristocracy. As with the question of female suffrage, she manifested more openness than did her politically ambitious husband.

Ambassador John Hays Hammond and Natalie Harris's attendance at the coronation of George V, in 1911, allowed them to deepen their acquaintance

with elements of the British aristocracy and also exposed them anew to
the latest scientific thinking on issues of race in English society, including
that in the burgeoning field of eugenics. The contours of analytical and
evidence-based thinking about race had a certain appeal for the Hammonds,
whose Southern attitudes and beliefs were readily compatible with notions
of social Darwinism. What modern America and its elite lacked, however,
were female-led initiatives capable of transmitting such progressive, scientific thinking throughout society.

There was already a small and shaky scientific platform to build on back
at home. In 1904, the Carnegie Institution of Washington funded the study
of genetics at Cold Spring Harbor, in New York, and just two years later
a 'Race Betterment Foundation' had been established in Michigan. After
the couple's return from the coronation, Harris began corresponding with
Charles Davenport at Cold Spring Harbor, collecting and studying the latest scientific literature from both sides of the Atlantic until, by 1913, she was
ready to launch a classic Hammond-style, top-down initiative.[25]

She convened a meeting of the most influential women in Washington
and formed a group devoted to promoting 'healthy marriages'. In her own
words, and as recorded for a general readership:

> Thus came about the organization of a class composed of women
> who are politically and socially of the highest placed in the nation – a
> class virtually in the White House. This class includes Mrs Woodrow
> Wilson, wife of the President of the United States; Mrs William
> Jennings Bryan, wife of the Secretary of State, Mrs Justice Hughes
> and others in the cabinet circle.[26]

By June 1913, members of this ginger group were ready to make their initiative public at an event hosted by Mrs Hammond in Washington, attended by
400 people. Elnora Folkmar, a hygienist, addressed the meeting and, among
other measures, advocated physical examination of couples prior to the
granting of marriage licences, and that consideration be given to the idea
of segregating and sterilising those considered mentally or physically unfit
for marriage.[27]

Undaunted by the relatively tepid public response, Natalie Harris pushed
on, penning two articles – one in the *Times-Dispatch*, in Richmond, in July
of that year, and the other in *Harper's Bazaar*, in October. Using the motto
of the Washington group – 'Make the Stock Better' – she was determined
both to educate people about the dangers posed by unregulated, genetically
inferior unions and to show that, unlike other causes championed by idealists, eugenics could be 'practical' in ways that benefited the public purse in
a capitalist economy. 'There must be purity at the source of the race stream,'

she reminded readers of *Harper's*, while those of the *Times-Dispatch* learnt that 'Eugenics impresses upon us that our immigration laws should restrict the immigration of stocks unfit to blend with the American population'.[28]

Here again, Natalie Harris was slightly in advance of her husband's thinking, or more willing to go public with it than he. Genetics, too, could be a matter of dollars and cents. No less than 20 per cent of the budget of the state of New York, she estimated, was wasted on dealing with people with 'a criminal bias or feeble-mindedness'. 'The greatest need of today as to education,' argued Harris, was 'how to increase biological capital'. The new lessons and 'practical' approach she was advocating as public policy were not lost on Jack Hammond.

When articles in leading popular journals still did not cause the penny to drop, Harris used a meeting of the American Association for the Prevention of Infant Mortality, in November 1913, to drive home the message. 'Woman, rather than man, has always been conserver of racial purity,' she told her audience, and then went on to share her dream: 'I believe there should be a great national organization for the promotion of practical eugenics.' As a direct result of her efforts, 'A committee was appointed to meet the eugenics committee of the American Breeder Association' that had been formed years earlier.[29]

Natalie Harris's growing interest in eugenics and related issues continued when she became a senior committee member of the American Genetics Association, in 1914.[30] But the times were against her. The outbreak of war and the emergence of more immediate problems, such as those associated with the Militia of Mercy, leached her enthusiasm. American eugenics had to wait until the mid-1920s before it was served by a more focused and influential national association and the advent of many state policies now considered shameful in American history.[31]

Natalie Harris's interests in race and social engineering were broadly in keeping with those of her husband. Hammond, proudly Anglo-Saxon, was an engineer who sought not only to organise mining equipment in order to maximise production and profits, but also to align men and women to the emerging industrial world in ways that were compatible with his racial thinking and notions of social Darwinism.

His quest for comprehensive, if not total, control of the social and economic lives of white miners via the company store and bunkhouse, and his opposition to 'socialistic' trade unions, dated back to at least the time of the strikes in the Coeur d'Alene in 1892. In South Africa, in the mid-1890s, he suggested that black miners could be more effectively controlled by drawing wives and children into self-contained villages capable of reproducing new generations of resident cheap labour on-site. And, when that failed and the migrant labour system still did not deliver workers in adequate numbers after the Anglo-Boer War (1899–1902), he became an advocate of the enslavement of Africans for underground work. Nor were his pre-1914 views on African Americans, as we have noted, enlightened; 'My southern heritage made me sympathetic to the Southerner's attitude to the negro politically and socially,' he wrote.[32]

Hammond was relatively forthcoming about his attitudes and prejudices regarding Africans, African Americans and, for that matter, Mexicans – dark or swarthy people at the far end of the spectrum of racial evolution – who worked, in the main, in remote and rural colonial settings on mines or plantations he controlled. He was, however, more careful to conceal his views about supposedly genetically-suspect or 'undesirable' immigrants of East European origin, white men and women making their way into the mainstream of industrialising urban America. But, like his wife, Hammond fretted about the cultural and genetic Trojan horses already within the gates and, like her, was careful to encode his reservations.

The need for concealing underlying attitudes in language that was not overtly focused on ethnicity while simultaneously advocating changes to immigration policies was brought home to Hammond in 1911. He and members of the Jewish community in New York City, led by Jacob Schiff, got into a public wrangle about the role that Jewish bankers had played in the Russo-Japanese War (1904–1905), the promotion of economic coopera-tion between the United States and Russia, and the issuing of passports to poor Russian Jews hoping to emigrate to the US.[33]

Schiff was of the view that Hammond, an admirer of the Tsar who had twice visited Russia (in 1898 and 1910) as an unofficial 'special industrial adviser' to assess investment possibilities, was exercising undue influence over President Taft on the passport issue, and that the administration was willing to let considerations of trade triumph over questions of social justice. Taft was forced to do some fast talking to limit the public damage and then had to intervene privately, in unconvincing fashion, to protect the name and reputation of his 'good friend' Jack Hammond.[34]

Some of Hammond's friends, as he was quick to remind Schiff, were Jews, but one of his best friends was not, and was never far from anti-Semitism. Edward House complained to Woodrow Wilson about 'how ubiquitous Jews were, one stumbled over them at every move and they were so per-sistent it was impossible to avoid them'.[35] If Hammond ever shared those views, the Schiff contretemps taught him to steer clear of such overt formu-lations, but his underlying reservations about the unsuitability of unnamed ethnic European immigrants matched his wife's early interest in eugenics.

If Natalie Harris wanted 'healthy marriages' by ensuring that the genetic sluices were kept clean at domestic source – under license and within the household – then her ambitious engineering husband wanted to control the very watershed from which the streams issued. In 1921, with the war past and a wave of new immigrants readying itself to catch a first glimpse of the Statue of Liberty, Hammond tapped into a new debate and advocated the erection of an 'Ellis Island' in Europe, so as to 'weed out undesirables' at source.[36]

By the time Hammond and Jeremiah Jenks got round to publishing *Great American Issues* two years later, Hammond had given the matter more thought. Writing in the wake of the great Red Scare of 1919–1921, he was driven to even more radical solutions. His deeply rooted fear of 'Bolshevists' and socialists, harking back to fraught experiences in Idaho in 1892 and the imaginary terrors of the Witwatersrand, in 1895, prompted him to seek to 'exclude persons who are undesirable on political or social grounds'.[37] He and Jenks were well in line with much popular sentiment around these issues. The essential element in the entire controversy, he and Jenks argued, 'is that of assimilability of races materially divergent from the white race'.[38] In 1924, the Johnson-Reed Act halted all immigration from Asia, restricted that from Africa, and imposed national quotas on immigrants from almost all Eastern and Southern European countries.

A significant part of America was beginning to think like the Hammonds in a world becoming increasingly wary of enemies within and without. If the Hammonds had their way, then the United States would be led by a strongman not unlike a Díaz in Mexico, or a Mussolini in Italy, and become genetically, politically, racially and socially free of almost all 'undesirable' people and ideologies.

That, then, was the picture of the future as seen by the Hammonds. For Jack Hammond, a part of this desire for action and the need to be seen to be trying to shape or reshape the emerging world order derived from the challenges, hopes and fears unleashed by the First World War. It was hardly of a piece with his youthful experiences on the frontier, but here, yet again, he felt the need to show courage and manliness, commitment and innovation, and patriotism.

But, by the time war broke out, in 1914, Hammond was 60 years old. It was no longer as easy as it had once been to manifest bravery through action and deeds, as he had done as a young man in Mexico and later, at a distance, during his South African misadventure. Like many in the elite, he was originally of the view that there was no need for America to enter the war, moved to a position advocating 'military preparedness' and finally accepted that US involvement had become unavoidable.[39]

As with Natalie Harris, his evolving position was matched by appropriate actions, and Hammond became a member of several associations and committees making direct or indirect contributions to the American war effort. But, as befitted a man who saw himself as an unsung hero out of the

Old West, and as the President of the New York-based Rocky Mountain Club – his 'Eastern Home for Western Men' – Hammond, Fred Burnham, Theodore Roosevelt and others were very critical of a Wilson administration that was in no rush to enter the war. The Rocky Mountain Club became an instrument not only for Hammond and his Republican friends to burnish their reputations as men of action and courage, but also for them to revitalise a self-perpetuating elite network based on the friendship of frontier types, scouts and former military men.

In January 1917, Hammond, sensing the chance of killing two birds with one stone, organised a banquet in honour of Herbert Hoover, whom he hardly knew at the time, but who was collecting funds for Belgian relief. The dinner and the effort that followed were most successful and, within two months, the Club's 1 200 members helped raise over $3 million for the cause.[40] But while men of action, one-time cowboys, game hunters and soldiers were not scornful of fund-raising it was, in truth, an activity more readily associated with women's movements, and Roosevelt and Hammond wanted a great deal more.

Several weeks before America entered the war, in April 1917, Roosevelt and Hammond decided that the Club could be bent to more masculine and patriotic purposes and enlisted the services of Fred Burnham to help recruit a volunteer army that would, if necessary, be privately funded.[41] Western men, largely Republican in their political sympathies, some of them veterans of the Spanish-American War, would assist in the recruitment of four divisions of men to fight in France. But the President was unwilling to be upstaged; after a few sharp exchanges between Roosevelt and Woodrow Wilson, recruitment ceased and the four Rocky Mountain divisions never materialised.

Hammond, however, was not unduly dismayed by this development, which, perhaps understandably, he chose not to record in the 800 pages of his two-volume autobiography. Indeed, he managed to salvage a measure of private satisfaction from what was a public failure. The Rocky Mountain Club wartime initiative helped breach the gap that had opened up between him and Roosevelt at the time of the Bull Moose movement, and which had not only sunk President Taft's chances of re-election, but seriously divided the Grand Old Party.

By the time the war had ended, Hammond and Roosevelt were back on good terms, and four days before he died, on 6 January 1919, Roosevelt wrote the Hammonds a warm letter wishing them a Happy New Year. In October that same year, Hammond paid homage to Teddy's memory by hosting a dinner at New York City's Waldorf Astoria Hotel, at which, in the presence of a thousand members of the Rocky Mountain Club, he unveiled a portrait of Roosevelt dressed in 'Western Cowboy Costume'.[42] By then

Hammond's mind was firmly focused on the question of how his own career would be recalled, and was hard at work repositioning himself for a portrait by Clio that would bring out his own virtues as a cowboy-capitalist revolutionary with deep roots west of the Rockies.

Hammond's cooperative venture with the gung-ho American journalist, Richard Harding Davis, had resulted in the publication in New York City, in 1897, of *Dr Jameson's Raiders vs the Johannesburg Reformers*. The purpose of that book, published shortly before the outbreak of the Spanish-American War, was to exonerate the Reformers, and Hammond in particular, of the charge of cowardice because of their failure to ride to the rescue of the ill-disciplined Dr Jameson.

Even after Hammond's return to America, in 1899, many Americans, including influential Republicans such as Roosevelt, continued to see him as an agent of Cecil Rhodes and a lackey of the British Empire. It took a lot of hard political work by both the Hammonds, throughout the Anglo-Boer War and for half a decade thereafter, to shake off the worst of that unflattering image. Yet, despite that, Hammond could never quite rid himself of the feeling that, in certain quarters of the American establishment, he was still seen as a tool of British imperialism. It was part of the price that he paid for his remarkably Anglophile sentiments.

But as the Allies slowly gained control over the Central Powers and drove the First World War towards its conclusion, Hammond sensed a new opportunity to undo the last of the damage that the Jameson Raid had done to his reputation all those years ago. With America and Britain closer than they had been for more than a hundred years, and the Germans roundly hated throughout the English-speaking world, it was a good time to present the Jameson Raid, the Anglo-Boer War and the First World War as *all* having been driven by the designs of the Kaiser and therefore but parts of a single continuum. If only readers could be persuaded that the origins of the Jameson Raid lay squarely within the ambit of Germany's ambition to build a world empire, then Hammond's role in those events could be seen as being far-sighted and pre-emptive in ways that presaged much later Anglo-American cooperation in the First World War.

Richard Harding Davis had shown Hammond to be a brave man of high principle during the Jameson Raid. Now some new journalist, yet to be identified, would have the chance of casting him as an early and shrewd observer of German imperial ambitions as played out in southern Africa, in 1895–1899. It would also do Hammond no harm, at a time when military men ruled the social roost, to remind Americans of his own military ambitions and achievements at a time when he was still adventurous and physically strong. Old soldiers never die. The real question was, who should his new chronicler of the Raid be?

The lot fell to a Manchester-born journalist and lecturer who was a man's man – a onetime sailor, traveller and later a specialist in colonial studies – Alleyne Ireland. Ireland, who had once worked for Joseph Pulitzer, had not only reviewed Harding Davis's little book on the Jameson Raid most favourably, but had also written on the Anglo-Boer War in a way that suggested a safe pair of hands.[43] Moreover, Ireland had written approvingly of Taft's role in the Philippines and shared the Hammonds' new interest in the role of 'heredity' in public life.[44]

As with Harding, who had helped patch up his tattered reputation in the late 1890s, what Hammond now was in search of was a big name with an established following to tell his version of the Jameson Raid, in fluent prose, in a serious, reputable journal with an intelligent readership. *The North American Review*, with its venerable New England roots and focus on culture, was a fine choice. 'The True Story of the Jameson Raid as Related to Me by John Hays Hammond', by Alleyne Ireland, appeared in the August and September issues of the *Review* in 1918.[45]

The 'hook' within this contrived approach to the history of the Raid, a stridently anti-German angle, started in the opening line of the article and ended 20 lines later, recalling the Kaiser's telegram to President Kruger in which he congratulated Kruger for having successfully seen off the raiders. Ireland pinned this tiny tail to the donkey by suggesting that it was only through the telling of Hammond's tale that the telegram might be 'assigned its proper place in the dark record of Germany diplomacy'. The articles must have met with some approval because, weeks later, Hammond claimed that the clamour for copies was such that he had decided to have them republished as a 'little volume' at his own expense.

The truth behind the publication of the 'little volume', however, was a good bit more complicated. *The Truth Behind the Jameson Raid* was written 'by John Hays Hammond, as related to Alleyne Ireland', with Ireland now very much in the back seat – and for good reason. Having sniffed success via the articles, Hammond was now intent on extracting even more personal gain from the tale. What he wanted from the American elite was no less than full, retrospective exculpation for the questionable role that he had played in in the Jameson Raid 23 years earlier. And he knew how to get it.

The ink had hardly dried on the *North American Review* version of the Raid before Hammond called in several personal favours from five of the most prominent East Coast Americans he knew: former President William Taft; James Cardinal Gibbons, Archbishop of Baltimore; Oscar Straus, former Secretary of Commerce and Labor in Roosevelt's cabinet; Arthur Hadley, close friend and President of Yale University; and his long-standing Cape Ann neighbour and White House insider, Colonel Edward House. Hammond solicited letters of support for the new work from them, but since they almost certainly knew little about the Jameson Raid other than what they had been told by him or had read in the *Review*, he clearly suggested that they, too, might want to situate their endorsements of 'The Truth' by concentrating on the 'German' angle.

When the book, published by Marshall Jones of Boston, appeared, late in 1918, it duly boasted copies of the letters received from the famous five. The problem was, however, that three of the respondents had been so infected with war fever that their endorsements, when linked to the narrower terrain of the Jameson Raid, looked a trifle barmy. Taft, on his way to being Chief Justice, got the client's briefing almost perfectly. 'It is well to have the facts clearly brought out to show the attitude of Germany, which was of a piece with her foreign policy before and since, and the high purpose of those who were the first movers toward the freedom of the Transvaal,' he wrote. But then Taft added the rider that Hammond was longing for – 'and whose course is eminently justified by the result'. The Archbishop of Baltimore, too, did passably well, suggesting that the Jameson Raid had been one of those 'intrigues which flourished in so many parts of the world previous to the World War, and which have been looked upon as part of the preparation for the present struggle to secure world domination by the Central Powers'.[46]

Hadley and Straus, however, got a bit carried away. Straus saw Hammond's tale of the Jameson Raid as furnishing 'additional evidence of the Kaiser's unconscionable methods and of the German *kultur* of fraud and perversion'. But Hadley, another Hopkins Grammar School alumnus, felt that the events that played themselves out in Johannesburg in 1895, first and foremost, threw 'light on the attempt of the German emperor to establish a new world hegemony, if not an actual world empire', and told Hammond that 'you have done good service in contributing the testimony of an eyewitness to this chapter of history'. Only Colonel House was not fully taken in, and, although an old friend, was not going to provide any hostages to fortune. He confined himself to just two sentences. 'I am glad that you are giving to the public "The True Story of the Jameson Raid",' he wrote. 'It was one of the most dramatic incidents in history, and its consequences have been of such far-reaching importance that the world will be eager to know the facts.'[47]

What the wider public made of the book and its endorsement is not known because it appears to have attracted no reviews. But, from Hammond's point of view, the entire exercise was rendered worthwhile because he had been publicly vindicated by a man destined to be the highest judge in the land. Hammond's gratitude and the true purpose behind his 'little volume' became evident in the closing paragraphs of the book. In words that revealed as much as they concealed, he wrote:

> As I look back after the twenty years upon the events I have described, my conscience justifies the part I played in them. Given the same conditions I would again act as I then acted, and should again be sustained by the firm conviction that I was striving to the best of my ability to maintain and to extend those imperishable principles of fair play which are in a peculiar sense the heritage of the British Empire and the United States.[48]

In Hammond's many accounts – verbal and written – it was the first time since his failed attempt to start a 'revolution' (by 1918, after the Bolshevik Revolution and the Red Scare, a far more dangerous word to use in America) in Johannesburg that his conscience had been called into play. Although by his account his conscience was not clean, it fully justified his folly. Tens of thousands of British troops, along with the thousands of Boer soldiers and their wives and children who had died in the Anglo-Boer War, along with all the Africans and others of colour who nobody had kept count of, might have been less sanguine.

The apparently unchallenged reception that Hammond's contrived 1918 version of the Jameson Raid got in America pointed to a new, younger, reading public – one that was either largely unconcerned by its past imperialist excesses or those of Britain, the new-found ally and friend of the United States. All this contrasted quite sharply with the criticism that Hammond had endured in the wake of the Raid and that had caused him and Natalie to undergo a period of voluntary exile in England before risking a return to America. It was all quite reassuring, if not downright gratifying. Old-timers, men and women drawn from his own cohort, no longer cared much about his record as a dangerous capitalist-revolutionary, while younger folk saw him largely as an old adventurer, a quirk of history.

It was precisely the sort of calm and promising political environment in which to drive home the image of himself as a pioneer of enormous importance who, over a lifetime, had interacted with the great and good across two continents doing extraordinary things that were ethically neutral and to the economic benefit of all concerned – big business, capitalist entrepreneurs and the millions of indigenous people who got to work for them. Hammond, who never stopped telling the boys in his youth clubs that what mattered was not the cards that you were dealt with but how you played the hand, was not about to spurn an ace.

Building on the *North American Review* and 'little volume' initiatives of 1918, Hammond prepared himself for a second intervention, broadly of the same type, and designed to reposition himself in the minds of the reading public. The new article, which he was sufficiently confident to pen for himself, would serve overlapping purposes. First, it would educate readers about the wider African context in which he had undertaken his work and introduce them to some of the legendary men with whom he had had the privilege of interacting. The greater the achievements of his heroes, the better it would speak of him; it would be fame by association. Second, the article would test the market for such tales and help prepare for the writing of his lengthy autobiography.

'South African Memories: Rhodes-Barnato-Burnham' by John Hays Hammond appeared in *Scribner's Magazine* in March 1921.[49] Hammond was in good company in ways that mattered most to him. Rhodes was the load-bearing pillar of a eulogy. He was, of course, a 'great admirer of America and the Americans' – perhaps one in particular? Rhodes had been 'frantic with anxiety' about the well-being of Hammond and the other conspirators in the Raid, when, in fact, he remained remarkably aloof and distant for several months, and so on. No matter. Rhodes had 'been surpassed by no man in any generation in the qualities that inspire admiration and make for greatness in the highest sense of the word'. Rhodes also passed the greatest test of imperialism: 'No Roman emperor ever won a greater extent of territory.'[50]

Barnato, Hammond's earliest mentor in South Africa, got a favourable but not unqualified report. 'Barney was a financial genius' but some thought he was 'not over-scrupulous' – nothing too far off the stereotypical Jew there, then. Fred Burnham, however, posed a bit of a problem, not least of all because Hammond had never clapped eyes on him in Africa. Indeed, Hammond only really got to know the Major at the time of the Yaqui delta investment. It did not matter, Burnham was far too valuable to let go of.

Unlike Hammond's two other heroes, the Major was alive and well, an American legend that many readers would recognise, and the new Burnham Exploration Company was going like the clappers, promising millions of dollars in dividends. With a bit of judicious name-dropping and jiggling with some phrases, the Major's South African experiences could be lined up next to those of Hammond, the missing author. Thus, 'Rhodes often spoke to me of Burnham in terms of high appreciation', and when Rider Haggard asked whether he actually knew Burnham, 'I replied that, oddly enough, I had never met him, though, of course, I knew him very well by reputation and, in common with all other Americans in South Africa'.[51]

As with the articles in the *Review*, the new piece in *Scribner's* and *Great American Issues*, Hammond's views appear to have been swallowed almost whole by the East Coast reading elite. There were few if any critics in sight.[52] Hammond's repositioning of himself in history, a process that he had been working on from the moment that Jameson had jumped the gun on that fatal day back in Pitsani, thanks to Davis and Ireland, was going extremely well. Clio and her younger followers were proving to be forgetful – a wonderful, yet necessary, step on the way to forgiveness.

Thus encouraged, Hammond continued to draft the chapters of his auto-biography but, still not believing his luck, continued to test bits and pieces of it out on the public whenever he got the chance. Thus, in 1925, as his 70th birthday approached, he gave Louise Boardman a sweetheart interview to run in the *Brooklyn Daily Sun* and a set of six 'exclusive' interviews to the *Freeport New York Daily Review*. It was enough to make a man, even someone like him, exceptionally proud.

It certainly moved the members of the Rocky Mountain Club, of which he was the one and only chairman, to remember to laud his achievements on the day he turned 71. Over a thousand guests, with Jack Hammond as guest of honour, packed into the Great Ballroom at the Waldorf Astoria Hotel to hear of his 'greatness and genius'.[53] But so auspicious an occasion could not be confined to Manhattan, let alone America, and the organising committee, on which Chief Justice Taft was happy to serve, organised no less than ten other celebratory dinners in centres around the world – includ-ing London, Manila, San Francisco, Tokyo and several others. President Coolidge sent congratulations and over 10 000 other written tributes were received, while *Time* magazine moved to honour him with a cover portrait and an article headed 'Unique' in its 10 May 1926 edition. Two years later the Rocky Mountain Club was disbanded. Western man, it seemed – and one very special one – had long since conquered the East Coast of the United States, if not much of the world.

A millionaire prophet and sage in a society that, second only to God, worshipped material progress and wealth, Hammond's image was safe and secure. In the eyes of a generation with a memory that barely reached back to the turn of the century, he had, by dint of hard work and the help of friends everywhere, from the National Press Club to the White House, rid himself of all stains of colonialism, imperialism and racism. He was a grey-haired old man notable for his altruism, statesmanlike behaviour and wisdom. He was a speaker in great demand, happy to give of his knowledge at gatherings rang-ing from commencement addresses to occasions of national importance.

When the aviator Charles Lindbergh flew non-stop and solo across the Atlantic Ocean from New York to Paris, in 1927, President Coolidge did not hesitate to place 'John Hays Hammond, adventurer in his youth, noted min-ing engineer and millionaire philanthropist' in charge of the celebrations in Washington. It was the sort of occasion that allowed for a bit of amnesia, poetic licence and a lot of sloppy journalism. It was going to be 'the great-est show on earth', featuring a splendid motorcade, and, unsurprisingly, 'the greetings committee will invite John Hays Hammond, engineer of South African Boer War fame who will ride with Lindbergh'. Asked what les-sons Lindbergh's achievement might hold for ordinary people, Hammond expanded on the usual virtues that underwrote success but had a special message for those still in college: 'one of the greatest enemies of success,' he warned them, 'is conceit.'[54]

Natalie Harris, suffering from an undisclosed illness, died in 1931. By a cruel twist of fate, given her interest in eugenics and heredity, she and Jack were denied grandchildren. Harris, their eldest son, and Richard Pindle, the youngest, who became a noted composer, appear never to have married. Their middle son, John Hays Hammond Jnr, a successful inventor and bon vivant, or so it would seem, helped camouflage his homosexuality by marrying a society divorcée whom his mother, a stickler for propriety, never approved of. The Hammonds' only daughter, Natalie, found it impossible to settle on a husband, or possibly one acceptable to her parents, despite being engaged seven times.

Jack Hammond spent the closing years of his life reading and writing in the study of his palatial residence, 'Lookout', on Boston's North Shore. When his autobiography appeared, in 1935, it was received not to critical acclaim but as an informative and interesting work by a cowboy-knight who had started out his life in modest circumstances and gone on to become an exceedingly rich and well-connected man. It must have been pleasing to have finally lain to rest the charges of conspiracy and cowardice that had haunted him ever since that day, in 1895, when Dr Jameson had disregarded his explicit orders not to cross the border and embarked on the ill-fated Raid. In his last days, Jack pottered about in Gloucester, stopping to swap tales with the harbour folk. When the fishermen got a bit carried away and told preposterous yarns, he would raise his hand and say, 'Wait a minute boys! Not quite so fast. Remember I can tell some "tall" stories myself.'[55] Indeed he could, and most of them lasted very well. John Hays Hammond died on 8 June 1936 having done as much as any man to set South Africa on a politically disastrous course for 100 years.

Conclusion

John Hays Hammond and the Jameson Raid read as American Imperial History

The manner and speed with which the Afrikaner political elite of the largely agrarian Boer republics was forced into the wider Anglophone world of the British Empire after the Anglo-Boer War of 1899–1902 contributes to the historical amnesia that bedevils a more rounded understanding of the past. Often content with the binary opposition of Boer and Brit, as posed in much of the historiography covering the period from the Jameson Raid to the advent of the Republic of South Africa, in 1961, most analysts have lost sight of a crucial, preparatory interlude in the 1890s. The door leading to the development of modern industrial mining in southern Africa was first forced ajar in 1895 by scores of American engineers-turned-mine-owning partners, and by one man in particular – John Hays Hammond.[1] Hammond's opportunism came in an epoch notable for the territorial expansion of the United States.[2] South Africa's racist economic and political development in the 20th century was born of Boer and British parents, but the confinement came at an important juncture in US history and an American midwife helped induce the breech-birth.

If we wish to overcome the constraints imposed on us by the existing imperial and nationalist histories and develop a better understanding of South Africa's arrival in the modern world, we need to become more attuned to the role the United States and its intermediaries played in the run-up to the long and troubled 20th century. A more nuanced reading of the Jameson Raid, one in which it is seen as constituting a part of American history and political adventurism in South Africa, presents us with one, potentially more profitable line of inquiry.

Mesmerised by the long shadows cast by the bloody encounters between

Boer and Brit in the South African countryside we have now forgotten how different, how very 'American', the continent's primary urban door to modernity – Johannesburg – was throughout the 1890s, in the formative years of what already was the world's greatest gold-mining industry. By 1894, John Hays Hammond was, one commentator noted, 'the virtual Czar of South African mining [sic]' and his presence greatly benefited US companies, including Fraser & Chalmers, General Electric, Ingersoll, Otis and Westinghouse.[3] In 1896, in the midst of a marked US economic recession, the Scientific American noted that 'The growth of the general export business to South Africa for the last few years has been little less than phenomenal,' doubling between 1892 and 1894 and easily exceeding $5 million each year after the boom in 1895.[4] 'The shops are full of the latest and best American machinery' run by 'American experts,' noted a reporter, 'erected by American mechanics'. 'The assayer hails from Grass Valley,' the 'cyanide man' from Alaska, the 'chlorination supervisor used to be a cow-puncher' and the 'battery manager is more at home in 'Frisco than Johannesburg'.[5]

A primary industry dominated by powerful American networks spawned commercial and retail analogues. 'Walk through the principal streets,' a British journalist, mirroring a concern of Cecil Rhodes's, noted, and you will find 'American insurance offices, American furniture shops, American bicycle agents, American candy stores, American quack doctors, American machinery makers, American timber merchants and American novelty stores'.[6] By 1899, there had been a 'gradual but effectual Americanization of the town and its surroundings' and the talk around and on the mines was often 'redolent of California rather than Cornwall'.[7]

The cultural echoes of this progressive Americanisation were to be heard up and down the Reef in the homes of mine managers as well as in many of town's demi-monde and working-class haunts. The fourth of July – Independence Day – 'was practically a general holiday in Johannesburg and the neighbourhood' as the 'Stars and Stripes' were celebrated with renditions of 'Hail Columbia' and, of course, the 'Star-Spangled Banner'.[8] By the mid-1890s the town's gambling and organised prostitution underworld was completely dominated by the 'American Club' run by 'Bowery Boys' drawn from New York's Lower East Side. In a town with a whiff of the Wild West about it, few ventured into its darker parts, and especially lower Commissioner Street, unarmed, and it was said that 'every man carries a gun in his hip pocket'.[9]

It was against this backdrop that, in 1895, John Hays Hammond played his part in persuading a tiny Boer fifth column in Pretoria, and a few mine managers and hundreds of American miners in Johannesburg, to support his poorly thought-through attempt at a coup d'état. If successful, he – as opposed to Rhodes and Jameson – hoped privately that it would lead to a change of government within the framework of a still independent Boer republic and possibly pave the way for a separate, semi-autonomous, constitutional dispensation for the Witwatersrand along the lines of that of the District of Columbia.[10] In order to appreciate what went into Hammond's planning, and in order to better understand how he set about mobilising many of his fellow countrymen for an armed uprising in a foreign country, it is necessary to understand some of the evolution of American political thought up to the time of Jameson's Raid.

The American Declaration of Independence (1776), and the overlapping Revolutionary War (1775–1783), predated the French Revolution (1789) by fully half a decade. For most Americans, the word 'revolution', right up to the Bolshevik Revolution of 1917, held positive connotations associated with armed anti-imperial and anti-monarchical struggles aimed at gaining political freedom under the rule of law within the framework of a constitutionally-bound republic. This somewhat idealistic and romantic view of radical change proved to be remarkably long-lived among Americans. It was also inextricably linked to their rapidly growing 'vision of national greatness'.[11]

Hammond was a veritable sponge when it came to using American ideology as official or unofficial US foreign policy in his personal pursuit of fame and fortune. He was particularly comfortable with notions of 'national greatness' and 'revolution' derived from the Declaration of Independence, and never more so than during his courtship of Rhodes and Jameson. In the run-up to the Raid, when the chances of staging a successful coup seemed reasonable, he never hesitated to cast himself and his co-conspirators as 'revolutionaries', albeit – as he put it much later – of a type that was more 'fascist' than 'Bolshevik'. It was only once the Raid itself had metamorphosed from force into farce that he hurriedly re-cast himself and his collaborators, American and Boer alike, as reformers or 'Progressive' sympathisers. Nor did he hesitate to term the hoped-for uprising in Johannesburg as a 'revolution', as did his wife, Natalie Harris, who did her best to help rehabilitate her husband's reputation in *A Woman's Part in a Revolution* (1897).

For anyone intent on mobilising American support for a coup d'état these revolutionary sentiments offered an obvious point of rhetorical entry. Hammond knew exactly what he was doing when he addressed a meeting of American miners who were already in his thrall as Consolidated Gold Fields employees, on 31 December 1895. 'All I am going to ask you,' he said, 'is one single question.' 'Don't you agree with me that we've now reached the same point as the signers of the Declaration of Independence when they announced that "it was their right and their duty to throw off a despotic government, and to provide new guards for their future security"?'[12]

'That is all there is to it,' Hammond thundered. Then, conflating this call to revolutionary action with another deep-seated American political reflex, recently activated during the dispute about Venezuelan goldfields between Britain and the United States (and to which we will return in due course), he went on: 'You won't find anything in the Declaration of Independence that limits this principle to latitude or longitude.' 'It's a clean-cut issue,' he said, 'to be faced by us Americans here and now.'[13]

But precisely because a call to revolutionary action by Americans went hand-in-hand with a commitment to republicanism, and some workers were wary of being drawn into an imperialist plot, he could not let the matter rest there, and so Hammond pushed on, addressing their underlying concerns. 'You know as well as I do,' said he, 'that we won't stand for having a British flag hoisted over Johannesburg', and 'You can rely on me that I'll shoot any man who hoists any flag but the Boer flag.' 'The assemblage applauded vigorously,' 150 miners 'pledged their support' for 'the revolutionary cause' and, thus primed for 'active service', duly signed on for the 'George Washington Corps'.[14]

When Hammond later courted journalist Richard Harding Davis to present his version of the Jameson Raid to a sceptical American public back home, the same revolutionary tradition was paraded. Davis suggested that the Rand Reformers 'were acting for the best good of the country in trying to overthrow the Boer government, as did the revolutionists of 1776 in our own country'.[15]

The fact was, however, that at the time of the Raid not all American miners were taken in, and some had long since detected what they suspected was to be a mine owners' revolution and fled town and country.[16] Most members of the Boer elite, who had considerable respect for America's anti-imperial struggle and who had been inspired by the United States Constitution when drafting their own founding laws, would not have been surprised by that flight. But more importantly, many ordinary Americans and Boers knew and appreciated that they shared an underlying commitment to independence and republicanism. Not all such support, however, was as clear-headed as it might have been. At the outbreak of the Spanish-American War, in 1898, on the West Rand there was for a time talk of raising a volunteer corps to support the Americans in an endeavour that was but marginally anti-colonial. Nevertheless, a few veterans from the Spanish-American War returned the favour when, in 1899, they joined Boer commandos to fight in the Anglo-Boer War.[17]

But, in 1895, American miners on the Witwatersrand were clearly right to doubt Hammond's public commitment to the Zuid-Afrikaansche Republiek because, in truth, just a little probing would have revealed that he was, in fact a deeply conflicted man. His respect for American independence and republicanism – genuinely held – barely shaded his quite remarkable admiration for the British crown, its aristocracy and the empire.

Indeed, it was Hammond's veneration of the British ruling class and its institutions that probably drew him into the orbit of Rhodes and Jameson in the first place. And it is only by appreciating how this over-developed trait in Hammond's peculiarly 'Southern' make-up came about that one can understand fully how it was that he, an American, joined an Englishman and a Scot in the great Jameson Raid conspiracy.

The Hammond family, which hailed originally from Kent, had, like a fair number of others in the slaveholding South, lived with a belief in its real or imagined British aristocratic connections over several generations.[18] For the males in the family, this fictive relationship affected their behaviour, demeanour and fantasies to the point where it sometimes appeared to float freely across the boundary separating the kingdom of the imagination and the real world, and it lent itself to a certain amount of affectionate teasing or, occasionally, outright ridicule.

The primary impetus for such airs and graces dated back to before the Revolutionary War, when a distant Hammond male forebear represented the British crown in Maryland, where the family first settled. This distant connection to the crown endured, and John Hay's father, RP Hammond, took it with him when he moved south to Arkansas prior to going on to West Point. During the Mexican-American War of 1846–1848 RP's pseudo-aristocratic pretensions were sufficiently on display for Robert E Lee, the future Confederate general, to chaff him with a memo addressed to 'Sir Richard'.[19] This, and related affectations, were passed on effortlessly from father to son and daughter. As a slip of a girl the artistically gifted Natalie Hammond, who went on to write a play about 'Queen Elizabeth of England' that was staged in New York City, handed her father a little book she had written, entitled 'The Adventures of Sir John Hammond', while her brother, the inventor John Hays Jnr, built a replica medieval English castle in Gloucester, Massachusetts, which still stands. It followed then that the crowning social achievement of Mr and Mrs John Hays Hammond Snr came when their friend, President William Taft, appointed Jack as Special Ambassador to represent the United States at the coronation of King George V and Queen Mary, in 1911. Dreams and delusions became indistinguishable.

But Jack Hammond's romantic attachment to English courtly life constituted merely one strand of the much stronger ideological mix that bound him, Rhodes and Jameson into a transatlantic view that not only patronised but also fatally underestimated the culture and resolve of their Afrikaner-Dutch political opponents in the southern Africa far interior.[20]

In an Anglophone universe dominated by notions of social Darwinism that supposedly determined the rank order of races across the globe, the three conspirators – Hammond, Jameson and Rhodes – shared a belief in the inherent superiority all things Anglo-Saxon.[21] Such 'Anglo-Saxon racism,' one analyst notes, 'developed as a self-conscious bond connecting Britons and Americans in the late nineteenth century, forged on their violent imperial frontiers and solidifying at points of Anglo-American social and intellectual contact.' Believing they were owners of a set of unique, interlocking 'free political values and institutions', many such Anglo-Saxons felt 'racially destined to spread empires of liberty'.[22]

Hammond, who continued to believe into the 20th century that the Boers, whose government he had sought to overthrow in the mid-1890s, were content to live in a state of 'semi-barbarism', and that Africans should be enslaved so as to solve the labour crisis leading up to the importation of Chinese labour for the Rand mines, in 1903, had contracted the virus of racism in especially virulent form.[23] In 1911, as soon as he was formally free of the restrictions placed on him after the failed coup, he lost no time in driving home the extent of the provocation that he and other mine owners had been made to endure at the hands of an 'inferior' Boer administration. At the time of the Raid, he said, President Kruger's impositions 'were such as no man of the Anglo-Saxon race would have tolerated' and 'the Americans had voted to take up arms against him'.[24]

Rhodes and Jameson's ideas about the supposed virtues of Anglo-Saxons and the inadequacies of Kruger and his countrymen are so well known that they scarcely bear repeating. 'Remember that you are born an Englishman,' Rhodes once asserted, 'and consequently you have won first prize in the lottery of life.' But it was Dr Jameson, a man whose affection for American men of action was matched only by his contempt for the Afrikaner-Dutch, whose Darwinist notions came to cost the conspiratorial trio most dearly of all. Any man who believed that it would take only 'five hundred men armed with *sjamboks*' – whips – to clear the republic of all Boer resistance, was unlikely to resist the temptation of setting off on a fully armed incursion when faced with a faltering coup.[25]

The point being made is that, as long as historians continue to see the 1894–1895 conspiracy arising almost exclusively from Rhodes and Jameson's friendship, and as being motivated by their imperial dreams and jingoistic notions, they will fail to appreciate that the machinations that led up to the Raid cut three ways rather than two, and that a good part of the bonding agent that held together the unlikely trio was the ideology of Anglo-Saxon superiority. The Jameson Raid can obviously be read in many ways but, in one sense, its deepest political origins can be seen as lying with three expansionists drawn from either side of the most economically advanced parts of the Atlantic world. The upheaval on the Witwatersrand may have been local and played itself out in the south, but some of the cognitive drivers behind the failed 'revolution' can be traced to the industrial north in a world becoming ever more globalised.

So, if we can set aside for a moment the imperial blindness that afflicts so many, we may be able see the Jameson Raid as more of a failed American-British cooperative attempt at a coup d'état centred on the Witwatersrand than as a pre-emptive, exclusively British initiative benefiting largely from a knowing wink and nod in distant Westminster. Once we have done that, we can also deepen our inquiry into the way that political thinking, as it evolved in the United States in the early and mid-19th century, influenced the principal architect of the 'revolution'.

Although America succeeded in striking off its imperial yoke in the Revolutionary War, the young nation was at pains to ensure its long-term economic interests and, more especially, its political integrity. After the Napoleonic Wars, the spectre of renewed attempts at colonisation in the New World saw America, growing rapidly in confidence, lay down a new, more expansive foreign policy.[26]

By the mid-19th century the Monroe Doctrine, born in the first instance largely of America's political concerns, in 1823, had assumed growing geo-economic importance for the United States as it industrialised and sought new and expanding markets for its products. As originally conceived, the doctrine, more clearly articulated in 1850, gave notice that any further attempts at colonisation in North or South America by European powers would be construed as acts of aggression and invite active contestation by the United States. Britain, with its own fears of Spanish ambitions in the western hemisphere, agreed to the new pronouncement and the United States, in turn, undertook not to intervene in the domestic matters of the northern transatlantic powers.

Marked economic recessions in 1873–1878, 1882–1885 and 1893–1897, however, imbued the Monroe Doctrine with an increasing commercial and industrial – as opposed to a political – logic as the US set about either capturing new markets, or holding on to existing ones, in Latin America and further west in the Pacific, including Hawaii.[27] It was thus hardly by chance alone that it was in the midst of an extremely serious economic downturn in the United States, in 1895, that the American President, Grover Cleveland, chose to bare his Monroe Doctrine teeth.

At a time when America was struggling to balance the demands that arose from its policy of bimetallism – using gold and silver reserves to back its currency – Cleveland could not have chosen a more pertinent issue on which to challenge Britain.[28] Nor, coincidentally, could he have picked a fight that was likely to resonate more powerfully with politically conscious Americans on the Witwatersrand, where several of the leading mining engineers had personal experience of working on the El Callao Mine in Venezuela and were thus well acquainted with the region.

The remote origins of the dispute between America and Britain, which reached crisis proportions in 1895–1896, lay in agreeing where precisely the internationally recognised boundary between British Guiana and Venezuela should be drawn. In 1894, Washington became alarmed when London arbitrarily extended the boundary in ways that encircled the mouth of the Orinoco River and threatened United States commercial interests.[29] In 1895, diplomatic exchanges across the Atlantic grew ever sharper when two forceful characters, Richard Olney and Lord Salisbury, assumed office as Secretary of State and Secretary of State for Foreign Affairs, respectively.[30] Matters drew to a climax in December 1895 – just days before Jameson slipped the tether that supposedly bound him to Hammond's say-so at Pitsani. By 17 December, it was clear that, if necessary, America was willing to go to war to defend Venezuelan territorial integrity and enforce United States dominance in the western hemisphere. Three days later, amid rumours of war, $170 million in value had been wiped off the New York Stock Exchange before the would-be belligerents came to their senses, backed down and agreed to try and find a peaceful resolution of the problem.[31]

For many United States citizens in Johannesburg, including politically ambitious ones such as Hammond who had no intention of seeing out their days in South Africa, Olney's brandishing of the Monroe Doctrine helped refocus political thinking. It limited Hammond's ability to mobilise American miners for a conflict that some suspected was being initiated on behalf of a cosmopolitan set of mine owners who, by and large, were more sympathetically disposed to Britain and its imperial interests than they were to the United States. 'On account of the recent trouble between England and the United States,' Hammond confessed to a journalist, 'Americans on the spot' were 'strongly averse to giving the Reform Movement an exclusively English complexion'.[32]

As importantly, although he never openly admitted to it being so, Olney's challenge to Salisbury – the very antithesis of Anglo-American cooperation – must have forced Hammond into a last gasp re-evaluation of the potential long-term personal political consequences of the conspiracy he had entered into with his imperialist friends, Rhodes and Jameson. Left stranded in mid-Atlantic by events over which he had no control, Hammond was forced to choose between the heavy-handed realities of the Monroe Doctrine at his back, and the appeal of romantic, knightly pretentions staring him in the face. It was most uncomfortable, and so he sought the middle ground, trying repeatedly to hold Jameson in check.

America's willingness to throw down the gauntlet to Britain, in 1895, and to claim its place as a force to be reckoned with in international affairs, was a new departure since, 'until the late 1880s, the United States was dealt with as a second-rate power'.[33] This new and threatening American posture, did not escape the notice of sharp-eyed observers in London, who not only sensed the shift in power but were willing to speculate about its possible ties to the Jameson Raid and the future of the Witwatersrand. On 26 March 1896, *The Sketch* informed readers that:

> At the moment Mr Hammond is a most interesting person, for he is an American citizen, and with the Monroe Doctrine extending all directions, perhaps even reaching Africa, not only are they beginning to sing in Washington –
> And shall Hays Hammond die?
> Then thirty thousand Yankee boys will know the reason why? but so necessary is he to the gold industry that he has been released on parole and allowed to go off to Johannesburg to look after the deep levels, on which the future of not only the Consolidated Goldfields, but of President Kruger depends.

The economic muscle underlying this new assertiveness had been in the making for at least five decades before the Raid. Taken together, these developments formed an important part of the backdrop against which Hammond and other US citizens planned and prepared for the urban uprising in Johannesburg. Many of the attitudinal prerequisites for a successful political revolution on the Rand, one that might usher in an extension of America's sphere of influence and see it embrace a sister republic, were in place by 1895.

The sense of American self-confidence that presaged and underlay the dramatic territorial expansion of the mid-1840s – notably in the annexation of Texas in 1845 – was perhaps best captured in a catchphrase first employed by a newspaper editor but which soon became part of general political discourse. In 1845, John O'Sullivan asserted that it was America's 'Manifest Destiny to overspread the continent allotted by Providence'. Not without contemporary critics, who sensed in it potential moral and political hazards, Manifest Destiny's proponents saw it as a mission, underwritten by God, sanctioning the spread of the American people and their institutions across the continent. Not even the Civil War (1861–1865) and the dispute over slavery could lay the concept to rest. By the mid-1880s, amid rapidly accelerating industrial growth, Manifest Destiny was once again employed to underwrite the extension of America's informal economic empire in the Gilded Age.[34]

John Hays Hammond (born in 1855) was, like many in his group of admiring mining engineers on the Witwatersrand in the mid-1890s, part of a cohort raised on the idea of Manifest Destiny. 'The world into which I was born,' he later recalled, was one in which 'frontiers were being extended on every hand.'[35] Both his father and the uncle who helped tutor him for the adventurous life, John 'Coffee' Hays, were Southerners, military men, shaped by the Mexican-American War before moving west to California. There, both veterans were rewarded with public office by President Franklin Pierce who alienated Northerners by accommodating the interests of Southern slave-owners. Hammond was infused with an expansionist ethos – before, during and after – the Jameson Raid. In his view, the American-led initiative in Johannesburg, in 1895, was one that could not be constrained by considerations of 'latitude or longitude', and, towards the end of his career, it will be recalled, an approving scribe described him as being 'at heart a good American imperialist'.[36]

The pursuit of Manifest Destiny was, however, never confined to those initiatives formally authorised by the United States government. Indeed, in antebellum America, Manifest Destiny came to have a decidedly aggressive, exceedingly ugly, and wholly unlawful side to it – an 'underworld' – that was closely associated with Southern expansionism in a world outgrowing legalised slavery.[37]

In the 1850s, undaunted by the provisions of the United States Neutrality Act of 1818, filibusters – 'American adventurers who raised or participated in private military forces that either invaded or planned to invade foreign countries with which the United States was formally at peace' frequently championed the underlying tenets of Manifest Destiny.[38] Filibustering, infused with romantic notions of chivalry and knightly behaviour that nestled within a nexus of Anglo-Saxon superiority, anti-Catholic Freemasonry and secret society activity, appealed to frustrated Southern imperialists. These ranged from the one-time Governor of Mississippi, John A Quitman, to thousands of under-employed urban men marginalised by plantation slave economies.[39]

Mid-19th century filibusters in the United States were usually cast as 'pirates' by their newspaper critics, and, significantly, that was the one-word description that Jameson, an admirer of things American, hoped most to avoid as a label for his lunatic caper.[40] It was a sensitivity that Hammond, who had more reason than most to want to avoid it should the conspiracy have gone wrong, would have encouraged in Jameson who, right up to the moment that he set out from Pitsani, still looked upon his new American friend as the very embodiment of manly action.

In retrospect, it is difficult to over-emphasise the extent and intensity of American filibustering activity during Hammond's formative years.[41] Almost every year between 1850 and the Civil War saw one or more American-led armed invasions around the Caribbean, in Central America or Mexico. The most notorious filibuster of the era, until he was executed in Honduras, in 1860, was Tennessee-born William Walker.[42] Walker was, if not a friend of Major RP Hammond and ex-Texas Ranger Hays, then well known to them.

In 1849, Walker, a medical doctor and lawyer-turned-journalist, left New Orleans and went to California. Based in San Francisco, Walker was soon active in press circles and, like RP Hammond, a member of the Democratic Party where they aligned themselves with the Broderick faction in state politics.[43] In 1853, emboldened by President Pierce's avowedly expansionist policy, Walker abandoned the pen for the sword and seven years of adventurism.[44]

Walker's point of departure was San Francisco, where RP Hammond was the Collector of Customs in the port and his brother-in-law, Colonel John 'Coffee' Hays the town's Sheriff. In 1853, Walker acquired the brig *Arrow* and put together an expeditionary force that was to invade Lower California and Sonora and establish the independent republic that would, allegedly, save the local populace from predatory attacks by indigenous Indians.[45] But, when federal authorities got to hear of Walker's scheme, they turned to the army to try and halt the excursion. The military's attempts to thwart Walker's departure, however, proved wholly unsuccessful. Believing that they had detected silent approval from their distant political patron on the East Coast, President Franklin Pierce – a suspicion that came to be shared by others – RP Hammond and Coffee Hays used their official positions to intervene and, as a consequence of their stalling legal manoeuvres, Walker and his filibusters got the time and space necessary to slip out of San Francisco Bay, reach Mexico and establish the short-lived 'Republic of Lower California' (1853–1854).[46]

So scandalously ineffectual were Hammond and Hays in discharging their official duties during the episode that they became the subject of a semi-formal complaint, even though Walker himself enjoyed such widespread, wholehearted support among the local populace that he was considered a hero.[47] When Walker was eventually brought to justice, in 1854, it took a San Francisco jury just eight minutes to acquit him, thereby priming him for further expansionist expeditions, including two in Central America, one of which earned him official recognition as the 'president' of a central American 'republic'. It is difficult not to see RP Hammond and Hays as having collaborated with Walker, even if they were not outspoken public supporters of the filibuster. It may also be significant that it was later rumoured that RP Hammond was also 'involved in filibustering in Nicaragua' – again probably with Walker.[48]

The idea that Jameson's Raid was not unlike a William Walker adventure in Central America was not lost on Hammond's fellow Americans. Fred Burnham suggested that, 'like Walker of Nicaragua', Jameson was a fine leader of men and that 'All the revolutionists forgave him his error of judgement'[49] – 'all', that is, except one.

American expansionism as embodied either directly through orthodox warfare, or indirectly, as attempted by filibusters, was firmly embedded in the political DNA of Southern males, and the family of the young John Hays Hammond was no exception. In his memoirs, Jack Hammond, Grand Master of Biography by Omission, was fulsome about his childhood memories of notable figures in San Franciscan history, including several involved in pivotal events that predated his birth, such as the famous 'Committee of Vigilance'. But, if there is a studied hush about the roles that his father and uncle played in the adventures of William Walker's filibusters, it pales beside the silence about the even more dramatic events that occurred in Jack Hammond's hometown around the outbreak of the Civil War, in 1861.

Neither the political loyalties of the Hammond family nor those of many other citizens in San Francisco – a city with a significant number of Southerners – could be taken as given after the cannon roared at Fort Sumter on 6 March 1861. RP Hammond and Coffee Hays, obvious targets of suspicion when it came to Confederate sympathies, were both made to swear oaths of neutrality before being allowed to go about their ceaseless personal pursuit of property and wealth. Not everyone, however, including other affluent citizens, were content to sit on the financial fence amid a moral crisis. Asbury Harpending, once a soldier of William Walker's, and other Southerners anxious to secure Californian gold for the Confederate cause, joined a secret 'Committee of Thirty', in which each of the conspirators swore to recruit 100 more stalwarts.

The principal obstacle to the Committee of Thirty's objective was a fellow Southerner and friend of RP Hammond's, General AS Johnston, the commander of the US Army's Pacific Department and the local military base. A few members of the Committee hoped that Johnston might be persuaded to support their conspiracy. But Harpending, perhaps suspecting that the highly principled General would not readily forsake his oath of loyalty to the Union while still serving, was more taken with the idea that Johnston be 'taken by surprise and subdued with force'.[50]

The Committee of Thirty hoped that, once Johnston had been neutralised, they could seize the arsenal at Benicia, and then the city of San Francisco itself, as a prelude to proclaiming a 'Pacific Republic' that would support the Southern cause. But Johnston got to hear of the plot prematurely, through the indiscretion of a lawyer friend, and made it clear that he was unwilling to be party to an act of treason while still an officer in the Union Army. Instead, he quit his office weeks later, made his way east and became one of the South's most respected Civil War generals. Harpending was arrested and imprisoned on Alcatraz for a few years before benefiting from an amnesty granted him by President Lincoln.[51]

Did the conspiracy in San Francisco to bring about a 'Pacific Republic' in 1861 provide six-year-old Jack Hammond with the ghostly template for the Jameson Raid and, if so, in what ways? At first glance it seems unlikely. An attempted coup centred on the grievances of primary industry, one financed largely by the premier of a neighbouring state who enjoyed the covert support of a member of the British cabinet and relied on the police of a company with a Royal Charter to back a 'revolution' so as to effect an imperial outcome, with the conscious or unwitting assistance of a fifth column in the capital city, obviously differed from Asbury Harpending's plot in several important respects.

Yet, when all is said and done, can the opposite possibly be true? That is, that the San Francisco plot of 1861, in its various logistical, political and tactical dimensions, was not the subject of intense debate and speculation in the Hammond family, with all its powerful Southern military connections, both at the time of the conspiracy and for years thereafter, and that it had *no* influence whatsoever on the Hammond conspiracy?

That seems even less likely. The centrality of gold to the economy and to the 1895 political plot, the planned abduction of President Kruger, the seizure of the arsenal at Pretoria, the forcible occupation of Johannesburg and the Witwatersrand, which would lie at the heart of a new constitutional dispensation overseen by a more compliant government in a reconfigured republic – all central components of the Jameson Raid conspiracy that bear the Americanised, highly personalised imprimatur of Hammond – almost all point unerringly to San Francisco. The deepest roots of what, in perverted historical shorthand, later became known as the 'Jameson Raid' lie in the United States with John Hays Hammond rather than in England with Rhodes or in Scotland with Dr Jameson.[52]

But if the *theory* that later helped inform Hammond's planning of how the coup d'état on the Witwatersrand should unfold came to him during a Californian adolescence, via his father and uncle, and which he almost certainly went on to sell to Rhodes and Jameson while on safari in Matabeleland in 1894, then most of his *practical* experience of the logistics, organisation and politics that might inform a 'revolution' was acquired in his late thirties, during the mining war in the Coeur d'Alene in the early 1890s. Hammond lost this bitterly contested industrial war with organised labour in Idaho, and when he fled to southern Africa, in 1893, he left bearing all the scars of battle.[53]

When Hammond took up a new position with Rhodes and Consolidated Gold Fields, in 1894, the bloody struggle between mine owners and labour in the Bitterroot Mountains was still much on his mind. Indeed, through the use of hand-picked proxies every bit as intransigent as he was, Hammond was still very much involved in shaping the starkly adversarial nature of American industrial relations well into the Gilded Age.

For Hammond, still a Coeur d'Alene mine owner and once president of the Idaho equivalent of the Witwatersrand Chamber of Mines, the key constraints to reaping super-profits from the mining of precious metals were twofold – high freight charges from rail companies and wage demands coming from organised labour imbued with revolutionary zeal. Hammond saw these impediments as looming equally large for the gold-mining industry in the Kruger republic, where a concessionary monopoly controlled rail tariffs and a newly formed union of white workers had already achieved a hugely significant victory by successfully scuppering a law framed to limit the theft of gold, in 1893.

Back in the Coeur d'Alene Hammond and Victor M Clement, his trusted lieutenant, had declared war on the rail companies and the workers. The struggle was waged through shutdowns and wage reductions enforced by private detective agencies, secret agents and spies, backed up by imported scabs armed with rifles smuggled in across the state lines. Crucially, the mine owners and private army had also enjoyed the covert support of General James F Curtis, a former member of the San Francisco Vigilance Committee who, as personal adviser to Idaho governor Norman Willey, was right at the heart of the state machinery. When all else failed, federal troops would – and did – come to the rescue of Idaho mine owners, who had assumed near-total control of the mining towns.

The more insidious, 'softer' part of the mine owners' war in Idaho had been fought with commensurate cunning and resolve. Newspapers had been bought and editors appointed to spread disinformation and propaganda that supported collaborators and undermined opponents. Charitable causes were manipulated to provide desirable outcomes while traders and shopkeepers, caught between the scissors of capital and labour, were coaxed into establishing 'Law and Order Leagues' up and down the valleys, creating, in effect, local vigilance committees.

In late 1894, when they set out on that fateful mining safari, Rhodes was downcast by the fading prospects of drawing the Zuid-Arikaansche Republiek into an economic federation and ultimately into the British Empire. Jameson, by contrast, was full of adrenaline and self-confidence as a result of the recent Maxim gun-driven defeat of the Ndebele. Hammond, a notorious blowhard, was unlikely to have held back when selling his credentials as a man capable of taking history by the scruff of the neck and imposing radical change. He provided an up-to-the-minute analysis of the ills and potential for a labour-led upheaval on the Witwatersrand in the mid-1890s – an account verified subsequently for the hesitant Rhodes via a gung-ho Jameson. More importantly, Hammond *knew* how to mount a conspiracy, how to seize a city, how to create a democratic republican state, and how to explain, in detail, right down to cross-border gun-running, what was needed to foment a 'revolution'.[54]

Rhodes sensed that Hammond was a skilled political surgeon, a man with practical knowledge and a good theoretical understanding of the anatomy of revolution. But he also knew that Hammond, a man with big personal investments in the Witwatersrand mines, was at least as politically ambitious as he was avaricious. It was a combination that frightened Rhodes far more than it excited him. Hammond was a man whose dreams centred on money and power, or any combination thereof. Left to his own devices in a heavily Americanised setting such as Johannesburg, Hammond was capable of leading an urban upheaval culminating in a republican dispensation that might thwart Rhodes's own plan for folding the Zuid-Afrikaansche Republiek into a united southern Africa that nestled within the folds of the British Empire. Like Hammond, then, but for reasons that were transmitted to him only indirectly, Rhodes, too, became haunted by the Coeur d'Alene war of 1892, Harpending's conspiracy to seize San Francisco in 1861, and of that city's 'Committee of Vigilance' of 1851.

It was Fred Hamilton, editor of *The Star*, who noted later that, throughout the latter part of 1895, it was John Hays Hammond who had hammered away at Rhodes, telling him that 'if he refused to come in the Uitlanders would go their own way'.[55] By August 1895 Rhodes sensed that his hold on the situation was increasingly tenuous. In a letter to the co-financier of the Raid, Alfred Beit, he spelt out his concerns. 'Now I fear,' he wrote, that 'those fellows may have a revolution and a successful revolution in spite of me.'[56] But who might 'those fellows' have been? They most certainly were not Corner House men, for Rhodes would have said so.

The result was that premier Rhodes, the most inherently cautious of the conspiratorial trio at the heart of the Jameson Raid, the man with most to lose by far, was left playing catch-up politics. In effect, Rhodes was forced to decide whether he should leave his chief engineer – a man indispensable to his own mining fortunes on the Witwatersrand – to his own devices and risk a possibly unpredictable political outcome in the Kruger republic, or whether he should co-opt him and try to harness his formidable radical, expansionist political impulses to his and Jameson's dreams of empire. It may well have been the American-admiring Jameson, the adventurous gambler, the poor man's Clive of India, that swung Rhodes in favour of a conspiracy focused actively on 'revolution'.

We *know* all this because Rhodes and Hammond could not have been clearer about these matters, and the definitive evidence has been there for historians to come to terms with for more than a hundred years. In 1900, Rhodes told his close friend, an executor of his will and ardent fellow imperialist, WT Stead, that *he* had not led the thinking that underpinned the ill-fated Jameson Raid, but that his hand had been forced by those on the spot – and probably just one man – and that the pressure of time had pushed him into what was a premature response:

> 'In fact', said Mr Rhodes to me when he was explaining how it was he came to make the one fatal blunder of his career, 'it seemed to me quite certain that if I did not take a hand in the game, the forces on the spot would soon make short work of President Kruger. Then I would be faced with an American Republic – American in the sense of being intensely hostile to and jealous of Britain – an American republic manned largely by Americans and *Sydney Bulletin* [militantly republican] Australians who cared nothing for the old flag. They would have all the wealth of the Rand at their disposal. The drawing power of the Uitlander Republic would have collected round it all the other Colonies. They would have federated with it as centre and we should have lost South Africa. To avert this catastrophe, to rope in the Uitlanders before it was too late I did what I did.'[57]

Nor was this the wisdom of disillusionment viewed through the perfection of hindsight. Less than a week after he had proffered his resignation as Prime Minister of the Cape Colony, on 12 January 1896, on a Sunday and with many other things still on his mind, Rhodes sat down to compose a lengthy handwritten cablegram for the mass-circulating newspaper *The World*, in New York City. He appealed for Anglo-American solidarity in the face of possible German hostility in the wake of the Raid. He left readers in no doubt as to the importance of the role that the transatlantic immigrants played in the Kruger republic. 'The new males outnumber the old by five to one,' he wrote, 'and are composed largely of Americans, including the principal mine managers.' 'In the Transvaal,' he continued, 'all my mine managers are Americans.' And lest anyone should miss the point he reminded them that foreigners owned 90 per cent of the country's wealth.[58]

It requires little historical imagination to know who Rhodes thought might be foremost among those most capable of ushering in a new republican dispensation, one 'manned by Americans'. That at a time, as previously noted, when 'politicians, intellectuals and businessmen' in the United States were actively 'redefining notational power as disembodied – that is, divorced from contiguous territorial expansion'.[59] Not surprising, then, that, amid so much other treachery, Rhodes and Jameson may have conspired privately to steal Hammond's urban 'revolution' from under his nose by getting the invaders with the Maxim guns to hoist the Union Jack over Johannesburg at the last, critical juncture. Indeed, it was the notorious 'Flag Question' that probably did most to cause the entire conspiracy to unravel in the end. And why would Rhodes and Jameson not do so? Hammond, by his own admission, had secrets that he had never shared with Rhodes and Jameson, including his intention to abduct Kruger and then 'negotiate', at gunpoint, a semi-autonomous status for the Witwatersrand modelled on the District of Columbia.

But Stead, aware that critics might consider Rhodes's comments about the threat of an 'American republic' arising from among the tailings of the goldfields as an impromptu, one-off flight of fancy, or a convenient *ex post facto* rationalisation for what had turned out to be a misadventure, was unwilling to entertain any such speculation, or to leave the subject hanging open-ended. So, in the very next paragraph, he wrote: 'Repeated conversations with Mr Rhodes, even as recently as last autumn [1901] found him unchanged in the conviction that the danger of an American Republic in South Africa justified his conspiracy.'[60] Nor would the annexation of Hawaii (1898) or the triumph of the United States in the Spanish-American War, which occurred between the Jameson Raid and the Anglo-Boer War, have set Rhodes's mind at rest. Indeed, they would only have confirmed his suspicions.

But could Rhodes the Colossus, Rhodes the Founder, Rhodes the Champion of Imperialism in southern Africa really have been placed on the political back-foot by just *one* American on the Rand? Was it really possible for the Big Man to have been *following*, rather than driving the attempt at a coup d'état? And, if so, why was it that it raised no eyebrows among his contemporaries? The answer seems to be that at least one of Rhodes's closest admirers had a good idea of what was happening and had identified *the* moving force behind the events, and it was indeed just one man.

In early January 1896, only days after his bet-hedging statement to the *Natal Mercury*, Ewald Esselen, in panic mode – or in a 'funk', to use the prevailing terminology – penned a note to WP Schreiner. Schreiner was not only a close friend and political intimate of many years' standing but also the very man whom Esselen had approached to facilitate the secondment of Andrew Trimble to the Republic at short notice in 1894. By the time Esselen wrote to him, Schreiner had resigned from his position as Attorney General in the Rhodes ministry as a result of Jameson's Raid.

On 20 January, Schreiner, who appears not to have known how very deeply implicated in the Rand conspiracy both Esselen and Trimble were, responded, 'My Dear Ewald,' in a revealing note that bared his political soul:

> I got your letter today and was glad to hear from you. I need scarcely say how entirely I sympathise with and share your feeling of the bitter position in which men like ourselves are placed in this dreadful business. You know well how firmly I have adhered to the principle of good faith in the relations between the States and Colonies – for

example in the 'drifts' matter I had no alternative but to insist upon a fair recognition of your rights. But under a scheme as we are learning the details of gives a terrible blow to our higher aspirations' ...

I have never had a deeper grief than has come upon me since the day we talked together in the Club. The wound is all the deeper and more serious because I loved, still love, the man Rhodes. *He has been more led than leader in this business in my opinion.* I will not now, even to you, name *a certain man*, whose continued presence in South Africa is in my opinion a menace to our natural and right development.[61]

It may be reasonably inferred that the man Schreiner had in mind and who wielded such extraordinary influence over Rhodes (and Jameson) was a bird of passage, a foreigner in southern Africa. And Schreiner's wording, as might be expected of an advocate and former parliamentary draftsman, conjures up the sort of phraseology that one might encounter in the preamble to legislation on the deportation of prohibited immigrants. The chasm between Rhodes's unnamed 'Americans' and Schreiner's 'certain man' is best bridged by just one name – Hammond.

Back in the Matabeleland bush, in late 1894, Hammond would have come across as the man on the spot with the unparalleled insight and organisational ability necessary to mount an armed insurrection, which, if necessary, Jameson could back up with a military force of last resort – as provided by federal troops in the Coeur d'Alene. Hammond might well succeed in helping Rhodes bring about a change of regime in Pretoria, producing a new Boer government led nominally by General Piet Joubert, who was less implacably opposed to the mine owners, and a possible progressive folding of the republic into the British Empire.[62] Rhodes and Alfred Beit would provide the necessary funding – Hammond was unwilling to risk so much as a penny of his own, already very considerable income – and Rhodes, as Premier of the Cape Colony would help position the British cabinet for suitably discreet assistance in the possibly serious upheavals that might take place. All that the originating conspiratorial trio lacked was the equivalent of a General James Curtis in Idaho – a well-placed sympathiser, an 'agent', working deep within the heart of the Kruger government who could keep the conspirators abreast of all Boer military and political developments and even influence policy.

Rhodes knew the man to play that role. He was a former political ally of his, once of the Afrikaner Bond in the Cape Colony, a fellow Freemason, a Joubert supporter, a lawyer of the highest standing well known in mining circles and President Kruger's recently appointed State Attorney, the man in sole charge of the Republic's secret service and its police force. His name was Ewald Esselen and not only would he back any change of government that might see General Joubert become President of the Republic but he would also bring with him a collaborator, a friend, the leading Afrikaner-Dutch newspaper editor in the capital, a man almost as fanatically opposed to Kruger as Rhodes himself, the charming, drug-addicted, mercurial Eugène Marais. Within weeks of the safari conspiracy being broadly agreed upon, out in the Matabeleland bush, Jameson was in Johannesburg meeting Esselen.[63]

In keeping with Rhodes's fear of a republic – which he may have shared privately with Jameson but which remained publicly unstated prior to the planned 'revolution' – Hammond was never in doubt that the political momentum driving events on the Witwatersrand derived from an American vanguard, led by him, in search of independence that might be underpinned by unenfranchised white workers.[64] Of the 64 members of the Reform Committee arrested after the Raid, seven were Americans, while two others – Richard Parker and Dr Wolff – had already escaped.[65]

Within months of Hammond's departure for London, in 1896, he persuaded his apologist, Richard Harding Davis, a great admirer of William Walker and the American filibustering tradition, that the majority of the members on the Reform Committee 'had no intention of turning the country over to the Queen'.[66] In his first major, overtly political, public speech after the legal conditions that had been imposed on him after the Raid had formally lapsed, to the Boston Clover Club, in November 1911, Hammond, always ready to denigrate Kruger, was at pains to underscore his republican credentials to sceptical countrymen aware of his underlying Anglophilia: 'It is said that we were acting under the British Flag. It is false.' 'Jameson,' he said, 'came into the fight against our [American] wishes.'[67] And, in 1918, Hammond drove home the point, saying that what he had wanted to do was to harness the revolutionary zeal of his countrymen to set up a 'truly representative democracy on the American model' – a model which, we now know, might also accommodate an arrangement for the Witwatersrand along the lines of the District of Columbia.[68]

But, all that duly noted, the hero-worshipping Hammond had an untrammelled – almost delusional – admiration for Rhodes's achievements as an 'Anglo-Saxon', as an imperialist and as a conqueror of 'savages'. Rhodes was, he suggested, 'A born master of men, he was at the same time practical, imaginative and even romantic'. What impressed Hammond most of all, however, was the sheer geographical extent of the colonies that Rhodes had added to the British Empire: 'No Roman Emperor ever won a greater extent of territory.'[69] Hammond, too, as we have already noted, was an expansionist, but for him it was the extension of American commerce, trade and industry that would deliver the fast-growing, informal empire of the United States in the 1890s.[70]

In southern Africa, as in Venezuela, the key to unlocking new territories for incorporation into the expanding American economic empire was gold and an increase in the number of mining engineers on the ground. On the Witwatersrand, an 'American Society' helped all manner of newcomers settle into 'self-described colonies'. But for Hammond such Americanisation was not to be left to market forces to deliver, something to be waited on passively; it had to be *actively* undertaken and consciously pursued so as to achieve the desired outcome. Thus, in mid-1894, even *before* his safari with Rhodes and Jameson, he wrote to Dr Rutherfoord Harris, Secretary of the British South Africa Company, recommending a Californian, Henry Butters, as the man who might lead 'the colonization of Mashonaland and Matabeleland by Americans'.[71]

It was from within this sticky nexus of attitudes and ideas about colonisation, expansionism, filibustering, Manifest Destiny, slavery, racial superiority and social Darwinism, all wrapped up in his own identity as a Southerner, that one has to understand the extent and nature of the defence mounted to prevent the death sentence imposed on Hammond being carried out for his role in the Jameson Raid. Hammond's Mississippi-born wife, Natalie, and her uncle, Confederate general Nathaniel Harris, activated a network of well-connected American businessmen, politicians and military men, individuals with strong roots in the Old South or the West to come to Hammond's rescue. This was supplemented with judicious appeals to more modern and progressive members of his Yale cohort in the Northeast.[72] Thus it was that, while President Grover Cleveland, a Democrat, was reluctant to intervene on Hammond's behalf personally, Secretary of State Richard Olney, once of Yale, was not.[73] In the final analysis, Hammond's neck was spared largely through the sophisticated statesmanship displayed by President Kruger; to the extent that he was saved by a political chorus orchestrated in the United States, the voices came from Yale, the Old South and the West.

We would be making a mistake, however, if we confined our attempt to understand the Jameson Raid by asking only what American ideas the ambitious Hammond brought to the globalising south without also having probed – albeit briefly – how his experiences of colonisation and expansionism in southern Africa were taken back to the United States and subsequently informed his interventions in that same part of Mexico that first excited the attentions of William Walker and his filibusters. John Hays Hammond may have assisted in making southern African history in ways that are crucial for the understanding of 1894–1895 and the political disasters that followed, in the form of the Anglo-Boer War, the British attempt at reconstruction and the coming of a racist Union of South Africa, but southern African experiences also helped make him and did a good deal to shape his imperialistic project in Mexico.

When Hammond eventually returned to America from self-imposed political exile in England, in 1899, the following winds generated by the Anglo-Boer War and the Spanish–American War enabled him to affect a softer ideological landing on home shores than would have been possible in the immediate wake of the Jameson Raid. With the contrived assistance of the influential Richard Harding Davis, who used factual and fictional accounts of his adventures to successfully refurbish his reputation as an adventurous, honourable and brave soldier of fortune fighting noble causes in distant settings, Hammond was ready to face new challenges in an unstoppable quest for fame and fortune.

The problem confronting Hammond and others, however, was that at some point in the last quarter of the 19th century America had apparently reached its geographical limits, with serious consequences for the character of its increasingly affluent population as well as their democratic practices and economic prospects. The situation, it seemed, was dire. In 1891, the historian Frederick Jackson Turner had begun to flesh out his thesis that an open frontier and landed settlement had been the primary driver underlying American democratic traditions and economic prosperity. In July 1893, just weeks after Hammond had fled the industrial war zone that he and Victor Clement had helped bring about in the Coeur d'Alene, Turner delivered the most dramatically influential refinement of his still unfolding argument at the World's Fair in Chicago. The effective closing of the frontier, Turner suggested, helped explain why it was that in the 1890s the United States was being tortured by growing agrarian unrest, violent industrial confrontations and ideological challenges tinged with foreign socialism.[74]

The Turner thesis, it has been convincingly argued, came to form an important part of the intellectual foundations of American expansionism in the most crucial decade of all – the 1890s. In his own voluminous writings, however, Hammond refused to give hostages to fortune and pointedly refused to acknowledge the existence of theorists of expansion despite the fact that he could not possibly have avoided their influence in the public spaces that he negotiated.[75] Several of Hammond's political heroes, including for many years Teddy Roosevelt, openly commended Turner for sharpening the debate around emerging issues of national importance. With a new consensus around expansionism emerging between important political and business leaders, as well as influential missionaries and military and naval strategists, the minds of the public, if not always those in the White House itself, were being prepared for far more aggressive forms of colonialism. While the horizons being targeted for possible expansion lay largely – but not solely – on the contiguous land mass, they would also no longer be contained within the borders of an informal empire.[76]

In 1900, Hammond was not yet ready to turn his back on the West. For a start, through two younger brothers and a cousin, William Hammond Hall, he remained connected to men whose public office could be harnessed to private profit-seeking by focusing on California's need for water to generate cheap hydroelectric power, feed its growing cities and irrigate otherwise relatively dry river valleys.[77] The family network focused on land-and-water projects, some of which were supported by capital raised through the same Witwatersrand mining houses that had contributed to Hammond's expanding fortune. Hammond's powerful personal network, too, was extended further when, in 1907, he – as president for life – founded the influential Rocky Mountain Club as 'an eastern home for western men'. Among the members of the club were dozens of the most notable American imperialists of the decade, including Alfred T Mahan, Fred Burnham and Teddy Roosevelt to name but three. It was not surprising, then, that Hammond came within an ace of winning the Republican Party's nomination as William Taft's vice presidential running mate in the 1908 election. In the end it mattered little since, in effect, Hammond became the unofficial Vice President of the United States.[78]

But, given the increasingly favourable domestic political climate – foreshadowed by his own machinations in southern Africa around the Jameson Raid – Hammond's eyes swung away from the long-favoured West towards Mexico, which he contemplated with an appetite for imperialism perhaps last matched by William Walker.

Hammond's interest in America's southern neighbour as a source of potential profit was not new. After all, he and Victor Clement had been there in the 1880s. But this time round they invested significant sums in mining ventures, all the while dragging a small but significant Jameson Raid tail behind them in the shape of 'Hammond men' – engineers known for their skill but, one might speculate, also for their clan loyalty and political outlook.[79]

But important as Hammond's personal holdings in mining and oil in Mexico were – and they became huge – one has to look elsewhere to uncover the full extent of his stubbornly imperialist outlook and see how his southern African experiences informed his renewed attempts at American colonisation, this time south of the Rio Grande. Indeed, the one project that seems to have been closer to his heart than his purse was first drawn to his attention by the man who had once been Jameson's chief scout for the British South Africa Company forces in the early 1890s, Major Frederick R Burnham.[80]

In 1909, just months before the outbreak of the Mexican Revolution, Burnham, who had acquired a concession in Sonora during the heyday of the Diaz dictatorship, persuaded Hammond and other partners to underwrite the flotation of the ill-fated Yaqui Delta Land and Water Company.

Hammond saw the vast estate, some 60 000 hectares in extent, as part of a colonisation scheme underpinned by American settlers locked into smaller-scale commercial farms, and hoped that, if the project proved successful, it might also become a winter holiday retreat for members of the wealthy East and West Coast elite whom he cultivated in his search for personal power.[81]

Increasingly unsettled times and revolutionary contestation of ownership, however, required the increasing militarisation of the company town and settler properties abutting the Yaqui River, in order to protect lives and safeguard investments. In Hammond's mind, developments on Mexican property originally acquired by concession from a dictator must have recalled Rhodes's British South Africa Company, itself based on a much-disputed concession supposedly granted by an African chief and which, through imperial magic, eventually mutated into a Royal Charter.

Burnham's physical presence on the estate reinforced a tendency on Hammond's part to sometimes see the Yaqui Delta Company as if through Rhodes's eyes. And as security on the estate deteriorated, Hammond tried to draw in yet another man with experience of southern African warfare, the Anglo-Boer War veteran General Ben Viljoen. In 1909, Hammond supported an unsuccessful attempt by the General to secure the position of Collector of Customs at El Paso – a border town long notorious for gun-smuggling. The always impecunious Viljoen nevertheless remained active in Mexico and, according to Hammond, benefited from many – unspecified – 'acts of friendship'.

In 1911, General Viljoen also had to grapple with Yaqui Delta Company interests when he failed to settle a dispute about land ownership with the indigenous Yaqui Indians. Burnham's response, in 1912, was to raise a private army of over 500 fully armed men that took up positions around the river. But a few months later, when that too, failed to stem the tide of Mexican resistance, Hammond attempted a self-aggrandising stunt inspired directly by southern African experiences of colonial warfare. Copying Rhodes, who, in 1896, had gone into the Matopos to parley for peace with Ndebele chiefs, Hammond and Burnham offered to ride into the Sierra Madre 'unarmed' and try to make peace with the Yaquis.[82] In a post-frontier America trying to cling to notions of courage and manliness in the face of growing affluence, Hammond had turned to 'Rhodesia' for inspiration, knowing that, other than Burnham, few if any of his countrymen would know from where exactly they had purloined their idea. But the initiative came to nothing and by 1916 the estate, eventually sold in 1927, was falling into disrepair.[83]

In retrospect, it is clear that John Hays Hammond was a dangerous, romantic, capitalist visionary. In a ceaseless quest to enhance his own influence or the power of his heroes on two continents, Hammond could be inspired by anything ranging from the San Francisco Vigilance Committee of 1851 and

William Walker's filibustering exploits of 1853–1854 to Asbury Harpending's attempt in 1861 to stage a coup d'état and create a 'Pacific Republic' at the outbreak of the Civil War and the British drive to colonise southern Africa in the 1890s. However, Hammond's drive for political influence was matched, if not surpassed, by his ruthless cultivation of the economic muscle necessary to enhance his quest for money and display of wealth.

In a never-ending effort to link financial and political power more effectively, Hammond bestrode the modern world, operating east or west of Greenwich, or north or south of the equator, with equal ease, and he did so in the twenty years – 1890 to 1910 – that, more than any other period, marked the expansion of the United States' formal and informal empires. Hammond took his experiences of capitalism in America during the Gilded Age to southern Africa, and then brought his southern African experiences back to North America in his attempts to further colonialism and imperialism in Mexico during its revolutionary epoch.

It is against this broad backdrop, then – that of American and global history – that Dr Jameson's Raid needs to interrogated anew and re-positioned in a way that transcends the narrow parameters hitherto imposed on it by British and South African historiography. Setting aside for the moment the initial, unsuccessful attempt to get the United States to annex Hawaii, in 1893, the Jameson Raid may, in fact, have been the very first explosive episode in a decade that witnessed America's greatest push to extend its formal and informal empires. Seen from that angle, Hammond's folly – Jameson's Raid – lies at one end of a spectrum that stretches from unsanctioned American adventurism in southern Africa, in 1895, to the formal annexation of Hawaii in 1898 and the Spanish-American War of 1898–1902.

South African history, as characterised in most of the existing literature, is seen as having been scarred by a series of catastrophic, interlinked events that are of a piece – the Jameson Raid, the Anglo-Boer War (1899–1902), the reconstruction regime of the post-war British administration (1902–1906) and the awkward handing-over of political power to Afrikaner nationalist governments (1907), followed by the almost indecent haste that characterised the South African Act of Union (1910). These events, and the betrayal of African rights that accompanied them, in turn laid the foundations for decades of increasing urban and rural segregation, which, after 1948, metamorphosed into the abomination of grand apartheid – the master plan for white racial domination of every single aspect of economic, political and social life.

Nothing can change that chain of historical events if that is how they are to be seen and threaded together. But, what *can* change and be debated anew is the strength of the explanatory value that we attach to each of the links in that chain of causality, and there is no better place to start the process of critical re-examination than right at the beginning.

That the Jameson Raid was, in essence, a conspiracy by urban capital-ists to overthrow a conservative rural elite rooted in a republic founded on agricultural production so as to further hasten, deepen and entrench the emerging privileges of an internationally owned gold mining industry is irrefutable. But, whereas in the past it has been accepted, in the main, that the origins of the attempted coup of 1895 lay almost entirely within a vec-tor mapped and led by Rhodes and Jameson, who, with the help of Joseph Chamberlain, were intent on achieving a political and economic outcome that would eventually find a home in the British Empire, that is no longer self-evident. But, even if we continue to accept that blinkered version of history it has to be refined so as to include the machinations of a small Boer fifth column, composed largely of urban Afrikaner professionals who were already reconciled to the notion of an economy that would no longer be agricultural-industrial but industrial-agricultural, and who were ready to give their political backing to the disaffected Vice President of the republic, General Piet Joubert.

More fundamentally, however, it now seems necessary to view the ideas underlying the Jameson Raid as emanating not only from those Rand min-ing capitalists who looked to the City and Downing Street, but also from an extremely powerful set of American engineers with huge personal holdings in the gold mines who were motivated by business and political interests in Washington, DC, and on Wall Street, and who were actively fashioning an informal empire for the United States in the 1890s.

The British conspirators behind the Jameson Raid always sought an imperial outcome as the end-product of their machinations, albeit one that would need additional sequencing after the installation of a more sympathetic 'provisional government' in a still-independent republic. The Americans, too, wished to see a more sympathetic Boer government in control of an independent republic, but they also wanted a special District of Columbia-like dispensation for the Witwatersrand that, in the fullness of time, might fall within the ambit of the United States' informal empire.

The Jameson Raid started out as a joint Anglo-American conspiracy precisely because both parties sought to install mutually agreed-upon col-laborators in a refashioned Boer government, but neither party was averse to treachery because, privately, they differed as to the end-result – the one wanting to see the Zuid-Afrikaansche Republiek formally incorporated into the British Empire and the other seeking to absorb it into an informal American empire that was on the very threshold of dramatic expansion.

And at the centre of this complicated, diverging, fatally flawed 'Anglo-Saxon' capitalist conspiracy stood a dreamy, cross-cultural industrial visionary – an extremely complex, ambitious and ruthless American entrepreneur, one mesmerised by the trappings of British aristocracy and its expanding empire. On the one hand, he hero-worshipped Rhodes and his supposedly civilising mission, while on the other he could slither back to America, read the contours of the corrupt Gilded Age and politically seduce a President who was incapable of formulating foreign policy, thereby allowing him to colonise, exploit and subvert Mexican independence.

His name was John Hays Hammond, and while in Kruger's republic he wore the attractive mask of American capitalism, efficiency and modernity. But those of us who are interested in understanding the Jameson Raid and tragic history of 20th-century South Africa should be warned not to look into the eyes of the man behind the mask, but instead to listen to how and what he had to say when he spoke; it was the voice of the Confederacy, of the Old South, of racism and slavery. In the short and the longer term, it may have mattered very little whether the American or the British version of the conspiracy of 1895 had succeeded; both pathways led to industrialisation and racial subjugation. The deepest roots of the South African tragedy lie as much in the northern hemisphere as do they in the southern.

Notes

INTRODUCTION

1 See JH Wilkins (ed), *The Great Diamond Hoax and other Stirring Incidents in the Life of Asbury Harpending* (San Francisco, 1913) – from Chapter 3 of an electronic version without page numbers.

2 In his late sixties, when working outside the framework of the law was less possible, Hammond laid out his views on what was needed and how it was best achieved in JH Hammond and JW Jenks, *Great American Issues: Political, Social and Economic (A Constructive Study)* (New York, 1923).

3 See I Colvin, *The Life of Jameson, Vol 1* (London, 1922), pp 306–314.

4 See JH Hammond, 'South African Memories: Rhodes-Barnato-Burnham', *Scribner's Magazine*, Vol LXIX, No 3, March 1921, pp 257–278.

5 On this crucial point, which demonstrates how Hammond rather than Rhodes was at the cutting edge of revolutionary thought on the Rand, see WT Stead, *The Americanisation of the World or The Trend of the Twentieth Century* (London, 1902), p 30.

6 On the changing political climate in the United States in the 1890s, see KL Hoganson, *Fighting for American Manhood: How Gender Politics Provoked the Spanish-American and Philippine-American Wars* (London, 1998).

7 The men behind the Jameson Raid, argued Davis, '… were acting for the best good of the country, in trying to overthrow the Boer Government, as did the revolutionists of 1776 in our own country, or as do the rebels in Cuba at the present day' – RH Davis, *Dr Jameson's Raiders vs The Johannesburg Reformers* (New York, 1897), p 15.

8 A Ireland, 'The True Story of the Jameson Raid as Related to me by John Hays Hammond', *The North American Review*, Vol 208, No 753 and 754, August and September 1918, pp 185–196 and 365–376.

9 *Electrical Engineer*, Vol 55, No 7, July 1936, p 835.

CHAPTER 1

1 The attitudes, beliefs and visions of the three men on the mining safari are all beautifully captured and preserved in JH Hammond, 'South African Memories: Rhodes-Barnato-Burnham', *Scribner's Magazine*, Vol LXIX, No 3, March 1921, pp 257–278 [hereafter Hammond, 'Memories'].

2 See I Colvin, *The Life of Jameson, Vol 1* (London, 1922), p 307 [hereafter Colvin, *Jameson 1*] and, on Hammond's trauma and inflated assessment of the revolutionary potential of the Witwatersrand in the mid-1890s, see below Chapters 10 and 11.

3 See especially Colvin, *Jameson 1*, pp 171–218.

4 As reported in the *Morning Oregonian*, 29 March 1902.

5 JH Hammond, *The Autobiography of John Hays Hammond, Vol 1*, (New York, 1935), p 290 [hereafter Hammond, *Autobiography 1*].

6 The British allowed the old Roman-Dutch legal system to remain in place in the Cape Colony in the early 19th century and, in 1844, the South African Republic – the

Zuid-Afrikaansche Republiek – in turn adopted Cape law – see HR Halho and E Kahn, *The South African Legal System and its Background* (Johannesburg, 1973), pp 575–578.

7 See the 'Introduction' to JG Kotzé, *Memoirs and Reminiscences* (Cape Town, 1934).

8 See CH Muller, 'Policing the Witwatersrand: A History of the South African Republic Police', unpublished DPhil thesis, Centre for Africa Studies, University of the Free State, 2016 [hereafter Muller, 'Policing the Witwatersrand']. See also, Chapter 10, 'Organised Crime in a Frontier Town: Johannesburg, the Kruger State and the Depression of 1889–1892' in C van Onselen, *Showdown at the Red Lion: The Life and Times of Jack McLoughlin, 1859–1910* (Cape Town, 2014) [hereafter van Onselen, *Showdown at the Red Lion*].

9 See C van Onselen, *Masked Raiders: Irish Banditry in Southern Africa, 1880–1889* (Cape Town, 2010), pp 30–32, 36–40 and 88–90 [hereafter van Onselen, *Masked Raiders*].

10 As a prominent Johannesburg attorney who later became a member of the 'Reform Committee' noted: 'In 1890, a conspiracy was on foot to seize the artillery barracks and magazines at Pretoria as well as the public offices and members of the Executive Committee.' FW Bell, *The South African Conspiracy or the Aims of Afrikanerdom* (London, 1900), p 11.

11 For the disapproval that such punishment excited in the minds of members of the Reform Committee and those who were implicated in the Jameson Raid conspiracy, and its use for political propaganda purposes by the mining houses, see, for example, 'Life in Gaol', JP FitzPatrick, *The Transvaal from Within: A Private Record of Public Affairs* (London, 1899), pp 160–177 [hereafter FitzPatrick, *Transvaal from Within*].

12 On the Kruger government's attempt to cope with the emergence of organised white crime and resistance in the prisons during the depression of 1889–1892, see Chapter 10 in van Onselen, *Showdown at the Red Lion* and van Onselen, *Masked Raiders*, pp 75–92.

13 See especially CT Gordon, *The Growth of Boer Opposition to Kruger, 1890–1895* (London, 1970), pp 102 and 108 [hereafter Gordon, *Boer Opposition*].

14 See, for example, Gordon, *Boer Opposition*, p 89.

15 South African National Library, Cape Town, Lord Henry de Villiers Collection, MSC7, Vol 10, File 3, Extract from a letter written by Lionel Phillips to Alfred Beit, Johannesburg, dated 26 March 1894. I am indebted to Johan Bergh for drawing this and other items relating to the Kruger administration to my attention.

16 See C van Onselen, *The Fox and the Flies: The World of Joseph Silver, Racketeer & Psychopath* (London, 2008), p 175.

17 See Gordon, *Boer Opposition*, pp 165–167. For the Jameson Raid conspirators' view of the mobilisation of men without the franchise and representation in the legislature see Hammond, *Autobiography 1*, p 314, and/or FitzPatrick, *Transvaal from Within*, pp 55–56.

18 Gordon, *Boer Opposition*, p 98.

19 *Ibid*, pp 16 and 254.

20 See, for example, FitzPatrick, *Transvaal from Within*, pp 47–50, or Hammond, *Autobiography 1*, pp 316–319.

21 For an overview of the period and its problems, see also 'The World the Mineowners Made' in C van Onselen, *New Babylon, New Nineveh: Everyday Life on the Witwatersrand* (Cape Town, 2001), pp 1–27 [hereafter van Onselen, *New Babylon, New Nineveh*].

22 On 'foreign Jews' and Gillingham, see, for example, Gordon, *Boer Opposition*, pp 10, 39 and 45; and on Gillingham, more generally, J Hyslop, *The Notorious Syndicalist. J.T. Bain: A Scottish Rebel in Colonial South Africa* (Johannesburg, 2004), pp 100–102 [hereafter Hyslop, *The Notorious Syndicalist*].

23 See Gordon, *Boer Opposition*, pp 63 and 70.

24 Bread, for example, cost three times what it cost in America, Australia or Europe; Gordon, *Boer Opposition*, p 32.

25 See Gordon, *Boer Opposition*, pp 21–23 and 100–110.

26 See especially Gordon, *Boer Opposition*, pp 111–126 and, from a reformist perspective, FitzPatrick, *Transvaal from Within*, pp 71–73.

27 For the wider context of this and other developments in working-class culture in Johannesburg during the early 1890s, see van Onselen, *Showdown at the Red Lion*, Chapter 13.

28 See EN Katz, *A Trade Union Aristocracy* (Johannesburg 1976), p 22, and HJ and RE Simons, *Class and Colour in South Africa, 1850–1950* (Harmondsworth, 1969), p 53 [hereafter Simons, *Class and Colour*].

29 Simons, *Class and Colour*, p 55.

30 For the context of 1889–1892, see 'The Parameters of Popular Support: Criminal Heroes, Outlaw Legends and Social Bandits' in van Onselen, *Masked Raiders*, pp 139–161; and van Onselen, 'Organised Crime in a Frontier Town: Johannesburg, the Kruger State and the Depression of 1889–1892', in *Showdown at the Red Lion*, Chapter 10.

31 On illicit gold theft, see van Onselen, *Showdown at the Red Lion*, Chapter 17; and for the concern that this type of activity elicited in the mind of one of the chief conspirators, FitzPatrick, *Transvaal from Within*, p 182. On the illicit sale of alcohol and organised prostitution see van Onselen, *New Babylon, New Nineveh*, pp 71–72 and 119–120.

32 See van Onselen, *Showdown at the Red Lion*, Chapter 17.

33 See Gordon, *Boer Opposition*, pp 17 and 97–98.
34 See especially TJ Makhura, 'The Neglected Role of the Boer-Bagananwa War in the Jameson Raid' in J Carruthers (ed), *The Jameson Raid: A Centennial Perspective* (Johannesburg, 1996), p 116 [hereafter Carruthers, *Centennial Perspective*]. See also Fitzpatrick, *Transvaal from Within*, pp 55–56.
35 See FE Garrett and EJ Edwards, *The Story of an African Crisis and of the Jameson Raid* (London, 1897), pp 34–35 [hereafter Garrett and Edwards, *African Crisis*]. It should be noted that such talk, which dated back to at least July 1894, would have fed directly into Hammond's Matabeleland campfire prognostications the following month.
36 See Hammond, *Autobiography 1*, pp 341–342.
37 See especially HJG Kamffer, '*Om een scherpe oog in't zeil te houden*: Die Geheime Diens in die Zuid-Afrikaansche Republiek', unpublished DPhil thesis, Potchefstroomse Universiteit vir Christelike Hoër Onderwys, 1999, Chapter 1, pp 51–71. See GN van den Bergh, 'Secret Service in the South African Republic, 1895–1900', *Military History Journal*, Vol 3, No 2, December 1974, pp 1–11 [hereafter van den Bergh, 'Secret Service']. On the 'Secret Service Fund' as a source of political friction, see Charles Leonard's famous 'manifesto', as reproduced in FitzPatrick, *Transvaal from Within*, p 285.
38 Hylsop, *The Notorious Syndicalist*, p 108.
39 Van den Bergh, 'Secret Service', p 3. At some point after October 1894, however, the very ambitious Esselen also became a leading member of a Boer fifth column that worked closely with the Jameson Raid conspirators – see below, Chapters 15–17.
40 See G Cuthbertson, 'A Century of the Raid' in Carruthers, *Centennial Perspective*, p 2.
41 Hammond, 'Memories', p 272. For early leaks about Jameson's Raid, see, for example, Garrett and Edwards, *African Crisis*, p 66.
42 See C Ash, *The IF Man. Dr Leander Starr Jameson: The Inspiration for Kipling's Masterpiece* (Solihull, 2012), p 233.
43 On bureaucratic infighting among members of the Boer elite in 1894–1895, see Muller, 'Policing the Witwatersrand', Chapter 3, pp 46–99. By August 1895, the coming clash was already being debated in the Volksraad and reported on in the Pretoria press; see Gordon, *Boer Opposition*, p 157.
44 See especially the section on 'The Policy of Force' in Charles Leonard's manifesto, as reproduced in FitzPatrick, *Transvaal from Within*, pp 289–290.
45 See Gordon, *Boer Opposition*, p 35 and, more especially, FitzPatrick, *Transvaal from Within*, pp 49–50.
46 Gordon, *Boer Opposition*, pp 45–46.
47 See entry on EA Esselen in CJ Beyers and

JL Basson (eds), *Dictionary of South African Biography, Vol 5* (Pretoria, 1987), pp 248–249.
48 On Esselen – a figure worthy of a biography – and 'Young South Africa' see, for example, Gordon, *Boer Opposition*, pp 30, 84, 186 and, perhaps especially, p 269. Gordon is of the opinion that 'Young South Africa' suffered an early demise but this may be open to question. As late as 1898, it was obviously still capable of reaching out to progressive young nationalists including JC Smuts's outstanding protégé, FRM Cleaver. On Cleaver and his career of fighting organised crime in Johannesburg in the late 1890s, see *A Young South African: A Memoir of Ferrar Mostyn Cleaver, Advocate and Fieldcornet* (Johannesburg, 1913), edited by 'His Mother'; and C van Onselen, 'The Modernising of the Kruger State: FET Krause and JC Smuts and the Struggle for the Control of the Johannesburg Public Prosecutor's Office, 1889–99', *Law and History Review*, Vol 21, No 3, Fall 2003, pp 483–525.
49 On Kotzé and the *Vierkleur* newspaper, see Gordon, *Boer Opposition*, pp 38–39 and 260–261. For the Chief Justice's views of the Kruger era, see Kotzé, *Memoirs and Reminiscences, Vol 2*.
50 See Chapter 10, 'Organised Crime in a Frontier Town: Johannesburg, the Kruger State and the Depression of 1889–1902' in van Onselen, *Showdown at the Red Lion*.
51 Gordon, *Boer Opposition*, pp 188–189.
52 Gordon, *Boer Opposition*, pp 79–83. Predictably, the Selati Railway Company scandal became a favourite topic for the Jameson Raid conspirators; see FitzPatrick, *Transvaal from Within*, pp 48–49.
53 Gordon, *Boer Opposition*, pp 98–111.
54 See Gordon, *Boer Opposition*, pp 229–245.
55 For the wider context, see van Onselen, *Showdown at the Red Lion*, Chapter 13.
56 FitzPatrick, *Transvaal from Within*, p 55.

CHAPTER 2

1 Notable exceptions are CT Keto, 'The Aftermath of the Jameson Raid and American Decision Making in Foreign Affairs, 1896', *Transactions of the American Philosophical Society*, New Series, Vol 70, No 8, 1980, pp 1–46; and LE Meyer, *The Farther Frontier: Six Case Studies of Americans and Africa, 1848–1936* (London, 1992), which, in Chapter 5, takes a close look at 'John Hays Hammond and the Jameson Raid: Engineering a Capitalist Revolution in South Africa', pp 128–159 [hereafter Meyer, *The Farther Frontier*].
2 See 'Inside History – Chief Agitators were Americans', *Evening Post* (New Zealand), Vol LXXXll, No 10, 19 November 1911.

3 See WT Stead, *The Americanisation of the World* (New York, 1902), pp 56–57 [hereafter Stead, *Americanisation of the World*]. On Rhodes's fears of a strong, independent republic, see also I Colvin, *The Life of Jameson, Vol 1* (London, 1922), p 312, and *Vol 2*, pp 14–15.

4 Part of the constitution of the Orange Free State was copied word for word from the Constitution of the United States; see H Giliomee, "'n Ideale Gemenebes in Afrika-Omstandighede": Die Vrystaatse Republiek, *1854–1900*' in D Langer, *Republiek van die Oranje-Vrystaat* (Pretoria, 2014), pp 15–16.

5 E Rosenthal, *Stars and Stripes in Africa* (Cape Town, 1968), p 129 [hereafter Rosenthal, *Stars and Stripes*].

6 HC Hillegas, *Oom Paul's People* (New York, 1900), Chapter 6 [no page numbers].

7 See R Rotberg and MF Shore, 'Rhodes CJ' in HCG Matthew and B Harrison (eds), *The Oxford National Dictionary of Biography* (Oxford, 2004), pp 596–597.

8 See JH Hammond, 'South African Memories: Rhodes-Barnato-Burnham', *Scribner's Magazine*, Vol LXIX, No 3, March 1924, p 276.

9 See CT Gordon, *The Growth of Boer Opposition to Kruger, 1890–1895* (London, 1970), p 141 [hereafter Gordon, *Boer Opposition*].

10 See especially Gordon, *Boer Opposition*, p 201 and pp 256–259. I am indebted to Johan Bergh for drawing my attention to Kotzé's letter to *De Volksstem* of 10 August 1892.

11 E de Waal, 'The Part Played by Americans on the Witwatersrand during the Period 1886–1899', unpublished MA dissertation, Department of History, Unisa, 1971, p 165 [hereafter de Waal, 'Americans on the Witwatersrand'].

12 See Chapter 6 of Hillegas, *Oom Paul's People*; and J Wardner, *Jim Wardner of Wardner, Idaho* (New York, 1900), p 126 [hereafter Wardner, *Jim Wardner*]. See also de Waal, 'Americans on the Witwatersrand', p 167.

13 Paragraph constructed from de Waal, 'Americans on the Witwatersrand', pp 166–167, Wardner, *Jim Wardner*, pp 127–128, and CC Spence, *Mining Engineers and the American West: The Lace-Boot Brigade* (New Haven 1970), pp 308–309 [hereafter Spence, *Lace-Boot Brigade*].

14 The leading importer of West Australian timber was W ('Karri') Davies, who became a prominent member of the Reform Committee. Davies was an imperialist and may not have been the type of *Sydney Bulletin* Australian nationalist that Rhodes feared, although 'he stepped easily into the small and intimate circle in which Rhodes revealed himself' – according to the *Sunday Times* (Perth), 2 January 1927. See also 'The Late Colonel Karri Davies – A Servant of Empire' elsewhere in the same edition of the

Perth *Sunday Times*. It may, therefore, have been other Australians, who had entered Johannesburg in some numbers after the depression of 1892, whom Davies knew and whom he may have conveyed to Rhodes as having been 'Sydney Bulletin nationalists' in the making.

15 See especially Chapter 11 in Hillegas, *Oom Paul's People*, for an account of timber imports from the USA.

16 See de Waal, 'Americans on the Witwatersrand', p 169.

17 Lingham's important role and influence in the development of Delagoa Bay and the Witwatersrand can be traced in articles in the *San Francisco Call*, 21 April 1897; *New York Times*, 11 July 1895; and the *New Zealand Herald*, 15 July 1899. See also JH Hammond, *The Autobiography of John Hays Hammond, Vol 1* (New York, 1935), p 303 [hereafter Hammond, *Autobiography 1*].

18 Wardner, *Jim Wardner*, p 127.

19 Interestingly, however, none of these shipping lines flew the American flag, which probably indicated the vagaries of passages that could not easily sustain two-way trade. See Hillegas, *Oom Paul's People*, Chapter 11; and Wardner, *Jim Wardner*, p 127.

20 See Rosenthal, *Stars and Stripes*, p 123; and C van Onselen, *Masked Raiders: Irish Banditry in Southern Africa, 1880–1899* (Cape Town, 2010), p 74 [hereafter van Onselen, *Masked Raiders*].

21 See Gordon, *Boer Opposition*, pp 17–18 and 95. For the State President's take on the spider scandal, see, for example, 'De Spijderkwestie', in *De Volksstem*, 13 April, 1891.

22 Hammond, *Autobiography 1*, p 263.

23 See especially Wardner, *Jim Wardner*, pp 126–128; and Hillegas, *Oom Paul's People*, Chapter 11.

24 Wardner, *Jim Wardner*, p 128.

25 Hammond, *Autobiography 1*, p 270.

26 *Ibid*, pp 270–271.

27 Stead, *Americanisation of the World*, pp 56–57.

28 Wardner, *Jim Wardner*, p 126.

29 De Waal, 'Americans on the Witwatersrand', p 173.

30 Hillegas, *Oom Paul's People*, Chapter 11.

31 See, for example, M Nkosi, 'American Mining Engineers in the Kimberley and Witwatersrand Mines circa the turn of the 20th Century', paper presented at the 9th International Mining History Congress, Johannesburg, 17–20 April 2012; and the retrospective on 'American Uitlanders said to Dominate in the Gold Fields', *Chicago Tribune*, 18 March 1900.

32 For the wider context, see Chapters 10 and 17 of C van Onselen, *Showdown at the Red Lion: The Life and Times of Jack McLoughlin, 1859–1910* (Cape Town, 2015).

33 *The Star*, 2 September 1893.

34 For examples of revolver use on and around the Witwatersrand, see F Vane, *Back to the Mines or Tailings from the Randt* (London, 1902), pp 122, 162 and 182; and FE Garrett and EJ Edwards, *The Story of an African Crisis and of the Jameson Raid* (London, 1897), p 125 [hereafter Garrett and Edwards, *African Crisis*].

35 See Hammond, *Autobiography 1*, p 31. Hammond, however, explicitly rejected the idea that Johannesburg could be compared with anything out of a Harte novel – see de Waal, 'Americans on the Witwatersrand', p 189.

36 See van Onselen, *Masked Raiders*, pp 45–46.

37 Hillegas, *Oom Paul's People*, Chapter 11.

38 See V Erlmann, 'Orpheus McAdoo and the Virginian Jubilee Singers in South Africa, 1890–1898', *Journal of Southern African Studies*, Vol 14, No 3, April 1988, pp 331–350.

39 See de Waal, 'Americans on the Witwatersrand', p 184, but, more especially, JT Campbell, *Songs of Zion: The African Methodist Episcopal Church in the United States and South Africa* (New York, 1995), pp 120–121 and 147–148.

40 As, for example, in Wakkerstroom; see J Cabrita, 'People of Adam: Divine Healing and Racial Cosmopolitanism in the Early Twentieth-Century Transvaal, South Africa', *Comparative Studies in Society and History*, Vol 57, No 2, April 2015, pp 1–36 [hereafter Cabrita, 'Divine Healing']; and de Waal, 'Americans on the Witwatersrand', pp 184–185.

41 See Cabrita, 'Divine Healing', p 14; and de Waal, 'Americans on the Witwatersrand', p 186.

42 On Natalie Hammond in high society in Washington, DC, including at least one other person drawn from her Johannesburg set of yesteryear, see 'New Social Bosses in the Nation's Capital', *Los Angeles Times*, 23 November 1913.

43 De Waal, 'Americans on the Witwatersrand', pp 45–46 and 189–190.

44 *Ibid*, p 190.

45 So, for example, Hammond is cast as a 'circumspect head engineer' by Meyer, in *The Farther Frontier*, p 135. Likewise, Jaffe, in her essay on 'John Hays Hammond' in J Carruthers (ed), *The Jameson Raid: A Centennial Perspective* (Johannesburg, 1996), p 221, casts Hammond's interest as an engineer as the primary motivation for his involvement in the Raid [hereafter Jaffe, 'John Hays Hammond'].

46 As well as powerful speculators; see especially 'A Mining Bubble that will Soon Burst', *San Francisco Chronicle*, 13 October 1895.

47 As quoted in Spence, *Lace-Boot Brigade*, p 133.

48 *Ibid*, p 274.

49 Republic of South Africa, Grahamstown, Rhodes University, Cory Library, Gold Fields Collection, MS 16 087, CD Rudd to Captain

EF Rhodes, 16 November 1894, and HEM Davies to EF Rhodes, 29 November 1894. See also Meyer, *The Farther Frontier*, pp 130–131.

50 Spence, *Lace-Boot Brigade*, p 307.

51 As quoted in Jaffe, 'John Hays Hammond', p 222.

52 As Hammond put it, 'Many of us were on the Rand only temporarily' – Hammond, *Autobiography 1*, p 317.

53 'Major Colman Gets a Fair Plum', *San Francisco Call*, Vol 112, No 67, 6 August 1912.

54 Some of this background is best traced in Spence, *Lace-Boot Brigade*, p 307. Curiously, this strong South African connection is not explored more fully in RH Peterson, *The Bonanza Kings: The Social Origins and Business Behaviour of Western Mining Entrepreneurs, 1870–1900* (London, 1971). Some idea of the background and wealth of the Butters family, for example, including that of Charles Butters's brother, Henry Butters, can be gleaned from 'Henry Butters, Famous Man of Millions, Dies', *San Francisco Call*, Vol 104, No 149, 27 October 1908.

55 See Spence, *Lace-Boot Brigade*, p 307. The same network can be traced in YGM Lulat, *United States Relations with South Africa: A Critical Overview from the Colonial Period to the Present* (New York, 2008), pp 34–35.

56 See de Waal, 'Americans on the Witwatersrand', p 51; and Hammond, *Autobiography 1*, p 330.

57 See, for example, Garrett and Edwards, *African Crisis*, p 60; and Hammond, *Autobiography 1*, p 320.

58 Spence, *Lace-Boot Brigade*, p 353.

59 These developments can be tracked, in a chapter on 'Prostitutes and Proletarians, 1886–1914', in C van Onselen, *New Babylon, New Nineveh: Everyday Life on the Witwatersrand, 1886–1914* (Cape Town, 2001), pp 109–164. Joseph Silver's career, including the part of it that played out in Johannesburg, is recounted in C van Onselen, *The Fox and the Flies* (London, 2008), pp 145–180.

60 On Rhodes's fears, see especially Stead, *Americanisation of the World*, pp 56–57.

61 United Kingdom, Oxford University, Bodleian Library, Rhodes House, John Hays Hammond Collection, Private Letter Book, 9 March 1896 to 5 June 1897, JH Hammond to P Bigelow Esq, 28 August 1896.

CHAPTER 3

1 For some insight into RP Hammond's business methods and probity, see 'Board of Audit after Facts', *San Francisco Call*, 27 May 1893; and PW Gates, *Land and Law in California: Essays on Land Politics* (West Lafayette, IN, 2002), p 82.

2 On RP Hammond's trajectory within the Democratic Party in city and state, see the retrospectives offered in the *Daily Alta*, Vol 42, No 13639, 3 January 1897, and the *Los Angeles Herald*, 12 August 1907. See also HH Bancroft, *History of California*, Vol 6 (San Francisco, 1888). The Broderick faction to which RP Hammond and the filibuster William Walker both belonged is also alluded to in RE May, *The Southern Dream of a Caribbean Empire* (Gainesville, FL, 2002), p 79 [hereafter May, *Southern Dream*].

3 For the wider context of RP Hammond's dismissal, see Chapter 5 of WT Sherman, *Memoirs of General W.T. Sherman, Vol 1* (New York, 1889).

4 Some of RP Hammond's background is to be found in JH Hammond's *The Autobiography of John Hays Hammond, Vol. 1* (New York, 1935), pp 1–32 [hereafter Hammond, *Autobiography 1*]. The best short overview of RP Hammond's career, however, is to be found in an obituary, 'At Three Score Years and Ten – Death of Police Commissioner RP Hammond', *San Francisco Call*, Vol 70, No 175, 29 November 1891 [hereafter 'RP Hammond', *San Francisco Call*, 1891]. These sanitised versions, however, have to be supplemented by readings from other sources. John Hays Hammond, predictably, was of the view that his father had a 'reputation for absolute integrity'; see Hammond, *Autobiography 1*, p 114.

5 See G Brechin, *Imperial San Francisco: Urban Power and Earthly Ruin* (Los Angeles, 2006), pp 81–82 [hereafter Brechin, *Imperial San Francisco*], which outlines how RP Hammond and 'Coffee' Hays, along with a cousin of John Hays Hammond, constituted the family members of a tightly knit economic operation.

6 See Hammond, *Autobiography 1*, pp 3–25.

7 'RP Hammond', *San Francisco Call*, 1891.

8 On the telling of such tales to the boy, see Hammond, *Autobiography 1*, p 9, and, on his maxim about law enforcement, p 81.

9 See especially GR Stewart, *Committee of Vigilance: Revolution in San Francisco, 1851* (Boston, 1964) [hereafter Stewart, *Committee of Vigilance*]; and, for the important roles of Coleman and Hays, Hammond, *Autobiography 1*, p 9.

10 For 'Coffee' Hays's dealings with the Vigilance Committee, see, for example, Stewart, *Committee of Vigilance*, pp 30 and 260–264.

11 Hammond, *Autobiography 1*, p 17.

12 See especially May, *Southern Dream*, p 3; and CJ Nolan (ed), *The Greenwood Encyclopedia of International Relations, Vol 2* (Westport, 2002), p 544.

13 See May, *Southern Dream*, pp 3–76, and, more generally, RE May, *Manifest Destiny's Underworld: Filibustering in Antebellum America* (Chapel Hill, NC, 2002) [hereafter May, *Manifest Destiny's Underworld*]. And, for a wonderfully detailed study of American expansionist dreams in Cuba, see R Paquette, *Sugar is Made with Blood: The Conspiracy of La Escalera and the Conflict between Empires over Slaves in Cuba* (Middletown, CT, 1990).

14 For the wider context, see also F Juda, 'California Filibusters: A History of their Expeditions into Hispanic America', *The Grizzly Bear*, Vol XXI, No 4, February 1919; and May, *Southern Dream*, pp 46–76.

15 See also B Harrison, *Agent of Empire: William Walker and the Imperial Self in American Literature* (Athens, GA, 2004), and, more particularly, p 193, where Walker's standing in US history is bemoaned by RH Davis, the journalist that JH Hammond later used to propagate his version of the Jameson Raid. On William Walker in San Francisco and his interactions with RP Hammond and 'Coffee' Hays in the 1850s, see May, *Manifest Destiny's Underworld*, pp 122, 125 and 133–134; and May, *Southern Dream*, pp 79, 83, 90, 178–181.

16 See WO Scroggs, *Filibusters and Financiers: The Story of William Walker and his Associates* (New York, 1916), Chapter 4, 'The Raid on Lower California'.

17 See May, *Southern Dream*, p 181.

18 See RK Wyllys, 'The Republic of Lower California', *Pacific Historical Review*, Vol 2, No 2, 1933, pp 194–213, and the works of May as cited immediately above, in notes 15 and 17. The likely importance of filibustering and the Walker incident to the emerging world view of John Hays Hammond is explored in greater detail in the Conclusion to this volume.

19 See RA Courtemanche, 'The Royal Navy and the End of William Walker', *The Historian*, Vol 30, No 3, May 1968, pp 35–365; and May, *Southern Dream*, pp 77–110.

20 See L Richards, *The California Gold Rush and the Coming of the Civil War* (New York, 2007), pp 230–235.

21 See Hammond, *Autobiography 1*, p 22.

22 JH Wilkins, *The Great Diamond Hoax and Other Stirring Incidents in the Life of Asbury Harpending* (San Francisco, 1913), p 29. The influence of the San Francisco conspiracy on Hammond's planning of the Jameson Raid is more fully explored in Chapter 11 below and in the Conclusion.

23 Hammond, *Autobiography 1*, pp 18–23.

24 These formative influences are recounted in Hammond, *Autobiography 1*, pp 26–30. Not showing cowardice became something of an obsession for Hammond; see, for example, *Autobiography 1*, p 163 and other examples below.

25 See, for example, Hammond, *Autobiography 1*, pp 82 and 162.

26 Hammond, *Autobiography 1*, p 188.

27 Hammond, *Autobiography 1*, p 195.

28 As quoted in CC Spence, *Mining Engineers and The American West: The Lace-Boot Brigade, 1849–1933* (New Haven, 1970), p 324 [hereafter Spence, *Lace-Boot Brigade*].

29 Spence, *Lace-Boot Brigade*, p 336; and, from Hammond's *Autobiography 1*, describing life in the Pretoria prison, at p 357, 'Captain Mein increased his reputation as a raconteur, and was usually surrounded by groups listening to his illimitable store of western mining anecdotes.'

30 See Spence, *Lace-Boot Brigade*, p 178, and LE Meyer, *The Farther Frontier: Six Case Studies of Americans and Africa, 1848–1936* (London, 1992), p 159.

31 R Rotberg, *The Founder: Cecil Rhodes and the Pursuit of Power* (Cape Town, 2002), p 508.

32 On the move to Yale and courses taken there, see Hammond, *Autobiography 1*, pp 33–41. Significantly, Hammond later went on, with JW Jenks as co-author, to publish *Great American Issues: Political, Social, Economic (A Constructive Study)* (New York, 1923).

33 Spence, *Lace-Boot Brigade*, p 259.

34 On Hammond's membership of the Freemasons – and his brother's disappointment that a fellow Mason, President Cleveland, appeared to be ineffective in obtaining clemency for Jack Hammond when he was under the death sentence see, 'RP Hammond's Sorrow', *San Francisco Call*, Vol 79, No 151, 26 April 1896.

35 'I heard that the Chicago fellows had gone to *Sigma Delta Chi*', wrote Hammond, 'and as I thought it would be a fine thing to know some Midwesterners well, I went along with them' – see Hammond, *Autobiography 1*, pp 38–48, pp 49–50 and 106. On JL Houghteling and his banking pedigree, see JW Leonard (ed), *The Book of Chicagoans: A Biographical Dictionary of Leading Living Men of the City of Chicago* (Chicago, 1905).

36 Hammond, *Autobiography 1*, p 85.

37 On social life at Freiberg, see Hammond, *Autobiography 1*, pp 63–71.

38 Hammond, *Autobiography 1*, p 72.

39 JH Hammond, *The Autobiography of John Hays Hammond, Vol 2* (New York, 1935), p 741.

40 Hammond, *Autobiography 1*, pp 72–73.

41 *Ibid*, p 73.

42 On the Cornish in the American West, see, for example, Spence, *Lace-Boot Brigade*, pp 366–367, and, on the Rand, P Payton, *Cornwall: A History* (Fowey, 2004), pp 231–232.

43 Hammond, *Autobiography 1*, p 182.

44 On this period, see Hammond, *Autobiography 1*, pp 85–94.

45 *Ibid*, p 107.

46 *Ibid*, p 108.

47 See WA Dym, 'Freiberg on the Frontier: Louis Janin, German Engineering and "Civilisation" in the American West', *Annals of Science*, Vol 68, No 3, 2011, pp 295–323.

48 For Hammond's approval, see *Autobiography 1*, p 109.

49 Hammond, *Autobiography 1*, p 116.

50 *Ibid*, p 115.

51 All of this is based on Chapters 7 and 8 of Hammond's *Autobiography 1*, pp 106–147.

52 Hammond, *Autobiography 1*, p 130. This was a ploy that Hammond was to use later during the Kruger government's attempt to commandeer Uitlanders during the Malaboch campaign of 1894. See also Chapter 10 below.

53 Hammond, *Autobiography 1*, p 129.

54 *Ibid*, p 137.

CHAPTER 4

1 See JH Hammond, *The Autobiography of John Hays Hammond, Vol 1* (New York, 1935), p 116 [hereafter Hammond, *Autobiography 1*].

2 For the way in which these issues played out in northern Idaho – in some ways a world apart – see MD Beal and MW Wells, 'Populism and Free Silver, 1890–1896' in *History of Idaho, Vol 2* (New York, 1959), pp 72–85 [hereafter Beal and Wells, 'Populism and Free Silver']. See also Chapter 2, 'The Silver Movement in the USA' in WJ Lauck, *The Causes of the Panic of 1893* (Boston, 1907).

3 On the founding of the Populist Party and its agricultural bases in the economy, see C Vann Woodward, *Tom Watson: Agrarian Rebel* (Oxford, 1979).

4 Beal and Wells, 'Populism and Free Silver', p 83.

5 Thus it was Hammond who helped win the Union Works the contract for the construction of the battleship USS *Oregon*, see LE Meyer, *The Farther Frontier: Six Case Studies of Americans and Africa, 1848–1936* (London, 1997), p 130.

6 Hammond, *Autobiography 1*, pp 145–146.

7 See especially Hammond, *Autobiography 1*, pp 160–165.

8 Hammond, *Autobiography 1*, p 148.

9 This initiative came on the back of 1886, when the mine was 'booming along' – see J Wardner, *Jim Wardner of Idaho* (New York, 1900), p 72; and for the recommendation of Clement, see Hammond, *Autobiography 1*, p 182. On the financing of the Bunker Hill & Sullivan Mines and Concentrator Co (BHS Co), see also RW Smith, *The Coeur d'Alene Mining War of 1892* (Corvallis, OR, 1961), p 24 [hereafter Smith, *The War of 1892*], and CC Spence, *Mining Engineers and The American West: The Lace-Boot Brigade, 1849–1933* (New Haven, 1970), p 273 [hereafter Spence, *Lace-Boot Brigade*].

10 Spence, *Lace-Boot Brigade*, pp 152–153.

11 Hammond, *Autobiography 1*, p 183.

12 For Hammond's role, see *Autobiography 1*, pp 186–187.

13 Spence, *Lace-Boot Brigade*, p 273.

14 This description of the district is taken, almost as is, from GE French, 'The Coeur d'Alene Riots, 1892', *Overland Monthly and Out West Magazine*, Vol 26, Issue 151, July 1895, pp 32–49 [hereafter French, 'Riots 1892'].

15 For community solidarity within the Coeur d'Alene – to the point of refusing help from outside the valleys – see, for example, 'An Awful Fire', *The Spokane Review*, 29 July 1890.

16 See WJ Gaboury, 'From State House to Bull Pen: Idaho Populism and the Coeur d'Alene Troubles of the 1890s', *Pacific Northwest Quarterly*, Vol LVIII, January 1967, pp 14–22 [hereafter Gaboury, 'State House to Bull Pen']; and French, 'Riots 1892', p 32.

17 See Spence, *Lace-Boot Brigade*, pp 152–153.

18 *Coeur d'Alene Mining Troubles*, Senate Document No 25, 1st Session of the 56th Congress of the United States of America, p 1, prepared by the President of the Federation of Western Miners, Butte, Montana, 15 October 1899 [hereafter Federation of Miners, *Coeur d'Alene Troubles*]. See also, Gaboury, 'State House to Bull Pen', pp 14–22.

19 Federation of Miners, *Coeur d'Alene Troubles*, p 2; and Gaboury, 'State House to Bull Pen', pp 14–22.

20 See Spence, *Lace-Boot Brigade*, p 153 and pp 205–206.

21 See Federation of Miners, *Coeur d'Alene Troubles*, p 2; and Gaboury, 'State House to Bull Pen', pp 14–22.

22 Gaboury, 'State House to Bull Pen', pp 14–22.

23 Smith, *The War of 1892*, p 29.

24 This inference may also be drawn from Federation of Miners, *Coeur d'Alene Troubles*, p 2.

25 See especially 'The Mine Owners Organize' in Smith, *The War of 1892*, pp 28–30.

26 See 'The Big Strike' and 'The Miners' Strike' in *The Spokane Review*, 9 and 21 August 1891. See also Smith, *The War of 1892*, pp 28–29.

27 On the early planning of the region-wide wage reductions, see JM Bartos, 'The Blight of the Federation: James McParland, the Pinkerton National Detective Agency and the Western Federation of Miners, 1892–1907', unpublished MA thesis, Montana State University, 2013, p 17 [hereafter Bartos, 'Pinkerton National Detective Agency'].

28 MD Beal and MW Wells, 'Martial Laws in the Coeur d'Alene' in the *History of Idaho, Vol 2* (New York, 1959), p 105 [hereafter Beal and Wells, 'Martial Law'].

29 Hammond, *Autobiography 1*, p 50.

30 As previously noted, albeit in another context, Spence, in *Lace-Boot Brigade*, at page 178, finds Hammond's portrayal of his role in the Coeur d'Alene war as 'biased and distorted'. It is a commendably diplomatic formulation. Other, more critical words spring to mind.

31 Federation of Miners, *Coeur d'Alene Troubles*, p 2.

32 Bartos, 'Pinkerton National Detective Agency', p 17.

33 See Hammond, *Autobiography 1*, p 191.

34 CA Siringo, *A Cowboy Detective: A True Story of Twenty-Two Years with a World Famous Detective Agency* (Chicago, 1912), p 136 [hereafter Siringo, *Cowboy-Detective*].

35 See Smith, *The War of 1892*, p 40; and Siringo, *Cowboy-Detective*, p 144.

36 Smith, *The War of 1892*, p 40.

37 Hammond suggests that RE Brown's initials were 'TB' – Hammond, *Autobiography 1*, p 341; while Smith, *The War of 1892*, p 40, wrongly suggests that he was 'William Brown'. His real name appears to have been Robert Edward Brown. Hammond may well have been correct in suggesting that he was, by that time, also an informer for the Kruger government, which would help account for some name-changing; see also E de Waal, 'The Part Played by the Americans on the Witwatersrand during the Period 1886–1899', unpublished MA thesis, Department of History, Unisa, 1971, pp 59–60.

38 'At Three Score Years and Ten', *San Francisco Call*, Vol 70, No 175, 29 November 1891.

39 See Hammond, *Autobiography 1*, p 114.

40 See Bartos, 'Pinkerton National Detective Agency', p 19; Gaboury, 'State House to Bull Pen', pp 14–22; and 'Will Close the Mines', *The Spokane Review*, 13 January 1892. For details about the increase in freight charges, which, while substantial, appear not to have been crippling, and the way that this might have impacted on the mining companies, see Smith, *The War of 1892*, p 32. It is worth noting that so bitter did the subsequent battles become that organised labour refused to concede that the upping of the rail tariffs had played *any* part whatsoever in the subsequent closure of the mines – seeing it only as an anti-union measure. The silences in the Federation of Miners, *Coeur d'Alene Troubles*, and in TA Hickey, *The Story of the Bull Pen at Wardner, Idaho* (New York, 1900), are all too obvious.

CHAPTER 5

1 See JM Bartos, 'The Blight of the Federation: James McParland, the Pinkerton National Detective Agency and the Western Federation of Miners, 1892–1907', unpublished MA thesis, Montana State University, 2013, p 17 [hereafter Bartos, 'Pinkerton National Detective Agency']. Bartos gives the date as 16 January 1892, while the union recorded it as 17 January 1892 – see *Coeur d'Alene Mining Troubles*, Senate Document No 25, 1st Session

of the 56th Congress of the United States of America, p 2, prepared by the President of the Federation of Western Miners, Butte, Montana, 15 October, 1899 [hereafter Federation of Miners, *Coeur d'Alene Troubles*], p 2.

2 See JH Hammond, *The Autobiography of John Hays Hammond, Vol 1* (New York, 1935), pp 189 and 190 [hereafter Hammond, *Autobiography 1*].

3 See Hammond, *Autobiography 1*, p 185; and RW Smith, *The Coeur d'Alene Mining War of 1892* (Corvallis, OR, 1961), p 504 [hereafter Smith, *The War of 1892*].

4 Hammond, *Autobiography 1*, p 191. See also GE French, 'The Coeur d'Alene Riots, 1892', *Overland Monthly and Out West Magazine,* Vol 26, Issue 151, July 1895, p 35 [hereafter French, 'Riots 1892'].

5 TA Hickey, *The Story of the Bull Pen at Wardner, Idaho* (New York, 1900), p 5 [hereafter Hickey, *The Bull Pen*].

6 See Smith, *The War of 1892*, p 28.

7 On the sympathy of the *Spokane Review* for the MOA, see Smith, *The War of 1892*, p 90.

8 These developments are best traced in Smith, *The War of 1892*, at pp 34–37. In the Federation of Miners, *Coeur d'Alene Troubles*, at p 2, however, it is claimed that miners' wages were to be reduced by $1 to $2.50 per day and those of other underground workers by 50 cents to $2 per shift. See also WJ Gaboury, 'From State House to Bull Pen: Idaho Populism and the Coeur d'Alene Troubles of the 1890s', *Pacific Northwest Quarterly*, Vol LVIII, January 1967, pp 14–22 [hereafter Gaboury, 'State House to Bull Pen'].

9 'The Miners' Union must Go', *Spokane Review*, 10 May 1892; and French, 'Riots 1892', p 33.

10 French, 'Riots 1892', p 34.

11 See especially French, 'Riots 1892', p 36; and, for the local political context, MD Beal and MW Wells, 'Populism and Free Silver, 1890–1896', in their *History of Idaho, Vol 2* (New York, 1959), pp 72–85 [hereafter Beal and Wells, 'Populism and Free Silver'].

12 French, 'Riots 1892', p 33.

13 See Smith, *The War of 1892*, p 54.

14 The merchant community, however, remained split – see Smith, *The War of 1892*, p 55.

15 As cited in CC Spence, *Mining Engineers and The American West: The Lace-Boot Brigade, 1849–1933* (New Haven, 1970), p 180 [hereafter Spence, *Lace-Boot Brigade*]. See also Smith, *The War of 1892*, p 94.

16 See Smith, *The War of 1892*, pp 52 and 77.

17 See French, 'Riots 1892', and, more particularly, HR Lamar, *Charlie Siringo's West: An Interpretative Biography* (Albuquerque, 2005), p 186.

18 Hammond, *Autobiography 1*, pp 189–191.

19 See Smith, *The War of 1892*, pp 56–58.

20 Smith, *The War of 1892*, p 69, and Spence, *Lace-Boot Brigade*, p 180.

21 On the already weakening position of the more conservative Knights of Labor, see Beal and Wells, 'Populism and Free Silver', pp 80–81.

22 This paragraph is based on material drawn from French, 'Riots 1892', pp 32–35, and Smith, *The War of 1892*, pp 55 and 68.

23 See Hammond, *Autobiography 1*, pp 192–193; and CA Siringo, *A Cowboy Detective: A True Story of Twenty-Two Years with a World Famous Detective Agency* (Chicago, 1912), p 138 [hereafter Siringo, *Cowboy-Detective*].

24 See Siringo, *Cowboy-Detective*, p 150.

25 See especially Smith, *The War of 1892*, pp 47–51.

26 See GR Stewart, *Committee of Vigilance: Revolution in San Francisco, 1851* (Boston, 1964), pp 244 and 305.

27 This paragraph is based on Gaboury, 'State House to Bull Pen', pp 14–22; French, 'Riots 1892', p 35; and Smith, *The War of 1892*, p 92.

28 Smith, *The War of 1892*, pp 48–49.

29 Siringo, *Cowboy-Detective*, p 144. The propaganda value of these seemingly shocking acts was not lost on Hammond, who later faithfully repeated them – Hammond, *Autobiography 1*, p 192.

30 See French, 'Riots 1982, p 33; and Smith, *The War of 1892*, p 56.

31 See Bartos, 'The Pinkerton National Detective Agency', p 12; French, 'Riots 1892', p 36; and Siringo, *Cowboy-Detective*, pp 145–147.

32 See French, 'Riots 1892', p 35; Gaboury, 'State House to Bull Pen', pp 14–22; and Smith, *The War of 1892*, p 65.

33 Siringo, *Cowboy-Detective*, pp 157–159.

34 French, 'Riots 1892', p 35.

35 For hatred of Esler and his provocation of the union, see, for example, Smith, *The War of 1892*, pp 65–66.

36 See KG Aiken, *Idaho's Bunker Hill: The Rise and Fall of a Great Mining Company* (Oklahoma, 2005), p 13 [hereafter Aiken, *Idaho's Bunker Hill*].

37 See Smith, *The War of 1892*, p 66.

38 See French, 'Riots 1892', p 32, for the valuation of the mine and Chapter 6 of J Harriman's *The Class War in Idaho: The Horrors of the Bull Pen* (New York, 1900).

39 Smith, *The War of 1892*, p 69. Most historians accept that the concentrator was stacked with explosives – but Smith, at p 69, citing union sources, warns that this may have been part of an attempt to discredit the union.

40 French, 'Riots 1892', p 38.

41 See Aiken, *Idaho's Bunker Hill*, p 13; and Smith, *The War of 1892*, pp 68–69.

42 Aiken, *Idaho's Bunker Hill*, p 13; and Smith, *The War of 1892*, pp 68–69.

43 Smith, *The War of 1892*, pp 71–72.
44 *Ibid*, p 75; see also French, 'Riots 1892', p 36. It is also worth noting how the union sent bogus telegrams to Governor Willey in Clement's name, asking for troops not to be sent to Wardner. French, 'Riots 1892', p 37.
45 Smith, *The War of 1892*, p 93.
46 Spence, *Lace-Boot Brigade*, pp 180–181.
47 See the labour breakdown at BHS Co, by nationality, as at February 1894, in Spence, *Lace-Boot Brigade*, pp 170–171.
48 JA Lukas, *Big Trouble: A Murder in a South Western Town Sets off a Struggle for the Soul of America* (New York, 2012), p 110.
49 See Smith, *The War of 1892*, pp 74–84.
50 See especially Gaboury, 'State House to Bull Pen', pp 14–22; and Hickey, *The Bull Pen*, pp 6–7. See also Smith, *The War of 1892*, pp 85–86.
51 See especially Smith, *The War of 1892*, pp 97–101.
52 See Smith, *The War of 1892*, p 119.
53 *Ibid*, pp 119–124.
54 Federation of Miners, *Coeur d'Alene Troubles*, p 2; French, 'Riots 1892', pp 42 and 49; Gaboury, 'State House to Bull Pen', pp 14–22; Hickey, *The Bull Pen*, p 7; and Smith, *The War of 1892*, pp 92–93.
55 French, 'Riots 1892', p 40.
56 *Ibid*, p 48.
57 See especially Gaboury, 'State House to Bull Pen', pp 14–22.
58 See Aiken, *Idaho's Bunker Hill*, p 9; and United States of America, Moscow, University of Idaho Library, Manuscript Group 367, Box and Folder Inventory Guide, Corporate History, Bunker Hill Company, as compiled by J Nielson, October 1994.
59 Gaboury, 'State House to Bull Pen', pp 14–22.
60 See Gaboury, 'State House to Bull Pen', pp 14–22; and especially Spence, *Lace-Boot Brigade*, p 181.
61 See Spence, *Lace-Boot Brigade*, p 181.
62 *Ibid*, p 178
63 United Kingdom, Oxford University, Bodleian Library, John Hays Hammond Papers, Private Letters, JH Hammond to FW Bradley, 8 November 1895.
64 See Federation of Miners, *Coeur d'Alene Troubles*, pp 2–4; Gaboury, 'State House to Bull Pen', pp 14–22; and Hickey, *The Bull Pen*, pp 2–3.
65 Spence, *Lace-Boot Brigade*, p 182.
66 See Hickey, *The Bull Pen*, p 4.

CHAPTER 6

1 See D Rhoodie, *Conspirators in Conflict: A Study of the Johannesburg Reform Committee and its Role in the Conspiracy against the South African Republic* (Cape Town, 1967), p 24 [hereafter Rhoodie, *Conspirators in Conflict*].
2 FW Bell, *The South African Conspiracy or the Aims of Afrikanerdom* (London, 1900), p 11.
3 See C van Onselen, *Masked Raiders: Irish Banditry in Southern Africa, 1880–1899* (Cape Town, 2010), pp 156–161 [hereafter van Onselen, *Masked Raiders*].
4 Van Onselen, *Masked Raiders*, pp 80–92.
5 *Ibid*, p 89.
6 On Gansl and Hammond and membership of the Pacific Union Club, see the *San Francisco, Oakland and Alameda Business Directory of 1880* and the *San Francisco Blue Book, 1889*. On RP Hammond's banking links and social prominence, see John Hays Hammond, *The Autobiography of John Hays Hammond, Vol 1* (New York 1935), pp 10–13 [hereafter Hammond, *Autobiography 1*].
7 N Ferguson, *The House of Rothschild: The World's Banker, 1849–1899* (New York, 2014), p 356; and J Cooper, *The Unexpected Story of Nathaniel Rothschild* (London, 2015), pp 73–74.
8 V Harlow and F Hamilton, 'Sir Frederic Hamilton's Narrative of Events Relative to the Jameson Raid', *The English Historical Review*, Vol 72, No 283, April 1957, pp 282 and 286 [hereafter Harlow and Hamilton, 'Jameson Raid'].
9 See FE Garrett and EJ Edwards, *The Story of an African Crisis and of the Jameson Raid* (London, 1897), p 49 [hereafter Garrett and Edwards, *African Crisis*].
10 See especially 'Randlords and Rotgut, 1886–1903', in C van Onselen, *New Babylon, New Nineveh: Everyday Life on the Witwatersrand, 1886–1914* (Cape Town, 2001), pp 47–108.
11 Hammond, *Autobiography 1*, pp 304–305.
12 *Ibid*, 'Introduction', p 5.
13 See HJ and RE Simons, *Class and Colour in South Africa, 1850–1950* (Harmondsworth, 1969), p 55.
14 See EA Cripps, 'Provisioning Johannesburg, 1886–1906', unpublished MA thesis, Department of History, Unisa, February 2012, pp 82–83.
15 See AK Hamilton Jenkin, *The Cornish Miner* (Devon, 1962, third edition), pp 289–291, 327, 331 [hereafter Hamilton Jenkin, *Cornish Miner*]; and C Mills, 'A Hazardous Bargain: Occupational Risk in Cornish Mining, 1875–1914', *Labour History Review*, Vol 70, No 1, April 2005, p 61 [hereafter Mills, 'A Hazardous Bargain'].
16 See especially Hammond, *Autobiography 1*, p 300.
17 United States of America, Yale University, New Haven, Connecticut, John Hays Hammond Snr Papers, Box lll, Letter Book ll, JH Hammond to RA Parker, Consulting Mining Engineer, Marquette, Michigan, 29 May 1895.
18 P Payton, *The Cornish Overseas: A History of*

Cornwall's 'Great Migration' (Dundurn, 2005), p 7 [hereafter Payton, *The Cornish Overseas*].

19 Garrett and Edwards, *African Crisis*, p 125.

20 As quoted in Rhoodie, *Conspirators in Conflict*, p 56.

21 Hamilton Jenkin, *Cornish Miner*, p 305.

22 On Cornish ideological predispositions, see Hamilton Jenkin, *Cornish Miner*, pp 289–291; and, on traditional mining contracts, see Mills, 'A Hazardous Bargain', p 54.

23 See Payton, *The Cornish Overseas*, p 364.

24 See especially J Hyslop, *The Notorious Syndicalist. JT Bain: A Scottish Rebel in Colonial South Africa* (Johannesburg, 2004), pp 125–126.

25 See 'George Herbert Farrar', in *Oxford Dictionary of National Biography*.

26 Rhoodie, *Conspirators in Conflict*, p 40.

27 See especially Hammond's bitter complaints in *Autobiography 1*, pp 317–318.

28 Note, for example, how it was immediately after the Matabeleland trip, during Rhodes's bad-tempered meeting with Kruger, that the issue of rail tariffs seemed to have driven Rhodes further down the road to revolution. See, for example, Harlow and Hamilton, 'Jameson Raid', pp 281 and 288.

CHAPTER 7

1 See above, Chapter 4.

2 See E de Waal, 'The Part Played by Americans on the Witwatersrand during the Period 1886–1899', unpublished MA thesis, Department of History, Unisa, 1971, pp 59–60 [hereafter de Waal, 'Americans on the Witwatersrand'].

3 See Chapter 8 of Mrs John Hays Hammond, *A Woman's Part in a Revolution* (London, 1897). Interestingly, like her husband, Natalie Harris either did not care, or did not know, what Mr Brown's first names were, incorrectly giving his initials as 'KB'. For confirmation of Brown's initials as RE, and his Coeur d'Alene role, see also CC Spence, *Mining Engineers and the American West: The Lace-Boot Brigade* (London, 1970), p 315.

4 See Letter to the Editor, *Standard & Diggers' News*, 27 December 1895, as quoted in de Waal, 'Americans on the Witwatersrand', pp 59–60.

5 JH Hammond, *The Autobiography of John Hays Hammond, Vol 1* (New York, 1935), pp 341–342 [hereafter Hammond, *Autobiography 1*]; and A Ireland, 'The True Story of the Jameson Raid as related to me by John Hays Hammond, Part 1', *The North American Review*, Vol 208, No 753, August 1918, p 195 [hereafter Ireland, 'The True Story'].

6 Ireland, 'The True Story', p 195.

7 See GN van den Bergh, 'Secret Service in the South African Republic, 1895-1900',

Military History Journal, Vol 3, No 2, December 1974, p 2; and, for the wider context, HJG Kamffer, '*Om een scherpe oog in't zeil houden*: Die Geheime Diens in die Zuid-Afrikaansche Republiek', unpublished DPhil thesis, Potchefstroomse Universiteit vir Christelike Hoër Onderwys, 1999, pp 51–71 [hereafter Kamffer, 'Die Geheime Diens'].

8 See Hammond, *Autobiography 1*, p 130.

9 On the poor outcome of the Rhodes-Kruger meeting, see, for example, V Harlow and F Hamilton, 'Sir Frederic Hamilton's Narrative of Events Relative to the Jameson Raid', *The English Historical Review*, Vol 72, No 283, April 1957, p 281 [hereafter Harlow and Hamilton, 'Jameson Raid']. As Harlow and Hamilton point out, on the same page, this disappointing outcome came in the wake of Rhodes also having been told by the British government that his ambitions to acquire Delagoa Bay could not be entertained. See also I Colvin, *The Life of Jameson, Vol 2* (London, 1922), pp 2–3 [hereafter Colvin, *Jameson 2*].

10 Harlow and Hamilton, 'Jameson Raid', p 281.

11 RI Rotberg, *The Founder; Cecil Rhodes and the Pursuit of Power* (Cape Town, 2002), p 526.

12 Hammond, *Autobiography 1*, p 294.

13 United Kingdom, Oxford University, Bodleian Library, Hammond Papers, JH Hammond to Captain EF Rhodes, 21 October 1895.

14 See Chapter 5 of JP FitzPatrick's *The Transvaal from Within* (London, 1899) [hereafter FitzPatrick, *Transvaal from Within*].

15 Hamilton's view was that 'in a fairly long life I have known fewer men who were better balanced – a good mind, a sound and agile physique, a sincere and sterling character, and a humour and real kindliness of heart which bubbled and shone through those twinkling eyes' – Harlow and Hamilton, 'Jameson Raid', p 287. It is not known whether Hamilton, like most journalists of the day and later, drank heavily. His is a description of Hammond that does not even remotely resemble that provided by others who knew him.

16 The only source of information about Bettington's early career appears to be a short article that he wrote for the magazine *South Africa* and which was subsequently reprinted in, among others, *The Clarence and Richmond Examiner* (New South Wales), 14 November 1896.

17 See Colvin, *Jameson 2*, pp 14 and 137.

18 Nor was this a secret; note, for example, how JT Bain approached the State Attorney, Ewald Esselen, in August 1894 to become a 'detective' at a time when the secret service was managed through the detective department. See J Hyslop, *The Notorious Syndicalist. JT Bain: A Scottish Rebel in Colonial*

South Africa (Johannesburg, 2004), p 108 [hereafter Hyslop, *The Notorious Syndicalist*]. On the rise of the secret service, see Kamffer, 'Die Geheime Diens', pp 36–70.

19 See Hammond, *Autobiography 1*, p 305, for his views on alcohol and black miners.

20 For the wider context, see C van Onselen, *The Small Matter of a Horse: The Life of 'Nongoloza' Mathebula, 1867–1948* (Pretoria, 2008).

21 For the background to these developments, see the following by C van Onselen: *Masked Raiders, New Babylon and New Nineveh: Everyday Life on the Witwatersrand, 1886–1914* (Cape Town, 2001), pp 90–91 and 109–156; and *Showdown at the Red Lion: The Life and Times of Jack McLoughlin, 1859–1910* (Cape Town, 2015), Chapters 10 to 15 [hereafter van Onselen, *Showdown at the Red Lion*]. On Ferguson's complicity in gold thefts, see CH Muller, 'Policing the Witwatersrand: A History of the South African Republic Police, 1886–1899', unpublished DPhil thesis, Centre of Africa Studies, University of the Free State, 2016, pp 264–276 [hereafter Muller, 'Policing the Witwatersrand'. And for the mine owners' outrage, see FitzPatrick, *Transvaal from Within*, p 64.

22 Hammond, *Autobiography 1*, p 81.

23 DE Schutte to Editor, *Standard & Diggers' News*, 11 October 1894; and Muller, 'Policing the Witwatersrand', pp 145–147.

24 Muller, 'Policing the Witwatersrand', pp 100–180.

25 See van Onselen, *Showdown at the Red Lion*, pp 266–281.

26 Rowland A Bettington to the Editor, *The Star*, 5 March 1895.

27 See van Onselen, *Masked Raiders*, pp 36–40.

28 *The Star*, 5 March 1895. See also 'Tonight's Meeting', *The Star*, 7 March 1895.

29 'Vigilance Committees – A Famous Association', *The Star*, 12 March 1895. See also Hammond, *Autobiography 1*, p 9.

30 As cited in Republic of South Africa (RSA), Pietermaritzburg Archives Repository (PAR), A 1297, EM Trimble Papers, folios 504–505.

31 For more of the context, see also Muller, 'Policing the Witwatersrand', pp 161–162; and 'The Police Situation', *The Star*, 10 March 1895.

32 Harlow and Hamilton, 'Jameson Raid', p 282.

33 *Ibid*.

34 *Ibid*, p 283.

35 RSA, Johannesburg, Brenthurst Library, Rhodes Papers, CJ Rhodes to Alfred Beit, Cape Town, letter dated 'August 1895' [hereafter, Brenthurst, Rhodes to Beit, August 1895].

36 See especially C van der Merwe, *Donker Stroom: Eugène Marais en die Anglo-Boereoorlog* (Cape Town, 2015), pp 23–74.

37 For the careers and pre-1895 political trajectories of all these politicians, see CT Gordon's indispensable *The Growth of Boer Opposition to Kruger, 1890–1895* (London, 1970).

38 As quoted in C Ash, *The IF Man. Dr Leander Starr Jameson: The Inspiration for Kipling's Masterpiece* (Solihull, 2012), pp 218–219.

39 Brenthurst, Rhodes to Beit, August 1895.

CHAPTER 8

1 Within this context note how removed CJ Rhodes and CD Rudd of Consolidated Gold Fields were from the Witwatersrand. Rhodes attempted to compensate for this by sending his brothers – first Ernest and then Frank – to run the Johannesburg offices. See RV Kubicek, *Economic Imperialism in Theory and Practice: The Case of South African Gold Mining Finance, 1886–1914* (Durham, 1979), p 102 [hereafter Kubicek, *Economic Imperialism*].

2 It is therefore doubly ironic that leading figures in the mining industry who, before 1895, were reluctant to underwrite the political reform programme of Charles Leonard's National Union, appropriated most of its pedigree once the planned urban insurrection began to fail.

3 See CW de Kiewiet, *The Anatomy of South African Misery* (London, 1956), pp 10–11.

4 For the importance of Stellaland and Goshen in the experience of Rhodes and, to a lesser extent, Jameson, and how the Boer freebooter republics helped shape Britain and the South African Republic's relationship in the mid-1880s, see I Colvin, *The Life of Jameson, Vols 1 and 2* (London, 1922), at pp 92–94 and 22, respectively [hereafter Colvin, *Jameson 1* or *2*].

5 See C van Onselen, *Masked Raiders: Irish Banditry in Southern Africa, 1880–1899* (Cape Town, 2010), p 225.

6 Hammond appears to have eventually dominated both Ernest and Frank Rhodes. On Ernest Rhodes, see Kubicek, *Economic Imperialism*, p 103 and, on Frank Rhodes, below.

7 A Ireland, 'The True Story of the Jameson Raid as Related to me by John Hays Hammond, Part 2', *The North American Review*, Vol 208, No 754, September 1918, p 365 [hereafter Ireland, 'The True Story, Part 2']. This high regard for Frank Rhodes's personal qualities was also that of Jameson's biographer, Colvin. Colonel Rhodes '… was an open, brave, honest charming English gentleman, without any idea in politics save that the British Empire was a cause worth fighting for, and that his younger brother was always right'. See Colvin, *Jameson 2*, p 86.

8 United Kingdom, Oxford University, Bodleian Library, Rhodes House, Hammond

Papers, JH Hammond to Sir John Willoughby, 26 November 1895.

9 Kubicek, *Economic Imperialism*, p 103. For the largely speculative dimension to the so-called Kaffir Boom of 1895, see especially IR Phimister, 'Frenzied Finance: Gold Mining in the Globalizing South, c. 1886–1896' in B Mountford and SD Tuffnell (eds), *Gold Rush: A Global History c. 1848–1910* (Oxford, forthcoming).

10 Hammond could often manipulate Rhodes, but not his principal partner in Consolidated Gold Fields, CD Rudd. Thus Hammond did not inform Rudd about his planned 'revolution' until very late in the day – see Kubicek, *Economic Imperialism*, pp 102–103. After the Jameson Raid, Rudd urged Hammond to resign from his position in the company voluntarily, but Hammond declined to do so. See United Kingdom, Oxford University, Bodleian Library, Rhodes House, CD Rudd to JH Hammond, 24 January 1896.

11 See FE Garrett and EJ Edwards, *The Story of an African Crisis and The Jameson Raid* (London, 1897), pp 49–50 [hereafter Garrett and Edwards, *African Crisis*].

12 V Harlow and FH Hamilton, 'Sir Frederic Hamilton's Narrative of Events Relative to the Jameson Raid', *The English Historical Review*, Vol 72, No 283, April 1957, pp 302–303 [hereafter Harlow and Hamilton, 'The Jameson Raid'].

13 For an outline of these developments see, for example, M Fraser and A Jeeves (eds), *All that Glittered: Selected Correspondence of Lionel Phillips, 1890–1924* (Cape Town, 1977), pp 3–6 [hereafter Fraser and Jeeves, *All that Glittered*].

14 The evidence on which this paragraph is based comes from Fraser and Jeeves, *All that Glittered*, and Mrs Lionel Phillips, *Some South African Recollections* (London, 1900) [hereafter Phillips, *South African Recollections*]. On the Phillips's home, see Fraser and Jeeves, *All that Glittered*, p 5. On Phillips's relaxed attitude towards corruption, see two letters to JB Taylor, dated 16 and 28 June 1893, at pages pp 52–55, and one to Nellmapius himself on 21 March, 1893, at pp 72–73. On Kruger's resentment of Phillips's alleged neglect of Nellmapius' widow, see Phillips to L Weinthal, 16 June 1894, at p 80 – all the aforementioned in Fraser and Jeeves, *All that Glittered*. On Phillips as the 'King of Johannesburg' and Kruger's alleged intense dislike of him, see Phillips, *South African Recollections*, p 76.

15 See C van der Merwe, *Donker Stroom: Eugène Marais en die Anglo-Boereoorlog* (Cape Town, 2015), pp 42–48.

16 Phillips, in turn, was prompted by one of his correspondents, Kann, to think about 'the formation of a sort of mines defence association' – see L Phillips to A Beit, London,

12 August 1894, in Fraser and Jeeves, *All that Glittered*, pp 80–81. But for the best possible insight into Lionel Phillips's mindset at the time, see Phillips, *South African Recollections*, pp 53–55.

17 Note, for example, how Hammond in his autobiography, when introducing some of the leading actors in the Jameson Raid, characterises Frank Rhodes as an 'officer with a distinguished military record', Charles Leonard as 'the head of the National Union' and George Farrar as 'an important mine owner', but Philips only as 'a partner in Wernher, Beit and Company' – JH Hammond, *The Autobiography of John Hays Hammond, Vol 1* (New York, 1935), pp 319–320 [hereafter Hammond, *Autobiography 1*].

18 Fraser and Jeeves, *All that Glittered*, Phillips to Beit, 16 June 1894, p 79.

19 Phillips, *South African Recollections*, pp 114–116.

20 *Ibid*, p 64.

21 See RI Rotberg, *The Founder: Cecil Rhodes and the Pursuit of Power* (Cape Town, 2002), p 508.

22 There may, of course, have been a smidgeon of Jack Hammond in FitzPatrick's fiction in the shape of 'Rocky Mountain Jack' in *Jock of the Bushveld* – see above, Chapter 2.

23 That, despite the fact that FitzPatrick's trip was long in the making and that Hammond almost never missed the opportunity to be seen in the company of the great and the good. See, for example, Republic of South Africa, Grahamstown, National English Language Museum, FitzPatrick Collection, Reuters, 'Interview regarding his trip to California', undated but almost certainly late 1920 and other, related, documents where the name of Hammond is conspicuous by its absence.

24 Hammond, suggest Harlow and Hamilton, 'was the acknowledged leader of the American community in Johannesburg' – Harlow and Hamilton, 'The Jameson Raid', p 283.

25 Parts of JH Jennings and HC Perkins's prior experience, largely in California and Venezuela, can be traced in CC Spence, *Mining Engineers and The American West: The Lace-Boot Brigade, 1849–1933* (London, 1970), at pp 22, 144, 268, 305, 314, 342 and 346 [hereafter Spence, *Lace-Boot Brigade*].

26 See Fitzpatrick, *The Transvaal from Within*, p 86.

27 In the case of Jennings see, for example, Spence, *Lace-Boot Brigade*, pp 314 and 346.

28 As quoted in E de Waal, 'The Part Played by Americans on the Witwatersrand during the Period 1886–1899', unpublished MA thesis, Department of History, Unisa, 1971, p 30 [hereafter de Waal, 'Americans on the Witwatersrand'].

29 Rhodes to Harris, 24 November 1895, as reproduced in Colvin, *Jameson 2*, pp 38–39

(emphasis added).

30 See Garrett and Edwards, *African Crisis*, p 67.

31 Hammond, *Autobiography 1*, p 337. You do not need to be a student of history or of literature – although it may help – to be struck by how closely, at this point in his memoirs, Hammond's narrative follows that of Percy FitzPatrick in *The Transvaal from Within* at p 86. 'They were received civilly enough', writes Hammond (p 337) while FitzPatrick notes that 'The President received them civilly' (p 86). Curiously enough, neither Hammond nor FitzPatrick felt free enough to name the men as Jennings and Perkins, even though sources at the time make it abundantly clear that it was indeed them. See also de Waal, 'Americans on the Witwatersrand', p 61: 'It is clear that Hammond wished to "discipline Hennen Jennings and HC Perkins …"'

32 E Rosenthal, *Stars and Stripes in Africa* (Cape Town, 1968), p 141.

CHAPTER 9

1 These paragraphs are based on I Colvin, *The Life of Jameson, Vols 1 and 2* (London, 1922), pp 1–10 [hereafter Colvin, *Jameson 1* or *2*]; and GS Fort, *Dr Jameson* (London, 1918), pp 121–123 [hereafter Fort, *Dr Jameson*].

2 Colvin, *Jameson 1*, pp 1–5.

3 As Fort puts it, Dr Jameson described his father as displaying a 'high and somewhat doctrinaire intellectuality' (p 49), and, while at Kimberley, Jameson cast the Boer diggers as 'mean cusses' because of the ways in which they exploited black and child labour (pp 60–61).

4 This paragraph is based on Colvin, *Jameson 1*, pp 8–11 and Fort, *Dr Jameson*, p 49. It is not clear from the two major biographies of Jameson, but worth speculating that 'Middleton' Jameson's name – like that of Leander Starr – was American-inspired. If Middleton's name was derived from that of the South Carolina plantation owner and prominent activist in the American Revolutionary War – Henry Middleton – it would point to more significant ties between the Jameson family and America than emerges from Colvin or Fort's work.

5 See Colvin, *Jameson 1*, p 11; and D Lowry, 'Sir Leander Starr Jameson', in HCG Matthew and B Harrison (eds), *Oxford Dictionary of National Biography* (Oxford, 2004), Vol 29, pp 756–761 [hereafter Lowry, 'Jameson', *Oxford Dictionary of Biography*].

6 The exact dates of this trip are difficult to determine from the standard biographies. It is interesting to note, however, that the Rev James King, who immersed himself in aspects of the Raid that others did not always pay

sufficient attention to, suggests, categorically, that Jameson had experienced some sort of breakdown in his own health and that the American visit was in 1875. See J King, *Dr Jameson's Raid: Its Causes and Consequences* (Manchester, 1896), p 177.

7 Colvin, *Jameson 1*, p 11.

8 *Ibid*, p 221.

9 Fort, *Dr Jameson*, p 52.

10 Colvin, *Jameson 1*, p 220.

11 See Fort, *Dr Jameson*, p 86.

12 See especially Fort, *Dr Jameson*, pp 173–174, and note how Fort emphasises 'high nervous tension', 'incessant travel', 'physical fatigue' and 'strained powers' – Jameson was clearly not well.

13 Colvin, *Jameson 1*, pp 38 and pp 79–80.

14 Jameson took charge of the administration of the country in April 1891 – see Fort, *Dr Jameson*, p 119.

15 On American involvement in the war of 1893, see also JH Hammond, 'South African Memories: Rhodes-Barnato-Burnham', *Scribner's Magazine*, Vol LXIX, No 3, March 1921, p 268 [hereafter Hammond, 'Memories'].

16 For Jameson's profound contempt of conventional military procedure, structure and tradition, see Colvin, *Jameson 1* and *2*, at pp 295 and 21, respectively. Ironically, Jameson's preference for leading men in formations not modelled on the British army or its traditions turned him into precisely the sort of figure that he did not wish to be seen as during the Raid – as a brigand, or a freebooter or, in his own words, as a 'pirate' – see especially Colvin, *Jameson 2*, pp 76–77.

17 T Pakenham, *The Scramble for Africa* (London, 1991), p 497.

18 Ironically, Hammond did not meet Burnham while he was in Africa. See United Kingdom, Oxford University, Bodleian Library, Rhodes House, Hammond Papers, JH Hammond to FR Burnham, Pasadena, California, 31 December 1896, in which Hammond writes, 'I have been desirous of meeting you for a long time; and hope that you will let me know when you come through London, so that I may have the pleasure of seeing you in person.' Hammond later helped Burnham make a fortune in developing Californian oil interests – see JH Hammond, *The Autobiography of John Hays Hammond, Vol 2* (New York, 1935), pp 735–755. For his tribute to Burnham, see Hammond, 'Memories', pp 257–278.

19 See, for example, Colvin, *Jameson 2*, pp 282–283.

20 *Ibid*, p 53.

21 On Heany's propensity for impulsive behaviour, behaviour of the sort that Jameson himself was prone to, see, for example,

'Captain Heany is Silent', *New York Times*, 8 March 1896, reporting on his marriage and behaviour in New York City.

22 A Kepple-Jones, *Rhodes and Rhodesia* (Pietermaritzburg, 1983), p 270.

23 Colvin, *Jameson 2*, p 53.

24 *Ibid*.

25 *Ibid*; and Fort, *Dr Jameson*, p 52.

26 See HM Hole, *The Jameson Raid* (London, 1930), p 102; and in E de Waal, 'The Part Played by Americans on the Witwatersrand during the Period 1886–1899', unpublished MA thesis, Department of History, Unisa, 1971, p 50 [hereafter de Waal, 'Americans on the Witwatersrand'].

27 See HA Wolff to Editor, *New York Times*, 27 November 1899; and the withering reply from GW van Siclen to the Editor later the same day.

28 Colvin, *Jameson 2*, pp 192–198; and Fort, *Dr Jameson*, p 119.

29 Colvin, *Jameson 1*, p 295.

30 *Ibid*, p 300.

31 FE Garrett and EJ Edwards, *The Story of an African Crisis and of the Jameson Raid* (London, 1897), p 29 [hereafter Garrett and Edwards, *African Crisis*].

32 See C van Onselen, *Masked Raiders: Irish Banditry in Southern Africa, 1880–1899* (Cape Town, 2010), p 226 [hereafter van Onselen, *Masked Raiders*].

33 C Danziger, *The Jameson Raid* (Cape Town, 1978), p 8 [hereafter Danziger, *The Jameson Raid*].

34 As quoted in Lowry, 'Jameson', *Oxford Dictionary of Biography*, p 759.

35 DM Schreuder and J Butler (eds), *Sir Graham Bower's Secret History of the Jameson Raid and the South African Crisis, 1895–1902* (Cape Town, 2004), p 48.

36 As quoted in Garrett and Edwards, *African Crisis*, p 196.

37 See D Rhoodie, *Conspirators in Conflict; A Study of the Johannesburg Reform Committee and its Role in the Conspiracy against the South African Republic* (Cape Town, 1967), p 105 [hereafter Rhoodie, *Conspirators in Conflict*].

38 See JH Hammond, *The Autobiography of John Hays Hammond, Vol 1* (New York, 1935), pp 251, 322 and 330 [hereafter Hammond, *Autobiography 1*].

39 The unhappiness that followed the Raid is explored in Chapter 12, below.

40 See, for example, Colvin, *Jameson 2*, pp 58–59; and Hammond, *Autobiography 1*, pp 320 and 331. There is a fine overview of Wolff's role in de Waal, 'Americans on the Witwatersrand', pp 49–51.

41 Colvin, *Jameson 1*, pp 118 and 142.

42 List of doctors taken from *The Otago Witness*, 7 May 1896. The hidden thread among most of the doctors was, of course, medical training

in Scotland – in particular, Aberdeen and Edinburgh. It should also be remembered that Ewald Esselen, too, started out as a medical student at Edinburgh. The many links of doctors to Jameson were thus geographical as well as professional. For the careers of some of the doctors involved, see especially JJ Harvie Pirie, 'Witwatersrand Medical Societies: A Historical Fragment', *The Journal of the Medical Association of South Africa* (BMA), 24 August 1929, pp 447–452.

43 See van Onselen, *Masked Raiders*, pp 226–227.

44 The Reform Committee consisted of '23 Englishmen, 16 South Africans, 9 Scots, 6 Americans, 2 Welshmen, 2 Germans, 1 Irishman, 1 Australian, 1 Dutchman, 1 Canadian, 1 Swiss and 1 Turk' – Danziger, *The Jameson Raid*, p 6.

45 Colvin, *Jameson 2*, p 14. Garrett is even less sparing of Charles Leonard: 'A less apt man to cast for the part of President by force of arms of an insurrectionary Republic it would be hard to find' – Garrett and Edwards, *African Crisis*, p 49.

46 For the wider context see C van der Merwe, *Donker Stroom: Eugène Marais en die Anglo-Boereoorlog* (Cape Town, 2015), pp 42–73. But see also Chapter 18, below.

47 On engineers see Colvin, *Jameson 2*, p 85; and on those with a background in journalism see above, Chapter 8.

48 See CC Spence, *Mining Engineers and the American West: The Lace-Boot Brigade* (London, 1970), pp 313–314.

49 For a list of the nationalities and occupations of those eventually committed for trial, see Rhoodie, *Conspirators in Conflict*, pp 96–98.

50 On the inability to draw in the Mercantile Association, see Rhoodie, *Conspirators in Conflict*, pp 67–68.

CHAPTER 10

1 V Harlow and FW Hamilton, 'Sir Frederic Hamilton's Narrative of Events Relative to the Jameson Raid', *The English Historical Review*, Vol 72, No 283, April 1957, p 302 [hereafter Harlow and Hamilton, 'The Jameson Raid'].

2 FE Garrett and EJ Edwards, *The Story of an African Crisis and of the Jameson Raid* (London, 1897), p 146 [hereafter Garrett and Edwards, *African Crisis*].

3 GS Fort, *Dr Jameson* (London, 1918), pp 159–160.

4 VR Markham, *South Africa Past and Present* (London, 1900), pp 129–130.

5 Jameson was clear that it was Hammond who set the tone for the Matabeleland discussions of 1894. See especially Vindex (F Verschoyle), *Cecil Rhodes: His Life and Political Speeches* (London, 1900), pp 460–462 [hereafter

Vindex, *Cecil Rhodes*].

6 I Colvin, *The Life of Jameson, Vol 1 and 2* (London, 1922), p 19–20 [hereafter Colvin, *Jameson 1* or *2*].

7 See above, Chapter 7, and, for the back story, C van Onselen, *Showdown at the Red Lion: The Life and Times of Jack McLoughlin, 1859–1910* (Cape Town, 2015).

8 See letters to the Editor from 'Citizen' and W Dodds, *The Star*, 6 and 8 March 1895. Although Dodds was coaxed or pushed into writing in support of the idea of a Vigilance Committee, it is noteworthy how, after this, both the self-styled 'revolutionaries' and the 'reform committee' could not get the shopkeepers to join their 'movement'. Hammonds and Clement, however, who knew from the Coeur d'Alene how important it was to get the traders on side in any public contestations, attempted to keep Dodds close to them. See NH Hammond, *A Woman's Part in a Revolution* (London, 1897), p 5.

9 *The Star*, 6 March 1895. For the full context of the so-called Kaffir Boom see IR Phimister, 'Frenzied Finance: Gold Mining in the Globalizing South, c. 1886–1896' in B Mountford and S Tuffnell (eds), *Gold Rush: A Global History, c 1848–1910* (Oxford, forthcoming) [hereafter Phimister, 'Frenzied Finance'].

10 Colvin, *Jameson 2*, p 21.

11 See WT Stead, *The Americanisation of the World* (London, 1901), pp 56–57 (emphasis added).

12 G Cuthbertson, 'A Century of the Raid' in J Carruthers (ed), *The Jameson Raid: A Centennial Retrospective* (Johannesburg, 1996), p 2.

13 On the 'frequent talks' between Jameson and Hammond, see Vindex, *Cecil Rhodes*, p 462.

14 This round of meetings is recorded in Colvin, *Jameson 2*, p 31.

15 Harlow and Hamilton, 'The Jameson Raid', p 290.

16 *Ibid*.

17 *Ibid*, pp 290–291.

18 See especially Colvin, *Jameson 2*, p 33.

19 Republic of South Africa, Johannesburg, Brenthurst Library, Rhodes Papers, CJ Rhodes to A Beit, dated only 'August 1895'.

20 FitzPatrick, as quoted in Colvin, *Jameson 2*, p 33, f/n 1.

21 On the closeness of Rhodes and Sir Hercules Robinson, see, among many others, Colvin, *Jameson 1*, p 106.

22 Colvin, *Jameson 2*, p 32.

23 *Ibid*, p 32; and JH Hammond, *The Autobiography of John Hays Hammond, Vol 1* (New York, 1935), pp 320–322 [hereafter Hammond, *Autobiography 1*].

24 *Ibid*, pp 320 and 322.

25 *Ibid*, p 322 [emphasis added]. See also A Ireland, 'The True Story of the Jameson Raid

as Related to me by John Hays Hammond', *The North American Review*, Vol 208, No 754, September 1918, p 367 [hereafter Ireland, 'The True Story', Part 2].

26 See especially RH Davis, *Dr Jameson's Raiders vs The Johannesburg Reformers* (New York, 1897), p 15.

27 Hammond, *Autobiography 1*, p 320.

28 'Our arms and ammunition were smuggled in by a small group of Americans ...' – Ireland, 'The True Story', Part 2, p 366.

29 See Hammond, *Autobiography 1*, pp 326–327.

30 See 'The Arming of Johannesburg' in Garrett and Edwards, *African Crisis*, pp 53–59.

31 Hammond, *Autobiography 1*, pp 307–308.

32 See CT Gordon, *The Growth of Boer Opposition to Kruger, 1890–1895* (London, 1970), pp 77–78.

33 For Hamilton's especially close monitoring of the market on the mistaken premise that a sliding market would bring about a waking in the consciousness of the working man, who might then be induced to take part in the planned insurrection, see Harlow and Hamilton, 'The Jameson Raid', pp 289–291.

34 See, RV Kubicek, *Economic Imperialism in Theory and Practice: The Case of South African Gold Mining Finance, 1886–1914* (Durham, 1979), p 25; but more especially Phimister, 'Frenzied Finance'; and E de Waal, 'The Part Played by Americans on the Witwatersrand during the Period 1886–1899', unpublished MA thesis, Department of History, Unisa, 1971, p 54.

35 For Hammond's misreading of the extent of possible Boer support for what turned out to be a failed 'revolution', see Hammond, *Autobiography 1*, pp 308–309; and Ireland, 'The True Story', Part 2, p 192.

36 See Garret and Edwards, *African Crisis*, p 11.

CHAPTER 11

1 As Jameson later noted, he was not always accorded the respect due to him: 'However, that was all due, I would acknowledge, to this abominable Raid. That was a bad blunder.' See GS Fort, *Dr Jameson* (London, 1918), p 219 [hereafter Fort, *Dr Jameson*].

2 All these comments are drawn from JH Hammond, *The Autobiography of John Hays Hammond, Vol 1* (New York, 1935), p 319 [hereafter Hammond, *Autobiography 1*].

3 CC Spence, *Mining Engineers and The American West: The Lace-Boot Brigade, 1849–1933* (London, 1970), p 178.

4 The need for 'adjustments' to the plan is part of a coded message that was to be passed on to Frank Rhodes by his brother – see United States of America, New Haven, Yale University Library, JH Hammond Papers, Box 1, Folder

10, JH Hammond to Captain E Rhodes, Cape Town, 14 October 1895.

5 Hammond, *Autobiography 1*, p 327.

6 In order to minimise his cutting-edge role in the plotting of a failed revolution, Hammond a little later took to claiming that seizing of the arsenal was among the 'tasks' allotted to me' – i.e. that, like a good soldier, he was merely carrying out orders; see A Ireland, 'The True Story of the Jameson Raid as Related to me by John Hays Hammond', Part 2, *The North American Review*, Vol 208, No 754, September 1918, p 366.

7 Hammond, *Autobiography 1*, p 328.

8 *Ibid*, p 327.

9 Republic of South Africa, Johannesburg, Brenthurst Library, Kelsey Papers 370/3/21, 17 May 1896. AA Kelsey's son, responsible for the deposition of the papers in the Brenthurst Library, DA Kelsey, suggested that the pages from which the quotation is drawn 'were either drafted by AA Kelsey or JH Hammond'. It seems clear, however, that the sentiment expressed is in line with the American Hammond's thinking and experience rather than that of the Englishman Kelsey.

10 See S Martin, 'Confederate Engineers in the American Civil War', *Engineer: The Professional Bulletin for Army Engineers*, October 2000.

11 WT Stead, *The Americanisation of the World or the Trend of the Twentieth Century* (London, 1902), pp 56–57 [hereafter Stead, *Americanisation*].

12 See Chapter 3 of JH Wilkins (ed), *The Great Diamond Hoax and Other Stirring Incidents in the Life of Asbury Harpending* (San Francisco, 1913). The Jameson Raid, too, was predicated on the need for the attack on the arsenal and abduction of the President to coincide with the Johannesburg uprising. Hammond, too, would have had good reason to be familiar with the arsenal at Benicia in San Francisco, because it was his father, RP Hammond, who had chosen its location while acting as a surveyor for the US government.

13 See L Richards, *The California Gold Rush and the Coming of the Civil War* (New York, 2007), p 231.

14 On the proposed ultimatum, the three days and the 'provisional government' – a nomenclature and structure more in keeping with a coup or a revolution than 'reform', see FE Garrett and EJ Edwards, *The Story of an African Crisis and of the Jameson Raid* (London, 1897), p 38 [hereafter Garrett and Edwards, *African Crisis*]. RH Davis, *Dr Jameson's Raiders vs The Johannesburg Reformers* (New York, 1897), p 18 [hereafter Davis, *Dr Jameson's Raiders*]; and LE Meyer, *The Farther Frontier: Six Case Studies of Americans and Africa* (London, 1992), pp 149 and 154 [hereafter Meyer, *Farther Frontier*].

15 See Fort, *Dr Jameson*, p 162. Note how, at the time of the publication of Fort's book, in 1908, Jack Hammond's secret plan-within-a-plan to abduct Kruger was already known but, at the time of the publication of Garrett and Edwards' *African Crisis*, in 1897, it had not yet been revealed by the only man who knew about it, Hammond.

16 Meyer, *Farther Frontier*, p 152.

17 United Kingdom, Oxford University, Bodleian Library, Rhodes House Library, John Hays Hammond Papers, JH Hammond to P Yeatman, 20 October 1895 [hereafter UK, Oxford, Hammond Papers].

18 UK, Oxford, Hammond Papers, JH Hammond to JB Lindley, 28 October 1895.

19 UK, Oxford, Hammond Papers, JH Hammond to the Rev H Forster, 2 September 1895; and JH Hammond to Sir John Willoughby, Bulawayo, 26 November 1895.

20 *Ibid*.

21 *Ibid*.

22 Hammond, *Autobiography 1*, p 330.

23 See Stead, *Americanisation*, pp 56–57.

24 For the background to this, see B Willan's outstanding *Sol Plaatje: A Biography* (Johannesburg, 1984), p 63.

25 See, for example, Garrett and Edwards, *African Crisis*, p 90. The estimate of 70 'Cape Boys and Kaffirs who drove Cape cart and ambulances' is recorded from an unsourced document cited in Davis, *Dr Jameson's Raiders*, p 21.

26 See Meyer, *Farther Frontier*, p 141 and Hammond, *Autobiography 1*, p 350.

27 Hammond, *Autobiography 1*, p 330.

28 See I Colvin, *The Life of Jameson Vol 2* (London 1922), pp 34–35 [hereafter Colvin, *Jameson 2*].

29 See Garrett and Edwards, *African Crisis*, p 47.

30 On Jameson's use of the word 'pirate', see Colvin, *Jameson 2*, pp 76–77; Davis, *Dr Jameson's Raiders*, p 51; Garrett and Edwards, *African Crisis*, p 98; V Harlow and FW Hamilton, 'Sir Frederic Hamilton's Narrative of Events Relative to the Jameson Raid', *The English Historical Review*, Vol 72, No 283, April 1957, p 294 [hereafter Harlow and Hamilton, 'The Jameson Raid'].

31 On the word 'filibuster' and its route into American discourse via the Spanish *filibustero* and its progress, in turn, from the Dutch *vrijbuiter* all the way back to 'pirate', see CJ Nolan (ed) *Greenwood Encyclopedia of International Relations, Vol 2* (Westport, CT, 2002) p 544. For Frank Rhodes's playing with the interchangeability of these terms in relation to Jameson's sensitivities and fear of being branded a 'pirate', see Davis, *Dr Jameson's Raiders*, p 51. None of this, however,

prevented Joseph Chamberlain, himself implicated in the plotting, from labelling the invasion as 'filibustering' – see EA Walker, 'The Jameson Raid', *Cambridge Historical Journal*, Vol 6, No 3, 1940, p 294.

32 See Hammond, *Autobiography 1*, p 325.

33 Harlow and Hamilton, 'The Jameson Raid', pp 293–294.

34 Meyer, *Farther Frontier*, p 142.

35 Garrett and Edwards, *African Crisis*, p 48.

36 See Hammond, *Autobiography 1*, pp 325–326.

37 Garrett and Edwards, *African Crisis*, p 48.

38 Hammond, *Autobiography 1*, p 328.

39 See GN van den Bergh, 'Secret Service in the South African Republic, 1895–1900', *Military History Journal*, Vol 3, No 2, December 1974.

40 As quoted in C Ash, *The IF Man. Dr Leander Starr Jameson: The Inspiration for Kipling's Masterpiece* (Solihull, 2012), p 233. On Bain's pro-Kruger sympathies, see J Hyslop, *The Notorious Syndicalist. JT Bain: A Scottish Rebel in Colonial South Africa* (Johannesburg, 2004).

41 See below, Chapter 19.

CHAPTER 12

1 See C van Onselen, *Showdown at the Red Lion: The Life and Times of Jack McLoughlin, 1859–1910* (Cape Town, 2015); and Chapter 7 above.

2 On Trimble and his background, see I Colvin, *The Life of Jameson, Vol 2* (London, 1922), pp 87–80 [hereafter Colvin, *Jameson 2*]. For the wider context of the contestation of both Esselen and Trimble's appointments see especially CH Muller, 'Policing the Witwatersrand: A History of the South African Republic Police, 1886–1899', unpublished DPhil thesis, Centre for Africa Studies, University of the Free State, February 2016, pp 100–180 [hereafter Muller, 'Policing the Witwatersrand'], or a poorly edited version in CH Muller, '"The Greatest State Scandal": Personality, Power and the South African Republic Police, 1886–1899', *South African Historical Journal*, Vol 68, No 1, 2016, pp 13–30.

3 See GN van den Bergh, 'Secret Service in the South African Republic, 1895–1900', *Military History Journal*, Vol 3, No 2, December 1974, p 3 [hereafter van den Bergh, 'Secret Service']. On Afrikaner-Dutch in the National Union, see also FE Garrett and EJ Edwards, *The Story of an African Crisis and of the Jameson Raid* (London, 1897), p 82 [hereafter, Garrett and Edwards, *African Crisis*]. And for the way that the conspirators worked at grooming Esselen, see, for example, the letter of Lionel Phillips to Alfred Beit, 12 August 1895, in M Fraser and A Jeeves (eds), *All that Glittered: Selected Correspondence of Lionel Phillips, 1890–1924*

(Cape Town, 1977), pp 80–83.

4 See especially Muller, 'Policing the Witwatersrand', p 174; and Chapter 5 of CT Gordon, *The Growth of Boer Opposition to Kruger, 1890–1895* (London, 1970). See also C Ash, *The IF Man. Dr Leander Starr Jameson: The Inspiration for Kipling's Masterpiece* (Solihull, 2012), p 216 [hereafter Ash, *The IF Man*]. Kruger's early – personal – opposition to the appointment of Trimble, a former member of the 6th Inniskilling Dragoons but who had not actively engaged Boer forces during the First Anglo-Boer War of 1880–1881, is noted in 'The Detective Inquiry', *The Star*, 8 May 1895. Trimble's background can also be traced in 'The Detective Inquiry', *The Star*, 17 May 1895.

5 See also entry on EA Esselen in CJ Beyers and JL Basson (eds), *Dictionary of South African Biography, Vol V*, (Pretoria, 1987), pp 248–249; and Muller, 'Policing the Witwatersrand', p 174.

6 See van den Bergh, 'Secret Service', p 3; and Muller, 'Policing the Witwatersrand', p 177.

7 See van den Bergh, 'Secret Service', p 3

8 See the detailed report carried in the *San Francisco Call*, Vol 79, No 56, 25 January 1896, which, in turn, is quoting from an undated issue of the Johannesburg *Standard & Diggers' News* of December 1895.

9 This, together with Brown's publicly stated opposition to an armed uprising, helps explain that fact that, after the Raid, Brown was found in possession of 22 rifles but was not prosecuted. See E de Waal, 'The Part Played by Americans on the Witwatersrand during the Period 1886–1899', unpublished MA thesis, Department of History, Unisa, 1971, p 60 [hereafter de Waal, 'Americans on the Witwatersrand'].

10 As quoted in Garrett and Edwards, *African Crisis*, p 4.

11 On Brown's politics, see de Waal, 'Americans on the Witwatersrand', pp 60 and 64.

12 As recorded in A Ireland, 'The True Story of the Jameson Raid as Related to me by John Hays Hammond, Part 1', *The North American Review*, Vol 208, No 753, August 1918, p 187. In his usual opportunistic way, Hammond, catering for a wartime readership, could not resist suggesting that among the secret agents there were 'many Germans'.

13 See de Waal, 'Americans on the Witwatersrand', pp 58–59.

14 See LS Meyer, 'John Hays Hammond and the Jameson Raid: Engineering a Capitalist Revolution in South Africa', in *The Farther Frontier: Six Case Studies of Americans and Africa, 1848–1936* (London, 1992), p 142 [hereafter Meyer, *Farther Frontier*].

15 See Garrett and Edwards, *African Crisis*, pp 64–65; and Colvin, *Jameson 2*, p 41.

16 In this context see also Garrett and Edwards, *African Crisis*, p 66.

17 Note Hammond's grudging admission that the smuggling of guns was 'the most difficult part of *their* [not 'my'] work' to RH Davis, in *Dr Jameson's Raiders vs The Johannesburg Reformers* (New York, 1897) p 15, emphasis added [hereafter Davis, *Dr Jameson's Raiders*].

18 See J Pinfold's entry on 'George Herbert Farrar' in L Goldman (ed), *Oxford Dictionary of National Biography* (Oxford, 2006).

19 '"Those men are funking it", he [Jameson] said. I'm going to stir them up".' That speech undoubtedly is the real reason for his remarkable action. He wanted the acclaim that would follow his invasion of the Transvaal, and he thought that the chance of his doing so was slipping from him through the half-heartedness of the men of Johannesburg – as quoted in Davis, *Dr Jameson's Raiders*, p 53.

20 Garrett and Edwards, *African Crisis*, p 65.

21 *Ibid*, p 64, where he describes the 120 as being made up only of 'old soldiers and others'.

22 On Hammond's say-so only months after the Raid, Davis, in *Dr Jameson's Raiders*, at p 22, describes some of those in the ranks as 'common adventurers and filibusters, men who, for reasons of their own, had sought a change of fortune in the unsettled country north of the Cape, and boys from the counties of England, sons of field labourers and farmers who had already seen a little "help yourself" fighting in the Kaffir and Matabele wars …'.

23 As quoted in the Rev J King, *Dr Jameson's Raid: Its Causes and Consequences* (Manchester, 1896), p 44 [hereafter King, *Jameson's Raid*].

24 The extracts taken from the unnamed trooper's letter are drawn from King, *Jameson's Raid*, pp 45–46.

25 See JH Hammond, *The Autobiography of John Hays Hammond, Vol 1* (New York, 1935), p 330 [hereafter Hammond, *Autobiography 1*].

26 On 28 December, Jameson telegraphed Cape Town, noting 'I stand to lose 50 good British South Africa Company's police – time expires and so on' – see Colvin, *Jameson 2*, p 50.

27 Among others – including Hammond, who points to desertion being a problem – see V Harlow and FH Hamilton, 'Sir Frederic Hamilton's Narrative of Events Relative to the Jameson Raid, *The English Historical Review*, Vol 72, No 283, April 1957, p 303 [hereafter, Harlow and Hamilton, 'The Jameson Raid']. Nor was the problem confined to Chartered Company men. As Colvin recounted it, '… time-expired Bechuanaland Police were threatening to resign and Jameson could not stop them'; Colvin, *Jameson 2*, p 51.

28 On 5 February 1896, Jameson told his brother Sam that, despite what had happened, he was on the 'most affectionate terms' with Frank Rhodes and Hammond – see Colvin,

Jameson 2, p 160. As we shall have occasion to note later, Hammond, with the larger ego of the two, and the sense that his Southern honour had been impugned by accusations of 'cowardice' for not having ridden out to assist Jameson in his hour of need, remained deeply resentful for years thereafter.

29 See Ash, *The IF Man*, p 227.

30 Garrett and Edwards, *African Crisis*, p 64. Read this in conjunction with Hammond, *Autobiography 1*, p 332.

31 Some of these problems date back to mid-November; see letter of that date from Jameson to Bobby White in Garrett and Edwards, *African Crisis*, pp 51–52.

32 Garrett offers a rather one-dimensional view in suggesting that Mein '… was as typical a Yankee as ever chewed tobacco …' – Garrett and Edwards, *African Crisis*, p 162. For Mein's background, see *San Francisco Call*, Vol 79, No 56, 25 January 1896; and Vol 87, No 165, 5 May 1900; entry for Thomas Mein (1838–1900) in the 'Alaska Mining Hall of Fame Foundation'; and CC Spence, *Mining Engineers and The American West: The Lace-Boot Brigade* (London, 1970), pp 23 and 336 [hereafter Spence, *Lace-Boot Brigade*]. On Mein's call to southern Africa, see, for example, de Waal, 'Americans on the Witwatersrand', pp 24–25.

33 Perhaps it is in this context that one has to view Louis Cohen's observations that he 'neither cared for fair political treatment nor fleas, Boer or British' – as cited in D Rhoodie, *Conspirators in Conflict* (Cape Town, 1967), p 69 [hereafter Rhoodie, *Conspirators in Conflict*].

34 Spence, *Lace-Boot Brigade*, p 336.

35 While Phillips entertained some early revolutionary thoughts, in late 1894 and the first quarter of 1895, he kept his distance from the Gold Fields revolutionaries until he was encouraged by Beit himself, probably at Rhodes's behest, to become more involved. See, among others, Rhoodie, *Conspirators in Conflict*, p 22.

36 See W LaFeber, *The New Empire: An Interpretation of American Expansion, 1860–1898* (London 1963), pp 242–248; and ER May, *Imperial Democracy: The Emergence of America as a Great Power* (New York, 1961), pp 34–42.

37 Among others see Garrett and Edwards, *African Crisis*, p 82.

38 See, among others, Rhoodie, *Conspirators in Conflict*, p 49. These were Garrett's 'well-meaning jingoes' – see Garrett and Edwards, *African Crisis*, pp 81–82.

39 Rhodes and Jameson's predictable commitment to raising the British flag above the Witwatersrand can be traced in Colvin, *Jameson 2*, p 44; and Garrett and Edwards, *African Crisis*, p 88.

40 Rhoodie, *Conflicted Conspirators*, p 50.

41 As quoted in Rhoodie, *Conflicted Conspirators*, p 69.
42 As quoted in Meyer, *Farther Frontier*, p 146.
43 Garrett and Edwards, *African Crisis*, p 82.
44 On Dodd's and others' fears, see Meyer, *Farther Frontier*, p 150.
45 Colvin, *Jameson 2*, pp 87–91.
46 Rhoodie, *Conflicted Conspirators*, pp 67–68.
47 On the loss of prestige felt by members of the Reform Committee after the Raid, see, for example, de Waal, 'Americans on the Witwatersrand', p 66.
48 See Harlow and Hamilton, 'The Jameson Raid', p 295.
49 Hammond, *Autobiography 1*, pp 334–335.
50 As recorded in Garrett and Edwards, *African Crisis*, p 73.
51 *Ibid*, p 74.
52 *Ibid*, p 74.
53 *Ibid*, pp 85–86.

CHAPTER 13

1   JH Hammond, *The Autobiography of John Hays Hammond, Vol 1* (New York, 1935), p 337 (emphasis added) [hereafter Hammond, *Autobiography 1*].
2   This paragraph is taken, almost in its entirety, from sources cited in E de Waal, 'The Part Played by Americans on the Witwatersrand during the Period, 1886–1899', unpublished MA thesis, Department of History, University of South Africa, 1971, pp 61–62 [hereafter de Waal, 'Americans on the Witwatersrand'].
3   E Garrett and EJ Edwards, *The Story of an African Crisis and of the Jameson Raid* (London, 1897), p 162 [hereafter Garrett and Edwards, *African Crisis*].
4   Hammond, *Autobiography 1*, p 337
5   I Colvin, *The Life of Jameson, Vol 2* (London, 1922), p 50 [hereafter Colvin, *Jameson 2*].
6   Hammond, *Autobiography 1*, p 333.
7   Garrett and Edwards, *African Crisis*, p 133.
8   *Ibid*, pp 138–139.
9   *Ibid*, p 207.
10 See 'Fled from the Transvaal', *Lawrence Daily World*, 10 February 1896.
11 See V Harlow and FR Hamilton, 'Sir Frederic Hamilton's Narrative of Events Relative to the Jameson Raid', *The English Historical Review*, Vol 72, No 283, April 1957, p 297 [hereafter Harlow and Hamilton, 'The Jameson Raid'].
12 Garrett and Edwards, *African Crisis*, p 125.
13 See Colvin, *Jameson 2*, p 11; Garrett and Edwards, *African Crisis*, p 125; and P Payton, *The Cornish Overseas: A History of Cornwall's 'Great Migration'* (Dundurn, 2005), p 7 [hereafter Payton, *The Cornish Overseas*].
14 See especially J Hyslop, *The Notorious Syndicalist. JT Bain: A Scottish Rebel in Colonial South Africa* (Johannesburg, 2004), pp 105–109.
15 As Mrs Hammond was perhaps not too sad to note: 'The Cornish miners were politely presented at Kimberley and other places en route with bunches of white feathers by the howling mob' – see f/n 2, of Chapter 2, in NH Hammond, *A Woman's Part in a Revolution* (London, 1897).
16 Republic of South Africa, Johannesburg, Brenthurst Library, AA Kelsey Papers, Notes contained in Folder 'A', apparently written on 30 December 1895.
17 See Payton, *The Cornish Overseas*, p 364.
18 See de Waal, 'Americans on the Witwatersrand', pp 63–64.
19 Hammond, *Autobiography 1*, p 338.
20 *Ibid*, p 339. Hammond's self-aggrandising memoirs have left a legacy of problems for American historians not fully *au fait* with South African history. Thus, while Sammy Marks was undoubtedly a Kruger informant and sympathiser, he was also the country's most prominent industrialist and can hardly be relegated to the role of being a 'spy' – see, for example, LE Meyer, 'John Hays Hammond and the Jameson Raid: Engineering a Capitalist Revolution in South Africa' in his *The Farther Frontier: Six Case Studies of a Americans and Africa, 1848–1936* (London, 1992), p 150 [hereafter Meyer, *Farther Frontier*].
21 Hammond, *Autobiography 1*, p 340.
22 See Garrett and Edwards, *African Crisis*, pp 142–146; and Colvin, *Jameson 2*, p 101.
23 Hammond, *Autobiography 1*, p 340.
24 See Chapter 9 above.
25 Hammond, the arch-conspirator, thus devoted a chapter of his memoirs to recasting events so as to cover his tracks and minimise recriminations for 'The Reform Movement' – see Hammond, *Autobiography 1*, pp 307–328. It is extraordinary how many historians have fallen, uncritically, for this 'spin' before the era of 'spin' in their renditions of events relating to the Jameson Raid, and have been content to write about the 'reform movement'. Equally amusing, in retrospect, are references to the 'national movement' and the 'provisional government' – see, for example, Garrett and Edwards, *African Crisis*, pp 166–168. Whose 'nation' exactly was this? And how could recent, self-styled 'reformers' – as opposed to 'revolutionaries' – *simultaneously* preside over a 'provisional government'? For those interested in the Jameson Raid such political terminology does not, in the first instance, make for accurate description. These terms need to be seen and analysed as representing aspirations rather than actualities, and more as indicators of the direction of short-term political developments than as accurate descriptors.
26 Hammond, *Autobiography 1*, p 319.
27 See, for example, Garrett and Edwards,

African Crisis, pp 166–168. Again, how mere 'reformers' – as opposed to hopeful 'revolutionaries' – could preside over a 'provisional government' was not explained.

28 See Meyer, *Farther Frontier*, p 149.

29 See Garrett and Edwards, *African Crisis*, pp 163–164.

30 On the brigades, see Garrett and Edwards, *African Crisis*, p 201.

31 See Colvin, *Jameson 2*, pp 88–89; Garrett and Edwards, *African Crisis*, p 169.

32 See especially, 'The Police Force', *The Star*, 8 January 1896; and J King, *Dr Jameson's Raid: Its Causes and Consequences* (London, 1896), p 125. For a complete list of the names of pugilists that served under Andrew Trimble, see Republic of South Africa, Pietermaritzburg, Pietermaritzburg Archive Repository (PAR), A 1297, EM Trimble Papers, folio 937.

33 See Garrett and Edwards, *African Crisis*, pp 165–168 and, more especially, the list reproduced on p 167.

34 Hammond, *Autobiography 1*, p 343.

35 *Ibid*, p 342.

36 *Ibid*, p 343.

37 *Ibid*, p 343; and Garrett and Edwards, *African Crisis*, p 131.

38 What Hammond failed to record, however, was the fact that, after the meeting, an 'American Citizens' Association' was formed – yet another structure in which he played no recorded role. Moreover, it was at about this time, too, that yet another American observer, Frank Norris, noted how those in the 'Reform Committee' began to lose their prestige and never regained it. See especially de Waal, 'Americans on the Witwatersrand', pp 65–66.

39 For another account of this meeting – but one not fully cognisant of all the interpersonal clashes and micro-politics at play – see de Waal, 'Americans on the Witwatersrand', pp 66–67.

40 For Hammond's take on this, see Hammond, *Autobiography 1*, p 343.

41 See Garrett and Edwards, *African Crisis*, pp 170–174.

42 The back story to this extraordinary development is recounted in Chapters 17 and 18 below.

43 See Republic of South Africa, Johannesburg, Brenthurst Library, AA Kelsey Papers, notes in Folder 'B'.

44 Hammond, *Autobiography 1*, p 344.

45 Garrett and Edwards, *African Crisis*, p 49.

46 *Ibid*, p 175.

47 See Colvin, *Jameson 2*, pp 74–75.

48 *Ibid*, pp 76–77; and Garrett and Edwards, *African Crisis*, p 177. In an article in *Vanity Fair*, 9 April 1896, Jameson was labelled as 'a raider, a freebooter and a filibuster' – see the text and cartoon by 'Spy' reproduced on

p 180 of J Carruthers (ed), *The Jameson Raid: A Centennial Perspective* (Johannesburg, 1996) [hereafter Carruthers (ed), *The Jameson Raid*].

49 Fred Hamilton, relatively cool-headed, later suggested that 'bad faith' could be detected at almost every level from as early as 26 December – Harlow and Hamilton, 'The Jameson Raid', p 297.

50 See IR Smith, 'Joseph Chamberlain and the Jameson Raid', pp 89–110 in Carruthers (ed), *The Jameson Raid*.

51 See Garrett and Edwards, *African Crisis*, p 180.

52 On the Chief Justice, see, among others, CT Gordon, *The Growth of Boer Opposition to Kruger, 1890–1895* (London, 1970); and on Kotzé's own love of intrigue, even though he came down on the side of Kruger during the Jameson Raid, see Garrett and Edwards, *African Crisis*, p 197.

53 See Colvin, *Jameson 2*, pp 96–98; and Garrett and Edwards, *African Crisis*, pp 175–176.

54 Hammond, *Autobiography 1*, p 346. See also Garrett and Edwards, *African Crisis*, p 183, where it is reported that Phillips also said that 'If necessary, they were prepared to continue the movement they had seen fit to commence with their guns'. In the late 19th century, gentlemen never lied, they 'bluffed'. Phillips, a poker player who could match the best of them, could, when the need arose, also 'bluff' with the best of them.

55 See Garrett and Edwards, *African Crisis*, pp 202–203; and Colvin, *Jameson 2*, pp 101–103.

56 Colvin, *Jameson 2*, p 99.

57 On Trimble as secret agent, see Chapter 19 below.

58 See Colvin, *Jameson 2*, p 99.

59 *Ibid*, pp 104–109; and Garrett and Edwards, *African Crisis*, pp 107–112.

60 See 'The Krugersdorp Battle', *Evening Post* (New Zealand), 31 January 1896.

61 It was the issue of cowardice that framed Hammond's first post-Raid public counteroffensive with his house-trained journalist of choice, Richard Harding Davis. His other initiatives will be discussed below. See RH Davis, *Dr Jameson's Raiders vs The Johannesburg Reformers* (New York, 1897) – starting at p 7 and ending on p 56.

CHAPTER 14

1 That felicitous formulation is, of course, not mine – it comes from S Trapido's seminal article, 'South African in a Comparative Study of Industrialization' in *The Journal of Development Studies*, Vol 7, No 3, 1971.

2 See JH Hammond, *The Autobiography of John Hays Hammond, Vol 1* (New York, 1935), pp 347–348 [hereafter Hammond,

Autobiography 1].

3 *Ibid*, p 348.

4 *Ibid*.

5 Any study of the crowds in Johannesburg during the Jameson Raid should start with J King, *Dr Jameson's Raid: Its Causes and Consequences* (Manchester, 1896), and pay some attention to pp 118–125.

6 This paragraph is based on Hammond, *Autobiography 1*, pp 348–349; I Colvin, *The Life of Jameson, Vol 2* (London, 1922), pp 137–139 [hereafter Colvin, *Jameson 2*]; and FE Garrett and EJ Edwards, *The Story of an African Crisis* (London 1897), pp 207–209 [hereafter Garrett and Edwards, *African Crisis*].

7 Colvin, *Jameson 2*, pp 138–139.

8 Hammond, *Autobiography 1*, p 349.

9 *Ibid*.

10 The exchanges between Chamberlain and British officials based in southern Africa at the time, including Sir Hercules Robinson, can be most readily traced in JP FitzPatrick's *The Transvaal from Within* (London, 1899), pp 126–141.

11 Garrett and Edwards, *African Crisis*, p 209.

12 *Ibid*, pp 209–210.

13 *Ibid*, p 211.

14 *Ibid*, p 215.

15 *Ibid*, p 217.

16 For Hammond's take on these events see Hammond, *Autobiography 1*, pp 351–352; and Garrett and Edwards, *African Crisis*, pp 219–221. What is clear from Garrett, however, is that Shippard and de Wet were also misled by Robinson. On Shippard as 'Father of Lies', see Colvin, *Jameson 2*, pp 141–142.

17 As reproduced in Garrett and Edwards, *African Crisis*, p 221.

18 *Ibid*, p 222. It is notable how, at that point in his own narrative, Hammond, too, back in full Anglophile mode and in search of any crumbs of imperial justice that might come his way, switches from the easy and familiar use of the term 'mob' to 'crowd'. See Hammond, *Autobiography 1*, p 352. The analogue is, of course, that when men are assembled in large numbers and are of a mind to follow their leaders they constitute 'crowds', but when they have, or develop a collective mind of their own they degenerate into 'mobs'. The future historian who studies the behaviour of the 'crowds' and 'mobs' in the Jameson Raid will draw these distinctions far more clearly than I have done so here.

19 Hammond, *Autobiography 1*, p 352. See also Garrett and Edwards, *African Crisis*, pp 222–223.

20 Garrett and Edwards, *African Crisis*, p 224.

21 *Ibid*, p 224.

22 *Ibid*, p 226.

23 *Ibid*, p 227.

24 *Ibid*, p 225.

25 See Colvin, *Jameson 2*, p 142.

26 Hammond, *Autobiography 1*, p 352.

27 *Ibid*, pp 352–323.

28 *Ibid*, p 353. Natalie Harris's version of her husband's arrest at Heath's Hotel has none of the cowboy movie elements that characterise Jack Hammond's account – no cards sent up to rooms, no brains being blown out, and no farewell drinks at the bar. Her version reads: 'We started up at a tap on the door. A friend to tell us the officer was waiting at the street entrance. I helped my husband into his coat and we kissed each other good-bye.' See NH Hammond, *A Woman's Part in a Revolution* (London, 1897), p 14.

29 As reproduced in Garrett and Edwards, *African Crisis*, p 231.

CHAPTER 15

1 Indeed, the seeds of the idea of taking over an entire town under arms may have first been planted in the minds of the brothers, Advocates Charles and James Leonard, arguably foremost of the imperialists and jingoes on the Witwatersrand, in the late 1880s and early 1890s. Their defence of 'social bandits' involved in acts of brigandage perpetrated by Irish deserters from the British armed forces can be traced in C van Onselen, *Masked Raiders: Irish Banditry in Southern Africa, 1880–1899* (Cape Town, 2010), pp 6–7, 157 and 227–228 [hereafter van Onselen, *Masked Raiders*]; and C van Onselen, *Showdown at the Red Lion: The Life and Times of Jack McLoughlin, 1859–1910* (Cape Town, 2015), pp 163, 178–179. The Leonards, said by some to be of Irish descent themselves, offer a direct, personal line linking the ideas that shaped the 'Irish Brigade', talk of armed incursion in the early 1890s and the urban revolution planned as the precursor to the 'Jameson Raid' in 1895. By the same token, it seems significant that it was after the opening of the Rand goldfields (1886), the occupation of Eureka City (1887) and the invasion of Johannesburg (1888) by the Irish Brigade that Dr WJ Leyds, first as State Attorney and, after 1889, as State Secretary, began allocating funds for a 'secret police' or 'secret service'. The primary focus of covert state inquiries in Johannesburg thus gradually shifted from being primarily 'criminal' (1886–1890) to being more 'political' in nature (1890–1894). This evolution can be traced in HJG Kamffer, '*Om een scherpe oog in't zeil te houden*: Die Geheime Diens in die Zuid-Afrikaansche Republiek', unpublished DPhil dissertation, Department of History, Potchefstroomse Universiteit vir Christelike Hoër Onderwys, 1999, at pp 31, 38, 43 and 45 [hereafter

Kamffer, 'Die Geheime Diens']. I am indebted to Carel van der Merwe for alerting me to this source. On the gold-recovery crisis see, for example, C van Onselen, *New Babylon, New Nineveh: Everyday Life on the Witwatersrand, 1886–1914* (Cape Town 2001), pp 3–6 [hereafter van Onselen, *New Babylon, New Nineveh*].

2 See Kamffer, 'Die Geheime Diens', p 61; and van Onselen, *Masked Raiders*, p 157.

3 On Bettington's background see above, Chapter 7; and, on his being spied upon, Kamffer, 'Die Geheime Diens', pp 64–68. This was of course replete with irony in that the agent, Taylor, was reporting to State Attorney Esselen, who was himself being pulled into the emerging 'Jameson Raid' conspiracy.

4 For the background of the Corner House during this period, see M Fraser and A Jeeves, *All that Glittered: Selected Correspondence of Lionel Phillips, 1890–1924* (Cape Town, 1977) [hereafter Fraser and Jeeves, *All that Glittered*]. On the corrupting influence of the company, see below.

5 On the importance of the Pretoria Club and the role of its various members, and more especially that of Eugène Marais, in what I have loosely termed the 'Spy Wars' here, see C van der Merwe's splendid *Donker Stroom: Eugène Marais en die Anglo-Boereoorlog* (Cape Town, 2015) [hereafter van der Merwe, *Donker Stroom*] and the classic that it successfully supplements with critical new findings, L Rousseau, *Die Groot Verlange: Die Verhaal van Eugène N Marais* (Pretoria, 2005) [hereafter Rousseau, *Groot Verlange*]. An imaginative account that links the Pretoria and Rand Clubs in the late 19th and early 20th centuries awaits its historian or a novelist.

6 See Chapter 8 above.

7 On the proximity of Phillips and Esselen at this time, see, for example, Phillips to J Wernher, 28 May 1894, in Fraser and Jeeves, *All that Glittered*, p 77.

8 Phillips to A Beit, 16 June 1894, in Fraser and Jeeves, *All that Glittered*, p 79.

9 See especially, Report No 10 of Taylor to Esselen, 6 October 1894, as rendered in f/ns 190 and 191 in Kamffer, 'Die Geheime Diens', p 53. For more on rifle associations at this time, see also p 63.

10 See Chapter 10 above.

11 Hammond's own interest in espionage networks on the Rand dates back to at least May 1894 when he identified the American, RE Brown as a 'spy' working for the Kruger government. See JH Hammond, *The Autobiography of John Hays Hammond, Vol 1* (New York, 1935), pp 319 and 341–342.

12 This early economic focus can be attributed to Rhodes's relatively late arrival as an investor on the Rand. See especially IR Phimister,

'Rhodes, Rhodesia and the Rand', *Journal of Southern African Studies*, Vol 1, No 1, pp 76–94.

13 See above, Chapter 11 and note 33.

14 There are only two passing references to Joubert and none whatsoever to Esselen in Hammond's *Autobiography*, 2 vols, (New York, 1935). Likewise, there are only single references to AW Malan and Marais – quite extraordinary given what we now know of both men's close involvement in events around the Raid.

15 See CT Gordon's seminal *The Growth of Boer Opposition to Kruger, 1890–1895* (London, 1970), pp 184–204 [hereafter Gordon, *Boer Opposition*].

16 See Gordon's persuasive analysis in *Boer Opposition*, pp 205–228.

17 *Ibid*, p 207 and pp 247–274; as well as Gordon's principal source – JA Mouton, 'Generaal Piet Joubert in die Transvaalse Geskiedenis', unpublished PhD dissertation, Department of History, University of Stellenbosch, 1949, pp 260–269. On Esselen's political radicalism, always ostensibly within constitutional bounds, see also van der Merwe, *Donker Stroom*, p 39.

18 See CJ Beyers and JL Basson (eds), *Dictionary of South African Biography, Vol 5* (Pretoria, 1987), pp 248–249) [hereafter Beyers and Basson (eds), *Dictionary of South African Biography*].

19 See I Colvin, *The Life of Jameson, Vol 2* (London, 1922), p 8.

20 See United Kingdom, Oxford University, Bodleian Library, Mss Afr.t.5m folio 103–104, CJ Rhodes to Esselen, 2 June 1887.

21 See J Scoble and HR Abercrombie, *The Rise and Fall of Krugerism* (New York, 1900), pp 66 and 79.

22 See L Phillips to A Beit, 12 August 1894, in Fraser and Jeeves, *All that Glittered*, p 81.

23 Esselen's attempts to scoop the position of State Attorney for himself during a cabinet reshuffle set off a political feud with Kruger that lasted six years. See Republic of South Africa, University of Cape Town (UCT), Jagger Library, BC 959, A11.5, Charles Cowen, undated, unpublished, 'Miscellany: Historical Reminiscences' – section on EA Esselen [hereafter RSA, UCT, Jagger Library, Cowen Miscellany]. The half-decade-long feud ended in 1894, when Kruger eventually appointed Esselen as State Attorney – see, for example, *De Express*, 2 March 1894.

24 See 'Transvaal Politics, Reviewed in England', *Natal Witness*, 16 December 1895. For more views on Esselen, see Beyers and Basson (eds), *Dictionary of South African Biography*, p 249; and, within this context also, Gordon, *Boer Opposition*, pp 185–186; and van der Merwe, *Donker Stroom*, pp 35–36.

25 See L Stanley and A Salter (eds), *The World's Greatest Question: Olive Schreiner's South*

African Letters, 1889–1920 (Cape Town, 2014), pp 123–124. I am indebted to Ian Phimister for drawing this letter to my attention.

26 RSA, UCT, Jagger Library, Cowen Miscellany – section on EA Esselen.

27 *Ibid.*

28 Gordon, *Boer Opposition*, p 186. See also Chapter 2 above.

29 Beyers and Basson (eds), *Dictionary of South African Biography*, p 248; and DW Crowley, 'The Crofter's Party – 1885 to 1892: The First British Independent Peoples' Political Party', *Scottish Historical Review*, Vol 35, 1956, p 6.

30 See the *New York Times* of 22 and 25 February 1900; the *Evening Star* (New Zealand), 9 April 1900; and 'Current Topics', *Daily Telegraph*, 25 August 1900.

31 Esselen opened a speech to his constituents in Potchefstroom, in 1892, by noting that 'during the last eight years the country had changed from an agricultural one to an industrial one. New conditions demanded new forms and methods'. See Gordon, *Boer Opposition*, p 159. On Esselen's liking for intrigue – something that he shared with Marais – see C Muller, 'Policing the Witwatersrand: A History of the South Africa Republic Police, 1886–1899', unpublished DPhil thesis, Centre for Africa Studies, University of the Free State, 2016, pp 100–180 [hereafter Muller, 'Policing the Witwatersrand'].

32 See Rousseau, *Groot Verlange*, pp 57, 63, 112 and 426; and van der Merwe, *Donker Stroom*, pp 28–29, 36, 45, 221–222 and 298.

33 See van der Merwe, *Donker Stroom*, p 56.

34 Likewise, it may be significant that Marais and Malan later fell out over the issue of how children in the prisoner of war camp in Bermuda during the Anglo-Boer War were allegedly treated; see AH Malan to the Editor, *Land en Volk*, 9 April 1903. Again, I am indebted to Carel van der Merwe for drawing my attention to this letter and for his guidance on several other aspects of Marais's early career.

35 On Esselen's drinking problems, see, for example, L Rousseau, *The Dark Stream: The Story of Eugène N Marais* (Cape Town, 1982), pp 48 and 100.

36 See, for example, Gordon, *Boer Opposition*, pp 42, 128 and 202.

37 Van der Merwe, *Donker Stroom*, pp 28–35.

38 See Rousseau, *Groot Verlange*, pp 51–61; and van der Merwe, *Donker Stroom*, pp 32–34.

39 See Gordon, *Boer Opposition*, pp 177 and 202. I am indebted to Fransjohan Pretorius for drawing my attention to the following sources from which this picture of AH Malan is constructed: J Malan, *Die Boere-Offisiere van die Tweede Vryheidsoorlog, 1899–1902* (Pretoria, 1990), p 104; R Mendelsohn, *Sammy Marks: 'The Uncrowned King of the Transvaal'* (Cape

Town, 1991), pp 127–128; SB Spies, *Methods of Barbarism?* (Cape Town, 1977), p 100; and PHS van Zyl, *Die Helde-Album: Verhaal en Fotos van Aanvoerders en Helde uit ons Vryheidstryd* (Johannesburg, 1944), p 163.

40 See Gordon, *Boer Opposition*, pp 201–202.

41 See LE van Niekerk, *Kruger se Regeterhand* (Cape Town, 2004), p 180. I am indebted to Carel van der Merwe for drawing my attention to the importance of this ongoing political connection between Malan and Marais.

42 See Gordon, *Boer Opposition*, pp 205–228.

43 *Ibid*, p 210; and, more pertinently, van der Merwe, *Donker Stroom*, p 70. After 1893, the possibility of armed rebellion or revolt were clearly in Marais's consciousness – something which, after 1894, would have helped draw him in the direction of Hammond's proposed Johannesburg-based 'revolution'.

44 These exchanges can be followed in Gordon, *Boer Opposition*, p 214.

45 See Gordon, *Boer Opposition*, pp 205–228; Rousseau, *Groot Verlange*, pp 73–74; and van der Merwe, *Donker Stroom*, p 41.

46 Gordon, *Boer Opposition*, pp 176–177.

47 See Kamffer, 'Die Geheime Diens', p 45, from which it would seem that Leyds was beginning to shift his focus from an exclusively criminal to a more politically informed threat to state security.

48 See Mrs Lionel Phillips (Florence), *Some South African Recollections* (London, 1900), p 78.

49 Fraser and Jeeves, *All that Glittered*, pp 36–37. Interestingly, the word 'corruption' fails to make an appearance in *All that Glittered*, despite the fact that Nellmapius was known to be a shady operator – see, for example, Gordon, *Boer Opposition*, p 18.

50 Gordon, *Boer Opposition*, pp 15–18; and van der Merwe, *Donker Stroom*, p 41.

51 See above, Chapter 2.

52 This, and much that follows, relies heavily on van der Merwe, *Donker Stroom*, pp 42–48.

53 Gordon, *Boer Opposition*, p 207.

54 See van der Merwe, *Donker Stroom*, p 47.

55 *Ibid*, pp 43–44.

56 *Ibid*, p 43.

57 At least one assault on Marais was recorded – see 'A Few Personal Notes', *The Mercury* (Hobart, Tasmania), 8 January 1896.

58 See van der Merwe, *Donker Stroom*, p 45.

59 *Ibid*, p 49.

60 See *Report of the Chamber of Mines 1894*, pp 123–124.

61 See especially *De Express*, 2 March 1895; and the *Transvaal Advertiser*, 15 March and 2 May 1895.

62 See Kamffer, 'Die Geheime Diens', p 52.

63 As cited in Gordon, *Boer Opposition*, p 235.

64 H Giliomee, *The Afrikaners: Biography of a People* (Charlottesville, 2003), p 238, citing JA

Coetzee's *Politieke Groepering in die wording van die Afrikaner Nasie* (Johannesburg, 1941), at p 317.

65 See entry on DJ Esselen in DW Kruger and CJ Beyers (eds), *Suid-Afrikaanse Biografiese Woordeboek, Deel 111* (Cape Town, 1977), p 287.

66 The first names of the Ueckermann brothers appear to be anglicised, barely disguised, versions of more likely Afrikaans-Dutch names such as 'Carl'. Carl Ueckermann was married to Eugène Marais's sister, Sophy, which made him a brother-in-law. On Sophy Ueckermann, see van der Merwe, *Donker Stroom*, p 51. On the Ueckermanns as undercover agents working for Esselen, see van Onselen, *New Babylon, New Nineveh*, pp 72 and 402, note 90; and Muller, 'Policing the Witwatersrand', pp 141 and 174. It would thus seem, then, that any secret information that Esselen and Marais shared during 1894–1895 was also, in part, cemented by Marais's distant family ties.

67 On Schröder and Marais, see Rousseau, *Groot Verlange*, p 76; and on his background, Kamffer, 'Die Geheime Diens', pp v, 8–9, 38 and 50. Schröder was investigating the notorious 'draadsaak' – and on him and Leonard see especially van der Merwe, *Donker Stroom*, p 46.

CHAPTER 16

1 See HJG Kamffer, '*Om een scherpe oog in't zeil te houden:* Die Geheime Diens in die Zuid-Afrikaansche Republiek', unpublished DPhil dissertation, Department of History, Potchefstroomse Universiteit vir Christelike Hoër Onderwys, 1999, p 52 [hereafter Kamffer, 'Die Geheime Diens'].

2 All this is well covered in Kamffer, 'Die Geheime Diens', pp 51–70. On Howcroft's initial covert operations and later move to criminal work in Johannesburg see also, 'The Detective Inquiry', *The Star*, 14 May 1895.

3 See Kamffer, 'Die Geheime Diens', pp 51–70 and, on Esselen – and indeed Kruger – being fully informed of gun-smuggling in Johannesburg by late August 1895, pp 82–83.

4 See GN van den Bergh, 'Secret Service in the South African Republic, 1895–1900', *Military History Journal*, Vol 3, No 2, December 1974.

5 The core conflict in the Johannesburg Detective Department was between LB Donovan and R Ferguson, who was Chief Detective in Johannesburg before his role fell away and, for much of 1895, was effectively replaced by Andrew Trimble. Some of this conflict as related to purely criminal matters can be traced in C van Onselen, *Showdown at the Red Lion: The Life and Times of Jack McLoughlin, 1859–1910* (Cape Town, 2015),

p 263 [hereafter van Onselen, *Showdown at the Red Lion*], and in 'The Detective Inquiry', as reported in *The Star* and more especially on 14 and 15 May 1895. But for the more important, wider political context, see CH Muller, '"The Greatest State Scandal": Personality, Power and the South African Republic Police, 1886–1896', *South African Historical Journal*, Vol 68, No 1, pp 13–30.

6 For WH Ueckermann's comments about Esselen's heavy drinking, see Republic of South Africa, South African National Archives (SANA), Pretoria, State Attorney (SP), Vol 81, File GR42/95, Sworn Affidavit of AF Brink, dated 18 May 1895. Brink, Trimble's secretary, was an Esselen loyalist and thus opposed to Ueckermann. On Ueckermann's transfer and resentment, see his evidence to 'The Detective Inquiry', *The Star*, 8 May 1895. For Ueckermann as the anchor of a pro-Kruger anti-Esselen grouping in the agencies, see Kamffer, 'Die Geheime Diens', p 90. Ueckermann and Trimble later became involved in a very public street-corner brawl.

7 Thus Kamffer notes how Esselen's unexpected resignation, in November 1895, disrupted the flow of incoming intelligence into the secret service at a 'critical juncture' – see Kamffer, 'Die Geheime Diens', p 89. That, too, may have been by chance but, given how the rest of the 'Progressive' core behaved it, may have been consciously calculated to have precisely that effect. And, if that is so, it may help explain why Hammond remained so silent about Trimble's role in the 'revolution'.

8 For contemporary fears that Trimble was a secret British agent receiving financial support from the Rhodes government, see GN van den Bergh, *Die Polisiediens in die Zuid-Afrikaansche Republiek* (Pretoria, 1980), pp 178–179 [hereafter van den Bergh, *Die Polisiediens*].

9 See RSA, KwaZulu-Natal, Pietermaritzburg Archives Repository (PAR), EM Trimble Papers, A.1297, folio 430 [hereafter RSA, PAR, EM Trimble Papers].

10 See CH Muller, 'Policing the Witwatersrand: A History of the South African Republic Police, 1886–1899', unpublished DPhil thesis, Centre for Africa Studies, University of the Free State, 2016, p 140 [hereafter Muller, 'Policing the Witwatersrand'].

11 This relationship if explored more fully below in Chapter 17.

12 See RSA, PAR, EM Trimble Papers, folio 867. Trimble's appointment was approved by Esselen as early as 18 November 1894 – see Trimble's evidence to 'The Detective Inquiry', *The Star*, 15 May 1895.

13 It is Colvin, Jameson's biographer, who points to Esselen's use of this back channel, see I Colvin, *The Life of Jameson, Vol 2* (London,

1922), pp 88 [hereafter Colvin, *Jameson 2*].

14 See RSA, PAR, EM Trimble Papers, folio 981.
    Not even Trimble's daughter, Edith, was aware
    of this Upington connection and it is only
    via Colvin, *Jameson 2*, p 88, that she, and we,
    learned of it.

15 By Trimble's own telling – see 'The Detective
    Inquiry', *The Star*, 18 May 1895.

16 See National Archives of South Africa
    (NASA), Pretoria, Transvaal Archive Bureau
    (TAB), Vol SP 463, E Esselen to Attorney
    General, Cape Town, 24 October 1894.

17 See, for example, RSA, University of Cape
    Town (UCT), Jagger Library, Leipoldt Papers,
    File 7, BC 317 (20), undated letter [almost
    certainly early 1895] from WP Schreiner to
    Esselen [hereafter RSA, UCT, Jagger Library,
    Leipoldt Papers].

18 See especially EA Esselen's letter of 29 May
    1893 to JH de Villiers, as cited in Part 1 of WG
    Schulze's, 'Melius de Villiers: A Biographical
    Sketch', undated, unpublished, manuscript,
    Unisa, Pretoria.

19 RSA, UCT, Jagger Library, Leipoldt Papers,
    BC94, D3.69, WP Schreiner to EA Esselen, 20
    January 1896.

20 See H Giliomee, *The Afrikaners: Biography of a
    People* (Charlottesville, 2003), p 238.

21 RSA, UCT, Jagger Library, Leipoldt Papers,
    BC94, D3.69, WP Schreiner to EA Esselen, 20
    January 1896.

22 See RSA, PAR, EM Trimble Papers, folio 442.

23 *Ibid*, folio 108.

24 For Esselen acting as a 'secret agent' for the
    British South Africa Company, in 1891, see
    Chapter 17 below.

25 For an earlier, 1888, case of a Kimberley
    detective being seconded to assist in the South
    African Republic, see Muller, 'Policing the
    Witwatersrand', p 74. It is worth stressing that
    all the relevant sources in the Cape Archives
    still do not yield a single line about Trimble's
    conditions of service or of a request for his
    secondment or an application for unpaid leave
    – that, while all the matching documents for
    other officers appear to be intact.

26 See Trimble's evidence in 'The Detective
    Inquiry', in *The Star*, 17 and 18 May 1895.

27 It is interesting to note that in Republic
    of South Africa (RSA), Cape Town, Cape
    Archives Bureau, Colonial Office CO Vol
    3784, Police Commissioner, Letters Received,
    1894, there appears to be no record of Trimble
    ever asking for, or having been granted, leave
    from the police.

28 Cape of Good Hope, House of Assembly,
    *Select Committee on the Jameson Raid into the
    Territory of the South African Republic, 1896*, p 76.

29 JH Hammond, *The Autobiography of John Hays
    Hammond, Vol 2* (New York, 1935), pp 406-408.

30 See Cape of Good Hope, House of Assembly,
    Select Committee on the Jameson Raid into the

Territory of the South African Republic, 1896.

31 On Upington's decision to prosecute Gardner
    Williams under a law that made provision for
    a fine instead of mandatory imprisonment,
    see, for example, the report carried in the *New
    Zealand Herald*, 14 April, 1896.

32 See Trimble's evidence, 'The Detective
    Inquiry', 18 May 1895.

33 Van den Bergh, *Die Polisiediens*, pp 178–179.

34 *Ibid*, p 178.

35 See Trimble's evidence, 'The Detective
    Inquiry', *The Star*, 18 May 1895.

36 On Green and Richards, see 'The Detective
    Inquiry', *The Star*, 17 May 1895.

37 For his achievements in this regard, see
    Colvin, *Jameson 2*, pp 40 and 90.

38 See evidence of HEO Green to 'The
    Detective Inquiry', *The Star*, 15 May 1895.

39 See evidence of HEO Green and A Trimble
    to 'The Detective Inquiry', *The Star*, 17 and
    18 May 1895.

40 See RSA, PAR, EM Trimble Papers, at folio
    312j and on Jameson's alleged love of female
    company, M Meredith, *Diamonds, Gold and
    War* (Johannesburg, 2007), p 121.

41 This paragraph is built around observations to
    be found in RSA, PAR, EM Trimble Papers,
    folios 108, 175, 867 and 871.

42 See RSA, PAR, EM Trimble Papers, folios 310
    and 312.

43 *Ibid*.

44 *Ibid*, folios 261–270 and 305.

45 See especially the evidence of HEO Green
    and A Trimble to 'The Detective Inquiry', as
    reported in *The Star* of 17 and 18 May 1895.

46 This connection is more fully probed in
    Chapter 19 below.

47 See Colvin, *Jameson 2*, pp 90 and 93.

48 See RSA, PAR, EM Trimble Papers, folios
    788 and 914.

49 *Ibid*, folios 90 and 1009.

50 Kamffer, 'Die Geheime Diens', p 92.

51 *Ibid*, p 75

52 See, for example, Chapter 18 below and
    note how confident Kruger was about his
    own sources of intelligence and security
    when Kotzé and van Niekerk, after talking
    to Joubert, went to inform the President
    that he might be abducted by the (then
    still unknown) force that Hammond had
    assembled at Irene.

53 See Chapter 13 above.

54 RSA, SANA, SS (State Secretary), Vol 4634,
    R 1856/95, R Ferguson to State President and
    the Executive Council, 11 February 1895.

55 On Ferguson's resignation – which in fact was
    predicated on political conflicts within the
    department and predated the murder at the
    Red Lion, but only surfaced after the murder
    of George Stevenson, see van Onselen,
    Showdown at the Red Lion, pp 282–298; and for
    Ferguson's letter of resignation, RSA, SANA,

SS Vol 4643, R 185/95, R Ferguson to the State President and Executive Council, 11 February 1895.

56 For Kruger's personal interest in how to go about getting information from wiretapping the telegraph, see, for example, D Blackburn and WW Caddell, *Secret Service in South Africa* (London, 1911), p 287.

57 Kamffer, 'Die Geheime Diens', p 48.

58 See WJ de Kock and DW Kruger (eds), *Dictionary of South African Biography, Vol 2* (Pretoria, 1972), entry on EJP Jorissen, pp 344–347.

59 On Jorissen's mission, see Kamffer, 'Die Geheime Diens', p 50; and, on the plausibility of such a mission in 1895, van Onselen, *Showdown at the Red Lion*, pp 249–265.

60 See Chapter 11 above.

61 See especially the evidence of ID de Vries and S Lombaard to 'The Detective Inquiry', as reported in the *The Star*, 8 May 1895.

62 See RSA, PAR, EM Trimble Papers, folios 571–572.

63 See Kamffer, 'Die Geheime Diens', p 75; and Muller, 'Policing the Witwatersrand', p 158.

64 RSA, UCT, Jagger Library, Leipoldt Papers, BC 94, D2.3, His Honour, SJP Kruger, State President to E Esselen, State Attorney, 29 May 1895.

65 See RSA, PAR, EM Trimble Papers, folios 788–795.

66 On Esselen's movements in December 1895 see Chapter 18 below; and on Trimble's brief exit from the Rand to Kimberley, see Muller, 'Policing the Witwatersrand', pp 180–181.

CHAPTER 17

1 JH Wilkins (ed), *The Great Diamond Hoax and Other Stirring Incidents in the Life of Asbury Harpending* (San Francisco, 1913), p 29. Hammond's initial foray in the direction was, of course, the Johannesburg Vigilance Committee, in early 1895, in which he, with the help of the editor of *The Star*, Fred Hamilton, held up the example of the famous San Francisco Vigilance Committee of 1851 for locals to consider. See Chapter 7 above.

2 The extent to which this was an accepted position can be traced in FE Garrett and EJ Edwards, *The Story of an African Crisis and of the Jameson Raid* (London 1897), p 38 [hereafter Garrett and Edwards, *African Crisis*].

3 See Chapter 12, note 9 above.

4 The telling phrase 'gold and maize' as already noted, is not mine but that of Stanley Trapido in his 'South Africa in a Comparative Study of Industrialization', *The Journal of Development Studies*, Vol 7, No 3, 1971, pp 309–320. On the aspirations of Esselen, Eugène Marais and other Progressives, see CT Gordon, *The*

Growth of Boer Opposition to Kruger, 1890–1895 (London, 1970) [hereafter Gordon, *Boer Opposition*].

5 See HJG Kamffer, '*Om een scherpe oog in 't zeil te houden*: Die Geheime Diens in die Zuid-Afrikaansche Republiek', unpublished DPhil dissertation, Department of History, Potchefstroomse Universiteit vir Christelike Hoër Onderwys, 1999, p 92 [hereafter Kamffer, 'Die Geheime Diens']. But, as we shall note later, it was not only the timing but the point of origin of Esselen's apologies – Cape Town – that are of interest; see below, Chapter 18.

6 For an overview of Esselen's early career, see 'Ewald Esselen, KC', *South African Law Journal*, No 321, 1906, pp 321–327.

7 The lack of so much as a footnote devoted to Jong Zuid-Afrika in contemporary historiography is a serious obstacle in our quest to develop an understanding of the emergence of a modernising strand in Afrikaner nationalism in the late 19th century that can take us beyond the more familiar outline of the theological roots of the ideology. The idea of developing a discussion group devoted to developing a progressive, radical, rational and scientifically informed approach to the analysis of contemporary problems appears to have originated with Esselen in 1890. Esselen, in turn, appears to have been inspired by the idea of Young Ireland and the interests and enthusiasm of men such as Gavin Brown Clark (an anti-imperialist and Scottish home rule advocate), whom Esselen had met during his student years in Edinburgh and London. Esselen had also met Karl Blind, the German revolutionary, an acquaintance of Karl Marx, in the early 1880s while assisting President Kruger in constitutional negotiations. The members of Jong Zuid-Afrika were suspected of harbouring revolutionary ideals in Pretoria in the early 1890s. See Gordon, *Boer Opposition*, p 186; K Blind, 'Problems of the Transvaal', *The North American Review*, Vol 162, No 473, April 1896, pp 457–472; and N Levy, *Jan Smuts: being a character sketch of General, the Honourable JC Smuts, KC, MLA, Minister of Defence, Union of South Africa* (London, 1917), p 48.

8 Republic of South Africa, University of Cape Town (UCT), Jagger Library, JC Smuts to E Esselen, 1 March 1897 [emphasis in the original].

9 On Rhodes helping out Esselen with a loan see United Kingdom, Oxford University, Bodleian Library, Mss.Afr.t.5, folio 103–104, CJ Rhodes to E Esselen, 2 June 1887; and, for the wider backdrop to Rhodes's political dealings, M Tamarakin, *Cecil Rhodes and the Cape Afrikaners: The Imperial Colossus and the*

Colonial Parish Pump (Abingdon, 1996).

10 See J Scoble and HR Abercrombie, *The Rise and Fall of Krugerism: A Personal Record of Forty Years in South Africa* (New York, 1900), pp 66 and 79 [hereafter Scoble and Abercrombie, *The Rise and Fall of Krugerism*]; and JP FitzPatrick, *The Transvaal from Within: A Private Record of Public Affairs* (London, 1899), p 64. The recording of this incident points to an intimate friendship between Esselen and FitzPatrick, as does Esselen's seeking out of FitzPatrick at the Pretoria Club in January 1896, after the Raid – see C van der Merwe, *Donker Stroom: Eugène Marais en die Anglo-Boereoorlog* (Cape Town, 2015), p 61 [hereafter van der Merwe, *Donker Stroom*].

11 See van der Merwe, *Donker Stroom*, pp 3–4; and I Colvin, *The Life of Jameson, Vols 1 and 2* (London, 1922), pp 200–201 [hereafter Colvin, *Jameson 1 or 2*].

12 See NG Garson, 'The Swaziland Question and a Road to the Sea', unpublished MA thesis, Department of History, University of the Witwatersrand, 1955, p 104.

13 An undated item drawn from the Flora Shaw collection, United Kingdom, Oxford University, Bodleian Library, MSS British Empire, S 590, Box 8, File No 3. I am indebted to Lucy McCann, Senior Archivist at the Bodleian, for helping me to place this item in its correct context. The emphasis is in the original.

14 See van der Merwe, *Donker Stroom*, p 35.

15 The official and principal interpreter in the October 1883 deliberations in London was, of course, Rev DP Faure – see G McCall Theal, *History of South Africa from 1873 to 1884* (London, 1919), p 154.

16 Scoble and Abercrombie, *The Rise and Fall of Krugerism*, p 172 (emphasis added). Scoble is probably a reliable source for this information because even before the Raid crisis was over his co-author, RH Abercrombie, confirmed that Esselen had frequently attended meetings hosted by what, in effect, was the local branch of the National Union – see *The Times* (London), 6 January 1896.

17 United Kingdom, Oxford University, Bodleian Library, Mss.Afr.s 228, C2A, folios 103–104, telegram from 'Comm.' to Premier, Cape Town, 4 March 1895.

18 Entry on DJ Esselen in DW Krüger and CJ Beyers (eds), *Suid-Afrikaanse Biografiese Woordeboek, Deel III*, (Cape Town, 1977), p 287 [hereafter Krüger and Beyers (eds), *Biografiese Woordeboek*].

19 Colvin, *Jameson 2*, pp 30–31 and especially footnote 1 on p 31.

20 See *The Colonies & India* (London), 3 August 1895, p 9.

21 See Krüger and Beyers (eds), *Biografiese Woordeboek*, p 287. On the 'drifts crisis', see

also Gordon, *Boer Opposition*, pp 78–79.

22 See Kamffer, 'Die Geheime Diens', especially pp 86–89.

23 Esselen's resignation had been mooted, in Johannesburg, as early as May 1895 once Kruger, Kock and Wolmarans – the conservative core of the Executive Council – began taking the fight to the State Attorney publicly over a series of issues relating to Esselen's portfolio. Principal among domestic problems was Esselen's insistence on retaining Trimble and the resulting 'Detective Inquiry' but, also on the list were other matters – a contested contract for providing clothing, the unpopular decision to transfer a public prosecutor from one district to another, and the question of an appropriate salary scale for the police. These issues can be traced most readily in 'Mr Esselen's Position' in *The Star*, 17 May 1895. On Esselen's eventual resignation, see 'Mnr Esselen's Bedanking', *Land en Volk*, 21 November 1895.

24 See *Semi-Weekly Express* (Terre Haute, IN), 3 January 1896.

25 See RSA, Pietermaritzburg Archive Repository (PAR), A. 1297, Edith May Trimble Papers (EM Trimble Papers), untitled biography of Andrew Trimble, folios 788–790 [hereafter RSA, PAR, EM Trimble Papers].

26 Intriguingly, in the draft biography of her father, Edith Trimble noted that Ewald Esselen was about to leave for 'Natal' but then crossed out the word and replaced it with 'Cape' – see RSA, PAR, EM Trimble Papers, p 788.

27 DJ Esselen was Acting State Secretary in the Boers' short-lived New Republic between 1884 and 1888. During this time he had represented the New Republic in high-level negotiations in Natal and, unsuccessfully, in London. See Krüger and Beyers (eds), *Biografiese Woordeboek*, pp 286–287.

28 See 'The Weenen Massacre', *Natal Witness*, 17 December 1895.

29 See, for example, *The Colonies & India*, 9 January 1896, p 9.

30 See also Chapter 19 below.

31 See CJ Muller, 'Policing the Witwatersrand: History of the South African Republic Police Force, 1886–1899', unpublished DPhil thesis, Centre for Africa Studies, University of the Free State, February 2016, p 188; and JA Mouton, *Generaal Piet Joubert in die Transvaalse Geskiedenis*, Archives Year Book for South African History (Parow, 1957), p 158 [hereafter Mouton, *Piet Joubert*].

32 RSA, Pretoria, South African National Archives (SANA), Leyds Archive, 1895–1896, Part I, p 165, telegram from Rorke to President Kruger, 31 December 1895, No 163, Esselen (Cape Town) to State President, Pretoria, 31 December 1895, No 165.

33 Garrett and Edwards, *African Crisis*, p 152.

34 See *Report of the Select Committee of the Cape of Good Hope House of Assembly on the Jameson Raid into the Territory of the South African Republic, March 1897*, evidence of WP Schreiner, pp 139–140.

35 See Conclusion below.

36 It seems that Edith Trimble took the name 'Stringer' – and the supposed meeting – from the generally well-researched fiction of John Presland [pseudonym of the Australian Gladys Skelton], *Dominion: A Novel of Cecil Rhodes and South Africa* (New York, 1925). It is difficult to know how seriously to weigh the evidence listed in the notes that immediately follow but Edith Trimble is a generally reliable source.

37 See RSA, PAR, EM Trimble Papers, folios 867[c] to 868.

38 *Ibid*, folio 869. Edith Trimble implies that this meeting took place on Christmas Day 1895, but that is clearly wrong – Jameson's invasion only took place on 29 December and 'Stringer' had little reason to be miserable to his core by as early as 25 December.

39 See Colvin, *Jameson 2*, pp 142–143.

40 *The Times* (London), 6 January 1896.

41 See van der Merwe, *Donker Stroom*, p 61.

42 See Chapter 19 below.

43 See van der Merwe, *Donker Stroom*, p 61.

44 Trimble appointees included Burgess, Wilson, Brink and Vosterlaak, at least two of whom were in Pretoria at one stage (Brink and Wilson); see evidence of LB Donovan, to the 'Detective Inquiry', *The Star*, 7 May 1895.

45 See Kamffer, 'Die Geheime Diens', p 91.

46 *Ibid*, pp 90 and 96.

47 See GN van den Bergh, *Die Polisiediens in die Zuid-Afrikaansche Republiek* (Pretoria, 1980), p 189.

48 Kamffer, 'Die Geheime Diens', p 84.

49 'Mnr Esselen's Bedanking', *Land en Volk*, 21 November 1895.

50 See Gordon, *Boer Opposition*, p 66, f/n 27.

51 As noted by 'Mede Republiekein' in a letter to the Editor of *Land en Volk*, 21 November 1895. In order to make sense of 'Mede Republikein's letter it should be placed against the background of events referred to in Gordon, *Boer Opposition*, at pp 181 and 236.

52 Colvin, *Jameson 2*, p 34.

53 See D Blackburn and WW Caddell, *Secret Service in South Africa* (London, 1911), note at p 287: 'Only once did the old man show any excitement. That was when he heard that Andrew Trimble had gone over to the Reformers, and was actually arming Uitlanders to fight burghers. Trimble had been the special protégé of Advocate Ewald Esselen. He got the President to consent to the appointment with difficulty. "I told you so," was Kruger's comment on hearing that the Chief Detective had turned traitor. He sent for Esselen, and that gentleman had a very warm quarter of an hour.'

54 There is endless debate among historians as to whether or not Marais and Malan's meeting with the 'reformers' was authorised by the Kruger government. I am of the view that it was not. In this I have chosen to follow the lead of the politically progressive-minded Chief Justice JG Kotzé, who was requested by the State President, along with two other judges, to attend the most important meetings of the Executive Council during December/January 1895/96 – see Sir John Gilbert Kotzé, *Memoirs and Reminiscences, Vol 2* (Cape Town, 1940), p 234 [hereafter Kotzé, *Memoirs*]. Unlike almost everyone else at the time who were present in one or other political capacity, the Chief Justice was present primarily in an advisory capacity and is unambiguous when retelling the tale: 'The members of the Reform Committee seem to have laboured under the impression that these two gentlemen [Marais and Malan] had been sent to make, as it were, from the side of the Government. But it was a quite mistaken notion on their part.' Independent to 'progressive' in his political thinking, Kotzé remained reasonably well disposed to Joubert and Malan. Indeed, he went out of his way to protect their reputation by discreetly failing to remind his readers of the extremely unpleasant exchange between Jorissen and Joubert about Malan which he had witnessed at first hand. Kotzé was, however, unforgiving of Marais who he characterised merely as editor of a 'strong anti-Government organ'.

55 See L Rousseau, *Die Groot Verlange: Die Verhaal van Eugène N Marais* (Pretoria, 1974), p 96, 'Genl. Joubert het intussen met sy belangrikste ondersteuners in verbinding gebly – Ewald Esselen, Eugène Marais en ander' [hereafter Rousseau, *Groot Verlange*].

56 See van der Merwe, *Donker Stroom*, pp 30–32 and 38–44.

57 See JH Hammond, *The Autobiography of John Hays Hammond, Vol 1* (New York 1935), p 343 [hereafter Hammond, *Autobiography 1*].

58 This previously elusive period in Marais's life is now captured more fully in van der Merwe, *Donker Stroom*, pp 76–87.

59 See van der Merwe, *Donker Stroom*, p 86.

60 See Mrs John Hays Hammond, *A Woman's Part in a Revolution* (London, 1897), Chapter 13, p 39. This hostility would only have been deepened by the knowledge that Joubert, in his attempt to put and keep distance between himself and the other Boer collaborators, had taken the unusually harsh view that the death sentence imposed on Hammond and the other leaders of the conspiracy should not be commuted. See Mouton, *Piet Joubert*, pp 167–168.

61 See van der Merwe, *Donker Stroom*, pp 51–53; and Rousseau, *Groot Verlange*, pp 92–95.

62 Marais and Falconer's relationship is well documented in van der Merwe, *Donker Stroom*, pp 49–50; on the opening of personal correspondence, see p 53.

63 Esselen's secret agents' interest in Fred Hamilton dated back to at least 1894. See RSA, National Archives (SANA), Pretoria, Staats Prokereur (SP), Vol 238, unsigned Report no '21', of 22 September 1894 containing a seating plan for a Transvaal National Union banquet as 'written out' by FH Hamilton.

64 Van der Merwe, *Donker Stroom*, p 54.

65 *Ibid*, pp 55–57.

66 This would also be of a piece with the disinformation – 'the little American bluff' – that Hammond later also passed on to Sammy Marks; see Hammond, *Autobiography 1*, p 339.

67 See van der Merwe, *Donker Stroom*, at p 57. Van der Merwe rightly draws attention to how, in affidavits, sworn on 10 January 1896 before State Attorney Coster, who was already taking an interest in the doings of Marais and Malan during the days of crisis, neither of them was willing to disclose the presence of the other on Monday 30 December. These silences – sins of omission – were recalibrated to match each other and set the record straight in a second set of sworn statements some weeks later.

68 See Colvin, *Jameson 2*, p 61.

69 On Marais as a self-described 'boy' at the time, see van der Merwe, *Donker Stroom*, p 56.

70 *Ibid*, pp 57–58 and, on the lack of Marais and Malan's credentials, Kotzé, *Memoirs*, p 234. Marais and Malan's visit to Johannesburg on Monday 30 December 1895 can only be read as having taken place with the government's knowledge, if not approval, if Joubert's personal, unofficial endorsement of the approval of Marais and Malan's visit is seen as constituting 'the government'. But Joubert's authority, even when acting on his own, in an official capacity – which in this case he was not, and of which there is no record – could hardly be interpreted as that of 'the government'. Joubert was in the government, but governmental approval or knowledge could not and did not reside solely in Joubert, even if Marais and Malan later found it convenient to conflate the two – as they did. This false and tedious elision has caused endless confusion and debate in the historical literature.

71 On Bailey, Wools-Sampson and Rutherfoord Harris as the nexus for this shipboard development, see Colvin, *Jameson 2*, pp 42–43. Colvin, however, suggests that neither Rhodes nor Jameson, both of whom were taken with the long-term idea of a confederation

of southern African states, were sufficiently impatient to have put about the idea of biting off the ZAR at one go and then seeing it digested into the British Empire. The fact is, of course, by that time – by his own telling to Stead a few years later – Rhodes was already fearful that Hammond and the Americans would triumph and then take the ZAR down a republican path that would jeopardise British interests in the long run; see WT Stead, *The Americanisation of the World* (New York, 1901), pp 56–57. Edmund Garret, who wrote earlier than Colvin, was clearly aware of this dimension of the problem at the time, and when he writes of an unnamed 'British jingo', in relation to imperial ambitions, is presumably referring to Aubrey Wools-Sampson – see Garrett and Edwards, *African Crisis*, pp 81–82.

72 On AH Malan's political status in 1894, if not 1895, see Gordon, *Boer Opposition*, p 177. Kruger, of course, was based on the farm Boekenhoutfontein.

73 On Dr Wolff's substantial role in laying out staging posts and provisions for Jameson and his men in the event of them being needed on the Rand, see Chapter 9 above. It could only have added to the underlying political ironies that JM Malan – who let part of his farm to the conspirators – was an arch-conservative and political supporter of Kruger's; see Gordon, *Boer Opposition*, pp 9–11. John Hays Hammond's shadow, too, can be seen flitting through the Rustenburg district, if not across Doornpoort itself, in October 1895 – see Cape of Good Hope, *Report of the Select Committee on the Jameson Raid into the Territory of the South African Republic*, A6-1896, Evidence of John Hays Hammond, p 235.

CHAPTER 18

1 See FE Garrett and EJ Edwards, *The Story of an African Crisis* (London, 1897), pp 142–146 [hereafter Garrett and Edwards, *African Crisis*]. Hammond's inability to deliver sufficient rifles to Johannesburg and the subsequent calling-off of the attack on the Pretoria arsenal also gave rise to great disaffection amongst fellow core conspirators – see JP FitzPatrick, *The Transvaal from Within: A Private Record of Public Affairs* (London, 1899), pp 126–139.

2 Garrett and Edwards, *African Crisis*, p 143.

3 *Ibid*, pp 143–144.

4 On Natalie Harris on this matter, see JH Hammond, *The Autobiography of John Hays Hammond, Vol 1* (New York, 1935) p 327 [hereafter Hammond, *Autobiography 1*]. On Clement, who was in on every aspect of American involvement in the planning of the uprising, this will have to be taken as an

article of faith and some of it can perhaps be read-off the proximity of Natalie Harris and Mrs Clement during the crisis itself – see NH Harris, *A Woman's Part in a Revolution* (London, 1987), p 12.

5 On Hammond's time-staggered disclosures about his private intention to abduct Kruger, see A Ireland, 'The True Story of the Jameson Raid as related to me by John Hays Hammond', *The North American Review*, Vol 208, No 754, September 1918, p 366; and then, only slightly more fully, in Hammond, *Autobiography 1*, pp 327–328 and p 340. In the former, written in 1918, Hammond was still keen to give the impression that the decision to abduct was a joint one and that his co-conspirators were fully informed about it, but in the latter, published in 1935, he acknowledged that he had kept this, his intention in this regard, 'very quiet'.

6 See Garrett and Edwards, *African Crisis*, p 145; and I Colvin, *The Life of Jameson, Vol 1* (London, 1922), p 101.

7 See Republic of South Africa (RSA), Pretoria, South African National Archives (SANA), SPR Vol 135/96, Sworn Statement by EN Marais, 10 January 1896. See also C van der Merwe, *Donker Stroom: Eugène Marais en die Anglo-Boereoorlog* (Cape Town, 2015), p 57 [hereafter van der Merwe, *Donker Stroom*].

8 See Marais's account of his later testimony in *Land en Volk*, 13 February 1896. All these events are well laid out in van der Merwe, *Donker Stroom*, pp 57–62.

9 RSA, Pretoria, South African National Archives (SANA), Leyds Archive, 1895–1896, Part I, p 165, Telegram from Rorke to President Kruger, 31 December 1895, and p 163, Esselen (Cape Town) to the State President, Pretoria, 31 December 1895.

10 On Jorissen as 'secret agent' see HJG Kamffer, '*Om een scherpe oog in 't zeil te houden:* Die Geheime Diens in die Zuid-Afrikaansche Republiek', unpublished DPhil dissertation, Department of History, Potchefstroomse Universiteit vir Christelike Hoër Onderwys, 1999, p 80 [hereafter Kamffer, 'Die Geheime Diens']. On Monday, 30 December 1895, and with State Secretary Leyds away in Europe, Kruger in effect co-opted three judges – Kotzé, Ameshoff and Jorissen – to serve as his closest advisers within a temporarily extended Executive Council. Like the Reform Committee, which remained almost in 'perpetual session' once the crisis broke, Kruger and his advisers met whenever necessary, right into January 1896. See JG Kotzé, *Memoirs and Reminiscences, Vol 2* (Cape Town, 1940), pp 233–234 [hereafter Kotzé, *Memoirs*]; and DW Krüger, *Paul Kruger, Deel ll* (Johannesburg, 1963), p 160 [hereafter Krüger, *Paul Kruger, Deel ll*].

11 Translated by the author from JA Mouton, *Generaal Piet Joubert in die Transvaalse Geskiedenis*, Archives Year Book for South African History (Cape Town, 1957), p 166 [hereafter Mouton, *Piet Joubert*].

12 Mouton, *Piet Joubert*, pp 166–167.

13 See van der Merwe, *Donker Stroom*, p 58 and L Rousseau, *Die Groot Verlange: Die Verhaal van Eugène N Marais* (Pretoria, 2005), p 92 [hereafter Rousseau, *Groot Verlange*].

14 Kamffer, 'Die Geheime Diens', p 94.

15 Garrett notes, '… Joubert, who had been accused of treason for not responding to urgent messages from the front, had actually given orders to the artillery to start, when the President interposed to stop it' – Garrett and Edwards, *African Crisis*, p 134.

16 On the price that the Jameson Raid exacted of Joubert's reputation as Commandant-General, see, for example, WJ Du Plooy, 'Die Militêre Voorbereiding en Verloop van die Jameson-Inval 1895/96', unpublished MA thesis, Department of History, University of Pretoria, 1958, pp 118–124 [hereafter Du Plooy, 'Militêre Voorbereiding']. Also, Mouton, *Piet Joubert*, p 168. See also Joubert's 'personal statement' as carried in *Land en Volk*, on 24 November 1897.

17 It is interesting to note in passing how Garrett – a Rhodes supporter – went out of his way to protect Hammond and Phillips in his rendition of what he called the 'Irene Mystery' in Garrett and Edwards, *African Crisis*, pp 142–146. His five-page chapter is filled with defensive interventions such as: 'it does not follow that the owner [Mrs Nellmapius letting to the Corner House people] was necessarily more cognisant of the way in which the property was to serve the revolution than worthy Volksraad member Malan was in the matter of Jameson's remount horses' (p 143) and 'that is the Irene Mystery, which there is *now* no harm in telling' (p 145 – emphasis added). The fact is that it is clear from a reading of Hammond's later (1918) confession about the planned abduction of Kruger that Garret himself was part of the cover-up at the time of his writing, in 1896, when the longer-term fate of Jameson, Hammond and the collaborators was not yet clear.

18 In this regard it is interesting to note, again in passing, just how successful Garrett was at leading subsequent Afrikaner historians astray about what happened at Irene – a siding where a train containing war equipment from Mashonaland had been noted earlier. The thought that there might be something untoward in Joubert and his son-in-law's behaviour and movements during that day was clearly beyond the pale for those interested in presenting only an orthodox,

nationalist, version of history – see, for example, GN van den Bergh, *Die Polisiediens in die Zuid-Afrikaansche Republiek* (Pretoria, 1980), p 192 and note; and Kamffer, 'Die Geheime Diens', p 95.

19 See also below.

20 Kotzé, *Memoirs*, p 238.

21 *Ibid*, pp 238–239.

22 *Ibid*, p 241.

23 *Ibid*, pp 239–241.

24 *Ibid*, p 240.

25 See Garrett and Edwards, *African Crisis*, p 147; and for credit being given to Joubert for his foresight in protecting the home of the State President, see Mouton, *Piet Joubert*, p 159.

26 *De Volksstem*, 26 February 1896.

27 See Du Plooy, 'Militêre Voorbereiding', p 94; and Hammond, *Autobiography 1*, pp 346–347. Here Hammond is, yet again, at pains to try to conceal the depth and nature of the Reformers' connection to Boer collaborators and merely describes Lace's companion on this futile mission as being 'a messenger'.

28 See Hammond, *Autobiography 1*, p 346; and A Ireland, 'The True Story of the Jameson Raid as related to me by John Hays Hammond, Part 1', *The North American Review*, Vol 238, No 753, August 1918, p 370.

29 On Marais's briefing of Joubert on that Monday night, and on the close contact between Joubert, Esselen and Marais during the crisis, see van der Merwe, *Donker Stroom*, p 58; and Rousseau, *Groot Verlange*, p 92.

30 Hammond, *Autobiography 1*, p 340 (emphasis added).

31 See, for example, the account of the 'Preliminary Examination' as carried in the *Oamouru Mail* (New Zealand) of 27 March 1896.

32 Van der Merwe sketches some of the context for the later scholarly disputation in *Donker Stroom*, pp 57–58. Krüger, *Paul Kruger, Deel II*, pp 162–163, for example, is adamant that Marais and Malan were never authorised to speak for the government and that it was entirely their own initiative that they decided to go to Johannesburg. That, too, is unlikely; they would probably have done so under advice from their mentor(s).

33 The 'Olive Branch' and 'official recognition' lines would appear to have been concocted at a meeting on Tuesday morning, 31 December 1895, between Marais and a senior member of the Reform Committee (almost certainly Hammond) whom FitzPatrick later also refused to name; see van der Merwe, *Donker Stroom*, p 58.

34 For the enactment of this fiction, much-needed and much-loved by Hammond, but which the government again pointedly ignored at the trial of the Reformers, see Hammond, *Autobiography 1*, pp 343–344.

35 'A little American bluff seemed indicated', Hammond, *Autobiography 1*, p 339; while van der Merwe's *Donker Stroom* offers a good number of examples of Marais's ability to craft lies instrumental enough to help him reach desirable outcomes over the short or longer term.

36 See Hammond, *Autobiography 1*, p 343; and van der Merwe, *Donker Stroom*, p 59.

37 As cited in J van der Poel, *The Jameson Raid* (Cape Town, 1951), p 114 [hereafter van der Poel, *Jameson*]. Rissik was not only Esselen's close friend but also his neighbour in Pretoria. On the Esselen-Rissik friendship see B Forsyth, 'The Pretoria Club: The Welcome of Lord Selborne to Pretoria, 14 May, 1905' – pp 25 and 49 [unpublished ms, 2015] [hereafter Forsyth, 'Pretoria Club'].

38 See van der Poel, *Jameson*, p 116; and, crucially, Mouton, *Piet Joubert*, p 159, note 10.

39 Compare the names of the government delegation as proposed by Malan and Marais in RSA, Pretoria, SANA, Leyds Archive, to the names of those who met with the Reformers and as recorded by Garrett and Edwards in *African Crisis*, p 175. For the background to the bitter conflict between Marais and Jan Kock, see van der Merwe, *Donker Stroom*, pp 46–47. Kruger may, of course, have known that, even though Rissik was a man of great integrity, he was also a friend of Esselen's and probably a Joubert supporter – see Forsyth, 'Pretoria Club' p 25. Moreover, Rissik was also an extremely active Freemason – see Forsyth, 'Pretoria Club', p 49.

40 The composition of the Reformers' delegation, headed by Phillips rather than Hammond, was clearly the outcome of some debate back in Johannesburg. Garrett, in diplomatic mode, at p 175 of *African Crisis*, described it as 'a representative rather than a personally powerful deputation'.

41 See Garrett and Edwards, *African Crisis*, p 176 (emphasis in the original).

CHAPTER 19

1 All that despite the fact that, late in 1897, Esselen went public about his intention to support Kruger ahead of Joubert in the forthcoming presidential election; see JA Mouton, *Generaal Piet Joubert in die Transvaalse Geskiedenis*, Archives Year Book for South African History (Parow, 1957), p 169 and note 2 on the same page. [hereafter Mouton, *Piet Joubert*].

2 See especially C van der Merwe's surgical probing of this in *Donker Stroom: Eugène Marais en die Anglo-Boereoorlog* (Cape Town, 2015), p 60 [hereafter van der Merwe, *Donker*

Stroom].

3 On Joubert's profound economic achievements, which left him with an estate worth in excess of a quarter of a million pounds sterling – derived from investments in mining and farming – see, for example, CT Gordon, *The Growth of Boer Opposition to Kruger, 1890–1895* (London, 1970), pp 246–247; and Chapter 20, 'Eknomiese Bedrywighede' in Mouton, *Piet Joubert*, pp 201–274.

4 Mouton, *Piet Joubert*, p 158.

5 See HJG Kamffer, 'Om een scherpe oog in't zeil te houden: Die Geheime Diens in die Zuid-Afrikaansche Republiek', unpublished DPhil thesis, Potchefstroomse Universiteit vir Christelike Hoër Onderwys, 1999, p 98. This appears to have been yet another instance of Kruger's tortoise philosophy coming to the fore.

6 See CJ Muller, 'Policing the Witwatersrand: History of the South African Republic Police Force, 1886–1899', unpublished PhD thesis, Centre for Africa Studies, University of the Free State, 2016, p 188 [hereafter Muller, 'Policing the Witwatersrand'].

7 See Mouton, *Piet Joubert*, p 167.

8 *Ibid*, pp 167–168.

9 *Ibid*. See also L Rousseau, *Die Groot Verlange: Die verhaal van Eugène N Marais* (Pretoria, 2005), pp 73 and 79 [hereafter Rousseau, *Groot Verlange*].

10 Mouton, *Piet Joubert*, pp 168.

11 On the suspicions around Marais, in Pretoria, through 1896 and his subsequent entry into social life in London, via the Hammonds, see van der Merwe, *Donker Stroom*, pp 62–67 and 76–87.

12 See, for example, in passing, Rousseau, *Groot Verlange*, p 101.

13 See Mouton, *Piet Joubert*, p 165.

14 *Ibid* (author's translation).

15 RSA, University of Cape Town (UCT), Jagger Library, Leipoldt Papers, BC 94, D3.40, JH Hofmeyr to E Esselen, 20 January 1896.

16 Republic of South Africa, Pretoria, South African National Archives, Transvaal Archives Bureau (TAB), Vol. W 123, Charles Leonard to Ewald Esselen Esq, Pretoria, 17 March 1896.

17 *Ibid*, Secretary to the Cabinet to Ewald Esselen, 2 May 1896, marked 'secret'.

18 RSA, Pietermaritzburg Archive Repository (PAR), A 1297, EM Trimble Papers, folio 935. I have been unable to trace the letter that Edith Trimble alludes to in an incomplete collection although there is another letter by Viljoen to the Editor, which appears in the edition of 28 March, 1896, that mentions neither Esselen nor Trimble.

19 See J Scoble and HR Abercrombie, *The Rise and Fall of Krugerism: A Personal Record of Forty Years in South Africa* (New York, 1900) p 111.

20 RSA, UCT, Jagger Library, Leipoldt Papers, B.C. 94–D3.22, F Dormer to E Esselen, 27 May 1898.

21 See I Colvin, *The Life of Jameson, Vol 2* (London, 1922), p 89 [hereafter Colvin, *Jameson 2*]; and RSA, PAR, EM Trimble Papers, folios 564 and 1010.

22 See RSA, PAR, EM Trimble Papers, folio 1010.

23 FE Garrett and EJ Edwards, *The Story of an African Crisis and of the Jameson Raid* (London, 1897), pp 266–267.

24 See Colvin, *Jameson 2*, p 89; Muller, 'Policing the Witwatersrand', pp 181–182; and RSA, PAR, EM Trimble Papers, folio 788.

25 The bill of over £1 300 run up by the agency for the payment of its detectives could not conceivably have been incurred only during the days of the Raid and must have covered most of December 1895; see RSA, PAR, EM Trimble Papers, folio 914.

26 Colvin, *Jameson 2*, p 89.

27 See RSA, PAR, EM Trimble Papers, folio 851.

28 *Ibid*, folio 1000.

29 On George Richards, see 'The Detective Inquiry', *The Star*, 17 May 1895; and, on his involvement with the Reform Committee, a report on 'The Transvaal' carried in the *Otago Witness*, 7 May 1896. On some of the wider connections, see also a summary of a talk by R Grosskopf on 'Freemasonary and the Jameson Raid' in the *Bulletin of the Boksburg and East Rand Historical Association*, No 191, November 2011.

30 See Colvin, *Jameson 2*, pp 90 and 101. Trimble clearly had somebody in the post office at Pretoria because, on one occasion, he also intercepted a telegram from Zeerust to President Kruger; see Colvin, *Jameson 2*, p 93. At this point one might also speculate how a newspaper editor, such as Marais, would have frequented the Pretoria post office and known the clerks. The clerks in Pretoria – and Kruger – were certainly familiar with espionage techniques, including wiretapping; see D Blackburn and WW Caddell, *Secret Service in South Africa* (London, 1911) p 287. Here, too, one might speculate about the role of Charles Rorke – the man who had been Esselen's secretary during the latter's term of office as State Attorney. Rorke started out his career working in the field of communications in the Cape Civil Service but had a strong interest in telegraphy, and during the Anglo-Boer War he served as a telegraphist for General PJ Joubert; see B Forsyth, 'The Pretoria Club – The Welcome of Lord Selborne to Pretoria, 24 April 1905', p 112 (unpublished ms).

31 See van der Merwe, *Donker Stroom*, pp 38 and 95, which draws attention to this aspect of Marais's character. Also, Rousseau, *Groot Verlange*, pp 30, 56–57 and 65–67.

32 On Esselen's affiliation to the Freemasons, see JP van der Merwe, 'Vrymesselary in die aangang tot die Suid-Afrikaanse Oorlog', Litnet.

33 See RSA, PAR, EM Trimble Papers, folio 1058.

34 Ibid, folios 1067–1068.

35 Ibid, folio 1066.

36 Ibid, folio 1069.

37 On this period, see RSA, PAR, EM Trimble Papers, folios 1057–1094; and The Inquirer and Commercial News (Perth), 22 May 1896.

38 See RSA, PAR, EM Trimble Papers, folios IIII and 1156–1162.

39 United Kingdom, Oxford University, Bodleian Library, Hammond Papers, Private Letter Book (PLB), 9 March 1896 to 5 June 1897 (1896–1897), from folio 1016 and folio 1044; it would seem that Cecil Rhodes and Trimble continued to have a business as well as a personal relationship for some time after the Raid.

CHAPTER 20

1 See especially G Roberts, The Confederate Belle (London, 2003) [hereafter Roberts, Confederate Belle].

2 Just as Hammond sought to align himself with the image of the cowboy and masculine hero emerging in the modern historical novel of the time, so his wife, too, was unwilling to be shackled by the roles traditionally accorded to American woman of the mid-19th century. In this respect both the behaviour and the personalised writings about the Jameson Raid of the Hammonds can be most profitably read against the background of the emerging American fiction of the times. See especially, A Kaplan, 'Romancing the Empire: The Embodiment of American Masculinity in the Popular Historical Novel of the 1890s', American Literary History, Vol 2, No 4 (Winter, 1990), pp 659–690, and, more especially, Kaplan's comments about 'cowboys' and 'new women', at pp 672–673 and pp 683–684.

3 In the case of the United States, see also JW Cash's evocative and enduring The Mind of the South (New York, 1991), p 67 [hereafter Cash, Mind of the South].

4 Natalie Harris Hammond, A Woman's Part in a Revolution (London, 1897), pp 30 and 41 [hereafter Harris, A Woman's Part]. On concepts of honour and the 'dread of dishonour' see Cash, Mind of the South, p 73; and Roberts, Confederate Belle, p 3.

5 Harris, A Woman's Part, p 39.

6 Jack Hammond described it as a 'large plantation' but I have been unable to find evidence suggesting that it was worked by a proportionately large number of slaves although it may have been; see JH Hammond, The Autobiography of John Hays Hammond, Vol 2 (New York, 1935), p 741.

7 See United States of America, Louisiana State University, Libraries Special Collection, Mss 3275, Biographical/Historical Notes, Harris (Nathaniel Harris and James WM) Papers.

8 On the importance of dancing and singing as part of the Southern Belle's repertoire of accomplishments, see Roberts, Confederate Belle, pp 15, 19 and 35.

9 Much of what follows is either taken from or heavily influenced by C Tshehloane Keto's 'The Aftermath of the Jameson Raid and American Decision Making in Foreign Affairs, 1896' in Transactions of the American Philosophical Society (Philadelphia), Vol 70, Part 8, 1980, pp 1–43 [hereafter Keto, 'Aftermath of the Raid'] which, despite minor editorial blemishes, remains a work of outstanding quality.

10 Keto, 'Aftermath of the Raid', pp 23–25.

11 Ibid, pp 24–25.

12 Ibid, p 28.

13 Ibid, especially, pp 7, 16, 28 and 39.

14 Ibid, pp 7, 14, 26 and 28; and JH Hammond, The Autobiography of John Hays Hammond, Vol 1 (New York 1935), p 361 [hereafter Hammond, Autobiography 1].

15 Keto, 'Aftermath of the Raid', pp 18–19.

16 Ibid, especially, pp 16–18 and 34.

17 Ibid, p 29.

18 See Hammond, Autobiography 1, p 361.

19 Keto, 'Aftermath of the Raid', p 22.

20 Ibid, p 26, f/n 15.

21 Ibid, p 33.

22 For the exact details see Keto, 'Aftermath of the Raid', pp 30–33.

23 On Houghteling, see Keto, 'Aftermath of the Raid', pp 25–27.

24 The parts played by Clement, Curtis and Wiltsee in the American campaign can be traced in Keto, 'Aftermath of the Raid', at pp 23, 25, 30, 31 and elsewhere. On RE Brown's shifting loyalties, but which Jack Hammond never forgave him for, see Harris, A Woman's Part, p 30, but, more especially, M Holloway, 'Dr Jimcrack and See-Saw Roads: Harold Bolce's "A Slump in Heroes"', English in Africa, Vol 18, No 2, October 1991, pp 68 and 75.

25 On Manion's role see, for example, Harris, A Woman's Part, pp 18 and 30; and Keto, 'Aftermath of the Raid', p 31.

26 See Keto, 'Aftermath of the Raid', pp 25 and 32.

27 For Jack Hammond's take on this, which conveniently concatenates events in January and May 1896, see Hammond, Autobiography 1, pp 360–361, and contrast it with Keto, 'Aftermath of the Raid', pp 35–36.

28 See Mrs Lionel Phillips, Some South African Recollections (London, 1900), p 114.

29 See especially, Hammond, *Autobiography 1*, pp 375, 378 and 397. At the latter point, Hammond joked that, 'my health began to mend almost from the moment I received the death sentence' – a sentence which was commuted to imprisonment within 24 hours of it having been passed.

30 Hammond, *Autobiography 1*, p 359.

31 *Ibid*, pp 356–357.

32 *Ibid*, p 357.

33 *Ibid*, p 358; and, more pertinently, Keto, 'Aftermath of the Raid', p 31.

34 Hammond, *Autobiography 1*, p 362.

CHAPTER 21

1 See Mrs Lionel Phillips, *Some South African Recollections* (London, 1900), p 173.

2 See JH Hammond, *The Autobiography of John Hays Hammond, Vol 1* (New York, 1935), pp 362–363 [emphasis in the original, hereafter Hammond, *Autobiography 1*]. Note how, a few years later, the favourable impression formed at this meeting between Natalie Harris and Kruger helped pave the way for a later audience with the President by Hammond; see JH Hammond, *The Autobiography of John Hays Hammond, Vol 2* (New York, 1935), pp 420–421 [hereafter Hammond, *Autobiography 2*].

3 See D Rhoodie, *Conflicted Conspirators: A Study of the Johannesburg Reform Committee and its Role in the Conspiracy against the South African Republic* (Cape Town, 1967), p 94 [hereafter Rhoodie, *Conflicted Conspirators*].

4 See Hammond, *Autobiography 1*, p 1; and E Garrett and EJ Edwards, *The Story of an African Crisis and of the Jameson Raid* (London, 1897), p 261.

5 See Natalie Harris Hammond, *A Woman's Part in a Revolution* (London 1897) p 24 [hereafter Harris, *A Woman's Part*].

6 See Hammond, *Autobiography 1*, p 371; and Harris, *A Woman's Part*, p 24.

7 See Hammond, *Autobiography 1*, p 371; and Harris, *A Woman's Part*, pp 24–25.

8 Hammond, *Autobiography 1*, p 372; and Harris, *A Woman's Part*, p 25.

9 See Harris, *A Woman's Part*, p 28; and Hammond, *Autobiography 1*, p 373.

10 Hammond, *Autobiography 1*, p 373.

11 *Ibid*, pp 373–376; Harris, *A Woman's Part*, p 29; and Rhoodie, *Conflicted Conspirators*, p 98. In the end JS Curtis never stood trial at all.

12 See Hammond, *Autobiography 1*, pp 374–375; and Harris, *A Woman's Part*, p 29.

13 Hammond, *Autobiography 1*, p 376. The fear here was Boer revenge for the Slachter's Nek Rebellion of 1815. The Hammonds might have been even more alarmed had they known that one the key figures involved in hanging the Boer rebels was Colonel JC Cuyler, an American who had remained loyal to the British during the Revolutionary War.

14 *Ibid*, pp 377–378.

15 *Ibid*, p 378.

16 *Ibid*, pp 378–379.

17 *Ibid*, pp 380–383; and Rhoodie, *Conflicted Conspirators*, pp 94–100.

18 That case, in 1891, included representations being made on behalf of two condemned Irishmen by the American Consul and the King of Portugal. See C van Onselen, *Masked Raiders: Irish Banditry in Southern Africa, 1880–1899* (Cape Town, 2010), pp 156–159 [hereafter van Onselen, *Masked Raiders*].

19 Hammond, *Autobiography 1*, p 382.

20 *Ibid*, pp 382–383; Harris, *A Woman's Part*, pp 324–235; and Rhoodie, *Conflicted Conspirators*, p 100.

21 See van Onselen, *Masked Raiders*, pp 156–159.

22 Hammond, *Autobiography 2*, pp 388–389.

23 *Ibid*.

24 *Ibid*, p 397.

25 See C Tshehloane Keto's 'The Aftermath of the Jameson Raid and American Decision Making in Foreign Affairs, 1896' in *Transactions of the American Philosophical Society* (Philadelphia), Vol 70, Part 8, 1980, p 37 [hereafter Keto, 'Aftermath of the Raid']; and Hammond, *Autobiography 1*, p 361. See also Harris, *A Woman's Part*, p 39. Hammond later, probably incorrectly, interpreted Olney's telegram as being what saved him and his co-conspirators from the hangman's noose; see, for example, 'Secret History. Americans in the Jameson Raid', *Manawatu Standard* (New Zealand), Vol XLI, Issue 9676, 29 November 1911, reporting on an event held in New York City. In fact, Kruger, aware of the political credibility that he had reaped from the reprieve of the Irish highwaymen (see above) was probably going to go down the path of commutation in any case.

26 Harris, *A Woman's Part*, p 39.

27 Perhaps the starkest example of this as regards Hammond's South African experience is the yarn he offers in his autobiography about an Irish prisoner named 'Sullivan', but which bears a startling resemblance to the real-life experiences of a member of the Irish Brigade, James Sutherland. Compare Hammond's tale, as set out in his *Autobiography 2*, pp 393–395, with the story of Sutherland as presented in van Onselen, *Masked Raiders*, p 152. See also comments by William Wallace Mein, son of Tom Mein, who had seen Hammond at work on the Rand, in CC Spence, *Mining Engineers and The American West: The Lace-Boot Brigade* (London, 1970), p 336, f/n 90.

28 See Harris, *A Woman's Part*, p 41 [emphasis added]; and Hammond, *Autobiography 2*, pp 400–401.

29 Keto, 'Aftermath of the Raid', pp 37–38.

30 Hammond, *Autobiography 2*, p 402.

31 *Ibid*, pp 402–403 [emphasis added].

32 *Ibid*, pp 403.

33 *Ibid*, pp 405–406.

CHAPTER 22

1 Despite many startling errors of fact, see J Teisch, '"Home is not so very far away": Californian Engineers in South Africa, 1868–1915', *Australian Economic History Review*, Vol 45, No 2, July 2005, p 146; or J Teisch, *Engineering Nature: Water, Development, & the Global Spread of American Environmental Expertise* (Chapel Hill, NC, 2011), pp 97–131.

2 As Garrett was quick to note, right from the outset of the failed attempt at effecting a coup, 'The two friends [Rhodes and Jameson] have been strikingly true to each other.' FE Garrett and EJ Edwards, *The Story of an African Crisis and of the Jameson Raid* (London, 1897), p 196. Hammond was equally grateful for Rhodes's loyalty and protection; see JH Hammond, *The Autobiography of John Hays Hammond, Vol 2* (New York, 1935), pp 415–417 [hereafter Hammond, *Autobiography 2*].

3 After several meetings that took place after Jameson's early release from prison on grounds of ill health, in late 1896 and in the company of Frank Rhodes, Hammond only ever saw Jameson again on two more occasions – once in the bush, in Rhodesia, and then at the coronation of George V in London, in 1911. None of these meetings appear to have been private, always with others present. See Hammond, *Autobiography 2*, p 414; and I Colvin, *The Life of Jameson, Vol 2* (London, 1922), pp 159–160 [hereafter Colvin, *Jameson 2*].

4 Hammond, *Autobiography 2*, p 410.

5 *Ibid*, pp 415–416, and Colvin's rather unconvincing suggestion that it might have been Rhodes's 'inordinate and paralysing shyness of emotion' that had held back Rhodes 'from an immediate meeting' once he did get to London. Colvin, *Jameson 2*, p 159.

6 See JH Hammond, *The Autobiography of John Hays Hammond, Vol 1* (New York, 1935), pp 330, 345 and 364 [hereafter Hammond, *Autobiography 1*].

7 As Jameson later put it, a good deal of his subsequent problems could be attributed to the 'abominable Raid. That was a bad blunder.' See GS Fort, *Dr Jameson* (London, 1918), p 218; and Hammond, *Autobiography 1*, p 369. There was, to my knowledge, no similar admission by Hammond, who attributed the failure of the revolution to Jameson alone.

8 See, for example, I Colvin, *The Life of Jameson, Vol 1* (London, 1922), p 144; Hammond,

Autobiography 1, p 368; and RH Davis, *Dr Jameson's Raiders vs The Johannesburg Reformers* (New York, 1897), p 8.

9 See J Darwin, *The Empire Project: The Rise and Fall of the British World System, 1830–1970* (Cambridge, 2009).

10 See W LaFeber, *The New Empire: An Interpretation of American Expansion, 1860–1898* (London, 1963), pp 1–61 [hereafter LaFeber, *New Empire*]; and, because of Hammond's later incorporation into a novel emblematic of the era, see especially, G Murphy, 'Democracy, Development and the Monroe Doctrine in Richard Harding Davis's *Soldiers of Fortune*', *American Studies*, Vol 42, No 2, (Summer 2001), pp 45–66; and its part-inspiration, A Kaplan, 'Romancing the Empire: The Embodiment of American Masculinity in the Popular Historical Novel of the 1890s', *American Literary History*, Vol 2, No 4, (Winter 1990), pp 659–690 [hereafter Kaplan, 'Romancing the Empire']. Neither Murphy nor Kaplan, however, appear to have been be aware of the fact that Robert Clay, the hero of *Soldiers of Fortune*, was based in good measure on the career of John Hays Hammond.

11 See, among others, LaFeber, *New Empire*.

12 Hammond suggested of Kruger, for example, that 'His impositions were such as no man of the Anglo-Saxon Race would have tolerated'. *Lewiston Daily Sun*, 25 November 1911. The idea of there being an Anglo-Saxon race that bridged the Atlantic was a central ideological strand in the mid-19th century that Hammond was raised in. For the broader context, see R Horsman, *Race and Manifest Destiny: The Origins of American Racial Anglo-Saxonism* (London, 1981), and, more especially, his essay on 'Romantic Racial Nationalism', pp 158–186 [hereafter Horsman, *Race and Manifest Destiny*].

13 See O Wister, 'The Evolution of the Cow-Puncher' in BM Vorphal (ed), *My Dear Wister: The Frederick Remington–Owen Wister Letters* (Palo Alto, 1972), pp 77–96; and, as importantly, RM Brown, 'Western Violence, Structure, Values, Myth', *The Western Historical Quarterly*, Vol 24, No 1 (February 1993), pp 4–20, in which Hammond is mentioned, by name, in f/n 9 on p 15.

14 See Kaplan, 'Romancing the Empire', pp 659–690.

15 See United Kingdom (UK), Oxford University, Bodleian Library, Hammond Papers, Private Letter Book, 9 March 1896 to 5 June 1897: Hammond to G Creighton Webb, 23 November 1896; and Hammond to FR Burnham, 31 December 1896.

16 See B Wyatt-Brown, *Southern Honor: Ethics and Behaviour in the Old South* (New York, 1982).

17 Much of what immediately follows is taken from M Holloway's, 'Dr. Jimcrack and See-

Saw Roads: Harold Bolce's "A Slump in Heroes'", *English in Africa*, Vol 18, No 2 (October 1991), pp 63–85 [hereafter Holloway, 'A Slump in Heroes'. The wider context is best traced in S Gray's comprehensive 'The Literature of the Jameson Raid' in J. Carruthers (ed), *The Jameson Raid: A Centennial Perspective* (Johannesburg, 1996), pp 21–53 [hereafter Carruthers (ed), *The Jameson Raid*].

18 Holloway, 'A Slump in Heroes', pp 79–80.

19 See, for example, a report on the Jameson Raid in the *Spokane Review* of 22 January 1896, which notes Bolce's presence in the Coeur d'Alene 'three or four years ago'.

20 See LE Meyer, *The Farther Frontier: Six Case Studies of Americans and Africa, 1848–1936* (London, 1992), p 151 [hereafter Meyer, *Farther Frontier*]. This should be offset against Hammond's complaint about the absence of a 'free press' in the South African Republic in the mid-1890s; see, for example, A Ireland, 'The Truth about the Jameson Raid as related to me by John Hays Hammond', *The North American Review*, Vol 208, No 753, August 1908, p 194.

21 Hammond, *Autobiography 2*, pp 409–410.

22 UK, Oxford University, Bodleian Library, Hammond Papers, Private Letter Book (PLB), 9 March 1896 to 5 June 1897 (1896–1897): Hammond to BF Hawksley Esq, 8 September 1896.

23 'It is preposterous,' Hammond blustered, 'to assert that a statesman of Chamberlain's acumen could have been party to the Raid. He would have realised how greatly that would embarrass Great Britain in her foreign relations.' Hammond, *Autobiography 1*, p 367. See also IR Smith, 'Joseph Chamberlain and the Jameson Raid' in Carruthers (ed), *The Jameson Raid*, pp 89–110. For Hammond's exoneration of Rhodes, see, for example, Hammond, *Autobiography 2*, pp 415–418.

24 Horsman, *Race and Manifest Destiny*, pp 1–6.

25 See Natalie Harris Hammond, *A Woman's Part in a Revolution* (London, 1897).

26 *Ibid*, p 10.

27 *Ibid*, p 12.

28 Hammond, *Autobiography 2*, p 415.

29 It was also a moment in Hammond's life when he spent a good deal of time in Bigelow's company, in England; see Hammond, *Autobiography 2*, p 434.

30 UK, Oxford University, Bodleian Library, Hammond Papers, PLB 1896–97, JH Hammond to Poultney Bigelow Esq, 28 August 1896.

31 'Book of the Day', *Chicago Tribune*, 17 October 1897

32 See Meyer, *Farther Frontier*, p 155. Becker was another of those who believed strongly in the link between liberty and the Anglo-Saxons;

see EN Gates, *Race and US Foreign Policy in the Age of Territorial and Market Expansion* (London, 2014), p 224.

33 UK, Oxford University, Bodleian Library, Hammond Papers, PLB 1896–97, JH Hammond to the Editor, *Engineering and Mining Journal*, 18 December 1896.

34 *Ibid*, JH Hammond to Miss Bushford, *Cosmopolitan Magazine*, New York, 31 December 1896.

35 *Ibid*, JH Hammond to Charles W Truslow Esq, 2 January 1897.

36 DJ Pisani, *From the Family Farm to Agribusiness: The Irrigation Crusade in California* (Oakland, 1984), p 186.

37 See RW Righter, *The Battle Over Hetch Hetchy: America's Most Controversial Dam and the Birth of Modern Environmentalism* (Oxford, 2005), p 80.

38 See, for example, 'W Hammond Hall', *Sacramento Daily Union*, Vol 93, No 6, 27 February 1897.

39 The family ties between Hall and Hammond, the fact that Hall was a hydraulic rather than a mining engineer by profession, not resident on the Rand and indirectly linked to Rhodes have not always been appreciated by historians. See, for example, S Marks and S Trapido, 'Lord Milner and the South African State', *History Workshop*, No 8, Autumn 1979, at pp 61–62. Hammond was unusually enthusiastic about the report of the commission, again without disclosing the role that his cousin had played in presenting evidence to it. See Hammond, *Autobiography 2*, pp 418–420.

40 See especially G Brechin, *Imperial San Francisco: Urban Power, Earthly Ruin* (Oakland, 2006), p 263; and Hammond, *Autobiography 2*, pp 479–488. The history of capital transfers between California, via its mining and other engineers, and southern Africa and the economic development of both between 1890 and 1914 has yet to be written.

41 See items in the *New York Times*, 16 April 1913, and the *San Francisco Call*, Vol 113, No 138, 17 April 1913.

42 See the entry on GC Webb, Bulletin of Yale University, *Obituary Record of Graduates Deceased during the Year ended July 1, 1948* (New Haven, 1949), p 5.

43 UK, Oxford University, Bodleian Library, Hammond Papers, PLB 1896–97, JH Hammond to G Creighton Webb Esq, 23 November 1896.

CHAPTER 23

1 For the background to the rise of some of those male journalists of the 1890s, who mixed fact and fiction in uneven proportions, including RH Davis, see, for example, P Wald,

MA Elliot and J Arac, *The American Novel* (Oxford, 2014), p 124.

2 See RH Davis, *Dr Jameson's Raiders vs The Johannesburg Reformers* (New York, 1897), p 7 [hereafter Davis, *Dr Jameson's Raiders*]; and JH Hammond, *The Autobiography of John Hays Hammond, Vol 2* (New York, 1935) pp 412–413 [hereafter Hammond, *Autobiography 2*].

3 Davis, *Dr Jameson's Raiders*, p 8; and Hammond, *Autobiography 2*, p 413 – where Holden's name is incorrectly rendered as 'Harry' rather than Henry.

4 Hammond, *Autobiography 2*, p 413.

5 *San Francisco Call*, Vol 80, No 98, 6 September 1896.

6 Hammond, *Autobiography 2*, p 433.

7 See Davis, *Dr Jameson's Raiders*, p 8.

8 *Ibid*, p 56.

9 See A Ireland, 'The True Story of the Jameson Raid as related to me by John Hays Hammond, Part 1', in the *North American Review*, Vol 208, No 753, August, 1918, pp 185–196; and Part 2, Vol 208, No 754, pp 365–376 [hereafter Ireland, *The Truth*]; also A Ireland, *The Truth of the Jameson Raid as related by John Hays Hammond to Me*. (Boston, 1918).

10 See Ireland, *The Truth*, pp 186 and 195. When not casting himself in a heroic role in some latter-day Western – a dream befitting a Californian – Hammond, the arch-conspirator, a member of secret societies and lover of political intrigue, could easily see himself as a victim of fiendish interrogators and spies. Thus it not only suited his book to cast Sammy Marks, the industrialist, as a Kruger 'spy' when it suited him – JH Hammond, *The Autobiography of John Hays Hammond, Vol 1* (New York, 1935), p 339 [hereafter Hammond, *Autobiography 1*] – but also, while in the Pretoria jail, which was not for very long, there were 'many attempts by Boer Secret Service Agents to extort confessions from us in order to involve Rhodes and in that way escape punishment ourselves' – Hammond, *Autobiography 2*, p 413.

11 'Among the New Books', *Chicago Tribune*, 19 January 1897.

12 'It was here [at Bickley] that he [Davis] not only developed his idea for his novel *Soldiers of Fortune*, but wrote part of it' – Hammond, *Autobiography 2*, p 433.

13 The most egregious of these failures is perhaps to be found in G Murphy, 'Democracy, Development and the Monroe Doctrine in Richard Harding Davis's *Soldiers of Fortune*', *American Studies*, Vol 42, No 2 (Summer 2001), pp 45–46.

14 Note, for example, the lacunae in Kaplan's 'Romancing the Empire' and Murphy, 'Soldiers of Fortune' – as cited in f/n 13 above – and S Gray, 'The Literature of the Jameson Raid', in J Carruthers (ed), *The Jameson Raid:*

A Centennial Perspective (Johannesburg, 1996), pp 21–53.

15 RH Davis, *Soldiers of Fortune* (first published 1897, but all page references here taken from Project Gutenberg version, eBook No 403, 2008), pp 34 and 59 [hereafter Davis, *Soldiers*].

16 Davis, *Soldiers*, p 58.

17 *Ibid*, pp 5–6, 8 and 117.

18 See, for example, Davis, *Soldiers*, pp 30 and 47.

19 See especially W LaFeber, *The New Empire: An Interpretation of American Expansion, 1860–1898* (London, 1963), pp 229–241.

20 Davis, *Soldiers*, p 78.

21 *Ibid*, pp 61, 66 and 91.

22 Hammond, *Autobiography 2*, p 433; and, for the wider context, E Löfroth, *A Word Made Safe: Values in American Best Sellers, 1895–1920* (Uppsala, 1983), more particularly Chapter 1, 'Overview: A Splendid World', pp 34–49.

23 Hammond, *Autobiography 2*, p 413.

24 I Colvin, *The Life of Jameson, Vol 2* (London, 1922), p 160.

25 See Hammond, *Autobiography 2*, p 415; and J Teisch, *Engineering Nature: Water, Development, & the Global Spread of American Environmental Expertise* (Chapel Hill, NC, 2011), pp 120–131.

26 Hammond, *Autobiography 2*, pp 420–421.

27 See especially the chapter on 'London Days' in Hammond, *Autobiography 2*, pp 430–453.

28 See C van der Merwe, *Donker Stroom: Eugène Marais en die Anglo-Boereoorlog* (Cape Town, 2015), p 79.

29 Hammond, *Autobiography 2*, p 437.

30 *Ibid*, pp 441–442.

31 See also C Ash, *The IF Man. Dr Leander Starr Jameson: The Inspiration for Kipling's Masterpiece* (Solihull, 2012).

32 Hammond, *Autobiography 2*, pp 446–447.

33 This is taken from an inscription Hammond made in a copy of Ireland's *The Truth about the Jameson Raid* and which he presented to Samuel W McCall, Governor of Massachusetts. The entry is taken from Catalogue No 112 of Clarke's Bookshop in Cape Town.

CHAPTER 24

1 See, for example, a report in the *Richmond Times-Dispatch*, 7 June 1908, which was quick to latch on to the differences.

2 WC Widener, *Henry Cabot Lodge in the Search for American Foreign Policy* (Los Angeles, 1980), p 230.

3 See JH Hammond, *The Autobiography of John Hays Hammond, Vol 2* (New York, 1935), p 447 [hereafter Hammond, *Autobiography 2*]. For the context of USA-South African Republic diplomatic relations at the time, see also RE Harrigan, *The New World Power: American Foreign Policy, 1898–1917* (Philadelphia, 2013), pp 191–192.

4 The *Corydon Democrat* (Indiana), 7 March 1900, for an account of a speech delivered by Hammond in Chicago, or the *San Francisco Call*, 23 November 1899.

5 JH Hammond, *The Transvaal Trouble* (New York, 1900).

6 Mrs John Hays Hammond, *The Boers and the Uitlanders* (San Francisco, 1901). See also NH Hammond, 'The Boers: A Woman's View', *Outlook*, 16 June 1900.

7 HJ Weeks to the Editor, *San Francisco Call*, No 2, 2 December 1899; and 'Native Boer' to the Editor, *Los Angeles Herald*, 7 December 1899. As late as 1902, Harvard undergraduates were still making it clear to Hammond that their sentiments were pro-Boer rather than pro-British; see *Cambridge Tribune*, Vol XXIV, No 48, 1902. Reservations about Hammond and his family dated back to the campaign waged to free him after the Raid. The Hammonds occasionally came under attack for the 'insidious power' they wielded. See, for example, 'San Francisco Papers and the Wars they Carry On', *Sacramento Daily Union*, Vol 91, No 63, 3 May 1896.

8 See 'Race War', *Chicago Tribune*, 13 October 1899.

9 See G Brechin, *Imperial San Francisco: Urban Power, Earthly Ruin* (London, 2006), pp 80–84 [hereafter Brechin, *Imperial San Francisco*]; and J Teisch, *Engineering Nature: Water Development, & the Global Spread of American Environmental Expertise* (Chapel Hill, NC, 2011), pp 13–50.

10 See Hammond, *Autobiography 2*, pp 735–739.

11 Brechin, *Imperial San Francisco*, p 82.

12 See item in the *New York Times*, 16 April 1913; 'Hall files suit for Large Amount', *San Francisco Call*, Vol 113, No 138, 17 April 1913; and Brechin, *Imperial San Francisco*, pp 267–269. Hammond's sanitised autobiography throws no further light on these events.

13 See Brechin, *Imperial San Francisco*, pp 267–269 and Hammond, *Autobiography 2*, pp 735–744.

14 Upon his return to the U.S.A. Hammond not only held an honorary position at Yale but also lectured on mining and metallurgy at Columbia, Harvard and Johns Hopkins universities. See *Prominent and Progressive Americans: An Encyclopaedia of Contemporaneous Biography* (New York, 1904).

15 See Hammond, *Autobiography 2*, pp 451, 495 and 516–517

16 *Ibid*, p 480.

17 Thus, via Hammond, Consolidated Gold Fields came to invest in Mexico – Hammond, *Autobiography 2*, p 747.

18 'John Hays Hammond visits Los Angeles', *Los Angeles Herald*, Vol XXXl, No 56, 26 November 1903.

19 See especially Chapter 4 of RH Davis, *The Congo and Coasts of Africa* (New York, 1907); A Hochschild, *King Leopold's Ghost: A Story of Greed, Terror and Heroism in Colonial Africa* (New York, 1999); and R Wuliger, 'America's Early Role in the Congo Tragedy', *The Nation*, 10 October 2007.

20 Hammond, *Autobiography 2*, p 541.

21 As in the matter of William Hall and other cases illustrating family problems, personal failure or vulnerability, Mark Twain and Plasmon find no place in Hammond's *Autobiography.*

22 'Sworn Jest by Mark Twain', *New York Times*, 17 October 1907.

23 As Hammond noted in his memoirs about his extensive collection of portrait photographs, 'I collected people, in a sense, people I had met and admired' – Hammond, *Autobiography 2*, p 706. There were – and are – less genteel, locker-room phrases that could be employed to describe Hammond's propensity to insert self among the famous, rich and powerful. See, for example, *The Princeton Union*, 18 June 1908, in which he is described as 'a hero worshipper' and as a man with a 'liking for men who have achieved'.

24 See H Hill, *Mark Twain: God's Fool* (Chicago, 2012), p 37.

25 *Ibid*, pp 103–104; and Court of Appeals of the State of New York, *Ashcroft v Hammond*, 197 NY 488 (NY 1910), Ralph W Ashcroft, Respondent v John H Hammond, Appellant, decided 15 February 1910.

26 Hammond, *Autobiography 2*, p 481.

27 *Ibid*, p 483.

28 See, for example, R Horsman, *Race and Manifest Destiny* (Cambridge, MA, 1981); and JP Spiro, *Defending the Master Race: Conservation, Eugenics and the Legacy of Madison Grant* (Lebanon, NH 2009), pp 4–6 [hereafter Spiro, *Defending the Master Race*].

29 See, for example, S Watts, *Rough Rider in the White House: Theodore Roosevelt and the Politics of Desire* (Chicago, 2003), pp 123–135 [hereafter Watts, *Rough Rider*].

30 As first argued by Nina Silber, and then presented by Watts in *Rough Rider*, at p 123.

31 RH Davis, *Soldiers of Fortune* (New York, 1906; reprinted as *Six Who Dared: The Lives of Six Great Soldiers of Fortune*, Tucson, AZ, 2007), p 96.

32 See, for example, BM du Toit, *Boer Settlers in the Southwest* (El Paso, 1995), Southwestern Studies No 101, p 23 [hereafter du Toit, *Boer Settlers*].

33 See especially JW Meijer, 'Generaal Ben Viljoen, 1868–1917', unpublished PhD thesis, Department of History, University of Pretoria, 1993, pp 11–93 [hereafter Meijer, 'Viljoen'].

34 See DW Krüger's entry on Viljoen, BJ in CJ Beyers (ed), *Dictionary of South African Biography, Vol lV* (Pretoria, 1981), pp 740–742, which provides a ready introduction to the general's extraordinary life. On Viljoen and

the founding of the 'Young Afrikaner Party' –
it never was a 'party' in the true sense – see D
Blackburn and WW Caddell, *Secret Service in
South Africa* (London, 1911), pp 15 and 18; also
Meijer, 'Viljoen', pp 33–34.

35 See also du Toit, *Boer Settlers*.

36 See J Biggers, *In the Sierra Madre* (Chicago,
2006), p 184 [hereafter Biggers, *Sierra Madre*].

37 J Dwyer, *The Agrarian Dispute: The
Expropriation of American-Owned Rural Land*
(Durham, 2009), p 23.

38 Biggers, *Sierra Madre*, p 184. See also the
'San Francisco Mail News' as carried in the
Otago Daily Times, Issue No 12680, 4 June
1903, which reports on the success of the
Boer mission to Mexico. In Viljoen's earliest
ventures south, however, he was preceded and
then partnered by Commandant WD Snyman
– see du Toit, *Boer Settlers*, pp 26–31.

39 See 'Boers becoming American Citizens', *El
Paso Herald*, 12 February 1906. The question
of bigamy became academic when he and
his first wife, Helena, were divorced shortly
after, in 1905; for the background to this, see
Meijer, 'Viljoen', pp 233–234.

40 Biggers, *Sierra Madre*, p 184; and *El Paso
Herald*, 12 February 1906.

41 On Madero's background see, for example,
LD Langley, *The Banana Wars: An Inner History
of American Empire, 1900–1934* (Lexington, KY,
1983), p 79.

42 See also Meijer, 'Viljoen', pp 235–239; and
more especially, du Toit, *Boer Settlers*, pp 41–54.

43 This character sketch of Viljoen is derived
largely from Meijer, 'Viljoen', pp 12–93. For
a fine, novelistic portrayal of Ben Viljoen
that rings true historically, see also S Loots,
Sirkusboere (Cape Town, 2011).

44 See Spiro, *Defending the Master Race*, p 5.

45 Hammond, *Autobiography 2*, p 710.

46 The dinner at the Waldorf Astoria Hotel
in New York City and a summary of the
speeches – some portraying Hammond as a
heroic 'Soldier of Fortune' in the Harding
Davis tradition and whose life had once been
on the line, can be found in *Engineering and
Mining Journal Press*, Vol 121, 8 May 1926.

47 See Hammond, *Autobiography 2*, p 532; and, on
Hammond's enthusiasm for the scheme, see
I Tyrrell, *Crisis of the Wasteful Nation: Empire
and Conservation in Theodore Roosevelt's America*
(Chicago, 2015), p 125.

48 As it happened, there were good legal reasons
behind Roosevelt's reluctance to send in
federal troops – see Hammond, *Autobiography 2*,
pp 491–494; and on Hammond and Roosevelt's
friendship, *The Spectator*, 29 April 1905.

49 See, for example, *The Country Herald*, 12 June
1908; and a report on Hammond and the
dispensing of patronage for services rendered
during the election of William Taft in the
Brooklyn Daily Eagle, 12 August 1909.

50 Hammond, *Autobiography 2*, pp 487–488.

51 *Ibid*, pp 500–525. For the terms of Hammond's
contract, including a 25 per cent interest
in all new mines – making him more part
mine owner than mere salaried official, see
KD Underwood, 'Mining Wars: Corporate
Expansion and Labor Violence in the Western
Desert, 1876–1920', unpublished DPhil thesis,
University of Nevada, 2009, p 147. See also
items in *The Auckland Star* (New Zealand), Vol
XXXIX, Issue 141, 13 June 1908, and the *Rock
Island Argus* (Illinois), Vol 57, No 3, 21 October
1907. His estimate of the value of his time,
rendered amid an economic recession, was
not beyond mockery from journalists; see, for
example, the *Los Angeles Herald*, 19 May 1908.

CHAPTER 25

1 JH Hammond, *The Autobiography of John
Hays Hammond, Vol 2* (New York, 1935), p 446
[hereafter Hammond, *Autobiography 2*].

2 *Ibid*, p 532.

3 Roosevelt, sensitive to the political problems
that came from playing golf rather than
engaging in cheaper, more popular forms of
recreation, often criticised Taft's liking for the
sport and, by implication one might suggest,
that of his most prominent golfing partner,
Hammond – see Hammond, *Autobiography
2*, p 540. It may, of course, not have been
golf that Roosevelt was criticising but Taft's
'golf cabinet' in which Hammond wielded
significant, perhaps a determinative, influence.

4 On Taft's 'golf cabinet', as opposed to Teddy
Roosevelt's 'tennis cabinet', see *Los Angeles
Herald*, Vol 36, No 329, 26 August 1909. For
Taft's men at play at brother Charles's ranch
in Texas, see *Rock Island Argus*, 19 October
1909. Also EJ Edwards, 'The Most Intimate
Friends of President Taft', *New York Times*, 29
May 1910.

5 Depending on your view of Hammond, the
coincidences and instrumentality behind this
friendship can be gauged from a reading of
Hammond, *Autobiography 2*, at pp 530–533.

6 *Ibid*, p 532.

7 G Brechin, *Imperial San Francisco: Urban
Power, Earthly Ruin* (Los Angeles, 2006), p 54
[hereafter Brechin, *Imperial San Francisco*].

8 See the *Rock Island Argus*, Vol 57, No 3, 21
October 1907; and, for more of the same,
'John Hays Hammond at Santa Barbara', *San
Francisco Call*, Vol 102, No 170, 17 November
1907; or 'King of the Wage Earners', *Los
Angeles Herald*, Vol 35, No 230, 19 May 1908.

9 Influential capitalists and big business were
never unduly discomfited by the Roosevelt
administration; see G Kolko, *The Triumph of
Conservatism* (New York, 2008), p 131.

10 For Hammond's view on this matter and

the need to be pragmatic, see Hammond, *Autobiography 2*, pp 578–579.

11 See, for example, Hammond's 1905 address to the American Academy of Political and Social Science predicting trouble with Japan and as reported in the *San Francisco Call*, Vol 97, No 131, 9 April 1905.

12 See, among others, ER May's influential and long-standing *Imperial Democracy: The Emergence of America as a Great Power* (New York, 1961), pp 8–9. More pertinently perhaps, it also fitted with Hammond's long-standing interests in shipbuilding, as epitomised by the Union Iron Works in San Francisco; see Brechin, *Imperial San Francisco*, pp 127–129 and 142–143.

13 For Taft's alleged 'shift' in regard to questions of independence for the Philippines, see, for example, items in the *New York Times* of 7 and 8 September 1915.

14 The serendipitous coincidence of Roosevelt's endorsement of Taft's candidature and Hammond's exit from the Guggenheims' business on grounds of 'poor health' can be tracked in Hammond, *Autobiography 2*, pp 524 and 533.

15 Hammond's resignation, first announced in late 1907, did not at first attract a great deal of press attention. See the *Daily Arizona Silver Belt*, 2 November 1907. It was, however, revisited in the first half of 1908; see, for example, 'Hammond Resigns', *Montreal Gazette*, 15 February 1908, and then had to be repeatedly confirmed as the Republican convention approached; see *Lawrence Daily World*, 4 June 1908; and *New York Times*, 7 June 1908. Hammond himself put his resignation as 'at the end of 1907' – Hammond, *Autobiography 2*, p 524.

16 See Hammond, *Autobiography 2*, pp 534–535. But, as is often the case and will be traced below, Hammond's memoirs are sometimes difficult to align with other independent evidence. Taft might indeed have encouraged Hammond's candidature – he had nothing to lose by so doing – but it was Hammond himself who was most seized by the idea of Vice President John Hays Hammond. Nor did he let go of the idea of high office very easily. The Florida *Evening Independent* suggested, on 1 March 1913, that 'Hammond, it is known, is very desirous of becoming the President of the United States Senate, having made a bid for it in 1908 when his candidacy was announced in Chicago'.

17 Robert Love, in the *Princeton Union*, 18 June 1908. Some observers found Hammond's interest in the vice-presidential nomination to be merely amusing; see *Times Dispatch*, No 17944, 7 June 1908.

18 Love, *Princeton Union*, 18 June 1908.

19 For the background of the de Young family,

see Brechin, *Imperial San Francisco*, pp 172–182 and 192–196.

20 *San Francisco Call*, Vol 104, No 9, 9 June 1908.

21 See 'Hammond Criticised', *Chicago Tribune*, 6 October 1908.

22 IZ Josephson to the Editor, *New York Times*, 5 June 1908.

23 See especially, G van Smith's report on 'Hammond Served on Platter by de Young Fails to Attract California's Political Gourmets', in *San Francisco Call*, Vol 104, No 15, June 1908 (emphasis added). See also *San Francisco Call*, Vol 104, No 18, 18 June 1908, for the delegation's resistance to de Young.

24 Hammond, *Autobiography 2*, pp 534–536.

25 *Ibid*, pp 556–558.

26 *Ibid*, p 542.

27 *Ibid*, p 544; and *New York Times*, 23 April 1911 (possible ambassadorship in Berlin), or the *Buffalo Courier*, 16 January 1912 (as possible French ambassador).

28 Hammond, *Autobiography 2*, p 538.

29 Some idea of the social life that the Hammonds constructed for themselves and enjoyed during the Taft presidency can be gauged from Hammond, *Autobiography 2*, pp 545–547; and DK Goodwin, *The Bully Pulpit: Theodore Roosevelt and the Golden Age of Journalism* (New York, 2013), p 559. On Hammond and the Sierra Madre Club, see, for example, items in the *Los Angeles Herald*, 22 September 1909 and 2 January 1910. On Mrs Hammond (née Natalie Harris), see especially 'Women who Count', *San Francisco Call*, Vol 110, No 95, 3 September 1911; and *New York Times*, 21 September 1912.

30 For Hammond – as in the cases of Barnato, Samuel Clemens and Rhodes – it was often the magnet of personal charisma and/or public profile that paved the way for a subsequent business relationship. It was a practice that worked more often than not. Hammond had not met Burnham prior to 1896, and certainly not while they were in Africa; see United Kingdom, Oxford University, Bodleian Library, John Hays Hammond Papers, Private Letter Book, 9 March 1896 to 5 June 1897, Hammond to Burnham, 31 December 1896. Hammond, however, had no qualms about later referring to Major Burnham as 'my old friend of South African days' – Hammond, *Autobiography 2*, p 565. Despite their being involved in a business venture in Mexico that dated back to 1909, it was only in the early 1920s that Hammond really became 'more intimately acquainted with Major Burnham'. That knowledge, too, was quickly realised for personal, reputational, gain; see JH Hammond, 'South African Memories: Rhodes-Barnato-Burnham', *Scribner's Magazine*, Vol LXIX, No 3, March 1921, pp 257–278.

31 The early, ugly history of the acquisition of the water rights and dispossession of the Yaquis can be traced in P van Wyk, *Burnham: King of Scouts: Baden-Powell's Secret Mentor* (Trafford, BC, 2003), pp 273–275. It was not a history that Burnham felt like repeating in his autobiographical account, which had an introduction by John Hays Hammond; see FR Burnham, *Scouting on Two Continents* (New York, 1926).

32 See J Biggers, *In the Sierra Madre* (Chicago, 2006), pp 159–160. On Viljoen's later move into New Mexico, see BM du Toit, *Boer Settlers in the Southwest* (El Paso, TX, 1995); and DV Meed, *Soldier of Fortune: Adventures in Latin America and Mexico with Emil Lewis* (Houston, 2002), p 62.

33 The tragic history of the Yaquis is outlined in J Dwyer, *The Agrarian Dispute: The Expropriation of American-Owned Rural Land* (Durham, 2009), p 23. The background of the Richardson family, Southerners, and their business connection to Hammond can be traced in MR Press Reference Library, *Western Edition, Notables of the West, Vol 1* (San Francisco, 1913), p 248, as transcribed, in 2009, by MR Pankey in *Los Angeles County Biographies* and in the *Arniston Star* (Arizona), 22 February 1931.

34 Hammond, *Autobiography 2*, p 741.

35 On the National Cotton Improvement Company and the linked General Cotton Securities Company, the rights to the 'Doremus Gin' and a libel suit brought by the 'Cotton King' against Hammond by Daniel Sully, see *New York Daily Tribune*, 11 March 1911; *New York Times*, 20 April 1911; and *Washington Herald*, 4 May 1911.

36 See *Los Angeles Herald*, Vol 36, No 17, 18 October 1908; and Hammond, *Autobiography 2*, pp 746–747.

37 See JM Hart, *Empire and Revolution: The Americans in Mexico since the Civil War* (Oakland, 2002), p 102; FN Magill (ed), *The 20th Century Go–N: Dictionary of World Biography, Vol 8* (London, 2014), p 1499; and D Nugent (ed), *Rural Revolt in Mexico: US Intervention and the Domain of Subaltern Politics* (Durham, NC, 1998), p 56.

38 Hammond, *Autobiography 2*, pp 747–748. See also, RF Himmelberg, *Antitrust and Regulation during World War One and the Republican Era, 1917–1932* (London, 1962), p 173; and SJ Randall, *United States Foreign Oil Policy since World War One: For Profits and Security* (Montreal, 2005), p 50.

39 Hammond, *Autobiography 2*, p 549.

40 See J Lurie, *William Howard Taft: The Travails of a Progressive Conservative* (Cambridge, 2011), pp 140–143 and 179–180; and the views of LL Gould on Taft and tariff reform as presented by KJA Miller, 'The William Howard Taft Presidency' in *The Annals of Iowa*, Vol 69, No

4, Fall 2010, pp 471–472. For Hammond's support and lobbying, see *Autobiography 2*, pp 553–556.

41 See Hammond, *Autobiography 2*, pp 556–561.

42 *Ibid*, p 550.

43 See CH Harris, *The Secret War in El Paso: Mexican Revolutionary Intrigue, 1906–1920* (Albuquerque, NM, 2009), pp 1–14.

44 On Díaz, see Hammond, *Autobiography 2*, pp 569–570; and on Mussolini, pp 724–725.

45 Hammond, *Autobiography 2*, pp 568–569.

46 *Ibid*, p 565.

47 On the border meeting between Burnham and Viljoen – men who had been on opposite sides in the Anglo-Boer War – see *The Arizona Republican*, 15 October 1909.

48 Hammond, *Autobiography 2*, pp 565–566.

CHAPTER 26

1 *Brooklyn Daily Eagle*, 1 April 1935.

2 On Woodrow Wilson's overt hostility to imperialism and his underlying sympathy for Mexicans marginalised by the Díaz administration and American capitalists, see, among others, LD Langley, *The Banana Wars: An Inner History of American Empire, 1900–1934* (Lexington, KY, 1983), pp 77–90 [hereafter Langley, *Banana Wars*]; and, even more pertinently in the case of Hammond and the Yaqui Delta Company, WR Edwards, 'The Protection of the American Lives and Property: The Sonora Crisis of 1915' (unpublished essay, 1993), drawn from his 'United States–Mexican Relations, 1913–1916: Revolution, Oil and Intervention', unpublished PhD thesis, Louisiana State University, 1971.

3 Langley, *Banana Wars*, p 78.

4 *Ibid*, pp 79–80.

5 JH Hammond, *The Autobiography of John Hays Hammond, Vol 2* (New York, 1935), p 571 [hereafter Hammond, *Autobiography 2*]; and for Hammond's championing of the 'practical' man see, for example, JH Hammond and JW Jenks, *Great American Issues: Political, Social, Economic (A Constructive Study)* (New York, 1923), p 2.

6 See MM Matthews, *The US Army on the Mexican Border: A Historical Perspective* (Kansas City, 2007), pp 60–61.

7 Hammond, *Autobiography 2*, pp 658–659.

8 *Ibid*, p 573.

9 See 'Revolt in Mexico', *Otago Daily Times*, 25 April 1911.

10 For Hammond's role in influencing those responsible for President Taft's private and public security, see, for example, Captain AW Butt's letter to his sister, 14 November 1909, as reproduced in AW Butt, *Taft and Roosevelt: The Intimate Letters of Archie Butt,*

Military Aide (Garden City, NJ, 1930); FM Garrett, *Atlanta and Environs: A Chronicle of its People and Events, 1880s–1930s* (Athens, GA, 2010), pp 578–579; and *San Francisco Call*, Vol 106, No 123, 1 October 1909. And, on the partial overlap between security personnel and the 'golf cabinet', see ME Shay, *Revered Commander, Maligned General: The Life of Clarence Rawson Edwards, 1859–1931* (Colombia, MO, 2011), p 85.

11 Hammond, of course, was less than mystified and simply saw himself as the beneficiary of patronage dispensed in return for his services to Taft and the Republican Party; see *Cornell Daily Sun*, Vol XXXll, No 86, 18 January 1912.

12 See especially the breathless section on 'Pageantry before the War' in Hammond, *Autobiography 2*, pp 588–600.

13 See, for example, the reprint of JW Cash's classic *The Mind of the South* (New York, 1991), with an outstanding introduction by B Wyatt-Brown, pp 65–74. 'By birth and ancestry Mrs Hammond is a Southern woman', and for Natalie Harris tracing her roots, back to the 'earliest Virginia colonial stock', see 'Women who Count', *San Francisco Call*, Vol 110, No 956, 3 September 1911.

14 See, among many others, the *Gazette Times*, 23 April 1911; *Rock Island Argus*, Vol 60, No 205, 13 June 1911; *San Francisco Call*, Vol 109, No 179, 28 May 1911 and Vol 110, No 24, 24 June 1911; or *Richmond Times-Dispatch* (Virginia) of 19 May and 23 June 1911.

15 Hammond, *Autobiography 2*, pp 594–597.

16 Speculation that Taft might not win nomination for a second term was evident within 18 months of his having assumed the presidency; see, for example, *Los Angeles Herald*, Vol 37, No 324, 21 August 1910. For the widening rift between Taft and Roosevelt, see especially Chapter 25 of DK Goodwin, *The Bully Pulpit: Theodore Roosevelt, William Howard Taft and the Golden Age of Journalism* (New York, 2013) [hereafter Goodwin, *The Bully Pulpit*].

17 See a report on the scheme carried in the *Brooklyn Daily Eagle*, 17 June 1911.

18 See Hammond, *Autobiography 2*, pp 741–743; and G Brechin, *Imperial San Francisco: Urban Power, Earthly Ruin* (Los Angeles, 2006), pp 228–229 [hereafter Brechin, *Imperial San Francisco*].

19 *Brooklyn Daily Eagle*, 17 June 1911.

20 See RM Utley, *Lone Star Lawmen: The Second Century of the Texas Rangers* (Oxford, 2007), p 10.

21 For Roosevelt's view, see HB Needham, 'Why Roosevelt opposes Taft', *Saturday Evening Post*, Vol 184, No 45, 4 May 1912.

22 See Hammond, *Autobiography 2*, pp 582–585.

23 See 'John Hays Hammond Raps Selfish Colonel', *San Francisco Call*, Vol 112, No 135,

13 October 1912; and JH Hammond, *Why I am for Taft* (Iowa, 1912).

24 See Hammond, *Autobiography 2*, pp 600–610; and *San Francisco Call*, Vol 112, No 2, 2 June 1912. On Hammond's long-standing and ever-expanding interest in international affairs, see JH Hammond, 'The Menace of Japan's Success', *Living Age*, No 240, 6 February 1904, pp 6273–6275; or JH Hammond, address on 'The Development of our Foreign Trade' to the American Association for the Advancement of Science, reprinted, under the same title, as an 11-page pamphlet in 1913. See also I Ruxton's translation of M Matusumura, *Baron Kaneko and the Russo-Japanese War, 1904–05: A Study in the Public Diplomacy of Japan* (Shinyudo, 2009), pp 304–305, for Hammond's positions on Russia and Japan; and J Israel, *Progressivism and the Open Door: America and China, 1905–1921* (Pittsburgh, 1971), p 83.

25 See *Evening Independent* (Florida), 1 March 1913.

26 Hammond, *Autobiography 2*, pp 600 and 610.

27 *Ibid*, p 584.

28 See Chapter 28, 'Bosom Friends, Bitter Enemies' in Goodwin, *The Bully Pulpit*; and from the Hammond-Taft perspective, Hammond, *Autobiography 2*, pp 585–586.

29 Hammond, *Autobiography 2*, p 658.

30 Thus he, Law, Belmont and Carnegie had experienced little difficulty in adjusting to and surviving Roosevelt's progressive, anti-trust administration. See G Kolko, *The Triumph of Conservatism* (New York, 2008), p 131.

31 Hammond, *Autobiography 2*, pp 661 and 757.

32 See Brechin, *Imperial San Francisco*, and, in this context, more especially, pp 200–244.

33 Indeed, Burnham took a few unnamed 'South African friends' with him to the Yaqui, which he was excited to consider as an active frontier; FR Burnham, *Scouting on Two Continents* (New York, 1926), with an introduction by JH Hammond, p 182 [hereafter Burnham, *Scouting*].

34 Burnham, *Scouting*, p 30.

35 Significantly, despite Hammond having written the introduction to his book, Burnham – allegedly wishing to avoid a two-volume autobiography – provides no account whatsoever of their private army on the Yaqui in *Scouting*. Smuggling men and guns across the USA-Mexican border was not the sort of tale that a man who prided himself on his law-abiding nature would have wanted recorded.

36 See Hammond, *Autobiography 2*, p 571; and on dissatisfaction with the Madero government in northwestern Mexico, for example, *Washington Herald*, 8 February 1912.

37 Just how strategic a position El Paso was became clear during US congressional hearings, in 1910, when it was established that

the Collector of Customs, who was in the pay of the government in Mexico City, was spying on Mexican refugees from the Díaz regime. See RF Acuña. *Corridors of Migration: The Odyssey of Mexican Laborers, 1600–1933* (Tucson, AZ, 2008), pp 139–140 [hereafter Acuña, *Corridors of Migration*]. See also DD Roma, *Ringside Seat to a Revolution: An Underground Cultural History of El Paso and Juárez, 1893–1923* (El Paso, TX, 2005).

38 Burnham, a scout for the British Army during the Anglo-Boer War of 1899–1902 was, around this time and with the active financial backing of Hammond, becoming increasingly comfortable in the company of former Boer notables, scouts and spies. By 1908, picking up on Roosevelt and Pinchot's lead on conservation, Burnham and Hammond were advocating a scheme to introduce South African 'deer' – eland – into the barren southwestern USA; see P van Wyk, *Burnham: King of Scouts: Baden-Powell's Secret Mentor* (Trafford, BC, 2003), p 450; and RH Davis, *Soldiers of Fortune* (New York, 1906; reprinted as *Six Who Dared: The Lives of Six Great Soldiers of Fortune*, Tucson, AZ, 2007), p 96. By 1910–1911, Burnham and Hammond included the Anglo-Boer War spy Frederick 'Fritz' Joubert (a nephew of General Piet Joubert's) in their circle of Washington, DC, lobbyists attempting – unsuccessfully – to get permission for, among other things, the importation of hippos – as a possible source of food – to the swamps of Louisiana. See especially *Boston Daily Globe*, 24 April 1910; *New York Times*, 17 April 1910; and *Lead Daily Call* (South Dakota), 2 March 1911.

39 I am indebted to Carel van der Merwe for providing me with the background to this election, which will be more fully covered in his forthcoming PhD study of Ben Viljoen at the University of Stellenbosch.

40 On Hammond's backing of Viljoen, see items in the *El Paso Herald* of 19 Nov. 1909, and 3 February and 4 March 1910.

41 See Hammond, *Autobiography 2*, pp 538 and 551; and on the outcome of the election in which Hammond could not deliver for his candidate, BM du Toit, *Boer Settlers in the Southwest* (El Paso, TX, 1995), pp 57–58 [hereafter du Toit, *Boer Settlers*].

42 See Hammond to the Editor, *El Paso Herald*, 8 January 1912.

43 Viljoen was one of many invited guests at a breakfast for Taft at the time of the border conference; see *El Paso Herald*, 16 October 1909. It is difficult to see how, other than via Hammond, such an invitation would have been issued. The presence of BJ Viljoen and others drawn from around Las Cruces, New Mexico, at the St Regis oilfield in San Antonio, Texas, is also noted in the *El Paso*

Herald, 26 October 1910. Again, Hammond was the person most likely to have provided these Boers with an introduction to Texas oilmen.

44 See du Toit, *Boer Settlers*, pp 62–64; *El Paso Herald*, 9 January 1911, and *The Press*, Vol LXVll, No 14096, 15 July 1911, with a report from a San Francisco correspondent dated 14 June.

45 On the Mexican Liberal Party and its political struggles in southern California and the Mexican Baja Peninsula see RG del Castillo, 'The Discredited Revolution: The Magonista Capture of Tijuana, 1911', *San Diego Historical Society Quarterly*, Fall 1908; and JHM Laslett, *Sunshine was Never Enough: Los Angeles Workers, 1880–2010* (Berkeley, 2012). Indeed, a Yaqui revolt was central to the Magonistas' revolutionary programmes in northwestern Mexico, in 1908; see also Acuña, *Corridors of Migration*, pp 138–139.

46 See *The Press*, Vol LXVll, No 14096, 15 July 1911.

47 See 'Madero warned that US may halt Mexican Anarchy', *Syracuse Herald*, 11 June 1911.

48 See A Knight, *The Mexican Revolution; Counter-Revolution and Reconstruction, Vol 2* (Lincoln, NB, 1990), pp 111–112.

49 See *El Paso Herald*, 8 November 1911; and du Toit, *Boer Settlers*, pp 64–65.

50 This paragraph is constructed from reports in the *El Paso Herald*, No 8, 1911, and du Toit, *Boer Settlers*, p 65.

51 See du Toit, *Boer Settlers*, p 65.

52 *Ibid*, p 65. On Viljoen's links to Guaymos, see also J Biggers, *In the Sierra Madre* (Chicago, 2006), pp 159–160.

53 See John Hays Hammond to the Editor, *El Paso Herald*, 8 January 1912.

54 Du Toit, *Boer Settlers*, pp 65–66. Viljoen not only lied about not taking the oath of allegiance while a Boer prisoner of war on St Helena but also later fraudulently took a loan from the post-war administration and later entered a bigamous marriage; see JW Meijer, 'Generaal Ben Viljoen, 1868–1917', unpublished PhD thesis, Department of History, University of Pretoria, 1993, pp 221, 228 and 234.

55 See a lengthy report taken from the *Evening Express* as carried in the *Chanute Daily Tribune* (Kansas), 23 April 1912. For some of the background to such an endeavour, see CH Harris and LR Sadler, 'The "Underside" of the Mexican Revolution: El Paso, 1912', *The Americas*, Vol 39, No 1, July 1982, pp 69–83.

56 See 'John Hays Hammond in War Zone', *Chicago Examiner*, Vol 12, No 31, 4 February 1912.

57 *Washington Herald*, 8 February 1912.

58 See items in the *Sausalito News*, 22 May 1912; and *Altoona Tribune*, 31 May 1912.

59 The background and context of this railroad development along the eastern shores of the Gulf of California can be traced in J Dwyer, *The Agrarian Dispute: The Expropriation of American-Owned Rural Land in Post-revolutionary Mexico* (Durham, 2009), pp 24–25; and JM Hart, *Empire and Revolution: The Americans in Mexico since the Civil War* (Berkeley, 2002), pp 102–103.

60 *Sausalito News*, Vol 28, No 39, 21 September 1912.

61 On Didapp's background and campaign to expose the capitalists see P Calvert, *The Mexican Revolution, 1910-1914: The Diplomacy of Anglo-American Conflict* (Cambridge, 1968), p 74 [hereafter Calvert, *The Mexican Revolution*].

62 See the *El Paso Herald*, 23 September 1912. The Didapp interview was reported on from coast to coast in America, but appears to have elicited no rebuttal from either Taft or Hammond. And, on the Anglo-American conflict about oil and other holdings at Mexico that formed the background to some of this corruption, see Calvert, *The Mexican Revolution*, pp 74–80.

63 Rhodes's unarmed negotiations with the Ndebele in the Matopos impressed Hammond and Burnham deeply. See JH Hammond, 'South African Memories; Rhodes-Barnato-Burnham', *Scribner's Magazine*, Vol LXlX, March 1921, p 274.

64 This political stunt was widely reported on throughout the United States; see, for example, *New York Times*, 12 January 1913; *Morning Oregonian*, 13 January 1913; or the *News-Record*, 13 January 1913, but the source of the inspiration, Rhodes, went unnoticed. The Rhodes-derived inspiration might not have ended there. Although the details of the planned offer by Hammond to the Yaquis is lost, at first glance it appears to have more than a passing similarity to Rhodes's notorious 1894 Glen-Grey Act in the Cape Colony; see Hammond, *Autobiography 2*, pp 744–745.

65 Older's editorial, as reproduced in *The Commoner* (Lincoln, NB), 7 February 1913.

66 Langley, *Banana Wars*, pp 80–83.

CHAPTER 27

1 On Hammond's noted 'hero-worshipping' propensities, see, for example, *New York Times*, 7 June 1908.

2 President Wilson's misgivings about American capitalists invested in Mexico are outlined in the principal sources employed in this chapter: WR Edwards, 'The Protection of American Lives and Property: The Sonora Crisis of 1915', which is derived from 'United States–Mexican Relations, 1913–1916: Revolution, Oil and Intervention', unpublished PhD thesis, Louisiana State University, 1971 [hereafter Edwards, 'The Sonora Crisis']; ES Rosenberg, 'Economic Pressures in Anglo-American Diplomacy, 1917–1918', *Journal of Inter-American Studies and World Affairs*, Vol 17, No 2, May 1975, pp 123–152; and CW Trow, 'Woodrow Wilson and the Mexican Interventionist Movement of 1919', *Journal of American History*, Vol 58, No 1, June 1971, pp 46–72.

3 Thus, while Hammond's Yaqui Delta Company saw the loss of some settler lives during the Mexican Revolution, the ASARCO company's mining and smelting operations, which he oversaw on behalf of the Guggenheims, did not lose one American life during the upheavals, 'and emerged in the 1920s more powerful than ever'; D Nugent (ed), *Rural Revolt in Mexico: U.S. Intervention and the Domain of Subaltern Politics* (Durham, NC, 1998), p 56 [hereafter Nugent (ed), *Rural Revolt*].

4 See JH Hammond, *The Autobiography of John Hays Hammond, Vol 2* (New York, 1935), p 742, for the size of the holdings, and p 747 for the origins lying in a 'colonization plan' [hereafter Hammond, *Autobiography 2*].

5 See reports carried in the *Asheville Citizen* and *Otago Daily Times*, 25 November 1913.

6 See *Richmond Times-Dispatch* (Virginia), 7 September 1915, or the *True Republican* (Illinois), 25 September 1915.

7 *New York Times*, 23 February 1916.

8 Thus, in late 1913, the *Pittsburgh Press* noted that 'Of course Mr Hammond (who seems to be the lobbyist-in-chief for special privilege in Washington) is bluffing when he threatens to allow spite to dictate his business interests'. Likewise, the *Day Book* (Chicago), Vol 3, No 174, 22 April 1914, referring by name to Hammond, Hearst, Rockefeller, Otis, and Guggenheim, suggested that 'It's worth millions to that bunch if they can stampede Uncle Sam into a war of conquest in Mexico'.

9 See CR Marchand, *The American Peace Movement and Social Reform, 1898–1914* (Princeton 2015), p 89 [hereafter Marchand, *The American Peace Movement*].

10 Hammond, *Autobiography 2*, pp 612–615.

11 See NJ Duke, 'An Internationalist's Place in History', unpublished PhD thesis, University of Florida, 1995.

12 See D Cortright, *Peace: A History of Movements and Ideas* (Cambridge, 2008), p 50.

13 J Israel, *Progressivism and the Open Door: America and China, 1905–1921* (Pittsburgh, 1971), p 83 [hereafter Israel, *Progressivism*].

14 See *New York Times*, 27 December 1914.

15 *Ibid*, 15 May 1915; and Hammond, *Autobiography 2*, pp 617–621.

16 For Hammond as part of a pressure group in

this regard, see *New York Times*, 1 June 1915.

17 WF Kuehl and LK Dunn, *Keeping the Covenant: American Internationalists and the League of Nations, 1920–1939* (Kent, OH, 1997), p 113; Hammond, *Autobiography 2*, pp 624–630. The sympathiser was Colonel EA House – see also below.

18 *Southside Observer* (New York), 4 February 1916.

19 *Brooklyn Daily Eagle*, 9 August 1925.

20 See Hammond, *Autobiography 2*, pp 635, 697, 715 and 760–762. PL Murphy, 'Sources and Nature of Intolerance in the 1920s', *Journal of American History*, Vol 51, No 1, June 1964, p 75, describes the National Civic Federation as being the home of 'professional patriots'. See also *St Petersburg Times* (Florida), 3 January 1917. For Hammond and, almost inevitably, Taft's involvement in the Boys Club Federation, see, for example, *The Rotarian*, Vol XVII, No 1, July 1920, p 18.

21 F Katz, *The Life and Times of Pancho Villa* (Stanford, 1998), p 313 [hereafter Katz, *Pancho Villa*].

22 JH Hammond, 'Wanted – A Foreign Trade Policy', *Annals of the American Academy of Political and Social Sciences*, Vol 84, July 1919, pp 153–158 [emphasis added]. By 1923, Hammond or his co-author had decided that using the word 'compel' was possibly unwise even though the basic sentiments remained unchanged. See JH Hammond and JW Jenks, *Great American Issues: Political, Social, Economic (A Constructive Study)* (New York, 1923), p 196.

23 Marchand, *The American Peace Movement*, p 89. Marchand is, however, also at pains to point out that, even then, those with a double agenda 'comprised only a small fraction of the businessmen in the New York Peace Society'.

24 Israel, *Progressivism*, p 84.

25 Note also the contrasting fates, in terms of human life, between the Yaqui Delta project and orthodox mining operations in this regard. See Nugent (ed), *Rural Revolt*, p 56; and note 3 above. For Hammond's notable interests in Mexico's oil, see SJ Randall, *United States Foreign Oil Policy since World War I: For Profits and Security* (Montreal, 2005), p 50.

26 See J Dwyer, *The Agrarian Dispute: The Expropriation of American-Owned Rural Land* (Durham, 2009), pp 23–24; JM Hart, *Empire and Revolution: The Americans in Mexico since the Civil War* (Berkeley, 2002), p 326; and A Okado, 'El impacto de la Revolución Mexicana: La Compañía Constructora Richardson en el Valle del Yaqui' (1905–1928), *Historia Mexicana*, Vol L, No 1, July–September 2000, p 97.

27 Hammond, *Autobiography 2*, pp 742–745.

28 One of the best overviews of the initial development of the scheme is to be found in *The Oasis* (Nogales, AZ), Second Series,

Vol XlV, No 181, 12 March 1910; but see also items in the *Lincoln Journal Star* (Nebraska), 22 June 1915, and the *Sunday Oregonian* (Portland) of 24 August 1917.

29 On Thornberry, see AP Henderson, *The Ninety-First: The First at Camp Lewis* (Washington, 1918), pp 306–309; and on Burnham between 1913 and 1917, P van Wyk, *Burnham: King of Scouts: Baden-Powell's Secret Mentor* (Trafford, BC, 2003), p 486.

30 Hammond, *Autobiography 2*, p 745.

31 *Ibid*, pp 631, 633.

32 *Ibid*, pp 629–630.

33 *Ibid*, p 633. On the Hammond-House relationship, see also WH Hobbs, *Leonard Wood Administrator, Soldier and Citizen* (New York, 1920), pp 157–158.

34 Hammond, *Autobiography 2*, p 633.

35 See, for example, F Katz, 'Pancho Villa and the attack on Columbus, New Mexico', *American Historical Review*, Vol 83, No 1, February 1978, pp 101–130.

36 There is an extensive primary and secondary literature on both the occupation of Veracruz and the 'Punitive Expedition'. See, for example, LD Langley, *The Banana Wars: An Inner History of American Empire, 1900–1934* (Lexington, KY, 1983), pp 91–114; and JM Cyrulik, 'A Strategic Examination of the Punitive Expedition into Mexico, 1916-1917', unpublished MMAS thesis, US Army Command and General Staff College, 2003; or Katz, *Pancho Villa*, pp 610–613.

37 See, for example, Hammond, *Autobiography 2*, p 667.

38 Hammond's last visitor on the day he died was Mrs Edward House, see *Ludington Daily News* (Michigan), 9 June 1936.

39 What follows relies almost totally on Edwards, 'The Sonora Crisis'; see note 2 above.

CHAPTER 28

1 On settler numbers in 1915, see WR Edwards, 'The Protection of American Lives and Property: The Sonora Crisis of 1915', which is derived from 'United States–Mexican Relations, 1913–1916: Revolution, Oil and Intervention', unpublished PhD thesis, Louisiana State University, 1971, p 6 [hereafter Edwards, 'The Sonora Crisis'].

2 Edwards, 'The Sonora Crisis', p 4.

3 *Ibid*, p 2.

4 *Ibid*, p 5; JM Hart, *Empire and Revolution: The Americans in Mexico since the Civil War* (Berkeley, 2002), p 345 [hereafter Hart, *Empire and Revolution*]; and, on Villa and the 'Yanqui protectorate', F Katz, 'Pancho Villa and the Attack on Columbus, New Mexico', *American Historical Review*, Vol 83, No 1, February 1978, p 112 [hereafter Katz, 'The Attack on

Columbus'].

5 As quoted in Edwards, 'The Sonora Crisis', p 1.

6 R Higgs, 'Who was Edward M. House'? – Newsletter of the Independent Institute, 13 August 2008.

7 Edwards, 'The Sonora Crisis', p 1.

8 F Katz, *The Life and Times of Pancho Villa* (Stanford, 1998), pp 505–506 [hereafter Katz, *Pancho Villa*]. Indeed, Canova's plotting with Mexican counterrevolutionary elements eventually cost him his position when he was, in effect, fired by the Secretary of State. See Katz, 'The Attack on Columbus', p 149, f/n 48.

9 Edwards, 'The Sonora Crisis', p 2.

10 *Ibid*, p 5.

11 *Ibid*; and Katz, *Pancho Villa*, p 504.

12 Edwards, 'The Sonora Crisis', p 3.

13 See *New York Times*, 1 June 1915; and, for the broader objective, Katz, *Pancho Villa*, p 313.

14 Edwards, 'The Sonora Crisis', p 4.

15 *Ibid*, p 5.

16 *Ibid*, p 6.

17 *Ibid*.

18 *New York Times*, 26 March 1916. For the wider context, see CW Trow, 'Woodrow Wilson and the Mexican Interventionist Movement of 1919', *The Journal of American History*, Vol 58, No 1 (June 1971), pp 46–72 [hereafter Trow, 'Mexican Interventionist Movement'].

19 In 1927, the journalist Max Stern was told by insiders that the initial developmental costs of the Yaqui estate, up to 1912, were of the order of $12 million; see 'Treacherous Yaquis and Tramp Bandits', *Pittsburgh Press*, 20 January 1927.

20 JH Hammond, *The Autobiography of John Hays Hammond, Vol 2* (New York, 1935), pp 746–747 [hereafter Hammond, *Autobiography 2*]; and, for the wider context, ES Rosenberg, 'Economic Pressures in Anglo-American Diplomacy in Mexico, 1917–1918', *Journal of Inter-American Studies and World Affairs*, Vol 17, No 2, (May 1975), p 123 [hereafter Rosenberg, 'Economic Pressures'].

21 Hammond, *Autobiography 2*, pp 695-96; and, for Hammond's willingness to back Fall's 1918 campaign for the Senate, DH Stratton, *Tempest over Teapot Dome: The Story of Albert B Fall* (Oklahoma, 1998), p 148 [hereafter Stratton, *The Story of Albert B Fall*].

22 See *The Advocate of Peace*, Vol 78, No 4, April 1916, pp 114–115.

23 Trow, 'Mexican Interventionist Movement', p 49.

24 *New York Times*, 5 March 1916. Fall's estimate of the number of men necessary to successfully occupy Mexico was in line with informed military opinions; see Katz, 'The Attack on Columbus', p 130.

25 See Trow, 'Mexican Interventionist Movement', p 50.

26 *Ibid*, p 61.

27 Rosenberg, 'Economic Pressures', pp 124–125.

28 See Rosenberg, 'Economic Pressures' pp 123–152 for the wider context; and, for the compliance of Hammond-owned operations, *Autobiography 2*, p 748. Hammond was a major player in Mexican oil; see SJ Randall, *United States Foreign Oil Policy since World War I: For Profits and Security* (Montreal, 2005), p 50.

29 Stratton, *The Story of Albert B Fall*, pp 147–148.

30 On the formation and background to these two organisations, see ML Davis, *Dark Side of Fortune: Triumph and Scandal in the Life of Oil Tycoon Edward L Doheny* (Berkley, 1998), p 119; LB Hall, *Oil, Banks and Politics: The United States and Post-revolutionary Mexico* (Austin, 2010), p 14; and Trow, 'Mexican Interventionist Movement', p 53. On the Yaqui Delta Company as a founding member of NAPARM, see *New York Times*, 30 January 1919; and, on Watriss, EJ Hindman, 'The United States and Alvaro Obregón: Diplomacy by Proxy', unpublished PhD thesis, Texas Technical University, 1972, pp 256–257. On Hammond-Watriss business ventures, see, for example, *Brooklyn Daily Eagle*, 12 October 1919; and on the Whitney-Watriss friendship, *New York Times*, 10 September 1915.

31 Trow, Mexican Interventionist Movement', pp 53–54; and WP Webb, *The Texas Rangers: A Century of Frontier Defense* (Austin, 2010), p xxi.

32 See f/n 13, in Trow, 'Mexican Interventionist Movement', p 51.

33 Trow, 'Mexican Interventionist Movement', pp 63–66.

34 *Ibid*, p 61.

35 *Ibid*, pp 69–71.

36 *Ibid*, pp 71–72.

37 See Hammond, *Autobiography 2*, pp 750–751.

38 *Ibid*, pp 752–753.

39 See Max Stern, 'Treacherous Yaqui Indians and Tramp Bandits', *Pittsburgh Press*, 2 January 1927

40 See, *The Spokesman-Review* (Spokane), 11 November 1927.

41 See the *Arniston Star* (Arizona), 22 February 1931; and Hart, *Empire and Revolution*, p 345.

42 See *El Paso Herald*, 12 June 1928.

43 See *Arniston Star* (Arizona), 22 February 1931 and P van Wyk, *Burnham: King of Scouts: Baden-Powell's Secret Mentor* (Trafford, BC, 2003), p 487.

CHAPTER 29

1 See JH Hammond, *The Autobiography of John Hays Hammond, Vol 1* (New York, 1935), p 79 and pp 190–196.

2 See columns by Will Rogers in the *Reading*

Eagle (Pennsylvania), 14 April 1935 and 21 May 1935.

3 See JH Hammond, *The Autobiography of John Hays Hammond, Vol 2* (New York, 1935), pp 753–754 [hereafter Hammond, *Autobiography 2*].

4 See *Courier Express* (Buffalo, NY), 2 November 1930.

5 *Ibid* [emphasis added].

6 Hammond's wife, Natalie Harris, died in 1931 – four years before Hammond. On his death he left the bulk of his fortune to his four children, none of whom appear to have had any offspring – and almost all of whom seem to have been, for want of a stronger term, somewhat eccentric.

7 See CE Neu, *Colonel House: A Biography of Woodrow Wilson's Silent Partner* (New York, 2015) [hereafter Neu, *Colonel House*].

8 *Boston Post*, 21 December 1920.

9 On the enduring Hammond-House friendship, see, for example, *Chicago Tribune*, 5 August 1931; and for Nikola Tesla's view of their closeness, even though the decade given is almost certainly incorrect, see also T Valone, *Harnessing the Wheelwork of Nature: Tesla's Science of Energy* (Kempton, IL, 2002), p 127. Hammond's importance in Republican politics remained considerable even after he made the mistake of backing the imperialist General Leonard Wood over Warren Harding at the 1920 convention; see *Wichita Daily Eagle*, 6 January 1921.

10 JH Hammond and JW Jenks, *Great American Issues: Political, Social and Economic (A Constructive Study)* (New York, 1923) [hereafter Hammond and Jenks, *Great American Issues*].

11 On Hammond, the commission and the times, see especially, RH Zieger, *Republicans and Labor: 1919–1929* (Lexington, 2015), pp 218–226.

12 See Hammond, *Autobiography 2*, pp 679 and 695.

13 *Ibid*, pp 446 and 693–694.

14 See, for example, 'Call John Hays Hammond Friend of Italy', *New York Times*, 1 February 1914; and *The Star and Sentinel* (Pennsylvania), 23 September 1915. For Natalie Harris's interest in the custodial care of cretins in Aosta, Italy, see a report on a speech delivered by her as carried in the *Australian Worker*, 13 November 1913, and Hammond's approval of Mussolini and his 'beneficent dictatorship' holding off communist advances and the decoration of the couple's son, Hammond, *Autobiography 2*, pp 724–725.

15 See the useful summary of Hammond's career in the *Lewiston Daily Sun*, 9 June 1936.

16 Hammond, *Autobiography 2*, p 712.

17 See items in *Richmond Times-Dispatch* (Virginia), 14 May 1911; *New Zealand Herald*, 20 May 1911; or *Rock Island Argus*, 13 June 1911.

18 *Wairapa Age*, Vol XXV, No 10713, 29 April 1914.

19 Such as hosting a lunch for 200 women, in 1916, at which the desirability of a world court was discussed as a means to further international peace see *Richmond Times-Dispatch*, 25 May 1916.

20 *San Francisco Call*, Vol 112, No 16, 11 June 1912.

21 See *Deseret News* (Salt Lake City), 22 May 1916; and *Fort Wayne News*, 24 May 1916.

22 See, for example, *Day Book* (Chicago), Vol 6, No 33, 4 November 1916; and *Reading Eagle*, 13 May 1917.

23 *New York Times*, 11 May 1917.

24 These developments can be traced in the *New York Times* of 29 November and 1 December 1917. The fate of the Militia after the departure of Natalie Harris is not clear.

25 For the wider context of American eugenics across the 20th century, see, among others, S Kuhl, *The Nazi Connection: Eugenics, the American Connection and German National Socialism* (New York; 2001); S Selden, 'Transforming Better Babies into Fitter Families: Archival Resources and the History of the American Eugenics Movements, 1908–1930', *American Philosophical Society*, Vol 149, No 2, 2005, pp 199–125. Mrs John Hays Hammond is located in another study – in MA Rembis, *Defining Deviance: Sex, Science, and Delinquent Girls* (Chicago, 2011), p 21.

26 Mrs John Hays Hammond, 'Why Washington Society Women study Genetics', *Richmond Times-Dispatch*, 6 July 1913. The choice of a newspaper based in Richmond, Virginia – the former capital of the Confederacy – as an outlet for the ideas of a self-consciously 'Southern' woman was presumably not entirely by chance.

27 See *Urbana Daily Courier*, 3 June 1913; and *Rock Island Argus* or *Wichita Daily Eagle* of 7 June 1913.

28 See also a report on Mrs John Hays Hammond address in 'Eugenics', *Australian Worker*, 13 November 1913.

29 *New York Times*, 16 November 1913.

30 See *Journal of Heredity*, Vol 5, No 8, 1914, p 340.

31 See note 23 above.

32 Hammond, *Autobiography 2*, p 541.

33 The origins of the conflict can be traced in *New York Times*, 18 November and 4 December 1911.

34 For the wider context of this storm see, among others, WC Askew, 'Efforts to Improve Russo-American Relations before the First World War: The John Hays Hammond Mission', *The Slavic and East European Review*, Vol 31, No 76 December 1952, pp 179–185; NW Cohen, *Jacob Schiff: A Study in American Jewish Leadership* (Lebanon, NH, 1999), p 149; and AJ Williams, *Trading with Bolsheviks: The Politics of East-West Trade, 1920–1939* (Manchester, 1992), p 18. On Taft's defence of

Hammond, see especially W Simon, *Presidents I Have Known from 1860–1918* (London, 1918), pp 319–320.

35 Neu, *Colonel House*, p 152.

36 *Morning Oregonian*, 10 February 1921.

37 Hammond and Jenks, *Great American Issues*, p 138.

38 *Ibid*, p 135.

39 On Hammond's evolving position as regards America's involvement in the First World War, see *New York Times*, 3 September 1915; and *Sausalito News,* 11 March 1916.

40 Hammond, *Autobiography 2*, p 710.

41 See T Roosevelt, *Foes of our Own Household* (New York, 1917), pp 341–345.

42 See Hammond, *Autobiography 2*, p 586; and *New York Times*, 28 October 1919.

43 See Ireland's review of the Jameson Raid as carried in *L'Abeille de la Nouvelle-Orléans*, 2 January 1900; and A Ireland, *The Anglo-Boer Conflict: Its History and Causes* (Boston, 1900).

44 On Ireland's growing disillusionment with democratic political system and interest in the role of heredity, see HL McBain's review of Ireland's *Democracy and the Human Equation* (New York, 1921) in *Political Science Quarterly*, Vol 36, No 4, December 1921, pp 690–692.

45 A Ireland, 'The True Story of the Jameson Raid as Related to me by John Hays Hammond, Part 1', *North American Review*, Vol 208, No 753, August 1918, pp 185–196; and Part 2, Vol 208, No 754, September 1918, pp 315–376.

46 See the preface in JH Hammond, *The Truth About the Jameson Raid, as Related to Alleyne Ireland* (Boston, 1918) [hereafter Hammond, *The True Story*].

47 Hammond, as cited in the preface of *The True Story*.

48 Hammond, *The True Story*, p 47.

49 JH Hammond, 'South African Memories: Rhodes-Barnato-Burnham', *Scribner's Magazine*, Vol LXIX, No 3, March 1921, pp 257–278.

50 *Ibid*, pp 262, 264 and 278.

51 *Ibid*, pp 260 and 275.

52 Thus, all that a critic in the *North American Review* could bring himself to say about Hammond and Jenks's *Great American Issues* was that it was a 'little dogmatic in tone' – *North American Review*, Vol 2145, No 788, 1 July 1921, pp 143–144. The date of the review would suggest that this was an issue that predated the republication of the work in 1923.

53 There is a good account of the proceedings in the *Engineering and Mining Journal Press*, Vol 121, 8 May 1926.

54 See items in *Day Book* (Chicago), 2 January 1927; *Pittsburgh Press*, 8 June 1927; and *Daily Sentinel* (Rome, NY), 6 May 1927.

55 Hammond, *Autobiography 2*, p 775.

CONCLUSION

1 The Jameson Raid was the progenitor of the Kruger government's Industrial Commission of Inquiry (1897) that saw the first systematic probing of the mining industry's grievances; see C van Onselen, *New Babylon, New Nineveh: Everyday Life on the Witwatersrand, 1886–1914* (Cape Town, 2001) pp 16 and 87. The 1897 commission also took extensive evidence from JH Hammond's cousin, WH Hall, at a time before the two men became estranged; see J Teisch, *Engineering Nature: Water, Development, & the Global Spread of American Environmental Expertise* (Chapel Hill, NC, 2011), pp 97–120.

2 On leading Americans such as V Clement, JH Hammond, T Mein, H Jennings, HC Perkins and E Wiltsee being highly incentivised as significant shareholders in Rand mines rather than mere engineers, see CC Spence, *Mining Engineers and the American West: The Lace-Boot Brigade* (New Haven, 1970), p 307 [hereafter Spence, *Lace-Boot Brigade*], and Chapter 2 above.

3 YGM Lulat, *United States Relations with South Africa: A Critical Overview from the Colonial Period to the Present* (New York, 2008), pp 36–37; and S Tuffnell, 'Engineering Inter-Imperialism: American Miners and the Transformation of Global Mining', *Journal of Global History*, Vol 10, Issue 1, March 2015, p 60 [hereafter Tuffnell, 'Inter-Imperialism'].

4 See 'Our Trade within Africa', *Scientific American*, 1896, p 391. Despite the prevailing depression, American investments abroad grew by about $250 million in the 1890s; see W LaFeber, *The New Empire: An Interpretation of American Expansion, 1860–1898* (London, 1963), p 179 [hereafter LaFeber, *New Empire*].

5 'American Uitlanders said to dominate in the Gold Fields', a report from the *Daily Mail* (London), reproduced in the *Chicago Tribune*, 18 March 1900. For the historical background to such movements, see, for example, Spence, *Lace-Boot Brigade*, p 305.

6 The classic statement about Rhodes's deep fear of an independent Boer republic under American sway, independent and therefore difficult to coax into an economic federation prior to an eventual assimilation into the British Empire, is to be found in WT Stead's *The Americanisation of the World or the Trend of the Twentieth Century* (London, 1902), pp 56–57 [hereafter Stead, *Americanisation*]; and, more generally, in R Hull, *American Enterprise in South Africa: Historical Dimensions of Engagement and Disengagement* (New York, 1990); and, in passing, in R Vinson, 'Citizenship over Race: African Americans in American-South African Diplomacy, 1890–1925', *Safundi: The Journal of South African and American Comparative Studies*, Issue 13/14,

April 2004, p 9 [hereafter Vinson, 'American-South African Diplomacy'].

7 *Chicago Tribune*, 18 March 1900.

8 *Ibid*; and, even more pertinently, 'An American', 'The Day we Celebrate', *Weekly Supplement, The Star*, 4 July 1896.

9 *Chicago Tribune*, 18 March 1900; but, for the context more fully described, see C van Onselen, *The Fox and the Flies* (London, 2008), pp 145–180; and *Showdown at the Red Lion: The Life and Times of Jack McLoughlin, 1859–1910* (Cape Town, 2015), pp 159–179 and 266–281.

10 See Chapter 11 above.

11 See MH Hunt, *Ideology and US Foreign Policy* (New Haven, 1987), pp 19–45 and 92–124.

12 JH Hammond, *The Autobiography of John Hays Hammond, Vol 1* (New York, 1935), p 343 [hereafter Hammond, *Autobiography 1*].

13 Hammond, *Autobiography 1*, p 343.

14 *Ibid*. The centrality of this 'revolutionary' defence in Hammond's thought can also be traced in A Ireland, 'The True Story of the Jameson Raid as related to me by John Hays Hammond', *North American Review*, Vol 208, No 753, Part 1, August 1918, p 186; and in Part 2, Vol 208, No 754, September 1918 [hereafter Ireland, 'Jameson Raid', Part 1 or Part 2].

15 See RH Davis, *Dr Jameson's Raiders vs The Johannesburg Reformers* (London, 1897), p 15 [hereafter Davis, *Jameson's Raiders*].

16 See, for example, the flight of WH Knight and his party two weeks before the Raid as recorded in the *Lawrence Daily World*, of 10 February 1896. See also Chapter 14, above, for the active, organised resistance of a few leading American engineers, including H Jennings, H Perkins and, of course, RE 'Barbarian' Brown of Coeur d'Alene fame.

17 See L Changuion, *Uncle Sam, Oom Paul, en John Bull: Amerika en die Anglo-Boere Oorlog* (Pretoria, 2001), p 26 [hereafter Changuion, *Uncle Sam*]; and, among several others, BN Brown, 'Americans who fought in the Anglo-Boer War', *Military History Journal* (South Africa), Vol 15, No 6, December 2011.

18 See WJ Cash's unsurpassed *The Mind of the South* (New York, 1991), at pp 67, 72 and 233–234.

19 Hammond, *Autobiography 1*, p 21.

20 This connection between Hammond and Rhodes in particular has also been noted at the American end. See, for example, G Brechin, *Imperial San Francisco: Urban Power, Earthly Ruin* (Berkeley, 2006), p 55 [hereafter Brechin, *Imperial San Francisco*].

21 The linkage between Anglo-Saxons and social Darwinism in the American context is traced in LaFeber, *New Empire*, pp 97–99.

22 See PA Kramer, 'Empires, Exceptions, and Anglo-Saxons: Race and Rule between the British and United States Empires,

1880–1910', *The Journal of American History*, Vol 88, No 4, March 2002, pp 1318 and 1322; and R Horsman, *Race and Manifest Destiny: The Origins of American Racial Anglo-Saxonism* (Cambridge, MA, 1981).

23 For Hammond and Rhodes's perception of the Boers living in a state of 'semi-barbarism', and the latter's noble drive to bring 'civilisation' to a backward people, see JH Hammond, 'South African Memories: Rhodes-Barnato-Burnham', *Scribner's Magazine*, Vol LXIX, No 3, March 1921, p 271 [hereafter Hammond, 'Memories']. It is against this broad ideological background, too, that one should read both Jack and Natalie Hays Hammond's early interest in eugenics, the appeal of racist thinking and the later acceptance of, if not liking for, fascism as embodied in the rise of Mussolini on the part of two male members of the family; see Chapter 29 above.

24 See, for example, 'John Hays Hammond Breaks Long Silence', *Lewiston Daily Sun*, 25 November 1911.

25 See M Meredith, *Diamonds, Gold and War: The Making of South Africa* (London, 2007), p 323.

26 See LaFeber, *New Empire*, p 4.

27 *Ibid*, p 8, but, more especially, pp 195, 257 and 262.

28 *Ibid*, pp 150–151 and 274. In Westminster, the Secretary of State for the Colonies, Joseph Chamberlain, saw British Guiana as 'potentially a new Transvaal' – see ER May, *Imperial Democracy; The Emergence of America as a Great Power* (New York, 1961) at pp 34, 44 and 254 [hereafter May, *Imperial Democracy*].

29 See also Tuffnell, 'Inter-Imperialism', p 65.

30 R Kagan, *Dangerous Nation: America and the World, 1600–1898* (London, 2006), p 368.

31 This account is based entirely on LaFeber's illuminating account in *New Empire*, pp 242–283. For the link between the Venezuelan crisis and the questions of personal courage and masculinity, evident in Davis's *Jameson's Raiders*, that became uppermost in Hammond's mind after the collapse of the coup, see also, KL Hoganson, *Fighting for American Manhood: How Gender Politics provoked the Spanish-American and Philippine-American Wars* (London, 1998), pp 16-17 [hereafter Hoganson, *Fighting for American Manhood*].

32 Ireland, 'Jameson Raid', Part 1, p 193.

33 See May, *Imperial Democracy*, pp 3–5.

34 See LaFeber, *New Empire*, pp 95–101; and RE May, *The Southern Dream of a Caribbean Empire* (Gainesville, FL, 2002), pp 21 and 81 [hereafter May, *Southern Dream*].

35 See JH Hammond, *The Autobiography of John Hays Hammond, Vol 2* (New York, 1935), p 757 [hereafter Hammond, *Autobiography 2*].

36 See *Brooklyn Daily Eagle*, 1 April 1895.

37 See especially RE May, *Manifest Destiny's*

Underworld: Filibustering in Antebellum America (Chapel Hill, NC, 2002 [hereafter May, *Filibustering*].

38 See May, *Filibustering*, pp xi, 3–4 and 53–54.

39 *Ibid*, pp xii, 84-85, 95-104 and 137-138.

40 *Ibid*, pp xii and 219; and Davis, *Jameson's Raiders*, pp 27 and 51, for Jameson not wanting to be cast as a 'pirate'. Again it is significant that the 'pirate' issue is addressed during the course of RH Davis's defending Hammond, who, he realised, might well be tarred with the same brush back in America.

41 See May, *Southern Dream*, p 3.

42 Walker's extraordinary career is especially well covered in May's *Filibustering*.

43 On Walker in San Francisco, see May, *Southern Dream*, p 79; and on RP Hammond, see 'History and Early Legislation' in *Daily Alta*, Vol 42, No 13639, 3 January 1887; and HH Bancroft, *History of California, Vol 6* (San Francisco, 1882), p 43.

44 On the Pierce administration's ambivalence about filibustering, see May, *Filibustering*, pp 119–123.

45 See RK Wyllys, 'The Republic of Lower California, 1853–54', *Pacific Historical Review*, Vol 23, June 1933, pp 194–213, and, on RP Hammond in particular, p 201.

46 RP Hammond and Coffee Hays's roles in Walker's dramatic departure from the port can be traced in May, *Filibustering*, at pp 125–127, 132–134 and 146–148.

47 See WO Scroggs, *Filibusters and Financiers: The Story of William Walker and His Associates* (London, 1916), p 49.

48 See PW Gates, *Land and Law in California: Essays on Land Policies* (West Lafayette, IN, 2002), p 82. I have been unable to find any corroborating evidence to back this rumour.

49 See FR Burnham, *Scouting on Two Continents* (New York, 1926), p 224.

50 As taken from JH Wilkins (ed), *The Great Diamond Hoax and Other Stirring Incidents in the Life of Asbury Harpending* (San Francisco, 1913), Chapter 4 – a work with no page numbers in its electronic format.

51 See Chapter 4 above; B McGinty, 'California in the Civil War', *Civil War Times Illustrated*, June 1981; and LL Richards, *The California Gold Rush and the Coming of the Civil War* (New York, 2007), pp 230–232.

52 Hammond is predictably silent about the San Francisco plot of 1861. Indeed, he could not even bring himself to mention Harpending by name in relation to the Great Diamond Hoax of 1872; see Hammond, *Autobiography 1*, p 171.

53 See above, Chapters 5–7.

54 In 1971, in an excellent MA thesis, E de Waal already pointed in this direction without being aware of the ways in which Hammond's consciousness had been, and was being,

shaped by events back in the Coeur d'Alene, Idaho; see E de Waal, 'The Part Played by Americans on the Witwatersrand during the Period 1886–1899', unpublished MA thesis, Department of History, Unisa, 1971, p 44.

55 V Harlow and F Hamilton, 'Sir Frederic Hamilton's Narrative of Events Relative to the Jameson Raid', *The English Historical Review*, Vol 72, No 283, April 1957, pp 282.

56 Republic of South Africa, Johannesburg, Brenthurst Library, Rhodes Papers, CJ Rhodes to Alfred Beit, Cape Town, letter dated 'August 1895'.

57 As cited in Stead, *Americanisation*, p 30.

58 See *The World*, Monday, 13 January 1896; and, for some misleading subsequent reporting of the same cable, the *Wairarapa Daily Times* (New Zealand), 15 January 1896, and *Border Watch* (South Australia), 18 January 1896.

59 See A Kaplan, 'Romancing the Empire: The Embodiment of American Masculinity in the Popular Historical Novel of the 1890s', *American Literary History*, Vol 2, No 4, Winter 1990, p 662 (emphasis in the original).

60 Stead, *Americanisation*, p 30.

61 RSA, University of Cape Town, Jagger Library, Leipoldt Papers, BC 94 D3.69, WP Schreiner to E Esselen, 20 January 1896 (emphasis added).

62 See H Giliomee, *The Afrikaners: Biography of a People* (Charlottesville, 2003), p 213; and, more particularly, on the same page, his reference to JA Coetsee, *Politieke Groepering in die wording van die Afrikaner Nasie* (Johannesburg, 1941), p 317.

63 See Chapters 12–16 above.

64 For Hammond as the chief conspirator, see, for example, Changuion, *Uncle Sam*, p 20; or LE Meyer, *The Farther Frontier: Six Case Studies of Americans and Africa, 1848–1936* (London, 1992), p 143.

65 Davis, *Jameson's Raiders*, p 15.

66 *Ibid*.

67 See *Meriden Morning Record* (Connecticut), 27 November 1911; and *Evening Post*, 29 November 1911. For the backlash that his remarks about Kruger engendered among well-placed critics, see *Sacramento Union*, No 36, 6 December 1911; and *El Paso Herald*, 16 December 1911.

68 Ireland, 'Jameson Raid', Part 1, p 187.

69 See Hammond, 'Memories', at pp 262, 265, 267 and 278.

70 See, for example, Vinson, 'American-South African Diplomacy', p 9.

71 Tuffnell, 'Inter-Imperialism', p 60.

72 Among these was the Anglophobic and bellicose Senator JT Morgan of Alabama, a former brigadier-general in the Army of the Confederacy – see C Tsehloane Keto, 'The Aftermath of the Jameson Raid and American Decision Making in Foreign Affairs, 1896',

Transactions of the American Philosophical Society, Vol 70, Part 8, 1980, p 24 [hereafter Keto, 'The Aftermath of the Jameson Raid'].

73 The campaign – and more especially the press campaign – mounted in the United States to come to Hammond's defence is, despite one or two editorial lapses, analysed in great depth and with considerable professional sophistication in Keto, 'The Aftermath of the Jameson Raid', pp 5–46.

74 See, for example, LaFeber, *New Empire*, pp 63–72.

75 Surprisingly, this includes JH Hammond and JW Jenks's work on *Great American Issues: Political, Social, Economic* (New York, 1923).

76 LaFeber, *New Empire*, p 150; but take note, too, of the important rider in May, *Imperial Democracy*, pp 267–270, in which he emphasises how 'Issues in Hawaii, China, Turkey, Venezuela had intruded almost of their own accord. Statesmen and politicians dealt with them according to their judgement of domestic, not foreign, conditions.'

77 In this broad context, the importance of John Hays Hammond as frontier entrepreneur, both before and after 1900, as well as his relative neglect by most historians, has been noted for some time. See, for example, JA Field Jnr, 'American Imperialism: The Worst Chapter in Almost any Book', *American Historical Review*, Vol 83, No 3, June 1978, p 645, note 2; and D Igler, 'The Industrial Far West: Region and Nation in the Late Nineteenth Century', *Pacific Historical Review*, Vol 69, No 2, May 2000, and especially pp 177–179. Some of these deficiencies have been addressed subsequently by Brechin's excellent *Imperial San Francisco*.

78 See above, Chapters 19–22.

79 Tuffnell, 'Inter-Imperialism', p 73.

80 Despite the fact that Hammond only became personally acquainted with Major Burnham relatively late in his own career, Burnham soon came to occupy a prime spot in Hammond's pantheon of heroes; see Hammond, 'Memories', pp 272–275.

81 See Chapters 19–22 above.

82 This bizarre stunt has to be seen against the issues explored in Hoganson's splendid *Fighting for American Manhood*, and, as importantly, as an understanding of the fact – as RH Davis had sought to counter in *Jameson's Raiders* – that the Jameson Raid had called Hammond's courage into question.

83 See Chapter 28 above.

A CAUTIONARY NOTE

1 D Judd, *The British Imperial Experience from 1765 to the Present* (London, 1912), p 159.

2 P Brendon, *The Decline and Fall of the British Empire* (London, 2008), p 191.

3 M Meredith, *Diamonds, Gold and War: The Making of South Africa* (London, 2007), p 311, although, to be fair, on the very next page, Meredith points directly to the importance of the Matabeleland mining safari.

4 See PJ Cain and AG Hopkins, *British Imperialism, 1688–2000* (London, 2002), p 323 [hereafter Cain and Hopkins, *British Imperialism*].

5 B Farwell, *The Great Boer War* (Barnsley, 2009), p 22.

6 W Beinart, *Twentieth Century South Africa* (Oxford, 2001), p 63.

7 Cain and Hopkins, *British Imperialism*, p 325.

8 E Longford, *Jameson's Raid: The Prelude to the Boer War* (Johannesburg, 1960), p ix.

9 TJ Makhura, 'Another Road to the Raid: The Neglected Role of the Boer-Bagananwa War as a Factor in the Coming of the Jameson Raid, 1894–1895', *Journal of Southern African Studies*, Vol 21, No 2, June 1995, pp 257–267.

10 C Saunders, 'Historiographical Aspects of the Jameson Raid' in J Carruthers (ed), *The Jameson Raid: A Centennial Perspective* (Johannesburg, 1996), p 239 [hereafter Carruthers (ed), *The Jameson Raid*].

11 The phrase comes from CT Gordon, *The Growth of Boer Opposition to Kruger, 1890–1895* (London, 1970), a uniquely valuable study that is surprisingly underutilised.

12 Just what can be done to stretch our understanding of the role that Afrikaners played in the events leading up to the Jameson Raid has been exceptionally well illustrated in C van der Merwe, *Donker Stroom: Eugène Marais en die Anglo-Boereoorlog* (Cape Town, 2015).

13 G Blainey, 'Lost Causes of the Jameson Raid', *The Economic History Review*, New Series, Vol 18, No 2 (1965), pp 350–366.

14 As always, there are a few laudable exceptions, including LE Meyer's 'John Hays Hammond and the Jameson Raid: Engineering a Capitalist Revolution in South Africa' in his *The Farther Frontier: Six Case Studies of Americans and Africa, 1843–1936* (London, 1992), pp 139–234; and, up to a point, J Jaffe's 'John Hays Hammond' in Carruthers (ed), *The Jameson Raid*, pp 211–226.

15 JH Hammond, *The Autobiography of John Hays Hammond*, Vols 1 and 2 (New York, 1935).

16 See RH Davis, *Dr Jameson's Raiders vs the Johannesburg Reformers* (New York, 1897); and A Ireland, 'The True Story of the Jameson Raid as Related to me by John Hays Hammond', Part 1, *The North American Review*, Vol 208, Nos 753, August 1918, pp 185–196, and Part 2, Vol 208, No 754, September 1918, pp 365–376.

A Cautionary Note

The Historiography of the Jameson Raid

It is reasonable to assume that after the elapse of more than one hundred years historians of the British Empire, Cecil Rhodes and the Jameson Raid would have reached an uneasy consensus about an event that was of cardinal importance in the subsequent economic development and political evolution of modern southern Africa. Some modern historians of empire, perhaps realising secretly that they are skating on thin historiographical ice, adopt a posture of supreme confidence as they glide across rickety explanation. All the more is the pity because that mock confidence appears to have discouraged new researchers and younger scholars from probing for new or questioning interpretations of the Jameson Raid. In truth, even a casual perusal of much of the literature will reveal a state of some confusion.

Let us ignore for the moment most of the 20th-century historiography of the Raid and concentrate on a half-dozen or so works that have appeared for the most part in the first decade of the 21st century, and then focus only on the role of the one man whom almost all believe was the *fons et origo* of just about every aspect of what was undoubtedly a seminal event – Cecil John Rhodes. According to a few historians such was Rhodes's imperial ambition and haste that he, almost single-handedly, generated the idea behind the Raid in the residence of the Cape Premier and then became not only the chief conspirator and principal financier of the plot, but also the man behind much of the logistical planning necessary to organise a coup d'état. By these accounts Rhodes was by nature a radical man, an imperial colossus as well as a managerial magician.

But let me not put words into the mouths of the professionals – let them

525

speak for themselves: 'Cecil Rhodes was the inspiration behind the episode. His ambition to topple the Kruger regime through armed intervention also arose from his unbridled ambition and his remarkable success hitherto.'[1] 'So, spirited on by an "innate Caesarism", he [Rhodes] plotted an armed coup against Kruger's regime.'[2] Bit of an ideological giveaway, that use of the term 'regime', but let us ignore it and push on. 'The conspiracy was hatched at Groote Schuur.'[3] Well, not really, but once again the underlying, one-man organising principle is there for the unwary to feed on. A few of the best historians are unwilling to accept the standard fare put out, but are then uncertain as to what then follows: 'To confine the explanation of this episode to Jameson or even to Rhodes is to adopt an excessively narrow view of causation.'[4] Quite so, but neither can a democracy of contributory factors take us much further.

In order to avoid the pitfalls that come with the crassest of 'great man' theories of history, authors are therefore pushed into trying to spread the explanatory load, but the results are not necessarily more convincing. Not convinced that Rhodes alone could come up with so radical an idea for imperial expansion, the blame shifts to unnamed members of the rag-tag Reform Committee who, it is claimed, first punted the idea of a revolution: 'Rhodes encouraged them. When they attempted to revolt he supplied them with arms, smuggling rifles and ammunition into the country in coal wagons and oil drums of the De Beers Company which he controlled.'[5] Revolt first, arms later. There appears to be a problem with the chronology here, as well as with an understanding of the genesis of the so-called Reform Committee, but no matter.

For all these reasons, historians remain understandably tentative as they search for the political mainspring underlying the failed revolution. But the resulting formulations can also be confusing. Consider the following: 'It was not a very British coup, but had more of the mark of settler politics.'[6] It is difficult to know what 'settlers' might mean in these circumstances, even if the underlying idea is sound, that is, if Jameson's Raid was indeed an imperial adventure gone wrong, it was not self-evidently 'British'. But if the Raid bore the mark of 'settler politics', how do we reconcile that with the suggestion from others that the attempted coup had a 'liberal tinge' to it. And, what to make of 'The Jameson Raid, had it succeeded, would have been welcomed in the republic'?[7] By whom exactly in 'the republic' – as opposed to the Rand – would it have 'been welcomed'?

Much of the latter-day academic bluster around the Raid rests on the foundation of decades of uninspired scholarship. The sense of exhaustion and frustration emanating from voluminous writings on the 'Jameson Raid' has now become almost palpable. But feelings of exasperation have been around for half a century and almost all sensible historians now do their best to avoid what has become a veritable black hole of boredom. Fifty years ago Elizabeth Longford introduced her book on the subject by inflicting a series of exclamation marks on her readers in the opening sentences of a work, warning all who ventured near that they were in danger of being sucked into a great nothingness of times past: 'What!', wrote she, 'Another book on the Jameson Raid!'[8] The warning may not have been enough to save her readers. Thirty years later, an African historian hovering on the edge of the Raid, Tlou Makhura, muttered that there was 'a certain sterility to the present debate'.[9] In 1995, total despair – not only about the past, but also about the *future* of the historiography – characterised a chapter offered to a 'Centennial Retrospective' marking the Raid:

> With new evidence unlikely to emerge, there may be no major rein-terpretations of the Raid in the future. As a precursor to the South African War, a seminal event in our history, the Raid will retain its importance, but most historians have shifted their attention to other wars, other raids, other cover-ups. It may well be that in another hundred years, someone thinking of surveying the historiography of the Raid over the century past will not find much to write about.[10]

That may, however, be an unnecessarily gloomy prediction. A lack of 'new evidence' should not, of its own accord, militate against the emergence of 'major reinterpretations'. As detectives working 'cold cases' know only too well, sometimes the mere act of getting fresh eyes to contemplate stale clues is enough to generate a new hypothesis, thus turning previously ignored or neglected lines of inquiry into new directions, and in the process of so doing generate new evidence. Facts and evidence, as postmodernists never tire of telling us, do not enjoy an independent existence; they are, in part, the product of the mind of the inquisitor. Just because a few brothers and sisters get carried away and then proceed to dispute the existence of *any* facts or evidence should not prevent us from understanding their reservations. What we need to do is to turn apparent weakness into strength since, to be sure, there *are* no limits to the inquisitive historical imagination. Looking askance at old conundrums and coming up with angled questions can make for new interpretations *and* evidence.

If that is true, then there is not much point now in going back and systematically unpacking all the previous approaches to the study of the Jameson Raid, which has given rise to a historiography widely accepted as being predictable, if not tedious. Instead, what follows are a few loosely connected points that may enhance the reader's appreciation of the existing good, bad and indifferent histories of the Jameson Raid and provide some understanding of my own approach to the subject when it came to writing this book. Here are a few discontents that informed my reading and research around the failed coup d'état.

First, it might help if we lost a bit of the 'gee whiz' air of amazement that surrounds some of the approaches to the study of the Jameson Raid. The incursion was indeed an event of great, arguably even seminal importance in the understanding of the history of southern Africa, but the study of it could perhaps be slightly better contextualised so as to help us widen our perspective. From the moment of the signing of the Sand River Convention, in 1852, right up to the outbreak of the South African War, in 1899, the borders of the Zuid-Afrikaansche Republiek (ZAR) underwent a never-ending process of adjustment and re-demarcation through armed confrontations and wars, diplomatic agreements or political settlements great and small. The point being that, in a Weberian sense, the legitimacy and power – of a state in the making, rather than an established state – was being challenged constantly at its margins, by Africans, by disgruntled Boers or by colonial and imperial powers seeking to defend or expand their holdings. For many the extent, let alone strength, of the northernmost Boer republic remained an unknown in 1895.

It was only in the 1870s that a formalised eastern border of sorts began to emerge between the ZAR and Portuguese East Africa, and it took another 25 years before that between the republic and neighbouring Swaziland was settled. In the southwest, Boers, tagged variously as 'filibusters' or 'mercenaries', and who were challenged by Rhodes, who was seeking to keep 'the road to the north' open, established the short-lived, independent republics of Stellaland and Goshen between 1882 and 1885. In 1891, the failed Adendorff trek saw another group of armed and marginalised Boers attempting to cross the Limpopo into territory supposedly under the control of Rhodes's British South Africa Company. It was a column of Jameson's company police that forced them to turn back, thereby contributing to his mounting arrogance and willingness to dismiss the Boers as worthy military opponents. In the northeast, where Chief Makhado's people had pushed back against progressive European encroachment, the VhaVenda polity was not fully conquered until as late as 1898. And, indeed, had it not been by chance that the invaders had neglected to cut one vital telegraph line, Jameson's border invaders may well have reached the Witwatersrand before they were detected and apprehended by Boer commandos.

With so much regional pushing and shoving going on around the outer rim of the South African Republic the notion of staging an armed incursion from land occupied by the Barolong, who had long-standing grievances of their own with Boer invaders, seems a bit less audacious or 'mad'. The very idea of staging a 'raid' was not entirely novel and, to a greater or lesser extent, was already reasonably well-embedded in the political subconscious of many in the trans-Vaal long before more exotic elements, deriving from experiences elsewhere, were readily grafted on to it.

Nor was the ZAR capable of easily enforcing its will on the settlements within its borders, even after the first significant gold deposits were discovered in the eastern part of the country, in the early 1880s. In 1887, 'Irish Brigade' brigands occupied Eureka City, a small mining town, for a week without any meaningful response from the state, and only months later members of the same murderous band effectively occupied inner Johannesburg for an entire weekend, eventually occasioning the first major reorganisation of the town's police force. A year later, in 1888, African prisoners suspected of murder were lynched in the mining hamlet of Steynsdorp. In 1891, in yet another incident that can be traced back to the 'Irish Brigade', parts of inner Pretoria had to be barricaded and the perimeters of the city carefully watched when white inmates threatened to seize control of the prison. The limits to ZAR state power were there for all to see, right up to the time of the Jameson Raid.

Second, the fact that the ZAR – without a standing army of note – and hardly a fully functioning entity in the mid-1890s, let alone one underpinned by an agricultural-industrial political economy able to come to terms with the changes necessary to become an industrial-agricultural complex, has sometimes eluded those studying the period. Having failed to come to terms with the underlying realities, some historians have then gone on to fall into the trap of reading history backwards – from, say the time of the Union, in 1910 – choosing to see the ZAR, before the Anglo-Boer War, as constituting a fully formed 'nation-state', thereby only further compounding the analytical problems that bedevil our understanding of both time and place. It is but a short slide from believing in the existence of the nation-state to accepting some of the more ideological notions about the birth and founding of the 'nation' in the face of external aggression and force.

It is precisely because the idea of the ZAR as constituting a nation-state by the mid-1890s has been accepted a touch uncritically, and because the Jameson Raid is often seen as being midwife to the birth of a nation, that so much of the history of the decade before the Anglo-Boer War has been cast in quasi-nationalist terms by Afrikaner, British and southern African historians writing in English. Instead of tracking the accelerated change taking place in the ZAR in the 1890s – a dynamic, unfolding process – historians have tended to accept that the state was fully formed, leaving them with a more or less static structural notion. These hidden assumptions, which tend to neglect the internal dynamics of the ZAR, come at some analytical cost.

If it is accepted that the ZAR was the complete article, already a 'nation-state', it tends to close off rather than open up avenues that might deepen our understanding of the crucial antebellum period. Instead of seeing the

Kruger government as fully in control of a Boer nation by 1895, as presiding over a strong state capable of easily seeing off an imperialist threat,
might we not be better served by viewing it as a weak government in an
underdeveloped state? Surely it makes sense to see the Jameson Raid itself,
as many have, as having given rise to a more unified Boer polity, stronger
government and a meaningful spurt in the development of the state?

If we take a one-dimensional view and accept uncritically the idea of
there being a strong and united ZAR before 1895, it saps the desire to
probe for schisms within Afrikaner society and fails to build on our existing
understanding of, in the words of CT Gordon, 'the growth of Boer political
opposition to Kruger'.[11] It was a mistake that the Jameson Raid conspirators
did not make. They spoke frequently of the need to work with 'Progressive'
elements in Pretoria, and talked of a 'provisional government', ushering
in an administration of national unity capable of turning an agricultural-
industrial state into one that was industrial-agricultural in its outlook. If
historians take *that* idea more seriously – and they should – it starts to
open the way to thinking the unthinkable, namely, who exactly among the
Afrikaner-Dutch in Pretoria might have been willing to collaborate with
the mine-owning conspirators and constitute a political fifth column for the
Jameson Raiders? Once again, the clues to the answer to that question have
been embedded in the literature for more than a century, in everything from
Edmund Garrett and EJ Edward's *The Story of an African Crisis* (1897) to John
Hays Hammond's *Autobiography* (1935).

An unwillingness to probe for the answers to those questions by Afrikaner
and English historians wearing nationalist or imperialist spectacles has diminished our ability to develop a more rounded understanding of the Jameson
Raid.[12] It has encouraged us to stick to the shallow distinction between
Boer and Brit – the comic-book cousins of 'nation' and 'state' – at precisely
the moment that we, as historians, should be wading into the deeper waters
of class, culture and ideologies of progress to establish the strength of any
undercurrents of collaboration. It is the often simple-minded distinction
drawn in the historiography between Boer and Brit that allows the Jameson
Raid to be seen almost exclusively as the 'prelude to the Boer War' and,
more corrosively still, to allow it to reduce the Afrikaner-Dutch – educated
and uneducated, urban and rural, alike – as mere victims of rampant British
imperialism and perfidious Albion – when, in truth, the situation was far
more complex and fluid.

The nation-state may, arguably, be a useful concept when studying
Europe, where the roots of the polity and the society often run as deep as
they do long. But in southern Africa, where both the nature and the shape
of the 'nation' and the 'state' has mutated constantly over little more than
a century, and where ongoing 'nation-building' exercises warn us that the

'nation-state' awaits its birth, historians may be better advised to *question* the notion rather than adopting it as a suitable tool for understanding the recent past. It is simply not good enough to see the Jameson Raid as pitting the British imperialists and/or the leading mine owners on the Rand against the Afrikaner-Dutch of the Kruger republic. That division has been reified and given rise to a binary opposition in the historiography that has narrowed our analysis at precisely the historical moment that incoming 'foreigners', 'uitlanders', including a significant number of American immigrants, were expanding the political repertoire.

Third, and as already noted tangentially, British and South African historians of various political persuasions, seduced by the entrenched binary opposition of Boer and Brit, have been unwilling to come to terms fully with the cosmopolitan nature of the Witwatersrand conspirators. It is as if most members of our guild have, for a century and more, been content to listen to a performance delivered by an ageing duo – imperialist and nationalist – when the score has clearly called for the voices of a trio. Historians of the American empire, almost without exception – despite the fact that one of their countrymen, John Hays Hammond, played a leading, if not *the* decisive, part in the planning of the Jameson Raid – have allowed this unsatisfactory situation to go unchallenged, despite the fact that it has long been known that the 1890s were central to the development of United States imperialism.

Intimidated by the dominant imperialist-nationalist dichotomy in southern Africa, most American historians have displayed little desire to explore possible connections between filibustering in the United States and the Jameson Raid of 1895, or to try and determine what the latter's relationship might be to the first, unsuccessful, attempt to annex Hawaii in 1893, or the coming of the Spanish-American War in 1898. Historians in the United States would do themselves a favour if, like their counterparts who are interested in the globalised British Empire, they showed more interest in the rise of the Witwatersrand goldfields as part of America's expanding informal empire during the economically troubled and explosive 1890s.

In terms of historical research, the consequences of working from so restrictive an imperialist-nationalist agenda have been predictable. Necessary as it might have been, a disproportionate amount of effort and time seems to have been devoted to finding, listening to and recording the voices of just two men: Cecil Rhodes, in Cape Town, and Joseph Chamberlain, in Westminster-Whitehall. Their diplomatic and culture-coded conversations, official and private, and so very English, are considered to be emblematic of what we are assured is still best heard as a British imperial misadventure, while a deaf ear is cocked in the direction of Hammond's louder and more direct American voice, which, in truth, came from the Deep South. As a result, what should be explored and experienced primarily as a capitalist conspiracy set within a complex triangular global setting gets reduced to a more predictable, tedious, two-way north-south process.

In 1965, half a century ago, exasperated by the preponderance of 'political' – for which read imperialist and nationalist – variations on a theme in the historiography, the Australian Geoffrey Blainey wrote what became if not the seminal, then a hugely influential, 'economic interpretation' entitled 'Lost Causes of the Jameson Raid'.[13] Blainey's sharp, some say too-sharply drawn, distinction between the owners of outcrop and deep-level mines assisted in determining more precisely who, when and why the principal figures became involved in a conspiracy to overthrow a state pressing ever more heavily on the changing cost structure of their companies. Blainey's insights, much loved by radical historians, undoubtedly elevated the debate around the Raid by suggesting how the possible underlying economic motivations of the mine owners who became involved in the plotting might be linked to the political outcomes they desired. It did not, however, take the debate as far forward as it might have because it, too, relied on a binary distinction, that between economics and politics, when what was needed most to enhance our understanding was a more integrated explanation, one of classic 'political economy'. As a stand-alone contribution, Blainey's essay leans towards economic reductionism and does not identify any clear-cut new direction for research precisely because it does not really offer us fully joined-up history. Who, where, why and when are clearly vital ingredients when coming up with more persuasive explanations, but history, and more especially the history of a political conspiracy, cries out for the addition of the question 'how'? *How* did the conspirators come by their ideas? What experiences past, or historical knowledge, went into the cognitive architecture underlying the plot? The latter are biographical, personal questions that take the analyst well beyond the oft-divided domains of 'economics' and 'politics'.

Here again, American historians, like many of their British and South African counterparts, have hesitated to probe the Jameson Raid from any, let alone new, perspectives. While that reluctance on the part of historians is understandable insofar as it relates to the Raid proper, which, after all, has a Scot, Dr Jameson, occupying centre stage, it is rather more puzzling when it comes to John Hays Hammond.[14] Hammond, known to have played a central role in the planning of the Jameson Raid, was one of four sentenced to death for his part in the attempted coup d'état and, at least as importantly, went on to occupy positions of great national importance in the economic, political and social life of the United States of America.

No biographer has ever been sufficiently attracted to Hammond's fascinating career and life to warrant the research and writing of an extended study. His two-volume *Autobiography*, seemingly so factual, comprehensive and reliable, appears to have discouraged critical scholarly inquiry.[15] More's the pity, because just beyond Hammond's irritatingly arrogant, narcissistic and self-serving story lie the crafted dissembling and strategic omissions that should make it a professional historian's delight. And, precisely because the attempted coup on the Rand became central to his life and self-perception, Hammond had already laid down two earlier vintages of his role in Jameson's Raid by the time he got around to writing the autobiography.

In 1897, Hammond relayed a first version of the attempted coup, one designed to emphasise personal courage and prepare the way for his return to the United States, to a renowned journalist and a novelist of the day, Richard Harding Davis. It was entitled *Dr Jameson's Raiders vs. the Johannesburg Reformers* and published as a booklet in New York City. The second, in 1918, piggy-backing on the First World War, was handled by another journalist, Alleyne Ireland, and appeared, in two parts, as 'The True Story of the Jameson Raid as Related to me by John Hays Hammond' in the influential and prestigious *North American Review*.[16] Both accounts appear to have been accepted as versions of the gospel by historians who, knowing better, should perhaps have probed them more systematically for change and continuity.

A more rigorous comparison of Hammond's three renditions of his involvement in the Raid, spread over forty years, but more especially 'The True Story' (and in that title lies a warning about how to approach *all* his versions), reveals just how deep the American's planning for the attempted coup d'état ran. If successful it was, as he and his wife later claimed, going to culminate in 'revolutionary' change. By Hammond's own telling and that which he dictated to his personal secretary, Arthur Kelsey, just 12 weeks after the failed uprising, his plans, not all of which he shared with his British-South African counterparts at the time, went well beyond what historians record about a conspiracy that they consistently cast in reformist rather than revolutionary terms. Hammond had a team of American miners, discharged from their positions for ill-discipline, on standby at Irene not only to help overrun the arsenal in Pretoria, but also to abduct the State President for 'negotiations' that would see a separate constitutional dispensation, along the lines of the District of Columbia, for the Witwatersrand goldfields. It is, for the most part, only Anglophone writers who share Edmund Burke's reservations about France in 1789 who have bought holus-bolus and uncritically into the belief that the Jameson Raid was a bad mistake of judgement, one that just happened to grow out of deep and genuinely held reformist sentiments of mine owners whose growth in profit margins was being threatened by the Kruger government's lopsided economic policies, which favoured burghers over Brits. That most certainly was *not* the view of the revolutionary in charge of the Rand uprising, the man who led the planning, controlled intelligence operations and oversaw the arms smuggling right up to the moment that he took fright when Jameson jumped the gun and let Lionel Phillips assume the political leadership of what was re-christened as a movement for reform.

There was a deliberate collapsing and confusing of the 'revolutionary' and 'reformist' trajectories of the Jameson Raid, led by the conspirators themselves, with Hammond – the goat with a bell around the neck – later being followed blindly by a troop of bleating historians. So successfully was this propaganda at the time that it soon became the dominant narrative in Anglophone circles; the conspirators, their silence proclaimed, had never been revolutionaries, just frustrated reformers whose legitimate aspirations were undone by an unfortunate miscalculation that had taken place on the Bechuanaland border. So keen were members of the Anglophone establishment at home and abroad to forget and conceal that reform-inclined English mine owners had once been led by an American with a 'revolutionary' agenda that, after a decent interval and the advent of the Union in 1910, the ideological tailors to British royalty were called in to fashion them the finest suits of imperial respectability. Abe Bailey became Sir Abe Bailey (1911); George Farrar became Sir George Farrar (1911); Percy FitzPatrick became Sir Percy FitzPatrick (1902); Lionel Phillips became Sir Lionel Phillips (1912); and even the blunderer-in-chief, Dr Jameson, became Premier of the Cape and Sir Leander Starr Jameson (1911). And, when President Taft appointed Hammond as the United States' Special Ambassador to the Court of St James's for the coronation of King George V and Queen Mary, in 1911, all was once again supposedly well across the Anglophone Atlantic world.

Those working their way through the historiography of the Raid will, however, be well aware that there were indeed Uitlander reformist political moves afoot in the ZAR some time before the Jameson Raid. Most such initiatives came from the National Union, well-served by yet more wolves in sheep's garb in the form of Rowland Bettington and the Leonard brothers, Charles and James. But, by late 1895, any public pretence at reform among the conspirators had long since given way to talk in private about the coming 'revolution', only for the original reformist vocabulary to be hastily reinstated after Jameson had let loose the horses and riders at Pitsani. Anybody reflecting upon the history of the events on the Witwatersrand in 1895 would be well advised to note, with great care, who precisely used the terms 'reform' and 'revolution' and where, when, why and how they were employed. The terms are simply *not* interchangeable, and to treat them as such is to fall for a mine owners' trick that went into circulation around 1895 and that persists in the historiography.

This brings us to a final point, one about Hammond's substantial body of writings and where they might fit into the picture of the Jameson Raid that emerges from most of the existing literature. Spread over the better part of half a century, Hammond's books and tightly directed interventions with the leading journalists of the day offer historians a unique opportunity to study, at considerable depth, how a life-changing event of international significance shaped the career the leading conspirator, whose ambitions briefly included running for the office of President of the United States of America. Hammond was raised in the American West, and by the early 1890s was active along the frontiers of southern African mining. After the failed Jameson Raid he spent several years in self-imposed exile, in London, restoring his damaged reputation before returning to the United States in 1899. From there he once again became actively involved in frontier politics, in Mexico, for two decades.

John Hays Hammond's various memoirs thus offer us a unique opportunity to track his thinking and behaviour as it relates to radical, if not revolutionary, spasms of capitalist development in several different frontier situations before, during and after the Jameson Raid. That alone makes him a subject worthy of the most serious interrogation for a full-scale biography by those fascinated by the history of industrial capitalism in the period leading up to the First World War. Even a partial glance into his life, however, such as that presented in this study, shows how Hammond's career can throw new light on subjects that are of national and international importance; he presents us with a sturdy and natural bridge for the writing of transnational history. And, as regards the literature on the Jameson Raid, Hammond's writings remind us in the starkest way possible that there is no need for us to hold our breath and wait for the emergence of new evidence before we re-examine events central to the making of the state in southern Africa. The real limits to writing revealing history lie as much with the historical imagination as they do with the absence or presence of evidence. The two can never be fully separated.

Select Bibliography

ARTICLES

Brown, RM, 'Western Violence, Structure, Values, Myth', *The Western Historical Quarterly*, Vol 24, No 1 (February 1993), pp 4–20.

Cabrita, J, 'People of Adam: Divine Healing and Racial Cosmopolitanism in the Early Twentieth-Century Transvaal, South Africa', *Comparative Studies in Society and History*, Vol 57, No 2 (April 2015), pp 1–36.

Dym, WA, 'Freiberg on the Frontier: Louis Janin, German Engineering and "Civilisation" in the American West', *Annals of Science*, Vol 68, No 3 (2011), pp 295–323.

French, GE, 'The Coeur d'Alene Riots, 1892', *Overland Monthly and Out West Magazine*, Vol 26, Issue 151 (July 1895), pp 32–49.

Gaboury, WJ, 'From State House to Bull Pen: Idaho Populism and the Coeur d'Alene Troubles of the 1890s', *Pacific Northwest Quarterly*, Vol LVIII (January 1967), pp 14–22.

Hammond, JH, 'South African Memories: Rhodes-Barnato-Burnham', *Scribner's Magazine*, Vol LXIX, No 3 (March 1921), pp 257–278.

Harlow, V and Hamilton, F, 'Sir Frederic Hamilton's Narrative of Events Relative to the Jameson Raid', *The English Historical Review*, Vol 72, No 283 (April 1957), pp 279–285.

Holloway, M, 'Dr Jimcrack and See-Saw Roads: Harold Bolce's "A Slump in Heroes"', *English in Africa*, Vol 18, No 2 (October 1991).

Igler, D, 'The Industrial Far West: Region and Nation in the Late Nineteenth Century', *Pacific Historical Review*, Vol 69, No 2 (May 2000), pp 159–192.

Ireland, A, 'The True Story of the Jameson Raid as Related to me by John Hays Hammond', *The North American Review*, Vol 208, No 753 and 754 (August and September 1918), pp 185–196 and 365–376.

Kaplan, A, 'Romancing the Empire: The Embodiment of American Masculinity in the Popular Historical Novel of the 1890s', *American Literary History*, Vol 2, No 4 (Winter 1990), pp 659–690.

Katz, F, 'Pancho Villa and the attack on Columbus, New Mexico', *American Historical Review*, Vol 83, No 1 (February 1978), pp 101–130.

Keto, CT, 'The Aftermath of the Jameson Raid and American Decision Making in Foreign Affairs, 1896' in *Transactions of the American Philosophical Society* (Philadelphia) Vol 70, Part 8 (1980), pp 1–43.

Kramer, PA, 'Empires, Exceptions, and Anglo-Saxons: Race and Rule between the

British and United States Empires, 1880–1910', *The Journal of American History*, Vol 88, No 4 (March 2002), pp 1315–1353.

Mills, C, 'A Hazardous Bargain: Occupational Risk in Cornish Mining, 1875–1914', *Labour History Review*, Vol 70, No 1 (April 2005), pp 53–71.

Muller, CH, '"The Greatest State Scandal": Personality, Power and the South African Republic Police, 1886–1899', *South African Historical Journal*, Vol 68, No 1 (2016), pp 13–30.

Murphy, G, 'Democracy, Development and the Monroe Doctrine in Richard Harding Davis's *Soldiers of Fortune*', *American Studies*, Vol 42, No 2 (Summer 2001), pp 45–66.

Phimister IR, 'Rhodes, Rhodesia and the Rand', *Journal of Southern African Studies*, Vol 1, No 1 (1974), pp 76–94.

Rosenberg, S, 'Economic Pressures in Anglo-American Diplomacy, 1917–1918', *Journal of Inter-American Studies and World Affairs*, Vol 17, No 2 (May 1975), pp 123–152.

Teisch J, '"Home is not so very far away": Californian Engineers in South Africa, 1868–1915', *Australian Economic History Review*, Vol 45, No 2 (July 2005), pp 139–160.

Trow, CW, 'Woodrow Wilson and the Mexican Interventionist Movement of 1919', *Journal of American History*, Vol 58, No 1 (June 1971), pp 46–72.

Tuffnell, S, 'Engineering Inter-Imperialism: American Miners and the Transformation of Global Mining', *Journal of Global History*, Vol 10, Issue 1 (March 2015), pp 53–76.

Van den Bergh, GN, 'Secret Service in the South African Republic, 1895–1900', *Military History Journal*, Vol 3, No 2 (December 1974).

Wyllys, RK, 'The Republic of Lower California', *Pacific Historical Review*, Vol 23, No 2 (June 1933), pp 194–213.

CHAPTERS IN BOOKS

Beal, MD and Wells, MW, 'Populism and Free Silver, 1890–1896' in *History of Idaho, Vol 2* (New York, 1959), pp 72–85.

Phimister, IR, 'Frenzied Finance: Gold Mining in the Globalizing South, c. 1886–1896' in B Mountford and S Tuffnell (eds), *Gold Rush: A Global History, c 1848–1910* (Oxford, forthcoming).

Wister, O, 'The Evolution of the Cow-Puncher' in BM Vorphal (ed), *My Dear Wister: The Frederick Remington–Owen Wister Letters* (Palo Alto, 1972), pp 77–96.

BOOKS

Acuña, RF, *Corridors of Migration: The Odyssey of Mexican Laborers, 1600–1933* (Tucson, AZ, 2008).

Aiken, KG, *Idaho's Bunker Hill: The Rise and Fall of a Great Mining Company* (Oklahoma, 2005).

Ash, C, *The IF Man. Dr Leander Starr Jameson: The Inspiration for Kipling's Masterpiece* (Solihull, 2012).

Bell, FW, *The South African Conspiracy or the Aims of Afrikanerdom* (London, 1900).

Biggers, J, *In the Sierra Madre* (Chicago, 2006).

Blackburn, D and Caddell, WW, *Secret Service in South Africa* (London, 1911).

Brechin, G, *Imperial San Francisco: Urban Power and Earthly Ruin* (Los Angeles, 2006).

Burnham, FR, *Scouting on Two Continents* (New York, 1926).

Calvert, P, *The Mexican Revolution, 1910–1914: The Diplomacy of Anglo-American Conflict* (Cambridge, 1968).

Carruthers, J (ed), *The Jameson Raid: A Centennial Perspective* (Johannesburg, 1996).

Cash, JW, *The Mind of the South* (New York, 1991).

Colvin, I, *The Life of Jameson, Vols 1 and 2* (London, 1922).

Cortright, D, *Peace: A History of Movements and Ideas* (Cambridge, 2008).

Danziger, C, *The Jameson Raid* (Cape Town, 1978).

Darwin, J, *The Empire Project: The Rise and Fall of the British World System, 1830–1970* (Cambridge, 2009).

Davis, RH, *Soldiers of Fortune* (New York, 1906; reprinted as *Six Who Dared: The Lives of Six Great Soldiers of Fortune*, Tucson, AZ, 2007).

Davis, RH, *Soldiers of Fortune* (New York, 1898).

Davis, RH, *Dr Jameson's Raiders vs the Johannesburg Reformers* (New York, 1897).

De Kiewiet, CW, *The Anatomy of South African Misery* (London, 1956).

Du Toit, BM, *Boer Settlers in the Southwest* (El Paso, TX, 1995).

Dwyer, J, *The Agrarian Dispute: The Expropriation of American-Owned Rural Land* (Durham, 2009).

FitzPatrick, JP, *The Transvaal from Within: A Private Record of Public Affairs* (London, 1899).

Fort, GS, *Dr Jameson* (London, 1918).

Fraser, M and Jeeves, A (eds), *All that Glittered: Selected Correspondence of Lionel Phillips, 1890–1924* (Cape Town, 1977).

Garrett FE and Edwards EJ, *The Story of an African Crisis and of the Jameson Raid* (London, 1897).

Gates, EN, *Race and US Foreign Policy in the Age of Territorial and Market Expansion* (London, 2014).

Gates, PW, *Land and Law in California: Essays on Land Politics* (West Lafayette, IN, 2002).

Giliomee, H, *The Afrikaners: Biography of a People* (Charlottesville, 2003).

Goodwin, DK, *The Bully Pulpit: Theodore Roosevelt and the Golden Age of Journalism* (New York, 2013).

Gordon, CT, *The Growth of Boer Opposition to Kruger, 1890–1895* (London, 1970).

Hamilton Jenkin, AK, *The Cornish Miner: an Account of his Life Above and Underground from Early Times* (Devon, 1962, third edition).

Hammond, JH, *The Autobiography of John Hays Hammond, Vols 1 and 2* (New York, 1935).

Hammond, JH, *The Truth About the Jameson Raid, as Related to Alleyne Ireland* (Boston, 1918).

Hammond, JH, *The Transvaal Trouble* (New York, 1900).

Hammond, NH, *A Woman's Part in a Revolution* (London, 1897).

Harrigan, RE, *The New World Power: American Foreign Policy, 1898–1917* (Philadelphia, 2013).

Harriman, J, *The Class War in Idaho: The Horrors of the Bull Pen* (New York, 1900).

Harris, CH, *The Secret War in El Paso: Mexican Revolutionary Intrigue, 1906–1920* (Albuquerque, NM, 2009).

Harrison, B, *Agent of Empire: William Walker and the Imperial Self in American Literature* (Athens, GA, 2004).

Hart, JM, *Empire and Revolution: The Americans in Mexico since the Civil War* (Berkeley, 2002).

Hickey, TA, *The Story of the Bull Pen at Wardner, Idaho* (New York, 1900).

Hill, H, *Mark Twain: God's Fool* (Chicago, 2012).

Hillegas, HC, *Oom Paul's People* (New York, 1900).

Hoganson, KL, *Fighting for American Manhood: How Gender Politics Provoked the Spanish-American and Philippine-American Wars* (London, 1998).

Horsman, R, *Race and Manifest Destiny: The Origins of American Racial Anglo-Saxonism* (Cambridge, MA, 1981).

Hull, R, *American Enterprise in South Africa: Historical Dimensions of Engagement and Disengagement* (New York, 1990).

Hyslop, J, *The Notorious Syndicalist. JT Bain: A Scottish Rebel in Colonial South Africa* (Johannesburg, 2004).

Israel, J, *Progressivism and the Open Door: America and China, 1905–1921* (Pittsburgh, 1991).

Kagan, R, *Dangerous Nation: America and the World, 1600–1898* (London, 2006).

Katz, EN, *A Trade Union Aristocracy* (Johannesburg, 1976).

Katz, F, *The Life and Times of Pancho Villa* (Stanford, 1998).

Kepple-Jones, A, *Rhodes and Rhodesia* (Pietermaritzburg, 1983).

King, J, *Dr Jameson's Raid: Its Causes and Consequences* (Manchester, 1896).

Knight, A, *The Mexican Revolution: Counter-Revolution and Reconstruction, Vol 2* (Lincoln, NB, 1990).

Kolko, G, *The Triumph of Conservatism* (New York, 2008).

Kotzé, JG, *Memoirs and Reminiscences* (Cape Town, 1934).

Krüger, DW, *Paul Kruger, Deel ll* (Johannesburg, 1963).

Kubicek, RV, *Economic Imperialism in Theory and Practice: The Case of South African Gold Mining Finance, 1886–1914* (Durham, 1979).

Kuehl, WF and Dunn, LK, *Keeping the Covenant: American Internationalists and the League of Nations, 1920–1939* (Kent, OH, 1997).

Langley, LD, *The Banana Wars: An Inner History of American Empire, 1900–1934* (Lexington, KY, 1983).

LaFeber, W, *The New Empire: An Interpretation of American Expansion, 1860–1898* (London, 1963).

Lamar, HR, *Charlie Siringo's West: An Interpretative Biography* (Albuquerque, 2005).

Löfroth, F, *A Word Made Safe: Values in American Best Sellers, 1895–1920* (Uppsala, 1983).

Lukas, JA, *Big Trouble: A Murder in a South Western Town Sets off a Struggle for the Soul of America* (New York, 2012).

Lulat, YGM, *United States Relations with South Africa: A Critical Overview from the Colonial Period to the Present* (New York, 2008).

Lurie, J, *William Howard Taft: The Travails of a Progressive Conservative* (Cambridge, 2011).

Marchand, CR, *The American Peace Movement and Social Reform, 1898–1914* (Princeton, 2015).

Markham, VR, *South Africa Past and Present* (London, 1900).

Matthews, MM, *The US Army on the Mexican Border: A Historical Perspective* (Kansas City, 2007).

May, ER, *Imperial Democracy: The Emergence of America as a Great Power* (New York, 1961).

May, RE, *Manifest Destiny's Underworld: Filibustering in Antebellum America* (Chapel Hill, NC, 2002).

May, RE, *The Southern Dream of a Caribbean Empire* (Gainesville, FL, 2002).

Meredith, M, *Diamonds, Gold and War: The Making of South Africa* (London, 2007).

Meyer, LE, *The Farther Frontier: Six Case Studies of Americans and Africa, 1848–1936* (London, 1992).

Mouton, JA, *Generaal Piet Joubert in die Transvaal Geskiedenis*, Archives Year Book for South African History (Parow, 1957).

Neu, CE, *Colonel House: A Biography of Woodrow Wilson's Silent Partner* (New York, 2015).

Nugent, D (ed), *Rural Revolt in Mexico: US Intervention and the Domain of Subaltern Politics* (Durham, NC, 1998).

Pakenham, T, *The Scramble for Africa* (London, 1991).

Paquette, R, *Sugar is Made with Blood: The Conspiracy of La Escalera and the Conflict between Empires over Slaves in Cuba* (Middletown, CT, 1990).

Payton, P, *The Cornish Overseas: A History of Cornwall's 'Great Migration'* (Dundurn, 2005).

Payton, P, *Cornwall: A History* (Fowey, 2004).

Peterson, RH, *The Bonanza Kings: The Social Origins and Business Behavior of Western Mining Entrepreneurs, 1870–1900* (London, 1971).

Phillips, Mrs Lionel, *Some South African Recollections* (London, 1900).

Pisani, DJ, *From the Family Farm to Agribusiness: The Irrigation Crusade in California* (Oakland, 1984).

Rhoodie, D, *Conspirators in Conflict: A Study of the Johannesburg Reform Committee and its Role in the Conspiracy against the South African Republic* (Cape Town, 1967).

Richards, L, *The California Gold Rush and the Coming of the Civil War* (New York, 2007).

Righter, RW, *The Battle Over Hetch Hetchy: America's Most Controversial Dam and the Birth of Modern Environmentalism* (Oxford, 2005).

Roberts, G, *The Confederate Belle* (London, 2003).

Roma, DD, *Ringside Seat to a Revolution: An Underground Cultural History of El Paso and Juárez, 1893–1923* (El Paso, TX, 2005).

Rosenthal, E, *Stars and Stripes in Africa* (Cape Town, 1968).

Rotberg, RI, *The Founder: Cecil Rhodes and the Pursuit of Power* (Cape Town, 2002).

Rousseau, L, *Die Groot Verlange: Die Verhaal van Eugène N Marais* (Pretoria, 1974).

Schreuder, DM and Butler, J (eds), *Sir Graham Bower's Secret History of the Jameson Raid and the South African Crisis, 1895–1902* (Cape Town, 2004).

Scoble, J and Abercrombie, RH, *The Rise and Fall of Krugerism: A Personal Record of Forty Years in South Africa* (New York, 1900).

Scroggs, WO, *Filibusters and Financiers: The Story of William Walker and His Associates* (New York, 1916).

Simons, HJ and Simons, RE, *Class and Colour in South Africa, 1850–1950* (Harmondsworth, 1969).

Siringo, CA, *A Cowboy Detective: A True Story of Twenty-Two Years with a World Famous Detective Agency* (Chicago, 1912).

Smith, RW, *The Coeur d'Alene Mining War of 1892* (Corvallis, OR, 1961).

Spence, CC, *Mining Engineers and the American West: The Lace-Boot Brigade* (New Haven, 1970).

Spiro, JP, *Defending the Master Race: Conservation, Eugenics and the Legacy of Madison Grant* (Lebanon, NH, 2009).

Stead, WT, *The Americanisation of the World or the Trend of the Twentieth Century* (London, 1902).

Stewart, GR, *Committee of Vigilance: Revolution in San Francisco, 1851* (Boston, 1964).

Stratton, DH, *Tempest over Teapot Dome: The Story of Albert B Fall* (Oklahoma, 1998).

Tamarakin, M, *Cecil Rhodes and the Cape Afrikaners: The Imperial Colossus and the Colonial Parish Pump* (Abingdon, 1996).

Teisch, J, *Engineering Nature: Water, Development, & the Global Spread of American Environmental Expertise* (Chapel Hill, NC, 2011).

Tyrrell, I, *Crisis of the Wasteful Nation: Empire and Conservation in Theodore Roosevelt's America* (Chicago, 2015).

Van den Bergh, GN, *Die Polisiediens in die Zuid-Afrikaansche Republiek* (Pretoria, 1980).

Van der Merwe, C, *Donker Stroom: Eugène Marais en die Anglo-Boereoorlog* (Cape Town, 2015).

Van der Poel, J, *The Jameson Raid* (Cape Town, 1951).

Van Onselen, C, *Showdown at the Red Lion: The Life and Times of Jack McLoughlin, 1859–1910* (Cape Town, 2015).

Van Onselen, C, *Masked Raiders: Irish Banditry in Southern Africa, 1880–1889* (Cape Town, 2010).

Van Onselen, C, *New Babylon, New Nineveh: Everyday Life on the Witwatersrand* (Cape Town, 2001).

Van Wyk, P, *Burnham: King of Scouts: Baden-Powell's Secret Mentor* (Trafford, BC, 2003).

Vindex (F Verschoyle), *Cecil Rhodes: His Life and Political Speeches* (London, 1900).

Wald P, Elliot, MA and Arac, J, *The American Novel* (Oxford, 2014).

Wardner, J, *Jim Wardner of Wardner, Idaho* (New York, 1900).

Watts, S, *Rough Rider in the White House: Theodore Roosevelt and the Politics of Desire* (Chicago 2003).

Webb, WP, *The Texas Rangers: A Century of Frontier Defense* (Austin, 2010).

Widener, WC, *Henry Cabot Lodge in the Search for American Foreign Policy* (Los Angeles, 1980).

Wilkins, JH, *The Great Diamond Hoax and Other Stirring Incidents in the Life of Asbury Harpending* (San Francisco, 1913).

Wyatt-Brown, B, *Southern Honor: Ethics and Behavior in the Old South* (New York, 1982).

UNPUBLISHED WORKS

Bartos, JM, 'The Blight of the Federation: James McParland, the Pinkerton National Detective Agency and the Western Federation of Miners, 1892–1907', MA thesis, Montana State University, 2013.

Cripps, EA, 'Provisioning Johannesburg, 1886–1906', MA thesis, Department of History, Unisa, February 2012.

Cyrulik, JM, 'A Strategic Examination of the Punitive Expedition into Mexico, 1916–1917', MMAS thesis, US Army Command and General Staff College, 2003.

De Waal, E, 'The Part Played by Americans on the Witwatersrand during the Period 1886–1899', MA dissertation, Department of History, Unisa, 1971.

Du Plooy, WJ, 'Die Militêre Voorbereiding en Verloop van die Jameson-Inval 1895/96', MA thesis, Department of History, University of Pretoria, 1958.

Edwards, WR, 'The Protection of American Lives and Property: The Sonora Crisis of 1915', derived from 'United States–Mexican Relations, 1913–1916: Revolution, Oil and Intervention', PhD thesis, Louisiana State University, 1971.

Kamffer HJG, '*Om een scherpe oog in't zeil te houden*: Die Geheime Diens in die Zuid-Afrikaansche Republiek', DPhil thesis, Potchefstroomse Universiteit vir Christelike Hoër Onderwys, 1999.

Meijer, JW, 'Generaal Ben Viljoen, 1868–1917', PhD thesis, Department of History, University of Pretoria, 1993.

Muller, CH, 'Policing the Witwatersrand: A History of the South African Republic Police, 1886–1899', DPhil thesis, Centre for Africa Studies, University of the Free State, 2016.

MANUSCRIPT SOURCES

Republic of South Africa, Johannesburg, Brenthurst Library, Rhodes Papers, CJ Rhodes to Alfred Beit, Cape Town, letter dated 'August 1895'.

Republic of South Africa, Grahamstown, National English Language Museum, FitzPatrick Collection, Reuters.

Republic of South Africa, Johannesburg, Brenthurst Library, Kelsey Papers 370/3/21, 17 May 1896.

Republic of South Africa, University of Cape Town (UCT), Jagger Library, BC 959,

A11.5, Charles Cowen, undated, unpublished, 'Miscellany: Historical Reminiscences'.

Republic of South Africa, National Archives of South Africa (SANA), Pretoria, Staats Prokereur (SP) Vol 238, unsigned Report no '21', of 22 September 1894 containing a seating plan for a Transvaal National Union banquet as 'written out' by FH Hamilton.

Republic of South Africa, Pretoria, South African National Archives (SANA), Leyds Archive, 1895–1896.

United States of America, Moscow, University of Idaho Library, Manuscript Group 367, Box and Folder Inventory Guide, Corporate History, Bunker Hill Company, as compiled by J Nielson, October 1994.

United Kingdom, Oxford University, Bodleian Library, MSS British Empire, S 590, Box 8, File No 3.

Acknowledgements and Thanks

L ike most academics, I have benefited from the institutional shelter and succour provided by various funding agencies and universities. I am indebted to the National Research Foundation for funding, and for support I received during my tenure as an Oppenheimer Fellow at the Hutchins Center for African & African American Research, Harvard University, where the research for this book commenced some years ago. The work could never have been brought to fruition, however, were it not for the generous backing and significant personal encouragement that I have received over many years from Profs Cheryl de la Rey and Robin Crewe at the University of Pretoria.

For the most part, archivists and librarians are a cheerful and helpful lot even though they are sometimes forced to frequent chambers that can be dark, dank and forbiddingly hushed. But, as I have learned over the decades, the finest among them can light up the dim recesses of a researcher's mind in ways that would shame the sun. Almost by definition the innermost history of a treasonous conspiracy is impossible to research to the satisfaction of the author. It is the tiniest of fragments that can set off an illuminating flash, and Lucy McCann at the Bodleian Library, Oxford University, Carson Holloway at Duke University and Clive Kirkwood of the Jagger Library at the University of Cape Town, along with Karen Harris at the University of Pretoria, have all helped me see more clearly. Jenny Duckworth, Rosemary Dixon-Smith and Cecilia Jacobs also devilled on my behalf in various archives in most profitable fashion.

In a country scarred by illiteracy and Third World economic management, it requires something special, even from those people inexplicably enthused by history, to transform breakfast talk into the magic of the printed and packaged form. Between them, in various combinations, my friends Jonathan Ball, Eugene Ashton and Jeremy Boraine have been performing that trick for two decades at considerable corporate, if not personal, cost. In this instance I have also benefited from the professional assistance of Mike Nicol, Alfred LeMaitre and Valda Strauss. As in the past, this volume is graced by maps produced by Philip Stickler.

A small army of historians have, at various points, tried to seal off the easiest approaches to my flanks in an attempt to protect me from my ignorance and prospective critics about things which, in truth, I know all too little about. Principal among the brave are: Ed Balleisen, Keith Beavon, Johan Bergh, Catherine Burns, Joel Cabrita, Jane Carruthers, Andy Cohen, John and Jean Comaroff, Richard Flockemann, Hermann Giliomee, Albert Grundlingh, John Higginson, Jon Hyslop, Elaine Katz, Robert Kaplan, Robert May, Donal McCracken, Diane McWorther, Cornelis Muller, Fransjohan Pretorius, Milton Shain, Karin Shapiro, Mordechai Tamarkin and André van der Walt. I would like to blame them for all errors of fact or interpretation in the work but, alas, the profession does not work like that. All the remaining errors, flaws and problems are thus mine. Damn.

On long marches such as this one, it's the voices of the friends closest to you, and the words of encouragement they are wont to chant, that do most to keep the head up and the feet moving forward. Peter Bruce, Jim Campbell, James Clarke, Gordon Forbes, Bobby Godsell, Mark Henning, Bill Johnson, Lize Kriel, Bruce Murray, Gail Nattrass, Patrick Pearson, Karel Schoeman, June Sinclair, Richard Steyn, Peter Sullivan and, more than most, Tim Couzens have all helped by engaging me in extraordinarily stimulating discussions spread over a very long time.

It is those scouting for what may lie ahead, by way of potentially lethal hazards, that are called on to do the hardest professional work of all through having to read and comment on draft formulations or questionable facts. Andrew Offenburger and Carel van der Merwe, consummate professionals that they are, have saved me from errors of fact and nudged me towards more sophisticated interpretations. My greatest debts lie with Paul la Hausse de Lalouvière and Ian Phimister, fine historians who have been forced to accompany me on journeys not of their choosing.

I do not think that either my wife or our daughter and sons have ever known a time when I was not tucked away in some quiet spot reading or 'working on the book' during daylight hours. I am aware that it is a rather shoddy excuse to offer Belinda, Gareth, Jessica and Matthew in exchange for all their love and support over 40 years but, sadly, I have none other to give. My sister, Cheric, equally supportive, knows the problem all too well and can by now hum the tune and mouth the words.

But it's not all bad news. My father used to say, more in hope than anticipation I grant you, that 'this has to stop' whenever one of my obsessions threatened to spin out of control. Alas, when it came to writing history it never happened. There are, however, now other, more powerful factors at play. Who knows if there is to be another book?

And that reminds me how I am now increasingly liable to forget things. So, sincere apologies to those helpful souls whose assistance I have unintentionally failed to acknowledge.

Charles van Onselen
Parkview, Johannesburg
JANUARY 2017

Index